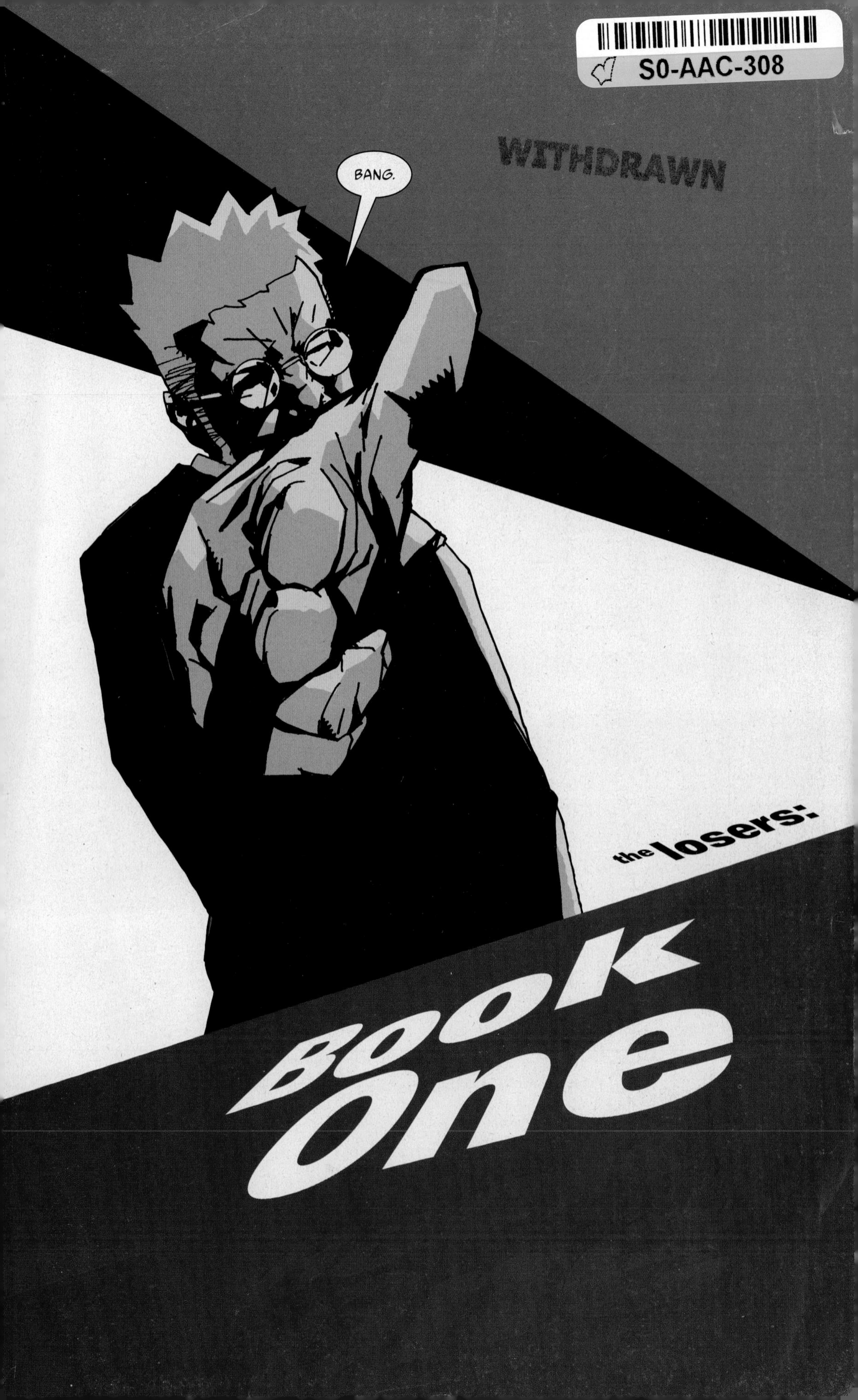
BANG.
the losers:
BOOK one

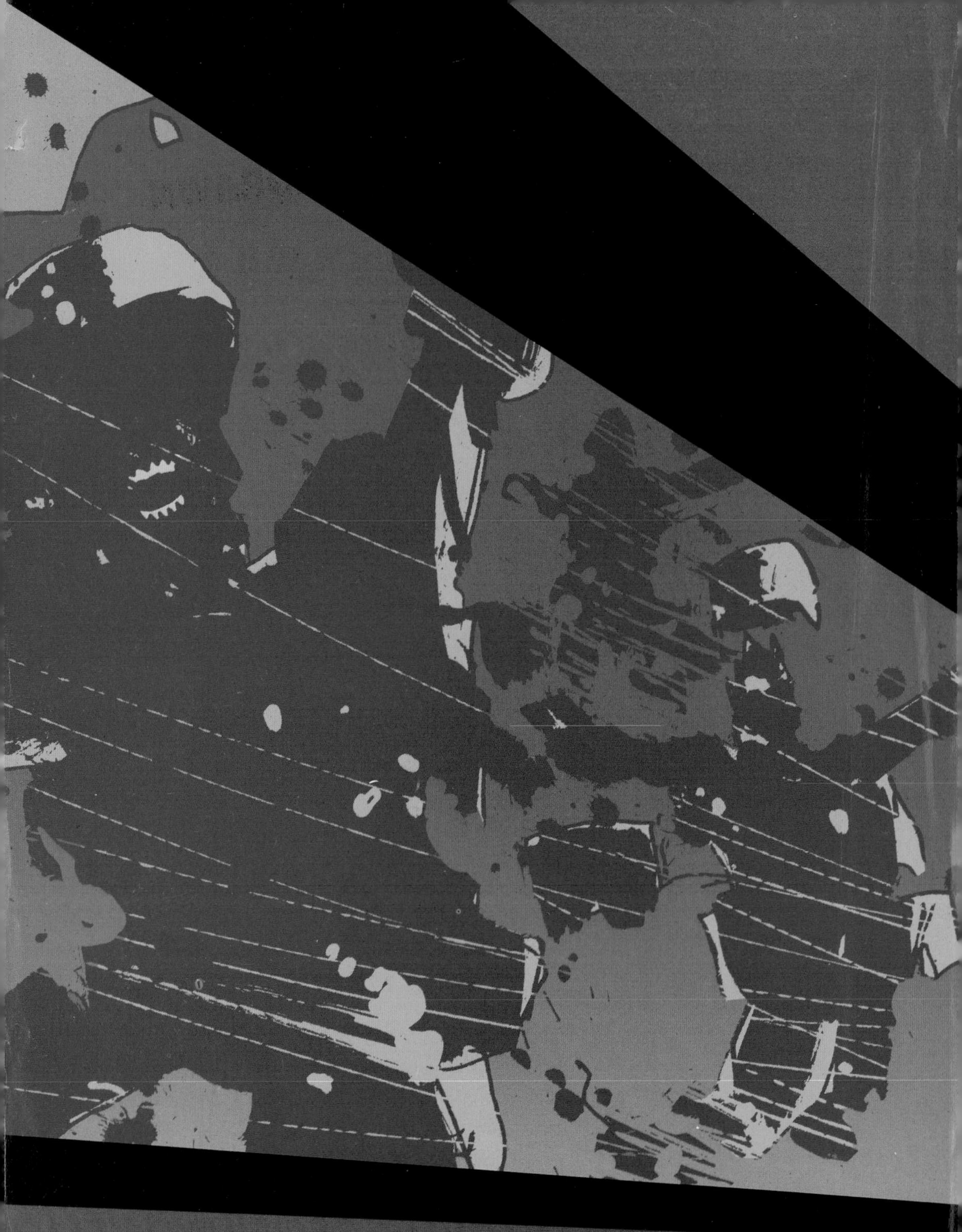

lee loughridge COLORIST

clem robins LETTERER

jock ORIGINAL SERIES COVERS

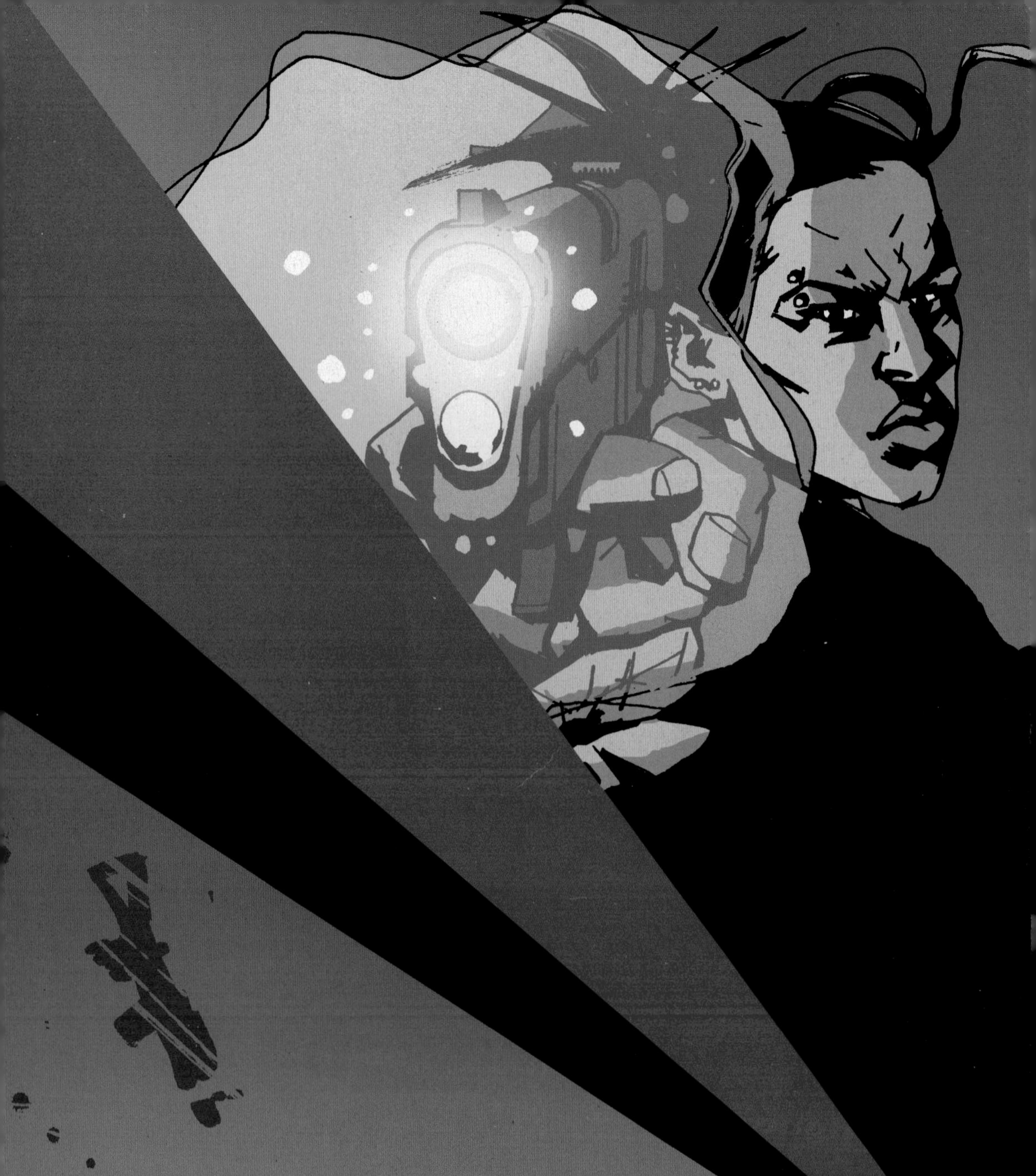

THE LOSERS

Book One

Written by **andy diggle**

Art by **jock** (issues 1-6, 9-12) & **shawn martinbrough** (issues 7-8)

Karen Berger SVP – Executive Editor **Will Dennis** Editor – Original Series **Zachary Rau** **Pornsak Pichetshote** Assistant Editors – Original Series
Georg Brewer VP – Design & DC Direct Creative **Bob Harras** Group Editor – Collected Editions **Scott Nybakken** Editor **Robbin Brosterman** Design Director – Books **Louis Prandi** Art Director

DC COMICS
Paul Levitz President & Publisher **Richard Bruning** SVP – Creative Director **Patrick Caldon** EVP – Finance & Operations **Amy Genkins** SVP – Business & Legal Affairs
Jim Lee Editorial Director – WildStorm **Gregory Noveck** SVP – Creative Affairs **Steve Rotterdam** SVP – Sales & Marketing **Cheryl Rubin** SVP – Brand Management

 DC Comics, 1700 Broadway, New York, NY 10019. A Warner Bros. Entertainment Company. Printed in Canada. Second printing. ISBN:978-1-4012-2733-3 Cover illustration by **Jock**.

SUSTAINABLE FORESTRY INITIATIVE
Certified Fiber Sourcing
www.sfiprogram.org
Fiber used in this product line meets the sourcing requirements of the SFI program. www.sfiprogram.org PWC-SFICOC-260

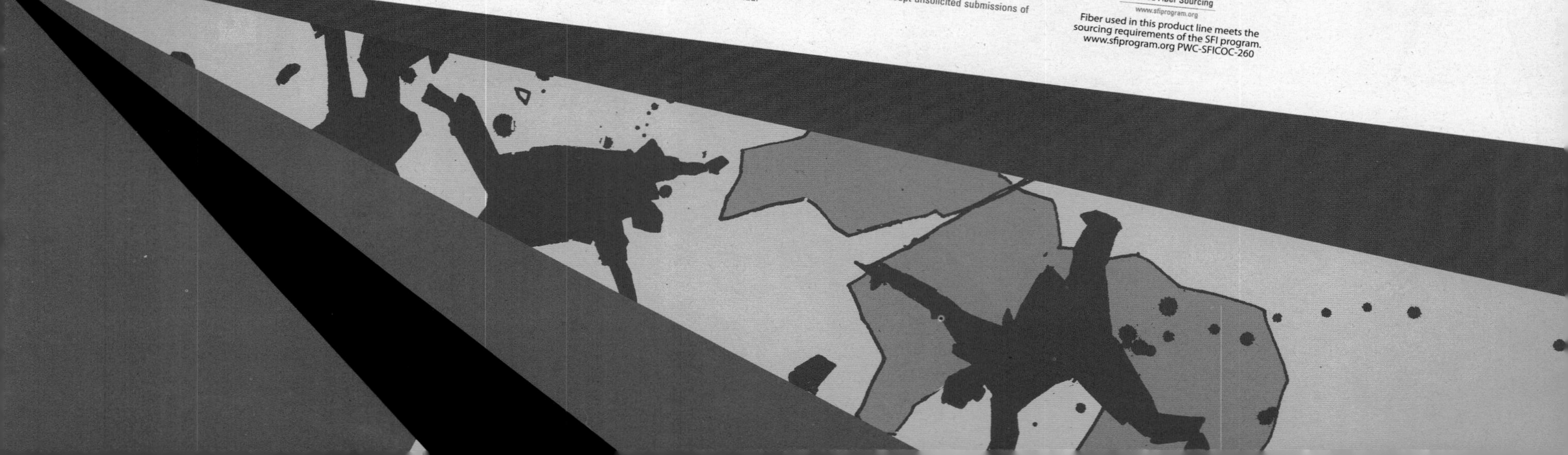

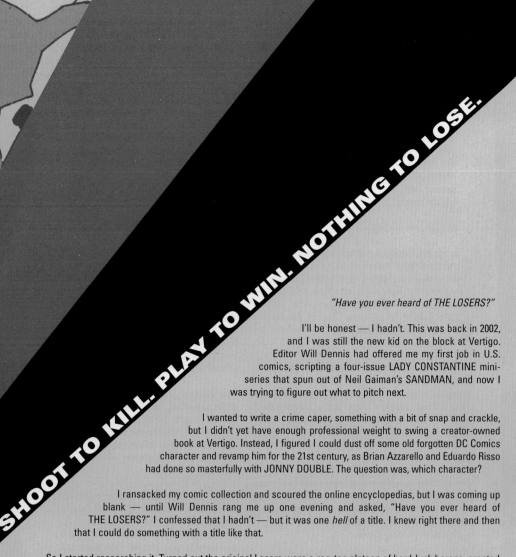

SHOOT TO KILL. PLAY TO WIN. NOTHING TO LOSE.

"Have you ever heard of THE LOSERS?"

I'll be honest — I hadn't. This was back in 2002, and I was still the new kid on the block at Vertigo. Editor Will Dennis had offered me my first job in U.S. comics, scripting a four-issue LADY CONSTANTINE mini-series that spun out of Neil Gaiman's SANDMAN, and now I was trying to figure out what to pitch next.

I wanted to write a crime caper, something with a bit of snap and crackle, but I didn't yet have enough professional weight to swing a creator-owned book at Vertigo. Instead, I figured I could dust off some old forgotten DC Comics character and revamp him for the 21st century, as Brian Azzarello and Eduardo Risso had done so masterfully with JONNY DOUBLE. The question was, which character?

I ransacked my comic collection and scoured the online encyclopedias, but I was coming up blank — until Will Dennis rang me up one evening and asked, "Have you ever heard of THE LOSERS?" I confessed that I hadn't — but it was one *hell* of a title. I knew right there and then that I could do something with a title like that.

So I started researching it. Turned out the original Losers were a rag-tag platoon of hard-luck heroes, created by writer Robert Kanigher in the pages of various DC World War II comics of the 1960s and '70s. And as a kid who pretty much learned to read with British war comics like *Battle*, *Warlord* and *Commando Picture Library*, I loved the idea of revamping the title.

There was just one problem: the Losers were dead.

According to DC Comics continuity, they were killed during the closing stages of the war while taking down a German missile site. I could have written a flashback story set before their deaths, but where's the drama in that? And that's when it hit me — *what if they didn't really die?* What if they were just missing in action, presumed K.I.A. — but the bodies were never found? And what if this rag-tag platoon of disgruntled ex-service-men got back together in the '50s for one last mission...?

Almost immediately, the rough outline of a snappy, high-concept crime caper downloaded itself straight into my skull, full of missing Nazi gold and German rocket scientists at Los Alamos and guys in sharkskin suits calling each other "Daddio." It was perfect.

I never even pitched it.

You see, Vertigo already had those bases covered with Garth Ennis' excellent WAR STORIES and Howard Chaykin and David Tischman's AMERICAN CENTURY, a '50s-era crime series. It seemed there was no place at Vertigo for the original Losers...

So I just took the title and tossed the rest.

To this day, I've still never read a single issue of the original LOSERS. I just took DC's trademarked title and ran with it, cooking up something completely new for them. New characters, new premise, new story. The one thing that did survive from my own '50s-era concept was the idea of disgruntled ex-servicemen, listed as K.I.A., re-teaming after the war to pull a heist.

And in the interests of full disclosure, I did include two tips of the hat to Robert Kanigher's team. We both had characters called "Clay." Maybe my Frank Clay is the grandson of Sarge Clay; or maybe it's just a coincidence. And while the original Losers had a dog called Pooch, that became the call-sign of Linwood Porteous, my team's transport specialist.

So I pitched Vertigo my new, contemporary version of THE LOSERS, a four-issue military heist caper that owed more to *Three Kings* and *The Way of the Gun* than it did to the blazing combat comics of old. And Vertigo liked it — enough that they asked me to re-tool it into an ongoing series.

Now this was one of those good problems; but it was a problem nonetheless. The thing about a heist caper is that it's *finite*. They plan the job; they pull the job; it either works or it doesn't, and that's that. How do you keep a story like that going indefinitely?

What I needed was an *ongoing series* of capers. What I needed was something to tie them all together.

What I needed was a bad guy.

Remember this was back in 2002, when America was still raw from 9/11 and George W. Bush was at the height of his popularity — on his home turf, at least. The Neo-Cons were holding the reins of power, and they were already using the worst terrorist atrocity in American history as an excuse to further their openly-stated agenda — namely, regime change in Iraq. The message coming out of Washington was, "If you're not with us, you're against us." It was called "unpatriotic" to question the actions of those in power, even as they tore up the Constitution that safe-guarded the very freedoms they were sworn to protect.

I've never liked being told what to do, or what to think, and that's just one of the many, many reasons I would have made a lousy soldier; but I have enormous respect for the men and women of the military. What must it have been like for them, being told to give their lives for a lie?

That's where I found the theme for my new version of THE LOSERS:

Sometimes, being a patriot means refusing to follow orders.

And that's how I came up with Max, the ultimate Neo-Conservative power player; Rumsfeld meets Blofeld. He's the guy who tried to have the Losers rubbed out, when all they were doing was fighting for their country and trying to save innocent lives. In my "ongoing series of capers," the Losers would be fighting to clear their names from Max's secret C.I.A. death list. If they wanted their lives back, they'd have to *steal* them.

Now it wasn't just a throwaway caper; it was *about* something. I wanted to try and marry the sheer kinetic entertainment value of Hollywood action movies with the paranoid smarts and social relevance of a '70s-era political conspiracy thriller. Aim high, miss high, that's my motto.

Most of all, THE LOSERS was my man-crush love letter to Shane Black, the screenwriter of *Lethal Weapon, The Last Boy Scout, The Long Kiss Goodnight* and more recently *Kiss Kiss Bang Bang* — and, let us not forget, the bespectacled joker in Arnie's squad who was first to be eviscerated by the *Predator*. Along with John Wagner and James Cameron, he's one of the reasons I wanted to become a writer in the first place, and to write stories that *move* — even on the printed page. I wanted to write a comic for people who don't read comics, but love a great action movie. A comic you could put into the hands of the average Joe — someone who doesn't even know that such things as comic shops *exist*, let alone would ever set foot inside one — and he'd *get* it, and get a kick out of it.

I'll leave you to judge whether we succeeded.

Looking back on it all now, I appreciate how lucky I was. Lucky to be in the right place at the right time. Lucky that editor Will Dennis was brave enough — or dumb enough — to take a chance on a couple of unknown British creators. But most of all, I was lucky to be working with Jock.

None of this would have happened without him.

I'd first met Jock when I was an editor at 2000 AD, and we worked together on my first published comics work — a sci-fi crime caper called LENNY ZERO. We just clicked, right from the start; he instinctively knew how to make the images in my head, and in my scripts, pop out and smack you in the face. His talent for page design is unparalleled.

More than anyone, Jock is the guy responsible for breathing life into the Losers, giving each of them a distinctive visual signature that makes them instantly recognizable — from Pooch's paunch to Cougar's hat to the curly cord that's perpetually sticking out from behind Jensen's ear.

And damn, he made those images *move* — just like they did in my head.

So now it's years later, and we're in that strange transition period between THE LOSERS being history — we wrapped the series in 2006 — and it becoming a whole new thing, with the movie adaptation bringing our story to a wider audience than we ever could have imagined.

It's been a strange experience, watching our baby go through the Hollywood machine. Jock and I visited the set of *The Losers* movie in Puerto Rico during the final days of filming, and it was downright surreal, seeing these characters we'd dreamt up walking and talking and blowing shit up. Looking *exactly* the way Jock designed them, saying lines I wrote, pulling heists that I planned out in meticulous detail while sitting in front of the computer in my spare bedroom all those years ago.

Of course, our Losers smoke and swear and fight the power a damn sight harder than those guys in the movie...

But hey, that's why I love comics.

— Andy Diggle
November 2009
www.AndyDiggle.com

Andy Diggle is a freelance comic-book writer. Formerly the editor of the legendary British sci-fi comics magazine 2000 AD, *he now has over a dozen graphic novels in print.*

His work includes THE LOSERS, BATMAN, HELLBLAZER, SWAMP THING, ADAM STRANGE and GREEN ARROW: YEAR ONE for DC Comics; Daredevil, Thunderbolts and Dark Reign: Hawkeye for Marvel; Judge Dredd vs. Aliens, Snow/Tiger and Lenny Zero for 2000 AD; and Guy Ritchie's Gamekeeper for Virgin Comics, the film adaptation of which is currently in development at Warner Bros.

He lives in the U.K. with his wife, two children and a clinical addiction to Call of Duty: Modern Warfare 2.

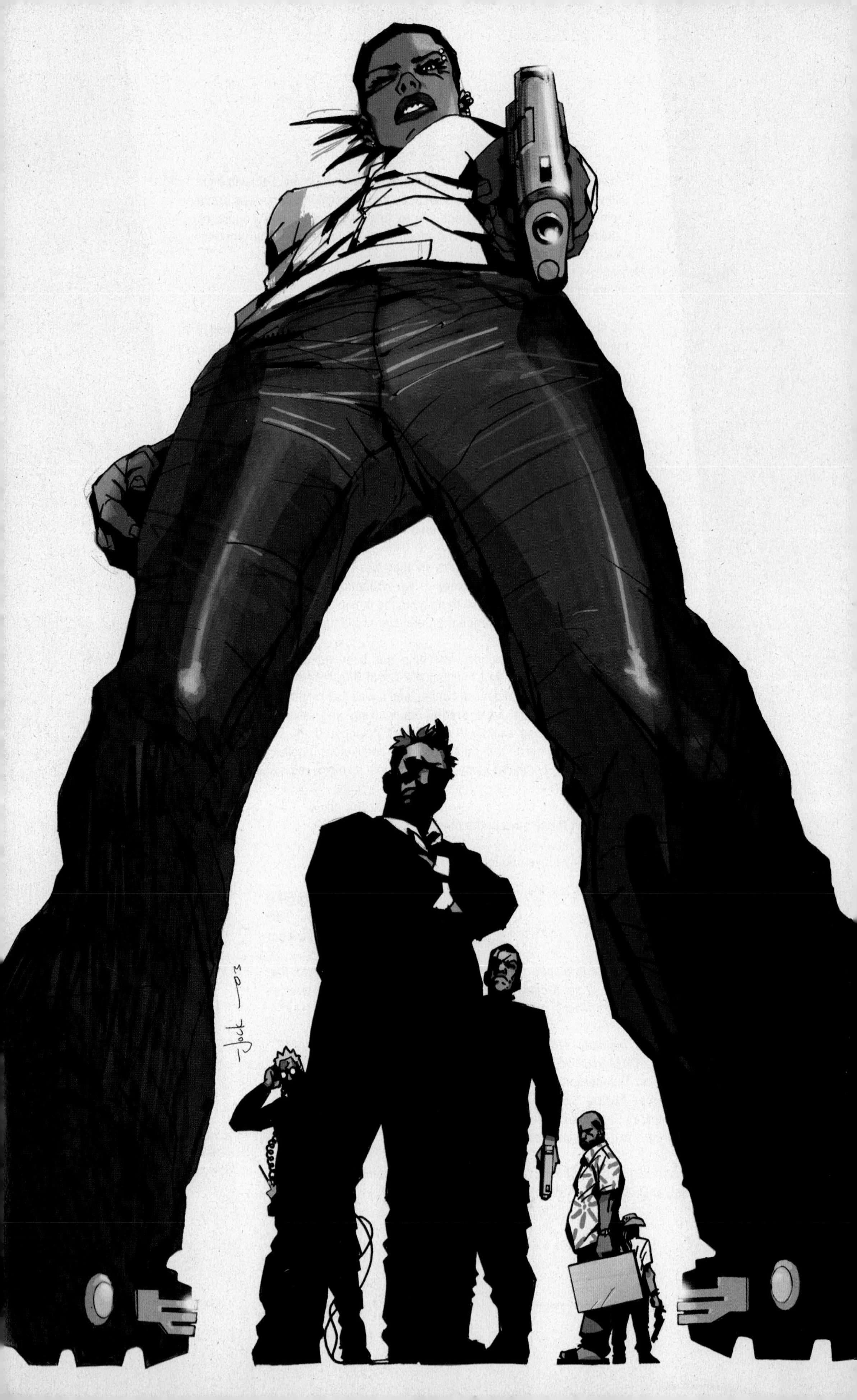

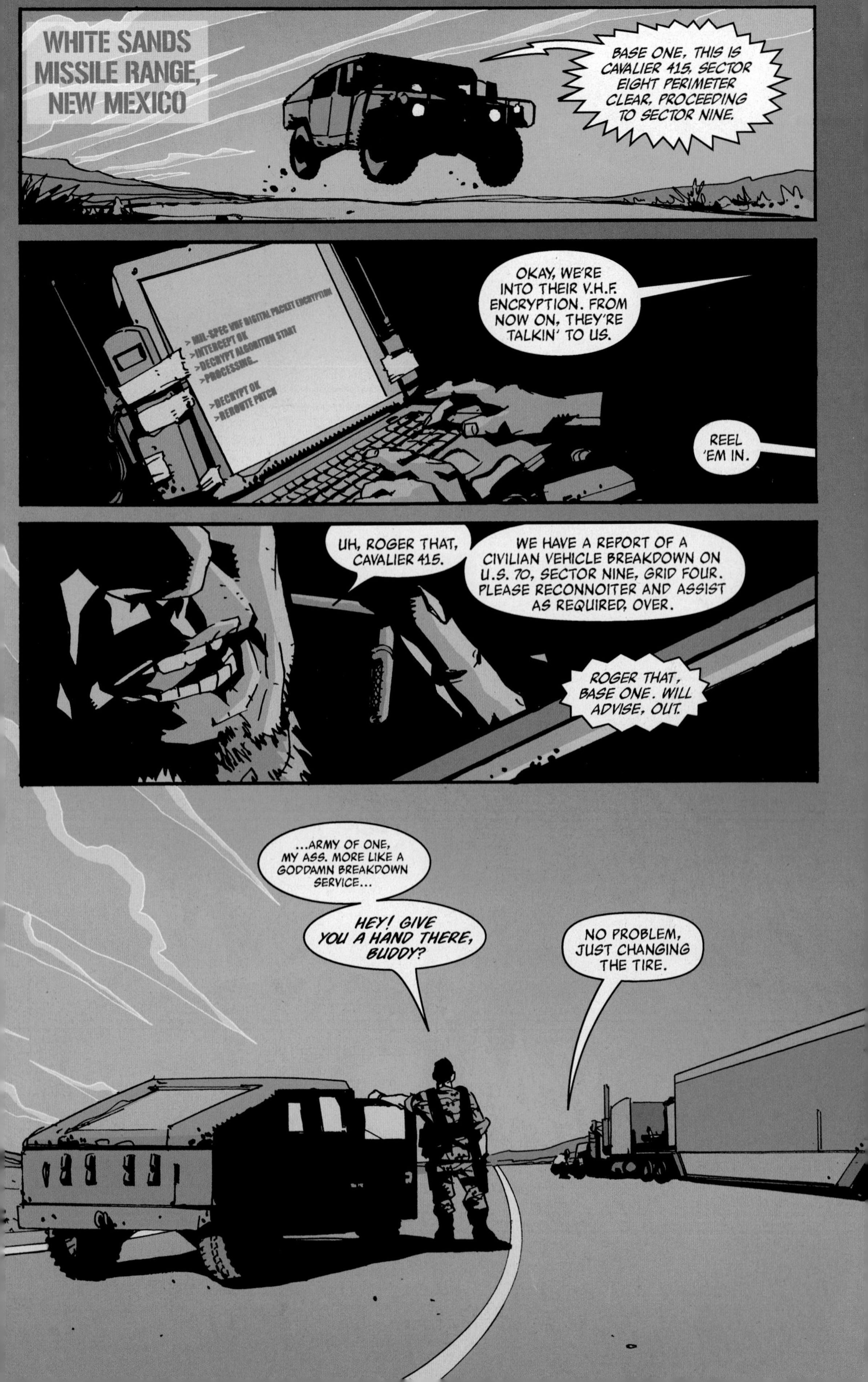
WHITE SANDS MISSILE RANGE, NEW MEXICO
BASE ONE, THIS IS CAVALIER 415, SECTOR EIGHT PERIMETER CLEAR, PROCEEDING TO SECTOR NINE.
MIL-SPEC VHF DIGITAL PACKET ENCRYPTION
>INTERCEPT OK
>DECRYPT ALGORITHM START
>PROCESSING...
>DECRYPT OK
>REROUTE PATCH
OKAY, WE'RE INTO THEIR V.H.F. ENCRYPTION. FROM NOW ON, THEY'RE TALKIN' TO US.
REEL 'EM IN.
UH, ROGER THAT, CAVALIER 415.
WE HAVE A REPORT OF A CIVILIAN VEHICLE BREAKDOWN ON U.S. 70, SECTOR NINE, GRID FOUR. PLEASE RECONNOITER AND ASSIST AS REQUIRED, OVER.
ROGER THAT, BASE ONE. WILL ADVISE, OUT.
...ARMY OF ONE, MY ASS. MORE LIKE A GODDAMN BREAKDOWN SERVICE...
HEY! GIVE YOU A HAND THERE, BUDDY?
NO PROBLEM, JUST CHANGING THE TIRE.

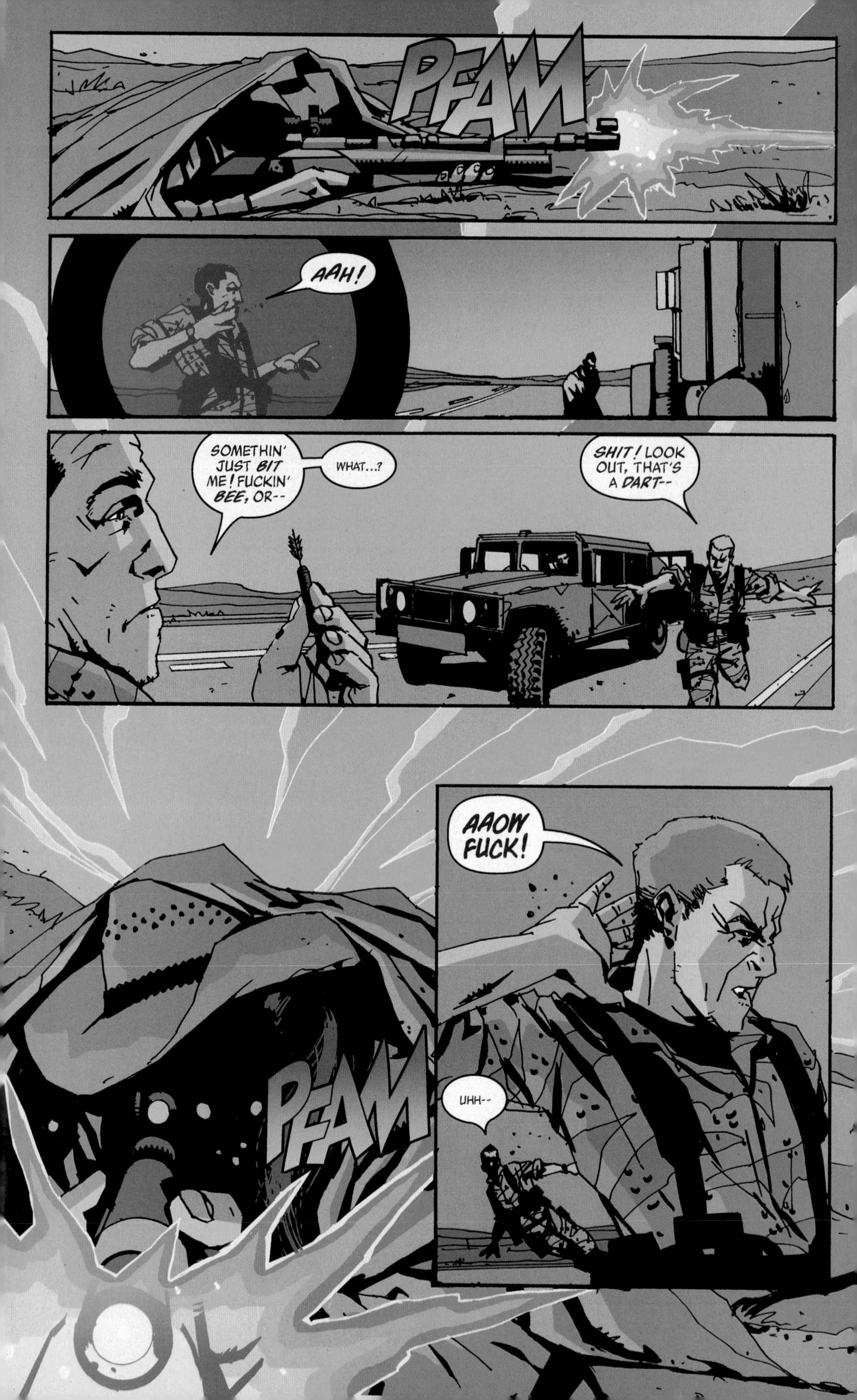
PFAM
AAH!
SOMETHIN' JUST BIT ME! FUCKIN' BEE, OR--
WHAT...?
SHIT! LOOK OUT, THAT'S A DART--
AAOW FUCK!
PFAM
UHH--

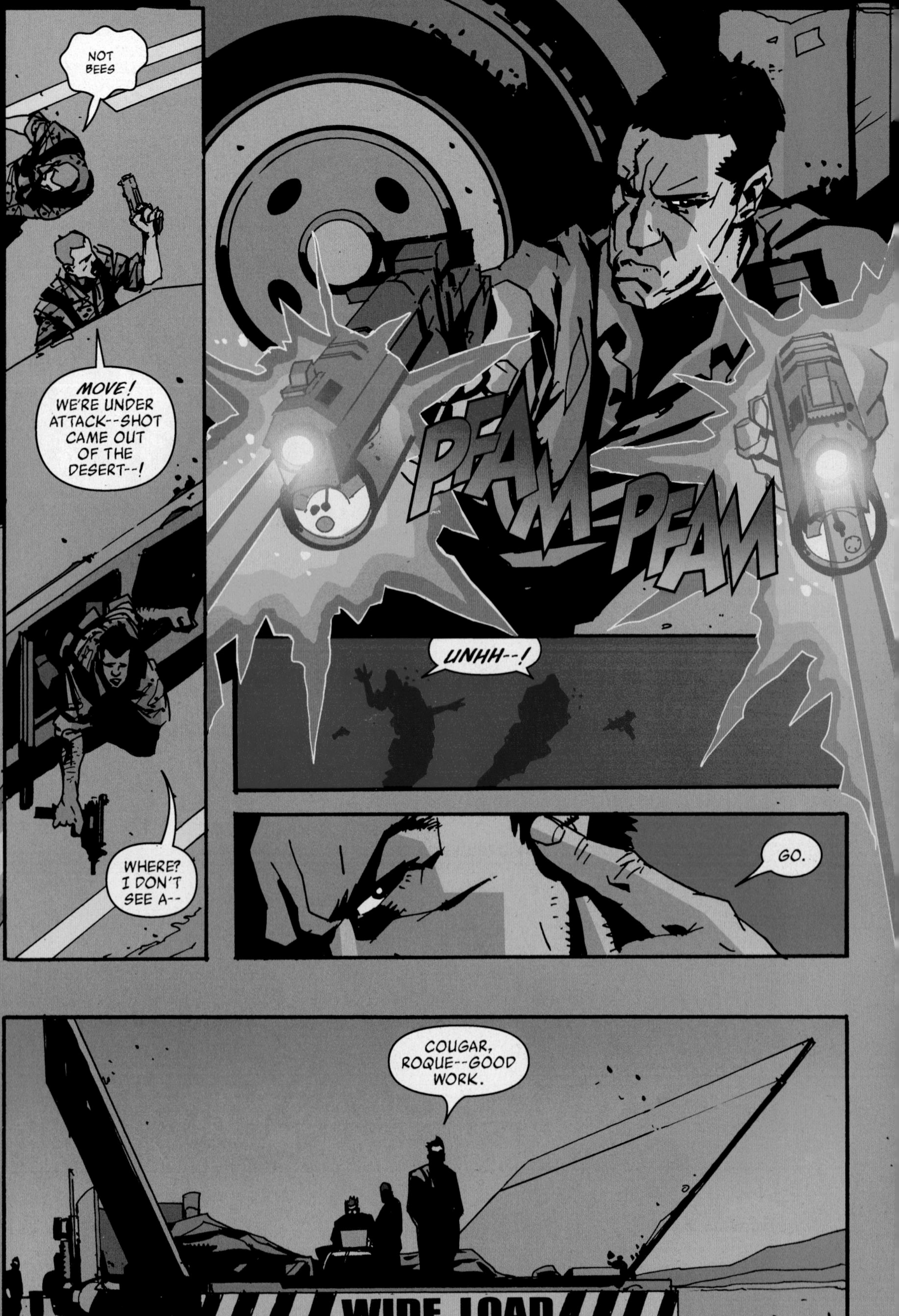
NOT BEES
MOVE! WE'RE UNDER ATTACK--SHOT CAME OUT OF THE DESERT--!
WHERE? I DON'T SEE A--
PFAM PFAM
UNHH--!
GO.
COUGAR, ROQUE--GOOD WORK.
WIDE LOAD

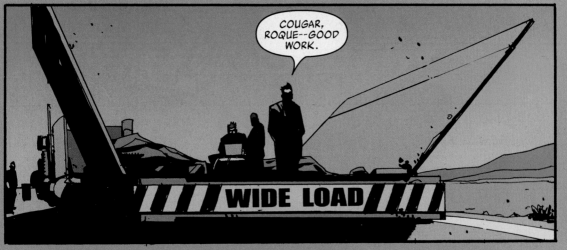

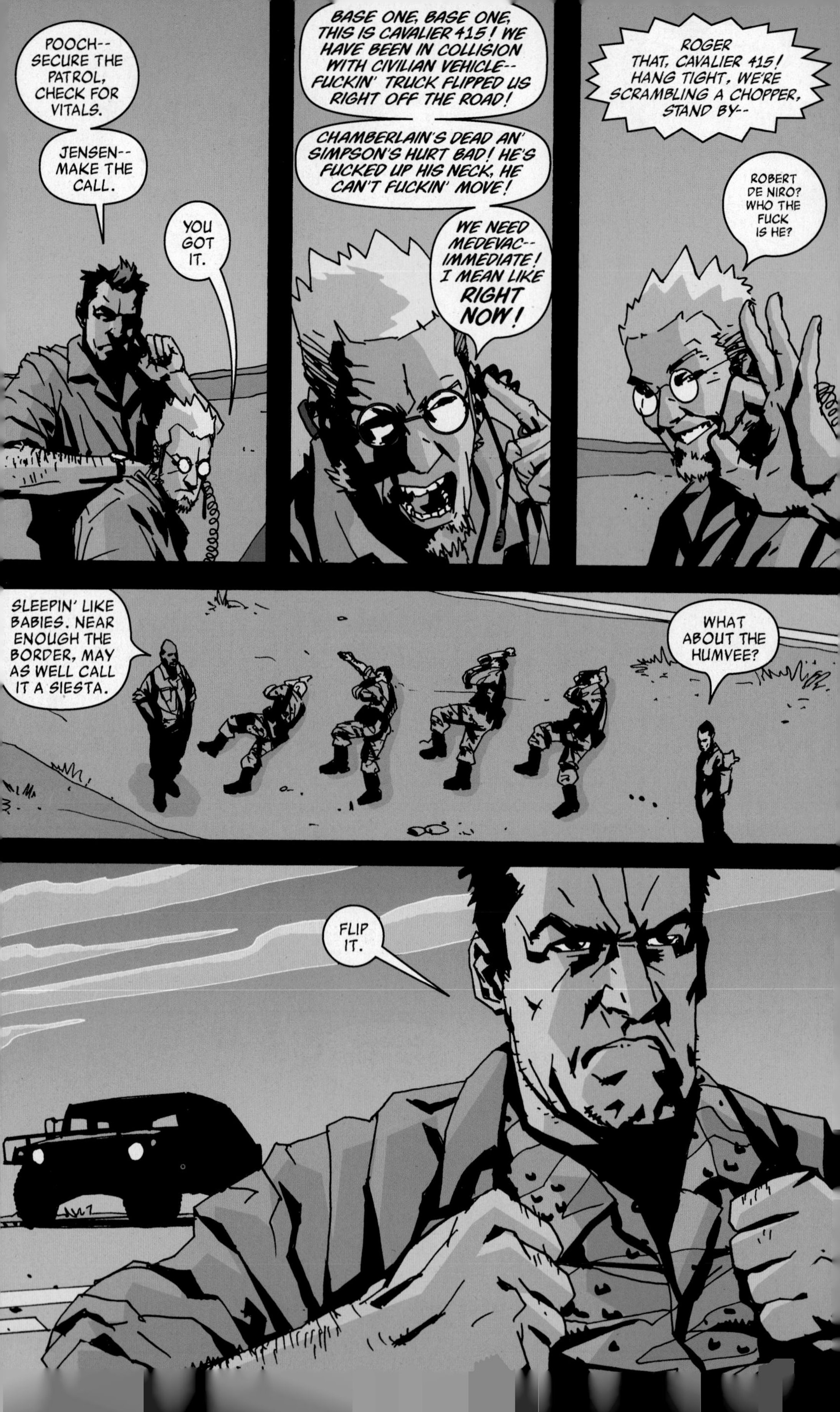
POOCH-- SECURE THE PATROL, CHECK FOR VITALS.
JENSEN-- MAKE THE CALL.
YOU GOT IT.
BASE ONE, BASE ONE, THIS IS CAVALIER 415! WE HAVE BEEN IN COLLISION WITH CIVILIAN VEHICLE-- FUCKIN' TRUCK FLIPPED US RIGHT OFF THE ROAD!
CHAMBERLAIN'S DEAD AN' SIMPSON'S HURT BAD! HE'S FUCKED UP HIS NECK, HE CAN'T FUCKIN' MOVE!
WE NEED MEDEVAC-- IMMEDIATE! I MEAN LIKE RIGHT NOW!
ROGER THAT, CAVALIER 415! HANG TIGHT, WE'RE SCRAMBLING A CHOPPER, STAND BY--
ROBERT DE NIRO? WHO THE FUCK IS HE?
SLEEPIN' LIKE BABIES. NEAR ENOUGH THE BORDER, MAY AS WELL CALL IT A SIESTA.
WHAT ABOUT THE HUMVEE?
FLIP IT.

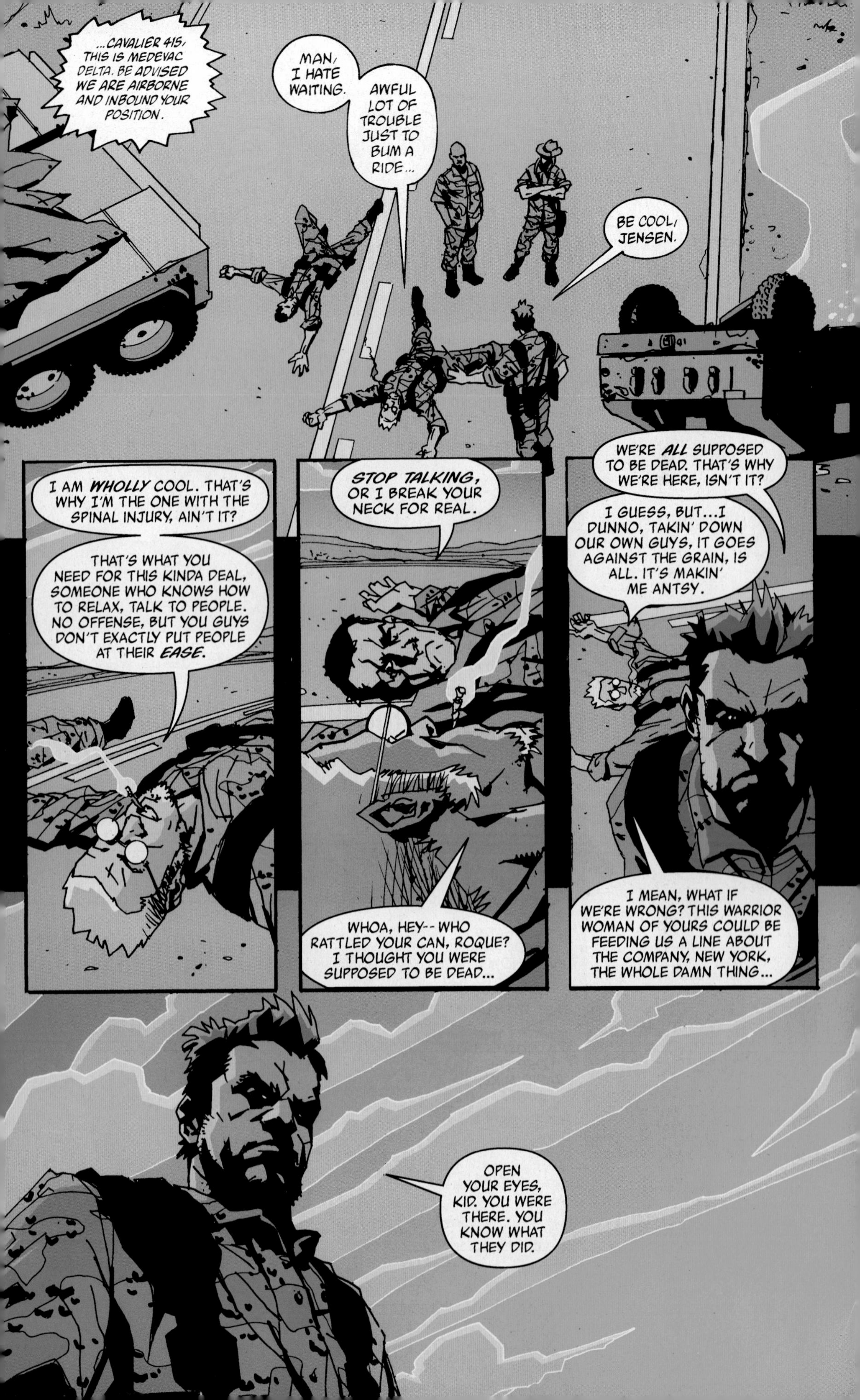
...CAVALIER 415, THIS IS MEDEVAC DELTA. BE ADVISED WE ARE AIRBORNE AND INBOUND YOUR POSITION.
MAN, I HATE WAITING.
AWFUL LOT OF TROUBLE JUST TO BUM A RIDE...
BE COOL, JENSEN.
I AM WHOLLY COOL. THAT'S WHY I'M THE ONE WITH THE SPINAL INJURY, AIN'T IT?
THAT'S WHAT YOU NEED FOR THIS KINDA DEAL, SOMEONE WHO KNOWS HOW TO RELAX, TALK TO PEOPLE. NO OFFENSE, BUT YOU GUYS DON'T EXACTLY PUT PEOPLE AT THEIR EASE.
STOP TALKING, OR I BREAK YOUR NECK FOR REAL.
WHOA, HEY-- WHO RATTLED YOUR CAN, ROQUE? I THOUGHT YOU WERE SUPPOSED TO BE DEAD...
WE'RE ALL SUPPOSED TO BE DEAD. THAT'S WHY WE'RE HERE, ISN'T IT?
I GUESS, BUT...I DUNNO, TAKIN' DOWN OUR OWN GUYS, IT GOES AGAINST THE GRAIN, IS ALL. IT'S MAKIN' ME ANTSY.
I MEAN, WHAT IF WE'RE WRONG? THIS WARRIOR WOMAN OF YOURS COULD BE FEEDING US A LINE ABOUT THE COMPANY, NEW YORK, THE WHOLE DAMN THING...
OPEN YOUR EYES, KID. YOU WERE THERE. YOU KNOW WHAT THEY DID.

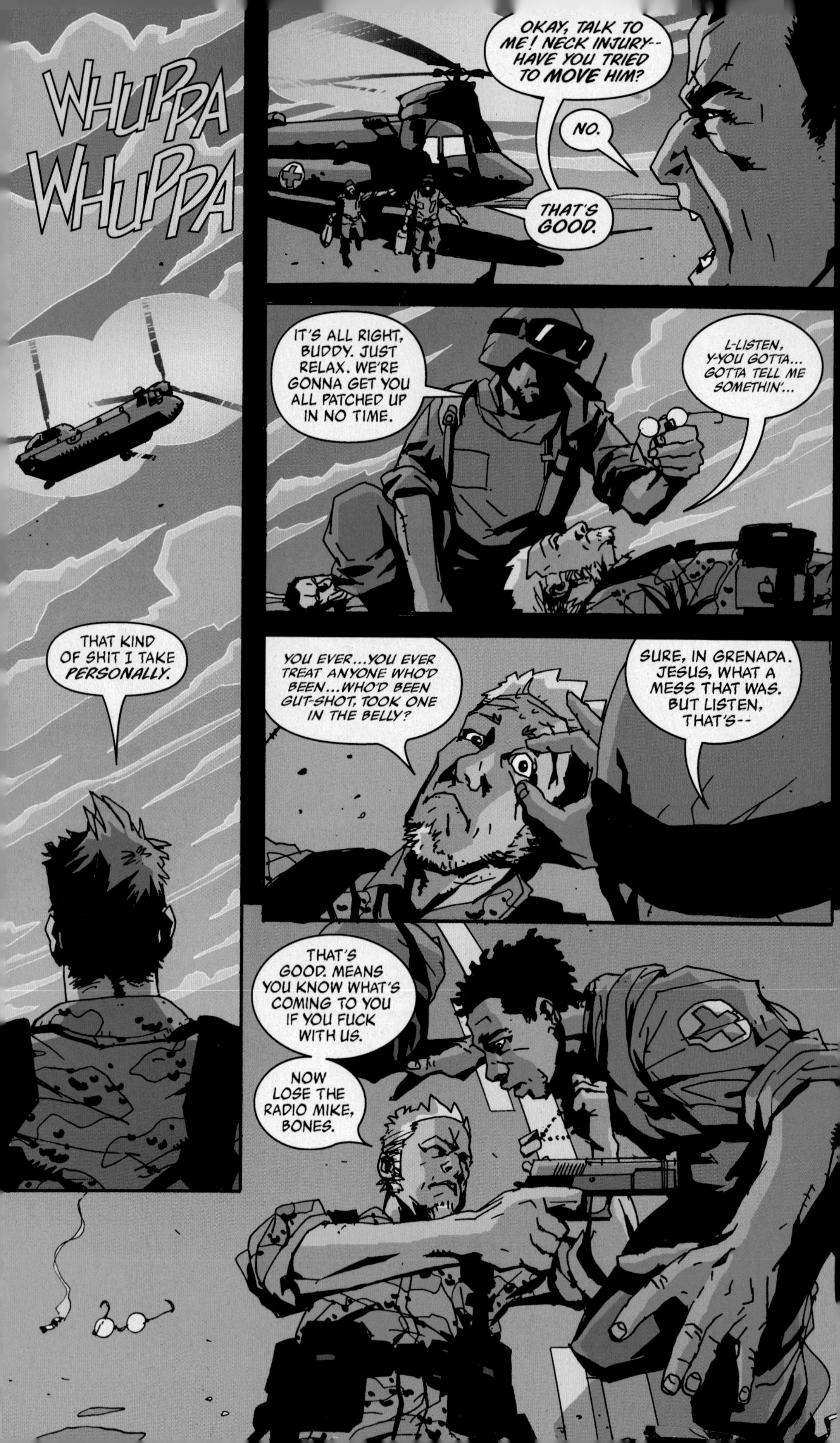
WHUPPA WHUPPA
OKAY, TALK TO ME! NECK INJURY--HAVE YOU TRIED TO MOVE HIM?
NO.
THAT'S GOOD.
IT'S ALL RIGHT, BUDDY. JUST RELAX. WE'RE GONNA GET YOU ALL PATCHED UP IN NO TIME.
L-LISTEN, Y-YOU GOTTA... GOTTA TELL ME SOMETHIN'...
THAT KIND OF SHIT I TAKE PERSONALLY.
YOU EVER...YOU EVER TREAT ANYONE WHO'D BEEN...WHO'D BEEN GUT-SHOT, TOOK ONE IN THE BELLY?
SURE, IN GRENADA. JESUS, WHAT A MESS THAT WAS. BUT LISTEN, THAT'S--
THAT'S GOOD. MEANS YOU KNOW WHAT'S COMING TO YOU IF YOU FUCK WITH US.
NOW LOSE THE RADIO MIKE, BONES.

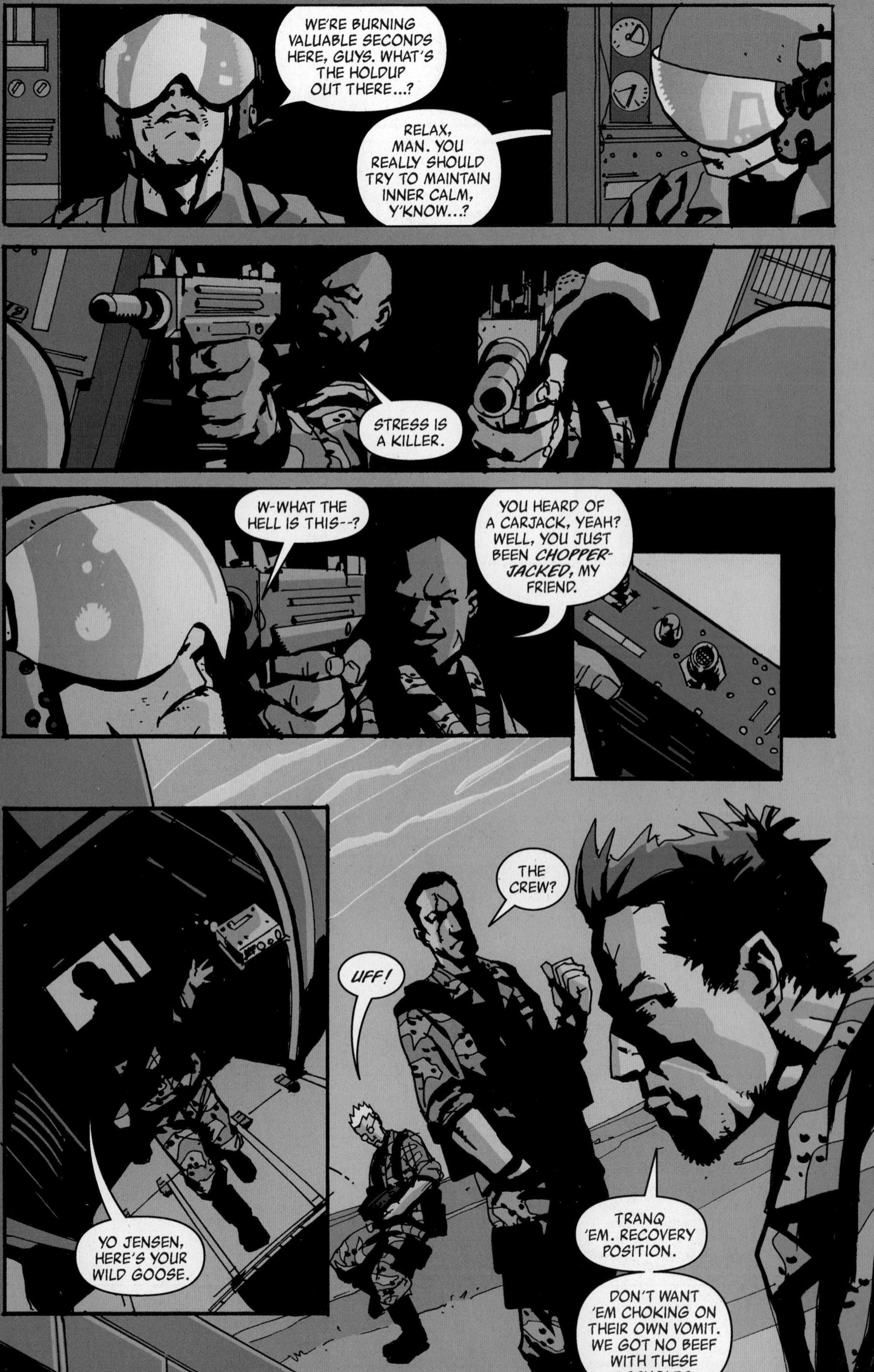

WE'RE BURNING VALUABLE SECONDS HERE, GUYS. WHAT'S THE HOLDUP OUT THERE...?
RELAX, MAN. YOU REALLY SHOULD TRY TO MAINTAIN INNER CALM, Y'KNOW...?
STRESS IS A KILLER.
W-WHAT THE HELL IS THIS--?
YOU HEARD OF A CARJACK, YEAH? WELL, YOU JUST BEEN *CHOPPER-JACKED*, MY FRIEND.
THE CREW?
UFF!
YO JENSEN, HERE'S YOUR WILD GOOSE.
TRANQ 'EM. RECOVERY POSITION.
DON'T WANT 'EM CHOKING ON THEIR OWN VOMIT. WE GOT NO BEEF WITH THESE ASSHOLES.

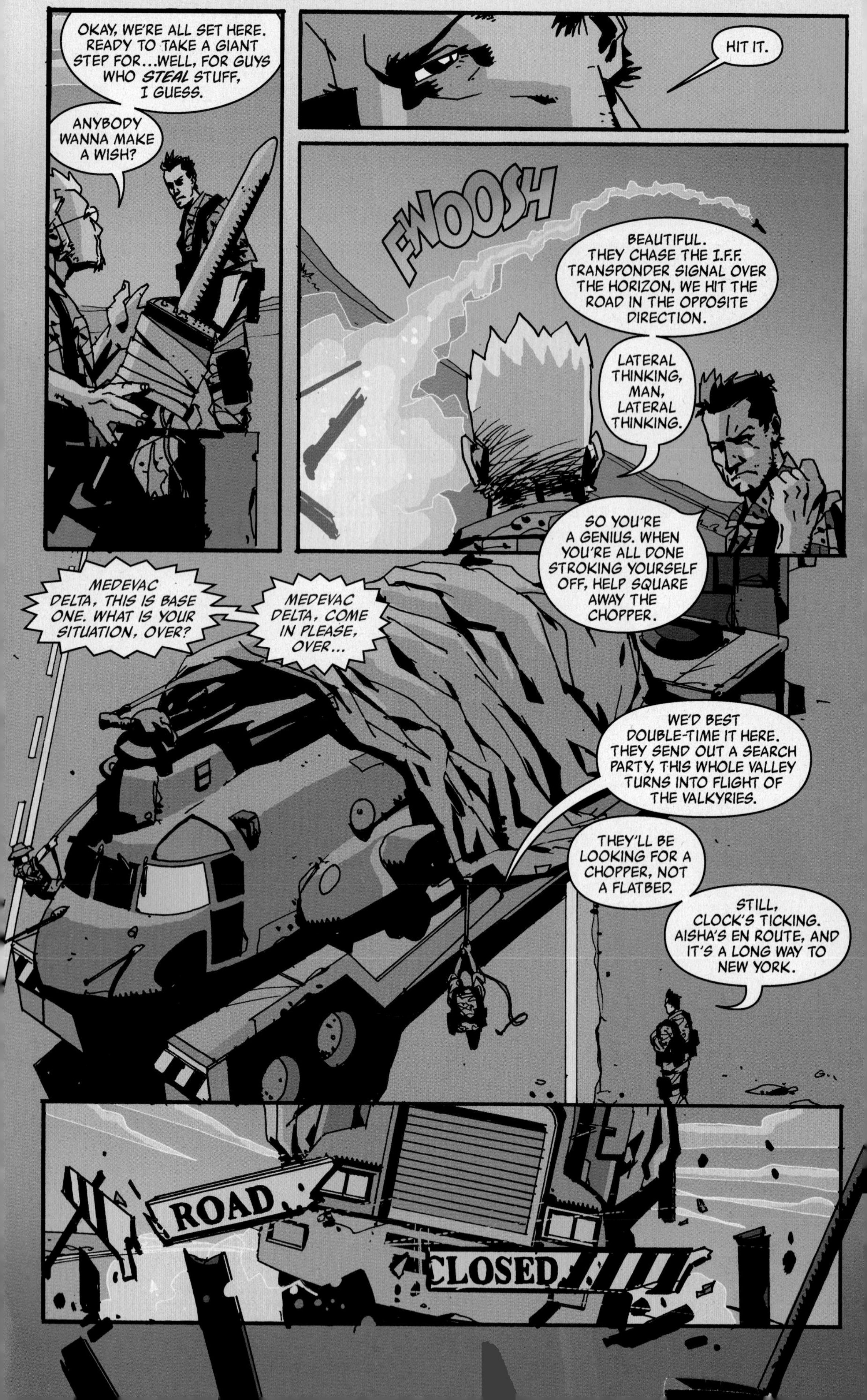
OKAY, WE'RE ALL SET HERE. READY TO TAKE A GIANT STEP FOR...WELL, FOR GUYS WHO *STEAL* STUFF, I GUESS.
ANYBODY WANNA MAKE A WISH?
HIT IT.
FWOOSH
BEAUTIFUL. THEY CHASE THE I.F.F. TRANSPONDER SIGNAL OVER THE HORIZON, WE HIT THE ROAD IN THE OPPOSITE DIRECTION.
LATERAL THINKING, MAN, LATERAL THINKING.
SO YOU'RE A GENIUS. WHEN YOU'RE ALL DONE STROKING YOURSELF OFF, HELP SQUARE AWAY THE CHOPPER.
MEDEVAC DELTA, THIS IS BASE ONE. WHAT IS YOUR SITUATION, OVER?
MEDEVAC DELTA, COME IN PLEASE, OVER...
WE'D BEST DOUBLE-TIME IT HERE. THEY SEND OUT A SEARCH PARTY, THIS WHOLE VALLEY TURNS INTO FLIGHT OF THE VALKYRIES.
THEY'LL BE LOOKING FOR A CHOPPER, NOT A FLATBED.
STILL, CLOCK'S TICKING. AISHA'S EN ROUTE, AND IT'S A LONG WAY TO NEW YORK.
ROAD
CLOSED

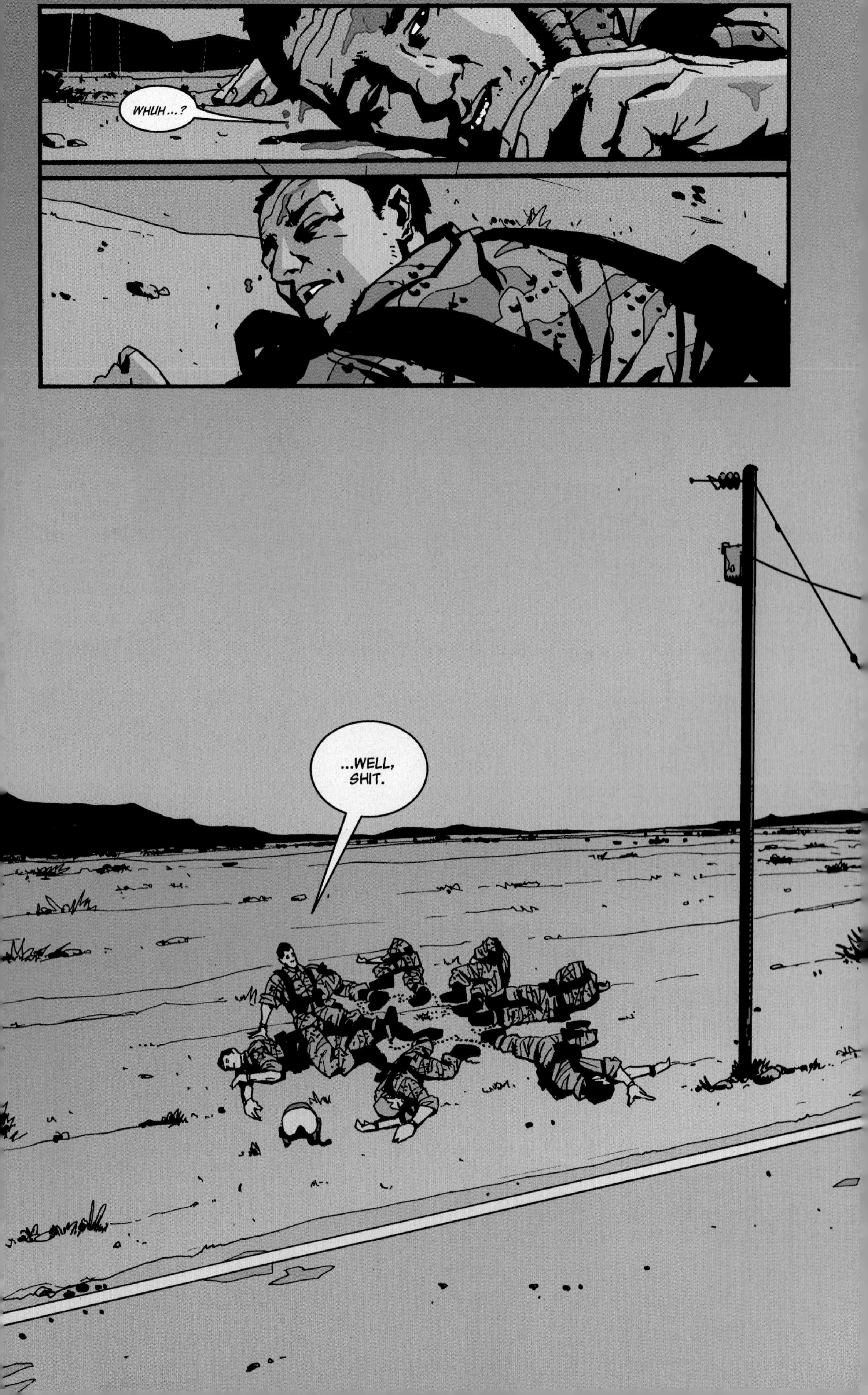
WHUH...?
...WELL, SHIT.

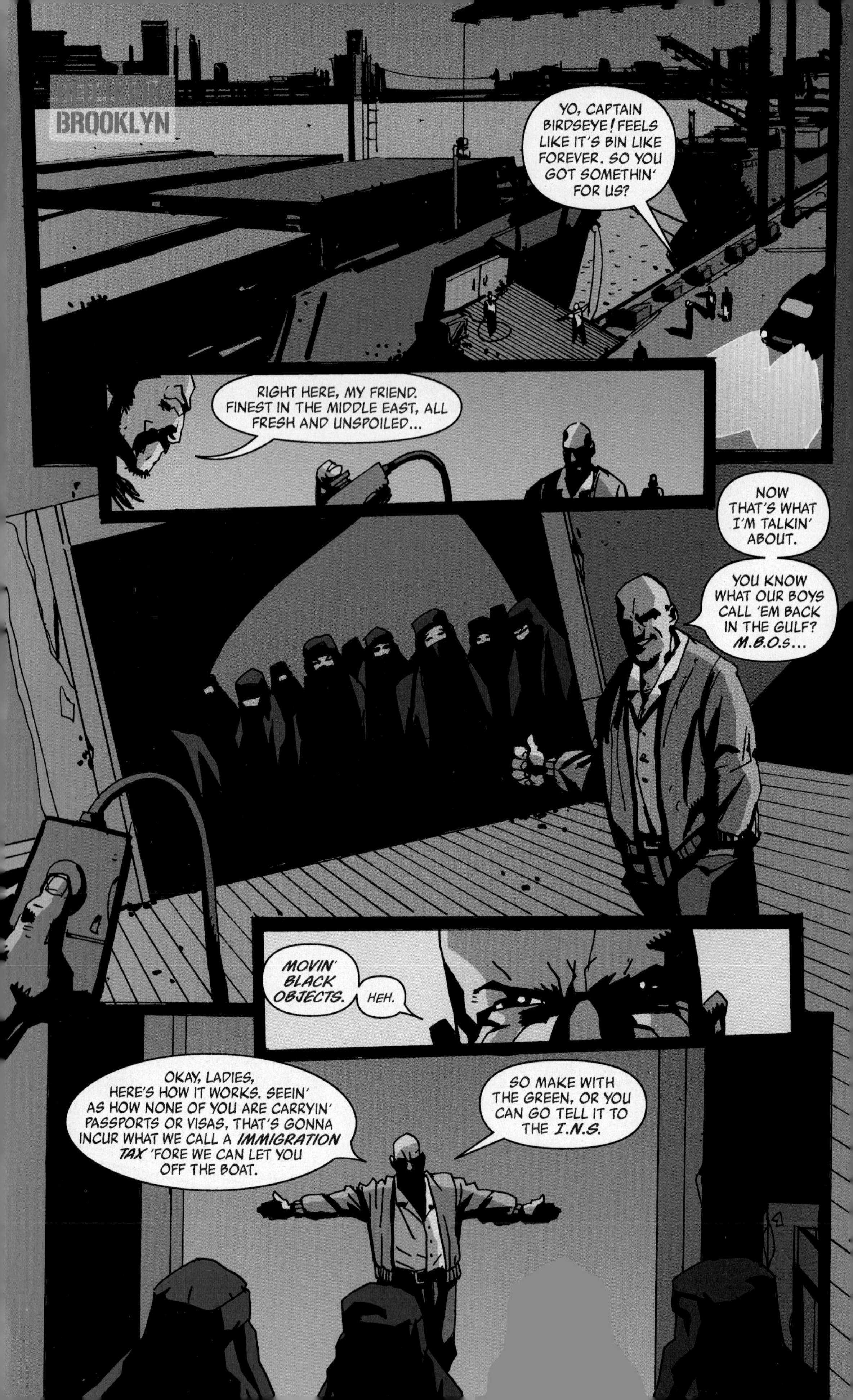
RED HOOK,
BROOKLYN
YO, CAPTAIN BIRDSEYE! FEELS LIKE IT'S BIN LIKE FOREVER. SO YOU GOT SOMETHIN' FOR US?
RIGHT HERE, MY FRIEND. FINEST IN THE MIDDLE EAST, ALL FRESH AND UNSPOILED...
NOW THAT'S WHAT I'M TALKIN' ABOUT.
YOU KNOW WHAT OUR BOYS CALL 'EM BACK IN THE GULF? *M.B.O.s...*
MOVIN' BLACK OBJECTS.
HEH.
OKAY, LADIES, HERE'S HOW IT WORKS. SEEIN' AS HOW NONE OF YOU ARE CARRYIN' PASSPORTS OR VISAS, THAT'S GONNA INCUR WHAT WE CALL A *IMMIGRATION TAX* 'FORE WE CAN LET YOU OFF THE BOAT.
SO MAKE WITH THE GREEN, OR YOU CAN GO TELL IT TO THE *I.N.S.*

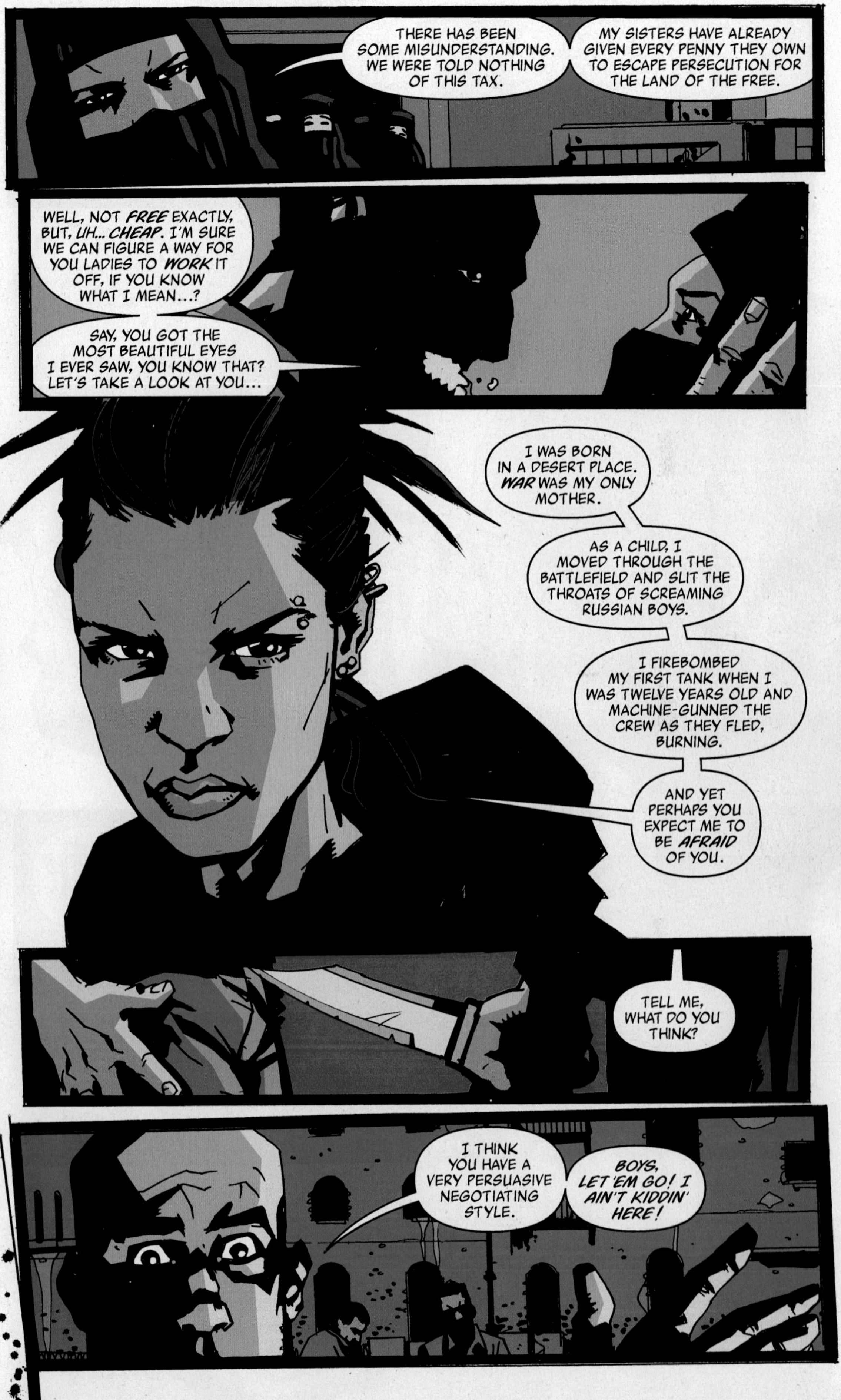
THERE HAS BEEN SOME MISUNDERSTANDING. WE WERE TOLD NOTHING OF THIS TAX.
MY SISTERS HAVE ALREADY GIVEN EVERY PENNY THEY OWN TO ESCAPE PERSECUTION FOR THE LAND OF THE FREE.
WELL, NOT *FREE* EXACTLY, BUT, *UH... CHEAP*. I'M SURE WE CAN FIGURE A WAY FOR YOU LADIES TO *WORK* IT OFF, IF YOU KNOW WHAT I MEAN...?
SAY, YOU GOT THE MOST BEAUTIFUL EYES I EVER SAW, YOU KNOW THAT? LET'S TAKE A LOOK AT YOU...
I WAS BORN IN A DESERT PLACE. *WAR* WAS MY ONLY MOTHER.
AS A CHILD, I MOVED THROUGH THE BATTLEFIELD AND SLIT THE THROATS OF SCREAMING RUSSIAN BOYS.
I FIREBOMBED MY FIRST TANK WHEN I WAS TWELVE YEARS OLD AND MACHINE-GUNNED THE CREW AS THEY FLED, BURNING.
AND YET PERHAPS YOU EXPECT ME TO BE *AFRAID* OF YOU.
TELL ME, WHAT DO YOU THINK?
I THINK YOU HAVE A VERY PERSUASIVE NEGOTIATING STYLE.
BOYS, LET 'EM GO! I AIN'T KIDDIN' HERE!

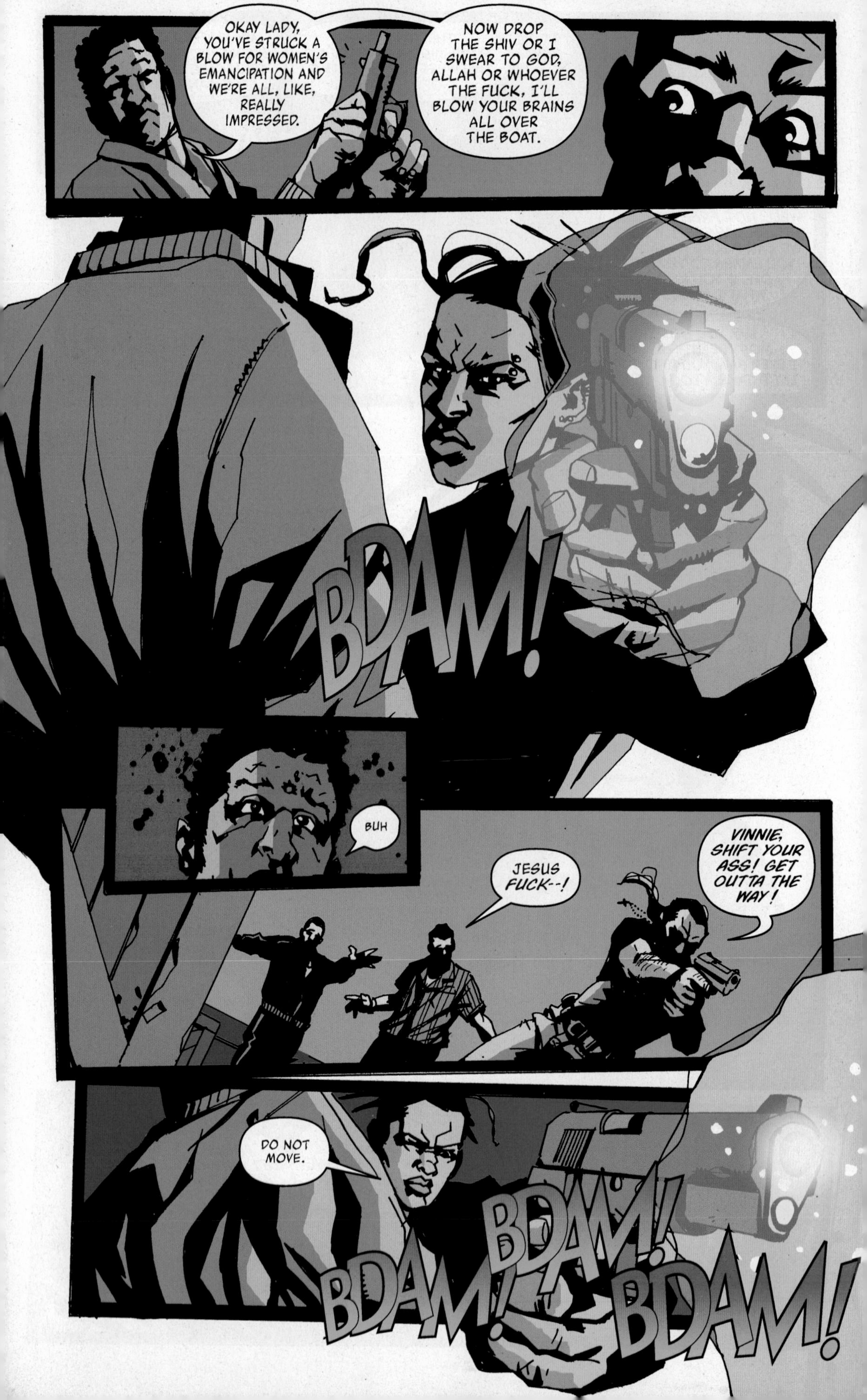
OKAY LADY, YOU'VE STRUCK A BLOW FOR WOMEN'S EMANCIPATION AND WE'RE ALL, LIKE, REALLY IMPRESSED.
NOW DROP THE SHIV OR I SWEAR TO GOD, ALLAH OR WHOEVER THE FUCK, I'LL BLOW YOUR BRAINS ALL OVER THE BOAT.
BDAM!
BUH
JESUS FUCK--!
VINNIE, SHIFT YOUR ASS! GET OUTTA THE WAY!
DO NOT MOVE.
BDAM!
BDAM!
BDAM!

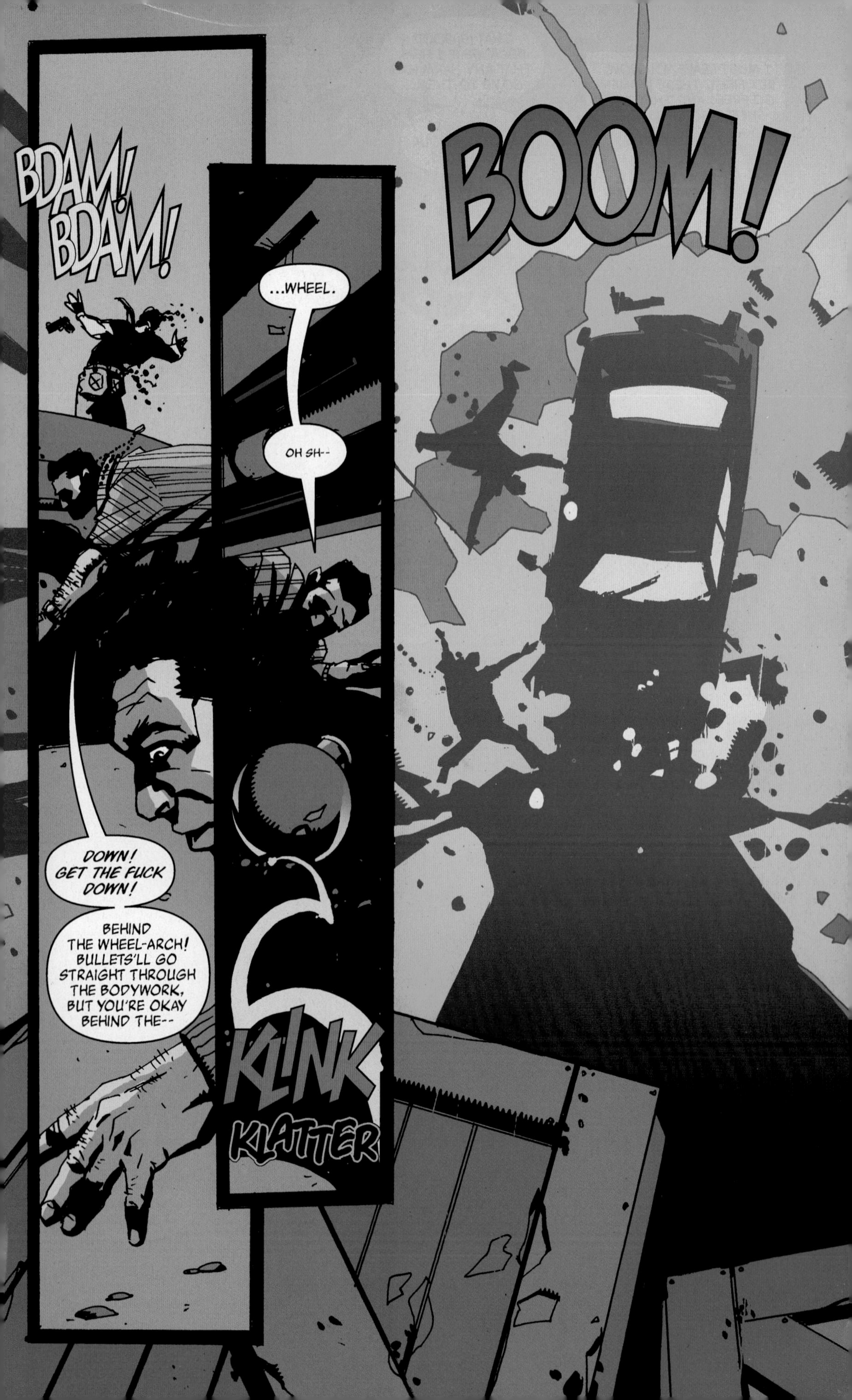
BDAM! BDAM!
...WHEEL.
OH SH--
DOWN! GET THE FUCK DOWN!
BEHIND THE WHEEL-ARCH! BULLETS'LL GO STRAIGHT THROUGH THE BODYWORK, BUT YOU'RE OKAY BEHIND THE--
KLINK
KLATTER
BOOM!

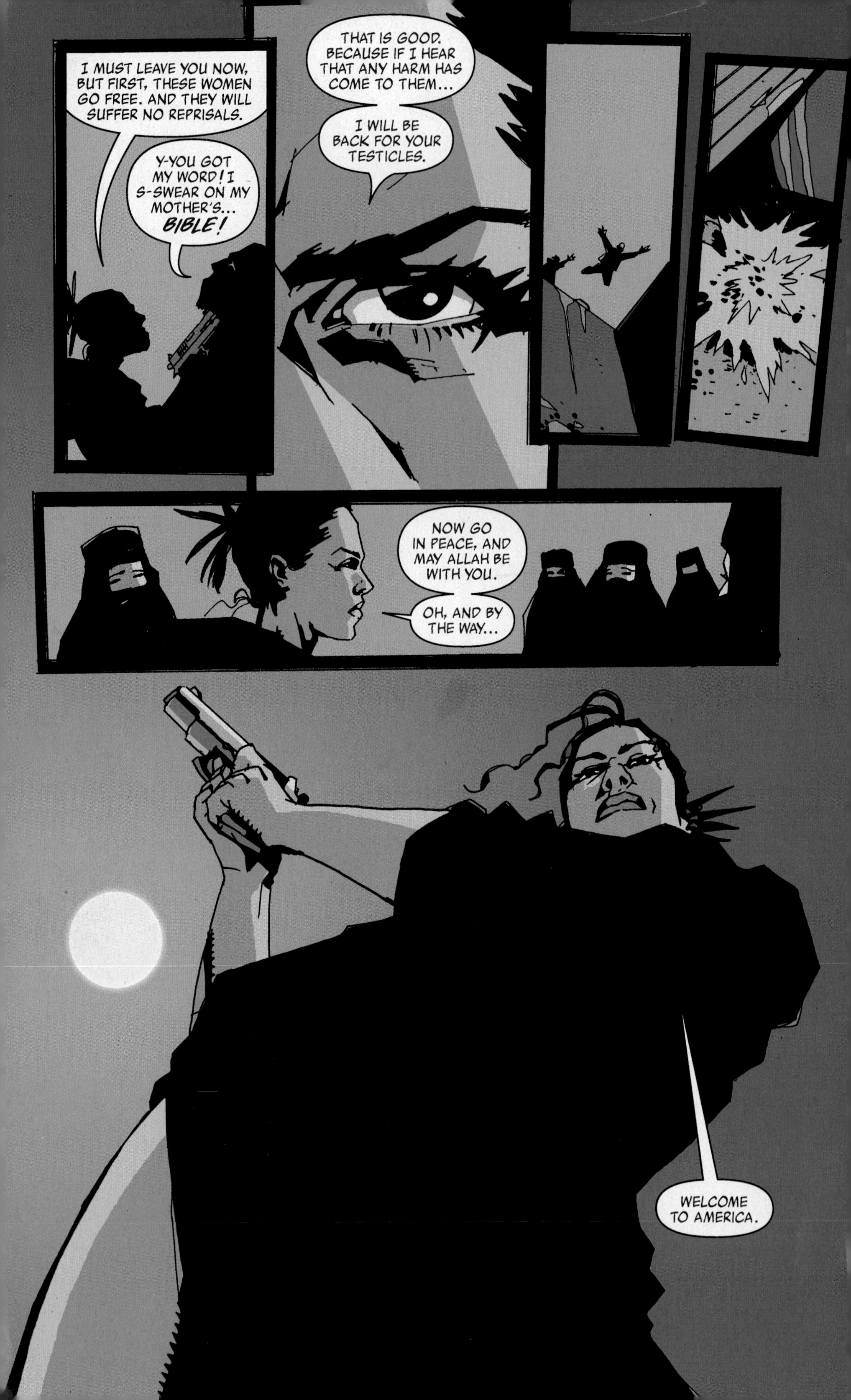

I MUST LEAVE YOU NOW, BUT FIRST, THESE WOMEN GO FREE. AND THEY WILL SUFFER NO REPRISALS.
Y-YOU GOT MY WORD! I S-SWEAR ON MY MOTHER'S... BIBLE!
THAT IS GOOD. BECAUSE IF I HEAR THAT ANY HARM HAS COME TO THEM...
I WILL BE BACK FOR YOUR TESTICLES.
NOW GO IN PEACE, AND MAY ALLAH BE WITH YOU.
OH, AND BY THE WAY...
WELCOME TO AMERICA.

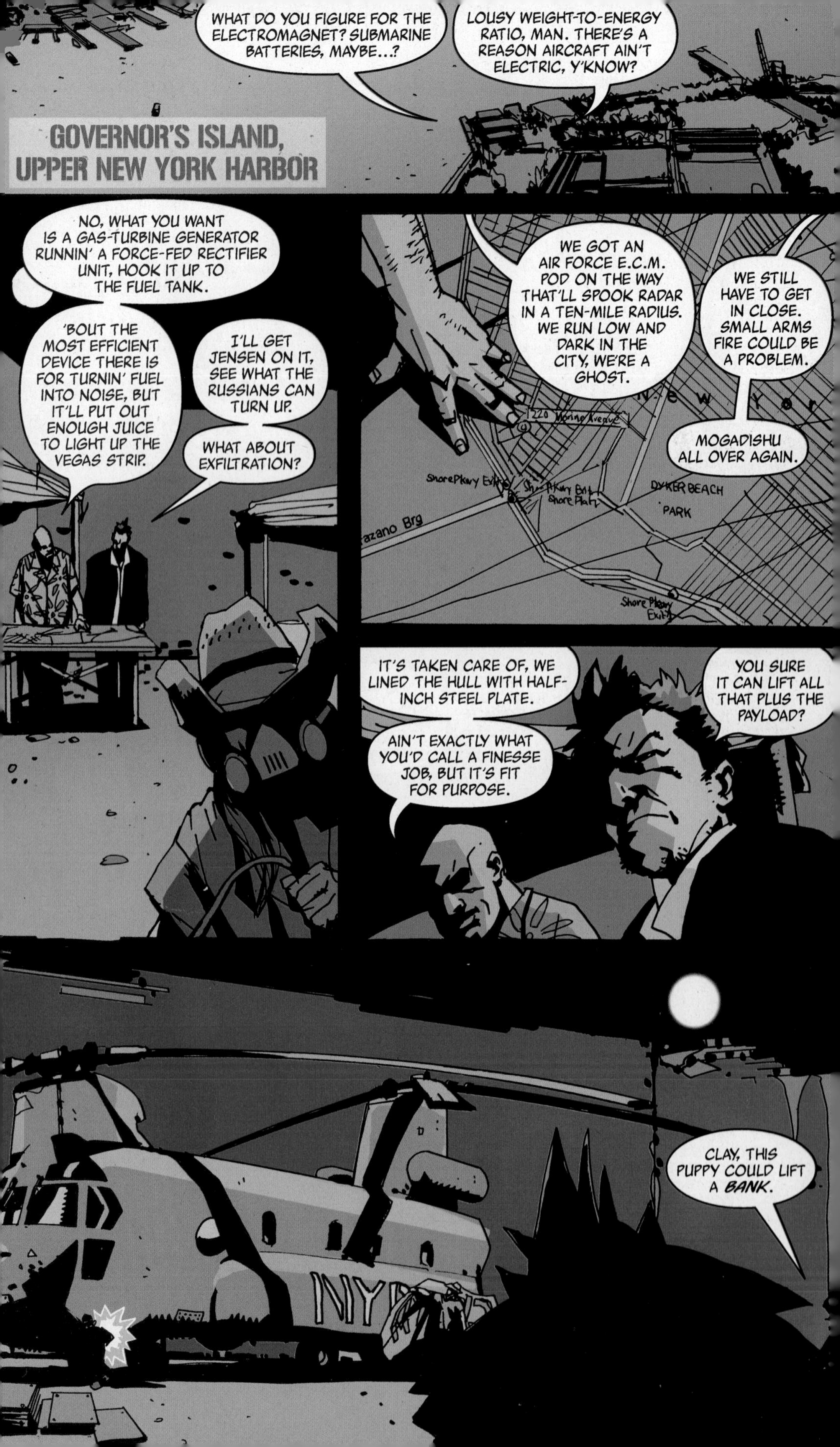

WHAT DO YOU FIGURE FOR THE ELECTROMAGNET? SUBMARINE BATTERIES, MAYBE...?
LOUSY WEIGHT-TO-ENERGY RATIO, MAN. THERE'S A REASON AIRCRAFT AIN'T ELECTRIC, Y'KNOW?
GOVERNOR'S ISLAND, UPPER NEW YORK HARBOR
NO, WHAT YOU WANT IS A GAS-TURBINE GENERATOR RUNNIN' A FORCE-FED RECTIFIER UNIT, HOOK IT UP TO THE FUEL TANK.
'BOUT THE MOST EFFICIENT DEVICE THERE IS FOR TURNIN' FUEL INTO NOISE, BUT IT'LL PUT OUT ENOUGH JUICE TO LIGHT UP THE VEGAS STRIP.
I'LL GET JENSEN ON IT, SEE WHAT THE RUSSIANS CAN TURN UP.
WHAT ABOUT EXFILTRATION?
WE GOT AN AIR FORCE E.C.M. POD ON THE WAY THAT'LL SPOOK RADAR IN A TEN-MILE RADIUS. WE RUN LOW AND DARK IN THE CITY, WE'RE A GHOST.
WE STILL HAVE TO GET IN CLOSE. SMALL ARMS FIRE COULD BE A PROBLEM.
MOGADISHU ALL OVER AGAIN.
220 Marine Avenue
Shore Pkwy Exit
Shore Pkwy Brk
DYKER BEACH PARK
azano Brg
Shore Pkwy Exit
IT'S TAKEN CARE OF, WE LINED THE HULL WITH HALF-INCH STEEL PLATE.
AIN'T EXACTLY WHAT YOU'D CALL A FINESSE JOB, BUT IT'S FIT FOR PURPOSE.
YOU SURE IT CAN LIFT ALL THAT PLUS THE PAYLOAD?
CLAY, THIS PUPPY COULD LIFT A *BANK*.

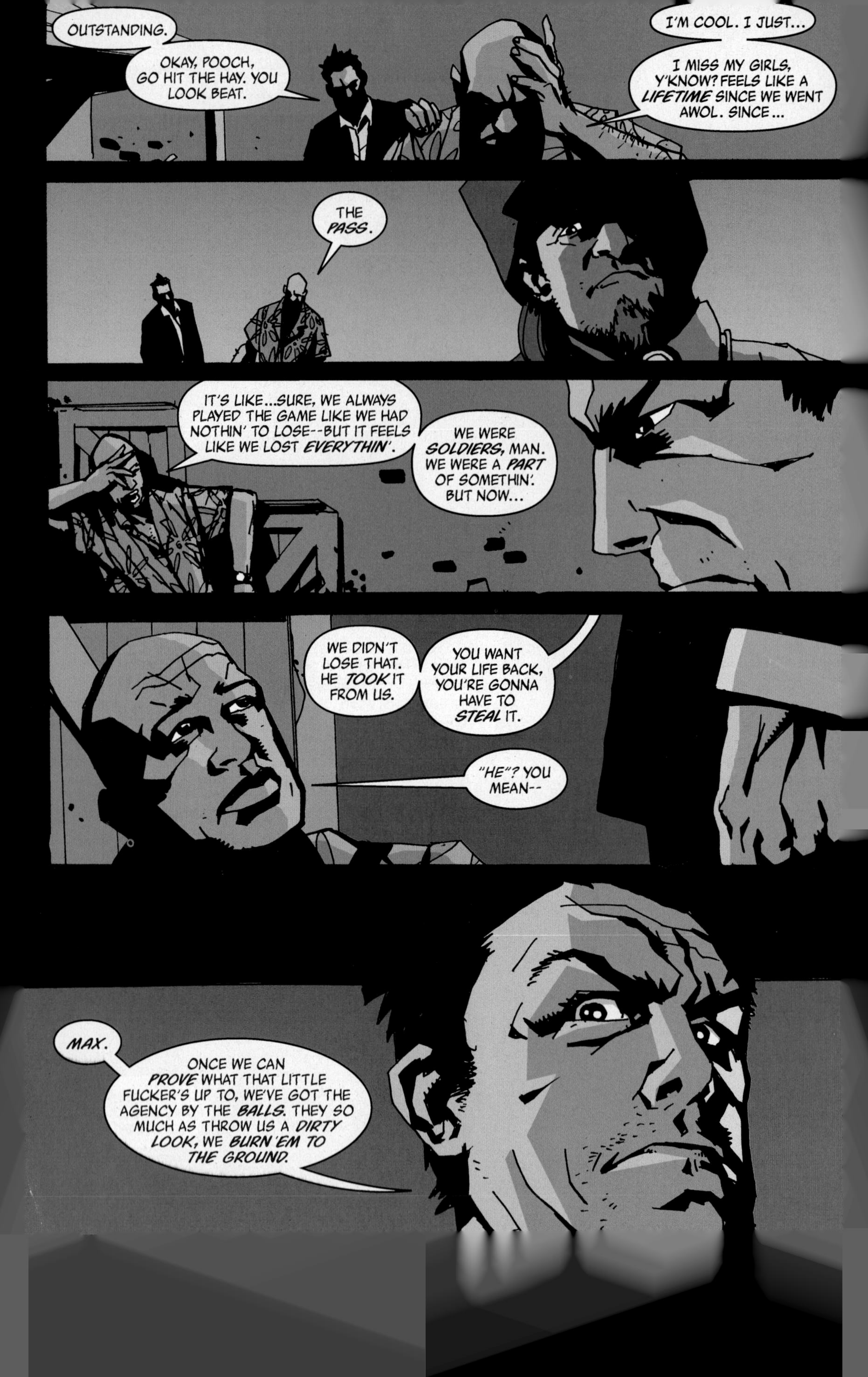
OUTSTANDING.
OKAY, POOCH, GO HIT THE HAY. YOU LOOK BEAT.
I'M COOL. I JUST...
I MISS MY GIRLS, Y'KNOW? FEELS LIKE A LIFETIME SINCE WE WENT AWOL. SINCE...
THE PASS.
IT'S LIKE...SURE, WE ALWAYS PLAYED THE GAME LIKE WE HAD NOTHIN' TO LOSE--BUT IT FEELS LIKE WE LOST EVERYTHIN'.
WE WERE SOLDIERS, MAN. WE WERE A PART OF SOMETHIN'. BUT NOW...
YOU WANT YOUR LIFE BACK, YOU'RE GONNA HAVE TO STEAL IT.
WE DIDN'T LOSE THAT. HE TOOK IT FROM US.
"HE"? YOU MEAN--
MAX.
ONCE WE CAN PROVE WHAT THAT LITTLE FUCKER'S UP TO, WE'VE GOT THE AGENCY BY THE BALLS. THEY SO MUCH AS THROW US A DIRTY LOOK, WE BURN 'EM TO THE GROUND.

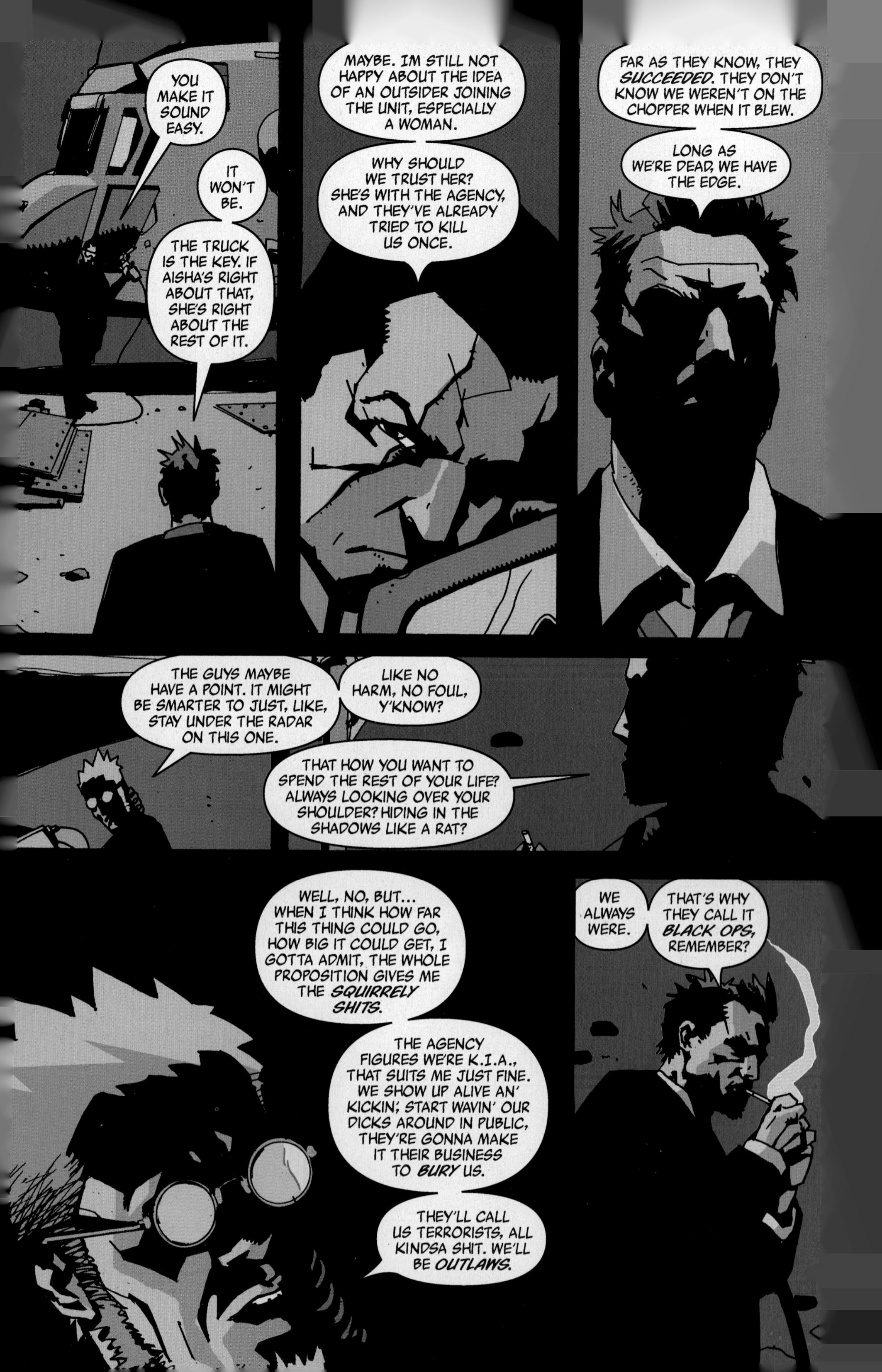
YOU MAKE IT SOUND EASY.
IT WON'T BE.
THE TRUCK IS THE KEY. IF AISHA'S RIGHT ABOUT THAT, SHE'S RIGHT ABOUT THE REST OF IT.
MAYBE. I'M STILL NOT HAPPY ABOUT THE IDEA OF AN OUTSIDER JOINING THE UNIT, ESPECIALLY A WOMAN.
WHY SHOULD WE TRUST HER? SHE'S WITH THE AGENCY, AND THEY'VE ALREADY TRIED TO KILL US ONCE.
FAR AS THEY KNOW, THEY *SUCCEEDED*. THEY DON'T KNOW WE WEREN'T ON THE CHOPPER WHEN IT BLEW.
LONG AS WE'RE DEAD, WE HAVE THE EDGE.
THE GUYS MAYBE HAVE A POINT. IT MIGHT BE SMARTER TO JUST, LIKE, STAY UNDER THE RADAR ON THIS ONE.
LIKE NO HARM, NO FOUL, Y'KNOW?
THAT HOW YOU WANT TO SPEND THE REST OF YOUR LIFE? ALWAYS LOOKING OVER YOUR SHOULDER? HIDING IN THE SHADOWS LIKE A RAT?
WELL, NO, BUT... WHEN I THINK HOW FAR THIS THING COULD GO, HOW BIG IT COULD GET, I GOTTA ADMIT, THE WHOLE PROPOSITION GIVES ME THE *SQUIRRELY SHITS*.
THE AGENCY FIGURES WE'RE K.I.A., THAT SUITS ME JUST FINE. WE SHOW UP ALIVE AN' KICKIN', START WAVIN' OUR DICKS AROUND IN PUBLIC, THEY'RE GONNA MAKE IT THEIR BUSINESS TO *BURY* US.
THEY'LL CALL US TERRORISTS, ALL KINDSA SHIT. WE'LL BE *OUTLAWS*.
WE ALWAYS WERE.
THAT'S WHY THEY CALL IT *BLACK OPS*, REMEMBER?

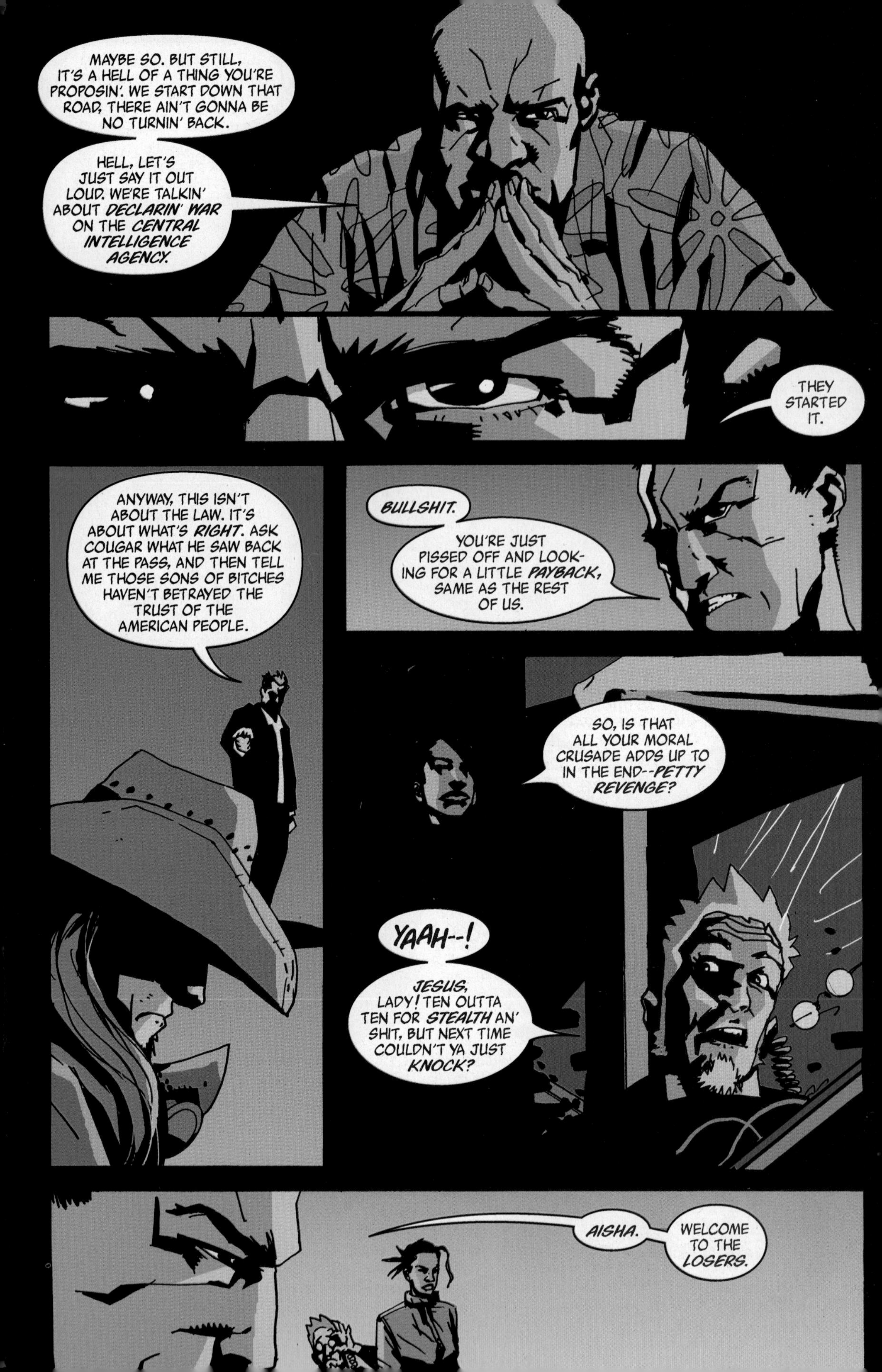
MAYBE SO. BUT STILL, IT'S A HELL OF A THING YOU'RE PROPOSIN'. WE START DOWN THAT ROAD, THERE AIN'T GONNA BE NO TURNIN' BACK.
HELL, LET'S JUST SAY IT OUT LOUD. WE'RE TALKIN' ABOUT DECLARIN' WAR ON THE CENTRAL INTELLIGENCE AGENCY.
THEY STARTED IT.
ANYWAY, THIS ISN'T ABOUT THE LAW. IT'S ABOUT WHAT'S RIGHT. ASK COUGAR WHAT HE SAW BACK AT THE PASS, AND THEN TELL ME THOSE SONS OF BITCHES HAVEN'T BETRAYED THE TRUST OF THE AMERICAN PEOPLE.
BULLSHIT.
YOU'RE JUST PISSED OFF AND LOOKING FOR A LITTLE PAYBACK, SAME AS THE REST OF US.
SO, IS THAT ALL YOUR MORAL CRUSADE ADDS UP TO IN THE END--PETTY REVENGE?
YAAH--!
JESUS, LADY! TEN OUTTA TEN FOR STEALTH AN' SHIT, BUT NEXT TIME COULDN'T YA JUST KNOCK?
AISHA.
WELCOME TO THE LOSERS.

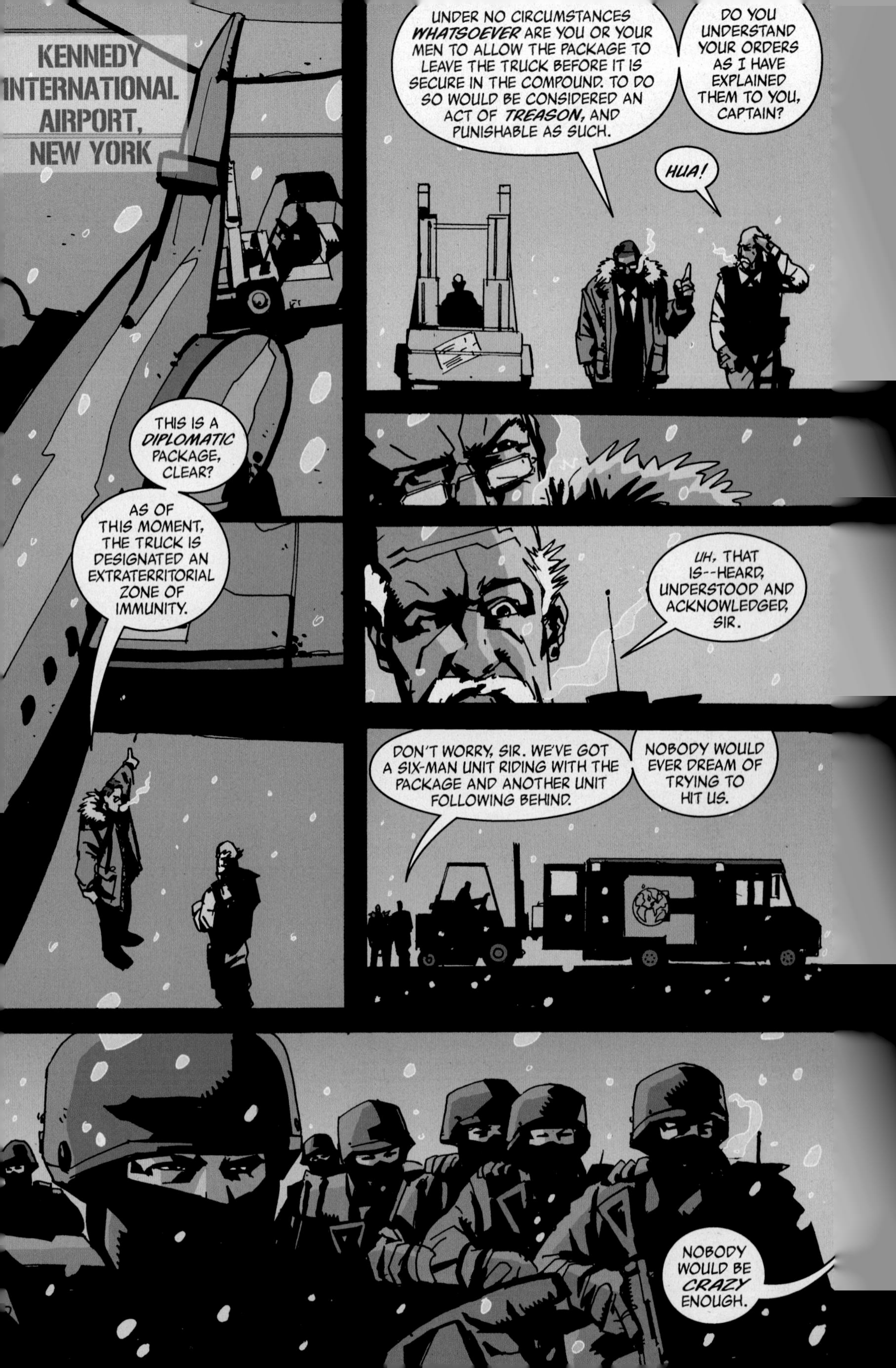
KENNEDY INTERNATIONAL AIRPORT, NEW YORK
UNDER NO CIRCUMSTANCES WHATSOEVER ARE YOU OR YOUR MEN TO ALLOW THE PACKAGE TO LEAVE THE TRUCK BEFORE IT IS SECURE IN THE COMPOUND. TO DO SO WOULD BE CONSIDERED AN ACT OF TREASON, AND PUNISHABLE AS SUCH.
DO YOU UNDERSTAND YOUR ORDERS AS I HAVE EXPLAINED THEM TO YOU, CAPTAIN?
HUA!
THIS IS A DIPLOMATIC PACKAGE, CLEAR?
AS OF THIS MOMENT, THE TRUCK IS DESIGNATED AN EXTRATERRITORIAL ZONE OF IMMUNITY.
UH, THAT IS--HEARD, UNDERSTOOD AND ACKNOWLEDGED, SIR.
DON'T WORRY, SIR. WE'VE GOT A SIX-MAN UNIT RIDING WITH THE PACKAGE AND ANOTHER UNIT FOLLOWING BEHIND.
NOBODY WOULD EVER DREAM OF TRYING TO HIT US.
NOBODY WOULD BE CRAZY ENOUGH.

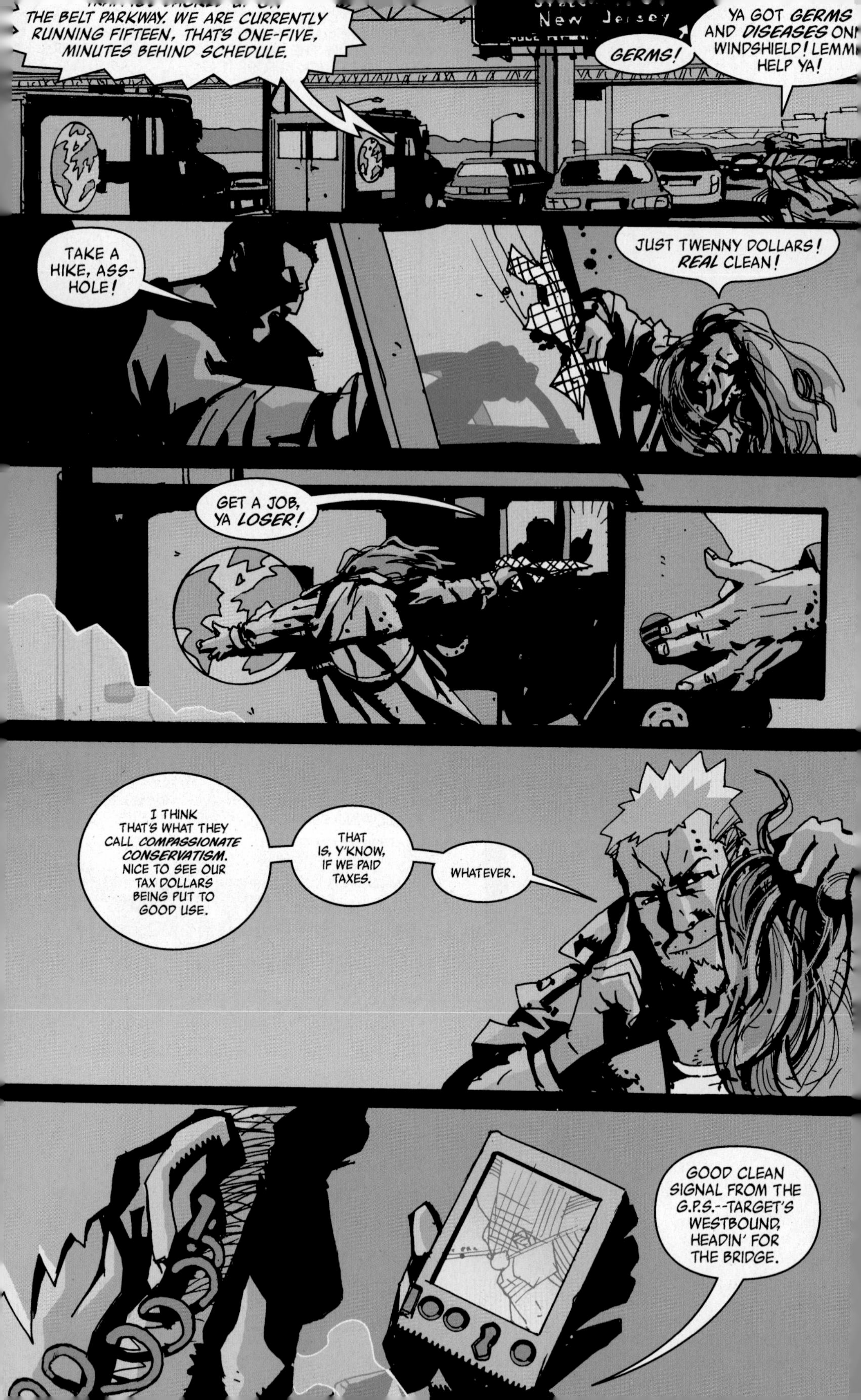
THE BELT PARKWAY. WE ARE CURRENTLY RUNNING FIFTEEN, THAT'S ONE-FIVE, MINUTES BEHIND SCHEDULE.
New Jersey
GERMS!
YA GOT GERMS AND DISEASES ONN WINDSHIELD! LEMM HELP YA!
TAKE A HIKE, ASS-HOLE!
JUST TWENNY DOLLARS! REAL CLEAN!
GET A JOB, YA LOSER!
I THINK THAT'S WHAT THEY CALL COMPASSIONATE CONSERVATISM. NICE TO SEE OUR TAX DOLLARS BEING PUT TO GOOD USE.
THAT IS, Y'KNOW, IF WE PAID TAXES.
WHATEVER.
GOOD CLEAN SIGNAL FROM THE G.P.S.--TARGET'S WESTBOUND, HEADIN' FOR THE BRIDGE.

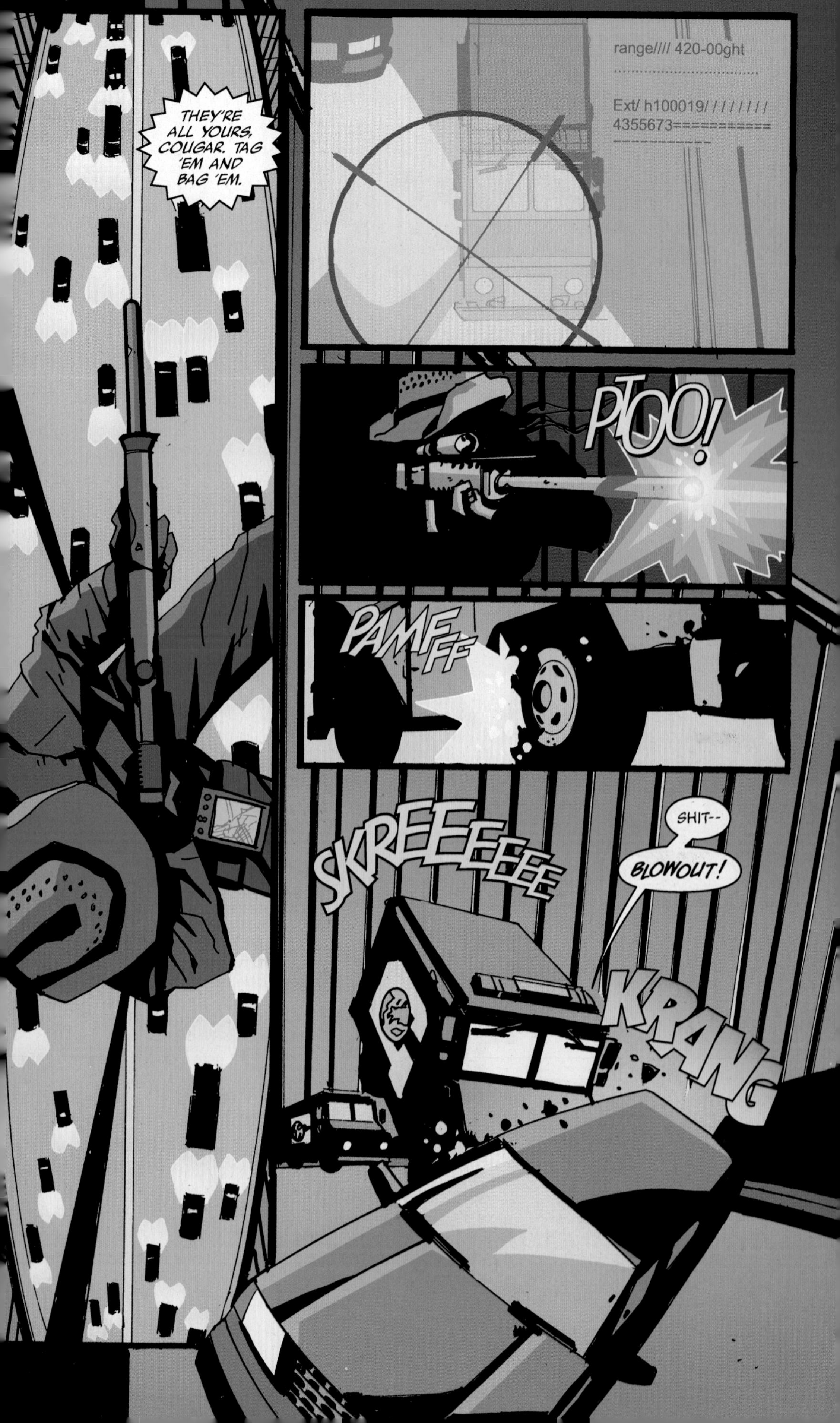
THEY'RE ALL YOURS, COUGAR. TAG 'EM AND BAG 'EM.
range//// 420-00ght
Ext/ h100019/ / / / / / / /
4355673===========
PTOOO!
PAMFFF
SKREEEEEEE
SHIT--
BLOWOUT!
KRANG

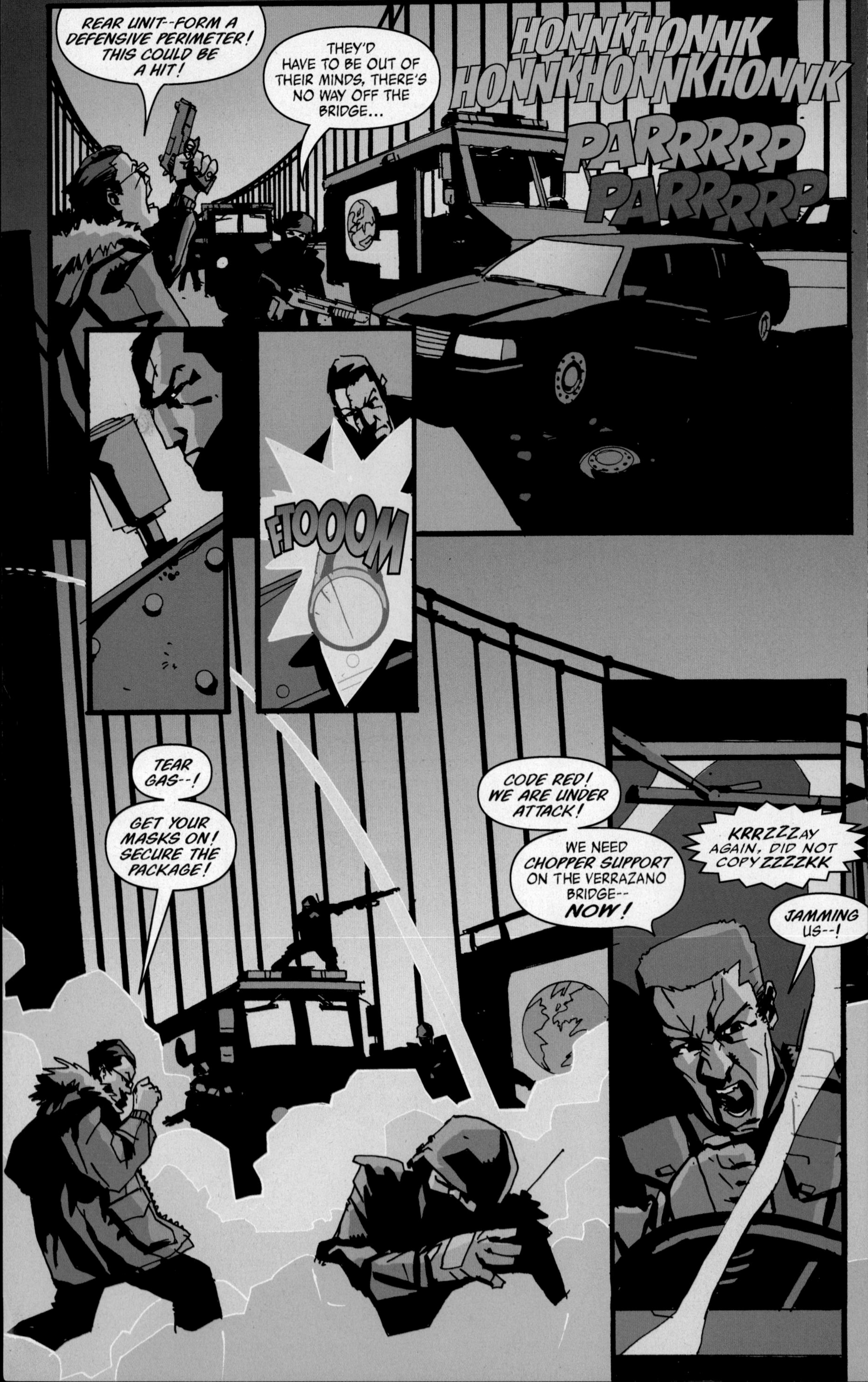
REAR UNIT--FORM A DEFENSIVE PERIMETER! THIS COULD BE A HIT!
THEY'D HAVE TO BE OUT OF THEIR MINDS, THERE'S NO WAY OFF THE BRIDGE...
HONNKHONNK
HONNKHONNKHONNK
PARRRRP
PARRRRP
FTOOOM
TEAR GAS--!
GET YOUR MASKS ON! SECURE THE PACKAGE!
CODE RED! WE ARE UNDER ATTACK!
WE NEED CHOPPER SUPPORT ON THE VERRAZANO BRIDGE-- NOW!
KRRZZZAY AGAIN, DID NOT COPYZZZZKK
JAMMING US--!

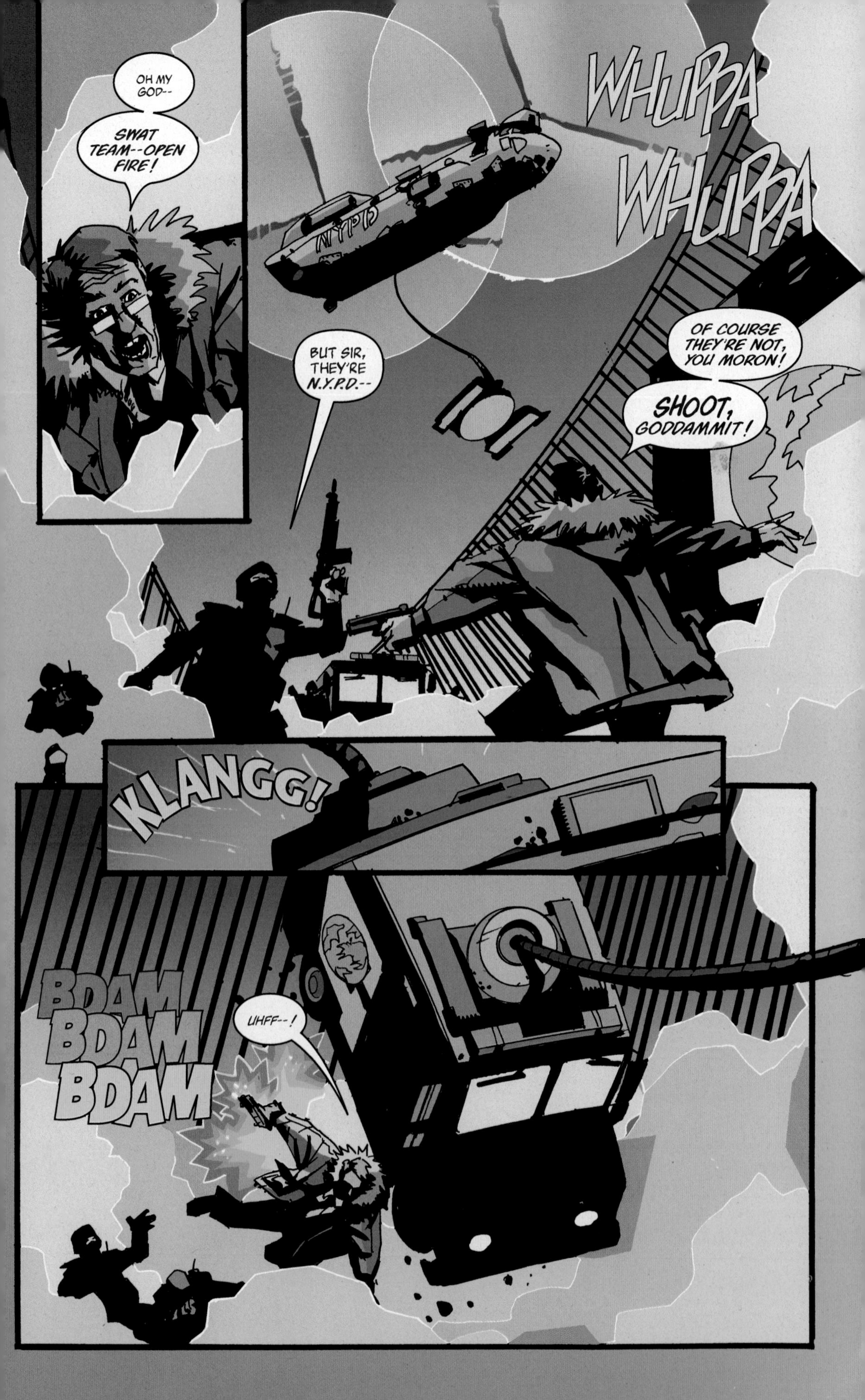
OH MY GOD--
SWAT TEAM--OPEN FIRE!
WHUPPA WHUPPA
BUT SIR, THEY'RE N.Y.P.D.--
OF COURSE THEY'RE NOT, YOU MORON!
SHOOT, GODDAMMIT!
KLANGG!
BDAM BDAM BDAM
UHFF--!

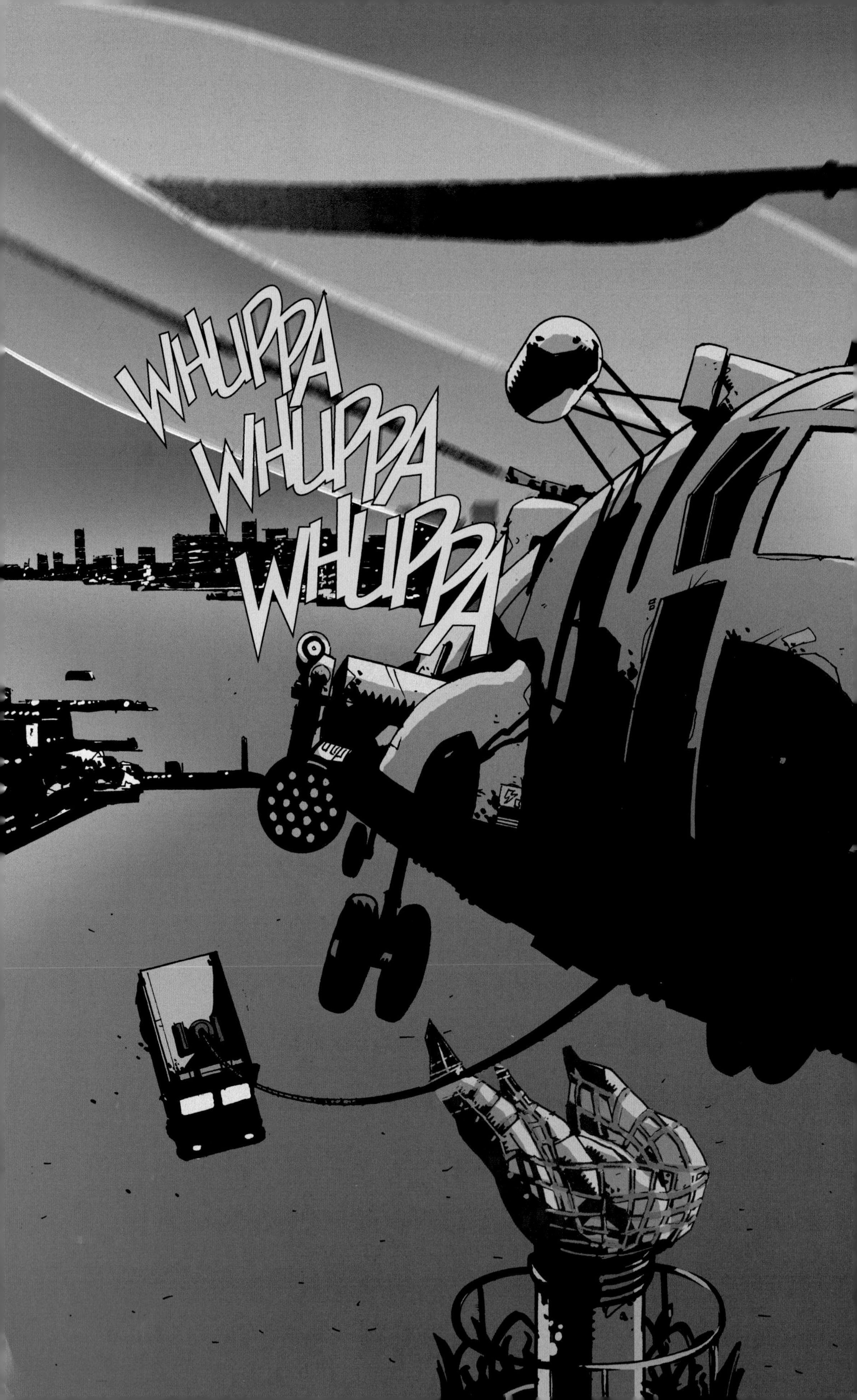
WHUPPA
WHUPPA
WHUPPA

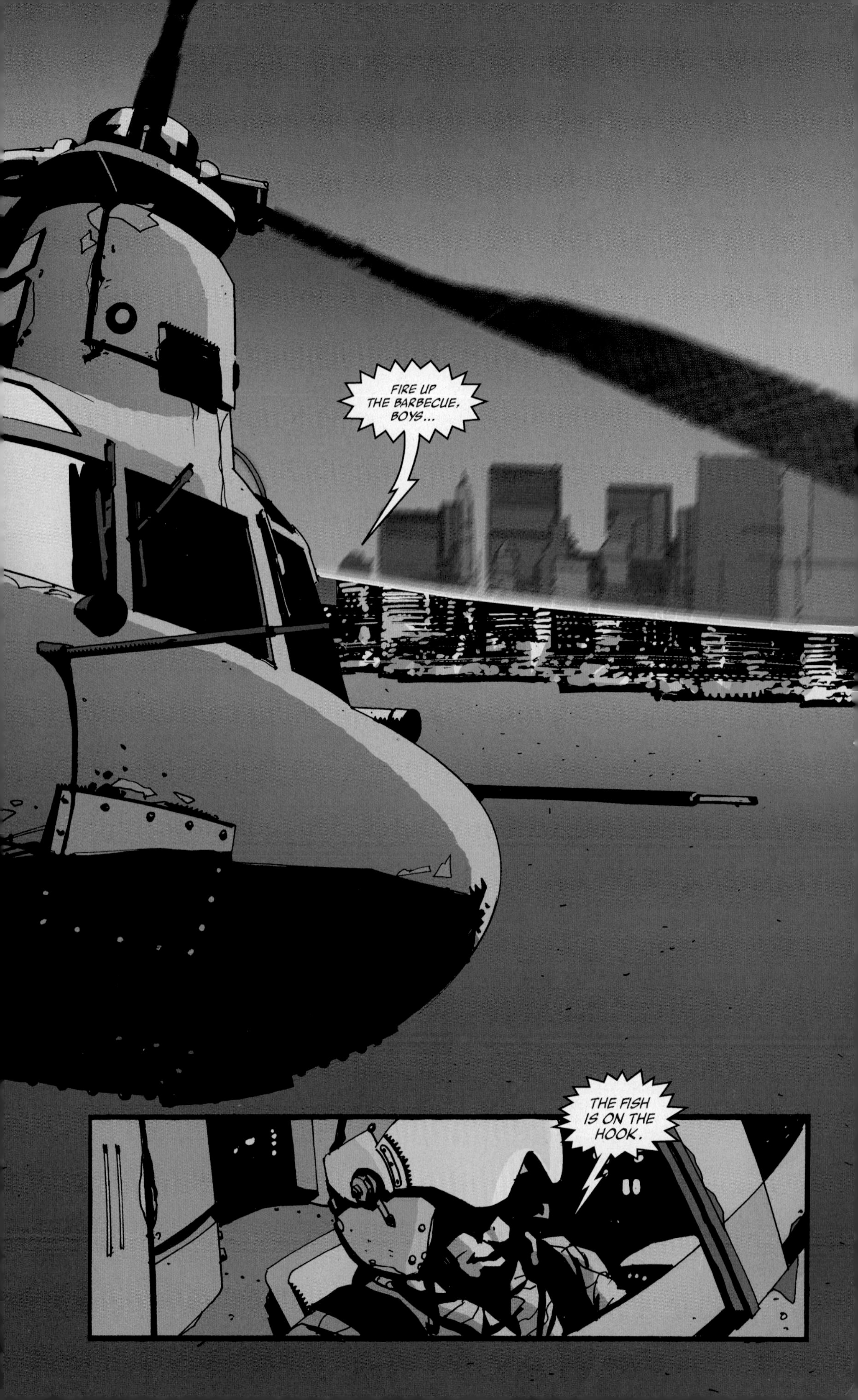
FIRE UP THE BARBECUE, BOYS...
THE FISH IS ON THE HOOK.

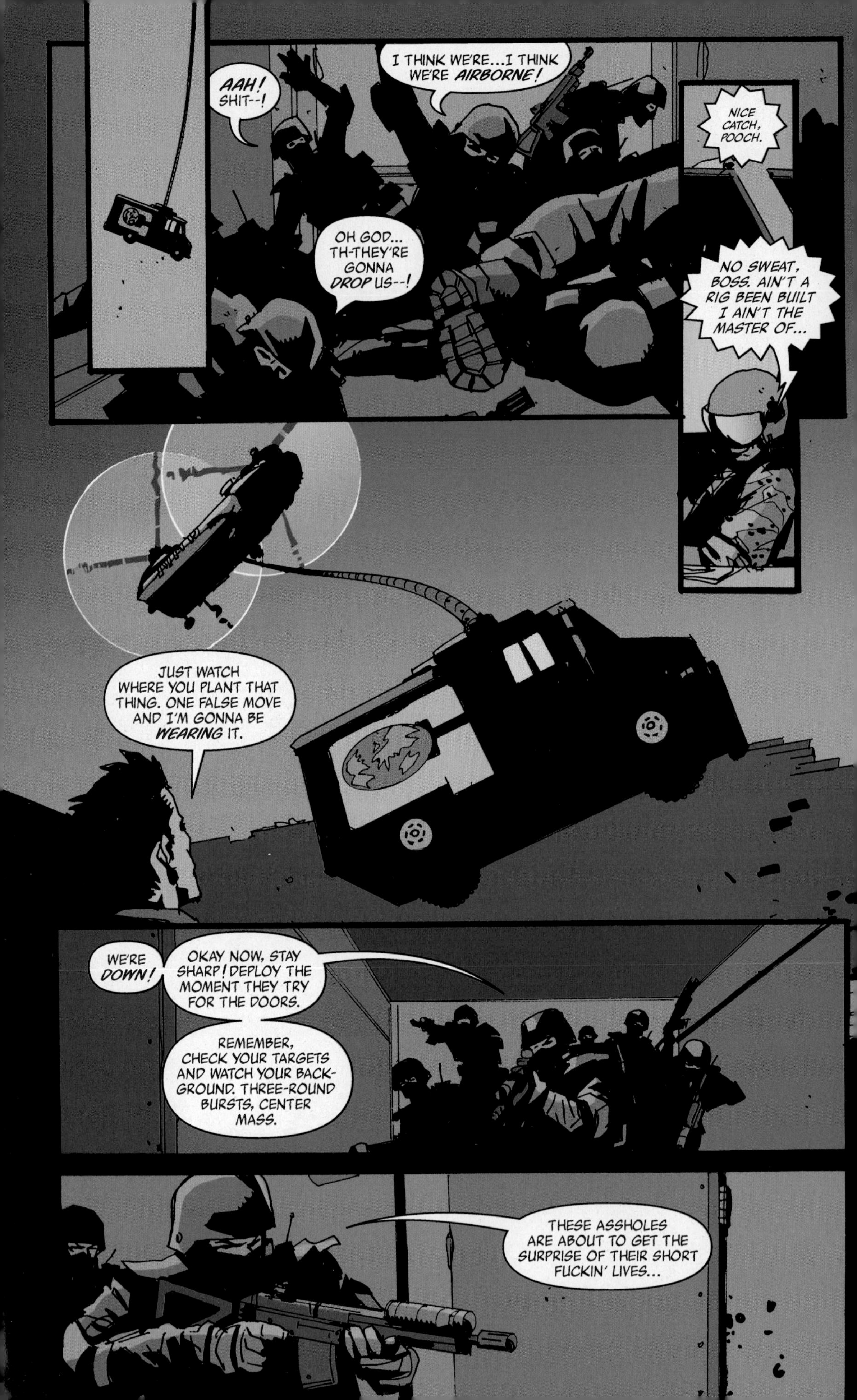
AAH! SHIT--!
I THINK WE'RE...I THINK WE'RE AIRBORNE!
OH GOD... TH-THEY'RE GONNA DROP US--!
NICE CATCH, POOCH.
NO SWEAT, BOSS. AIN'T A RIG BEEN BUILT I AIN'T THE MASTER OF...
JUST WATCH WHERE YOU PLANT THAT THING. ONE FALSE MOVE AND I'M GONNA BE WEARING IT.
WE'RE DOWN!
OKAY NOW, STAY SHARP! DEPLOY THE MOMENT THEY TRY FOR THE DOORS.
REMEMBER, CHECK YOUR TARGETS AND WATCH YOUR BACK-GROUND. THREE-ROUND BURSTS, CENTER MASS.
THESE ASSHOLES ARE ABOUT TO GET THE SURPRISE OF THEIR SHORT FUCKIN' LIVES...

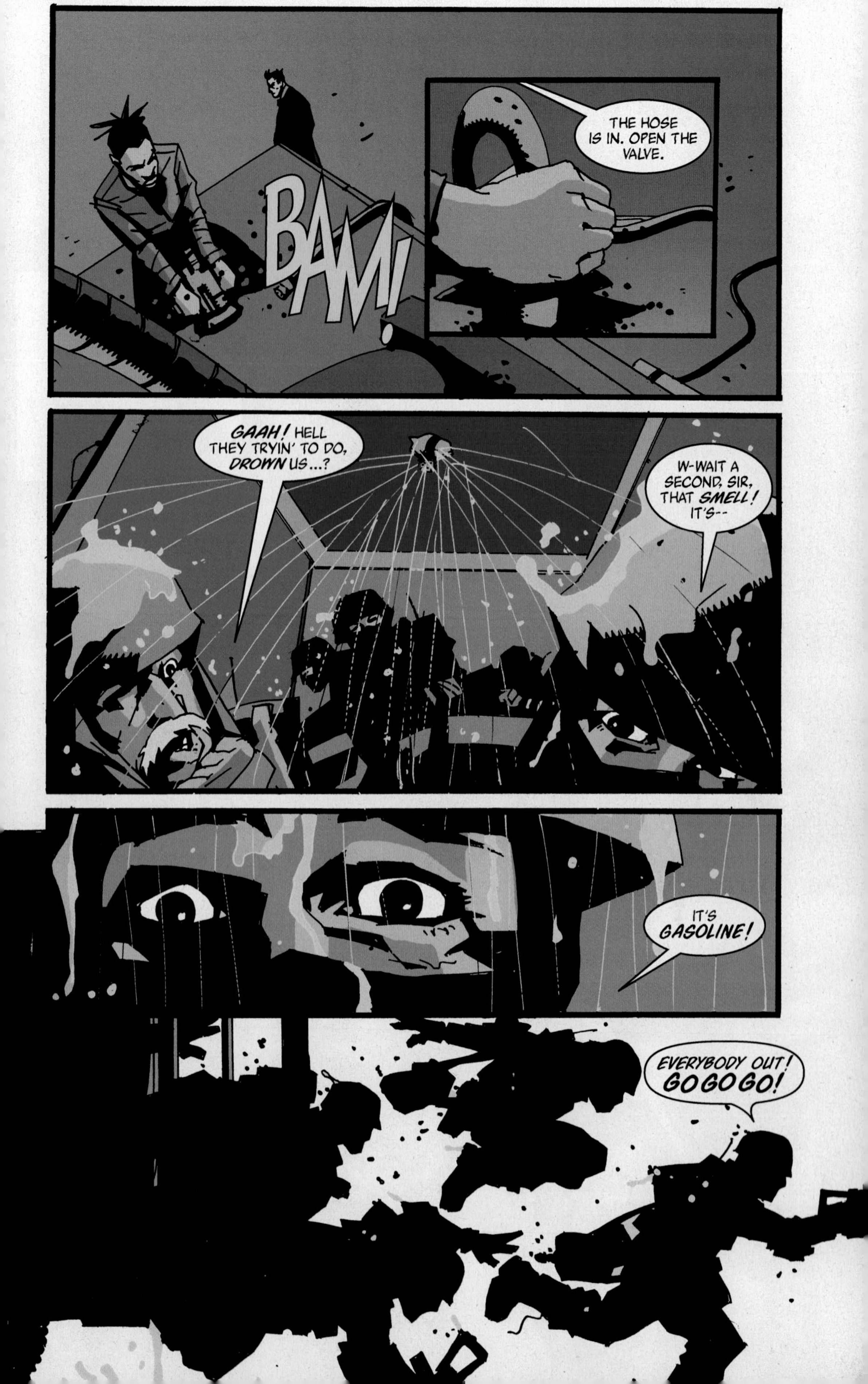
BAM!
THE HOSE IS IN. OPEN THE VALVE.
GAAH! HELL THEY TRYIN' TO DO, DROWN US...?
W-WAIT A SECOND, SIR, THAT SMELL! IT'S--
IT'S GASOLINE!
EVERYBODY OUT! GO GO GO!

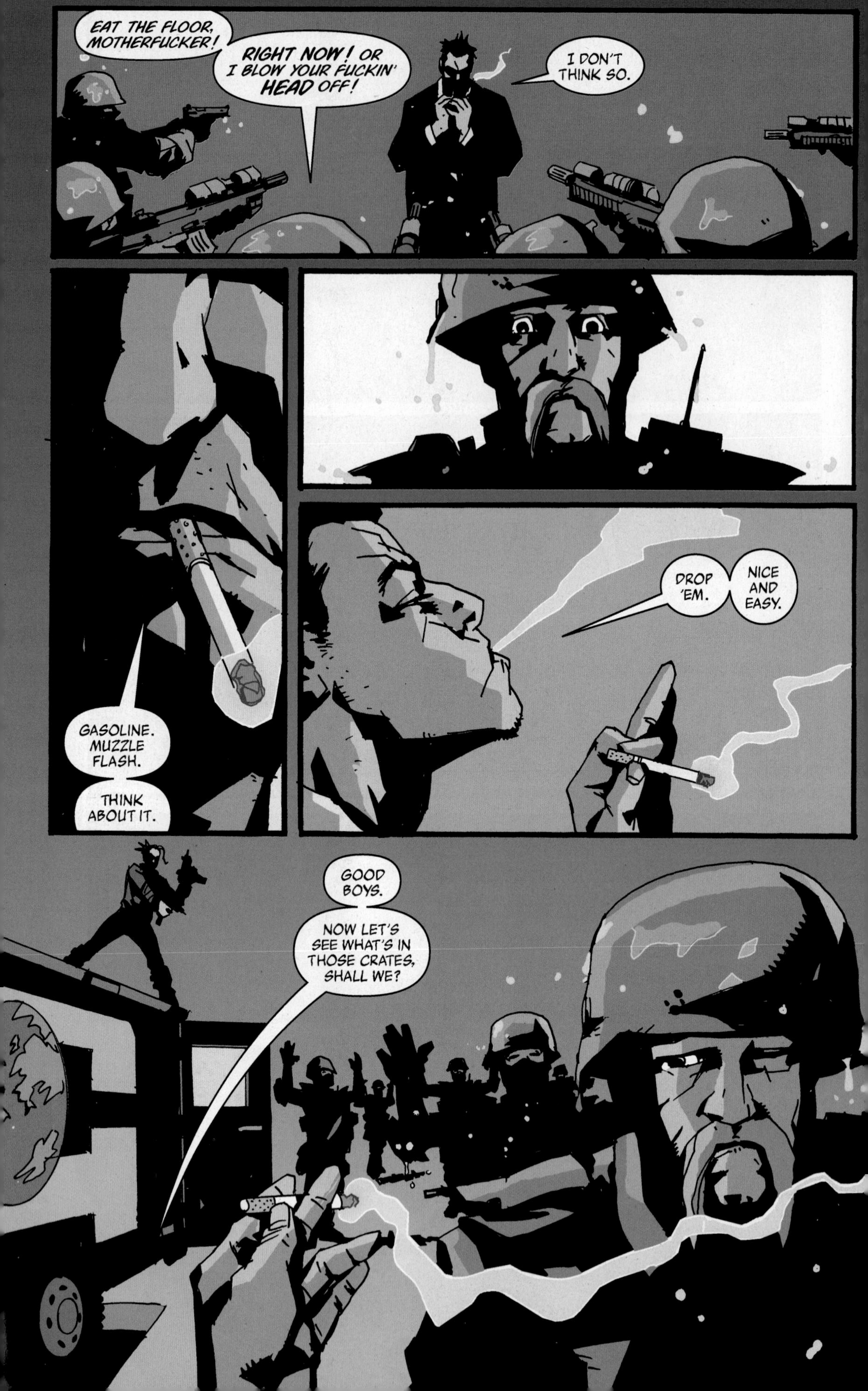
EAT THE FLOOR, MOTHERFUCKER!
RIGHT NOW! OR I BLOW YOUR FUCKIN' HEAD OFF!
I DON'T THINK SO.
GASOLINE. MUZZLE FLASH.
THINK ABOUT IT.
DROP 'EM.
NICE AND EASY.
GOOD BOYS.
NOW LET'S SEE WHAT'S IN THOSE CRATES, SHALL WE?

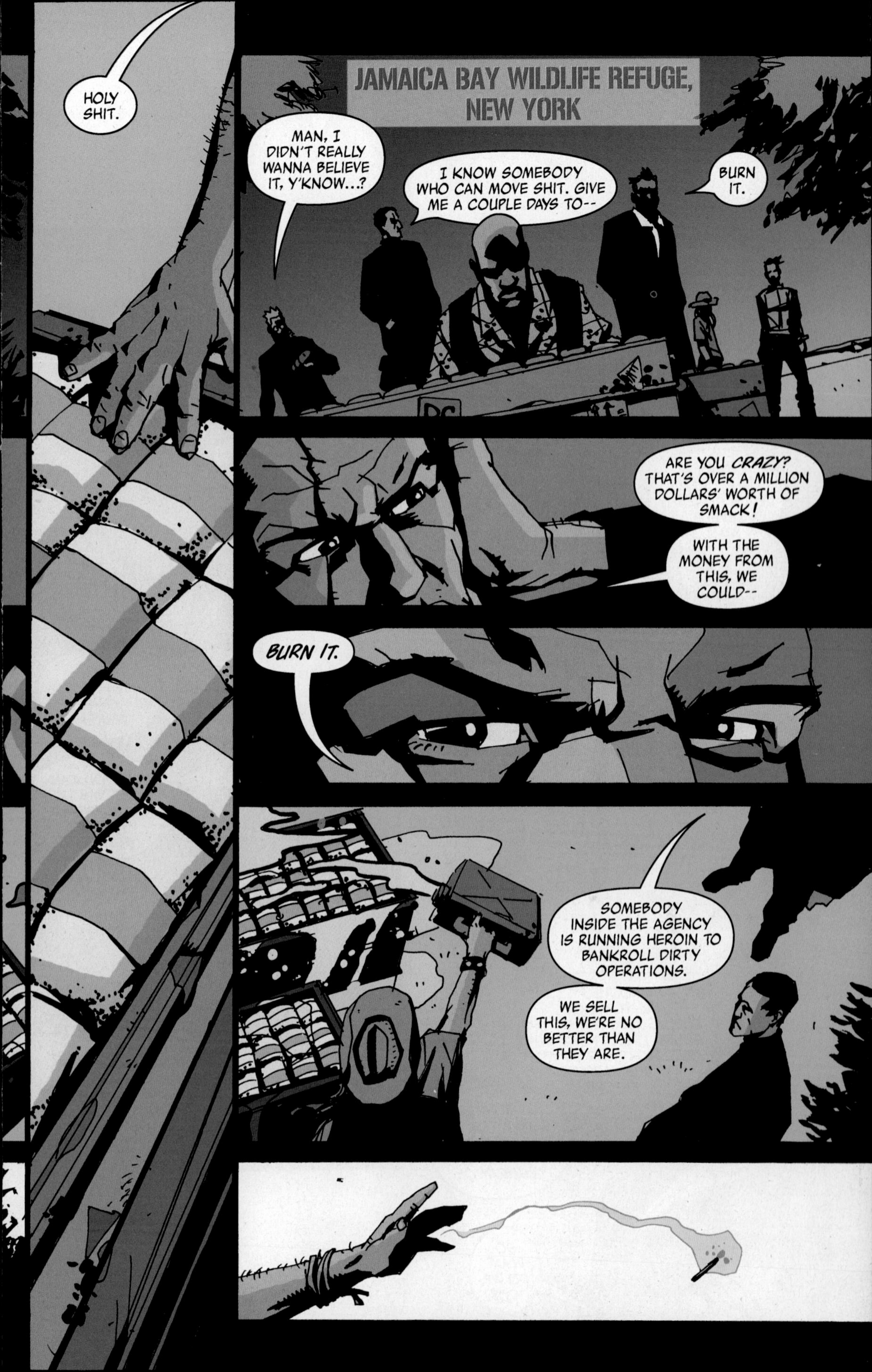
HOLY SHIT.
JAMAICA BAY WILDLIFE REFUGE, NEW YORK
MAN, I DIDN'T REALLY WANNA BELIEVE IT, Y'KNOW...?
I KNOW SOMEBODY WHO CAN MOVE SHIT. GIVE ME A COUPLE DAYS TO--
BURN IT.
ARE YOU CRAZY? THAT'S OVER A MILLION DOLLARS' WORTH OF SMACK!
WITH THE MONEY FROM THIS, WE COULD--
BURN IT.
SOMEBODY INSIDE THE AGENCY IS RUNNING HEROIN TO BANKROLL DIRTY OPERATIONS.
WE SELL THIS, WE'RE NO BETTER THAN THEY ARE.

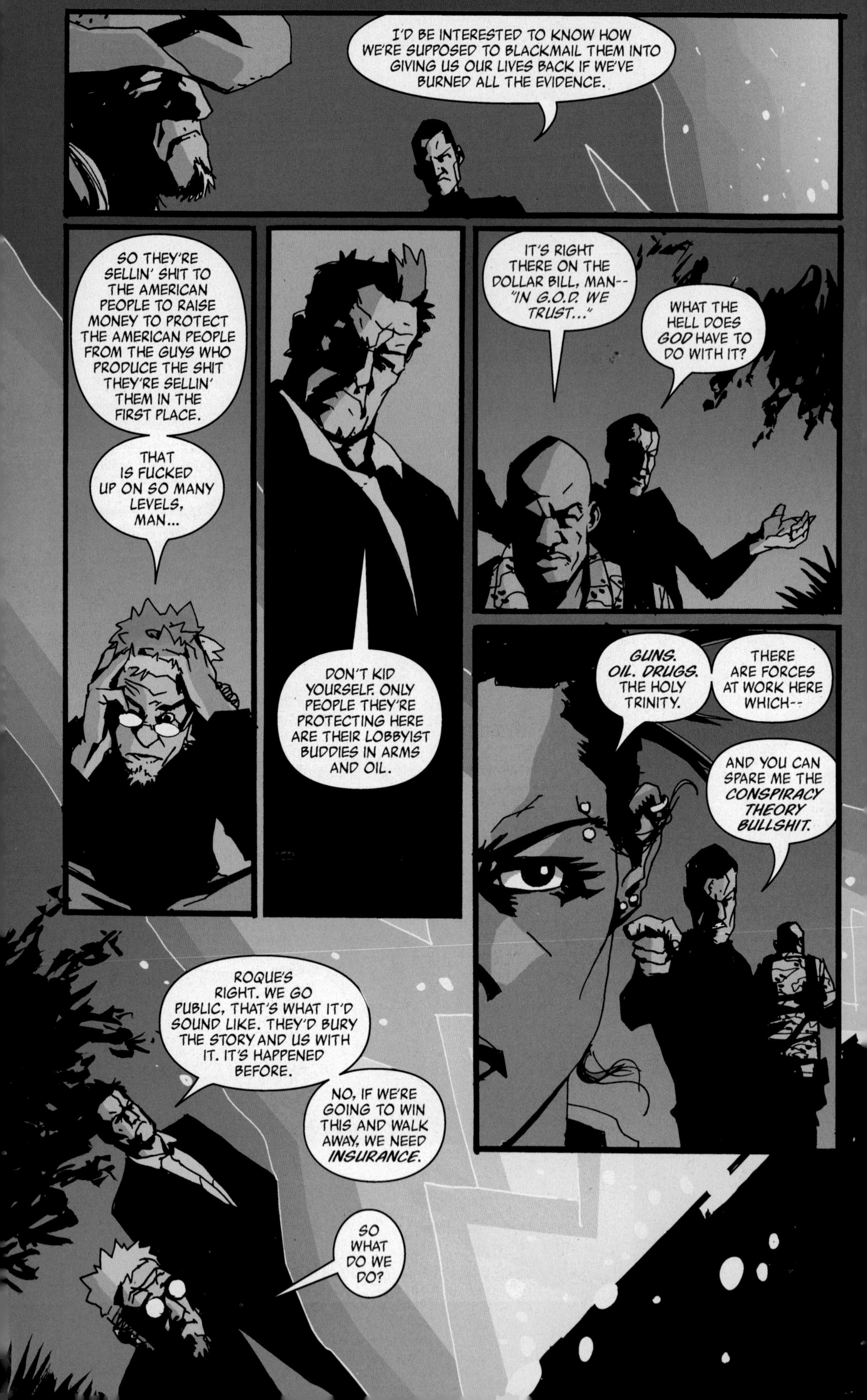
I'D BE INTERESTED TO KNOW HOW WE'RE SUPPOSED TO BLACKMAIL THEM INTO GIVING US OUR LIVES BACK IF WE'VE BURNED ALL THE EVIDENCE.
SO THEY'RE SELLIN' SHIT TO THE AMERICAN PEOPLE TO RAISE MONEY TO PROTECT THE AMERICAN PEOPLE FROM THE GUYS WHO PRODUCE THE SHIT THEY'RE SELLIN' THEM IN THE FIRST PLACE.
THAT IS FUCKED UP ON SO MANY LEVELS, MAN...
DON'T KID YOURSELF. ONLY PEOPLE THEY'RE PROTECTING HERE ARE THEIR LOBBYIST BUDDIES IN ARMS AND OIL.
IT'S RIGHT THERE ON THE DOLLAR BILL, MAN-- "IN G.O.D. WE TRUST..."
WHAT THE HELL DOES GOD HAVE TO DO WITH IT?
GUNS. OIL. DRUGS. THE HOLY TRINITY.
THERE ARE FORCES AT WORK HERE WHICH--
AND YOU CAN SPARE ME THE CONSPIRACY THEORY BULLSHIT.
ROQUE'S RIGHT. WE GO PUBLIC, THAT'S WHAT IT'D SOUND LIKE. THEY'D BURY THE STORY AND US WITH IT. IT'S HAPPENED BEFORE.
NO, IF WE'RE GOING TO WIN THIS AND WALK AWAY, WE NEED INSURANCE.
SO WHAT DO WE DO?

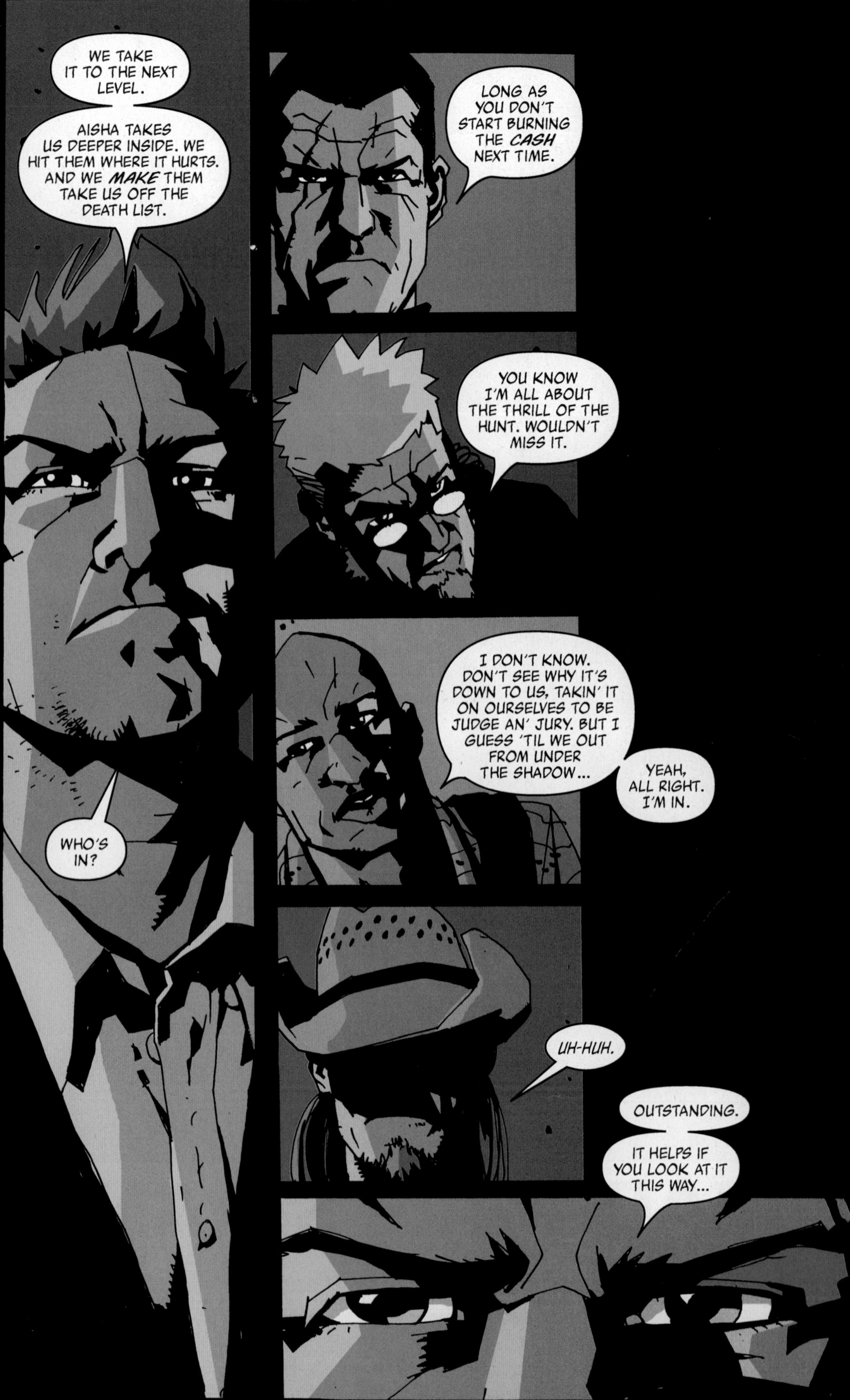
WE TAKE IT TO THE NEXT LEVEL.
AISHA TAKES US DEEPER INSIDE. WE HIT THEM WHERE IT HURTS. AND WE *MAKE* THEM TAKE US OFF THE DEATH LIST.
LONG AS YOU DON'T START BURNING THE *CASH* NEXT TIME.
YOU KNOW I'M ALL ABOUT THE THRILL OF THE HUNT. WOULDN'T MISS IT.
WHO'S IN?
I DON'T KNOW. DON'T SEE WHY IT'S DOWN TO US, TAKIN' IT ON OURSELVES TO BE JUDGE AN' JURY. BUT I GUESS 'TIL WE OUT FROM UNDER THE SHADOW...
YEAH, ALL RIGHT. I'M IN.
UH-HUH.
OUTSTANDING.
IT HELPS IF YOU LOOK AT IT THIS WAY...

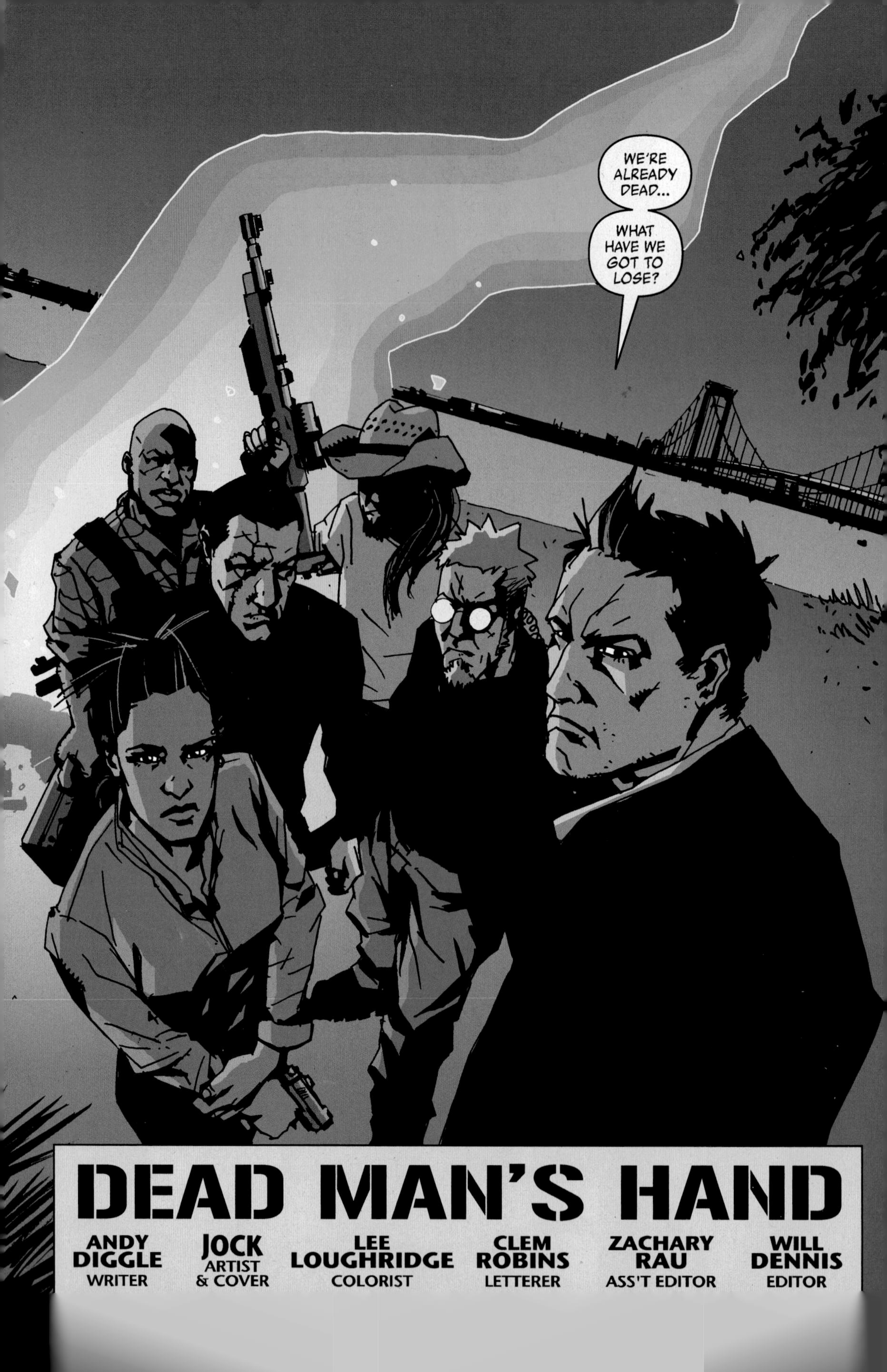
WE'RE ALREADY DEAD...
WHAT HAVE WE GOT TO LOSE?
DEAD MAN'S HAND
ANDY DIGGLE WRITER
JOCK ARTIST & COVER
LEE LOUGHRIDGE COLORIST
CLEM ROBINS LETTERER
ZACHARY RAU ASS'T EDITOR
WILL DENNIS EDITOR

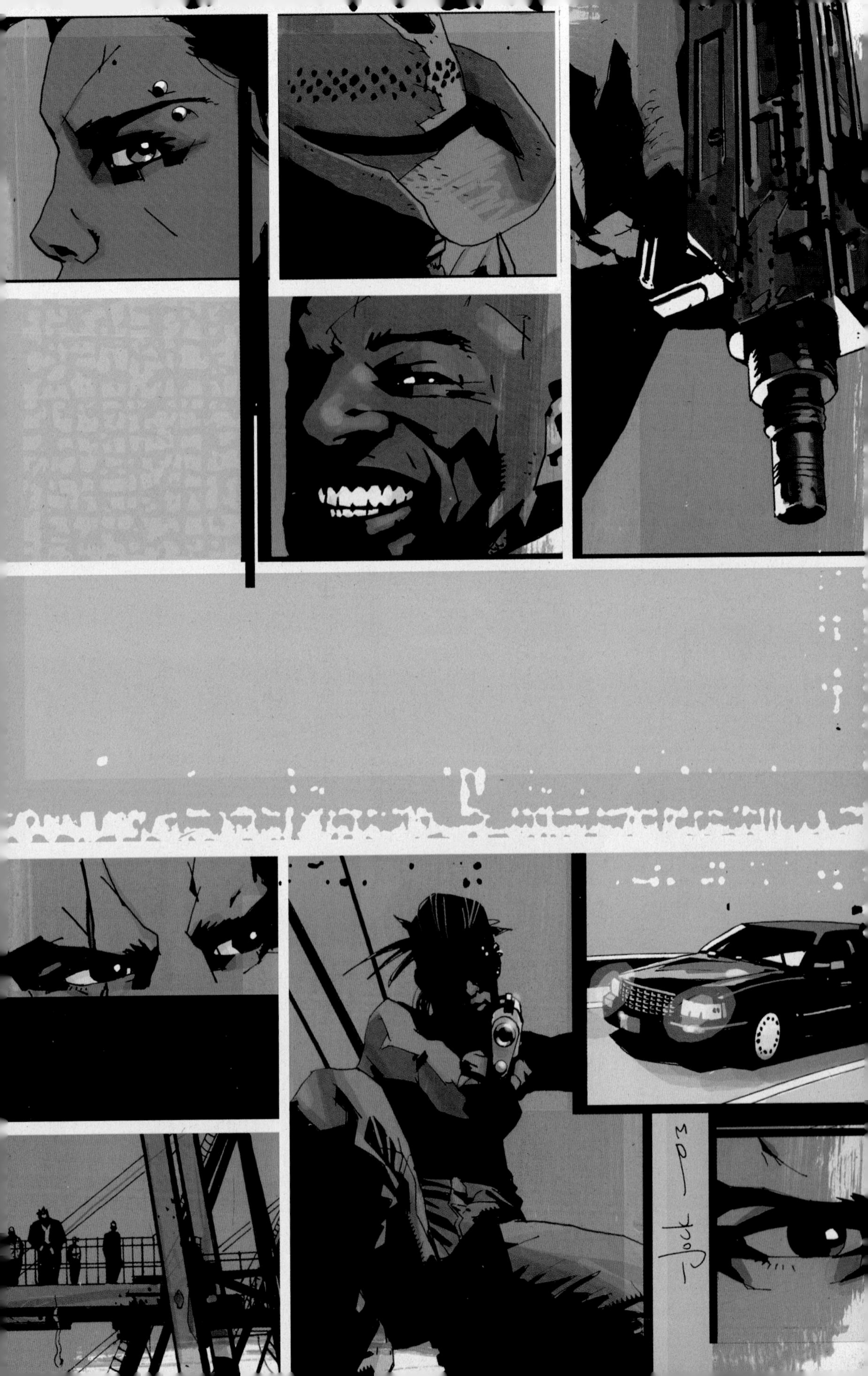
Jock — 03

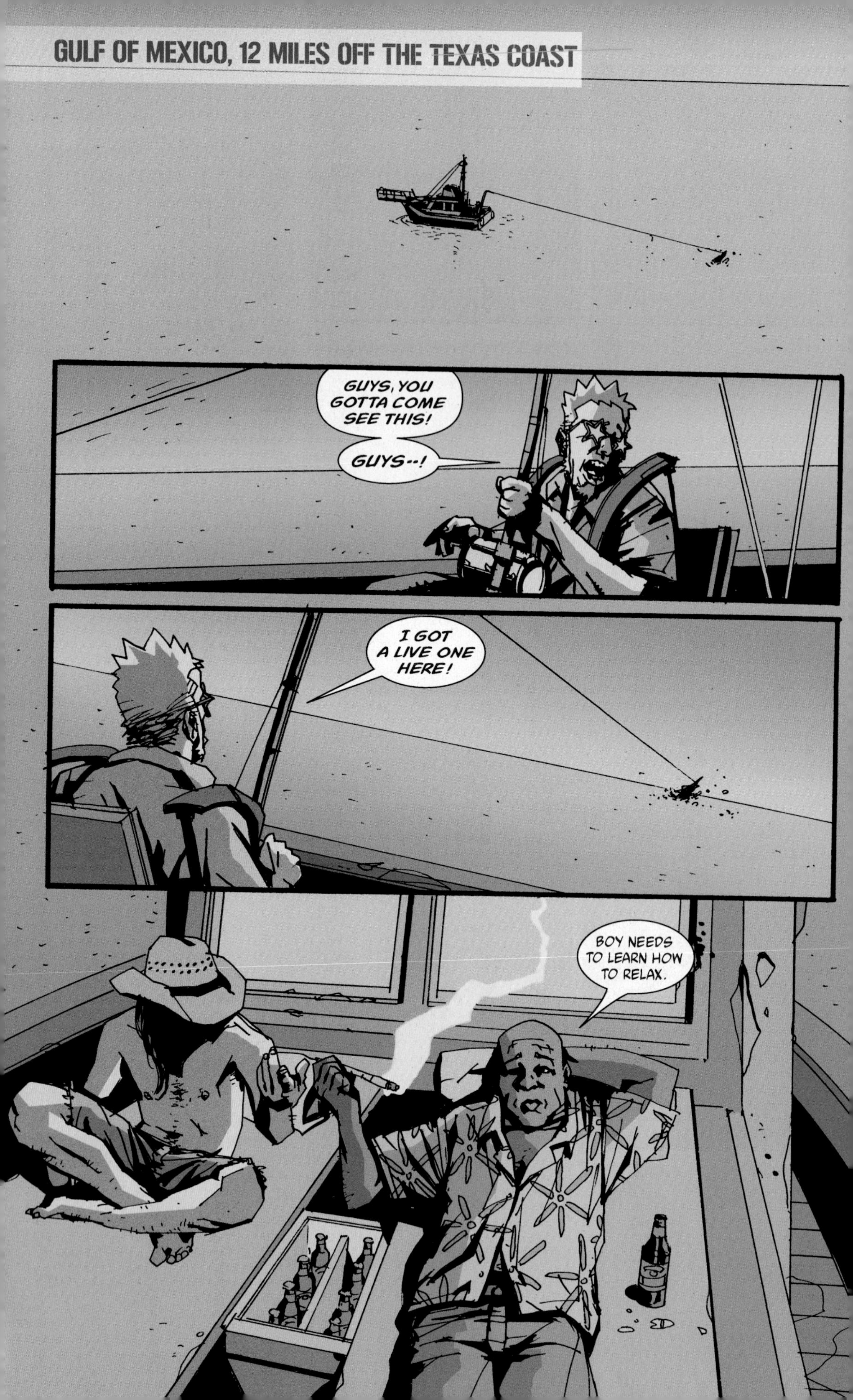
GULF OF MEXICO, 12 MILES OFF THE TEXAS COAST
GUYS, YOU GOTTA COME SEE THIS!
GUYS--!
I GOT A LIVE ONE HERE!
BOY NEEDS TO LEARN HOW TO RELAX.

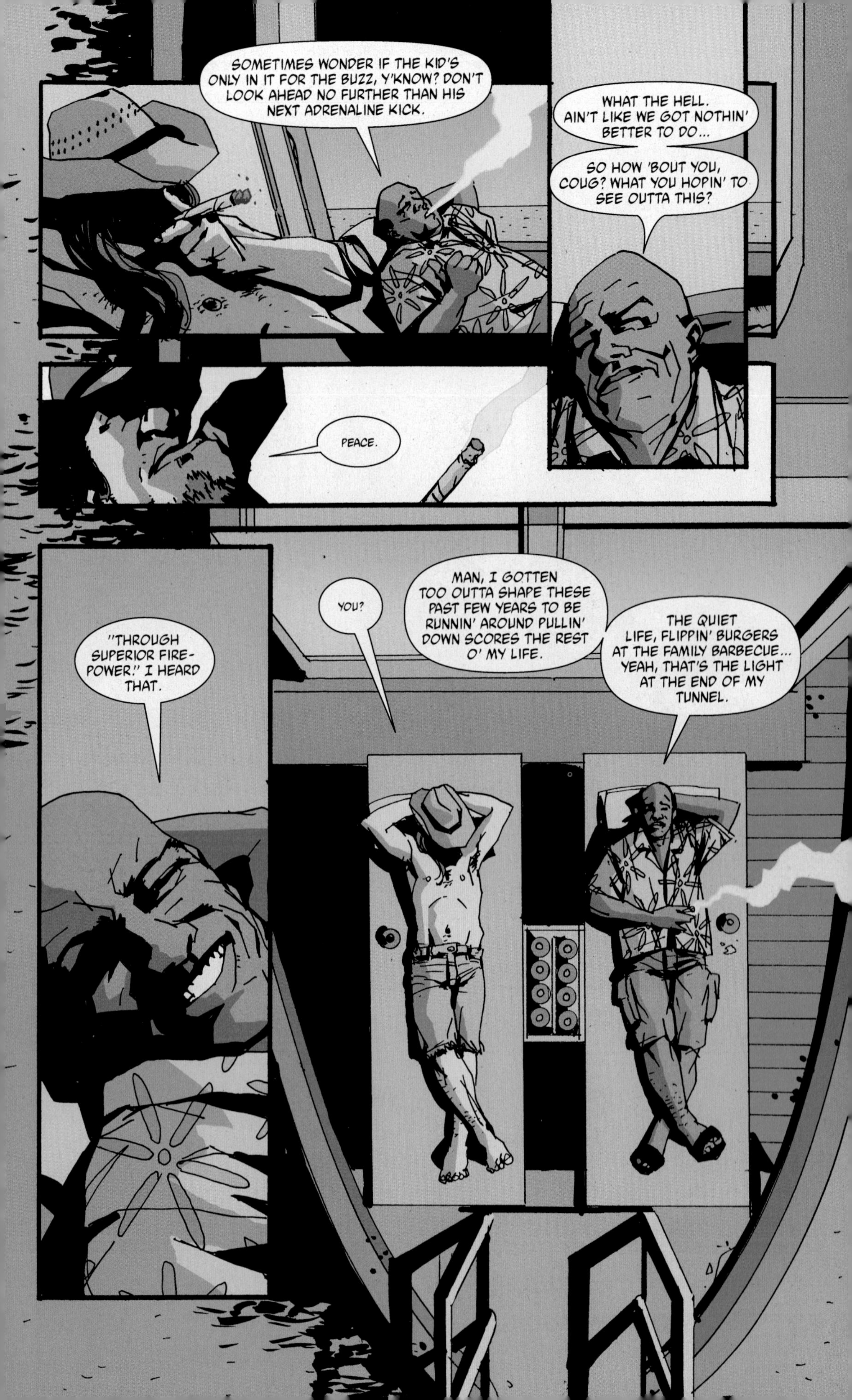
SOMETIMES WONDER IF THE KID'S ONLY IN IT FOR THE BUZZ, Y'KNOW? DON'T LOOK AHEAD NO FURTHER THAN HIS NEXT ADRENALINE KICK.
WHAT THE HELL. AIN'T LIKE WE GOT NOTHIN' BETTER TO DO...
SO HOW 'BOUT YOU, COUG? WHAT YOU HOPIN' TO SEE OUTTA THIS?
PEACE.
"THROUGH SUPERIOR FIRE-POWER." I HEARD THAT.
YOU?
MAN, I GOTTEN TOO OUTTA SHAPE THESE PAST FEW YEARS TO BE RUNNIN' AROUND PULLIN' DOWN SCORES THE REST O' MY LIFE.
THE QUIET LIFE, FLIPPIN' BURGERS AT THE FAMILY BARBECUE... YEAH, THAT'S THE LIGHT AT THE END OF MY TUNNEL.

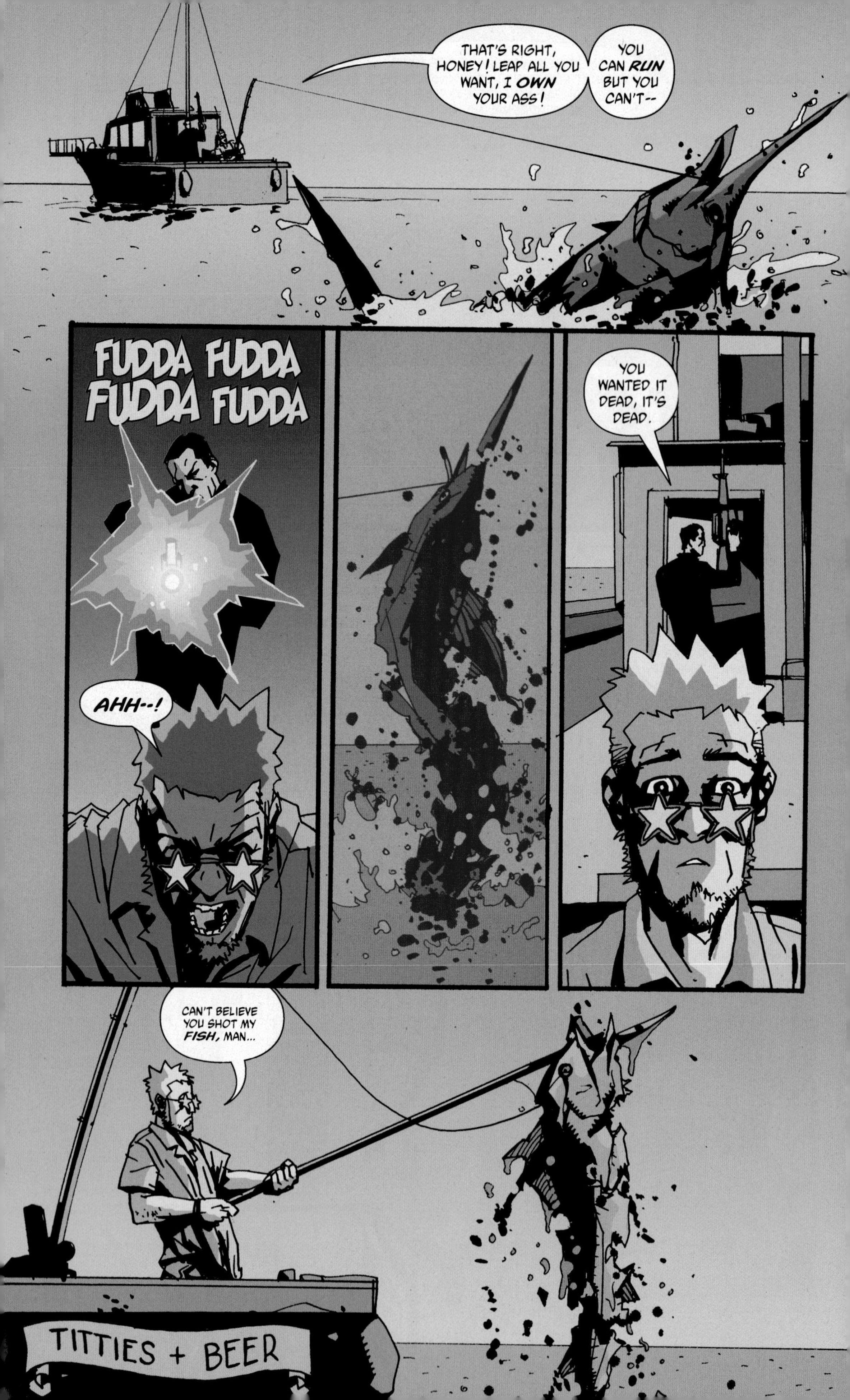
THAT'S RIGHT, HONEY! LEAP ALL YOU WANT, I OWN YOUR ASS!
YOU CAN RUN BUT YOU CAN'T--
FUDDA FUDDA FUDDA FUDDA
AHH--!
YOU WANTED IT DEAD, IT'S DEAD.
CAN'T BELIEVE YOU SHOT MY FISH, MAN...
TITTIES + BEER

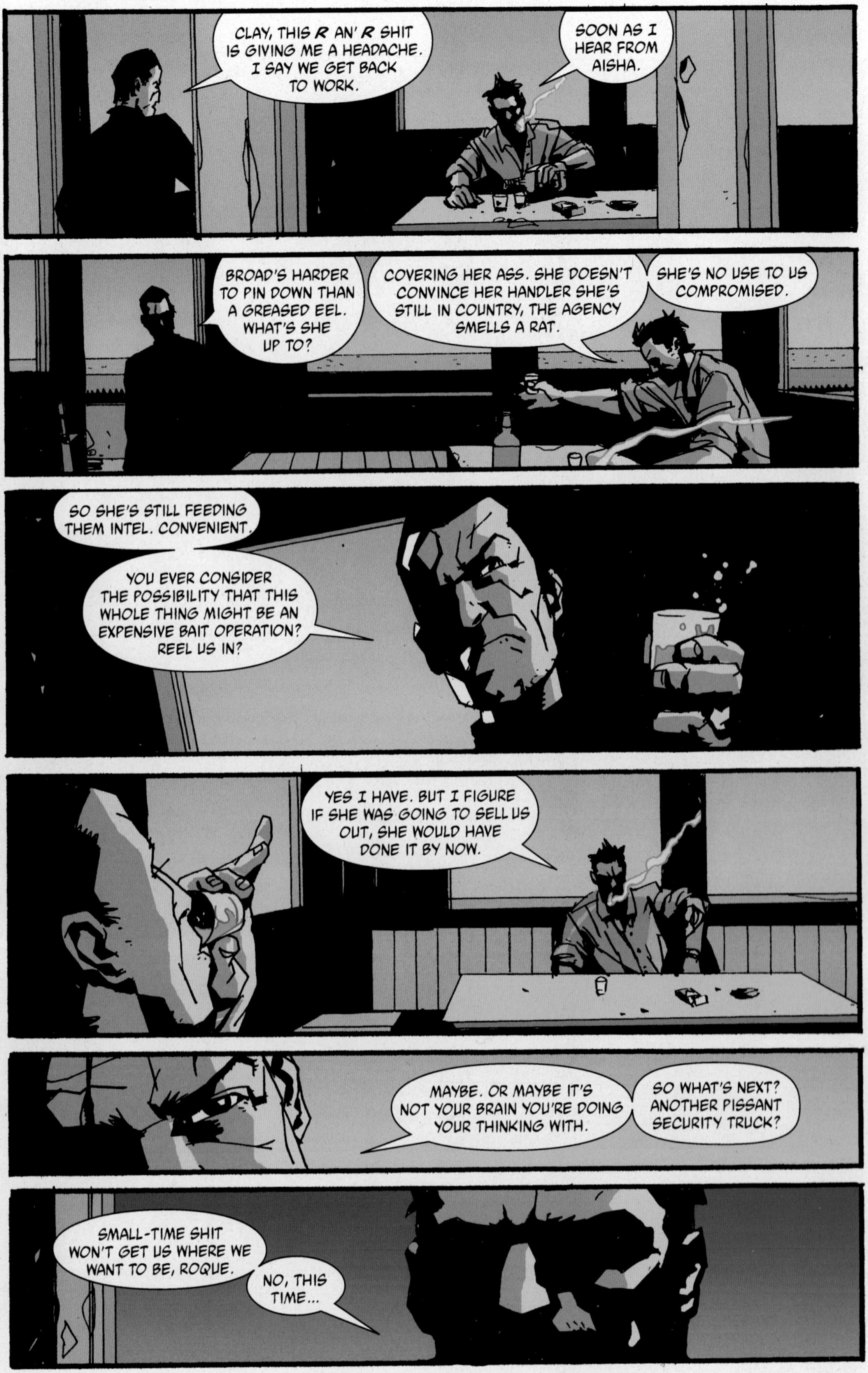
CLAY, THIS R AN' R SHIT IS GIVING ME A HEADACHE. I SAY WE GET BACK TO WORK.
SOON AS I HEAR FROM AISHA.
BROAD'S HARDER TO PIN DOWN THAN A GREASED EEL. WHAT'S SHE UP TO?
COVERING HER ASS. SHE DOESN'T CONVINCE HER HANDLER SHE'S STILL IN COUNTRY, THE AGENCY SMELLS A RAT.
SHE'S NO USE TO US COMPROMISED.
SO SHE'S STILL FEEDING THEM INTEL. CONVENIENT.
YOU EVER CONSIDER THE POSSIBILITY THAT THIS WHOLE THING MIGHT BE AN EXPENSIVE BAIT OPERATION? REEL US IN?
YES I HAVE. BUT I FIGURE IF SHE WAS GOING TO SELL US OUT, SHE WOULD HAVE DONE IT BY NOW.
MAYBE. OR MAYBE IT'S NOT YOUR BRAIN YOU'RE DOING YOUR THINKING WITH.
SO WHAT'S NEXT? ANOTHER PISSANT SECURITY TRUCK?
SMALL-TIME SHIT WON'T GET US WHERE WE WANT TO BE, ROQUE.
NO, THIS TIME...

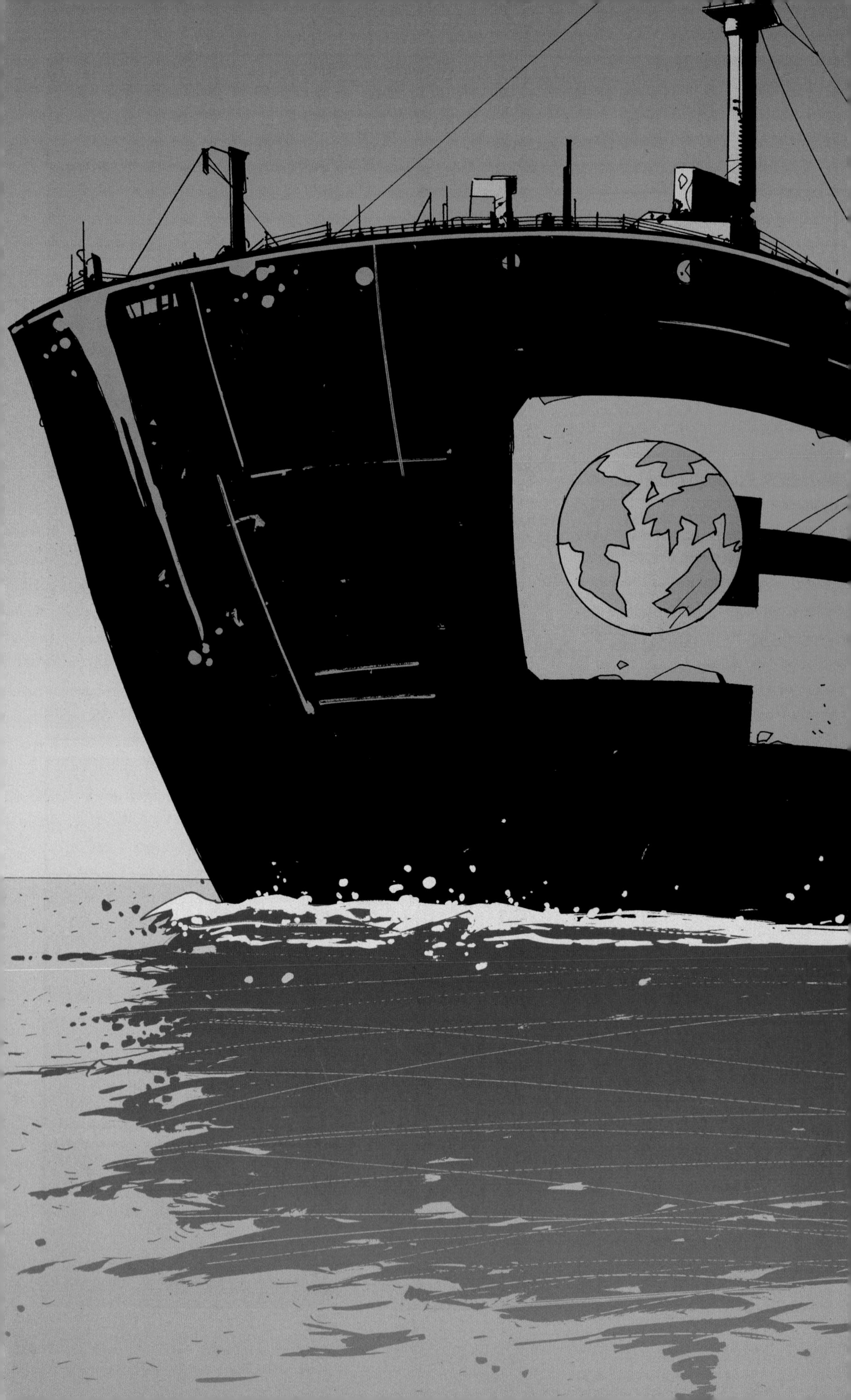

GOLIATH
PART ONE

ANDY DIGGLE, WRITER
JOCK, ARTIST & COVER

LEE LOUGHRIDGE, COLORIST
CLEM ROBINS, LETTERER
ZACHARY RAU, ASS'T EDITOR
WILL DENNIS, EDITOR

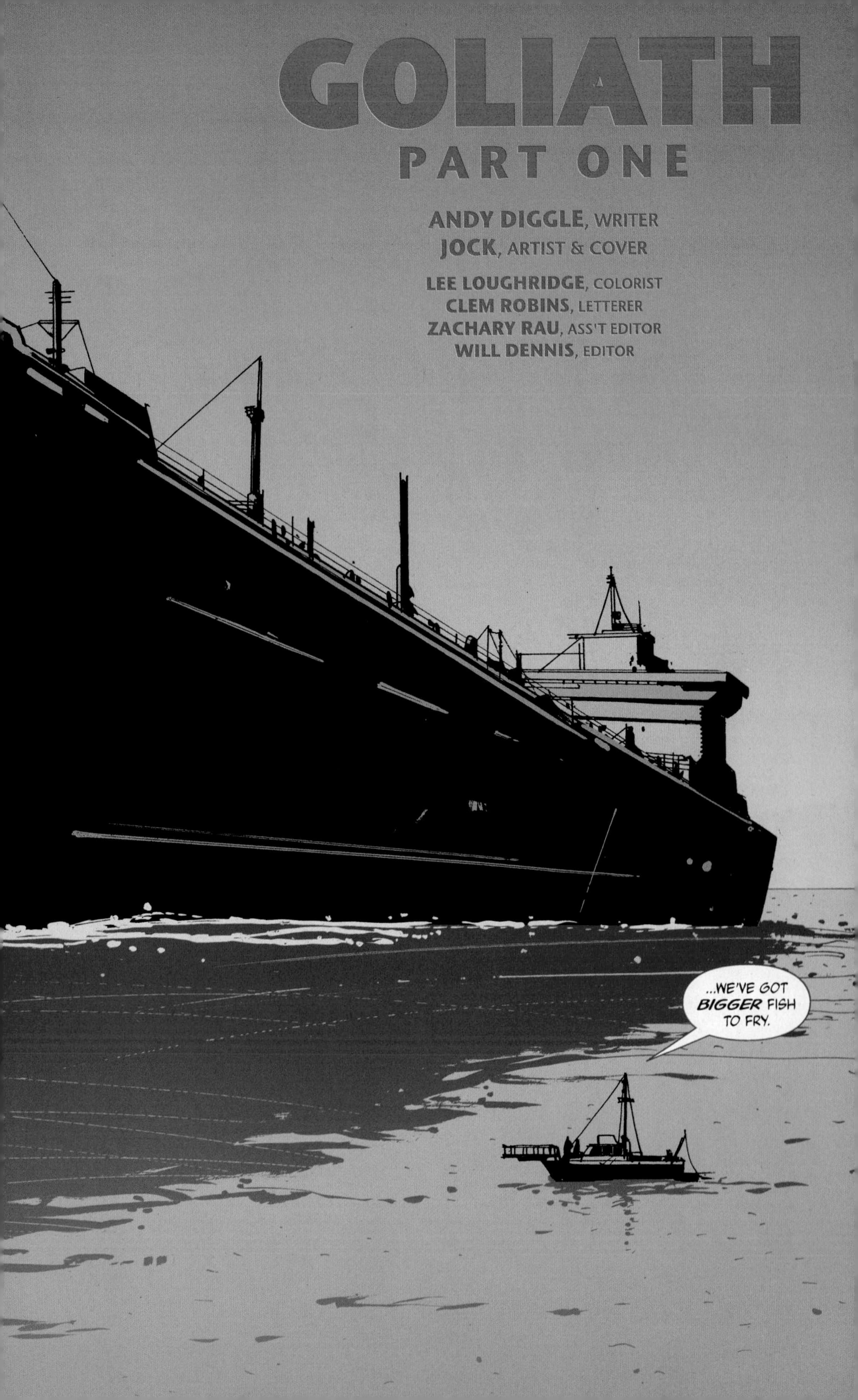
...WE'VE GOT *BIGGER* FISH TO FRY.

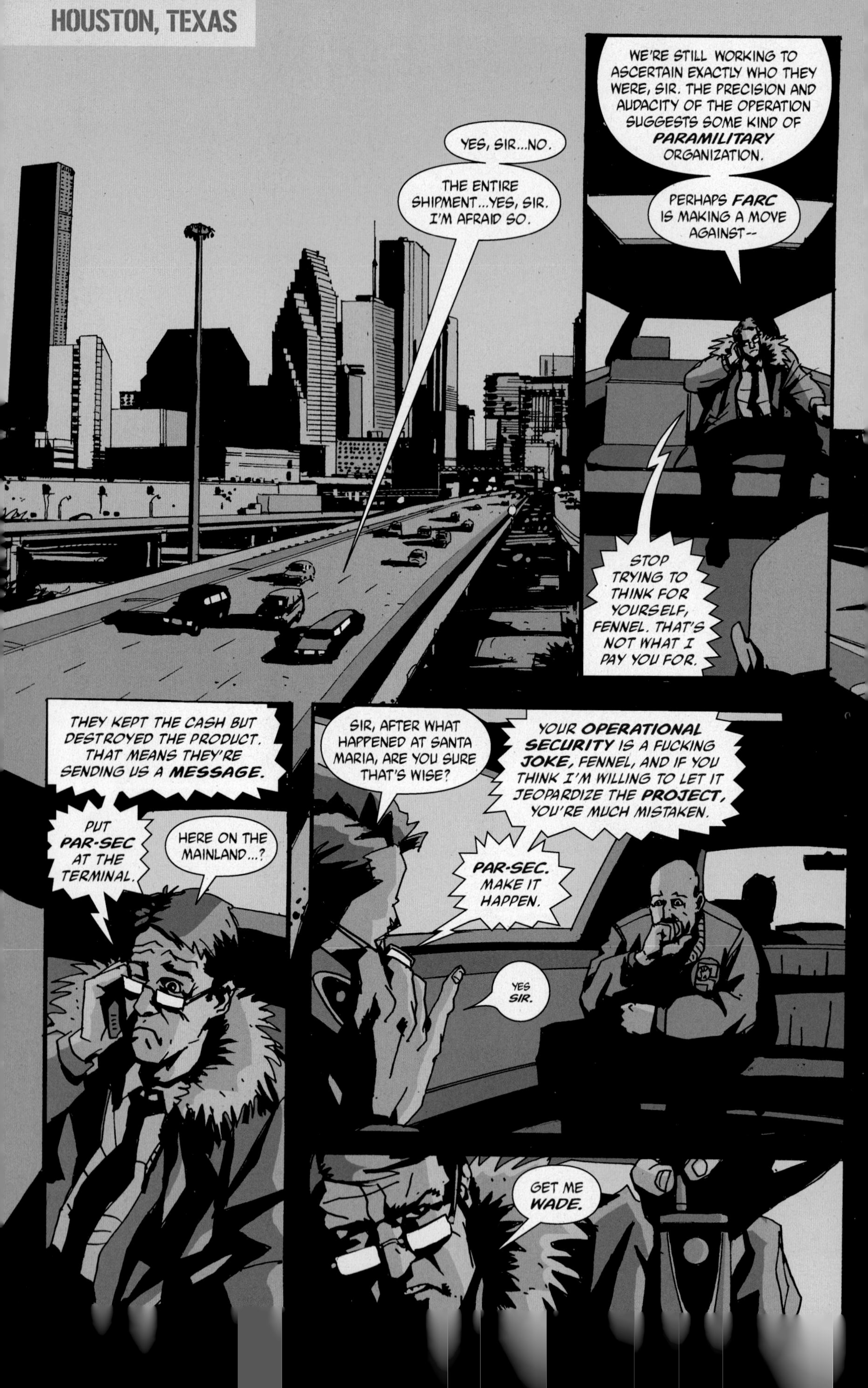
HOUSTON, TEXAS
YES, SIR...NO.
THE ENTIRE SHIPMENT...YES, SIR. I'M AFRAID SO.
WE'RE STILL WORKING TO ASCERTAIN EXACTLY WHO THEY WERE, SIR. THE PRECISION AND AUDACITY OF THE OPERATION SUGGESTS SOME KIND OF PARAMILITARY ORGANIZATION.
PERHAPS FARC IS MAKING A MOVE AGAINST--
STOP TRYING TO THINK FOR YOURSELF, FENNEL. THAT'S NOT WHAT I PAY YOU FOR.
THEY KEPT THE CASH BUT DESTROYED THE PRODUCT. THAT MEANS THEY'RE SENDING US A MESSAGE.
PUT PAR-SEC AT THE TERMINAL.
HERE ON THE MAINLAND...?
SIR, AFTER WHAT HAPPENED AT SANTA MARIA, ARE YOU SURE THAT'S WISE?
YOUR OPERATIONAL SECURITY IS A FUCKING JOKE, FENNEL, AND IF YOU THINK I'M WILLING TO LET IT JEOPARDIZE THE PROJECT, YOU'RE MUCH MISTAKEN.
PAR-SEC. MAKE IT HAPPEN.
YES SIR.
GET ME WADE.

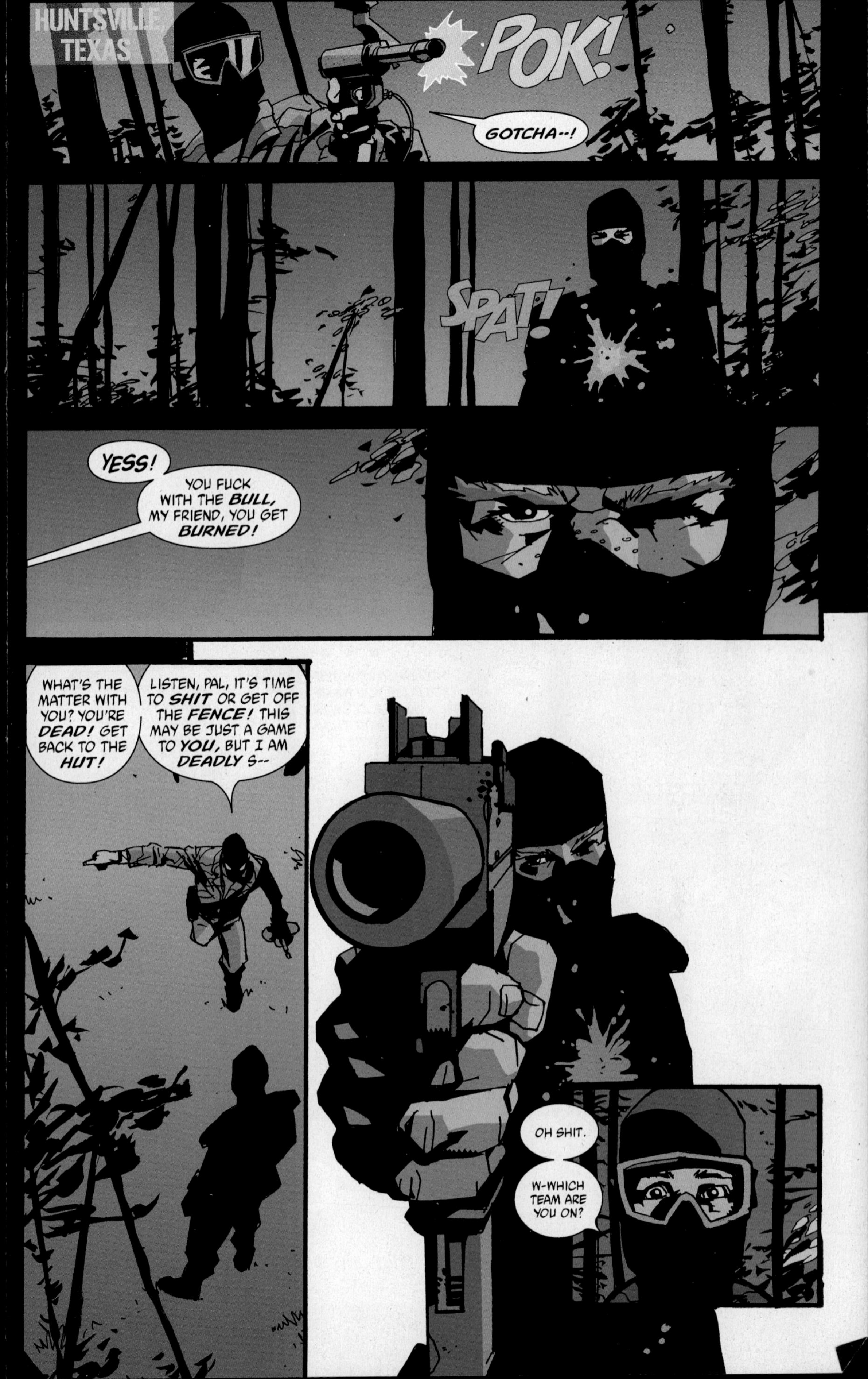
HUNTSVILLE TEXAS
POK!
GOTCHA--!
SPAT!
YESS!
YOU FUCK WITH THE BULL, MY FRIEND, YOU GET BURNED!
WHAT'S THE MATTER WITH YOU? YOU'RE DEAD! GET BACK TO THE HUT!
LISTEN, PAL, IT'S TIME TO SHIT OR GET OFF THE FENCE! THIS MAY BE JUST A GAME TO YOU, BUT I AM DEADLY S--
OH SHIT.
W-WHICH TEAM ARE YOU ON?

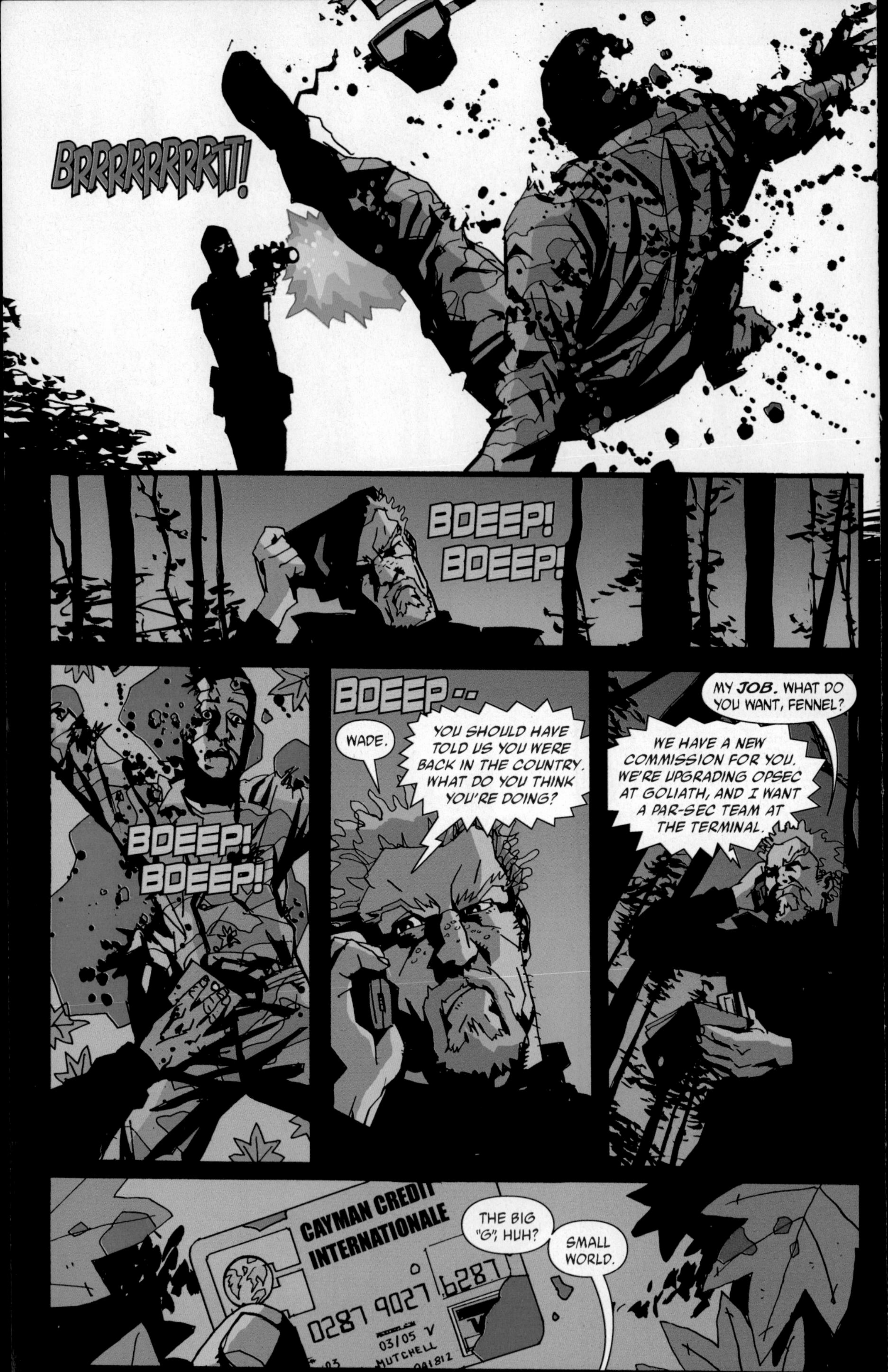
BRRRRRRRRTTT!
BDEEP! BDEEP!
BDEEP! BDEEP!
BDEEP..
WADE.
YOU SHOULD HAVE TOLD US YOU WERE BACK IN THE COUNTRY. WHAT DO YOU THINK YOU'RE DOING?
MY JOB. WHAT DO YOU WANT, FENNEL?
WE HAVE A NEW COMMISSION FOR YOU. WE'RE UPGRADING OPSEC AT GOLIATH, AND I WANT A PAR-SEC TEAM AT THE TERMINAL.
CAYMAN CREDIT INTERNATIONALE
0287 9027 6287
03/05
MUTCHELL
THE BIG "G", HUH?
SMALL WORLD.

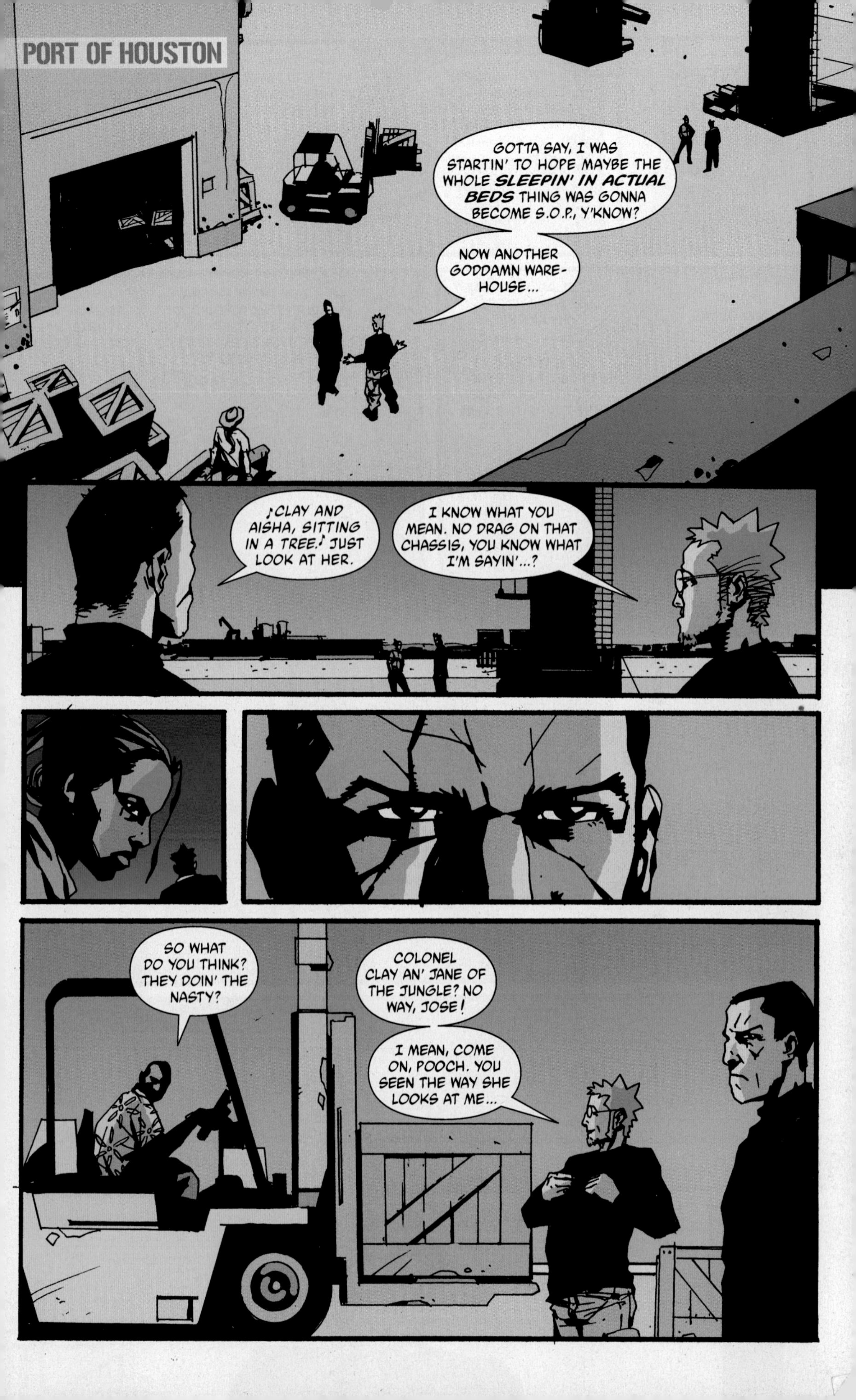
PORT OF HOUSTON
GOTTA SAY, I WAS STARTIN' TO HOPE MAYBE THE WHOLE SLEEPIN' IN ACTUAL BEDS THING WAS GONNA BECOME S.O.P., Y'KNOW?
NOW ANOTHER GODDAMN WARE-HOUSE...
♪CLAY AND AISHA, SITTING IN A TREE.♪ JUST LOOK AT HER.
I KNOW WHAT YOU MEAN. NO DRAG ON THAT CHASSIS, YOU KNOW WHAT I'M SAYIN'...?
SO WHAT DO YOU THINK? THEY DOIN' THE NASTY?
COLONEL CLAY AN' JANE OF THE JUNGLE? NO WAY, JOSE!
I MEAN, COME ON, POOCH. YOU SEEN THE WAY SHE LOOKS AT ME...

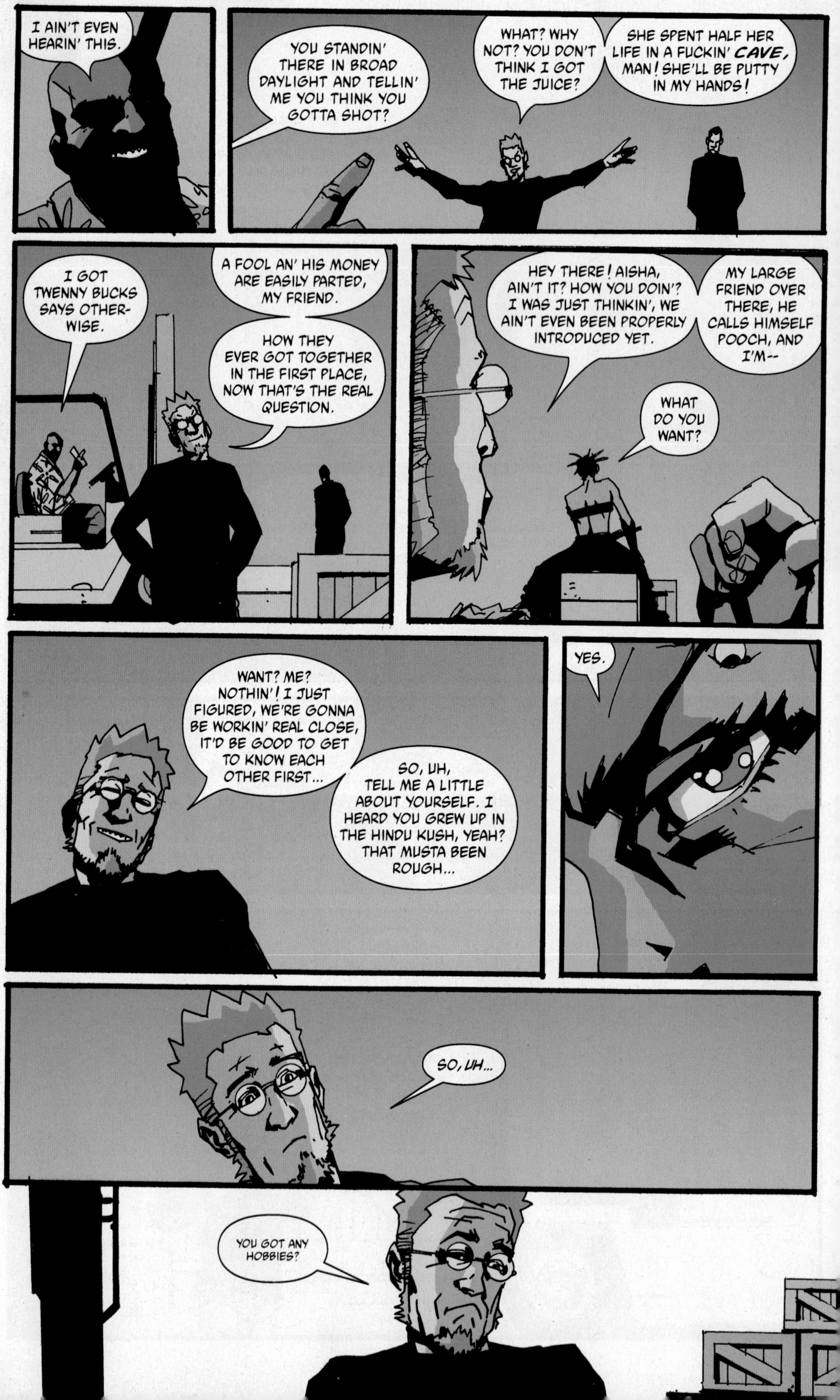
I AIN'T EVEN HEARIN' THIS.
YOU STANDIN' THERE IN BROAD DAYLIGHT AND TELLIN' ME YOU THINK YOU GOTTA SHOT?
WHAT? WHY NOT? YOU DON'T THINK I GOT THE JUICE?
SHE SPENT HALF HER LIFE IN A FUCKIN' CAVE, MAN! SHE'LL BE PUTTY IN MY HANDS!
I GOT TWENNY BUCKS SAYS OTHER-WISE.
A FOOL AN' HIS MONEY ARE EASILY PARTED, MY FRIEND.
HOW THEY EVER GOT TOGETHER IN THE FIRST PLACE, NOW THAT'S THE REAL QUESTION.
HEY THERE! AISHA, AIN'T IT? HOW YOU DOIN'? I WAS JUST THINKIN', WE AIN'T EVEN BEEN PROPERLY INTRODUCED YET.
MY LARGE FRIEND OVER THERE, HE CALLS HIMSELF POOCH, AND I'M--
WHAT DO YOU WANT?
WANT? ME? NOTHIN'! I JUST FIGURED, WE'RE GONNA BE WORKIN' REAL CLOSE, IT'D BE GOOD TO GET TO KNOW EACH OTHER FIRST...
SO, UH, TELL ME A LITTLE ABOUT YOURSELF. I HEARD YOU GREW UP IN THE HINDU KUSH, YEAH? THAT MUSTA BEEN ROUGH...
YES.
SO, UH...
YOU GOT ANY HOBBIES?

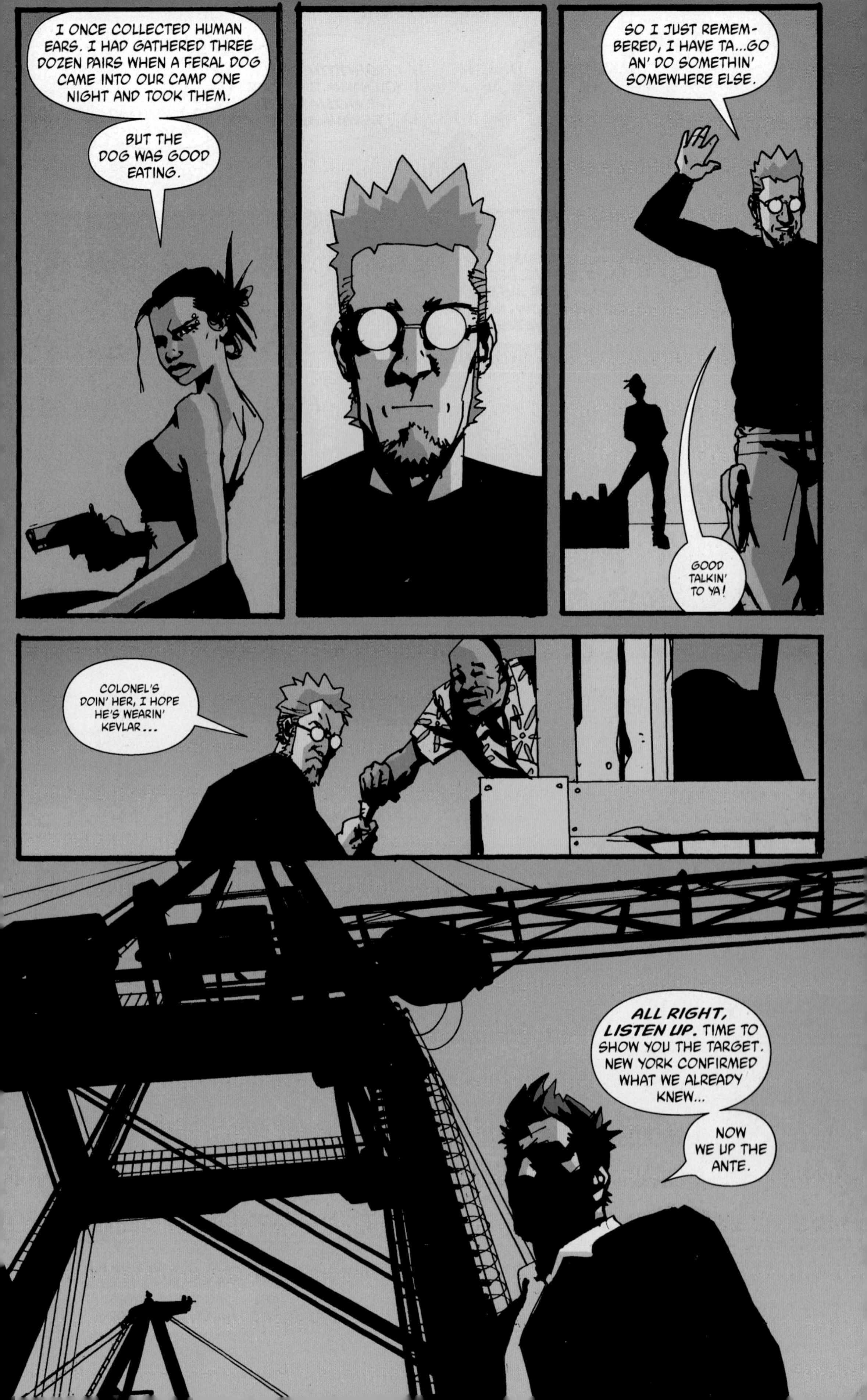
I ONCE COLLECTED HUMAN EARS. I HAD GATHERED THREE DOZEN PAIRS WHEN A FERAL DOG CAME INTO OUR CAMP ONE NIGHT AND TOOK THEM.
BUT THE DOG WAS GOOD EATING.
SO I JUST REMEMBERED, I HAVE TA...GO AN' DO SOMETHIN' SOMEWHERE ELSE.
GOOD TALKIN' TO YA!
COLONEL'S DOIN' HER, I HOPE HE'S WEARIN' KEVLAR...
ALL RIGHT, LISTEN UP. TIME TO SHOW YOU THE TARGET. NEW YORK CONFIRMED WHAT WE ALREADY KNEW...
NOW WE UP THE ANTE.

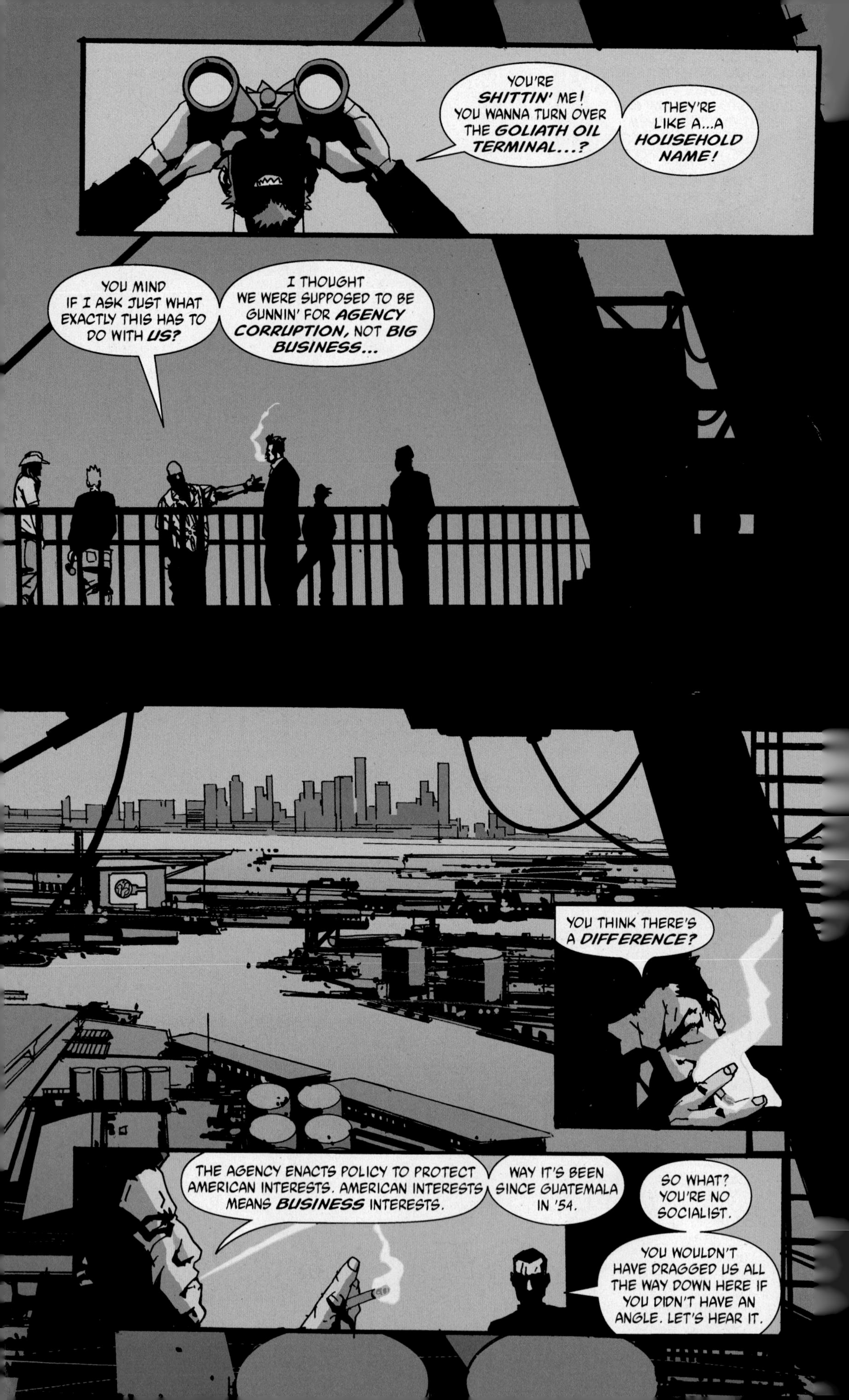
YOU'RE SHITTIN' ME! YOU WANNA TURN OVER THE GOLIATH OIL TERMINAL...?
THEY'RE LIKE A...A HOUSEHOLD NAME!
YOU MIND IF I ASK JUST WHAT EXACTLY THIS HAS TO DO WITH US?
I THOUGHT WE WERE SUPPOSED TO BE GUNNIN' FOR AGENCY CORRUPTION, NOT BIG BUSINESS...
YOU THINK THERE'S A DIFFERENCE?
THE AGENCY ENACTS POLICY TO PROTECT AMERICAN INTERESTS. AMERICAN INTERESTS MEANS BUSINESS INTERESTS.
WAY IT'S BEEN SINCE GUATEMALA IN '54.
SO WHAT? YOU'RE NO SOCIALIST.
YOU WOULDN'T HAVE DRAGGED US ALL THE WAY DOWN HERE IF YOU DIDN'T HAVE AN ANGLE. LET'S HEAR IT.

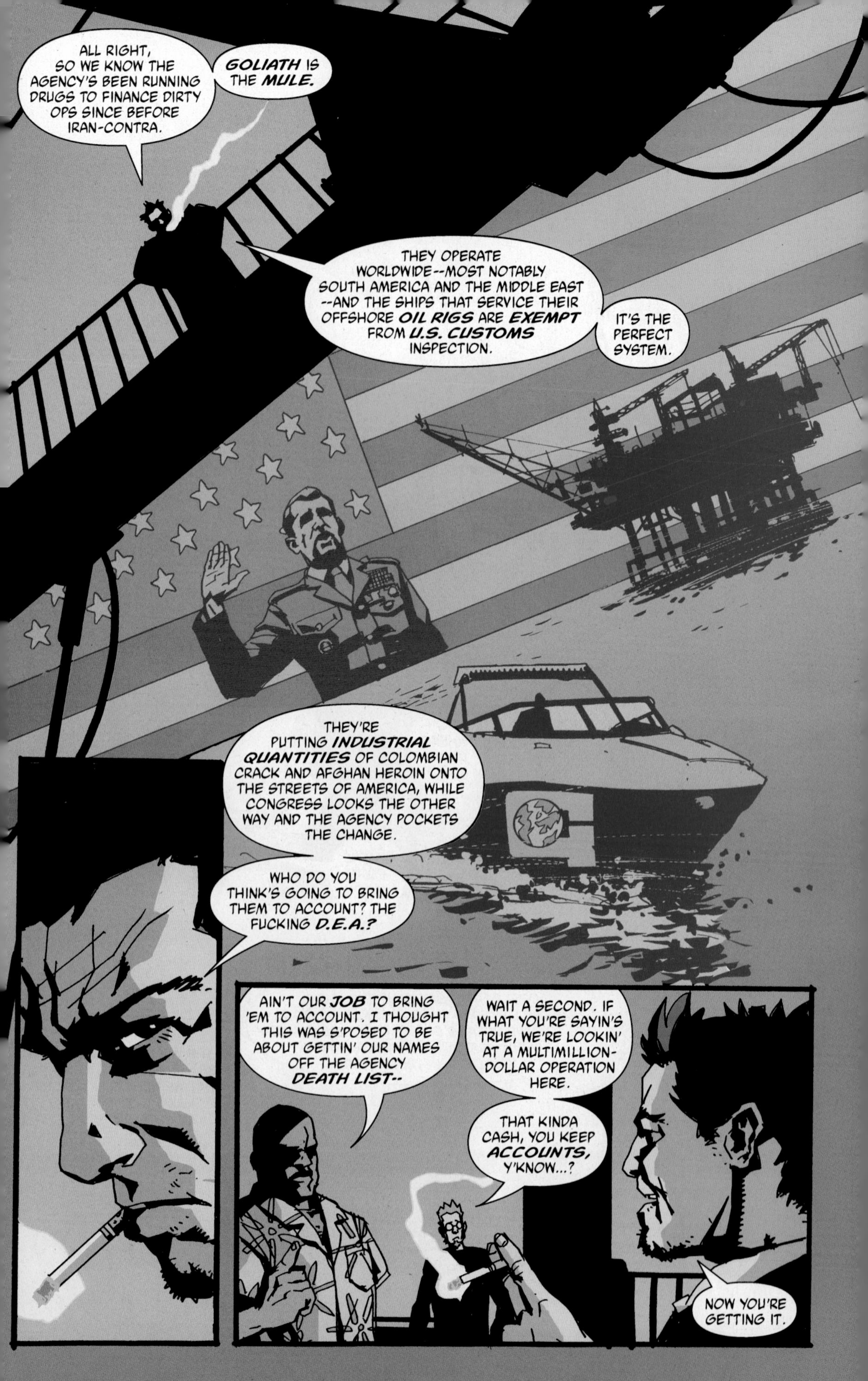
ALL RIGHT, SO WE KNOW THE AGENCY'S BEEN RUNNING DRUGS TO FINANCE DIRTY OPS SINCE BEFORE IRAN-CONTRA.
GOLIATH IS THE MULE.
THEY OPERATE WORLDWIDE--MOST NOTABLY SOUTH AMERICA AND THE MIDDLE EAST --AND THE SHIPS THAT SERVICE THEIR OFFSHORE OIL RIGS ARE EXEMPT FROM U.S. CUSTOMS INSPECTION.
IT'S THE PERFECT SYSTEM.
THEY'RE PUTTING INDUSTRIAL QUANTITIES OF COLOMBIAN CRACK AND AFGHAN HEROIN ONTO THE STREETS OF AMERICA, WHILE CONGRESS LOOKS THE OTHER WAY AND THE AGENCY POCKETS THE CHANGE.
WHO DO YOU THINK'S GOING TO BRING THEM TO ACCOUNT? THE FUCKING D.E.A.?
AIN'T OUR JOB TO BRING 'EM TO ACCOUNT. I THOUGHT THIS WAS S'POSED TO BE ABOUT GETTIN' OUR NAMES OFF THE AGENCY DEATH LIST--
WAIT A SECOND. IF WHAT YOU'RE SAYIN'S TRUE, WE'RE LOOKIN' AT A MULTIMILLION-DOLLAR OPERATION HERE.
THAT KINDA CASH, YOU KEEP ACCOUNTS, Y'KNOW...?
NOW YOU'RE GETTING IT.

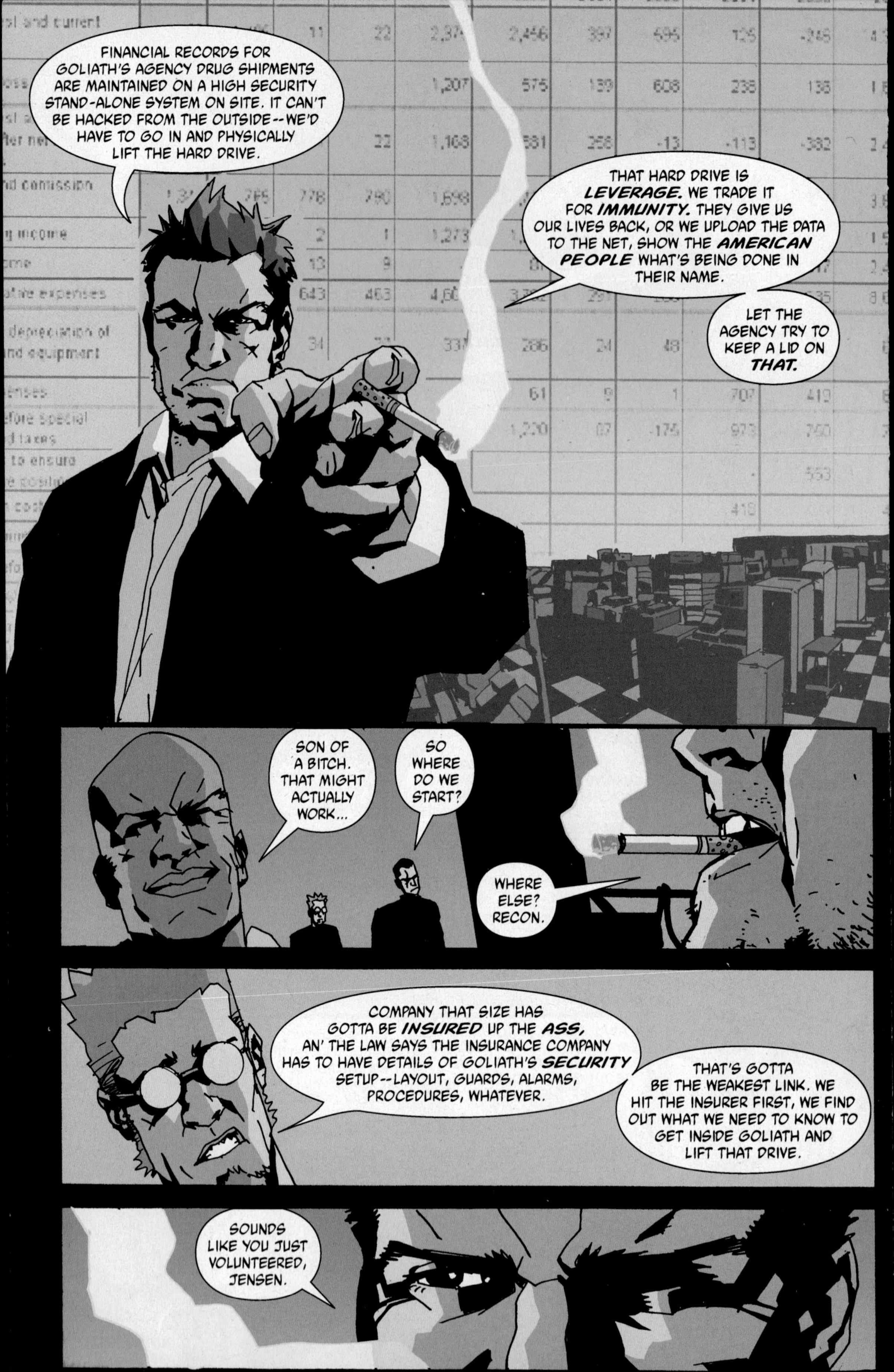
FINANCIAL RECORDS FOR GOLIATH'S AGENCY DRUG SHIPMENTS ARE MAINTAINED ON A HIGH SECURITY STAND-ALONE SYSTEM ON SITE. IT CAN'T BE HACKED FROM THE OUTSIDE--WE'D HAVE TO GO IN AND PHYSICALLY LIFT THE HARD DRIVE.
THAT HARD DRIVE IS *LEVERAGE.* WE TRADE IT FOR *IMMUNITY.* THEY GIVE US OUR LIVES BACK, OR WE UPLOAD THE DATA TO THE NET, SHOW THE *AMERICAN PEOPLE* WHAT'S BEING DONE IN THEIR NAME.
LET THE AGENCY TRY TO KEEP A LID ON *THAT.*
SON OF A BITCH. THAT MIGHT ACTUALLY WORK...
SO WHERE DO WE START?
WHERE ELSE? RECON.
COMPANY THAT SIZE HAS GOTTA BE *INSURED* UP THE *ASS,* AN' THE LAW SAYS THE INSURANCE COMPANY HAS TO HAVE DETAILS OF GOLIATH'S *SECURITY* SETUP--LAYOUT, GUARDS, ALARMS, PROCEDURES, WHATEVER.
THAT'S GOTTA BE THE WEAKEST LINK. WE HIT THE INSURER FIRST, WE FIND OUT WHAT WE NEED TO KNOW TO GET INSIDE GOLIATH AND LIFT THAT DRIVE.
SOUNDS LIKE YOU JUST VOLUNTEERED, JENSEN.

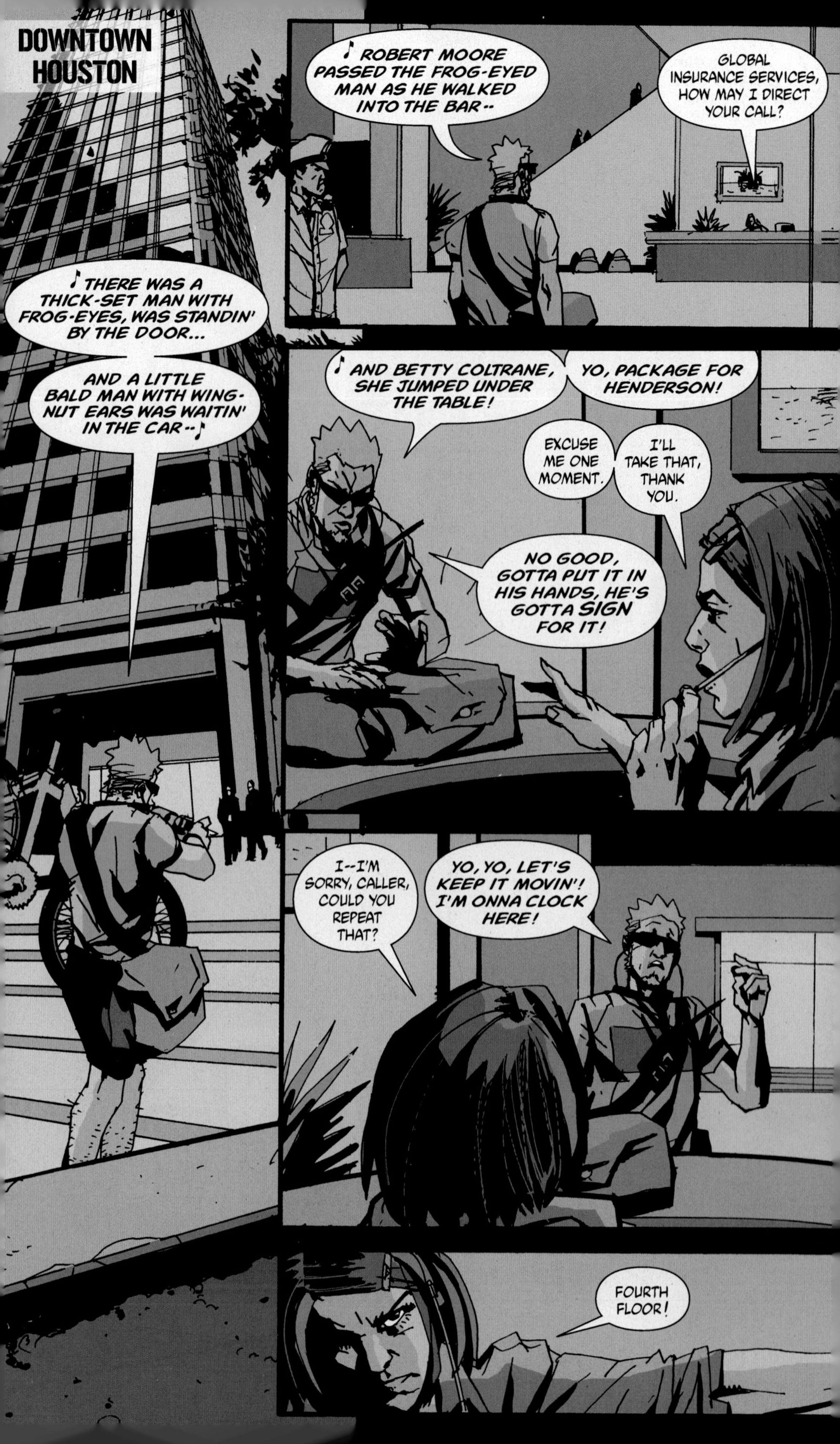
DOWNTOWN HOUSTON
♪ THERE WAS A THICK-SET MAN WITH FROG-EYES, WAS STANDIN' BY THE DOOR...
AND A LITTLE BALD MAN WITH WING-NUT EARS WAS WAITIN' IN THE CAR--♪
♪ ROBERT MOORE PASSED THE FROG-EYED MAN AS HE WALKED INTO THE BAR--
GLOBAL INSURANCE SERVICES, HOW MAY I DIRECT YOUR CALL?
♪ AND BETTY COLTRANE, SHE JUMPED UNDER THE TABLE!
YO, PACKAGE FOR HENDERSON!
EXCUSE ME ONE MOMENT.
I'LL TAKE THAT, THANK YOU.
NO GOOD, GOTTA PUT IT IN HIS HANDS, HE'S GOTTA SIGN FOR IT!
I--I'M SORRY, CALLER, COULD YOU REPEAT THAT?
YO, YO, LET'S KEEP IT MOVIN'! I'M ONNA CLOCK HERE!
FOURTH FLOOR!

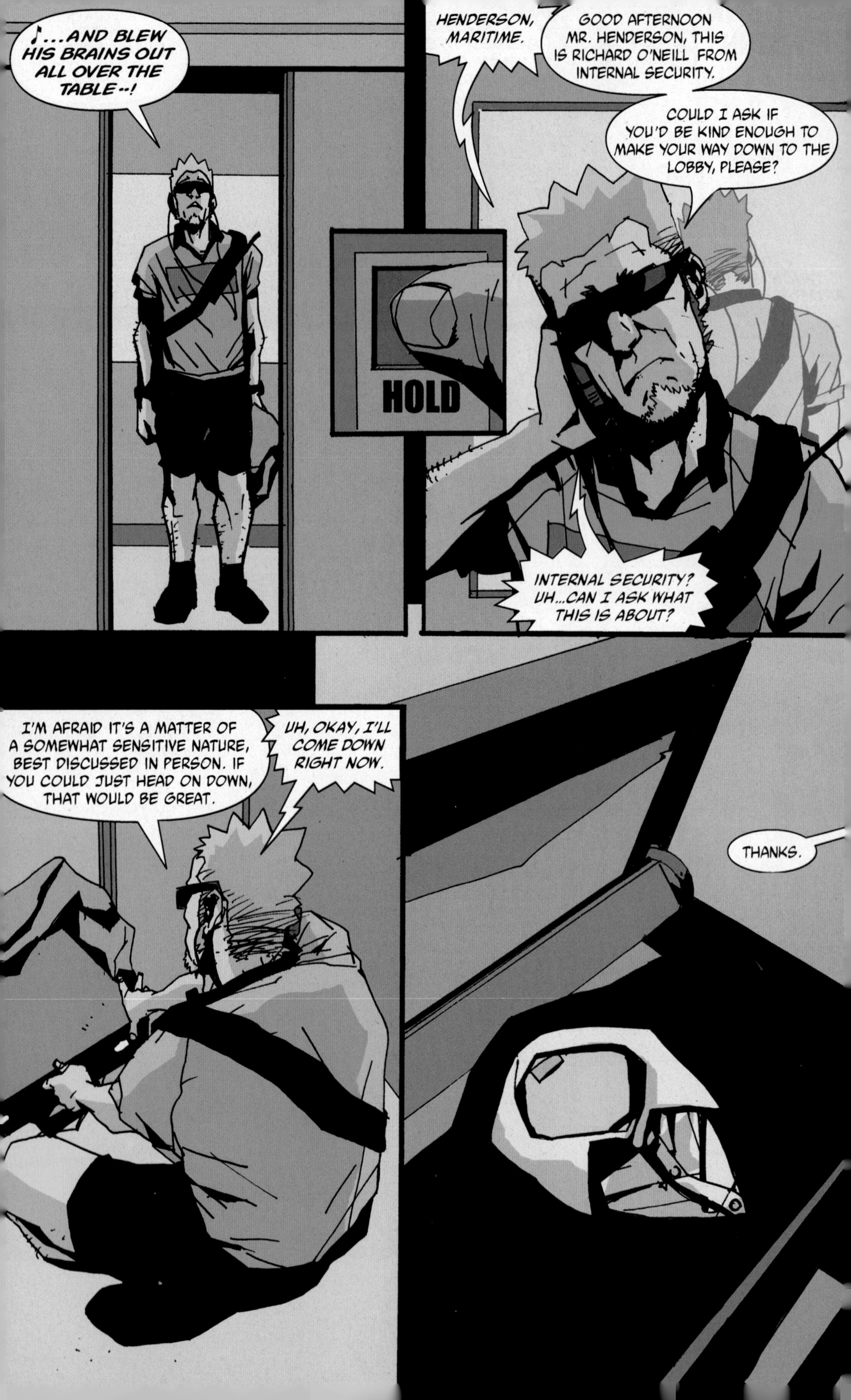
♪ ...AND BLEW HIS BRAINS OUT ALL OVER THE TABLE--!
HENDERSON, MARITIME.
GOOD AFTERNOON MR. HENDERSON, THIS IS RICHARD O'NEILL FROM INTERNAL SECURITY.
COULD I ASK IF YOU'D BE KIND ENOUGH TO MAKE YOUR WAY DOWN TO THE LOBBY, PLEASE?
HOLD
INTERNAL SECURITY? UH...CAN I ASK WHAT THIS IS ABOUT?
I'M AFRAID IT'S A MATTER OF A SOMEWHAT SENSITIVE NATURE, BEST DISCUSSED IN PERSON. IF YOU COULD JUST HEAD ON DOWN, THAT WOULD BE GREAT.
UH, OKAY, I'LL COME DOWN RIGHT NOW.
THANKS.

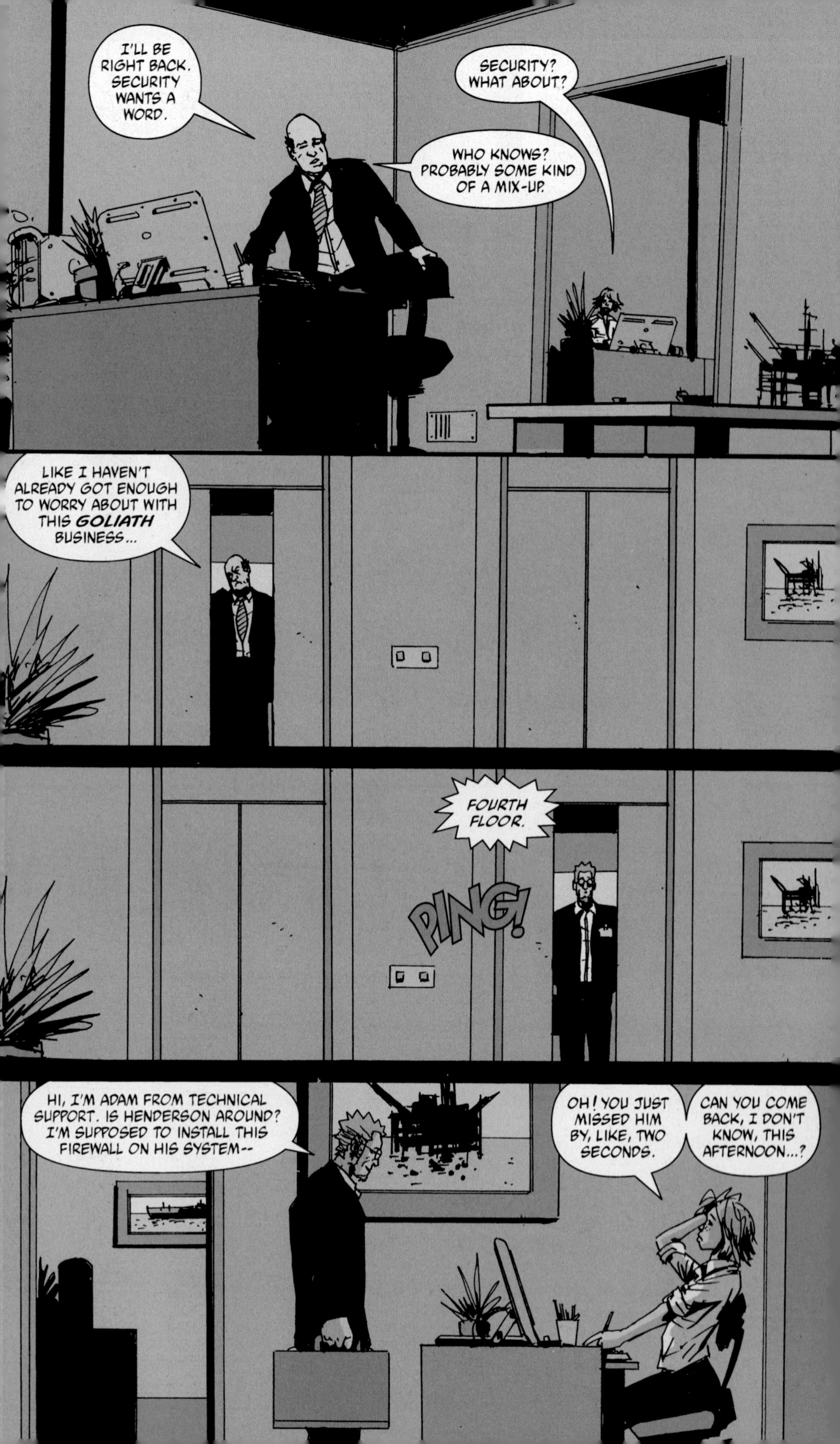
I'LL BE RIGHT BACK. SECURITY WANTS A WORD.
SECURITY? WHAT ABOUT?
WHO KNOWS? PROBABLY SOME KIND OF A MIX-UP.
LIKE I HAVEN'T ALREADY GOT ENOUGH TO WORRY ABOUT WITH THIS **GOLIATH** BUSINESS...
FOURTH FLOOR.
PING!
HI, I'M ADAM FROM TECHNICAL SUPPORT. IS HENDERSON AROUND? I'M SUPPOSED TO INSTALL THIS FIREWALL ON HIS SYSTEM--
OH! YOU JUST MISSED HIM BY, LIKE, TWO SECONDS.
CAN YOU COME BACK, I DON'T KNOW, THIS AFTERNOON...?

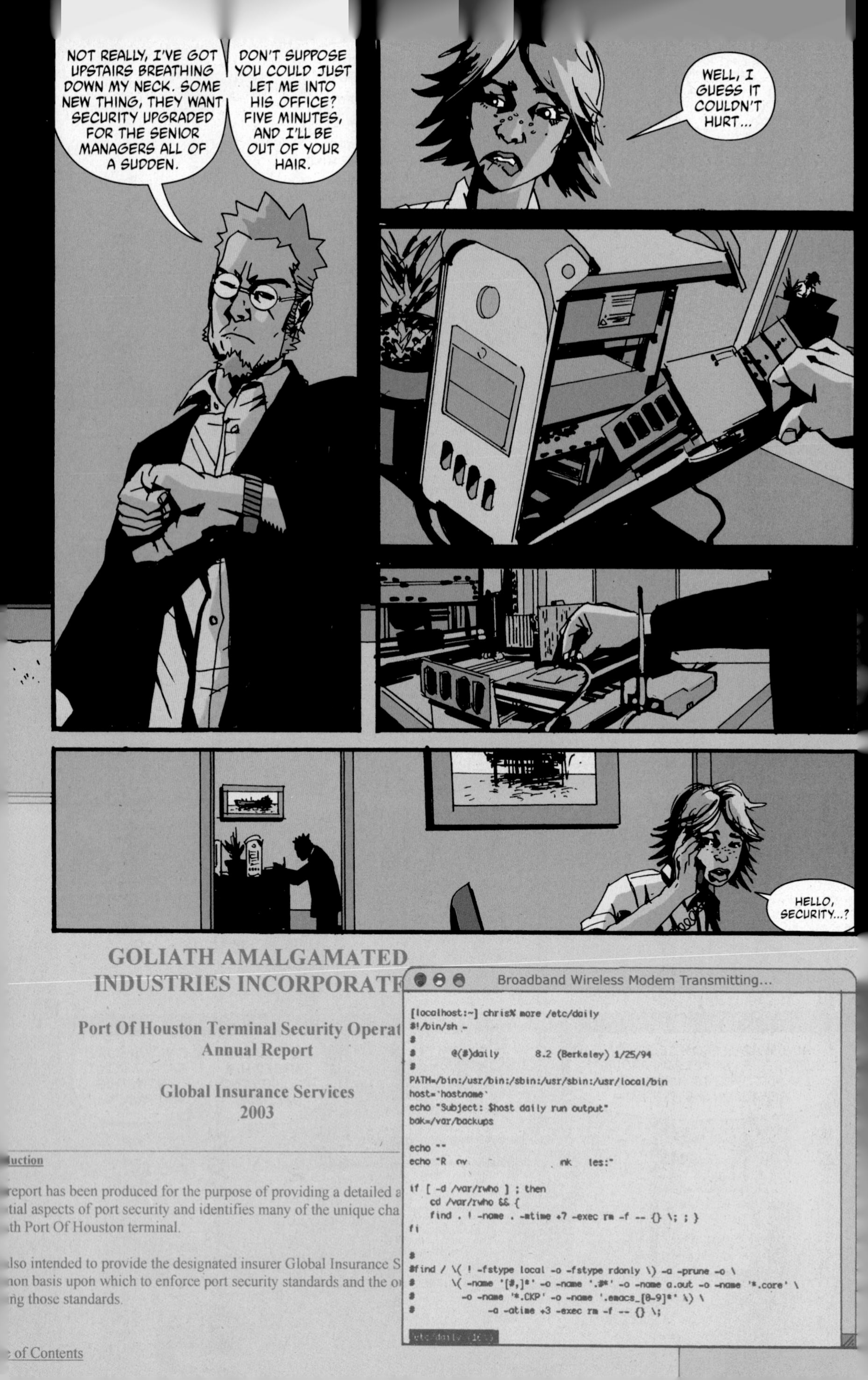
NOT REALLY, I'VE GOT UPSTAIRS BREATHING DOWN MY NECK. SOME NEW THING, THEY WANT SECURITY UPGRADED FOR THE SENIOR MANAGERS ALL OF A SUDDEN.
DON'T SUPPOSE YOU COULD JUST LET ME INTO HIS OFFICE? FIVE MINUTES, AND I'LL BE OUT OF YOUR HAIR.
WELL, I GUESS IT COULDN'T HURT...
HELLO, SECURITY...?
GOLIATH AMALGAMATED
INDUSTRIES INCORPORATE
Port Of Houston Terminal Security Operat
Annual Report
Global Insurance Services
2003
luction
report has been produced for the purpose of providing a detailed a
tial aspects of port security and identifies many of the unique cha
th Port Of Houston terminal.
lso intended to provide the designated insurer Global Insurance S
non basis upon which to enforce port security standards and the o
ng those standards.
of Contents
Broadband Wireless Modem Transmitting...
[localhost:~] chris% more /etc/daily
#!/bin/sh -
#
@(#)daily   8.2 (Berkeley) 1/25/94
#
PATH=/bin:/usr/bin:/sbin:/usr/sbin:/usr/local/bin
host=`hostname`
echo "Subject: $host daily run output"
bak=/var/backups
echo ""
if [-d /var/rwho] ; then
cd /var/rwho && {
find . ! -name . -mtime +7 -exec rm -f -- {} \; ; }
fi
#
#find / \(! -fstype local -o -fstype rdonly \) -a -prune -o \
\(-name '[#,]*' -o -name '.#*' -o -name a.out -o -name '*.core' \
-o -name '*.CKP' -o -name '.emacs_[0-9]*' \) \
-a -atime +3 -exec rm -f -- {} \;

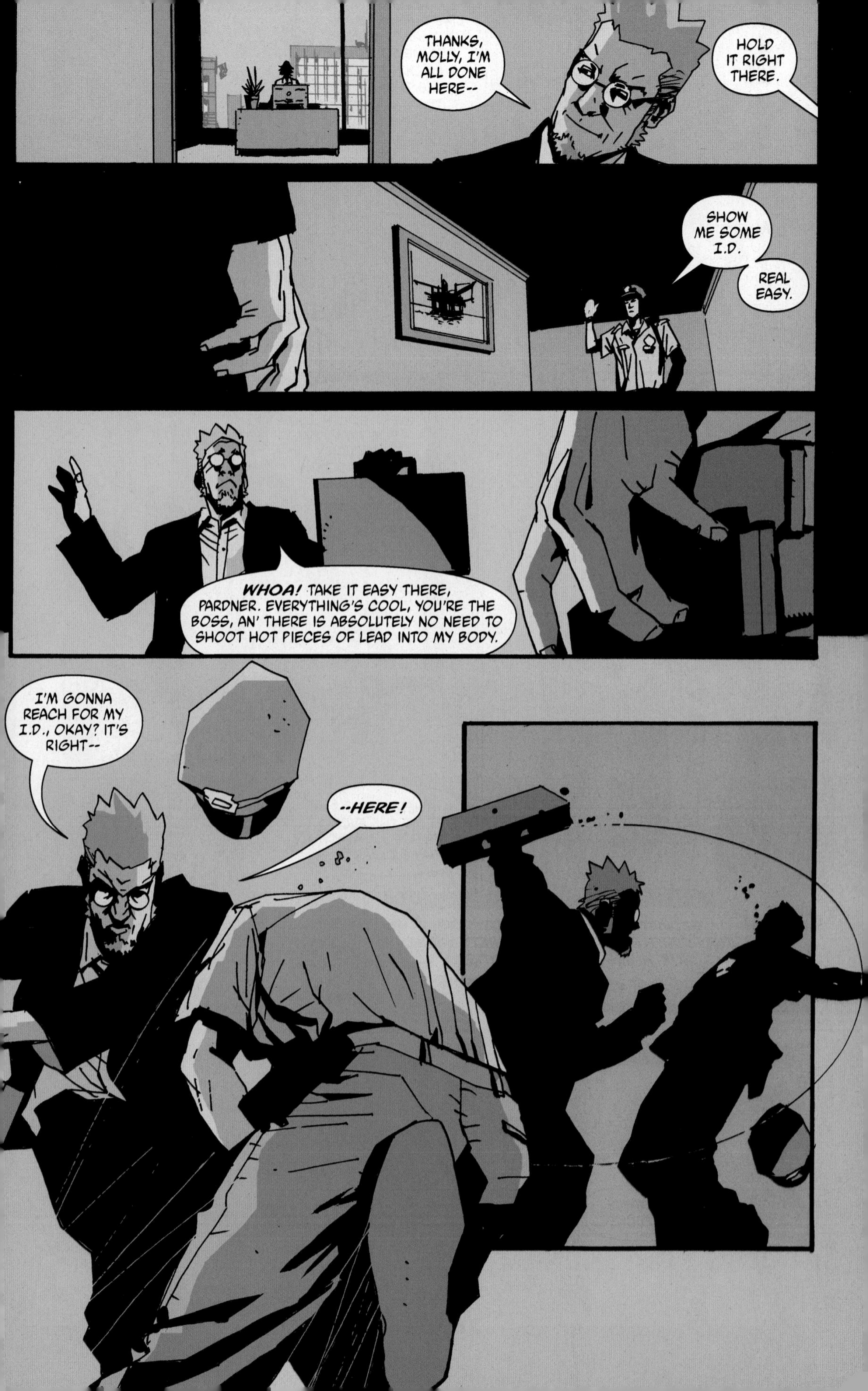
THANKS, MOLLY, I'M ALL DONE HERE--
HOLD IT RIGHT THERE.
SHOW ME SOME I.D.
REAL EASY.
WHOA! TAKE IT EASY THERE, PARDNER. EVERYTHING'S COOL, YOU'RE THE BOSS, AN' THERE IS ABSOLUTELY NO NEED TO SHOOT HOT PIECES OF LEAD INTO MY BODY.
I'M GONNA REACH FOR MY I.D., OKAY? IT'S RIGHT--
--HERE!

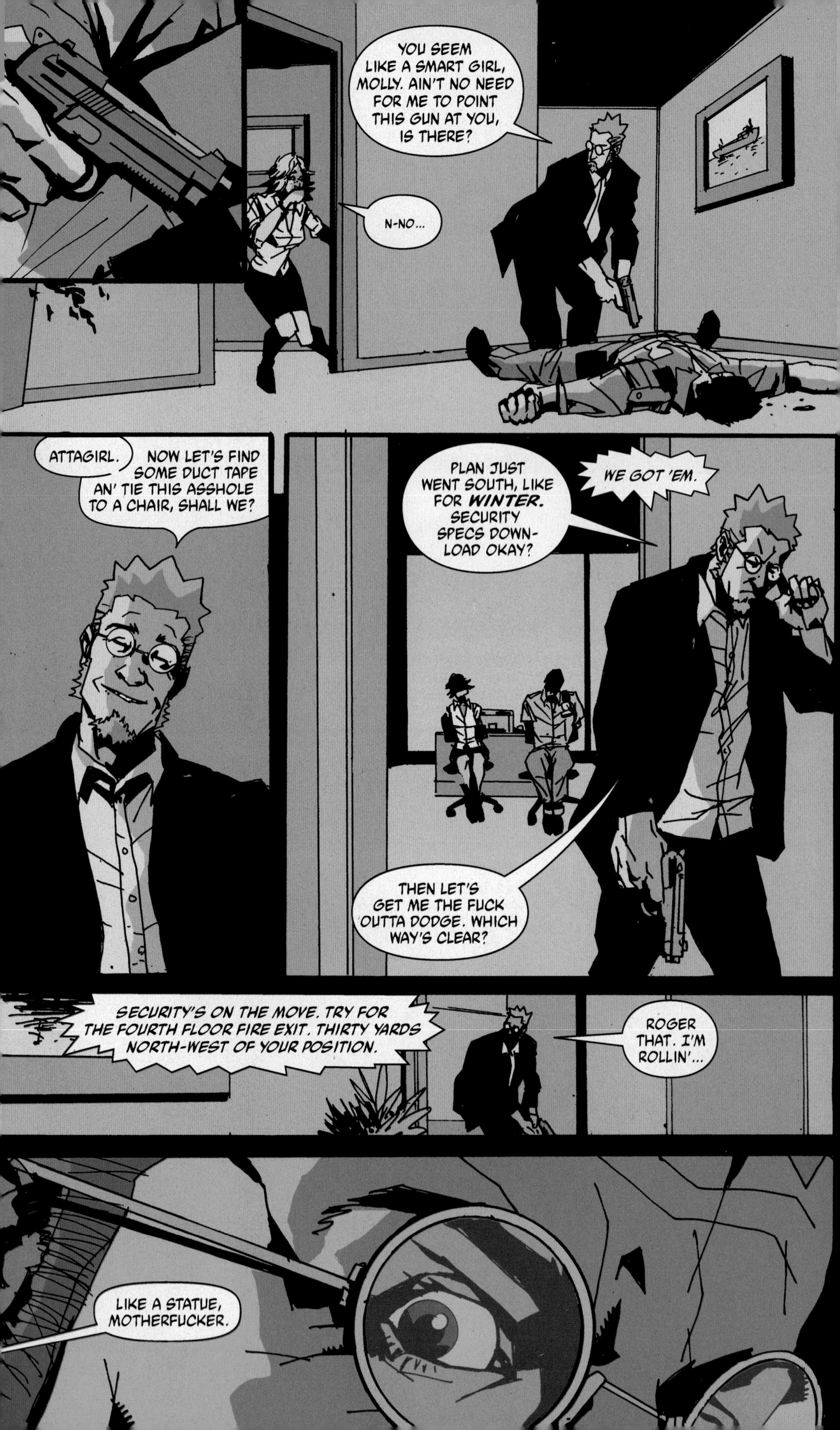
YOU SEEM LIKE A SMART GIRL, MOLLY. AIN'T NO NEED FOR ME TO POINT THIS GUN AT YOU, IS THERE?
N-NO...
ATTAGIRL.
NOW LET'S FIND SOME DUCT TAPE AN' TIE THIS ASSHOLE TO A CHAIR, SHALL WE?
PLAN JUST WENT SOUTH, LIKE FOR *WINTER.* SECURITY SPECS DOWN-LOAD OKAY?
WE GOT 'EM.
THEN LET'S GET ME THE FUCK OUTTA DODGE. WHICH WAY'S CLEAR?
SECURITY'S ON THE MOVE. TRY FOR THE FOURTH FLOOR FIRE EXIT. THIRTY YARDS NORTH-WEST OF YOUR POSITION.
ROGER THAT. I'M ROLLIN'...
LIKE A STATUE, MOTHERFUCKER.

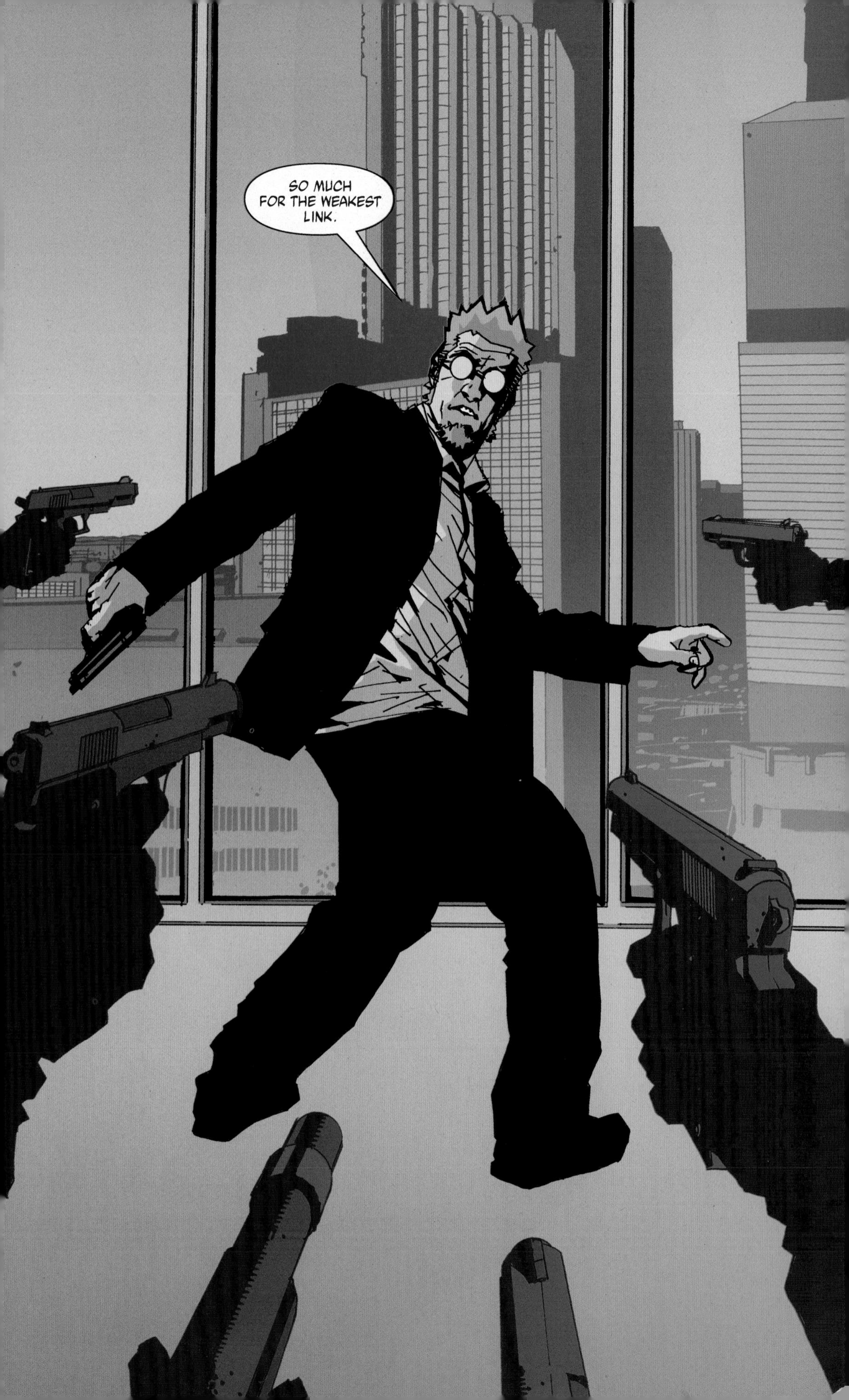
SO MUCH FOR THE WEAKEST LINK.

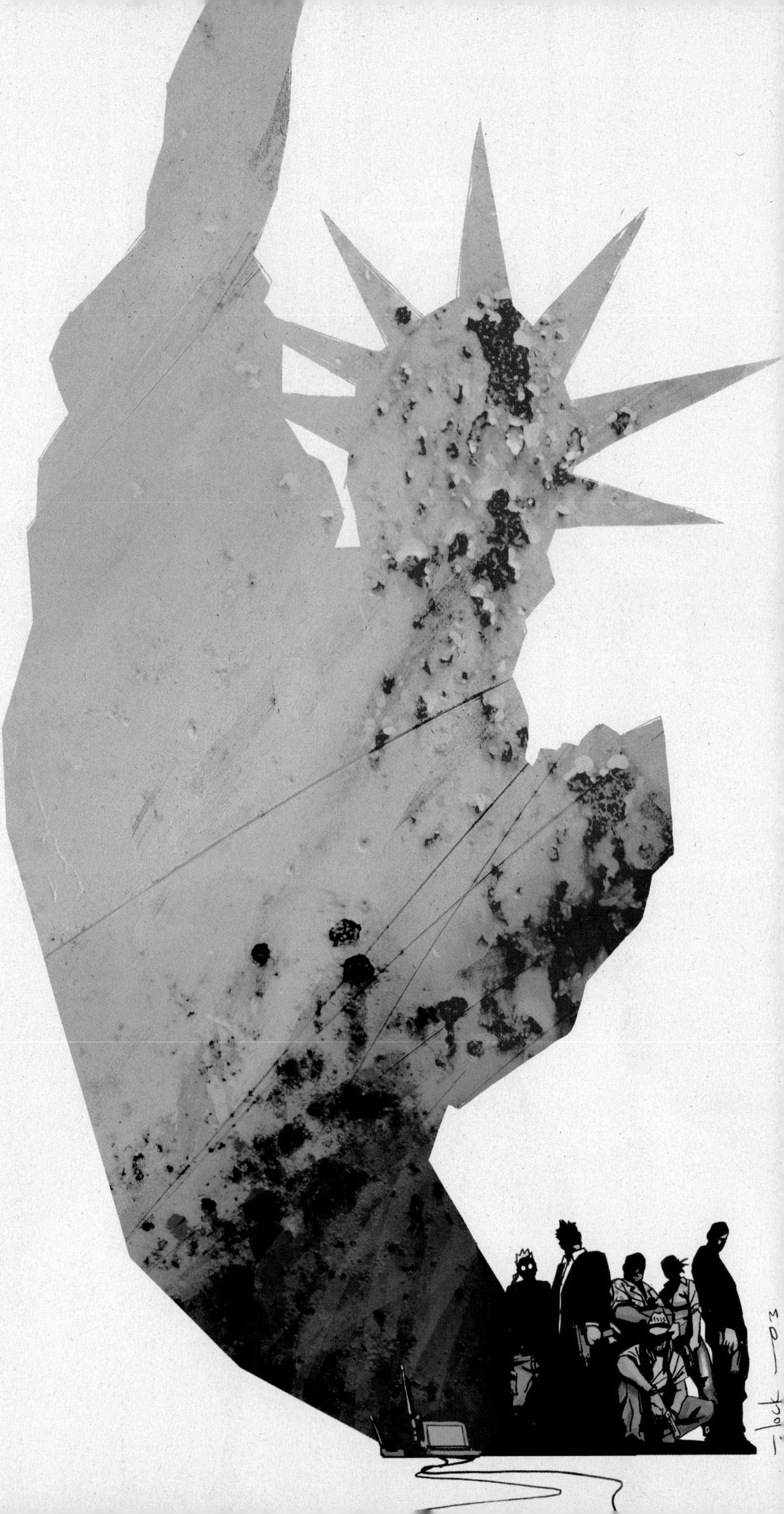

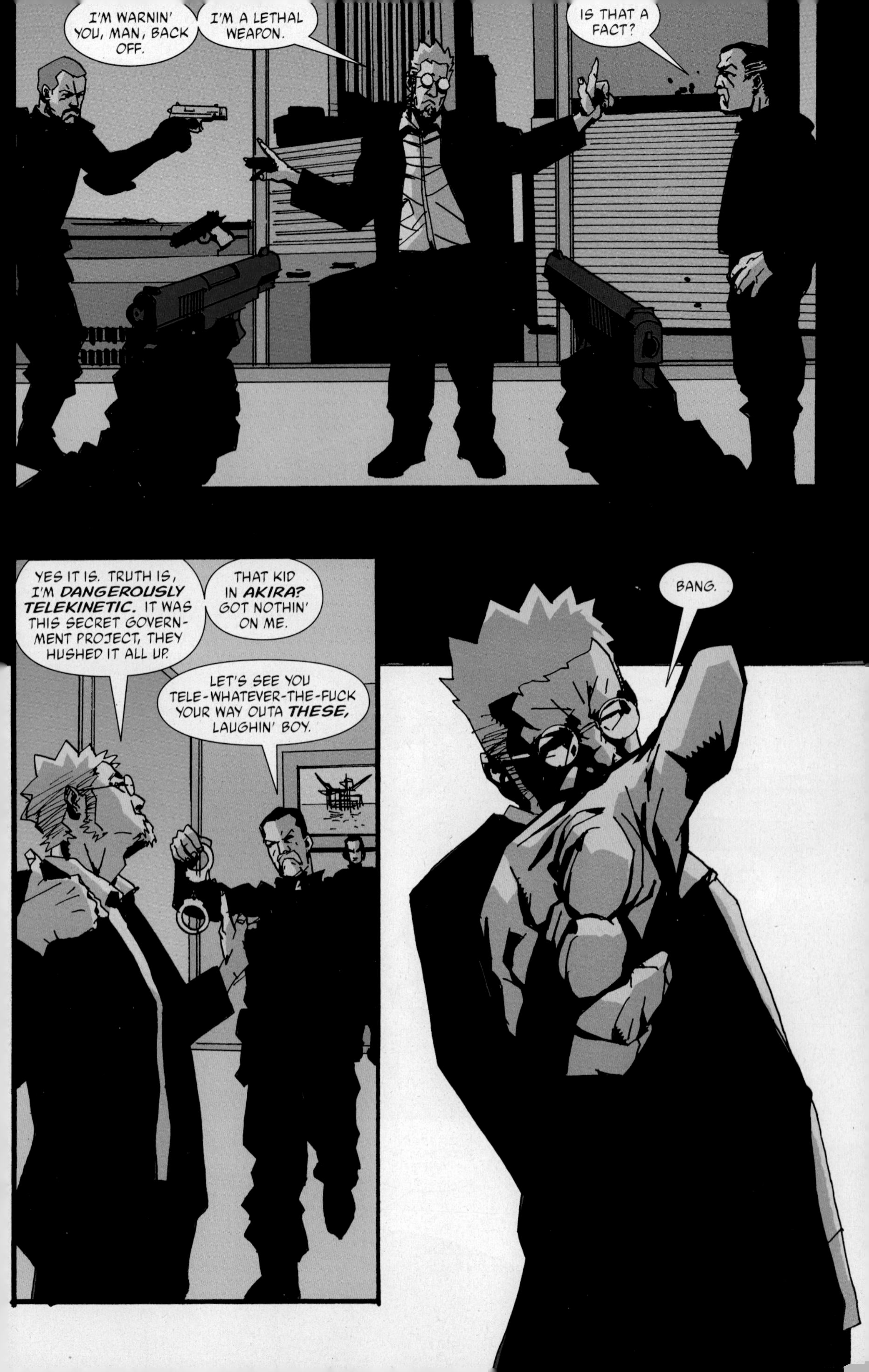
I'M WARNIN' YOU, MAN, BACK OFF.
I'M A LETHAL WEAPON.
IS THAT A FACT?
YES IT IS. TRUTH IS, I'M DANGEROUSLY TELEKINETIC. IT WAS THIS SECRET GOVERNMENT PROJECT, THEY HUSHED IT ALL UP.
THAT KID IN AKIRA? GOT NOTHIN' ON ME.
LET'S SEE YOU TELE-WHATEVER-THE-FUCK YOUR WAY OUTA THESE, LAUGHIN' BOY.
BANG.

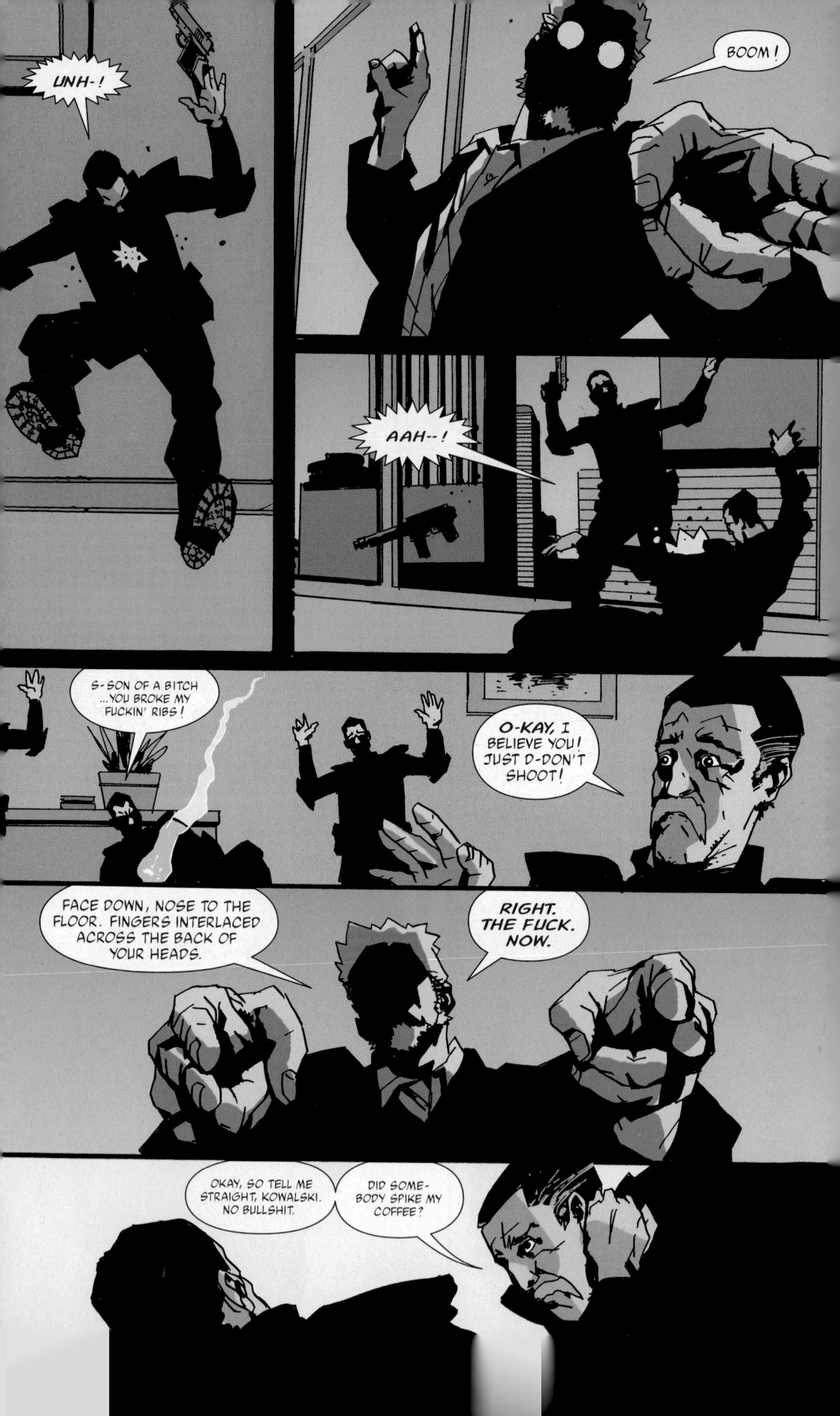
UNH-!
BOOM!
AAH--!
S-SON OF A BITCH ...YOU BROKE MY FUCKIN' RIBS!
O-KAY, I BELIEVE YOU! JUST D-DON'T SHOOT!
FACE DOWN, NOSE TO THE FLOOR. FINGERS INTERLACED ACROSS THE BACK OF YOUR HEADS.
RIGHT. THE FUCK. NOW.
OKAY, SO TELL ME STRAIGHT, KOWALSKI. NO BULLSHIT.
DID SOME-BODY SPIKE MY COFFEE?

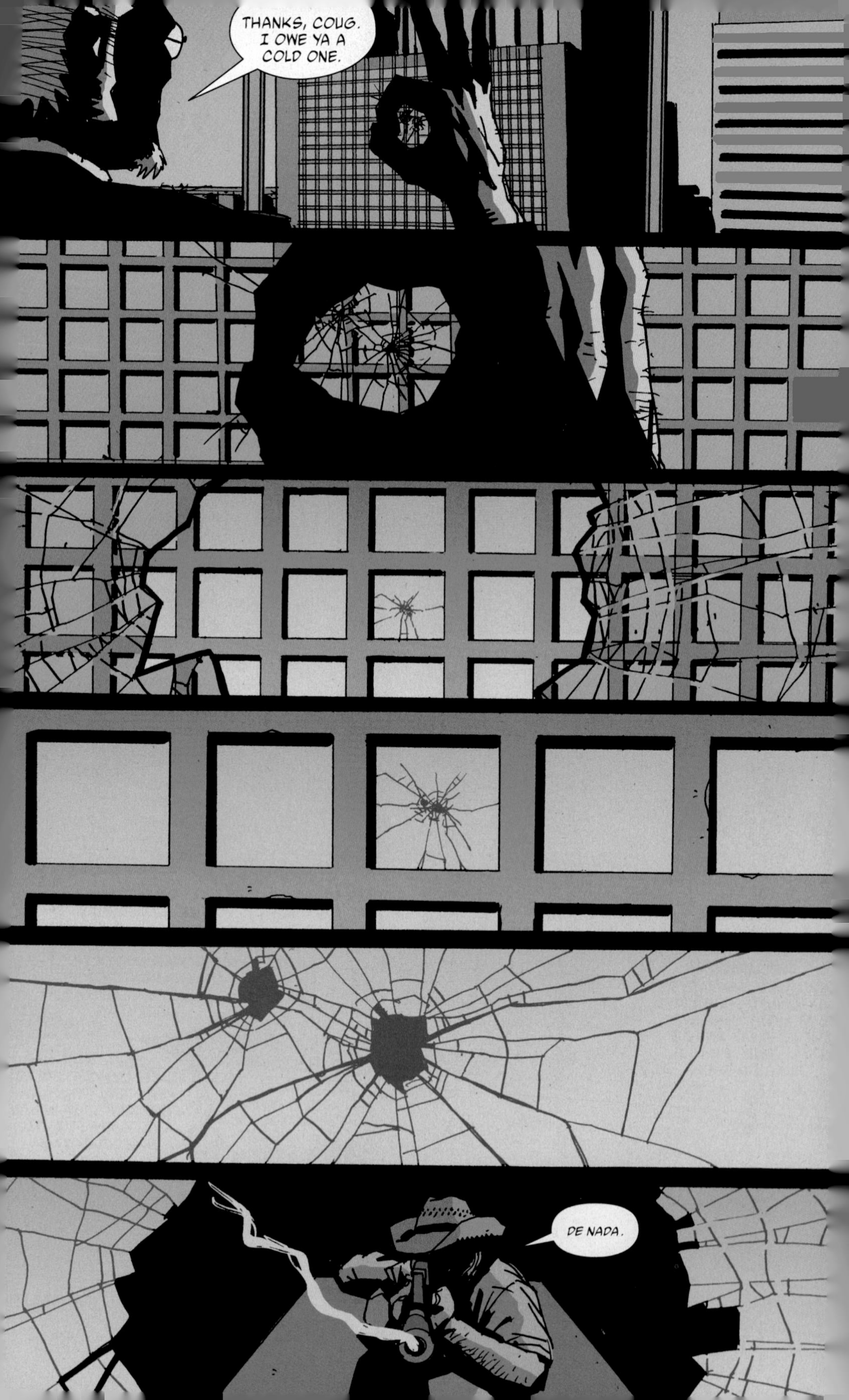
THANKS, COUG. I OWE YA A COLD ONE.
DE NADA.

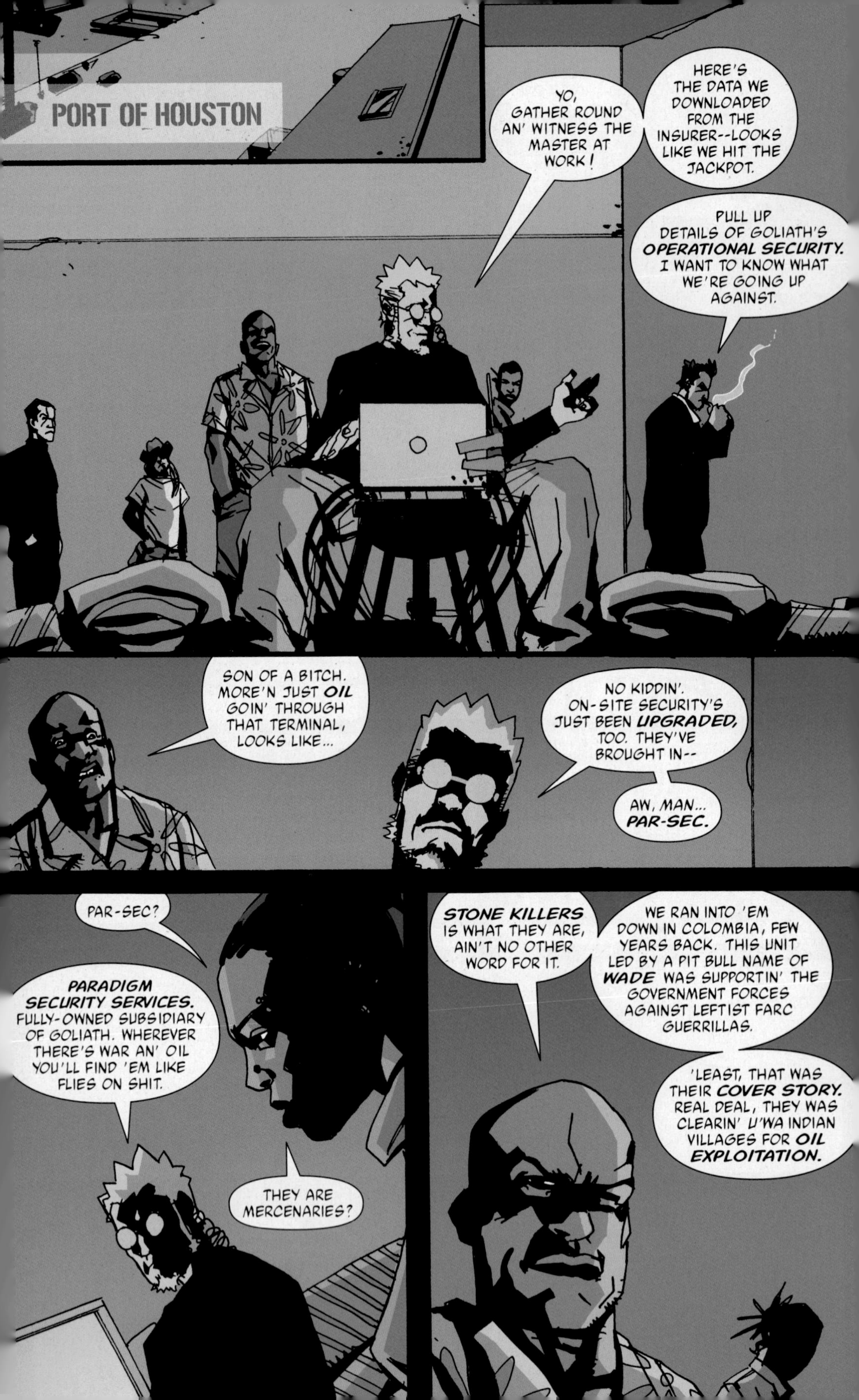
PORT OF HOUSTON
YO, GATHER ROUND AN' WITNESS THE MASTER AT WORK!
HERE'S THE DATA WE DOWNLOADED FROM THE INSURER--LOOKS LIKE WE HIT THE JACKPOT.
PULL UP DETAILS OF GOLIATH'S OPERATIONAL SECURITY. I WANT TO KNOW WHAT WE'RE GOING UP AGAINST.
SON OF A BITCH. MORE'N JUST OIL GOIN' THROUGH THAT TERMINAL, LOOKS LIKE...
NO KIDDIN'. ON-SITE SECURITY'S JUST BEEN UPGRADED, TOO. THEY'VE BROUGHT IN--
AW, MAN... PAR-SEC.
PAR-SEC?
PARADIGM SECURITY SERVICES. FULLY-OWNED SUBSIDIARY OF GOLIATH. WHEREVER THERE'S WAR AN' OIL YOU'LL FIND 'EM LIKE FLIES ON SHIT.
THEY ARE MERCENARIES?
STONE KILLERS IS WHAT THEY ARE, AIN'T NO OTHER WORD FOR IT.
WE RAN INTO 'EM DOWN IN COLOMBIA, FEW YEARS BACK. THIS UNIT LED BY A PIT BULL NAME OF WADE WAS SUPPORTIN' THE GOVERNMENT FORCES AGAINST LEFTIST FARC GUERRILLAS.
'LEAST, THAT WAS THEIR COVER STORY. REAL DEAL, THEY WAS CLEARIN' U'WA INDIAN VILLAGES FOR OIL EXPLOITATION.

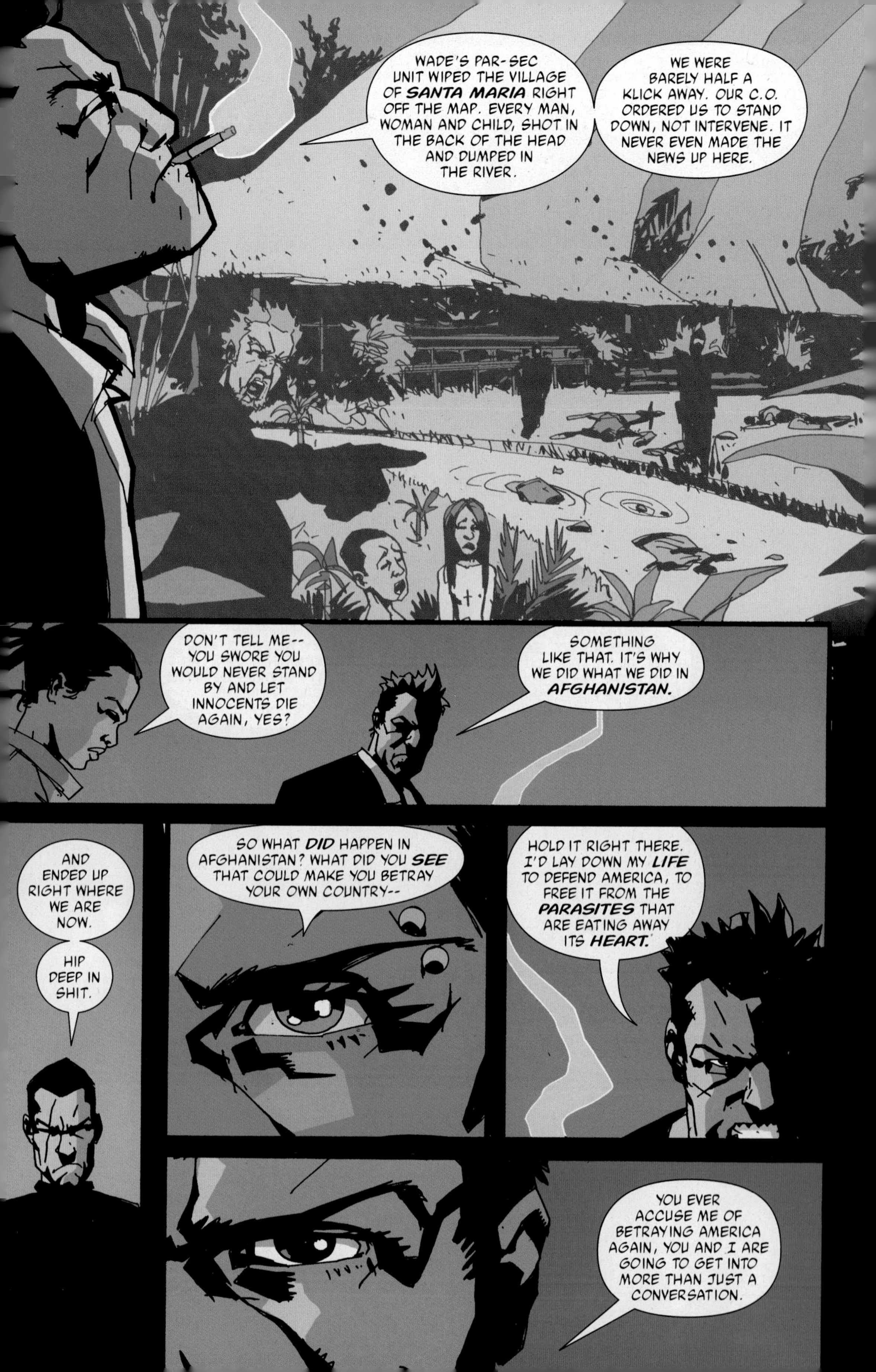
WADE'S PAR-SEC UNIT WIPED THE VILLAGE OF SANTA MARIA RIGHT OFF THE MAP. EVERY MAN, WOMAN AND CHILD, SHOT IN THE BACK OF THE HEAD AND DUMPED IN THE RIVER.
WE WERE BARELY HALF A KLICK AWAY. OUR C.O. ORDERED US TO STAND DOWN, NOT INTERVENE. IT NEVER EVEN MADE THE NEWS UP HERE.
DON'T TELL ME-- YOU SWORE YOU WOULD NEVER STAND BY AND LET INNOCENTS DIE AGAIN, YES?
SOMETHING LIKE THAT. IT'S WHY WE DID WHAT WE DID IN AFGHANISTAN.
AND ENDED UP RIGHT WHERE WE ARE NOW.
HIP DEEP IN SHIT.
SO WHAT DID HAPPEN IN AFGHANISTAN? WHAT DID YOU SEE THAT COULD MAKE YOU BETRAY YOUR OWN COUNTRY--
HOLD IT RIGHT THERE. I'D LAY DOWN MY LIFE TO DEFEND AMERICA, TO FREE IT FROM THE PARASITES THAT ARE EATING AWAY ITS HEART.
YOU EVER ACCUSE ME OF BETRAYING AMERICA AGAIN, YOU AND I ARE GOING TO GET INTO MORE THAN JUST A CONVERSATION.

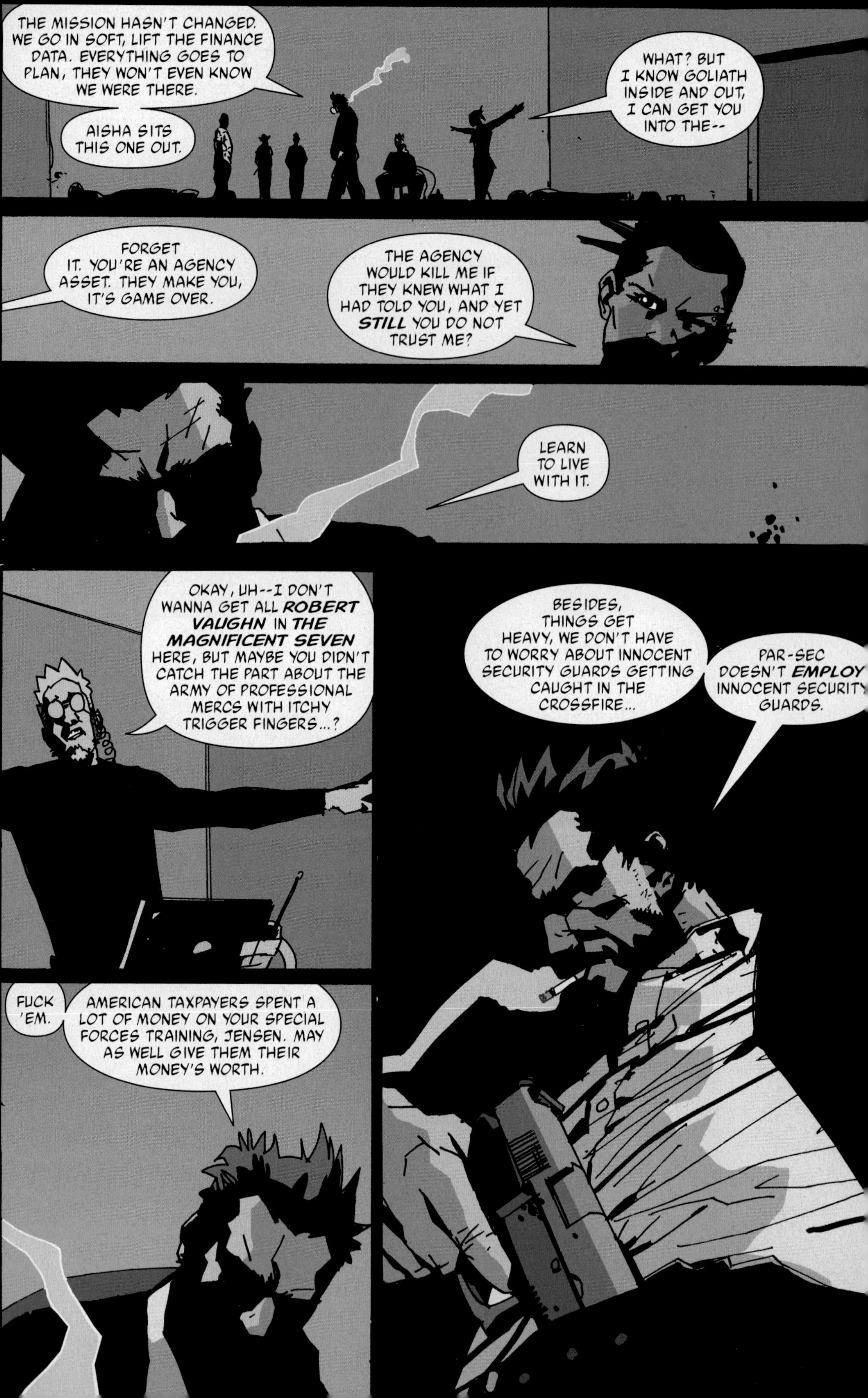
THE MISSION HASN'T CHANGED. WE GO IN SOFT, LIFT THE FINANCE DATA. EVERYTHING GOES TO PLAN, THEY WON'T EVEN KNOW WE WERE THERE.
AISHA SITS THIS ONE OUT.
WHAT? BUT I KNOW GOLIATH INSIDE AND OUT, I CAN GET YOU INTO THE--
FORGET IT. YOU'RE AN AGENCY ASSET. THEY MAKE YOU, IT'S GAME OVER.
THE AGENCY WOULD KILL ME IF THEY KNEW WHAT I HAD TOLD YOU, AND YET STILL YOU DO NOT TRUST ME?
LEARN TO LIVE WITH IT.
OKAY, UH--I DON'T WANNA GET ALL ROBERT VAUGHN IN THE MAGNIFICENT SEVEN HERE, BUT MAYBE YOU DIDN'T CATCH THE PART ABOUT THE ARMY OF PROFESSIONAL MERCS WITH ITCHY TRIGGER FINGERS...?
BESIDES, THINGS GET HEAVY, WE DON'T HAVE TO WORRY ABOUT INNOCENT SECURITY GUARDS GETTING CAUGHT IN THE CROSSFIRE...
PAR-SEC DOESN'T EMPLOY INNOCENT SECURITY GUARDS.
FUCK 'EM.
AMERICAN TAXPAYERS SPENT A LOT OF MONEY ON YOUR SPECIAL FORCES TRAINING, JENSEN. MAY AS WELL GIVE THEM THEIR MONEY'S WORTH.

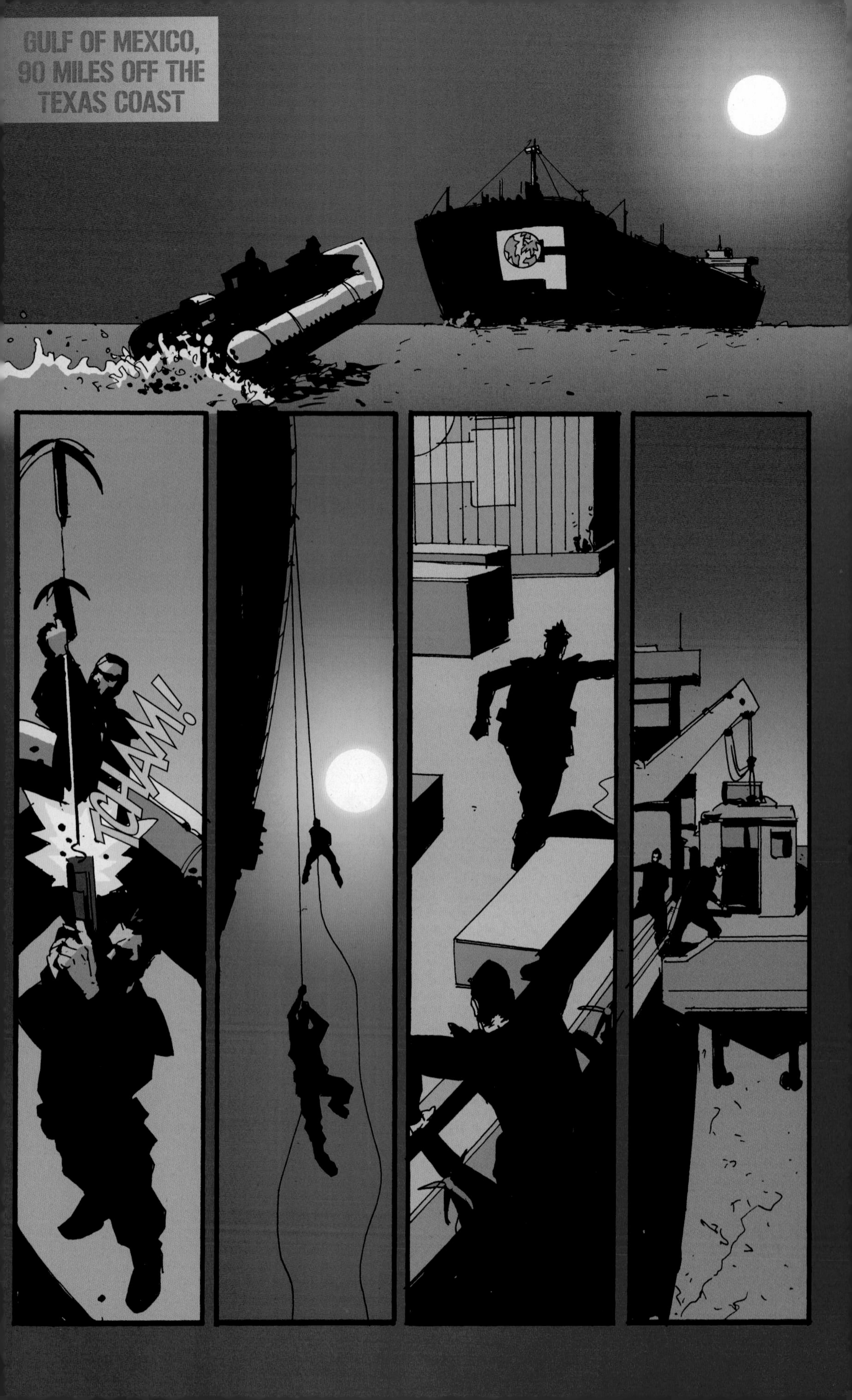
GULF OF MEXICO, 90 MILES OFF THE TEXAS COAST
TCHAM!

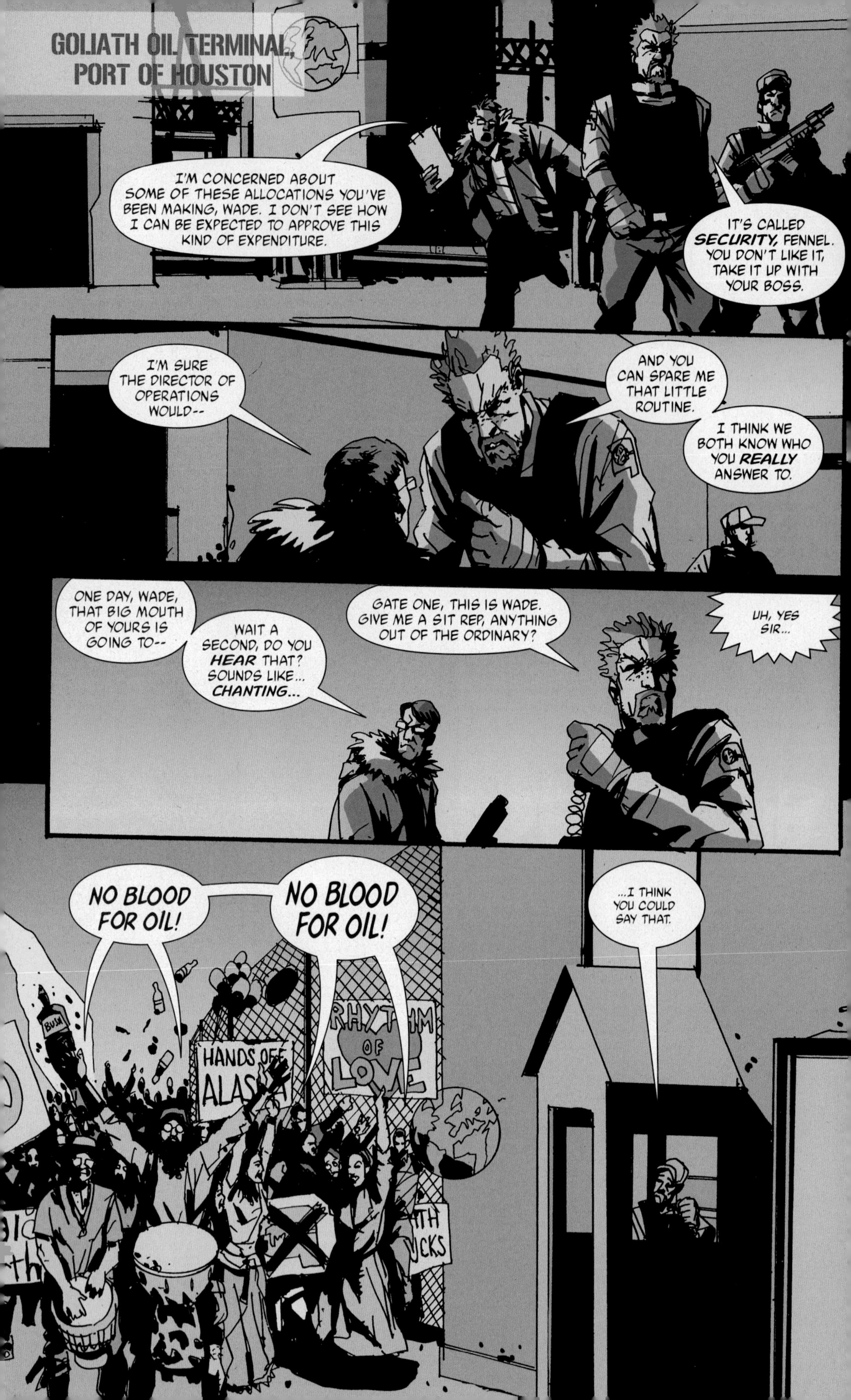
GOLIATH OIL TERMINAL, PORT OF HOUSTON
I'M CONCERNED ABOUT SOME OF THESE ALLOCATIONS YOU'VE BEEN MAKING, WADE. I DON'T SEE HOW I CAN BE EXPECTED TO APPROVE THIS KIND OF EXPENDITURE.
IT'S CALLED SECURITY, FENNEL. YOU DON'T LIKE IT, TAKE IT UP WITH YOUR BOSS.
I'M SURE THE DIRECTOR OF OPERATIONS WOULD--
AND YOU CAN SPARE ME THAT LITTLE ROUTINE.
I THINK WE BOTH KNOW WHO YOU REALLY ANSWER TO.
ONE DAY, WADE, THAT BIG MOUTH OF YOURS IS GOING TO--
WAIT A SECOND, DO YOU HEAR THAT? SOUNDS LIKE... CHANTING...
GATE ONE, THIS IS WADE. GIVE ME A SIT REP, ANYTHING OUT OF THE ORDINARY?
UH, YES SIR...
NO BLOOD FOR OIL!
NO BLOOD FOR OIL!
...I THINK YOU COULD SAY THAT.
HANDS OFF ALAS
RHYTHM OF LOVE

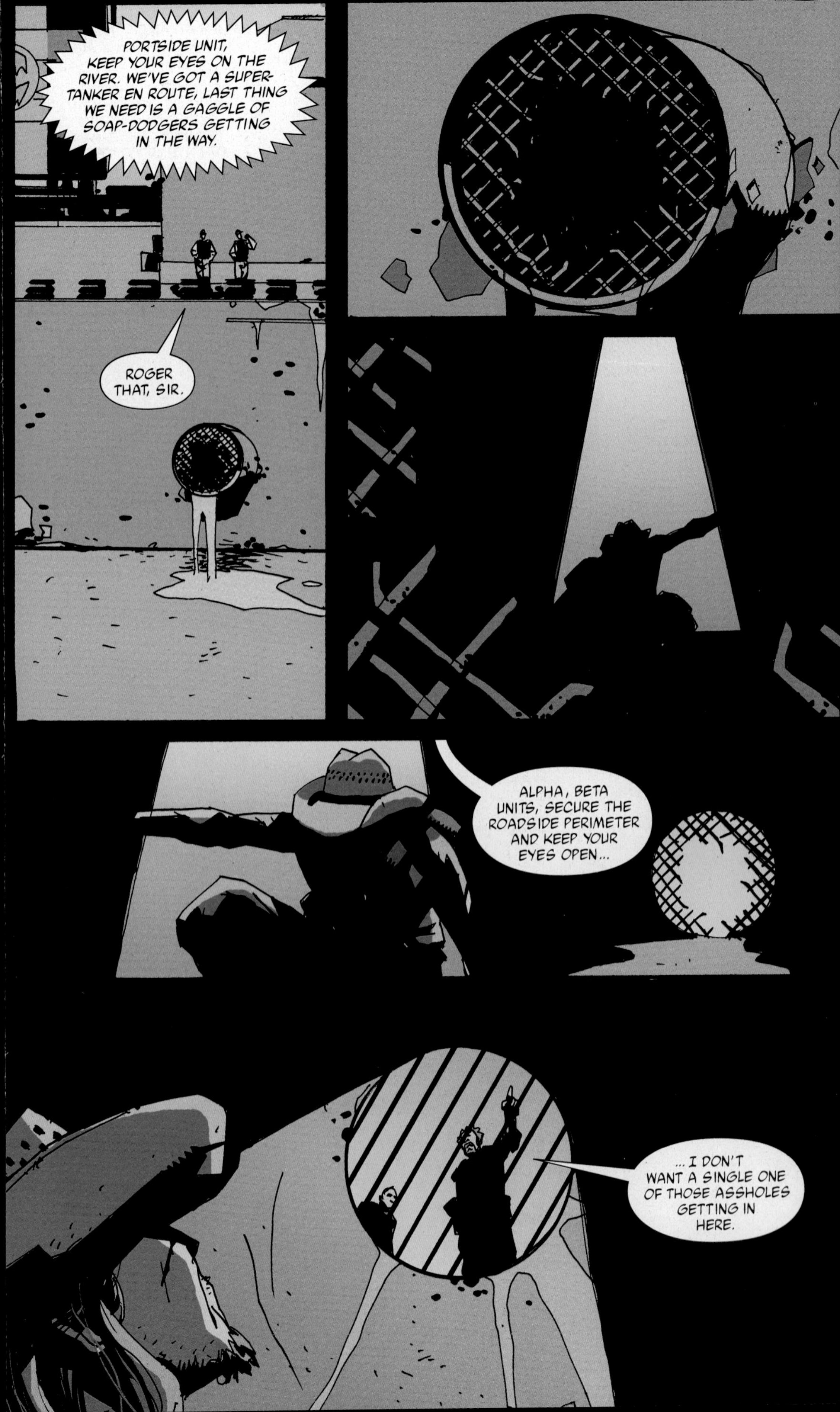
PORTSIDE UNIT, KEEP YOUR EYES ON THE RIVER. WE'VE GOT A SUPER-TANKER EN ROUTE, LAST THING WE NEED IS A GAGGLE OF SOAP-DODGERS GETTING IN THE WAY.
ROGER THAT, SIR.
ALPHA, BETA UNITS, SECURE THE ROADSIDE PERIMETER AND KEEP YOUR EYES OPEN...
...I DON'T WANT A SINGLE ONE OF THOSE ASSHOLES GETTING IN HERE.

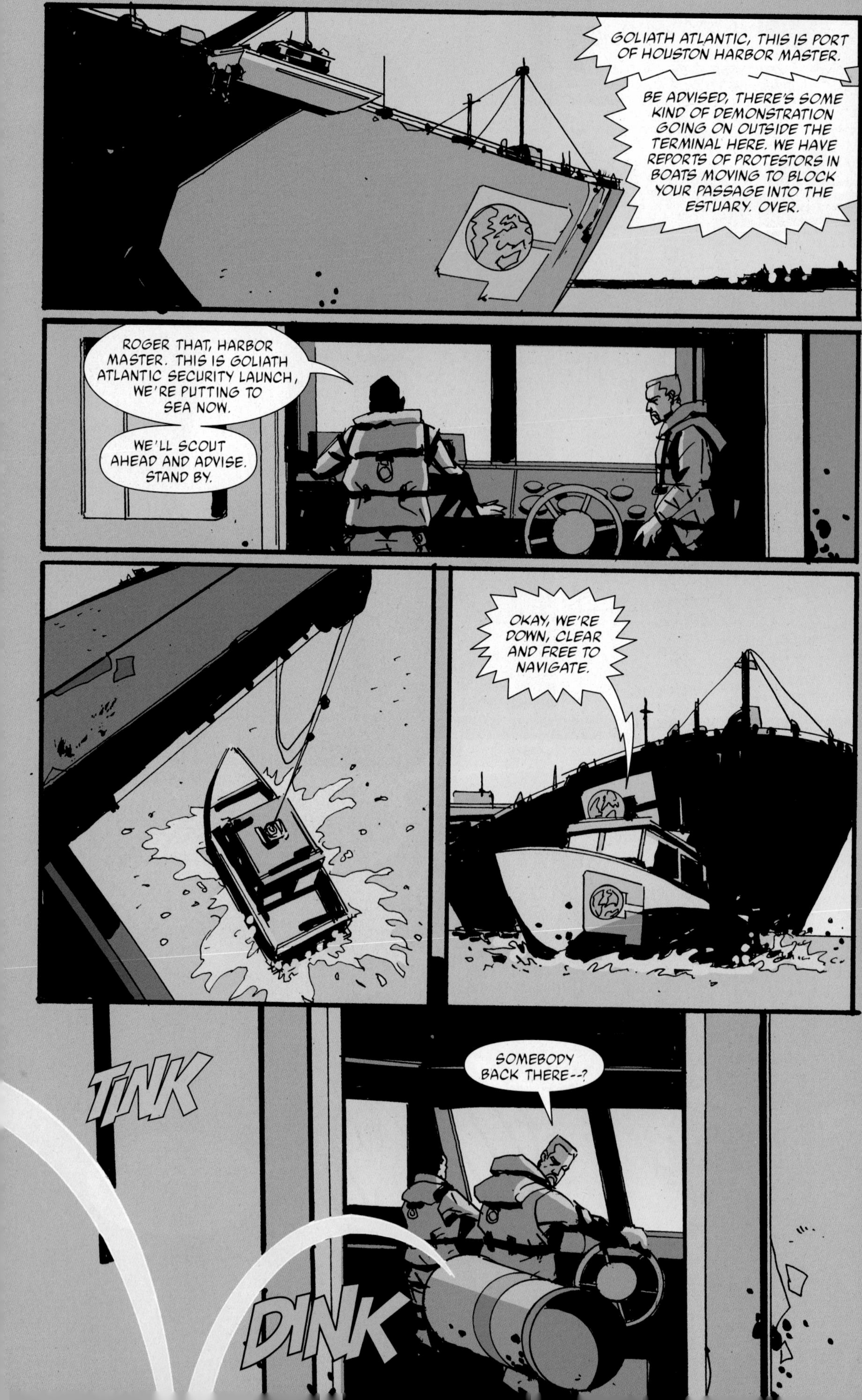
GOLIATH ATLANTIC, THIS IS PORT OF HOUSTON HARBOR MASTER.
BE ADVISED, THERE'S SOME KIND OF DEMONSTRATION GOING ON OUTSIDE THE TERMINAL HERE. WE HAVE REPORTS OF PROTESTORS IN BOATS MOVING TO BLOCK YOUR PASSAGE INTO THE ESTUARY. OVER.
ROGER THAT, HARBOR MASTER. THIS IS GOLIATH ATLANTIC SECURITY LAUNCH, WE'RE PUTTING TO SEA NOW.
WE'LL SCOUT AHEAD AND ADVISE. STAND BY.
OKAY, WE'RE DOWN, CLEAR AND FREE TO NAVIGATE.
TINK
SOMEBODY BACK THERE--?
DINK

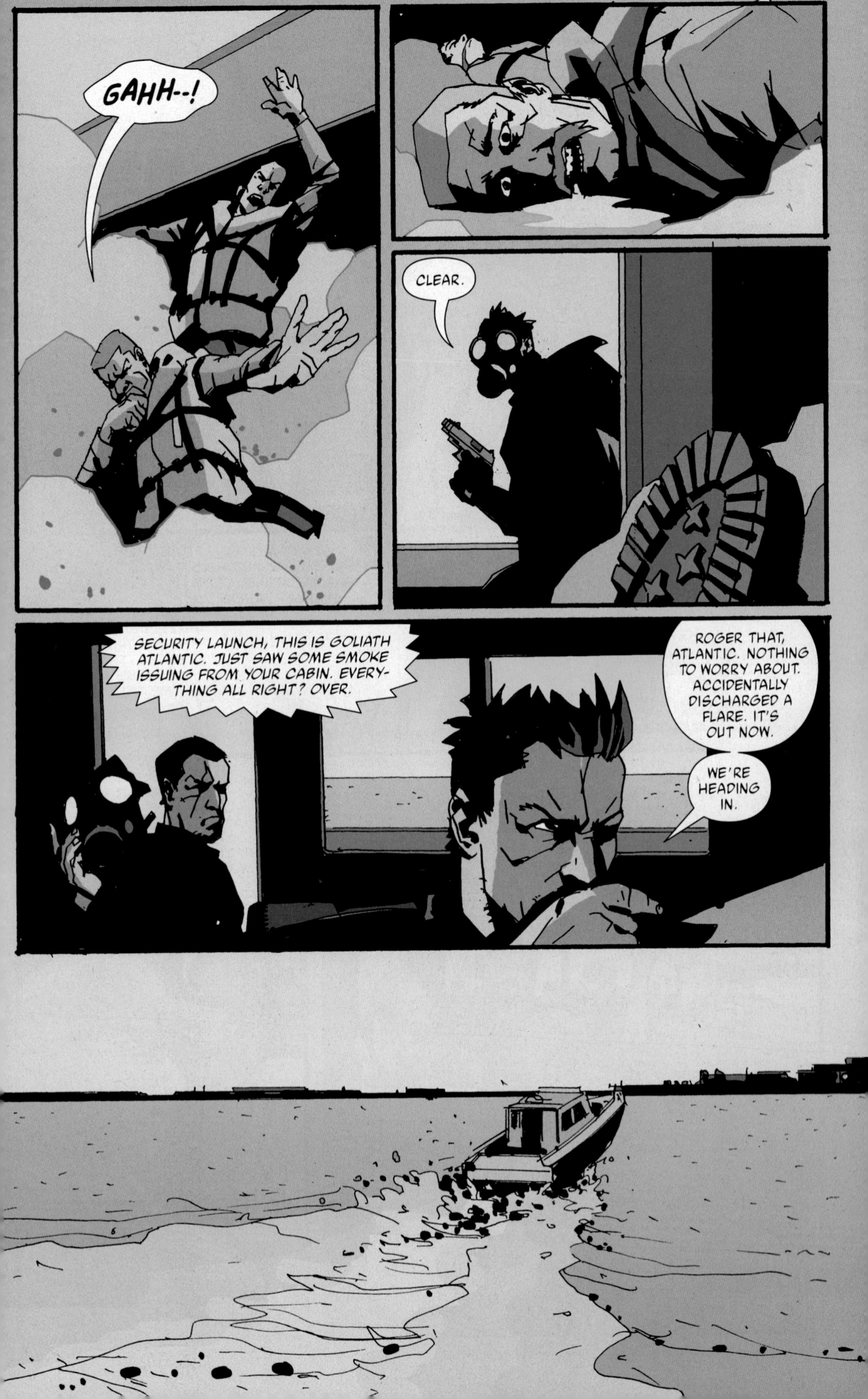
GAHH--!
CLEAR.
SECURITY LAUNCH, THIS IS GOLIATH ATLANTIC. JUST SAW SOME SMOKE ISSUING FROM YOUR CABIN. EVERYTHING ALL RIGHT? OVER.
ROGER THAT, ATLANTIC. NOTHING TO WORRY ABOUT. ACCIDENTALLY DISCHARGED A FLARE. IT'S OUT NOW.
WE'RE HEADING IN.

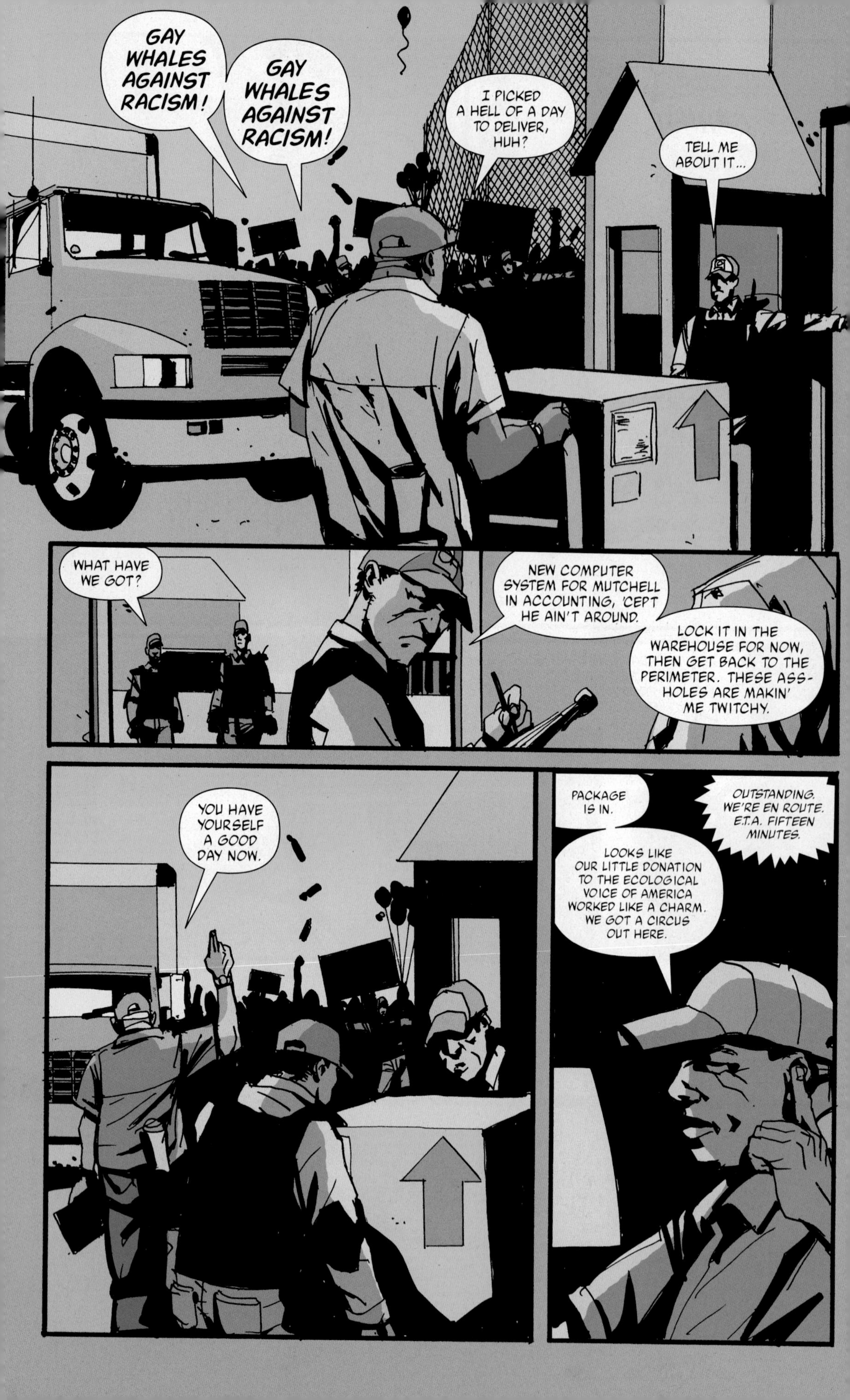

GAY WHALES AGAINST RACISM!
GAY WHALES AGAINST RACISM!
I PICKED A HELL OF A DAY TO DELIVER, HUH?
TELL ME ABOUT IT...
WHAT HAVE WE GOT?
NEW COMPUTER SYSTEM FOR MUTCHELL IN ACCOUNTING, 'CEPT HE AIN'T AROUND.
LOCK IT IN THE WAREHOUSE FOR NOW, THEN GET BACK TO THE PERIMETER. THESE ASS-HOLES ARE MAKIN' ME TWITCHY.
YOU HAVE YOURSELF A GOOD DAY NOW.
PACKAGE IS IN.
LOOKS LIKE OUR LITTLE DONATION TO THE ECOLOGICAL VOICE OF AMERICA WORKED LIKE A CHARM. WE GOT A CIRCUS OUT HERE.
OUTSTANDING. WE'RE EN ROUTE. E.T.A. FIFTEEN MINUTES.

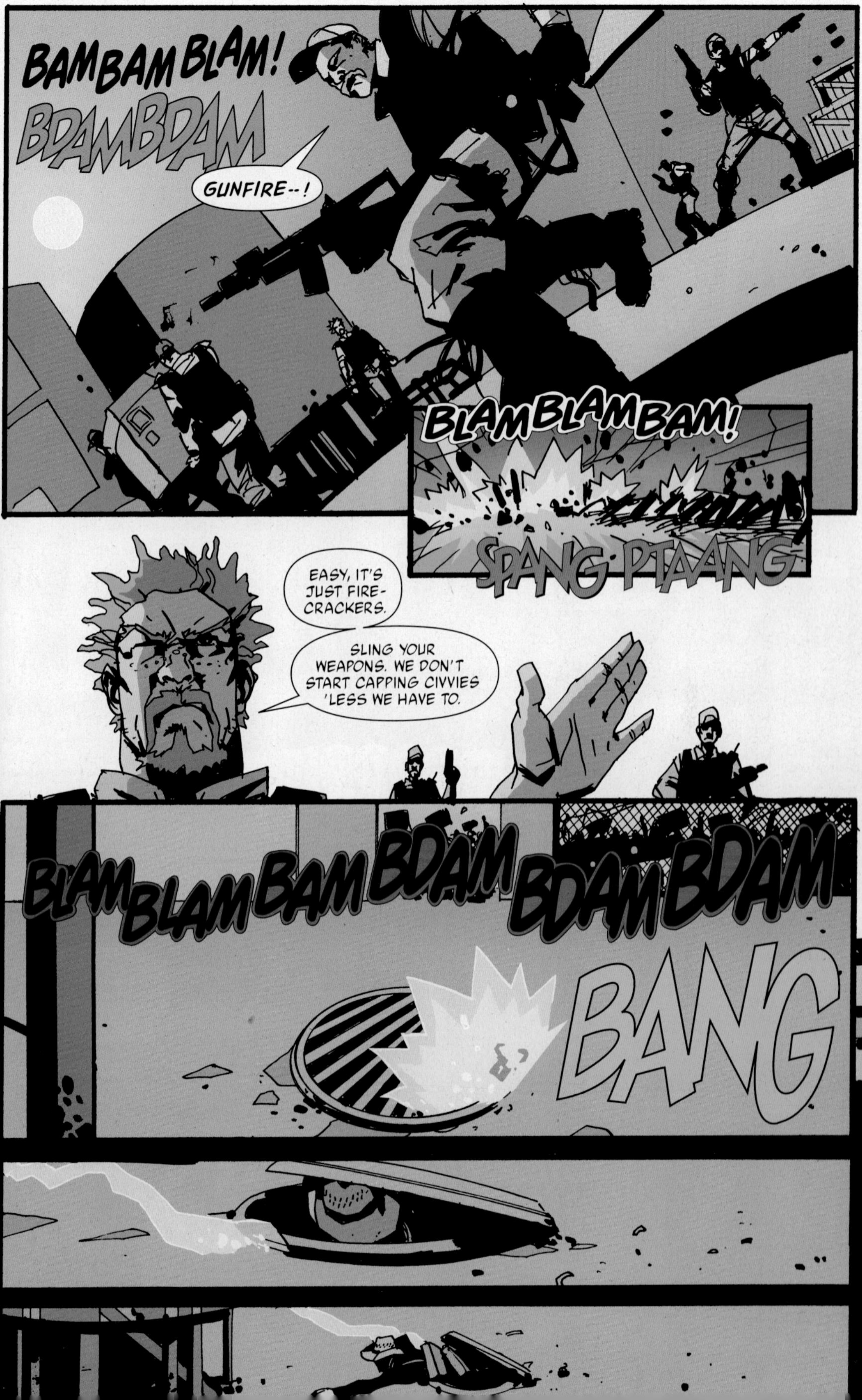

BAMBAMBLAM!
BDAMBDAM
GUNFIRE--!
BLAMBLAMBAM!
SPANG PTAANG
EASY, IT'S JUST FIRE-CRACKERS.
SLING YOUR WEAPONS. WE DON'T START CAPPING CIVVIES 'LESS WE HAVE TO.
BLAM BLAM BAM BDAM BDAM BDAM
BANG

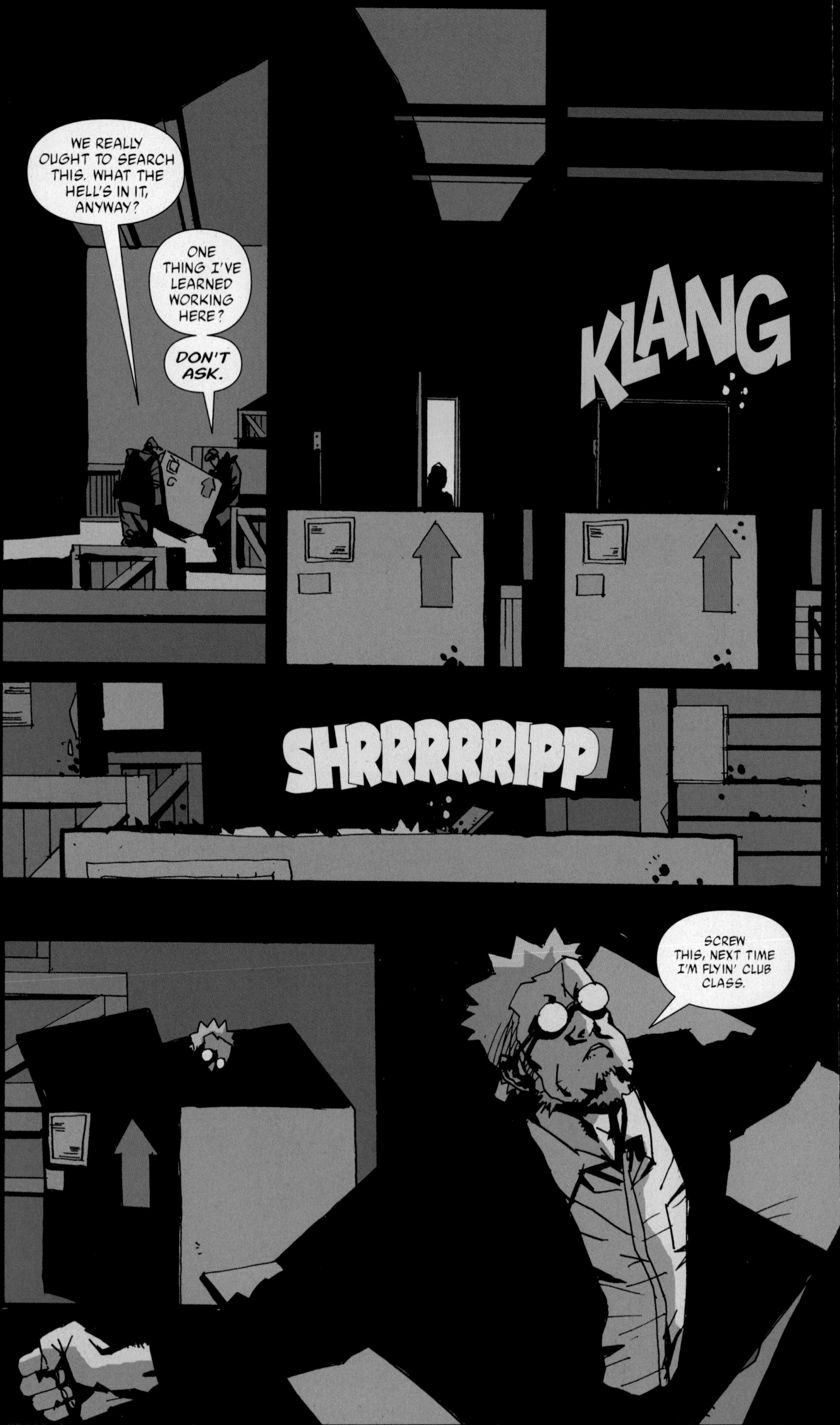
WE REALLY OUGHT TO SEARCH THIS. WHAT THE HELL'S IN IT, ANYWAY?
ONE THING I'VE LEARNED WORKING HERE?
DON'T ASK.
KLANG
SHRRRRRIPP
SCREW THIS, NEXT TIME I'M FLYIN' CLUB CLASS.

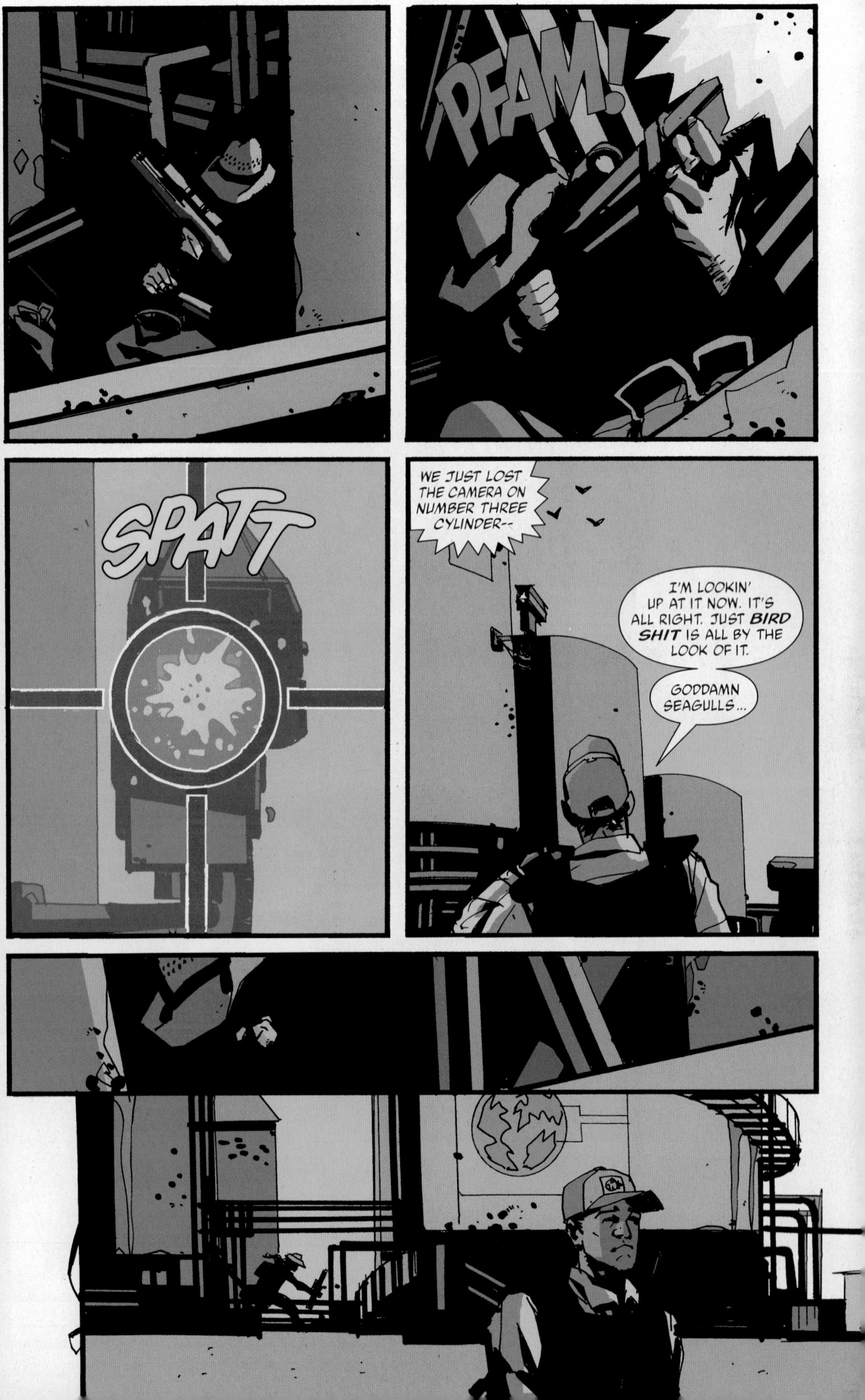
PFAM!
SPATT
WE JUST LOST THE CAMERA ON NUMBER THREE CYLINDER--
I'M LOOKIN' UP AT IT NOW. IT'S ALL RIGHT. JUST BIRD SHIT IS ALL BY THE LOOK OF IT.
GODDAMN SEAGULLS...

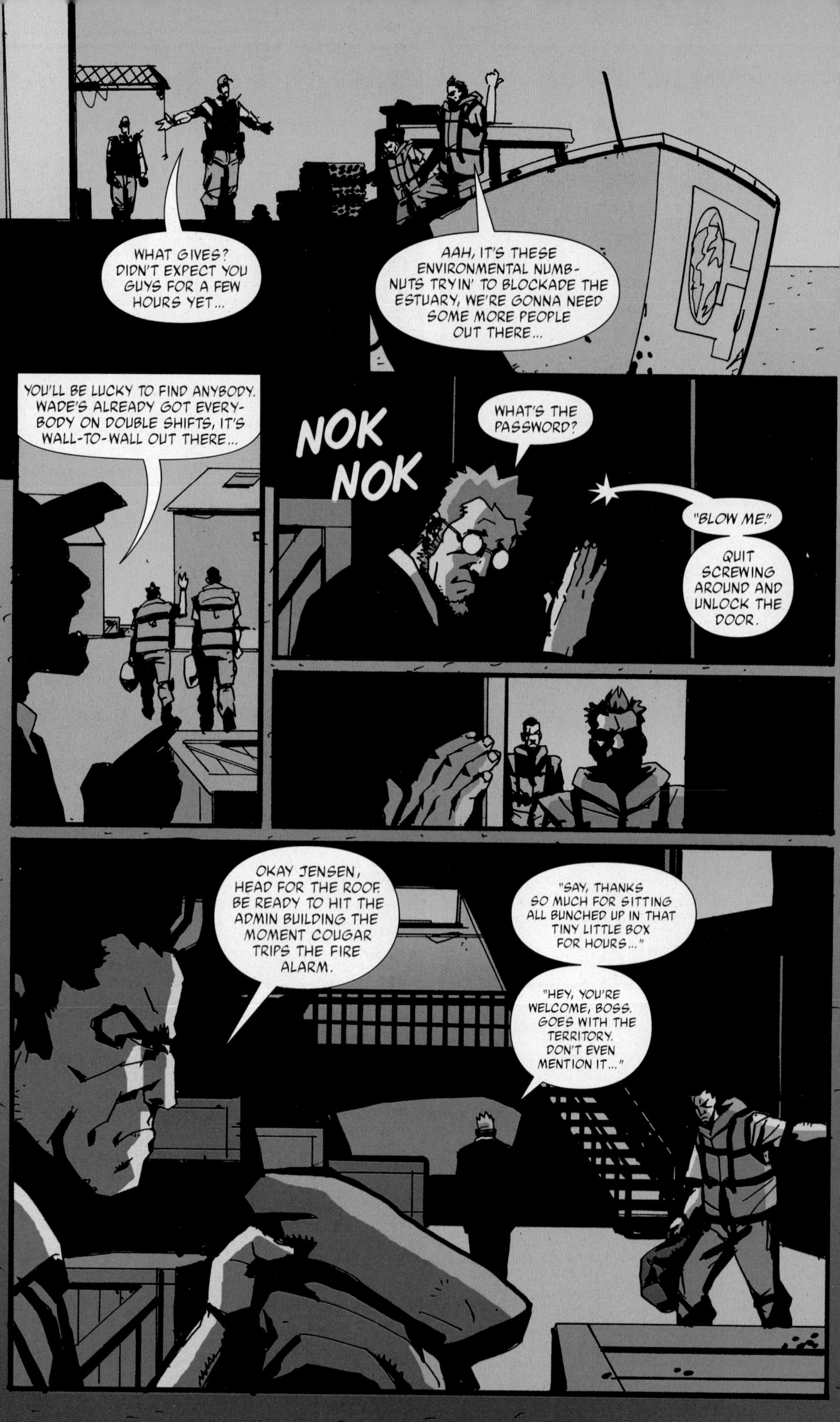
WHAT GIVES? DIDN'T EXPECT YOU GUYS FOR A FEW HOURS YET...
AAH, IT'S THESE ENVIRONMENTAL NUMB-NUTS TRYIN' TO BLOCKADE THE ESTUARY, WE'RE GONNA NEED SOME MORE PEOPLE OUT THERE...
YOU'LL BE LUCKY TO FIND ANYBODY. WADE'S ALREADY GOT EVERY-BODY ON DOUBLE SHIFTS, IT'S WALL-TO-WALL OUT THERE...
NOK NOK
WHAT'S THE PASSWORD?
"BLOW ME."
QUIT SCREWING AROUND AND UNLOCK THE DOOR.
OKAY JENSEN, HEAD FOR THE ROOF. BE READY TO HIT THE ADMIN BUILDING THE MOMENT COUGAR TRIPS THE FIRE ALARM.
"SAY, THANKS SO MUCH FOR SITTING ALL BUNCHED UP IN THAT TINY LITTLE BOX FOR HOURS..."
"HEY, YOU'RE WELCOME, BOSS. GOES WITH THE TERRITORY. DON'T EVEN MENTION IT..."

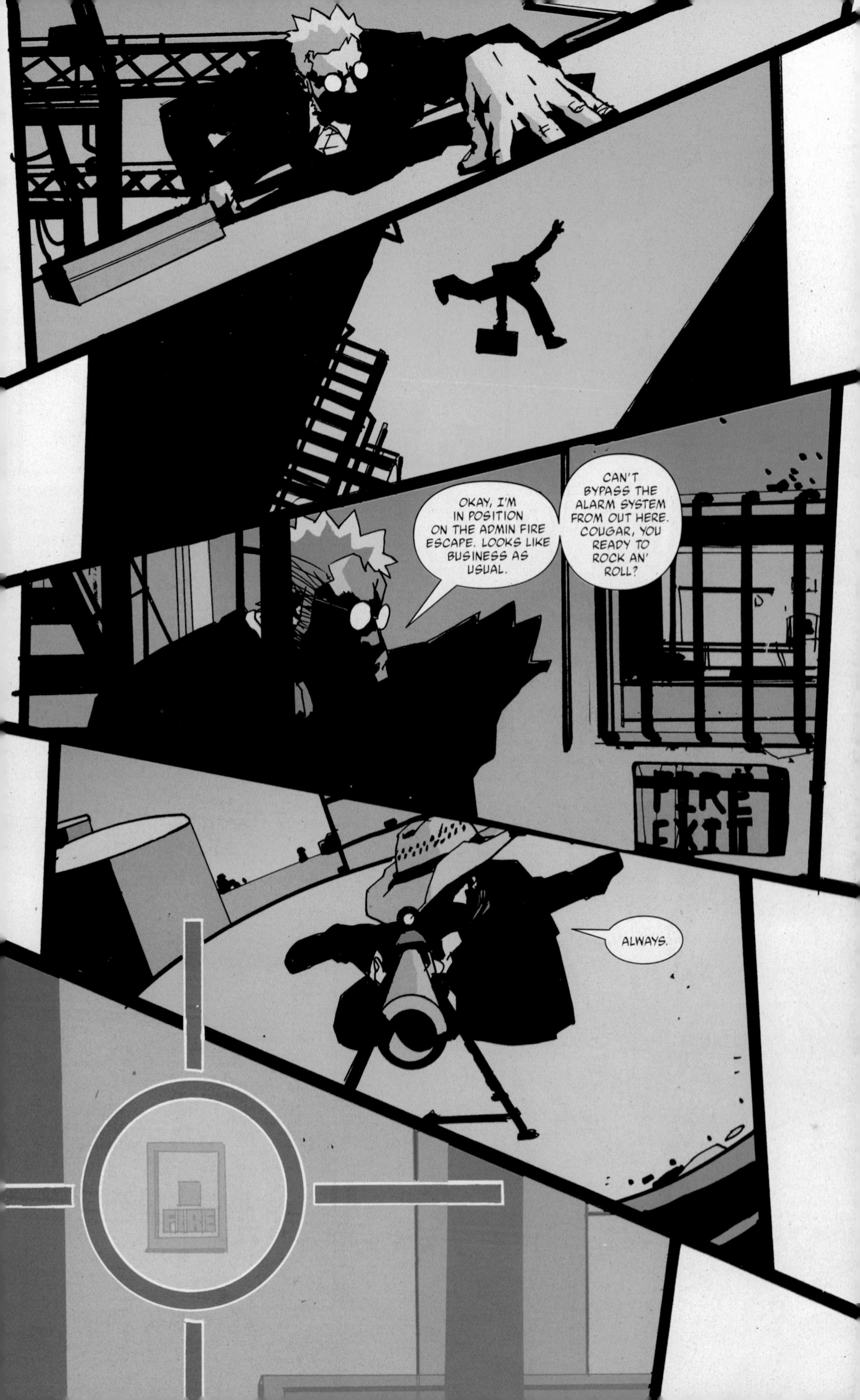
OKAY, I'M IN POSITION ON THE ADMIN FIRE ESCAPE. LOOKS LIKE BUSINESS AS USUAL.
CAN'T BYPASS THE ALARM SYSTEM FROM OUT HERE. COUGAR, YOU READY TO ROCK AN' ROLL?
FIRE EXIT
ALWAYS.
FIRE

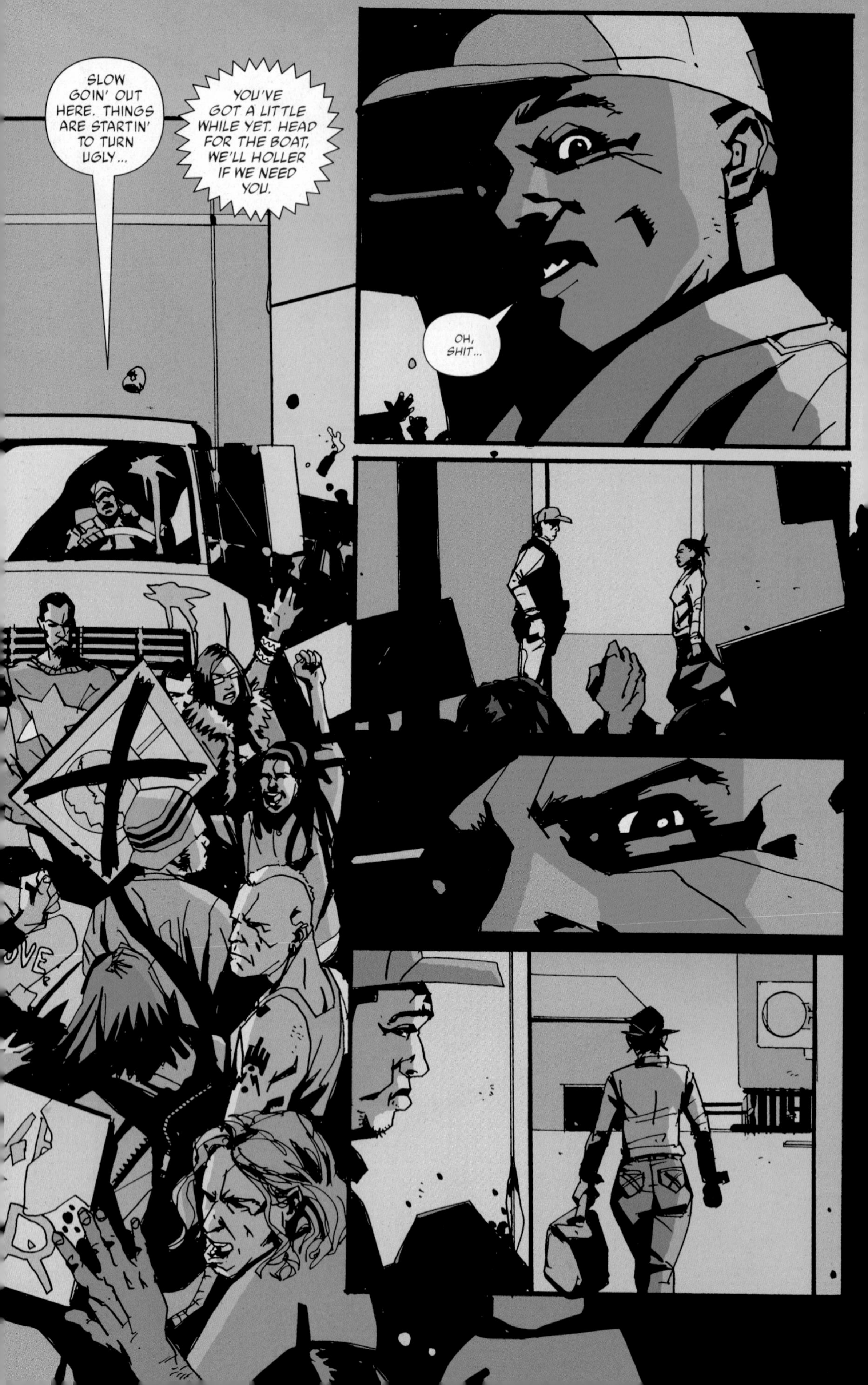
SLOW GOIN' OUT HERE. THINGS ARE STARTIN' TO TURN UGLY...
YOU'VE GOT A LITTLE WHILE YET. HEAD FOR THE BOAT, WE'LL HOLLER IF WE NEED YOU.
OH, SHIT...

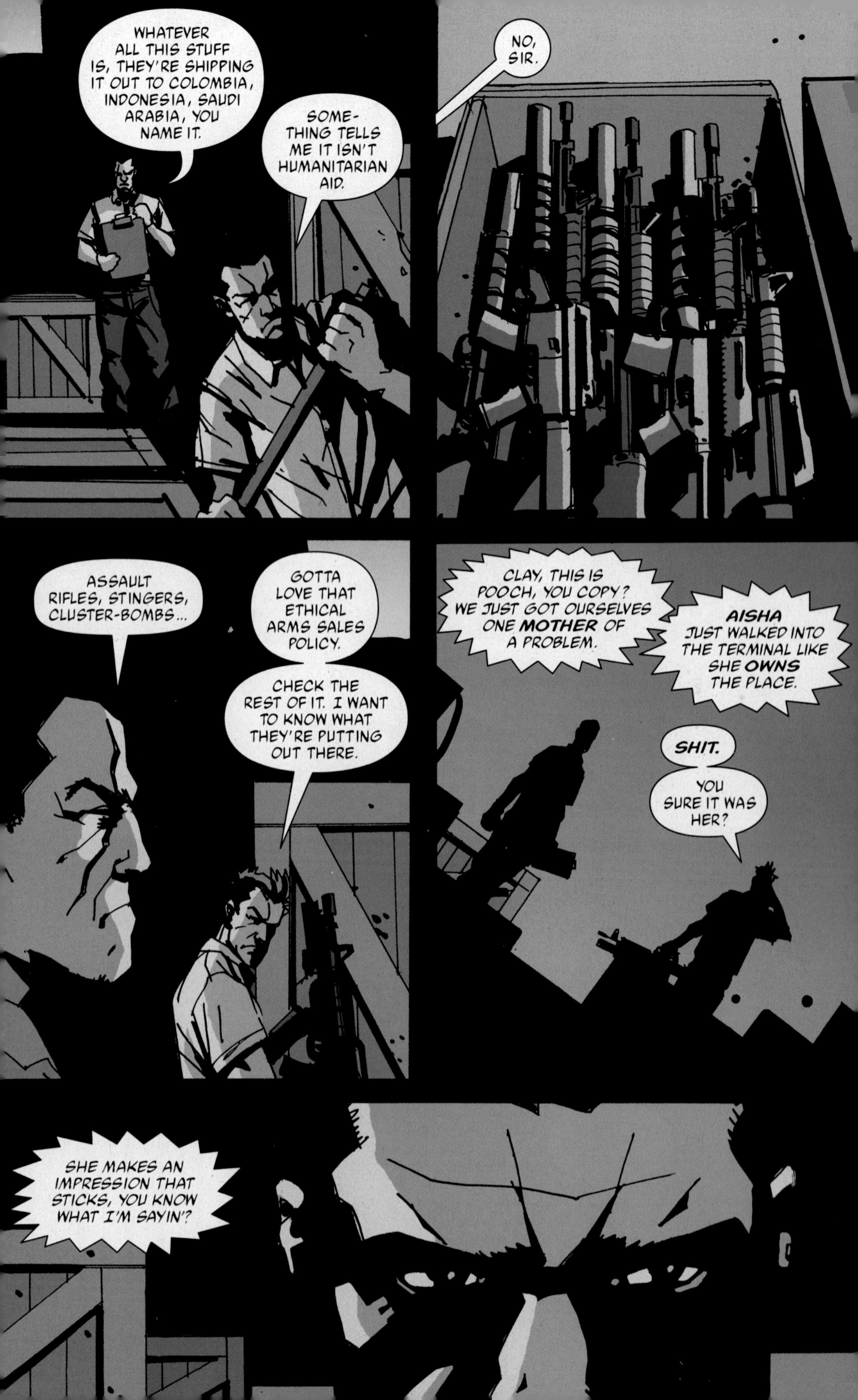
WHATEVER ALL THIS STUFF IS, THEY'RE SHIPPING IT OUT TO COLOMBIA, INDONESIA, SAUDI ARABIA, YOU NAME IT.
SOME-THING TELLS ME IT ISN'T HUMANITARIAN AID.
NO, SIR.
ASSAULT RIFLES, STINGERS, CLUSTER-BOMBS...
GOTTA LOVE THAT ETHICAL ARMS SALES POLICY.
CHECK THE REST OF IT. I WANT TO KNOW WHAT THEY'RE PUTTING OUT THERE.
CLAY, THIS IS POOCH, YOU COPY? WE JUST GOT OURSELVES ONE MOTHER OF A PROBLEM.
AISHA JUST WALKED INTO THE TERMINAL LIKE SHE OWNS THE PLACE.
SHIT.
YOU SURE IT WAS HER?
SHE MAKES AN IMPRESSION THAT STICKS, YOU KNOW WHAT I'M SAYIN'?

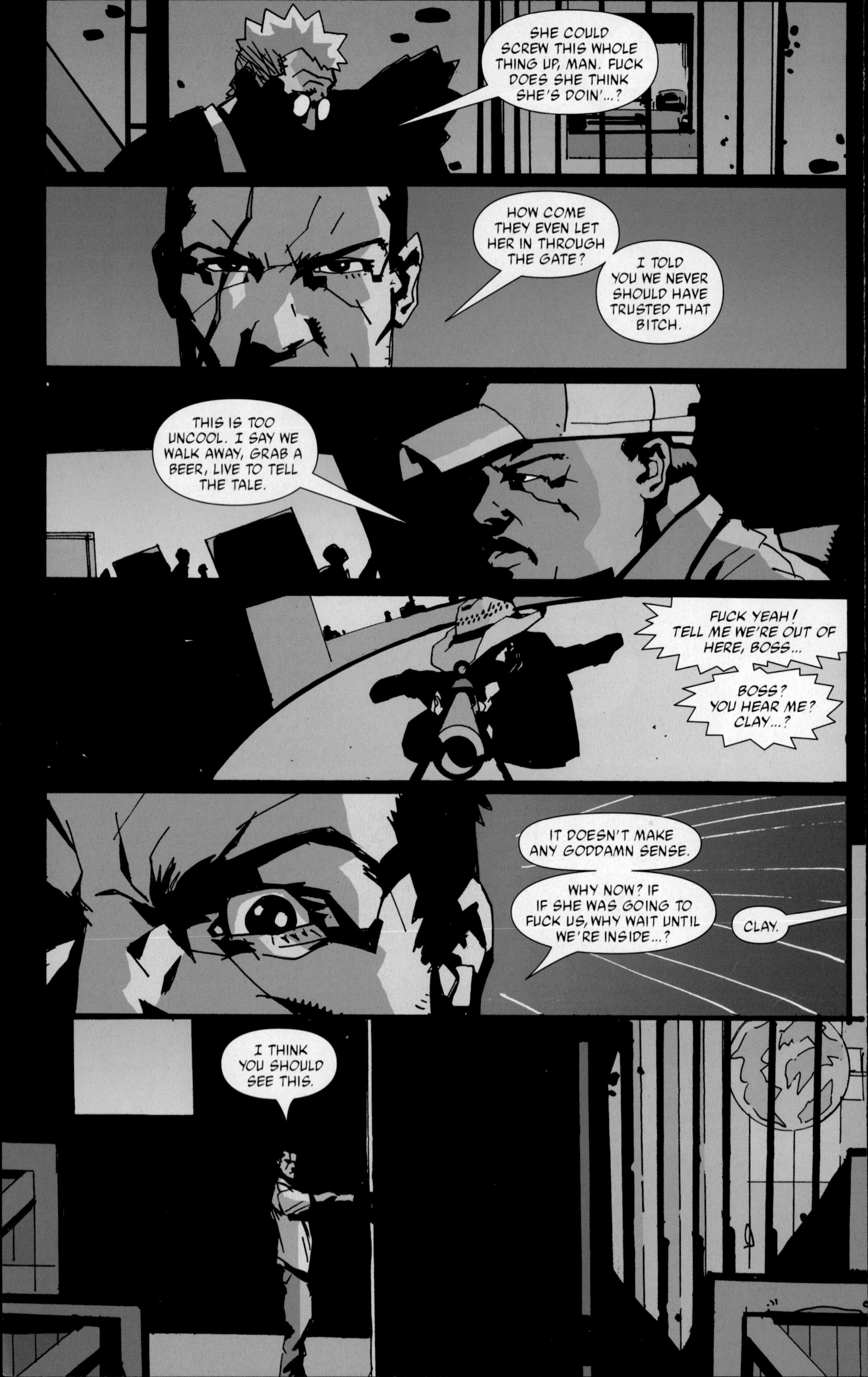
SHE COULD SCREW THIS WHOLE THING UP, MAN. FUCK DOES SHE THINK SHE'S DOIN'...?
HOW COME THEY EVEN LET HER IN THROUGH THE GATE?
I TOLD YOU WE NEVER SHOULD HAVE TRUSTED THAT BITCH.
THIS IS TOO UNCOOL. I SAY WE WALK AWAY, GRAB A BEER, LIVE TO TELL THE TALE.
FUCK YEAH! TELL ME WE'RE OUT OF HERE, BOSS...
BOSS? YOU HEAR ME? CLAY...?
IT DOESN'T MAKE ANY GODDAMN SENSE.
WHY NOW? IF IF SHE WAS GOING TO FUCK US, WHY WAIT UNTIL WE'RE INSIDE...?
CLAY.
I THINK YOU SHOULD SEE THIS.

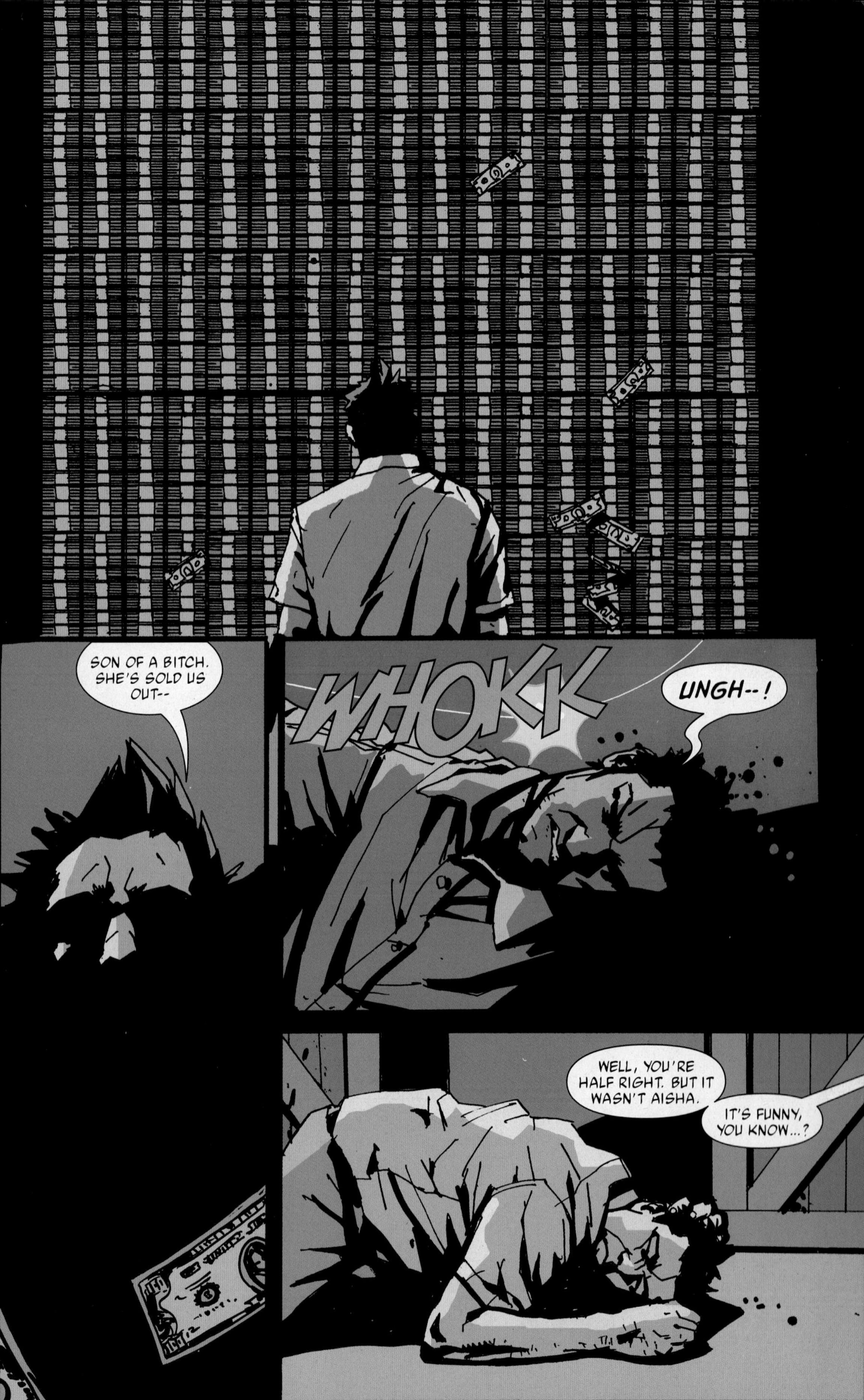
SON OF A BITCH. SHE'S SOLD US OUT--
WHOKK
UNGH--!
WELL, YOU'RE HALF RIGHT. BUT IT WASN'T AISHA.
IT'S FUNNY, YOU KNOW...?

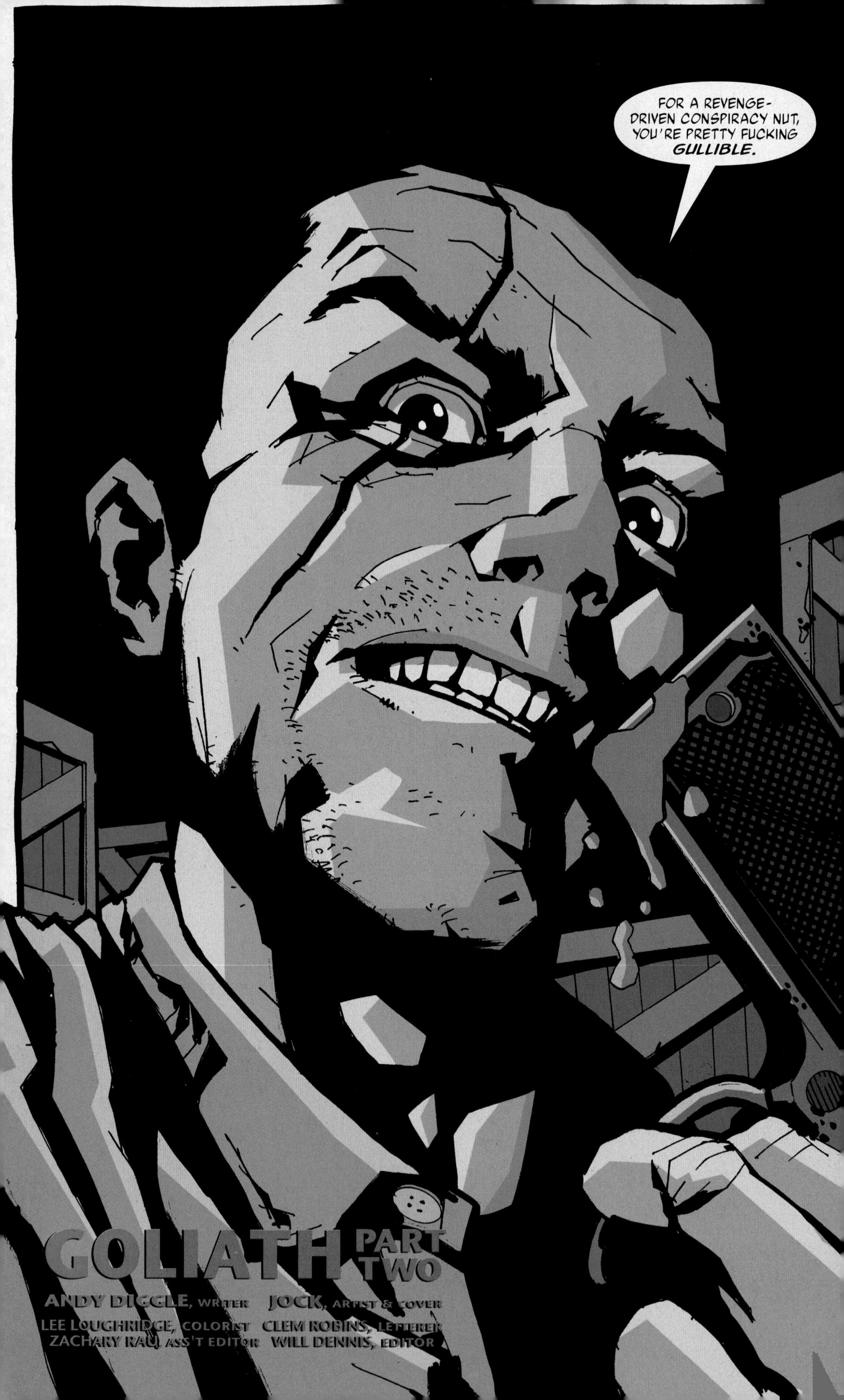
FOR A REVENGE-DRIVEN CONSPIRACY NUT, YOU'RE PRETTY FUCKING *GULLIBLE.*
GOLIATH PART TWO
ANDY DIGGLE, WRITER JOCK, ARTIST & COVER
LEE LOUGHRIDGE, COLORIST CLEM ROBINS, LETTERER
ZACHARY RAU, ASS'T EDITOR WILL DENNIS, EDITOR

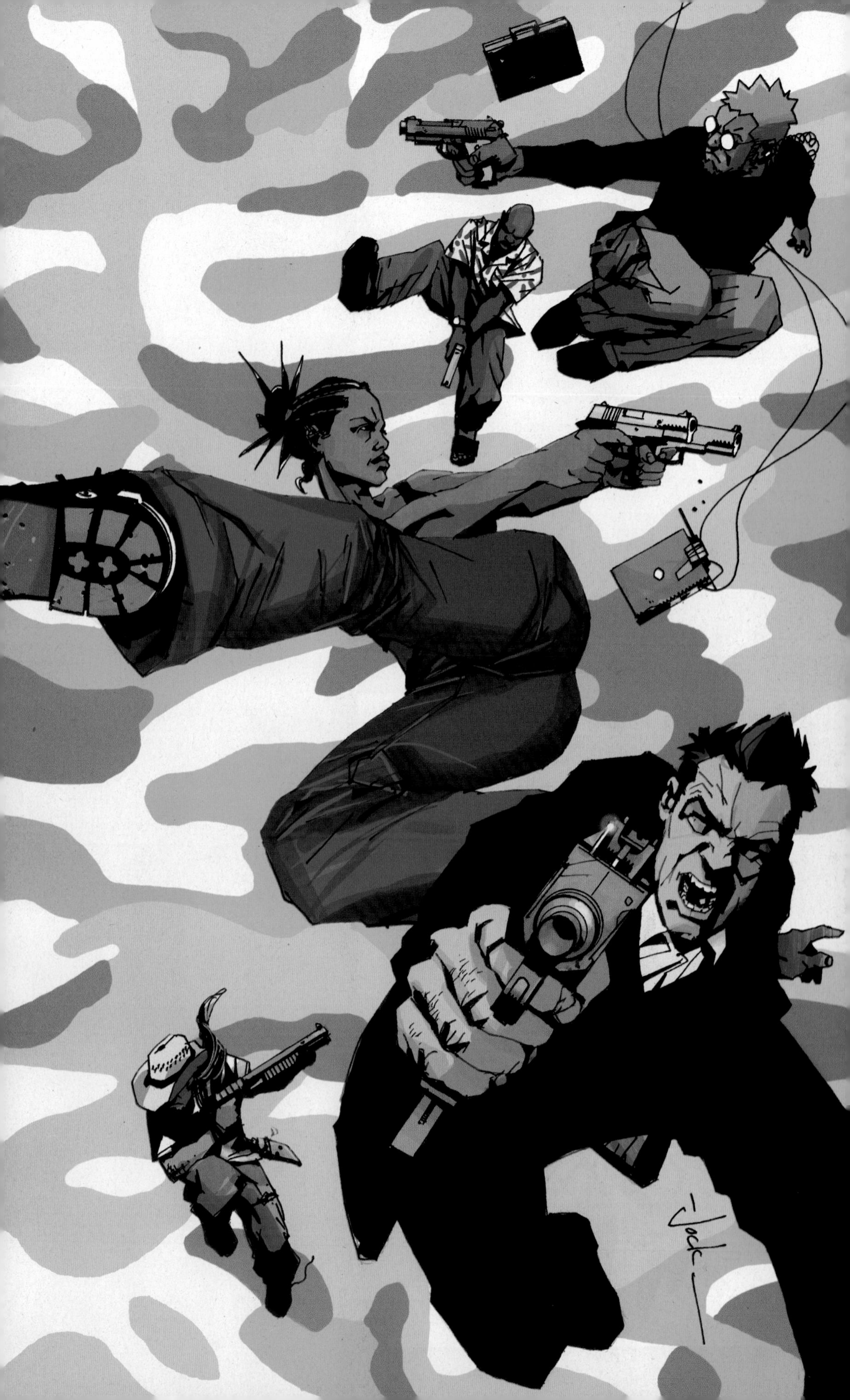
Jock

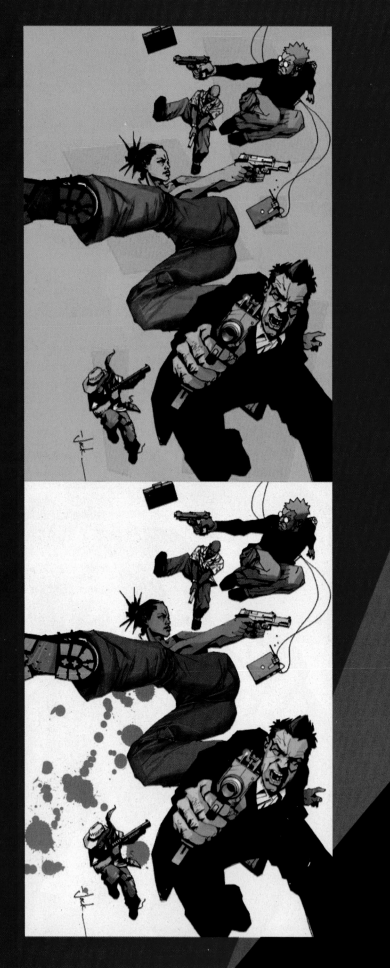

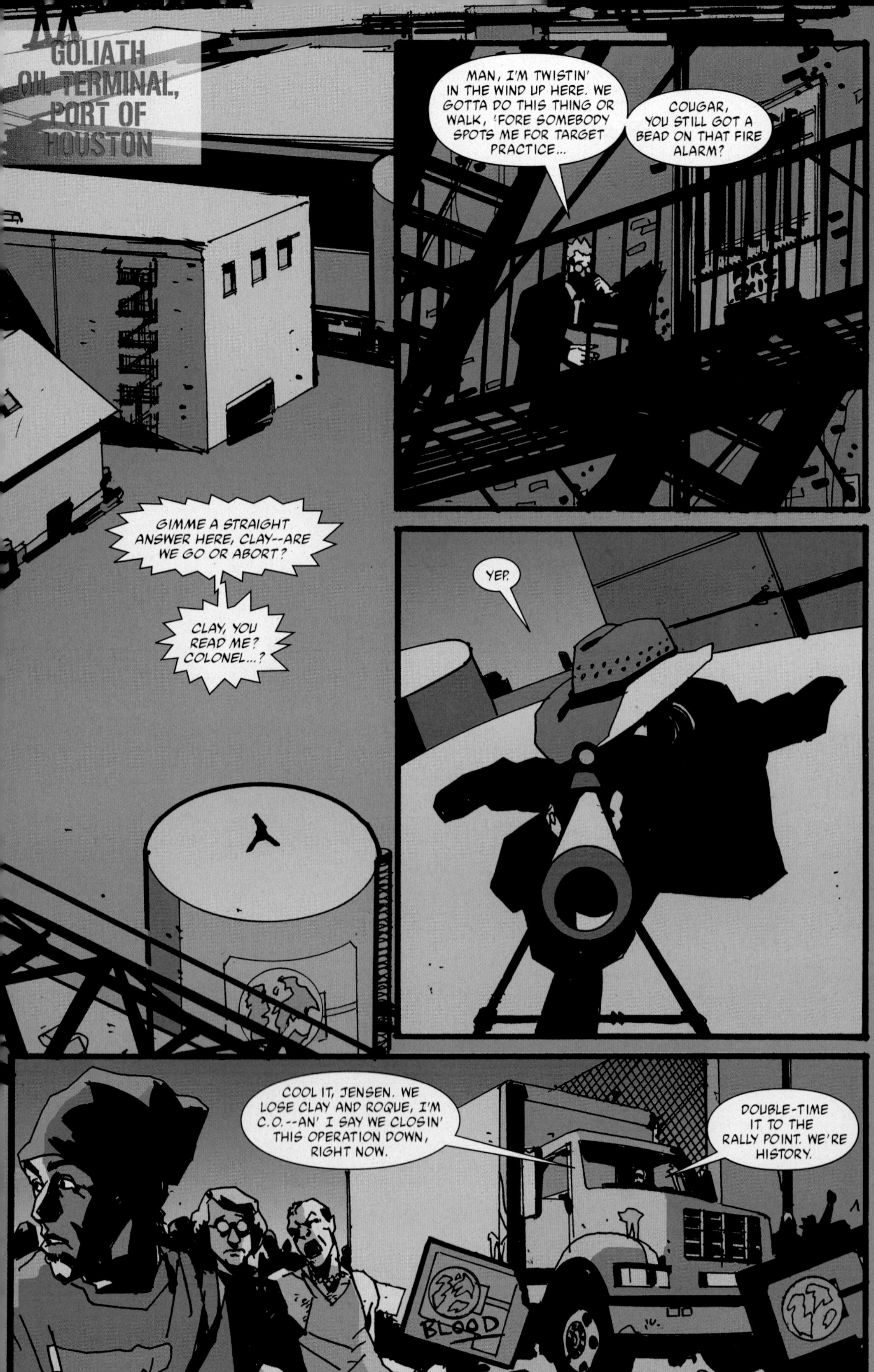
GOLIATH OIL TERMINAL, PORT OF HOUSTON
MAN, I'M TWISTIN' IN THE WIND UP HERE. WE GOTTA DO THIS THING OR WALK, 'FORE SOMEBODY SPOTS ME FOR TARGET PRACTICE...
COUGAR, YOU STILL GOT A BEAD ON THAT FIRE ALARM?
GIMME A STRAIGHT ANSWER HERE, CLAY--ARE WE GO OR ABORT?
CLAY, YOU READ ME? COLONEL...?
YEP.
COOL IT, JENSEN. WE LOSE CLAY AND ROQUE, I'M C.O.--AN' I SAY WE CLOSIN' THIS OPERATION DOWN, RIGHT NOW.
DOUBLE-TIME IT TO THE RALLY POINT. WE'RE HISTORY.
BLOOD

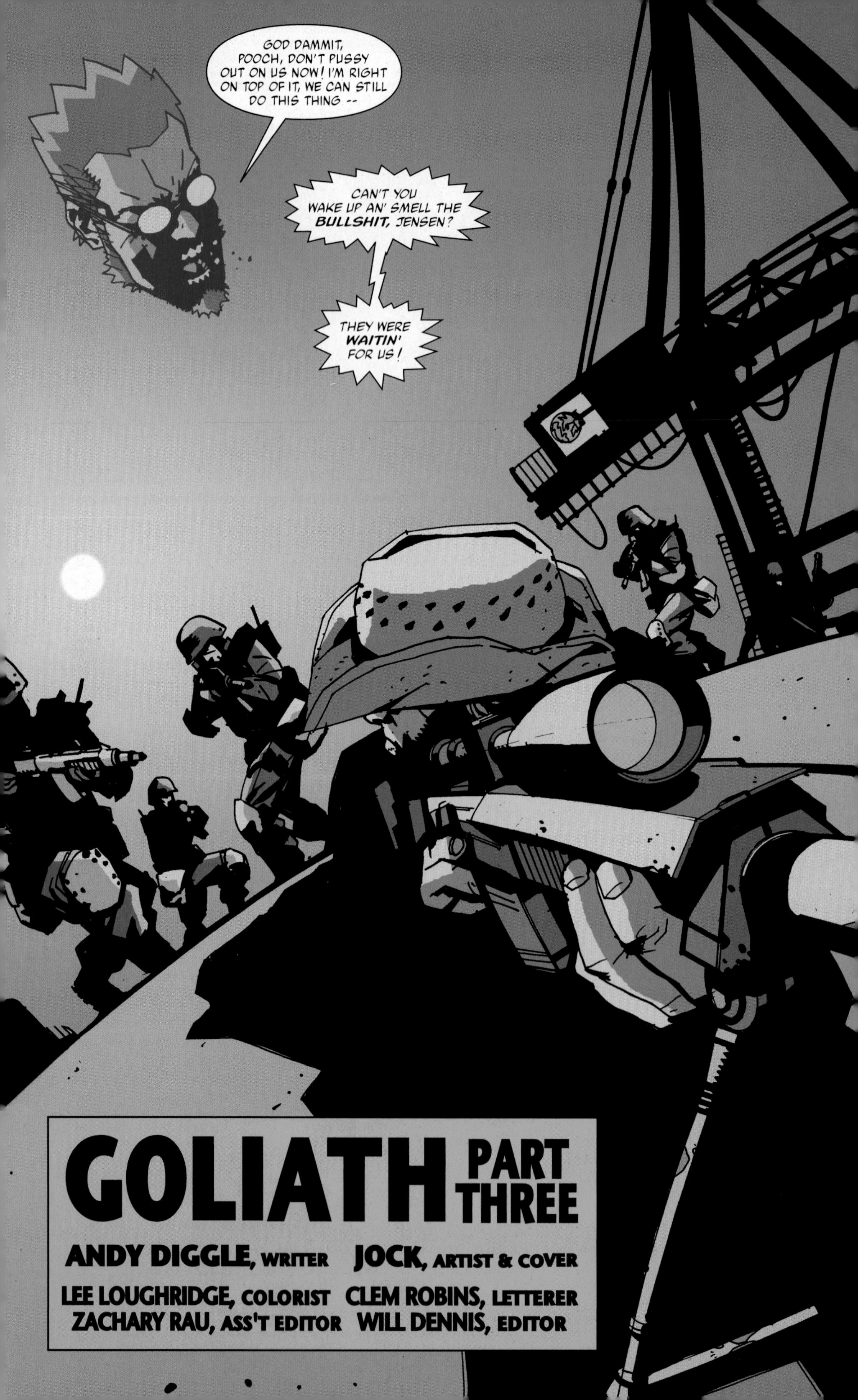
GOD DAMMIT, POOCH, DON'T PUSSY OUT ON US NOW! I'M RIGHT ON TOP OF IT, WE CAN STILL DO THIS THING --
CAN'T YOU WAKE UP AN' SMELL THE BULLSHIT, JENSEN?
THEY WERE WAITIN' FOR US!
GOLIATH PART THREE
ANDY DIGGLE, WRITER JOCK, ARTIST & COVER
LEE LOUGHRIDGE, COLORIST CLEM ROBINS, LETTERER
ZACHARY RAU, ASS'T EDITOR WILL DENNIS, EDITOR

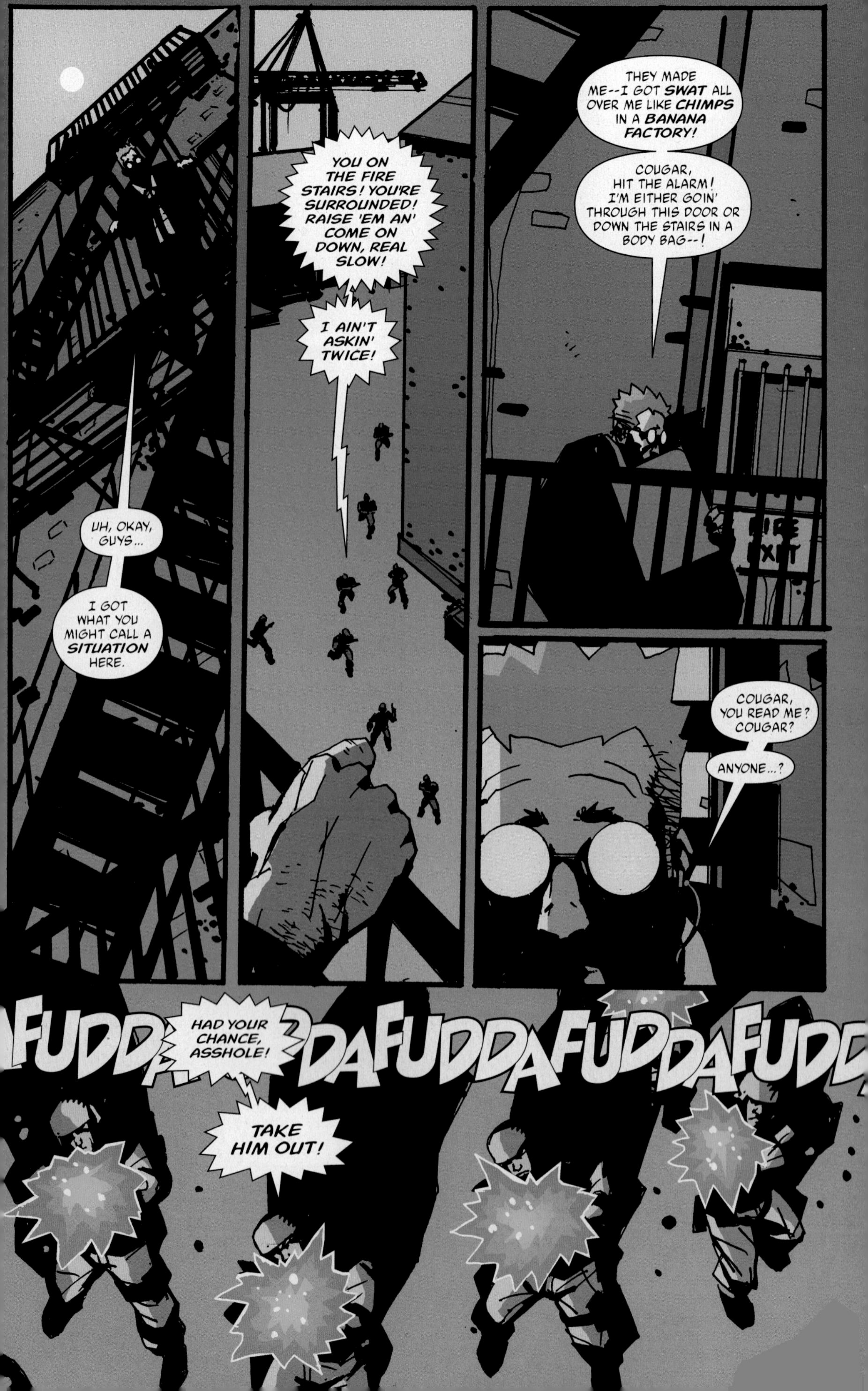
UH, OKAY, GUYS...
I GOT WHAT YOU MIGHT CALL A SITUATION HERE.
YOU ON THE FIRE STAIRS! YOU'RE SURROUNDED! RAISE 'EM AN' COME ON DOWN, REAL SLOW!
I AIN'T ASKIN' TWICE!
THEY MADE ME--I GOT SWAT ALL OVER ME LIKE CHIMPS IN A BANANA FACTORY!
COUGAR, HIT THE ALARM! I'M EITHER GOIN' THROUGH THIS DOOR OR DOWN THE STAIRS IN A BODY BAG--!
COUGAR, YOU READ ME? COUGAR?
ANYONE...?
HAD YOUR CHANCE, ASSHOLE!
TAKE HIM OUT!
DAFUDDAFUDDAFUDDAFUDD

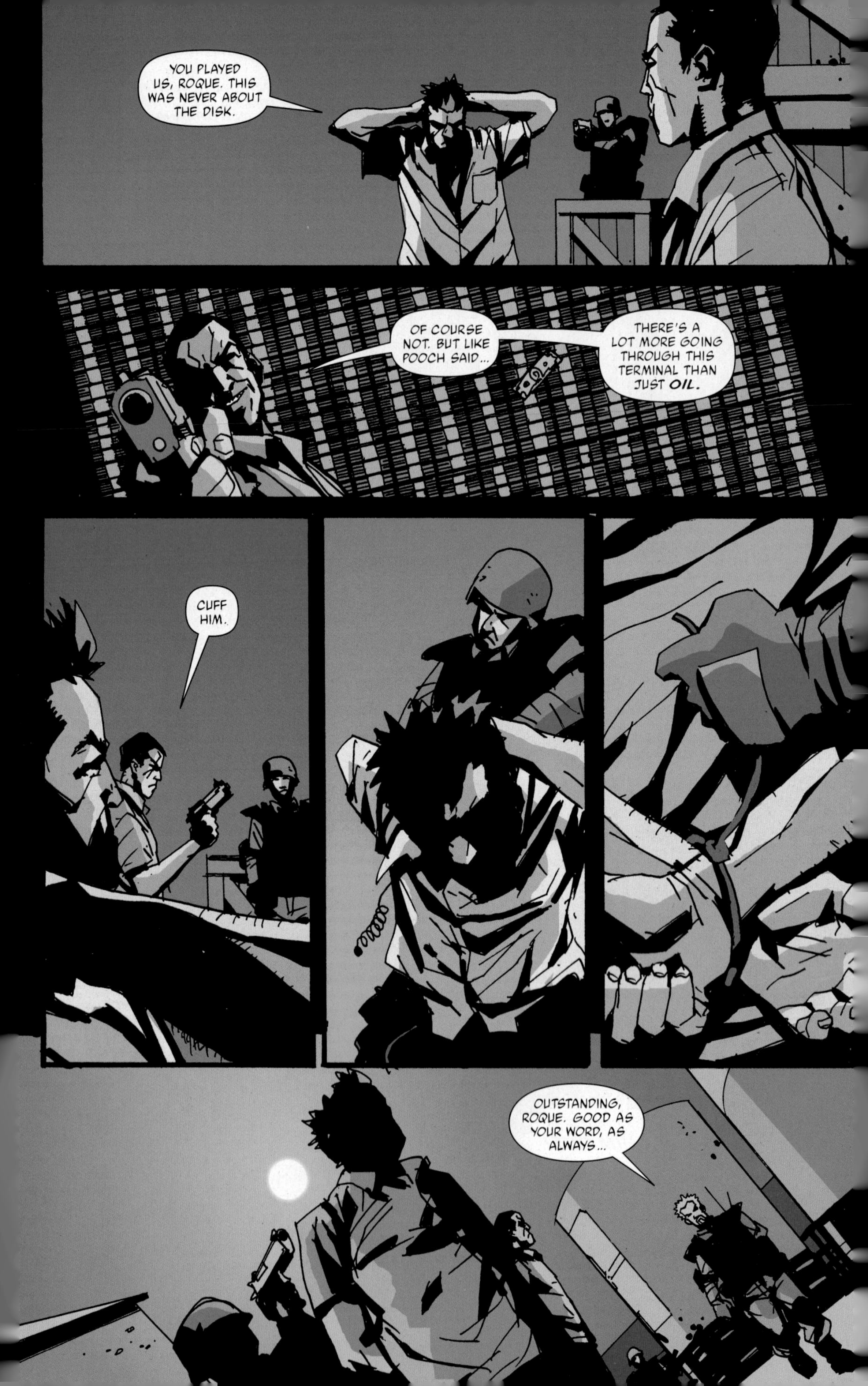
YOU PLAYED US, ROQUE. THIS WAS NEVER ABOUT THE DISK.
OF COURSE NOT. BUT LIKE POOCH SAID...
THERE'S A LOT MORE GOING THROUGH THIS TERMINAL THAN JUST OIL.
CUFF HIM.
OUTSTANDING, ROQUE. GOOD AS YOUR WORD, AS ALWAYS...

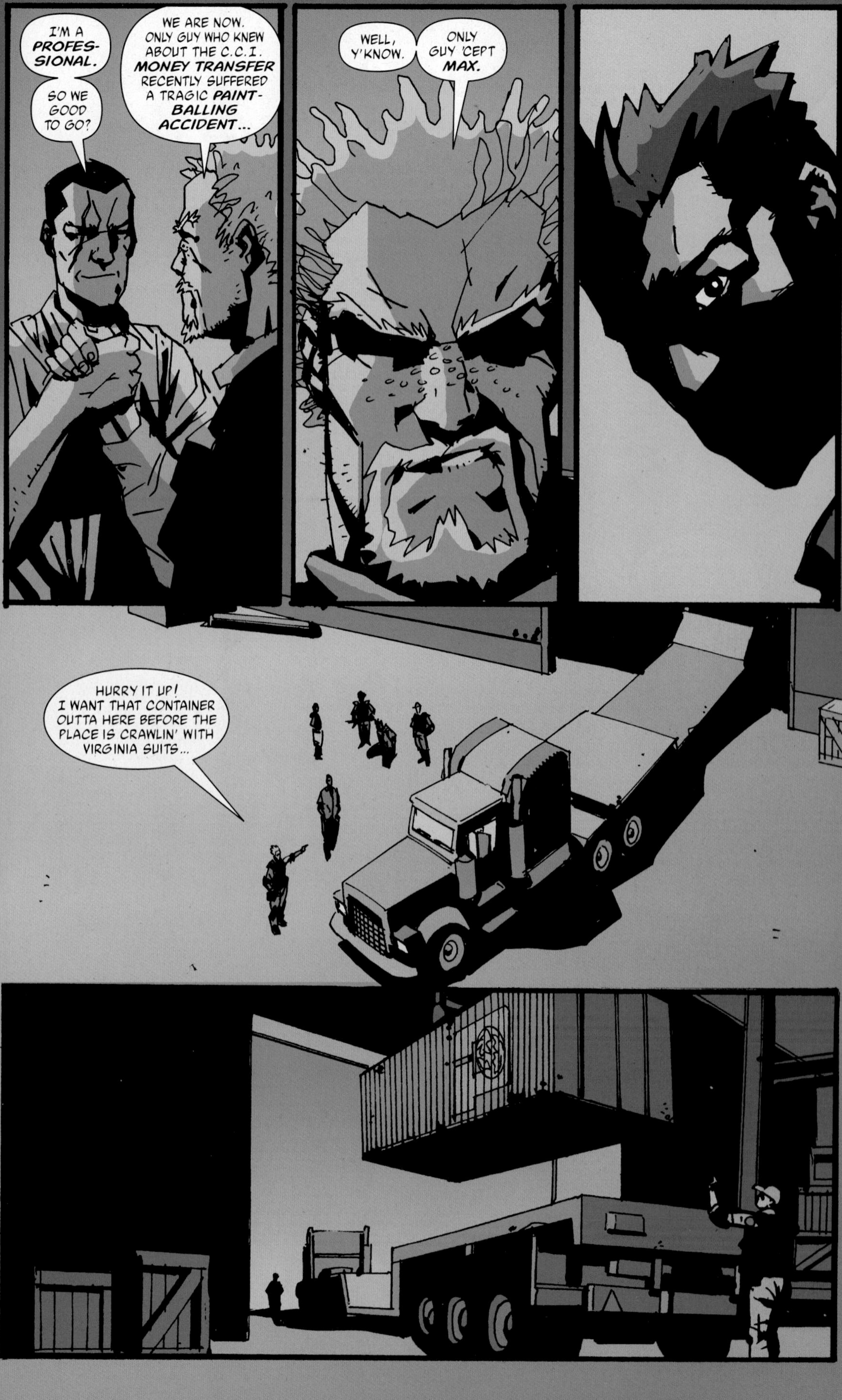
I'M A PROFES-SIONAL.
SO WE GOOD TO GO?
WE ARE NOW. ONLY GUY WHO KNEW ABOUT THE C.C.I. MONEY TRANSFER RECENTLY SUFFERED A TRAGIC PAINT-BALLING ACCIDENT...
WELL, Y'KNOW.
ONLY GUY 'CEPT MAX.
HURRY IT UP! I WANT THAT CONTAINER OUTTA HERE BEFORE THE PLACE IS CRAWLIN' WITH VIRGINIA SUITS...

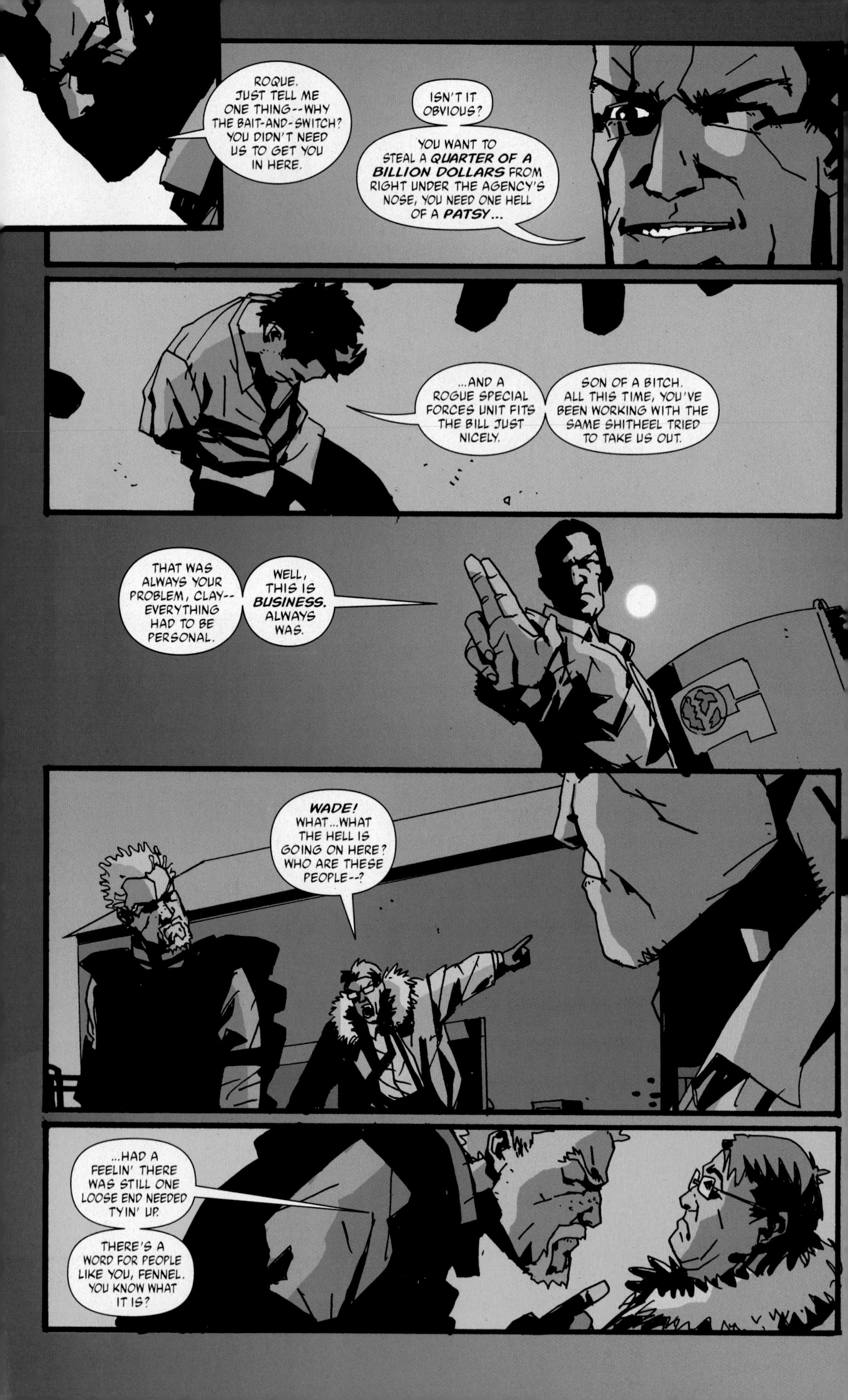
ROGUE. JUST TELL ME ONE THING--WHY THE BAIT-AND-SWITCH? YOU DIDN'T NEED US TO GET YOU IN HERE.
ISN'T IT OBVIOUS?
YOU WANT TO STEAL A **QUARTER OF A BILLION DOLLARS** FROM RIGHT UNDER THE AGENCY'S NOSE, YOU NEED ONE HELL OF A **PATSY...**
...AND A ROGUE SPECIAL FORCES UNIT FITS THE BILL JUST NICELY.
SON OF A BITCH. ALL THIS TIME, YOU'VE BEEN WORKING WITH THE SAME SHITHEEL TRIED TO TAKE US OUT.
THAT WAS ALWAYS YOUR PROBLEM, CLAY-- EVERYTHING HAD TO BE PERSONAL.
WELL, THIS IS **BUSINESS.** ALWAYS WAS.
WADE! WHAT...WHAT THE HELL IS GOING ON HERE? WHO ARE THESE PEOPLE--?
...HAD A FEELIN' THERE WAS STILL ONE LOOSE END NEEDED TYIN' UP.
THERE'S A WORD FOR PEOPLE LIKE YOU, FENNEL. YOU KNOW WHAT IT IS?

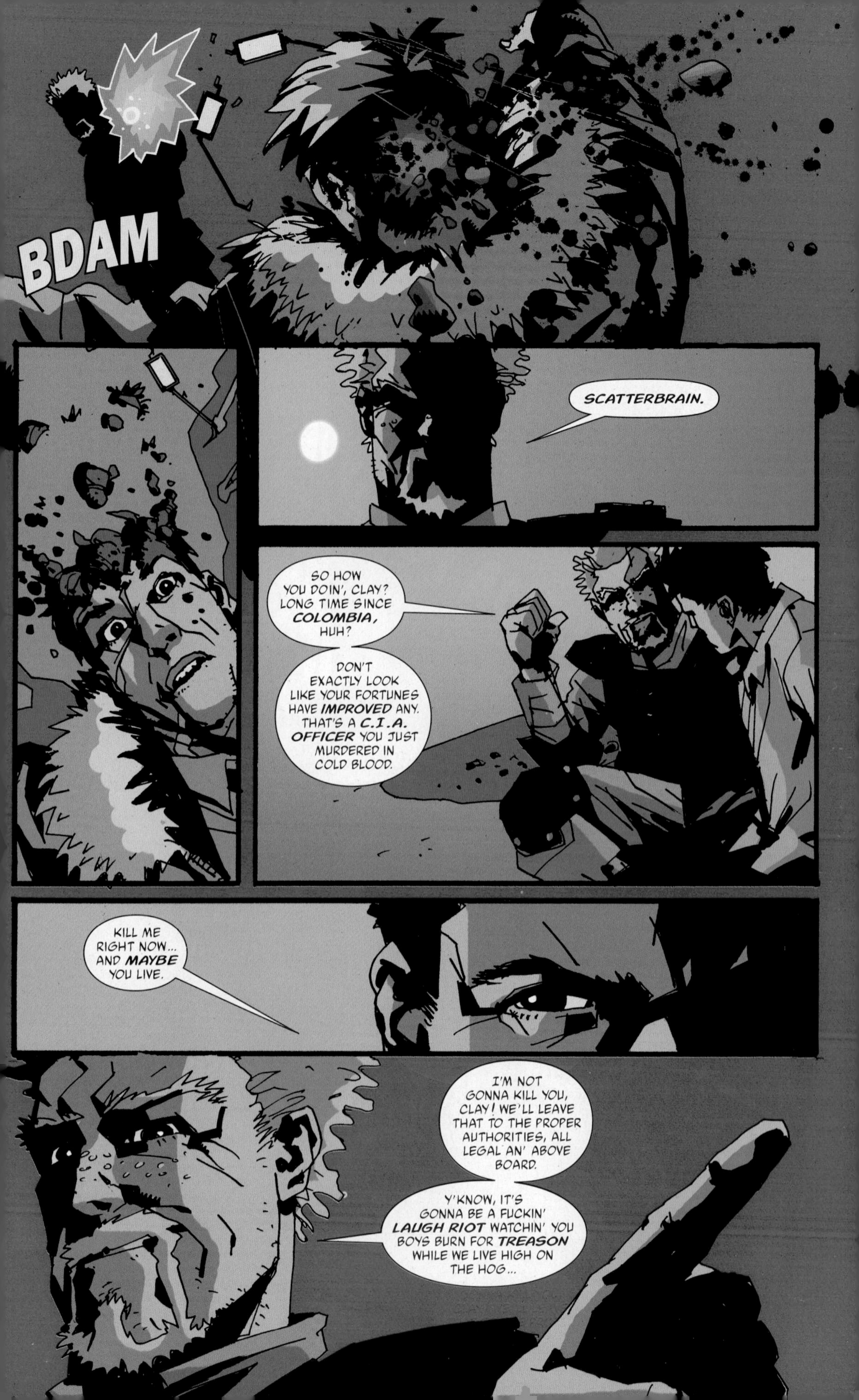
BDAM
SCATTERBRAIN.
SO HOW YOU DOIN', CLAY? LONG TIME SINCE **COLOMBIA,** HUH?
DON'T EXACTLY LOOK LIKE YOUR FORTUNES HAVE **IMPROVED** ANY. THAT'S A **C.I.A. OFFICER** YOU JUST MURDERED IN COLD BLOOD.
KILL ME RIGHT NOW... AND **MAYBE** YOU LIVE.
I'M NOT GONNA KILL YOU, CLAY! WE'LL LEAVE THAT TO THE PROPER AUTHORITIES, ALL LEGAL AN' ABOVE BOARD.
Y'KNOW, IT'S GONNA BE A FUCKIN' **LAUGH RIOT** WATCHIN' YOU BOYS BURN FOR **TREASON** WHILE WE LIVE HIGH ON THE HOG...

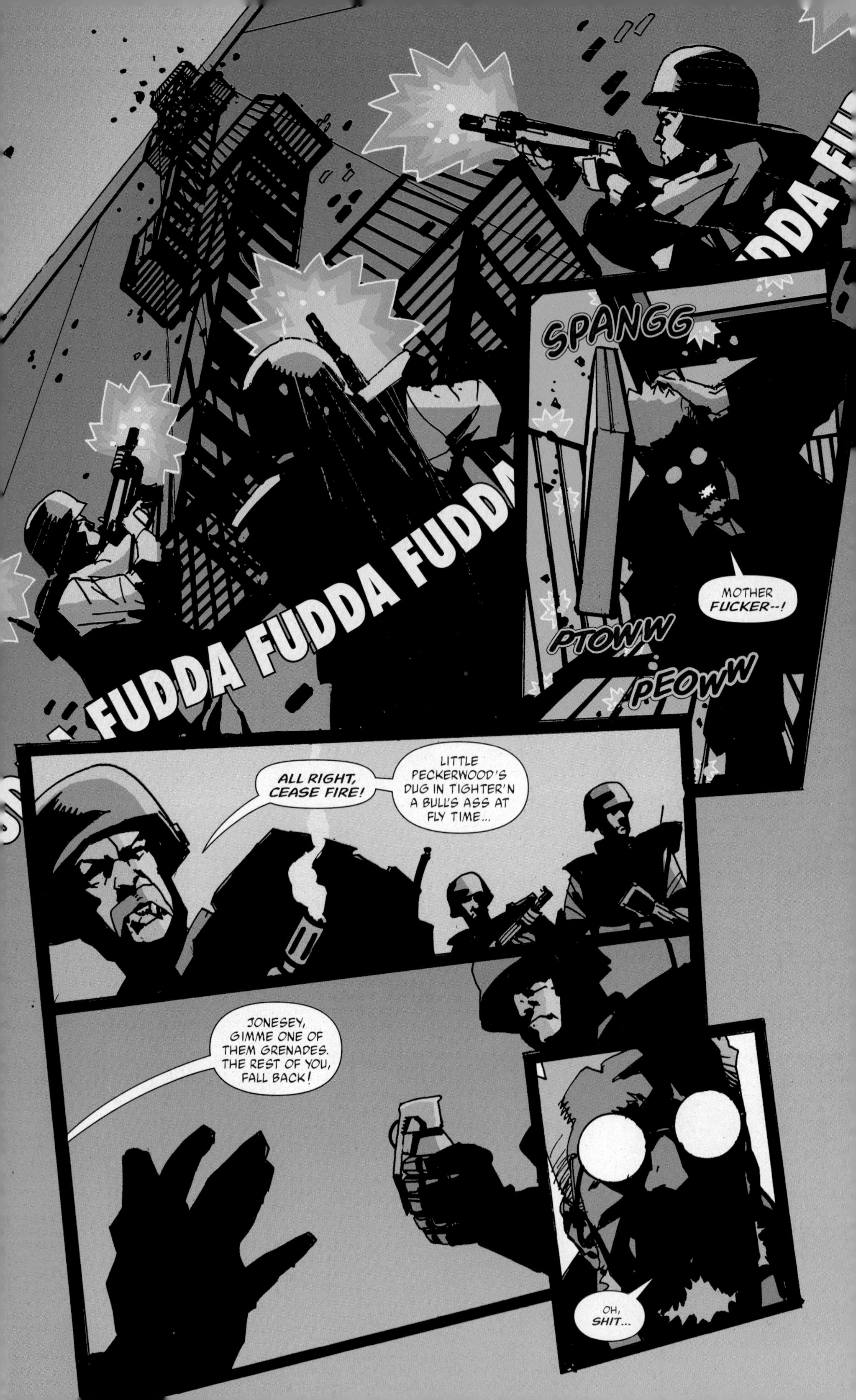
FUDDA FUDDA FUDDA FUDDA
SPANGG
MOTHER FUCKER--!
PTOWW
PEOWW
ALL RIGHT, CEASE FIRE!
LITTLE PECKERWOOD'S DUG IN TIGHTER'N A BULL'S ASS AT FLY TIME...
JONESEY, GIMME ONE OF THEM GRENADES. THE REST OF YOU, FALL BACK!
OH, SHIT...

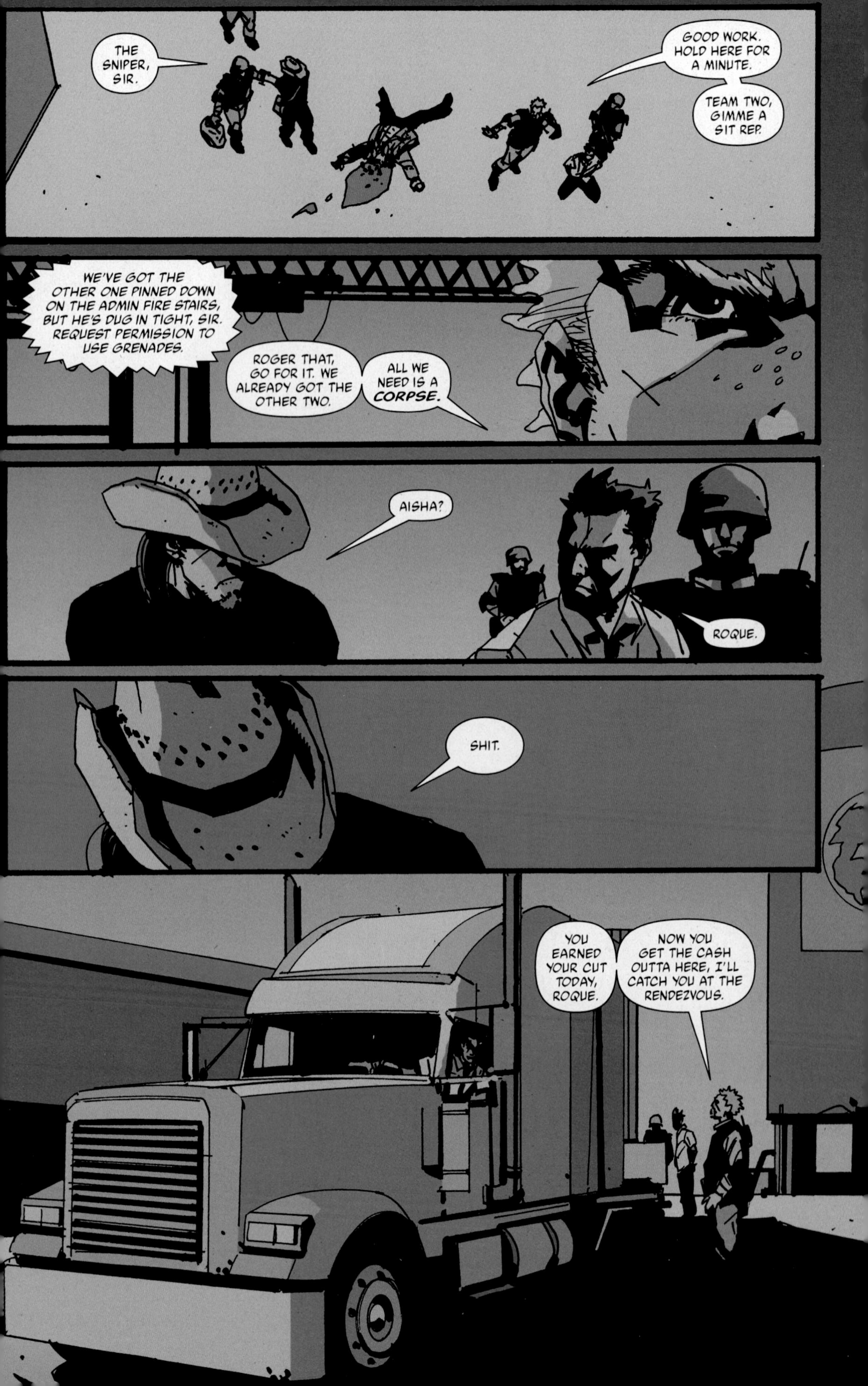
THE SNIPER, SIR.
GOOD WORK. HOLD HERE FOR A MINUTE.
TEAM TWO, GIMME A SIT REP.
WE'VE GOT THE OTHER ONE PINNED DOWN ON THE ADMIN FIRE STAIRS, BUT HE'S DUG IN TIGHT, SIR. REQUEST PERMISSION TO USE GRENADES.
ROGER THAT, GO FOR IT. WE ALREADY GOT THE OTHER TWO.
ALL WE NEED IS A CORPSE.
AISHA?
ROQUE.
SHIT.
YOU EARNED YOUR CUT TODAY, ROQUE.
NOW YOU GET THE CASH OUTTA HERE, I'LL CATCH YOU AT THE RENDEZVOUS.

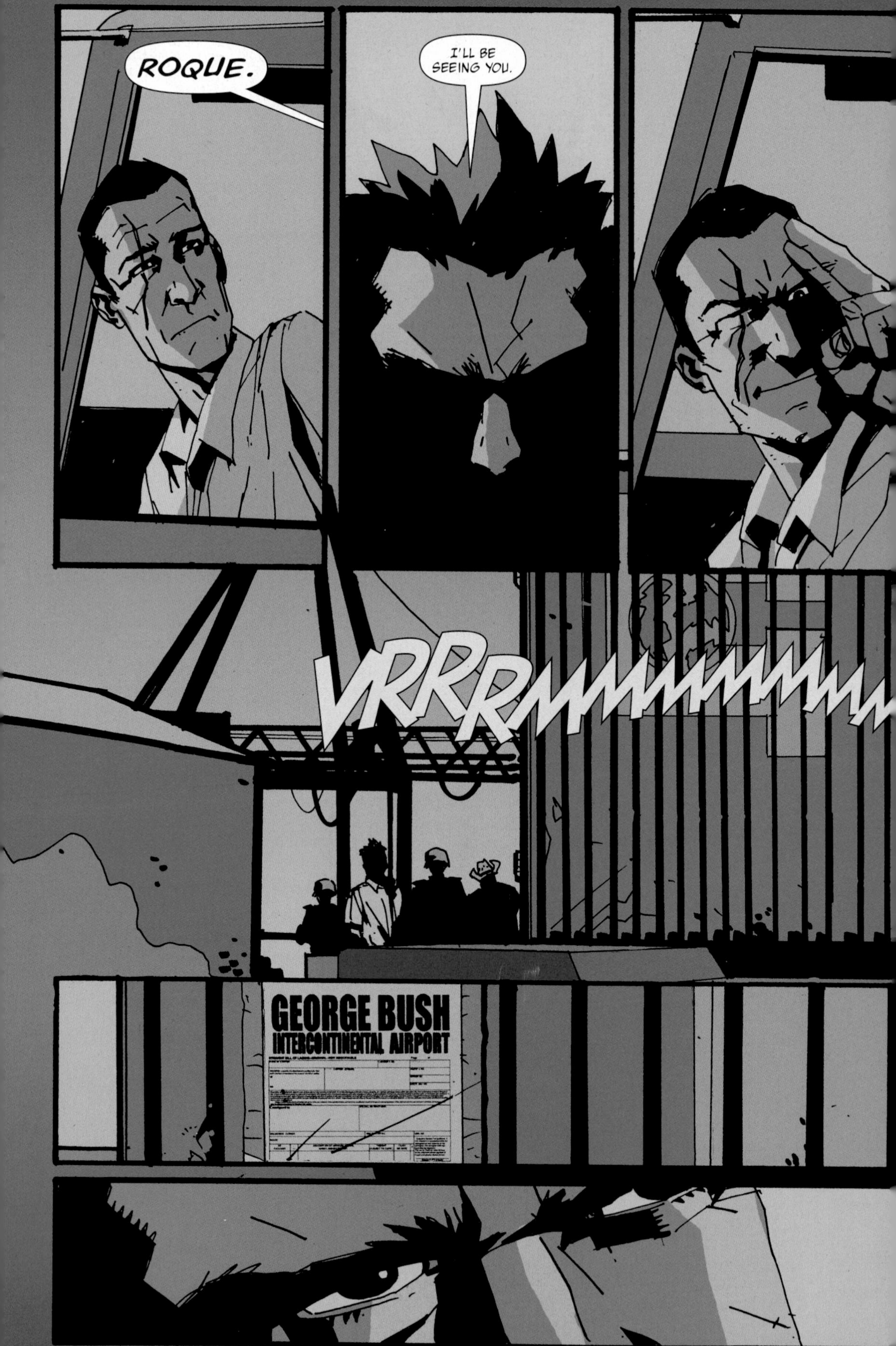
ROQUE.
I'LL BE SEEING YOU.
VRRRMMMMMMMM
GEORGE BUSH
INTERCONTINENTAL AIRPORT

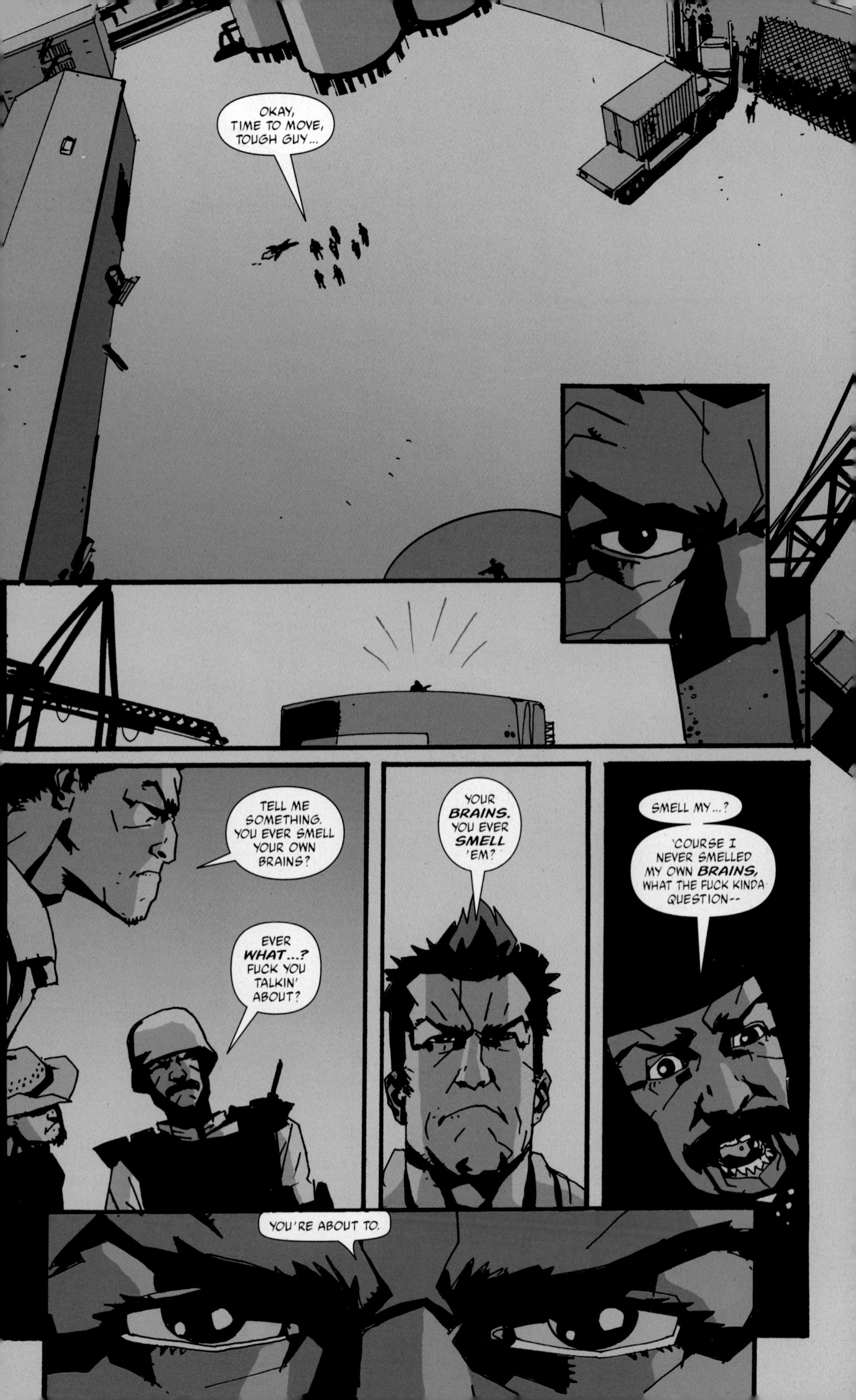
OKAY, TIME TO MOVE, TOUGH GUY...
TELL ME SOMETHING. YOU EVER SMELL YOUR OWN BRAINS?
EVER WHAT...? FUCK YOU TALKIN' ABOUT?
YOUR BRAINS. YOU EVER SMELL 'EM?
SMELL MY...?
'COURSE I NEVER SMELLED MY OWN BRAINS, WHAT THE FUCK KINDA QUESTION--
YOU'RE ABOUT TO.

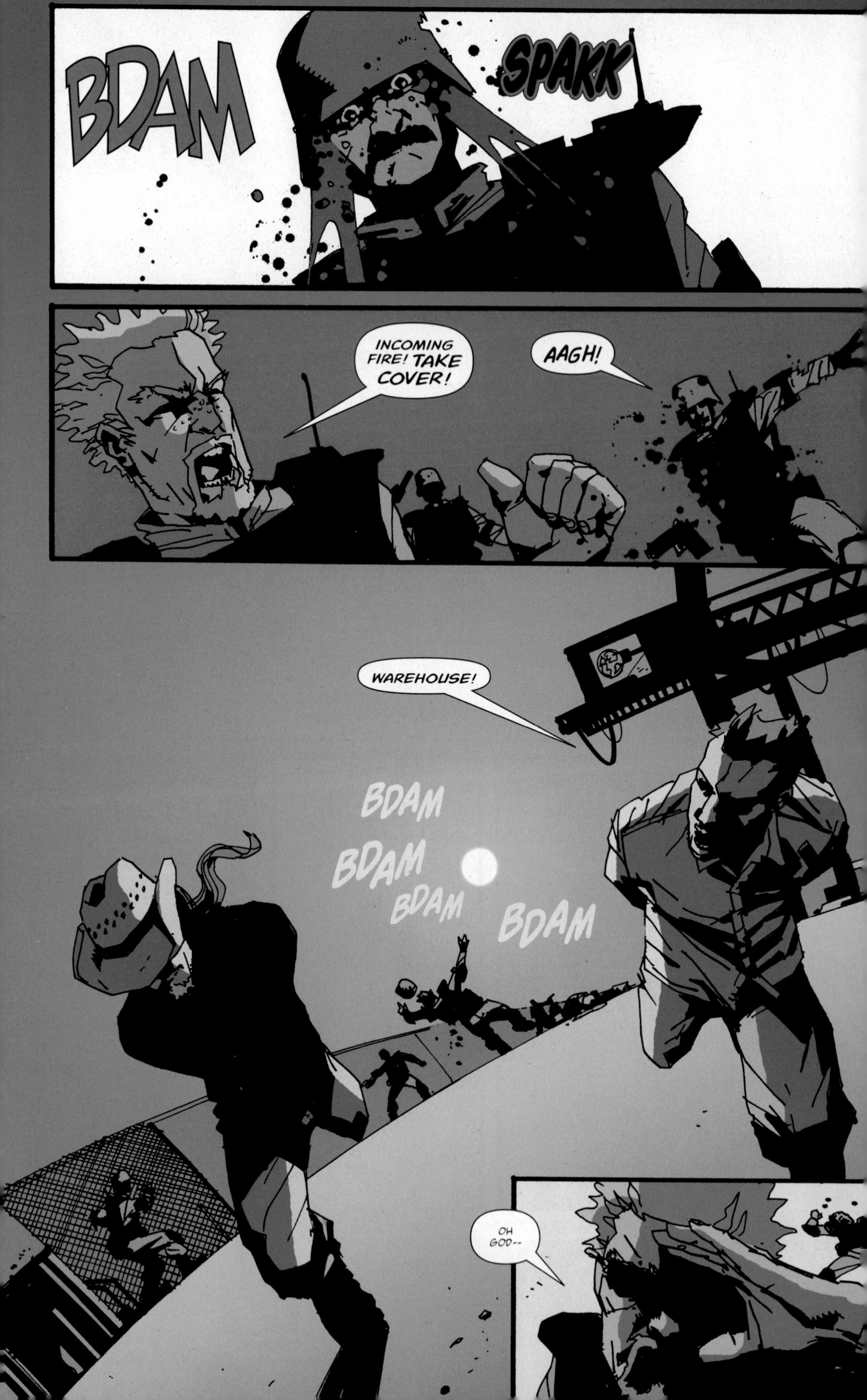
BDAM
SPAKK
INCOMING FIRE! TAKE COVER!
AAGH!
WAREHOUSE!
BDAM
BDAM
BDAM
BDAM
OH GOD--

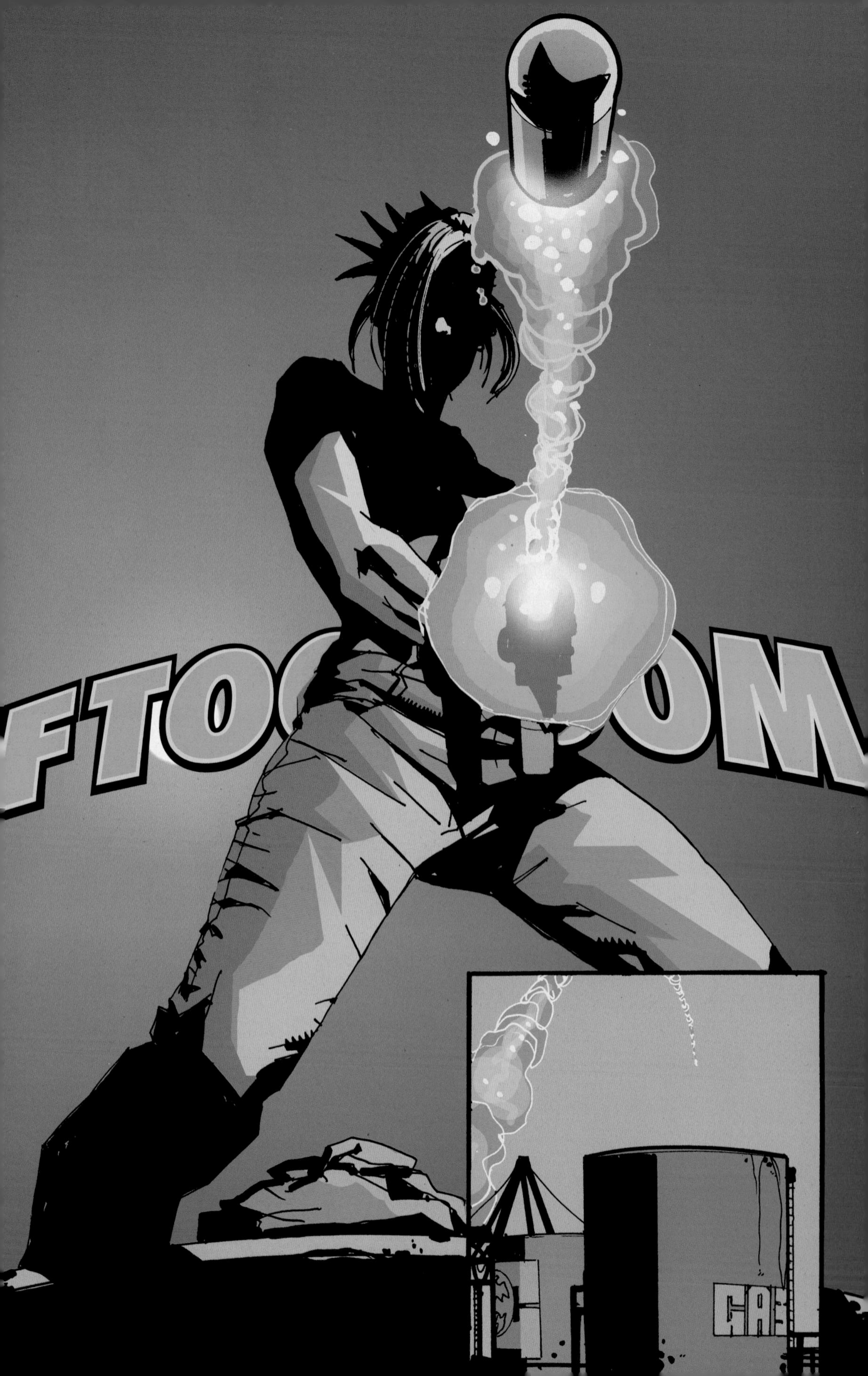

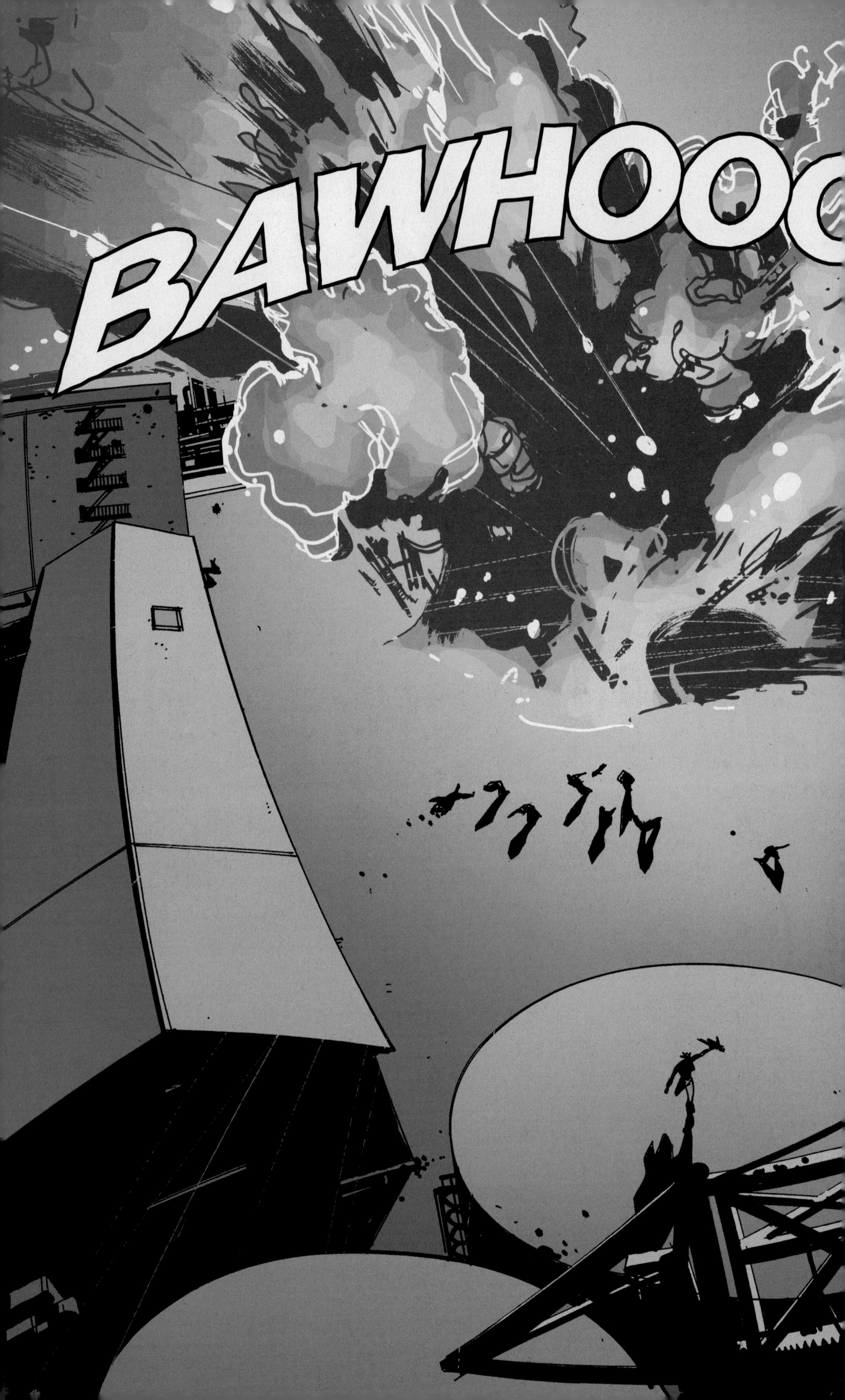
BAWHOOO

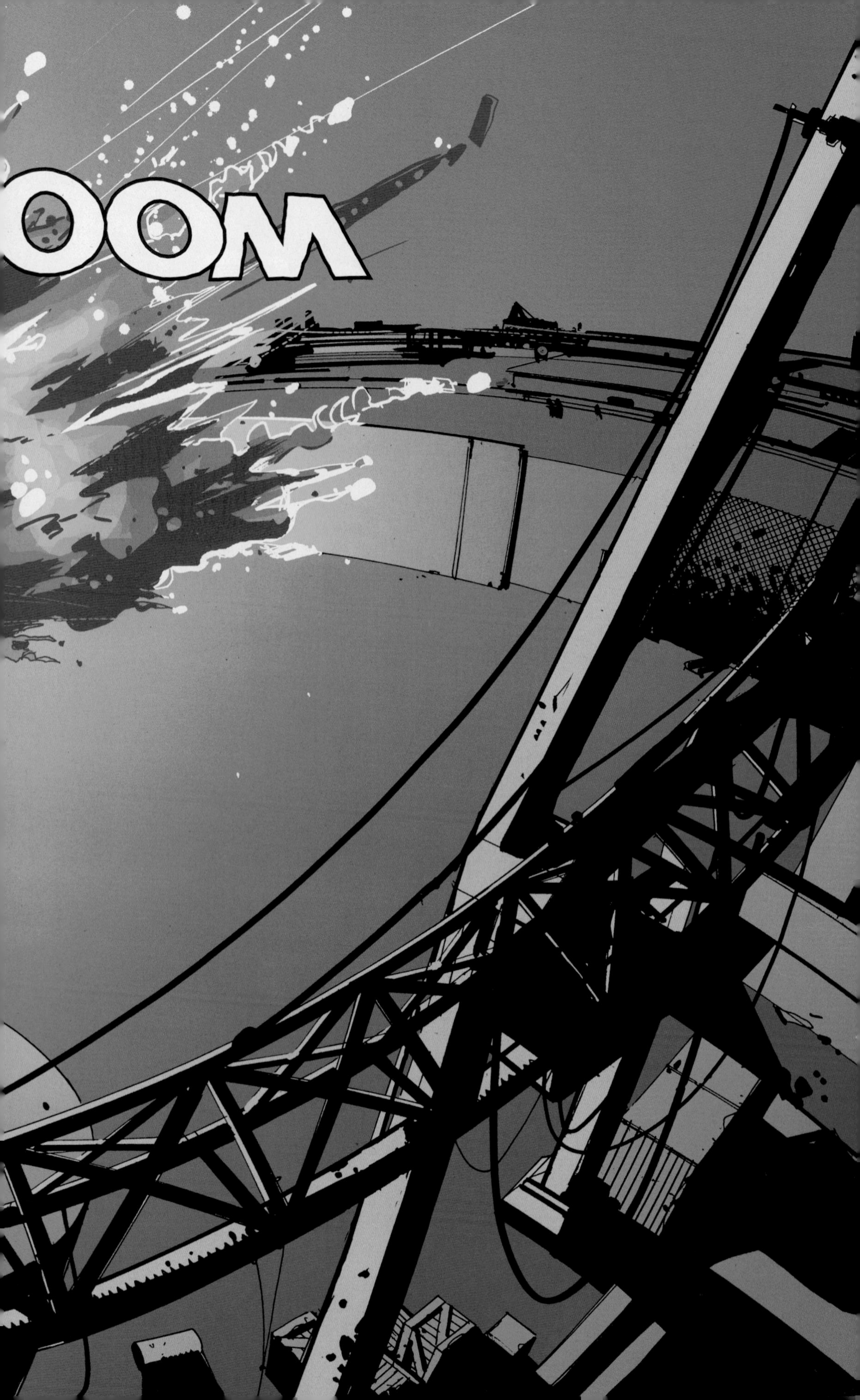
OOM

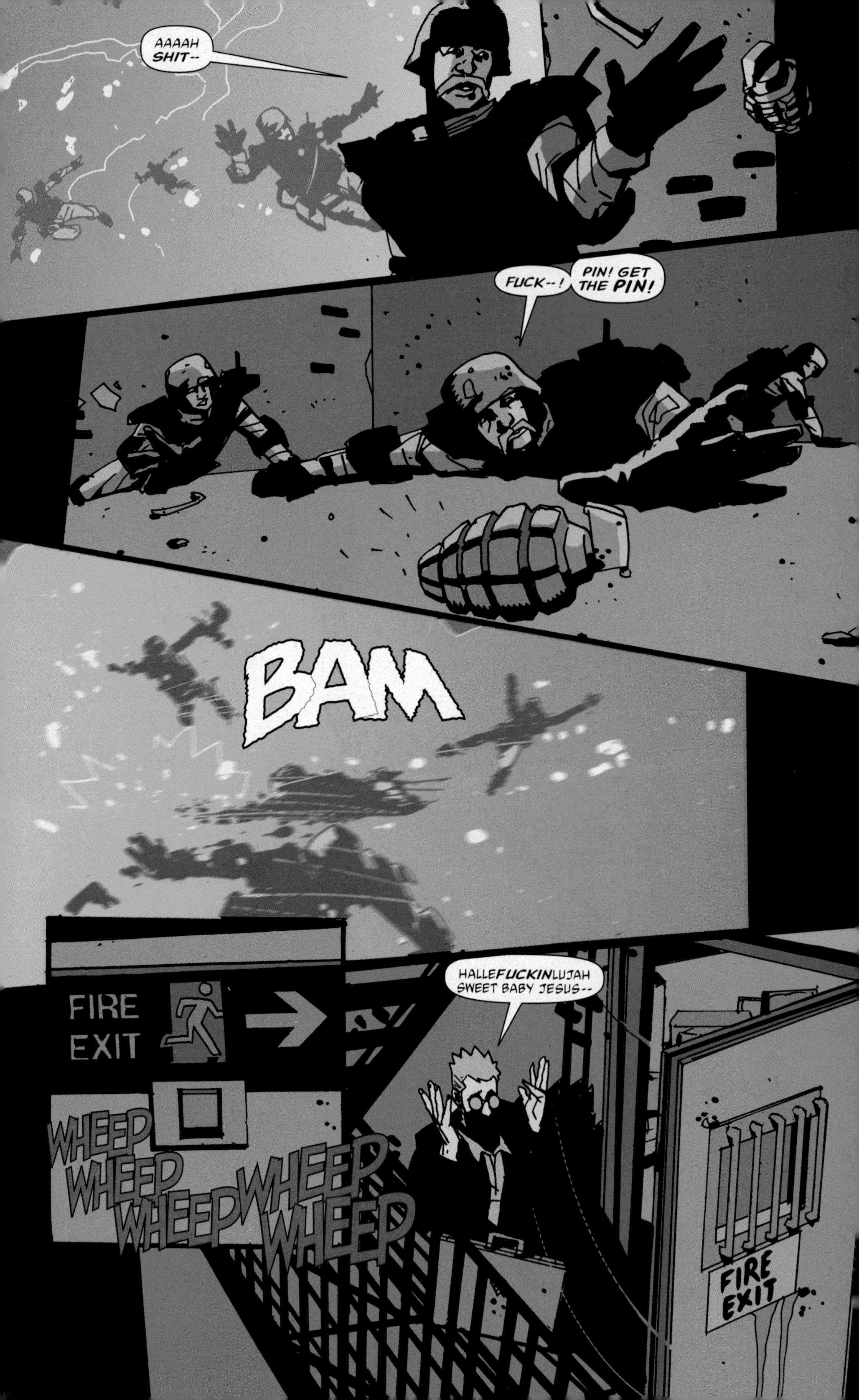
AAAAH SHIT--
FUCK--!
PIN! GET THE PIN!
BAM
FIRE EXIT
HALLEFUCKINLUJAH SWEET BABY JESUS--
WHEEP WHEEP WHEEP WHEEP WHEEP
FIRE EXIT

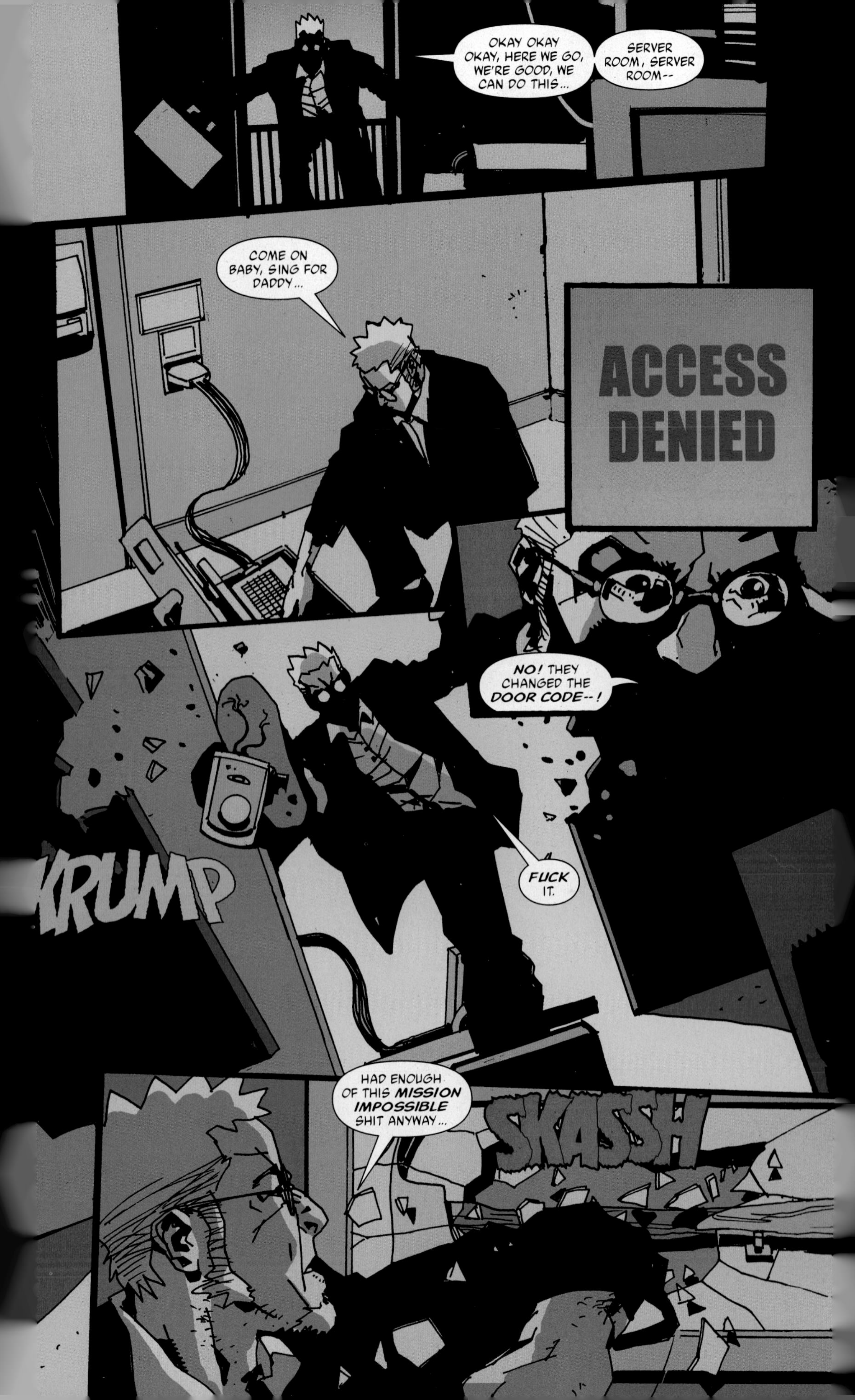
OKAY OKAY
OKAY, HERE WE GO, WE'RE GOOD, WE CAN DO THIS...
SERVER ROOM, SERVER ROOM--
COME ON BABY, SING FOR DADDY...
ACCESS DENIED
NO! THEY CHANGED THE DOOR CODE--!
KRUMP
FUCK IT.
HAD ENOUGH OF THIS MISSION IMPOSSIBLE SHIT ANYWAY...
SKASH

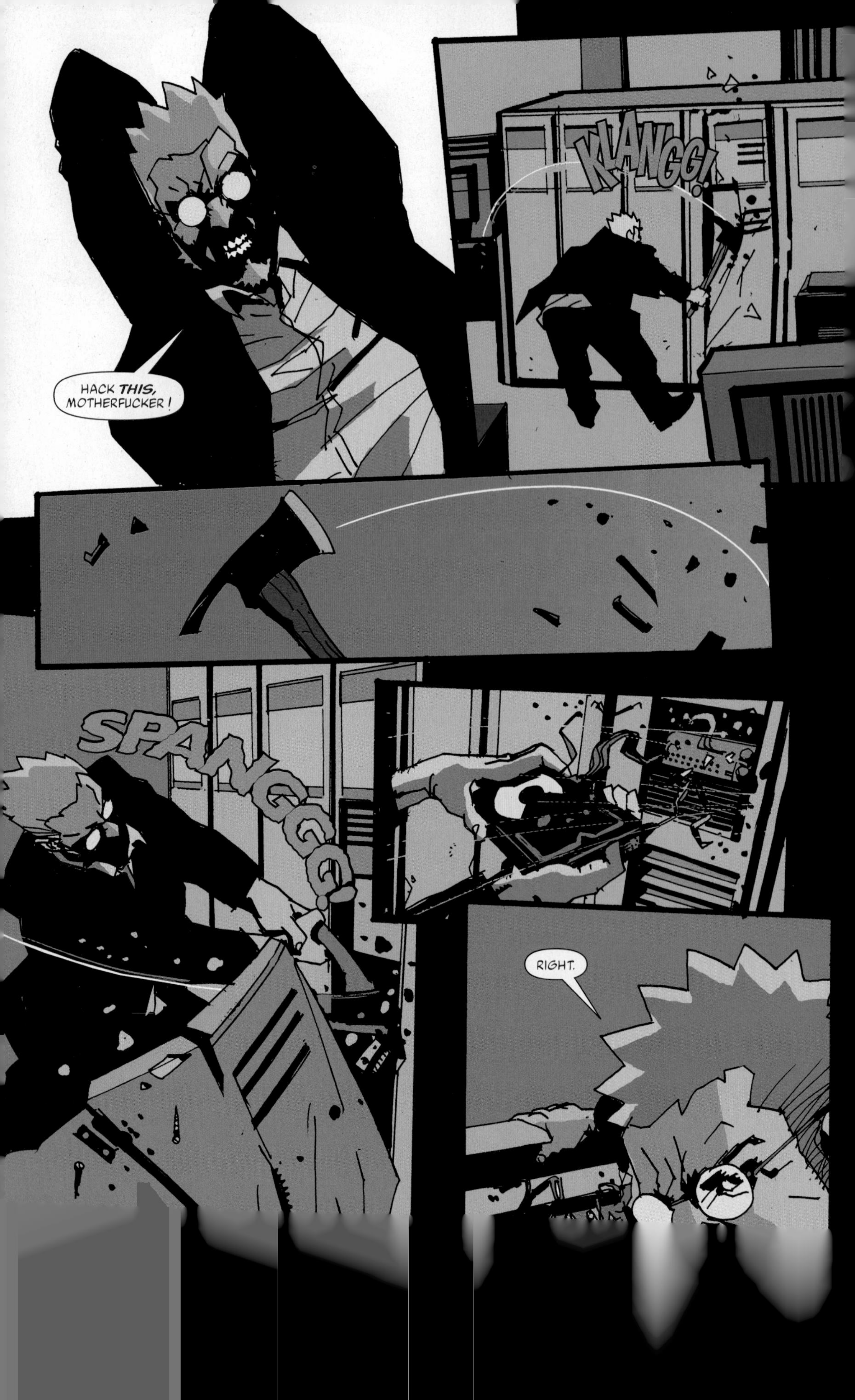
HACK THIS, MOTHERFUCKER!
KLANGG!
SPANGGG
RIGHT.

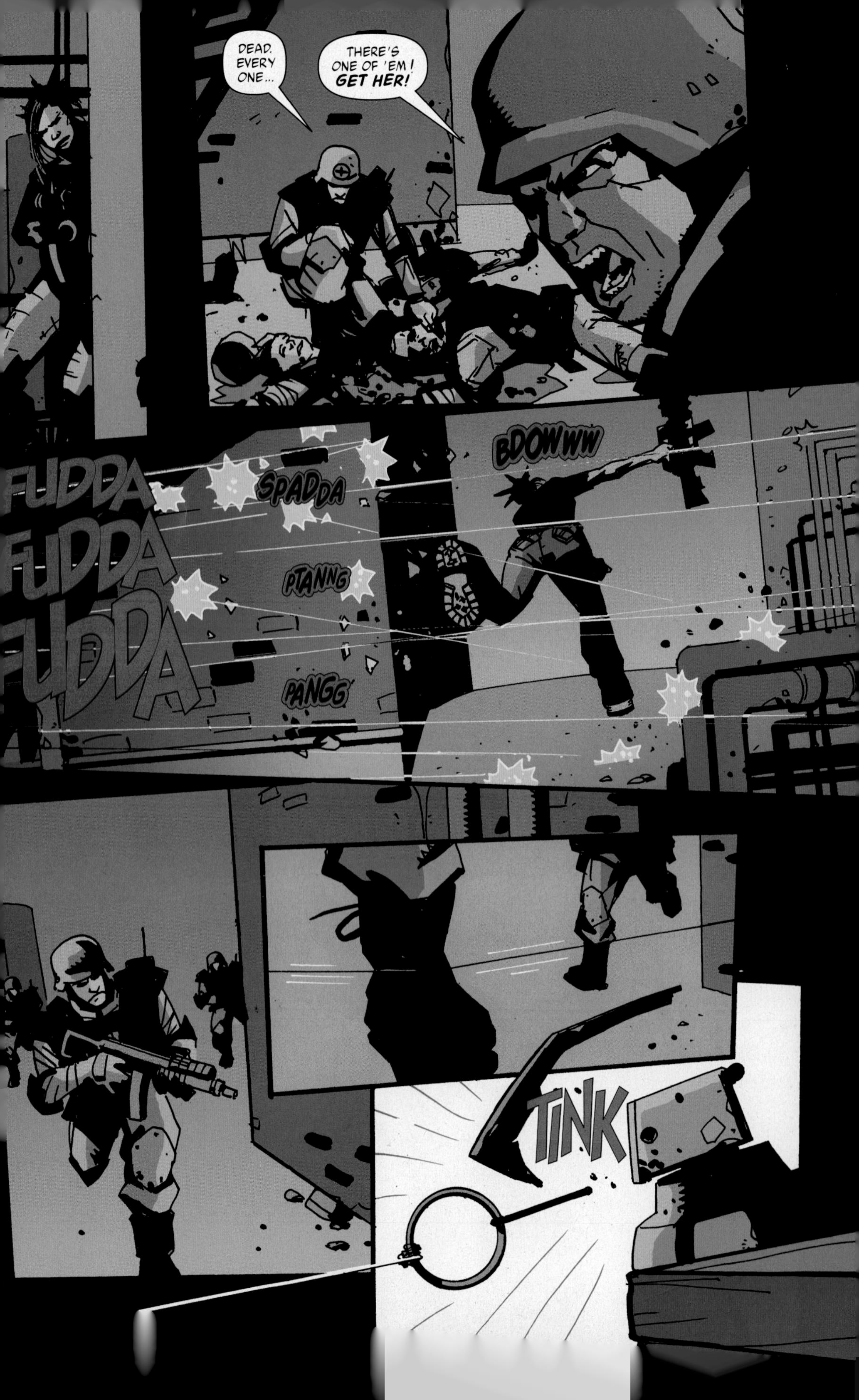

DEAD. EVERY ONE...
THERE'S ONE OF 'EM! GET HER!
FUDDA FUDDA FUDDA
SPADDA
PTANNG
PANGG
BDOWWW
TINK

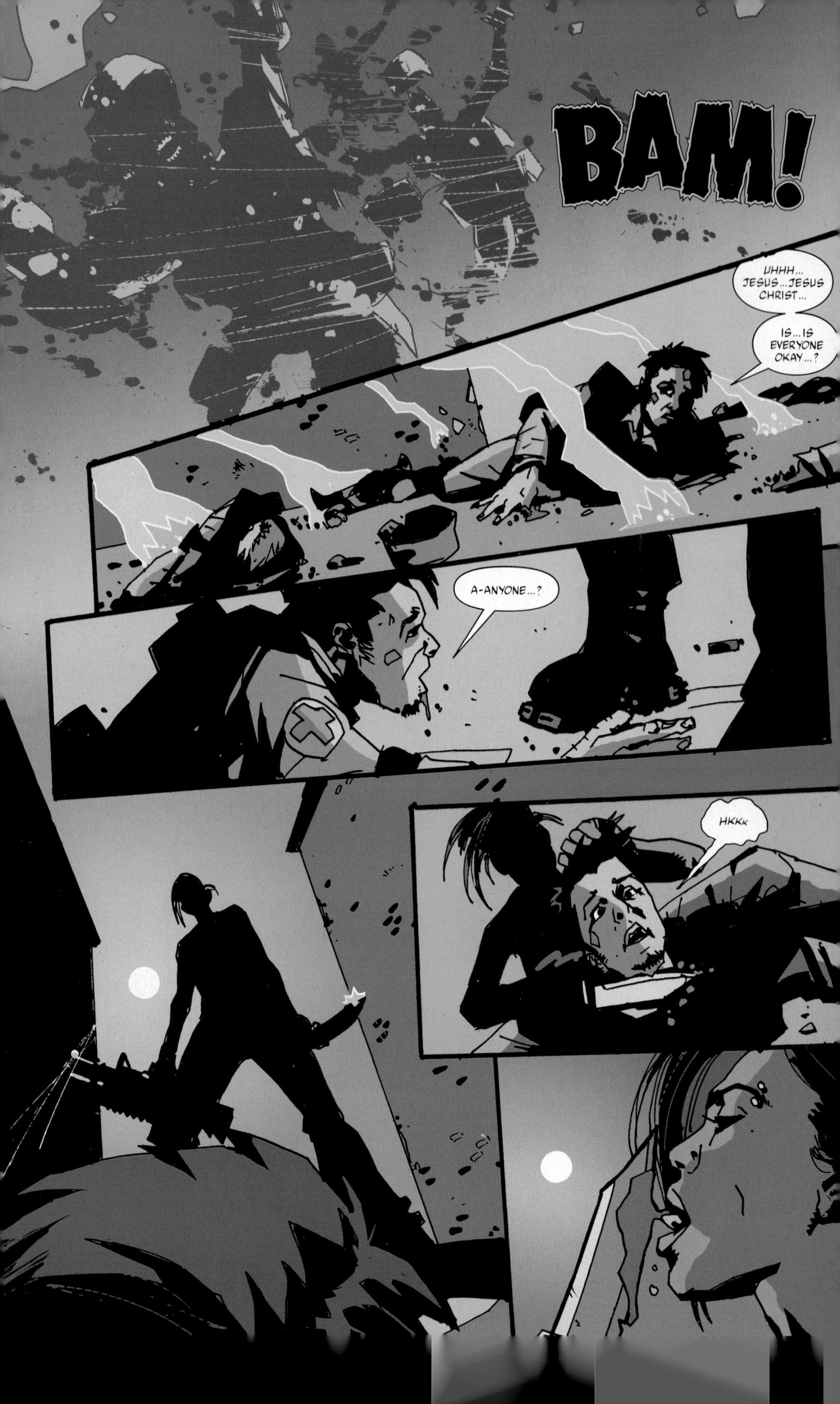
BAM!
UHHH... JESUS...JESUS CHRIST...
IS...IS EVERYONE OKAY...?
A-ANYONE...?
HKKK

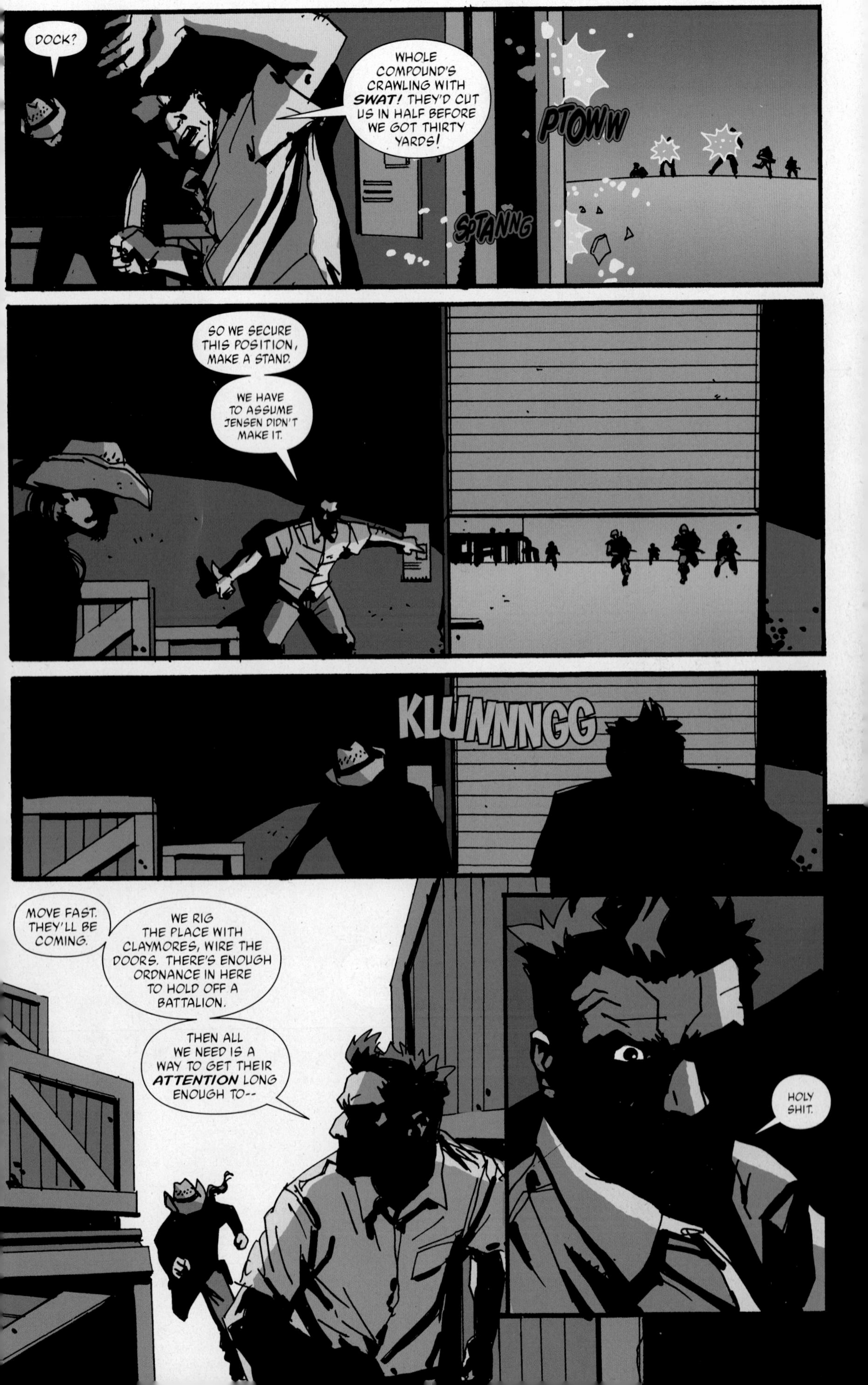
DOCK?
WHOLE COMPOUND'S CRAWLING WITH SWAT! THEY'D CUT US IN HALF BEFORE WE GOT THIRTY YARDS!
PTOWW
SPTANNG
SO WE SECURE THIS POSITION, MAKE A STAND.
WE HAVE TO ASSUME JENSEN DIDN'T MAKE IT.
KLUNNNGG
MOVE FAST. THEY'LL BE COMING.
WE RIG THE PLACE WITH CLAYMORES, WIRE THE DOORS. THERE'S ENOUGH ORDNANCE IN HERE TO HOLD OFF A BATTALION.
THEN ALL WE NEED IS A WAY TO GET THEIR ATTENTION LONG ENOUGH TO--
HOLY SHIT.

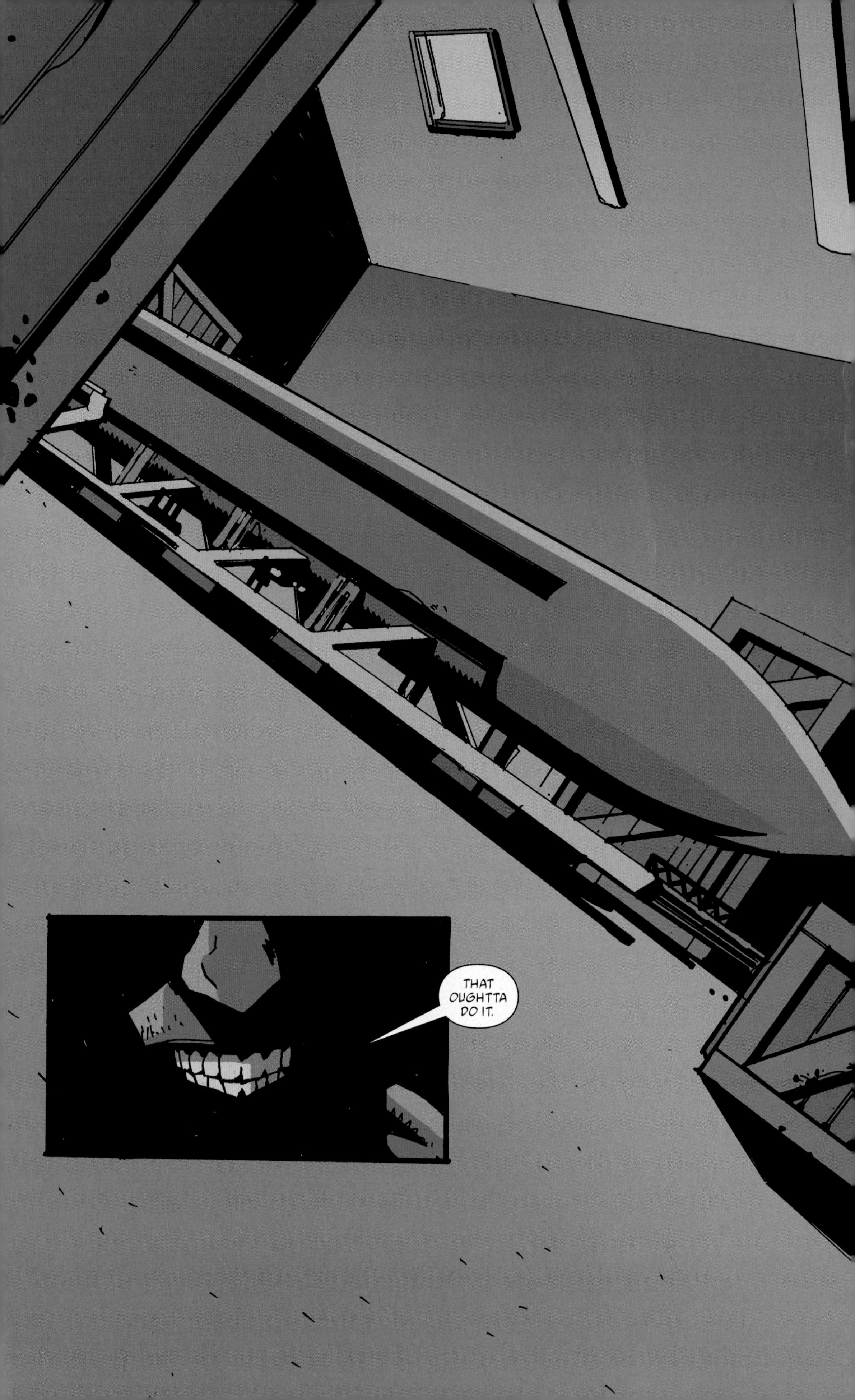
THAT OUGHTTA DO IT.

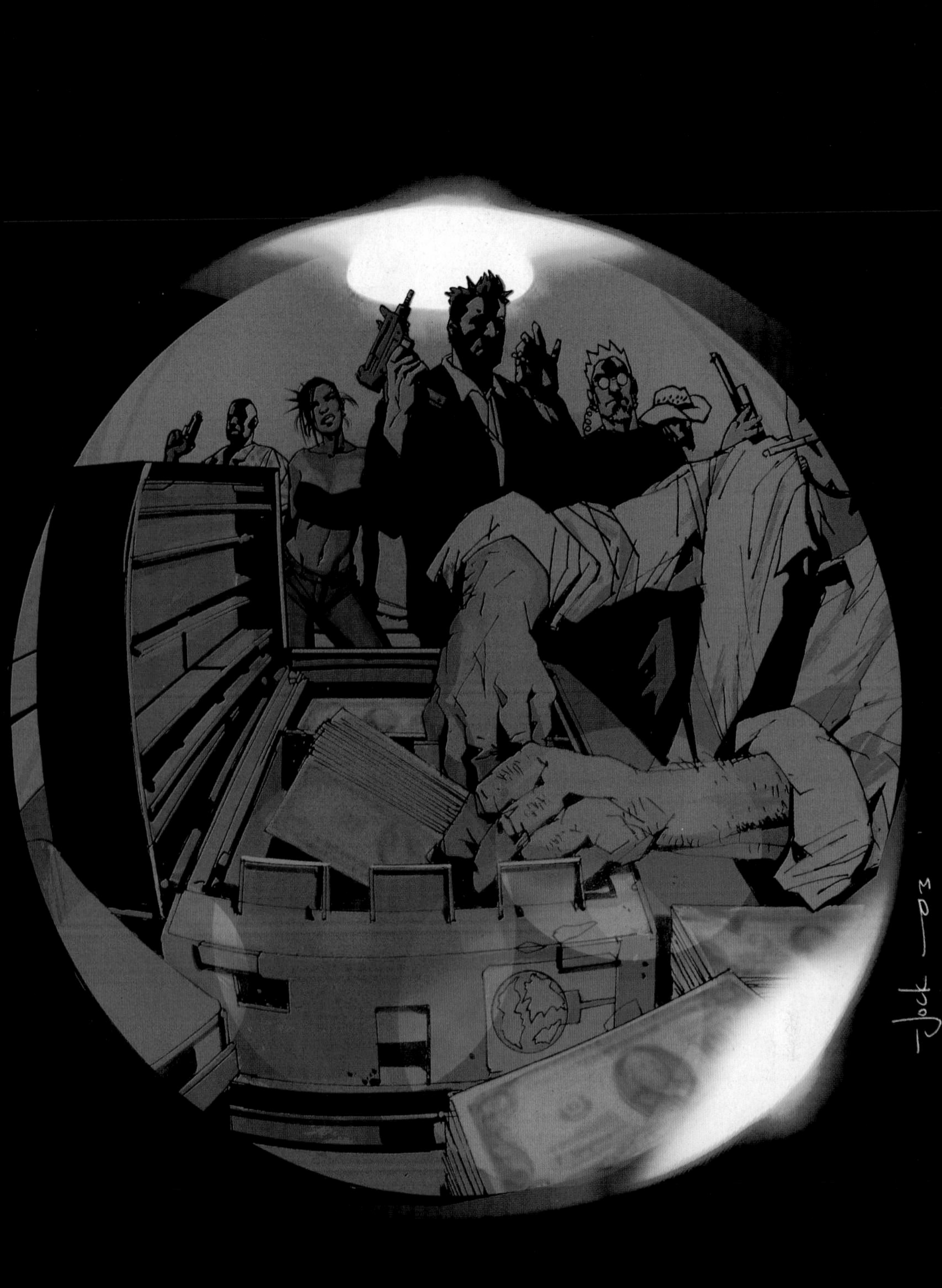

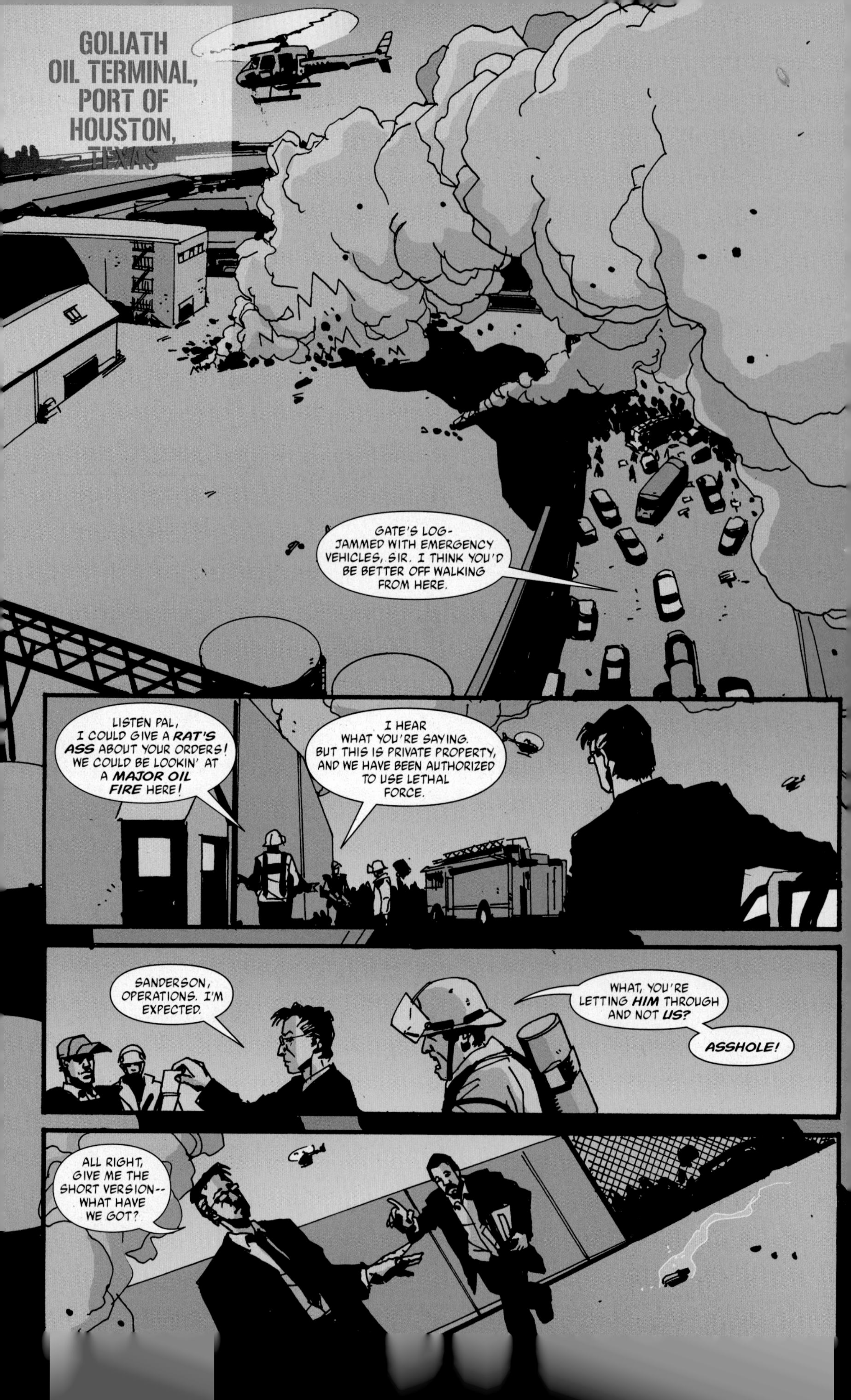
GOLIATH OIL TERMINAL, PORT OF HOUSTON, TEXAS
GATE'S LOG-JAMMED WITH EMERGENCY VEHICLES, SIR. I THINK YOU'D BE BETTER OFF WALKING FROM HERE.
LISTEN PAL, I COULD GIVE A RAT'S ASS ABOUT YOUR ORDERS! WE COULD BE LOOKIN' AT A MAJOR OIL FIRE HERE!
I HEAR WHAT YOU'RE SAYING. BUT THIS IS PRIVATE PROPERTY, AND WE HAVE BEEN AUTHORIZED TO USE LETHAL FORCE.
SANDERSON, OPERATIONS. I'M EXPECTED.
WHAT, YOU'RE LETTING HIM THROUGH AND NOT US?
ASSHOLE!
ALL RIGHT, GIVE ME THE SHORT VERSION--WHAT HAVE WE GOT?

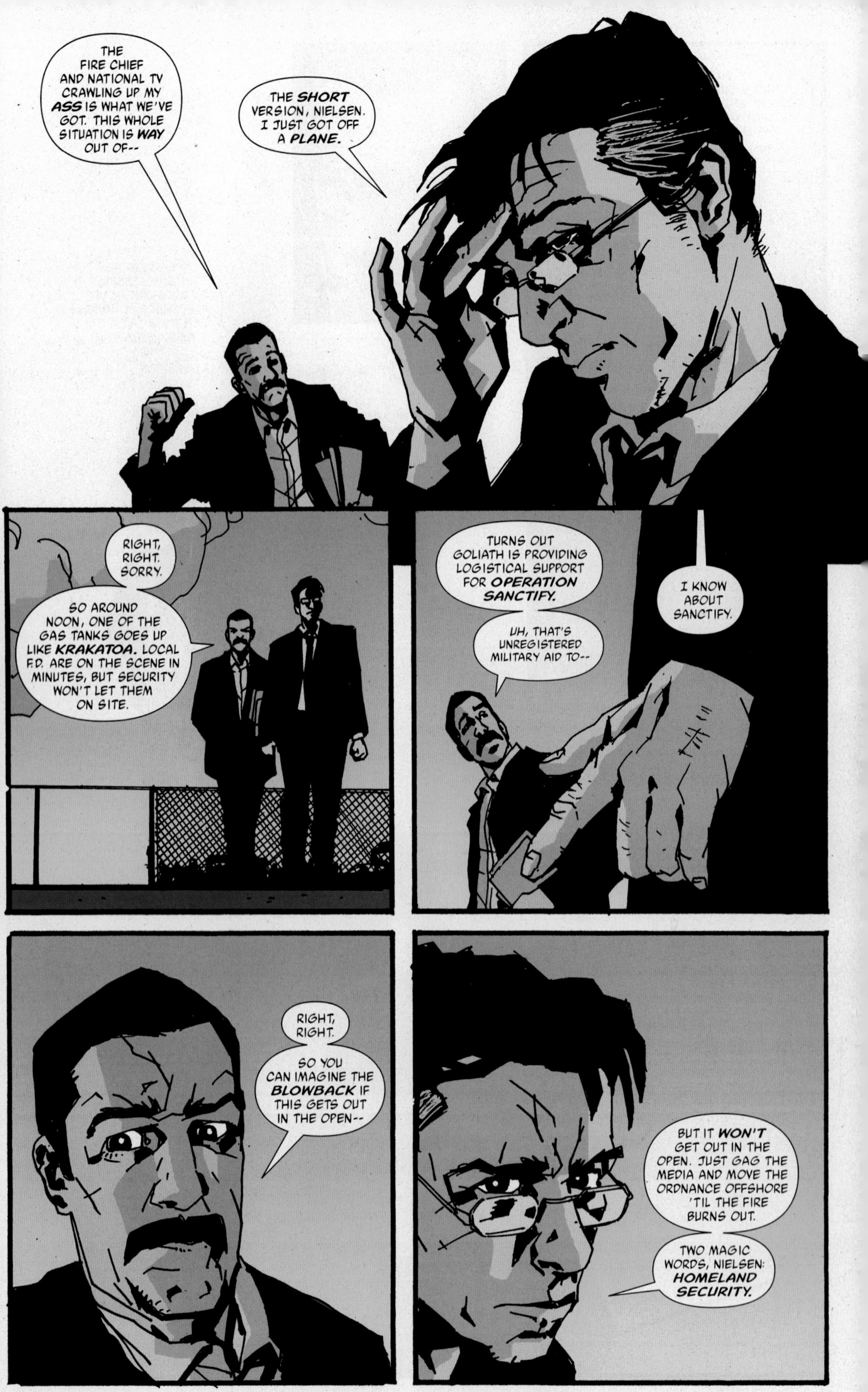
THE FIRE CHIEF AND NATIONAL TV CRAWLING UP MY ***ASS*** IS WHAT WE'VE GOT. THIS WHOLE SITUATION IS ***WAY*** OUT OF--
THE ***SHORT*** VERSION, NIELSEN. I JUST GOT OFF A ***PLANE.***
RIGHT, RIGHT. SORRY.
SO AROUND NOON, ONE OF THE GAS TANKS GOES UP LIKE ***KRAKATOA.*** LOCAL F.D. ARE ON THE SCENE IN MINUTES, BUT SECURITY WON'T LET THEM ON SITE.
TURNS OUT GOLIATH IS PROVIDING LOGISTICAL SUPPORT FOR ***OPERATION SANCTIFY.***
UH, THAT'S UNREGISTERED MILITARY AID TO--
I KNOW ABOUT SANCTIFY.
RIGHT, RIGHT.
SO YOU CAN IMAGINE THE ***BLOWBACK*** IF THIS GETS OUT IN THE OPEN--
BUT IT ***WON'T*** GET OUT IN THE OPEN. JUST GAG THE MEDIA AND MOVE THE ORDNANCE OFFSHORE 'TIL THE FIRE BURNS OUT.
TWO MAGIC WORDS, NIELSEN: ***HOMELAND SECURITY.***

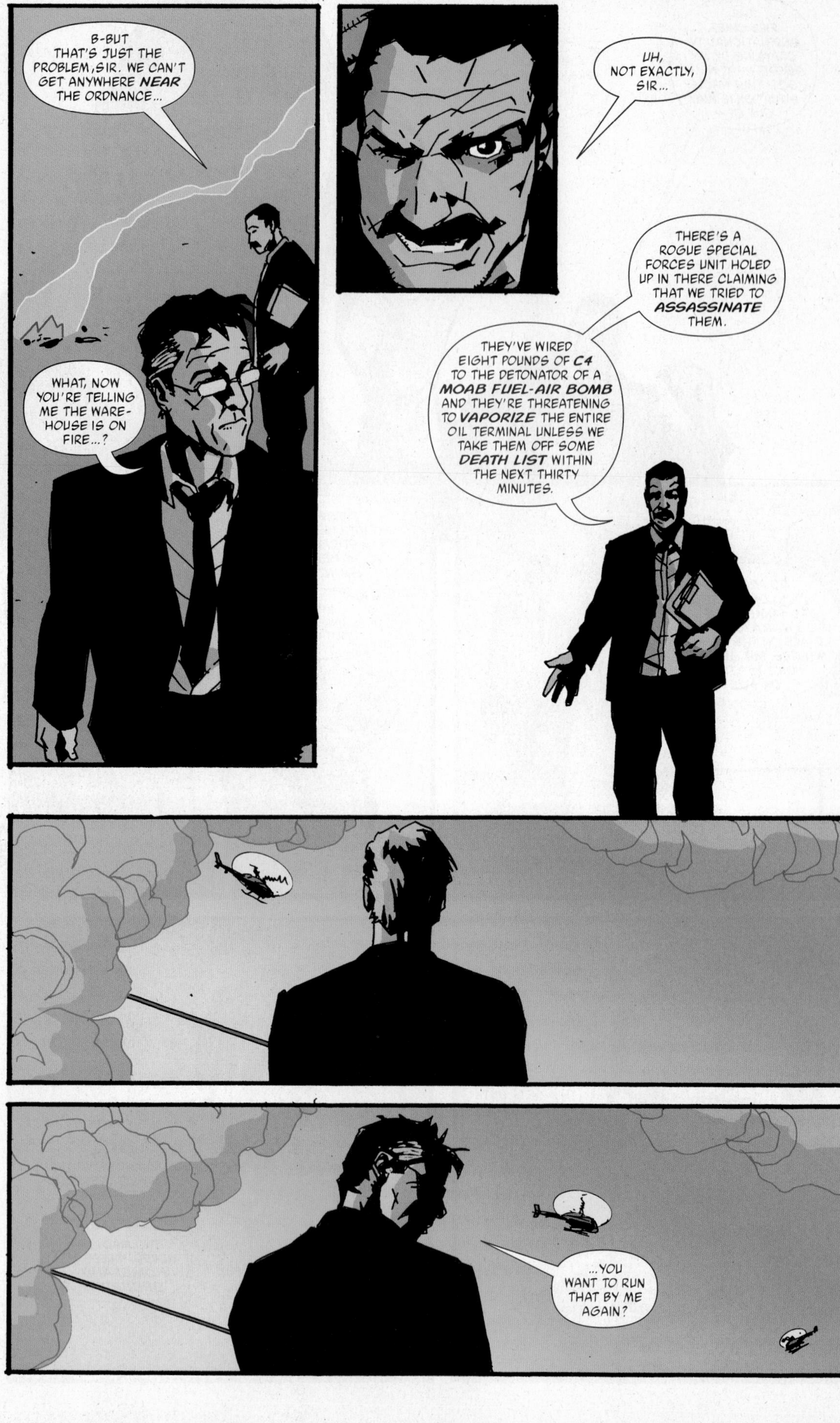
B-BUT THAT'S JUST THE PROBLEM, SIR. WE CAN'T GET ANYWHERE NEAR THE ORDNANCE...
WHAT, NOW YOU'RE TELLING ME THE WARE-HOUSE IS ON FIRE...?
UH, NOT EXACTLY, SIR...
THERE'S A ROGUE SPECIAL FORCES UNIT HOLED UP IN THERE CLAIMING THAT WE TRIED TO ASSASSINATE THEM.
THEY'VE WIRED EIGHT POUNDS OF C4 TO THE DETONATOR OF A MOAB FUEL-AIR BOMB AND THEY'RE THREATENING TO VAPORIZE THE ENTIRE OIL TERMINAL UNLESS WE TAKE THEM OFF SOME DEATH LIST WITHIN THE NEXT THIRTY MINUTES.
...YOU WANT TO RUN THAT BY ME AGAIN?

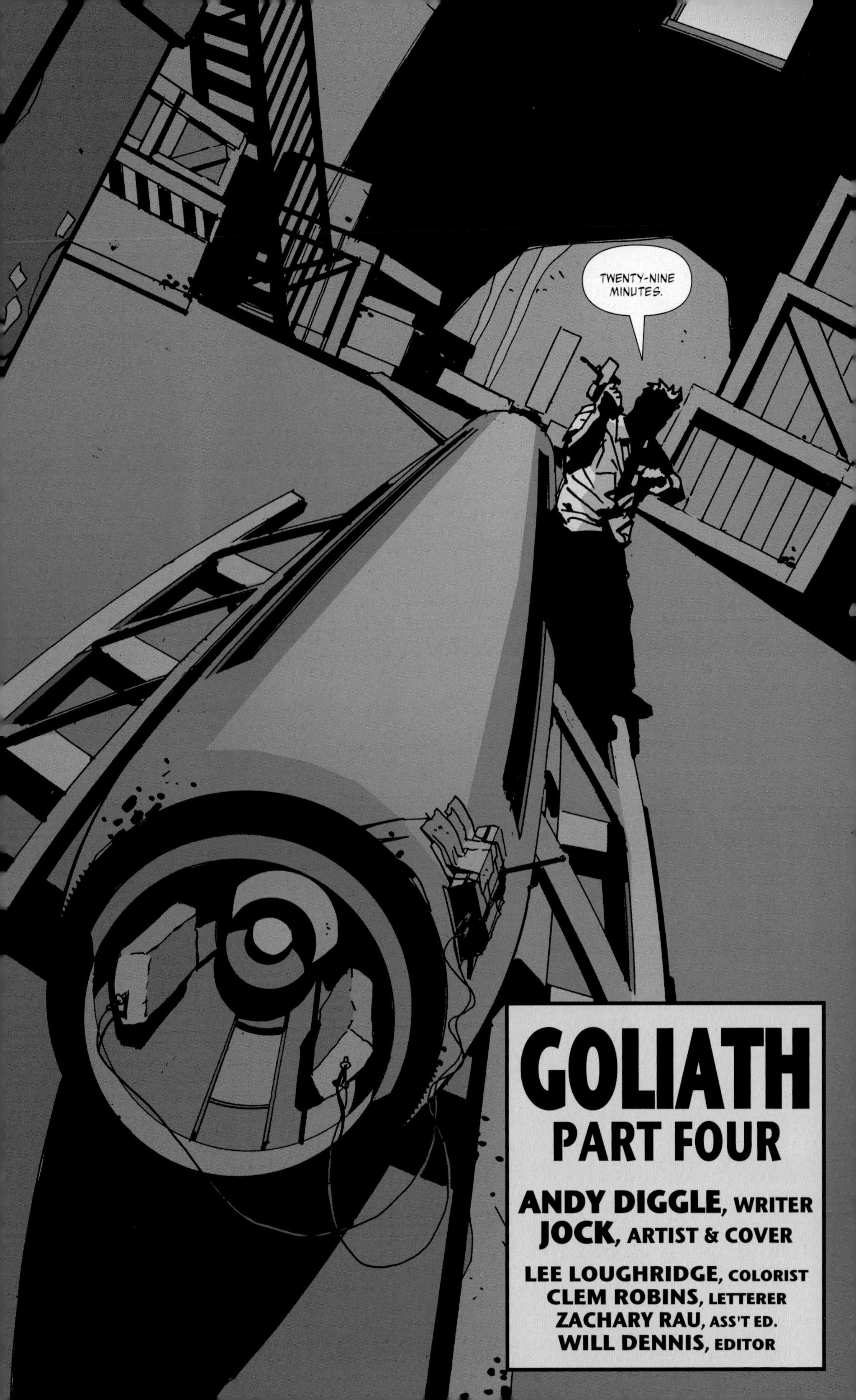
TWENTY-NINE MINUTES.
GOLIATH
PART FOUR
ANDY DIGGLE, WRITER
JOCK, ARTIST & COVER
LEE LOUGHRIDGE, COLORIST
CLEM ROBINS, LETTERER
ZACHARY RAU, ASS'T ED.
WILL DENNIS, EDITOR

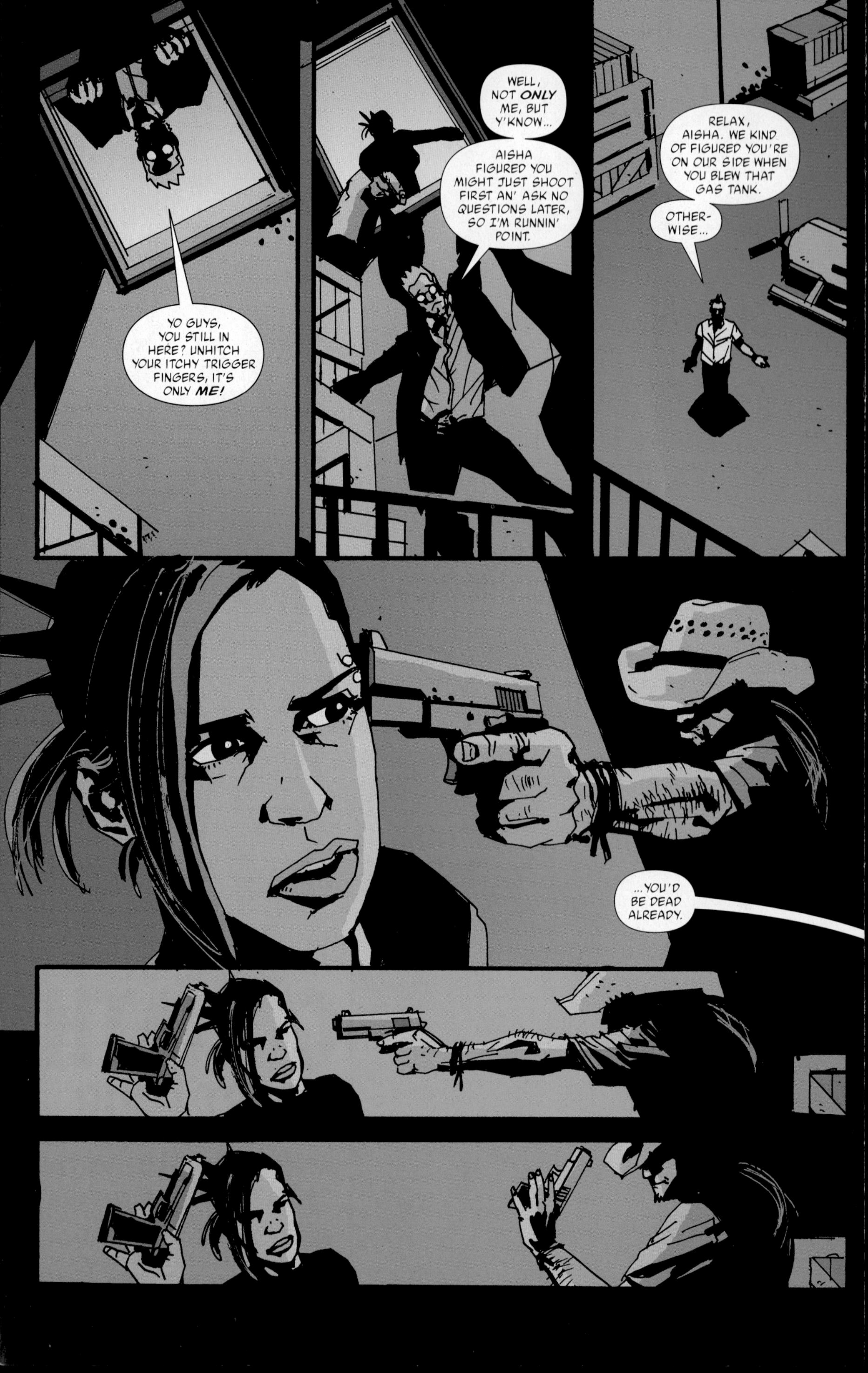
YO GUYS, YOU STILL IN HERE? UNHITCH YOUR ITCHY TRIGGER FINGERS, IT'S ONLY ME!
WELL, NOT ONLY ME, BUT Y'KNOW...
AISHA FIGURED YOU MIGHT JUST SHOOT FIRST AN' ASK NO QUESTIONS LATER, SO I'M RUNNIN' POINT.
RELAX, AISHA. WE KIND OF FIGURED YOU'RE ON OUR SIDE WHEN YOU BLEW THAT GAS TANK.
OTHER-WISE...
...YOU'D BE DEAD ALREADY.

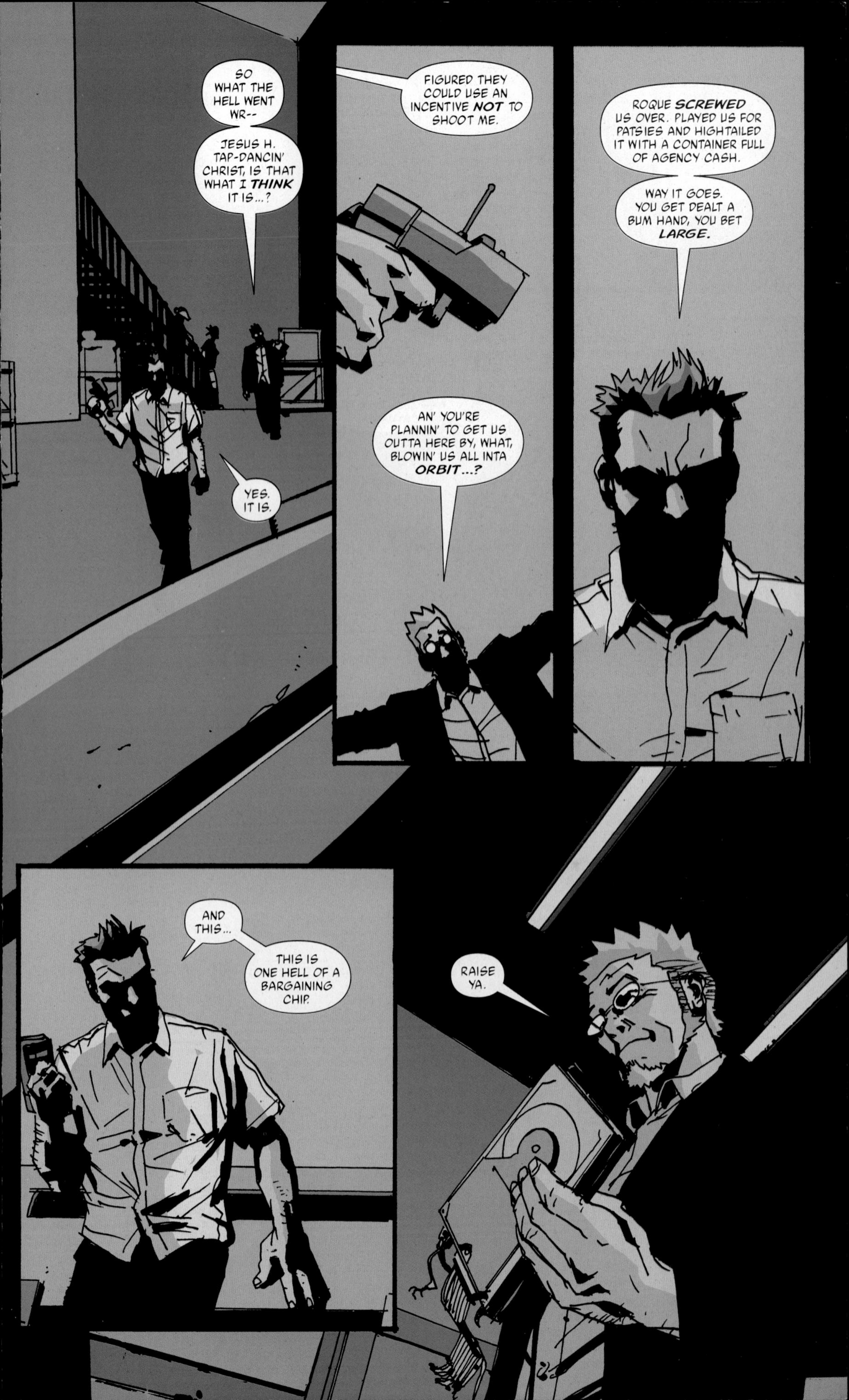

SO WHAT THE HELL WENT WR--
JESUS H. TAP-DANCIN' CHRIST, IS THAT WHAT I *THINK* IT IS...?
YES. IT IS.
FIGURED THEY COULD USE AN INCENTIVE *NOT* TO SHOOT ME.
AN' YOU'RE PLANNIN' TO GET US OUTTA HERE BY, WHAT, BLOWIN' US ALL INTA *ORBIT...?*
ROQUE *SCREWED* US OVER. PLAYED US FOR PATSIES AND HIGHTAILED IT WITH A CONTAINER FULL OF AGENCY CASH.
WAY IT GOES. YOU GET DEALT A BUM HAND, YOU BET *LARGE.*
AND THIS...
THIS IS ONE HELL OF A BARGAINING CHIP.
RAISE YA.

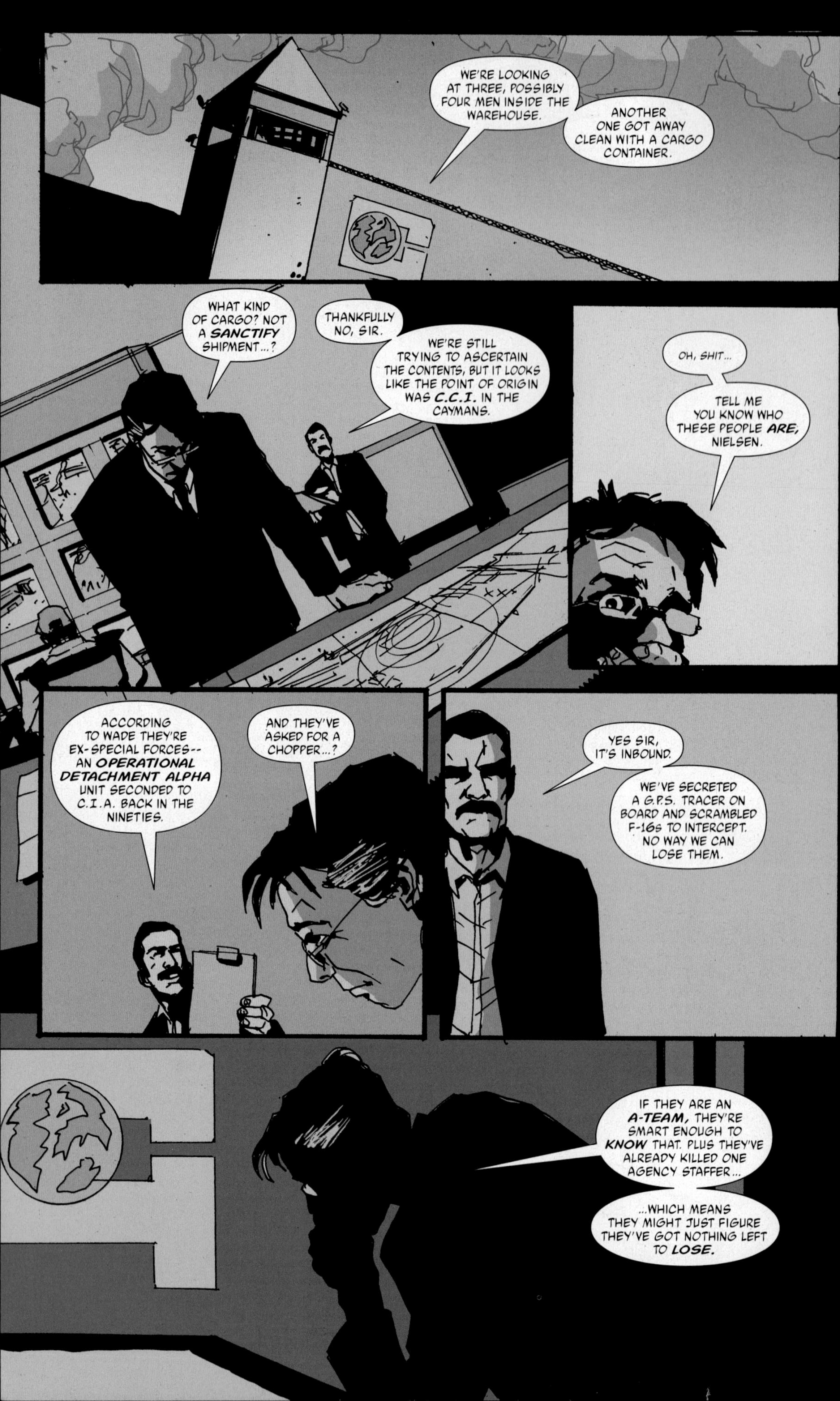
WE'RE LOOKING AT THREE, POSSIBLY FOUR MEN INSIDE THE WAREHOUSE.
ANOTHER ONE GOT AWAY CLEAN WITH A CARGO CONTAINER.
WHAT KIND OF CARGO? NOT A SANCTIFY SHIPMENT...?
THANKFULLY NO, SIR.
WE'RE STILL TRYING TO ASCERTAIN THE CONTENTS, BUT IT LOOKS LIKE THE POINT OF ORIGIN WAS C.C.I. IN THE CAYMANS.
OH, SHIT...
TELL ME YOU KNOW WHO THESE PEOPLE ARE, NIELSEN.
ACCORDING TO WADE THEY'RE EX-SPECIAL FORCES--AN OPERATIONAL DETACHMENT ALPHA UNIT SECONDED TO C.I.A. BACK IN THE NINETIES.
AND THEY'VE ASKED FOR A CHOPPER...?
YES SIR, IT'S INBOUND.
WE'VE SECRETED A G.P.S. TRACER ON BOARD AND SCRAMBLED F-16s TO INTERCEPT. NO WAY WE CAN LOSE THEM.
IF THEY ARE AN A-TEAM, THEY'RE SMART ENOUGH TO KNOW THAT. PLUS THEY'VE ALREADY KILLED ONE AGENCY STAFFER...
...WHICH MEANS THEY MIGHT JUST FIGURE THEY'VE GOT NOTHING LEFT TO LOSE.

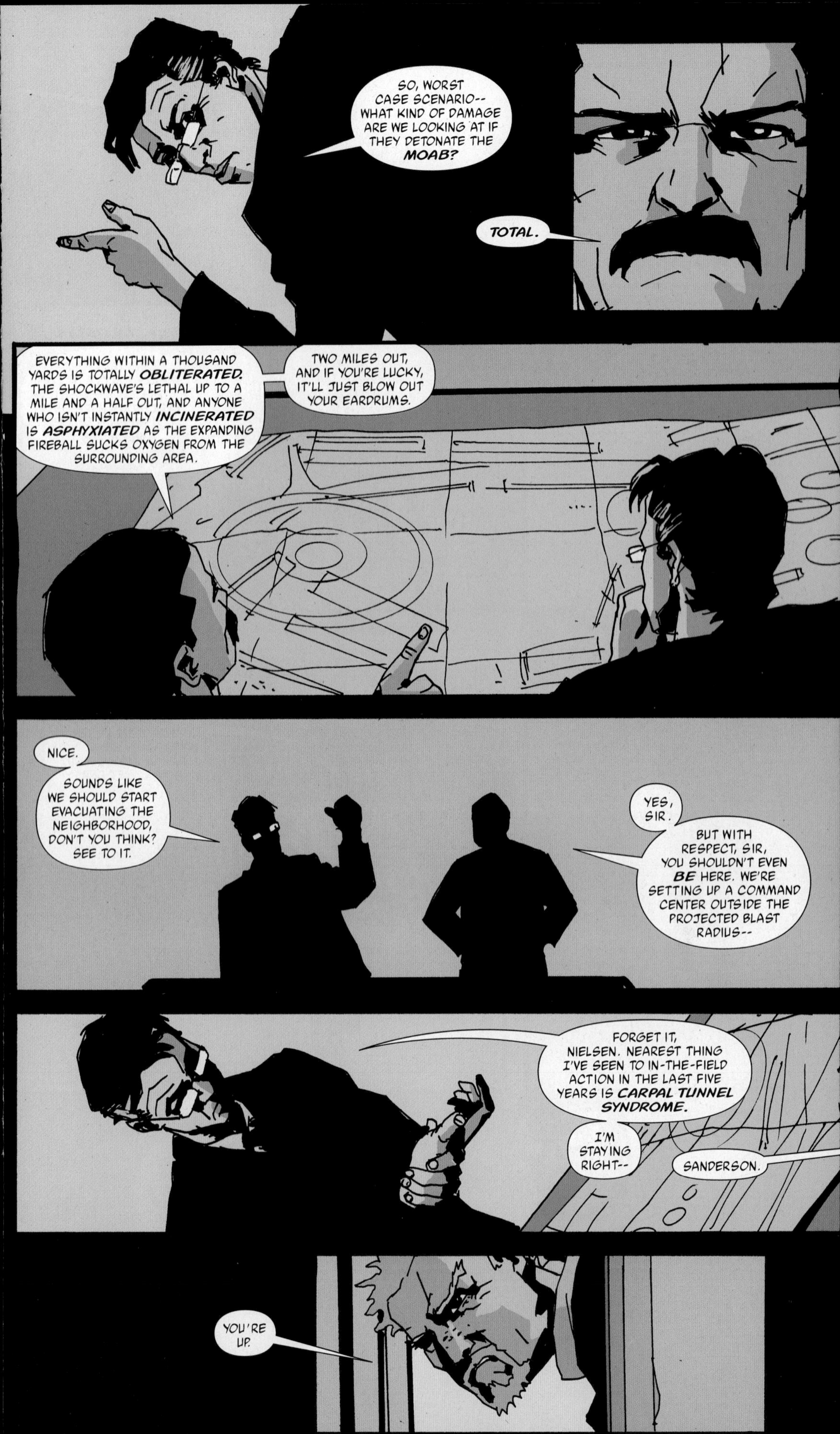
SO, WORST CASE SCENARIO-- WHAT KIND OF DAMAGE ARE WE LOOKING AT IF THEY DETONATE THE MOAB?
TOTAL.
EVERYTHING WITHIN A THOUSAND YARDS IS TOTALLY OBLITERATED. THE SHOCKWAVE'S LETHAL UP TO A MILE AND A HALF OUT, AND ANYONE WHO ISN'T INSTANTLY INCINERATED IS ASPHYXIATED AS THE EXPANDING FIREBALL SUCKS OXYGEN FROM THE SURROUNDING AREA.
TWO MILES OUT, AND IF YOU'RE LUCKY, IT'LL JUST BLOW OUT YOUR EARDRUMS.
NICE.
SOUNDS LIKE WE SHOULD START EVACUATING THE NEIGHBORHOOD, DON'T YOU THINK? SEE TO IT.
YES, SIR.
BUT WITH RESPECT, SIR, YOU SHOULDN'T EVEN BE HERE. WE'RE SETTING UP A COMMAND CENTER OUTSIDE THE PROJECTED BLAST RADIUS--
FORGET IT, NIELSEN. NEAREST THING I'VE SEEN TO IN-THE-FIELD ACTION IN THE LAST FIVE YEARS IS CARPAL TUNNEL SYNDROME.
I'M STAYING RIGHT--
SANDERSON.
YOU'RE UP.

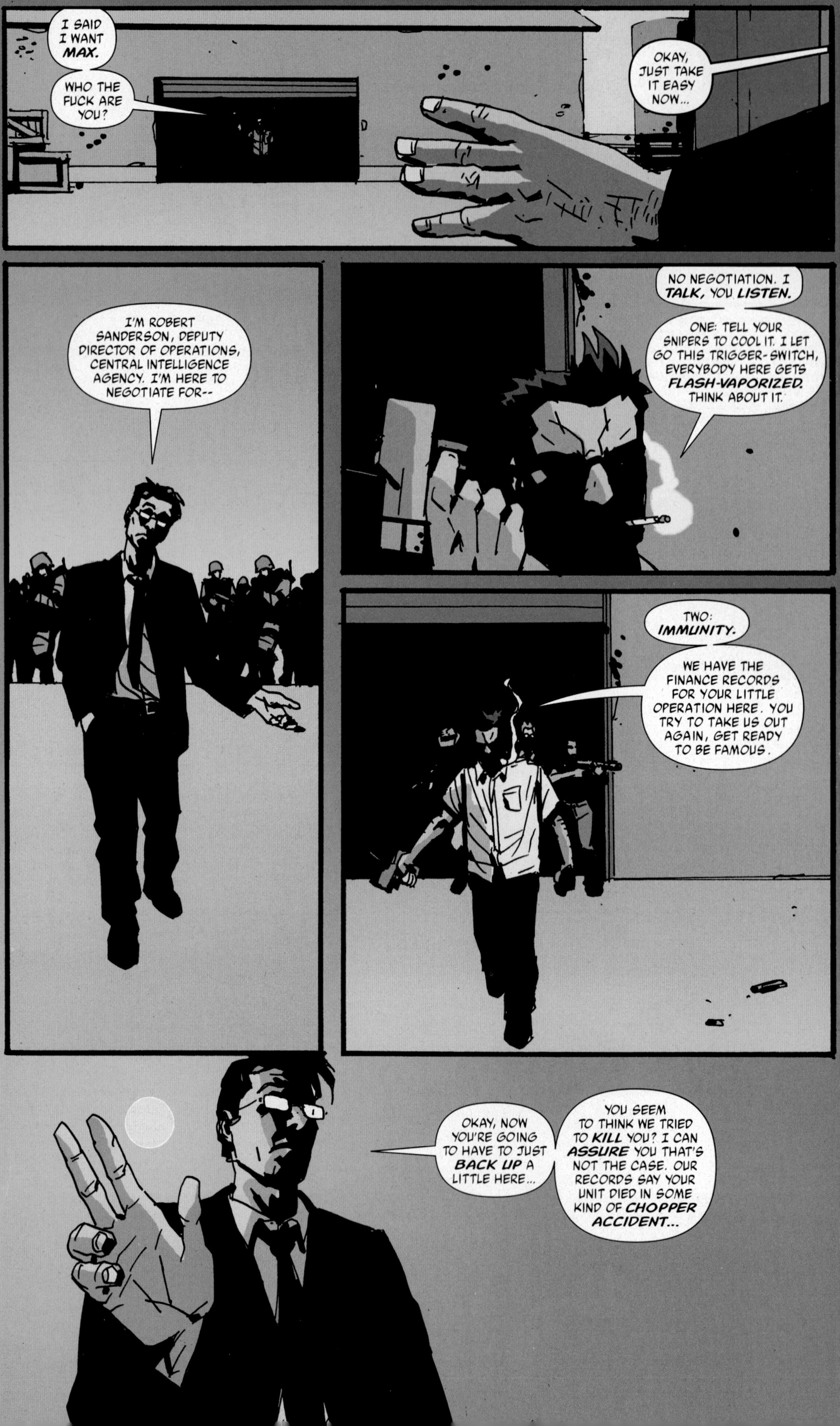
I SAID I WANT MAX.
WHO THE FUCK ARE YOU?
OKAY, JUST TAKE IT EASY NOW...
I'M ROBERT SANDERSON, DEPUTY DIRECTOR OF OPERATIONS, CENTRAL INTELLIGENCE AGENCY. I'M HERE TO NEGOTIATE FOR--
NO NEGOTIATION. I TALK, YOU LISTEN.
ONE: TELL YOUR SNIPERS TO COOL IT. I LET GO THIS TRIGGER-SWITCH, EVERYBODY HERE GETS FLASH-VAPORIZED. THINK ABOUT IT.
TWO: IMMUNITY.
WE HAVE THE FINANCE RECORDS FOR YOUR LITTLE OPERATION HERE. YOU TRY TO TAKE US OUT AGAIN, GET READY TO BE FAMOUS.
OKAY, NOW YOU'RE GOING TO HAVE TO JUST BACK UP A LITTLE HERE...
YOU SEEM TO THINK WE TRIED TO KILL YOU? I CAN ASSURE YOU THAT'S NOT THE CASE. OUR RECORDS SAY YOUR UNIT DIED IN SOME KIND OF CHOPPER ACCIDENT...

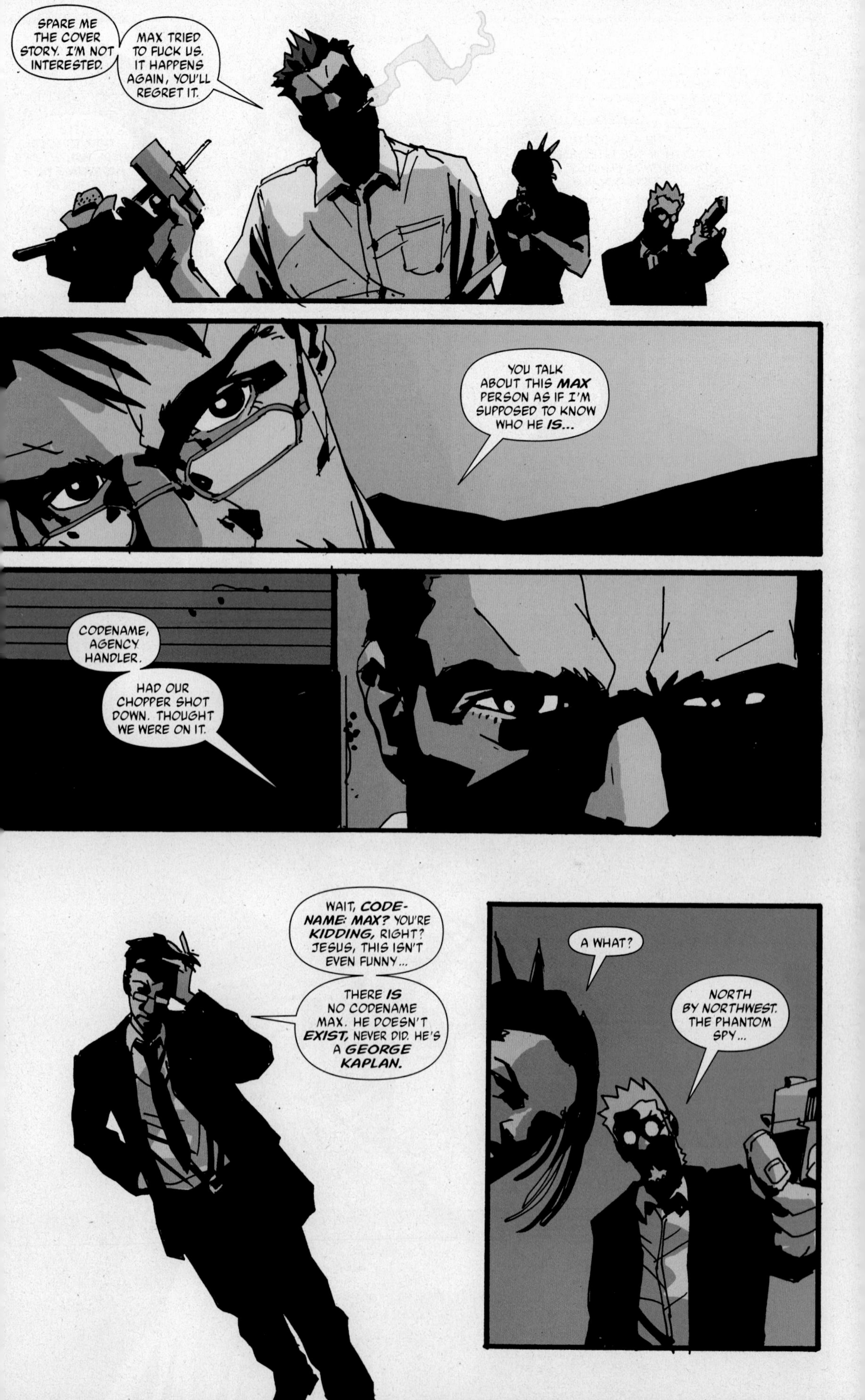
SPARE ME THE COVER STORY. I'M NOT INTERESTED.
MAX TRIED TO FUCK US. IT HAPPENS AGAIN, YOU'LL REGRET IT.
YOU TALK ABOUT THIS MAX PERSON AS IF I'M SUPPOSED TO KNOW WHO HE IS...
CODENAME, AGENCY HANDLER.
HAD OUR CHOPPER SHOT DOWN. THOUGHT WE WERE ON IT.
WAIT, CODE-NAME: MAX? YOU'RE KIDDING, RIGHT? JESUS, THIS ISN'T EVEN FUNNY...
THERE IS NO CODENAME MAX. HE DOESN'T EXIST, NEVER DID. HE'S A GEORGE KAPLAN.
A WHAT?
NORTH BY NORTHWEST. THE PHANTOM SPY...

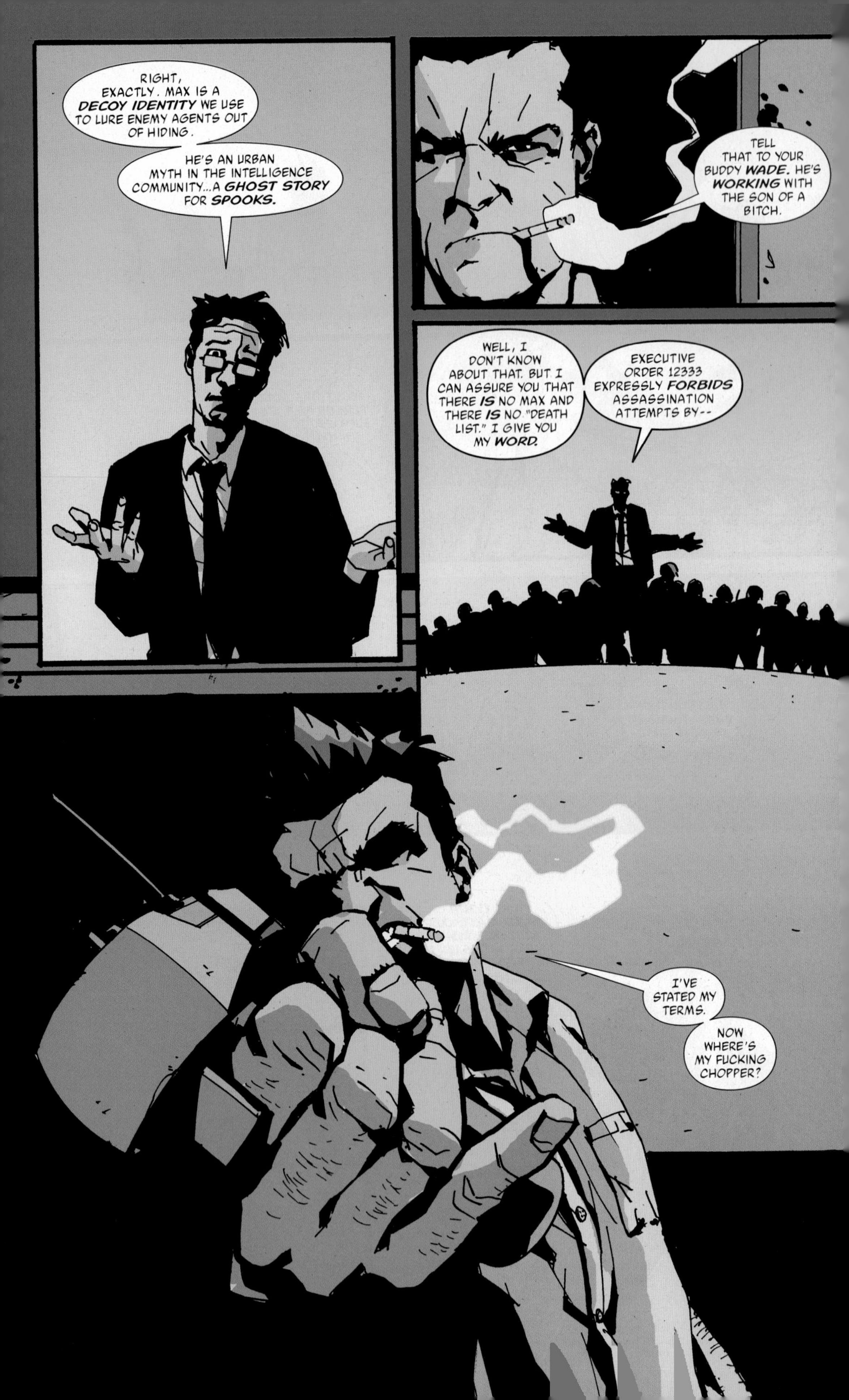
RIGHT, EXACTLY. MAX IS A DECOY IDENTITY WE USE TO LURE ENEMY AGENTS OUT OF HIDING.
HE'S AN URBAN MYTH IN THE INTELLIGENCE COMMUNITY...A GHOST STORY FOR SPOOKS.
TELL THAT TO YOUR BUDDY WADE. HE'S WORKING WITH THE SON OF A BITCH.
WELL, I DON'T KNOW ABOUT THAT. BUT I CAN ASSURE YOU THAT THERE IS NO MAX AND THERE IS NO "DEATH LIST." I GIVE YOU MY WORD.
EXECUTIVE ORDER 12333 EXPRESSLY FORBIDS ASSASSINATION ATTEMPTS BY--
I'VE STATED MY TERMS.
NOW WHERE'S MY FUCKING CHOPPER?

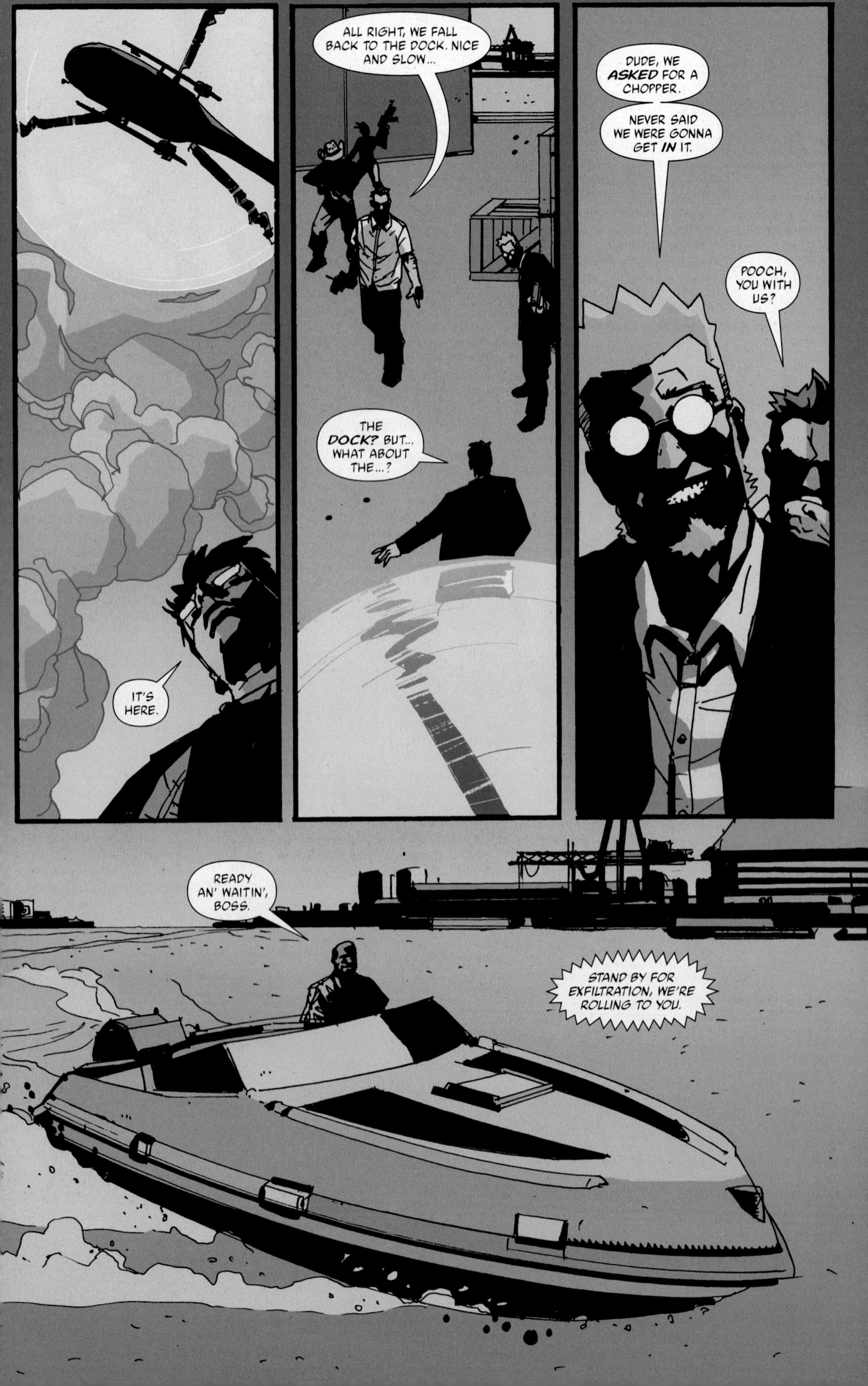
IT'S HERE.
ALL RIGHT, WE FALL BACK TO THE DOCK. NICE AND SLOW...
THE DOCK? BUT... WHAT ABOUT THE...?
DUDE, WE ASKED FOR A CHOPPER.
NEVER SAID WE WERE GONNA GET IN IT.
POOCH, YOU WITH US?
READY AN' WAITIN', BOSS.
STAND BY FOR EXFILTRATION, WE'RE ROLLING TO YOU.

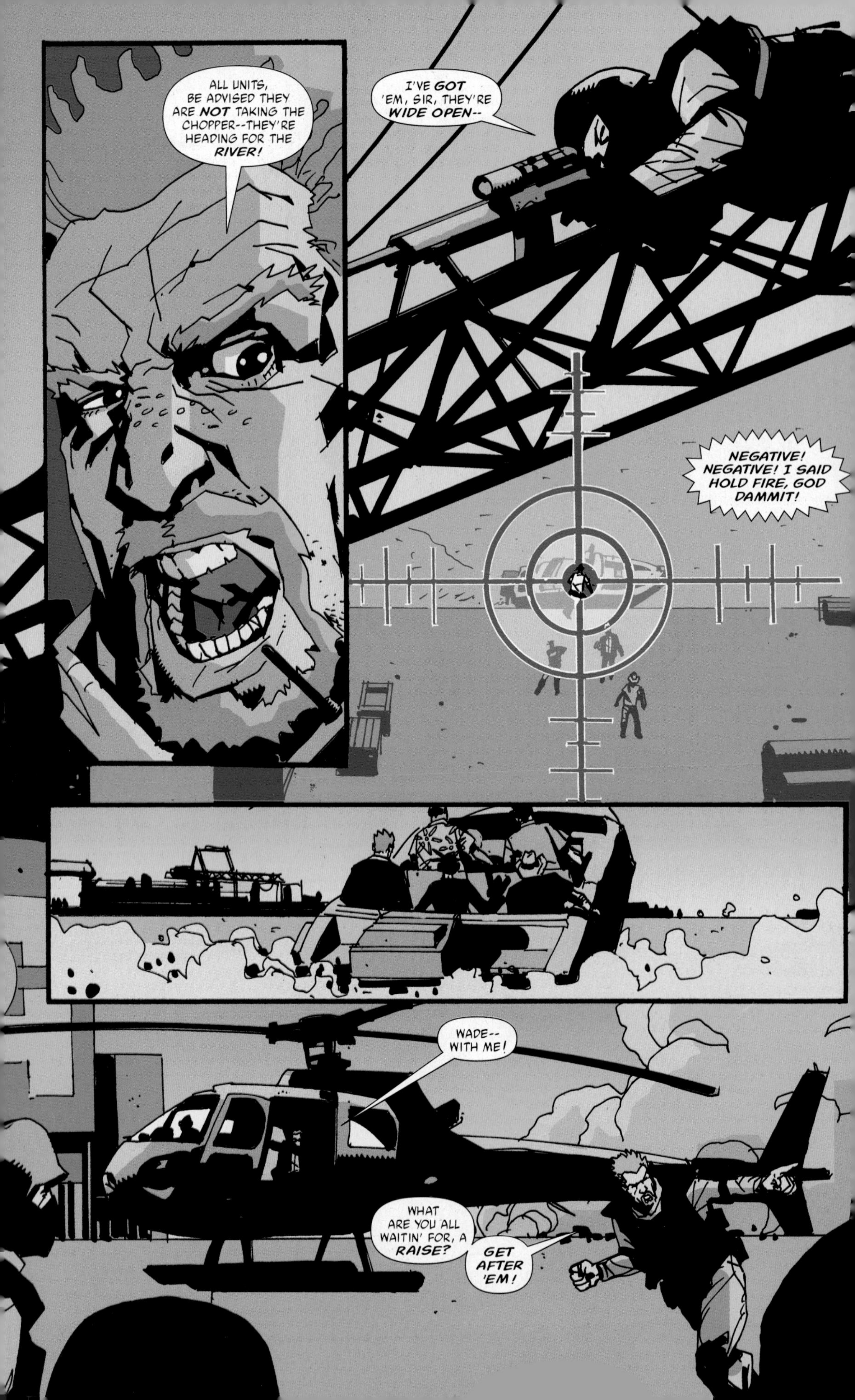
ALL UNITS, BE ADVISED THEY ARE **NOT** TAKING THE CHOPPER--THEY'RE HEADING FOR THE ***RIVER!***
I'VE **GOT** 'EM, SIR, THEY'RE ***WIDE OPEN--***
NEGATIVE! NEGATIVE! I SAID HOLD FIRE, GOD DAMMIT!
WADE-- WITH ME!
WHAT ARE YOU ALL WAITIN' FOR, A ***RAISE?***
GET AFTER 'EM!

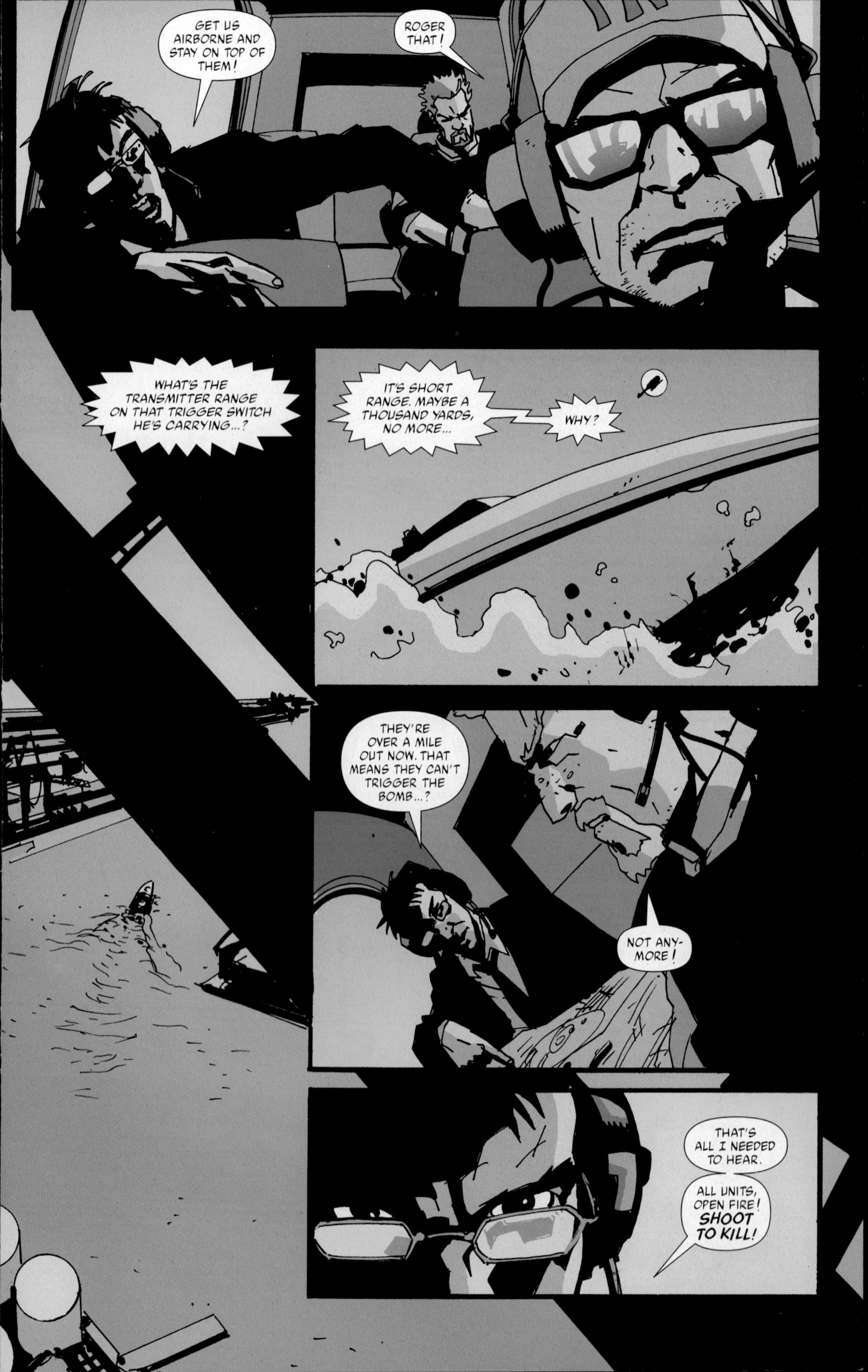
GET US AIRBORNE AND STAY ON TOP OF THEM!
ROGER THAT!
WHAT'S THE TRANSMITTER RANGE ON THAT TRIGGER SWITCH HE'S CARRYING...?
IT'S SHORT RANGE. MAYBE A THOUSAND YARDS, NO MORE...
WHY?
THEY'RE OVER A MILE OUT NOW. THAT MEANS THEY CAN'T TRIGGER THE BOMB...?
NOT ANY-MORE!
THAT'S ALL I NEEDED TO HEAR.
ALL UNITS, OPEN FIRE! SHOOT TO KILL!

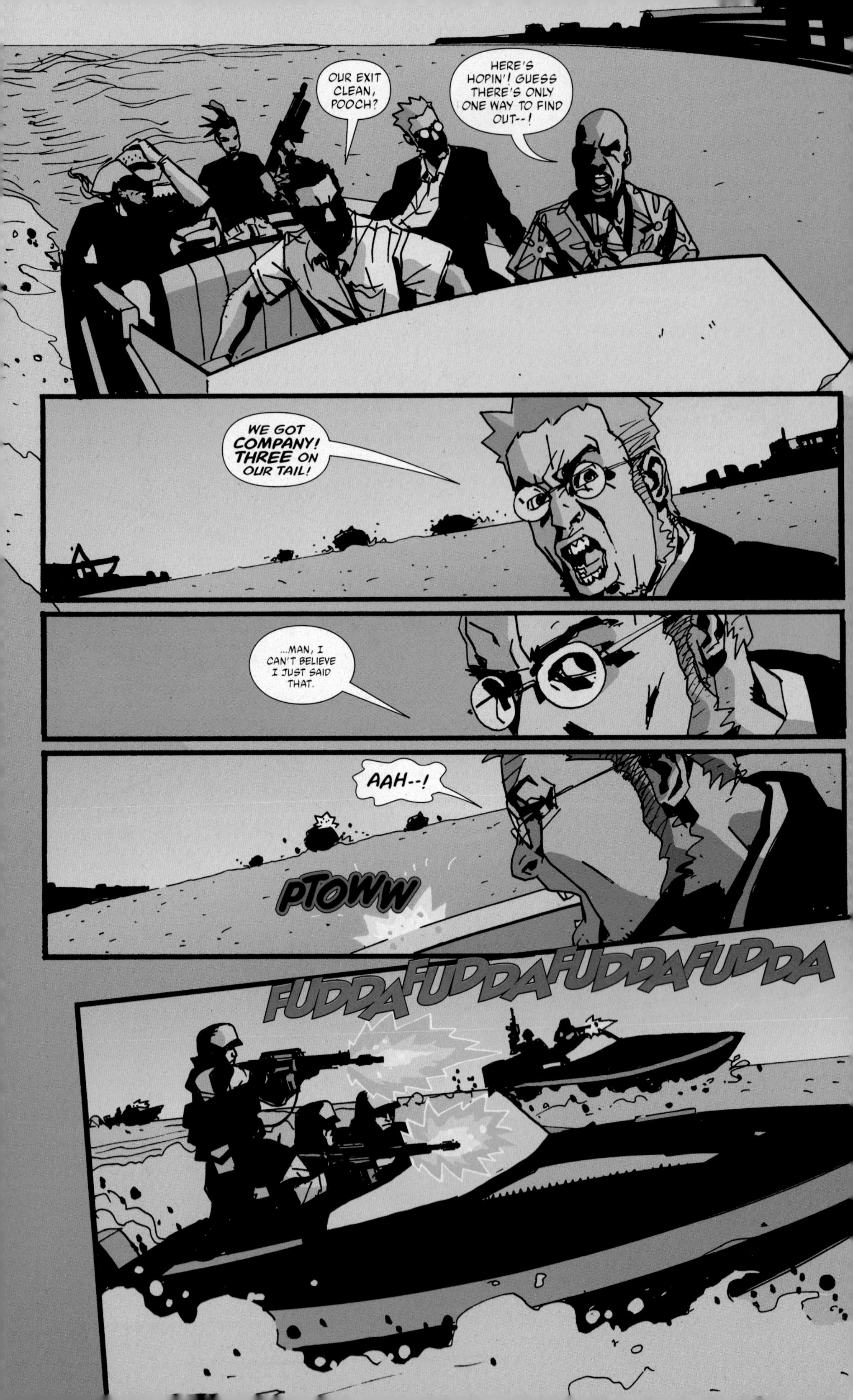
OUR EXIT CLEAN, POOCH?
HERE'S HOPIN'! GUESS THERE'S ONLY ONE WAY TO FIND OUT--!
WE GOT COMPANY! THREE ON OUR TAIL!
...MAN, I CAN'T BELIEVE I JUST SAID THAT.
AAH--!
PTOWW
FUDDAFUDDAFUDDAFUDDA

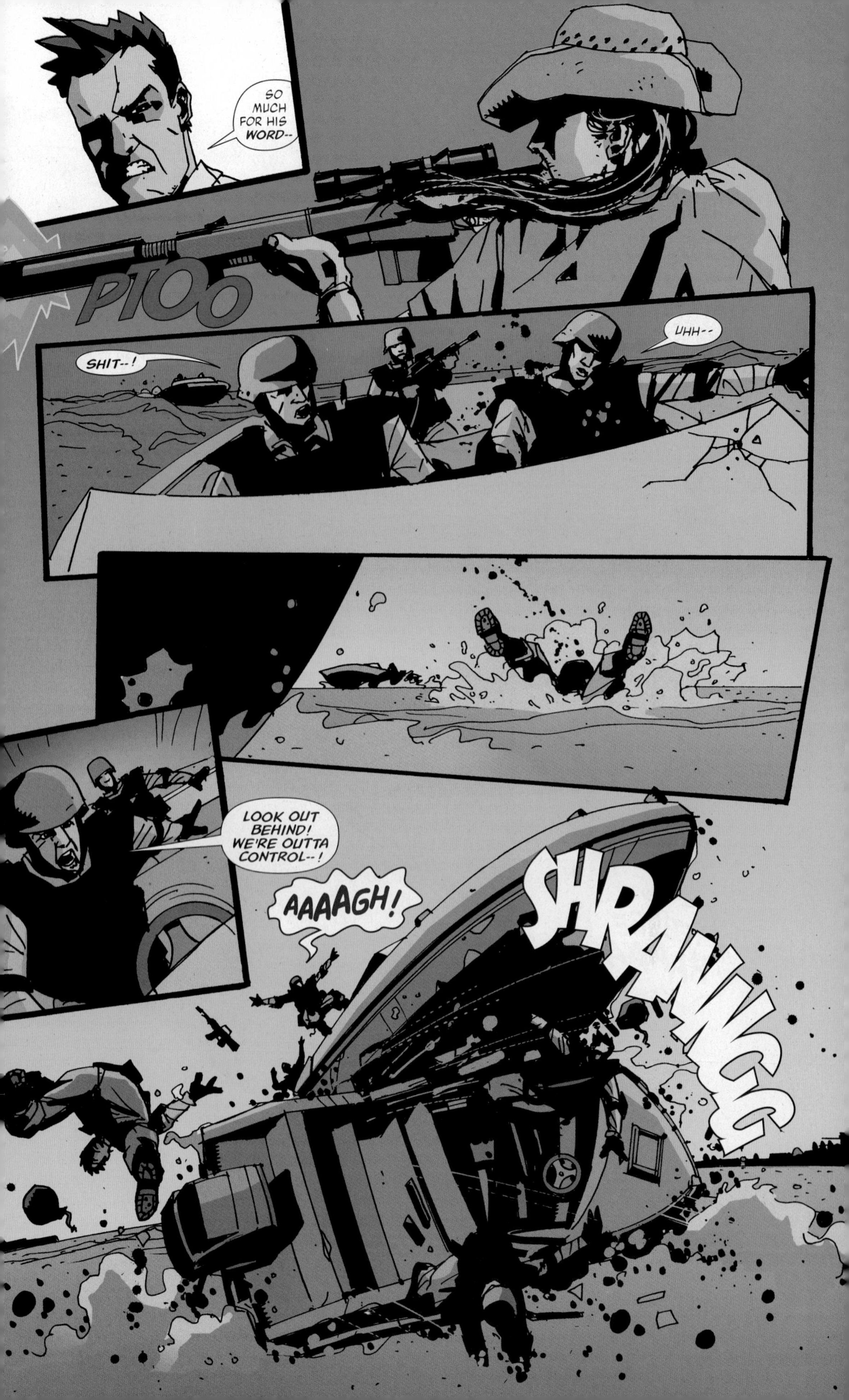
SO MUCH FOR HIS WORD--
PTOO
SHIT--!
UHH--
LOOK OUT BEHIND! WE'RE OUTTA CONTROL--!
AAAAGH!
SHRANNGG

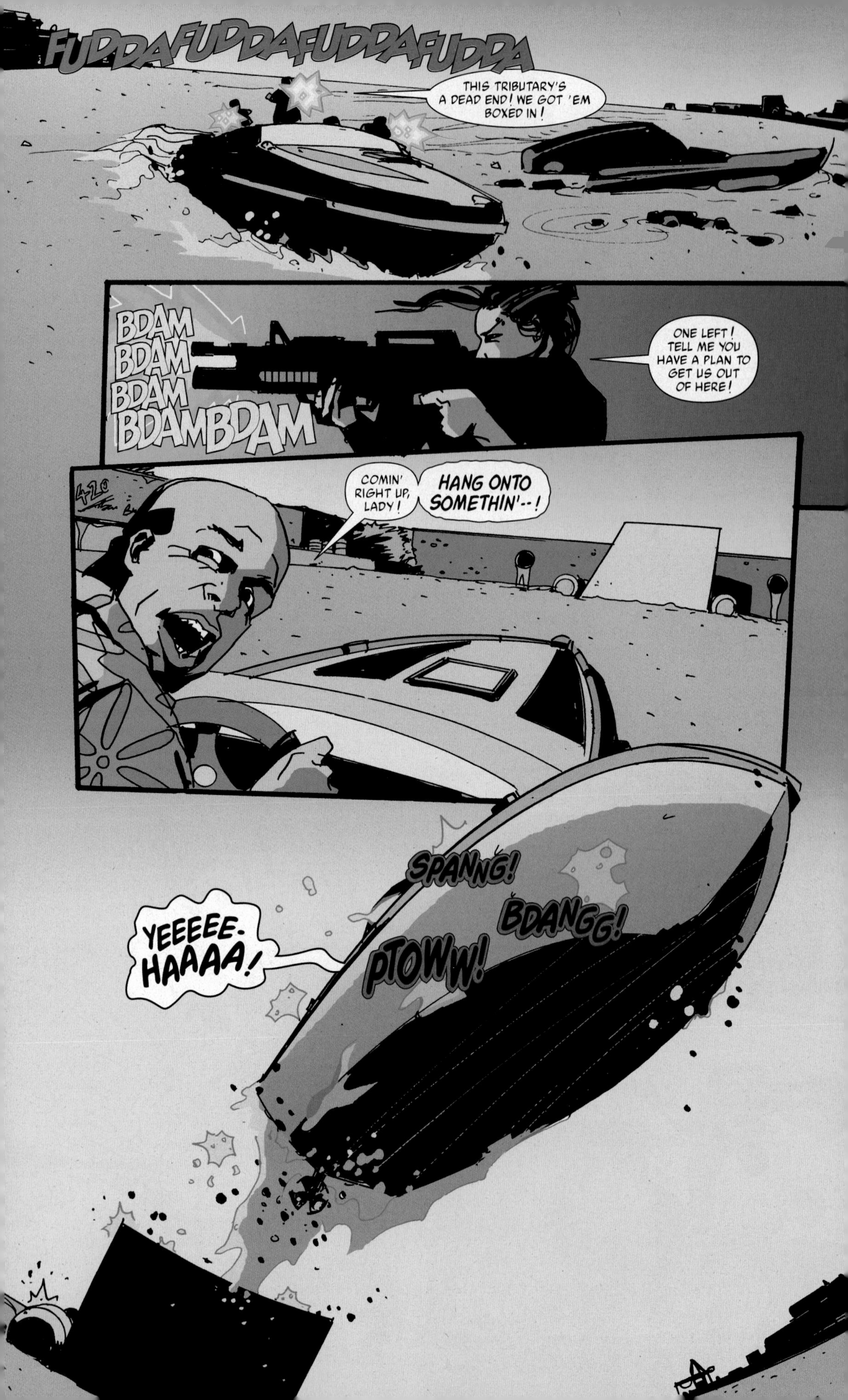
FUDDAFUDDAFUDDAFUDDA
THIS TRIBUTARY'S A DEAD END! WE GOT 'EM BOXED IN!
BDAM BDAM BDAM BDAMBDAM
ONE LEFT! TELL ME YOU HAVE A PLAN TO GET US OUT OF HERE!
COMIN' RIGHT UP, LADY!
HANG ONTO SOMETHIN'--!
SPANNG!
BDANGG!
PTOWW!
YEEEEE-HAAAA!

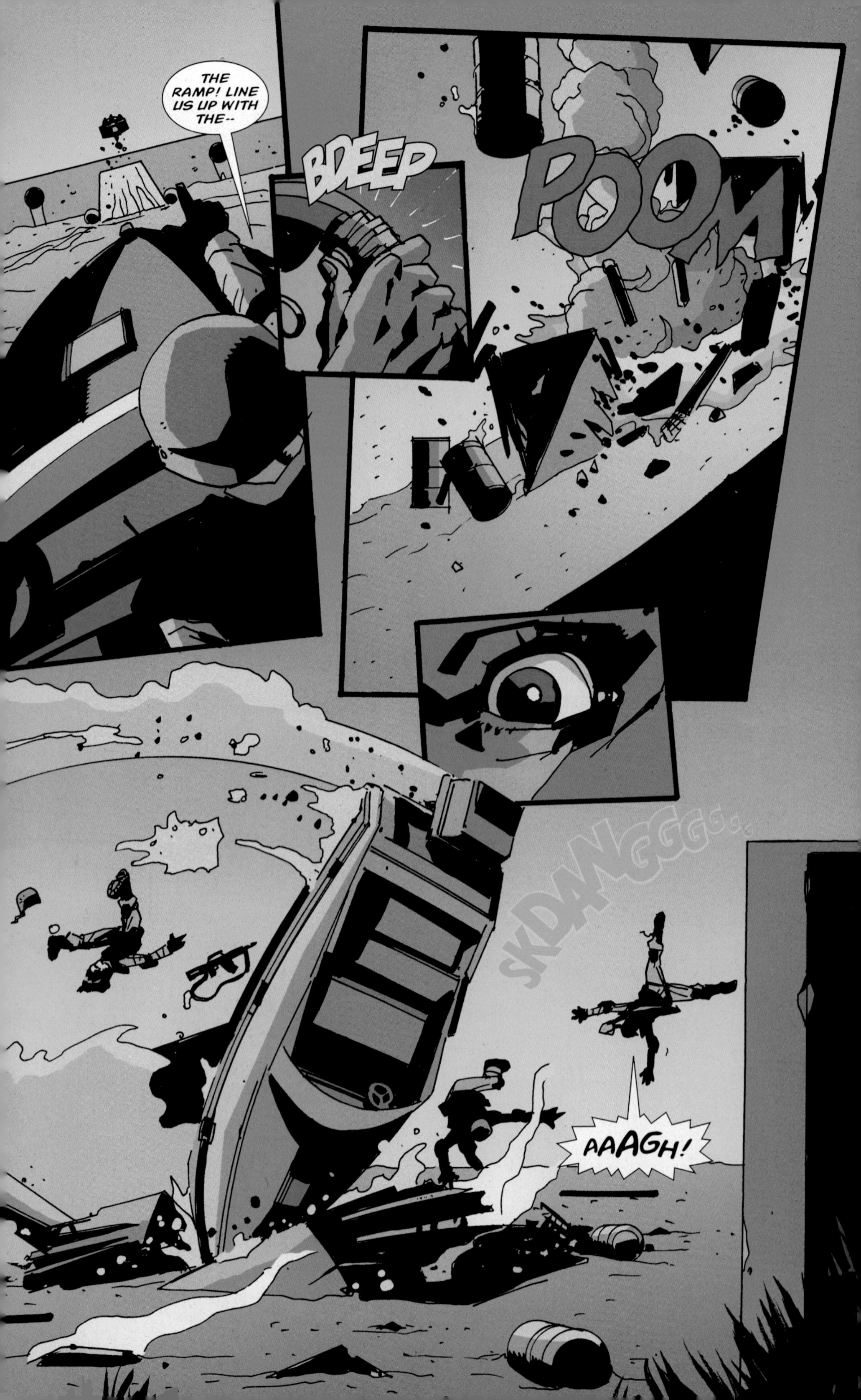
THE RAMP! LINE US UP WITH THE--
BDEEP
POOM
SKDANGGGG
AAAGH!

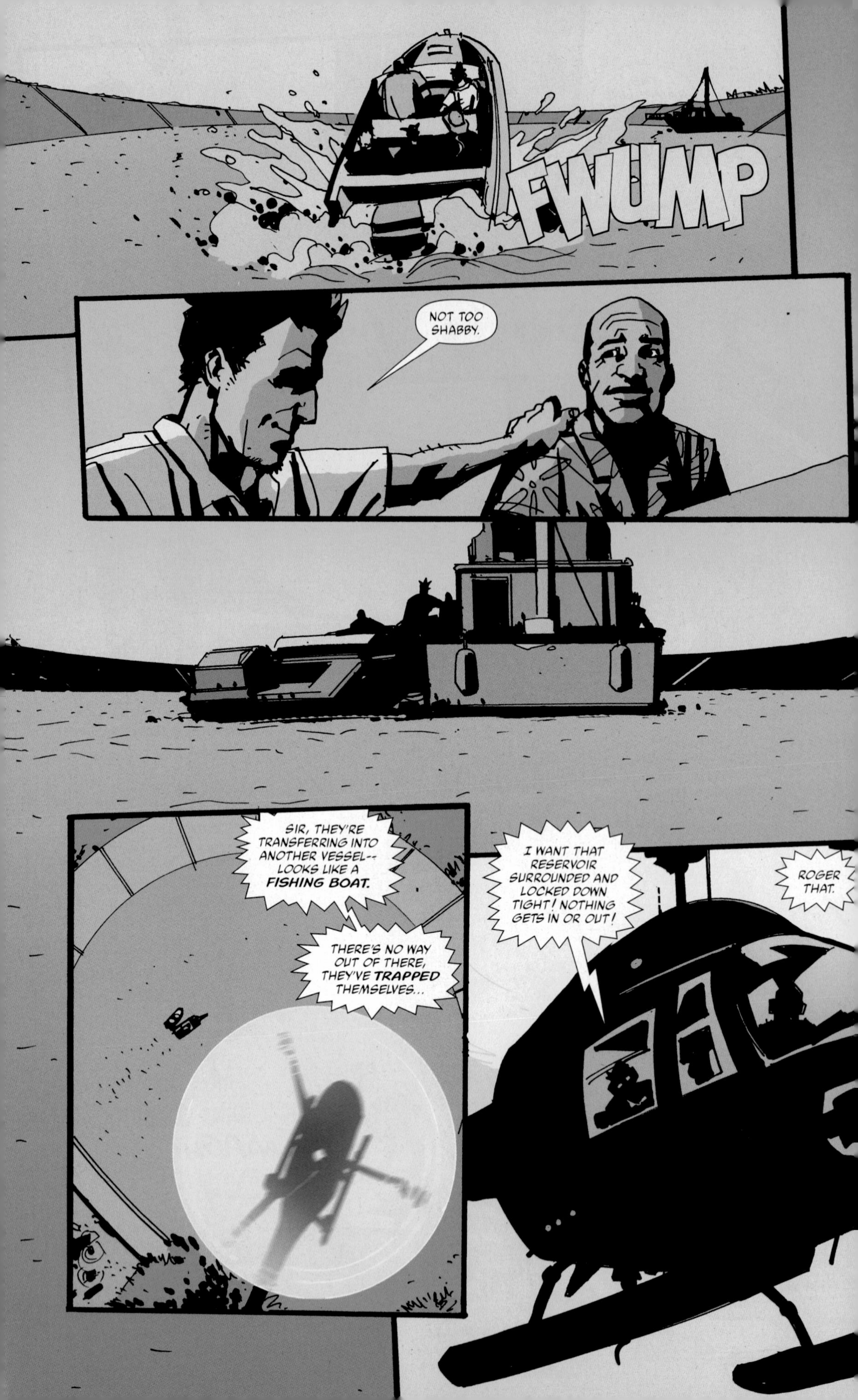
FWUMP
NOT TOO SHABBY.
SIR, THEY'RE TRANSFERRING INTO ANOTHER VESSEL-- LOOKS LIKE A FISHING BOAT.
THERE'S NO WAY OUT OF THERE, THEY'VE TRAPPED THEMSELVES...
I WANT THAT RESERVOIR SURROUNDED AND LOCKED DOWN TIGHT! NOTHING GETS IN OR OUT!
ROGER THAT.

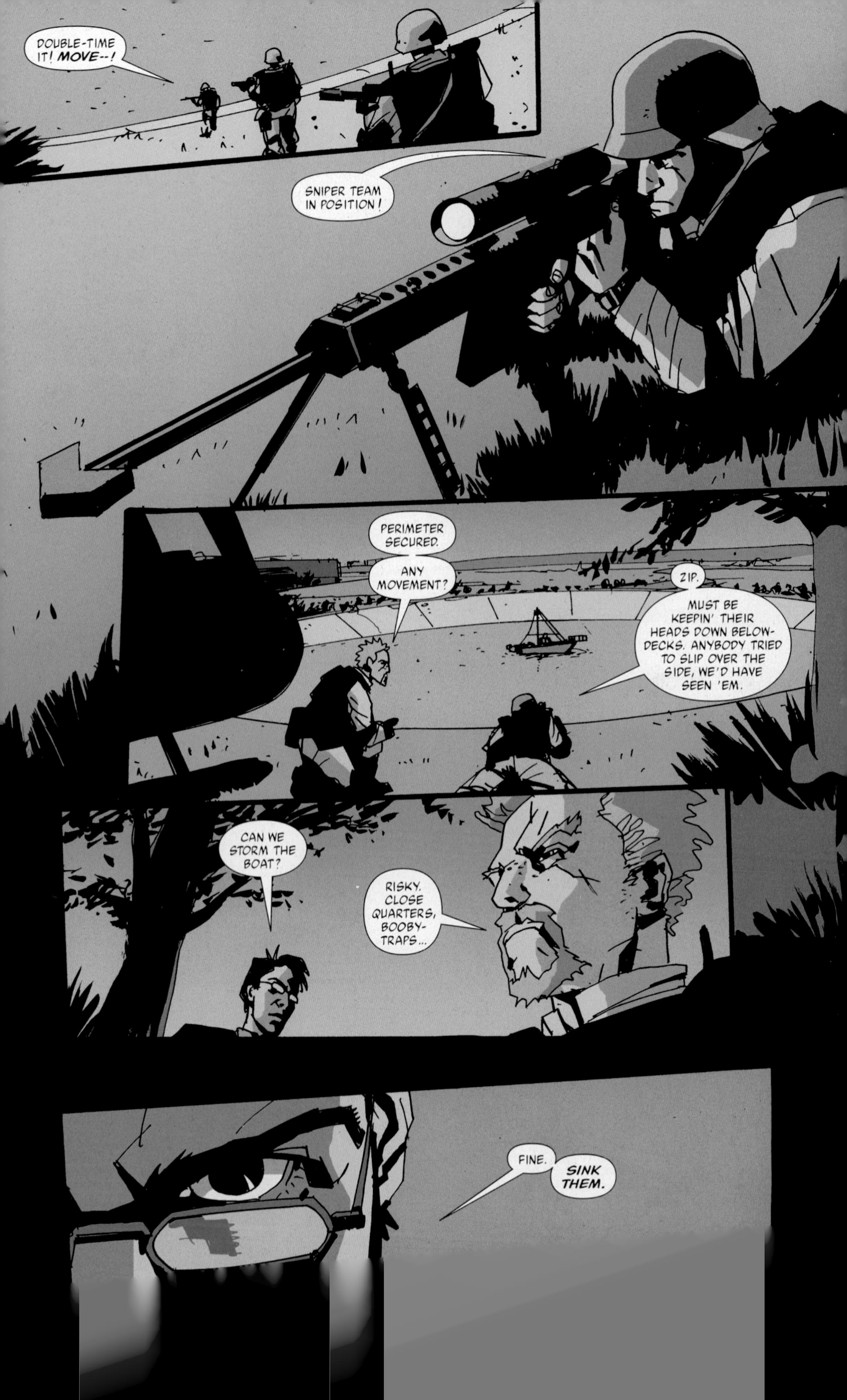
DOUBLE-TIME IT! MOVE--!
SNIPER TEAM IN POSITION!
PERIMETER SECURED.
ANY MOVEMENT?
ZIP.
MUST BE KEEPIN' THEIR HEADS DOWN BELOW-DECKS. ANYBODY TRIED TO SLIP OVER THE SIDE, WE'D HAVE SEEN 'EM.
CAN WE STORM THE BOAT?
RISKY. CLOSE QUARTERS, BOOBY-TRAPS...
FINE.
SINK THEM.

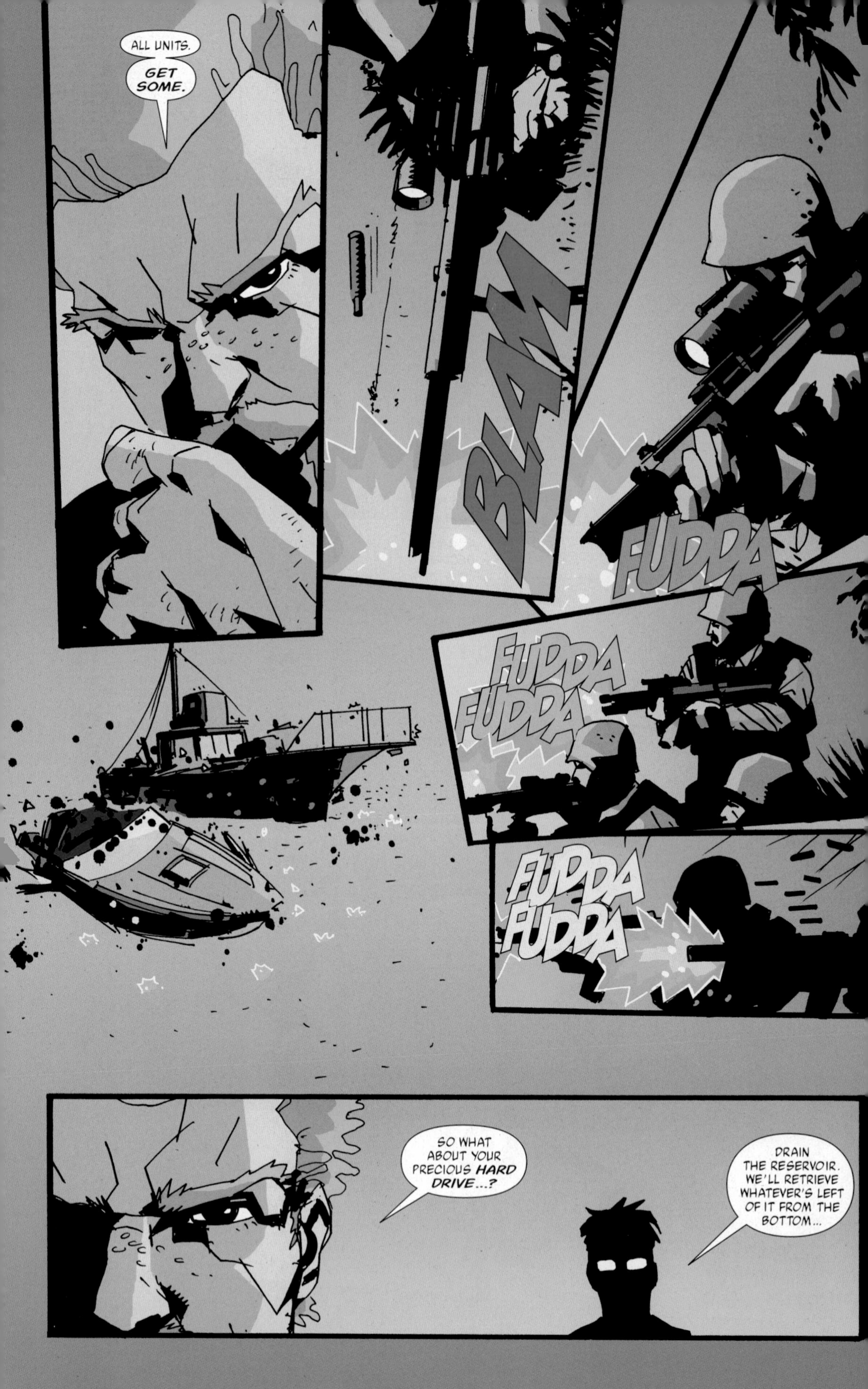
ALL UNITS.
GET SOME.
BLAM
FUDDA
FUDDA FUDDA
FUDDA FUDDA
SO WHAT ABOUT YOUR PRECIOUS HARD DRIVE...?
DRAIN THE RESERVOIR. WE'LL RETRIEVE WHATEVER'S LEFT OF IT FROM THE BOTTOM...

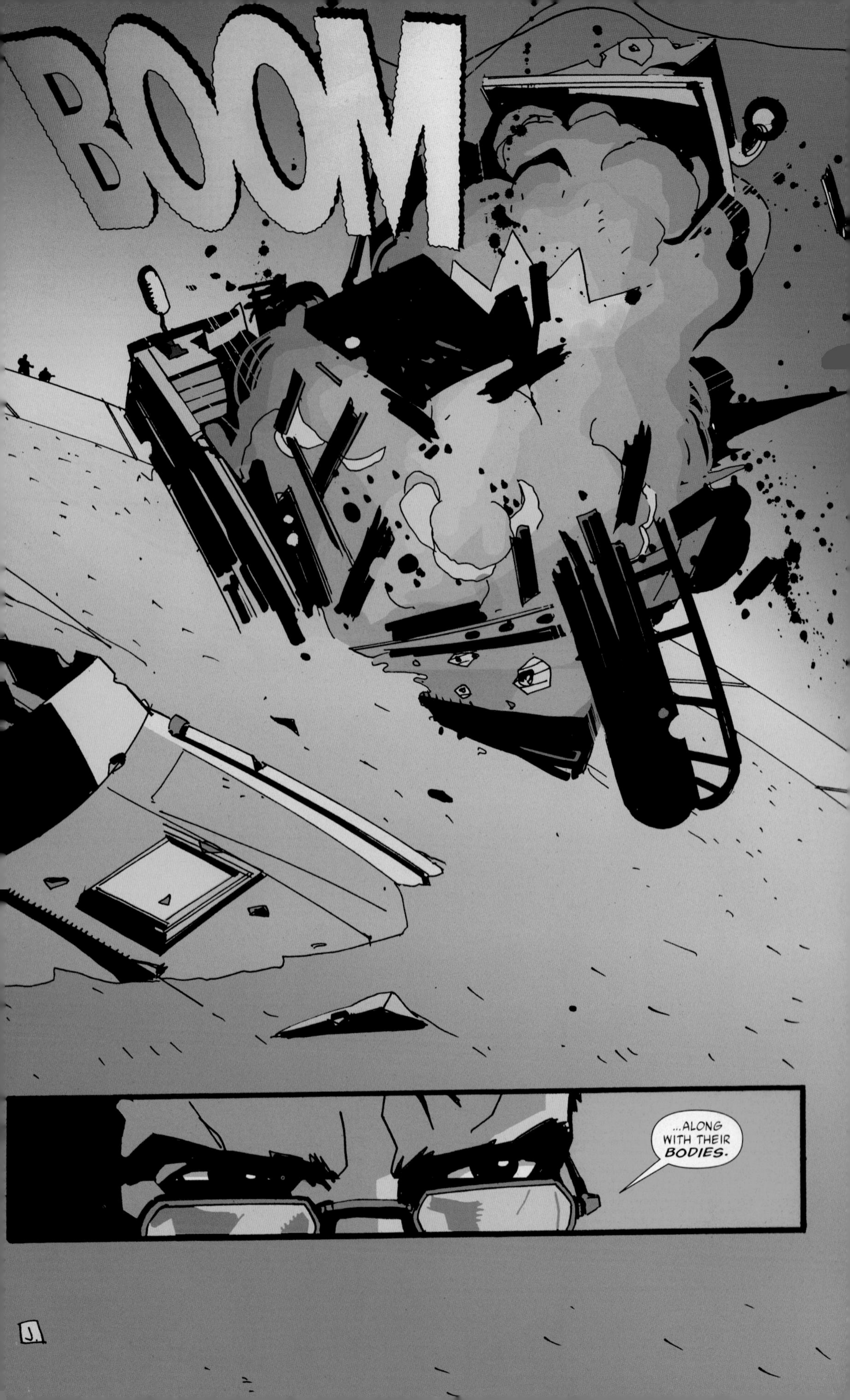
BOOM
...ALONG WITH THEIR BODIES.
J.

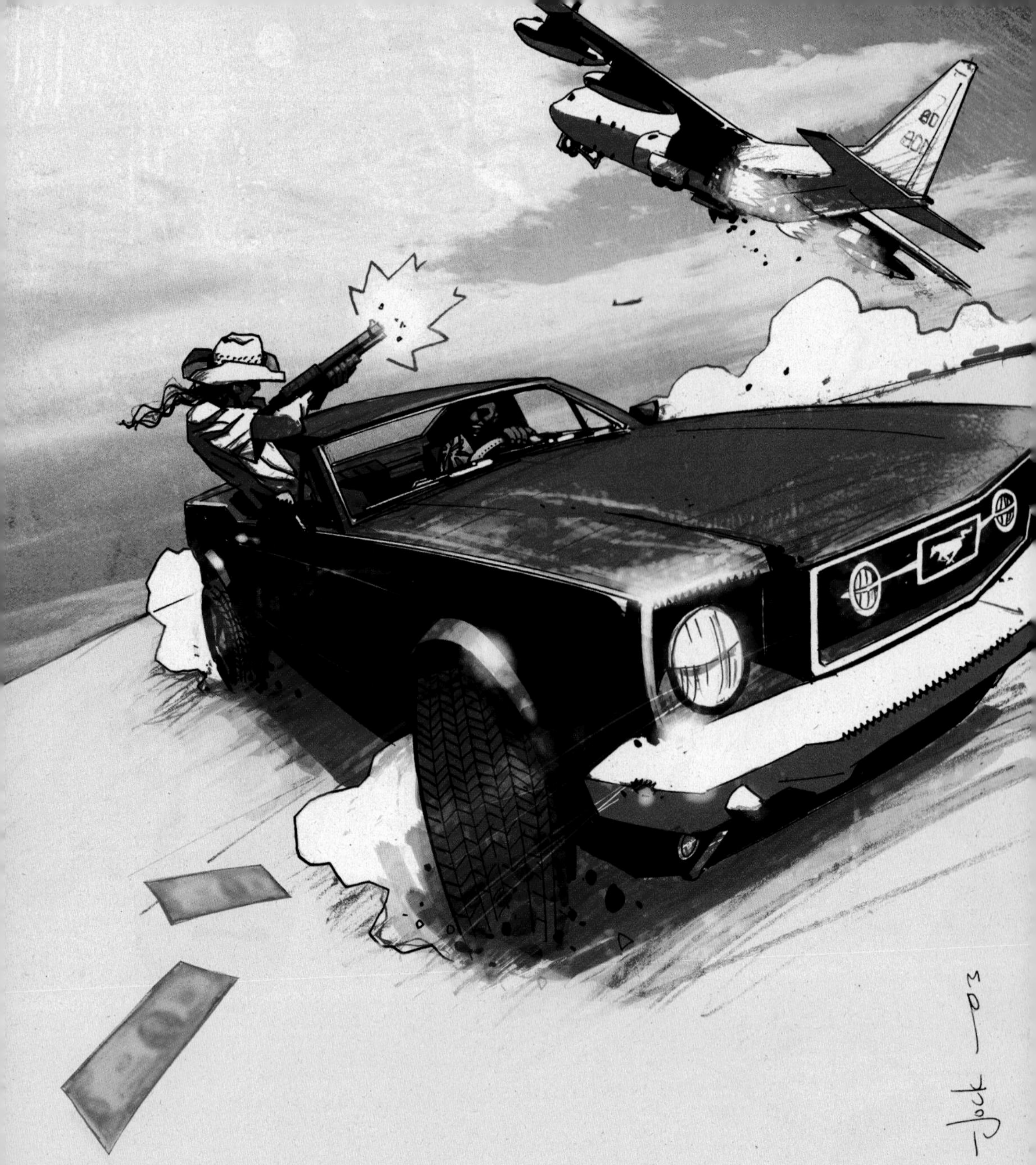

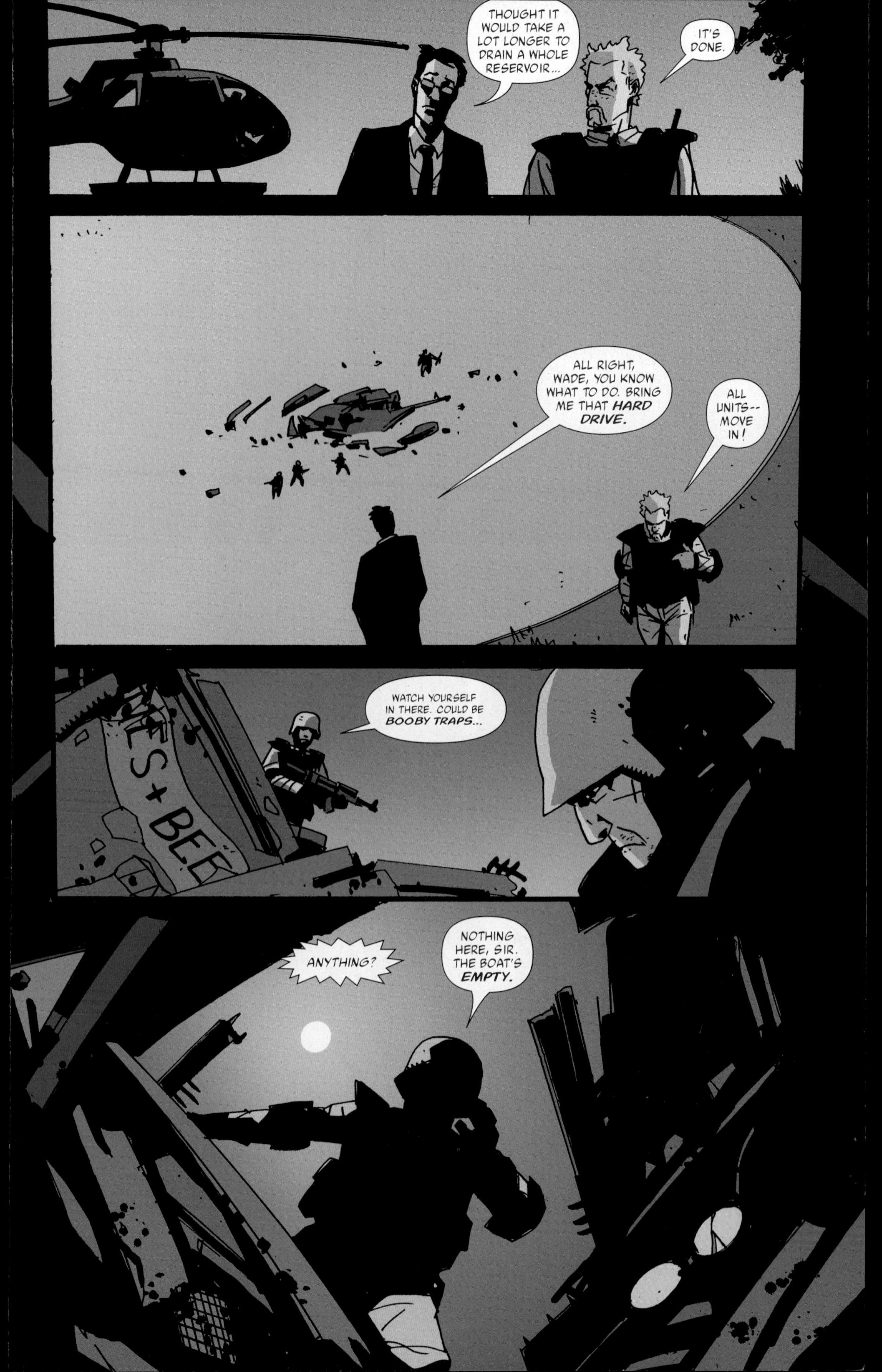
THOUGHT IT WOULD TAKE A LOT LONGER TO DRAIN A WHOLE RESERVOIR...
IT'S DONE.
ALL RIGHT, WADE, YOU KNOW WHAT TO DO. BRING ME THAT HARD DRIVE.
ALL UNITS-- MOVE IN!
WATCH YOURSELF IN THERE. COULD BE BOOBY TRAPS...
ANYTHING?
NOTHING HERE, SIR. THE BOAT'S EMPTY.

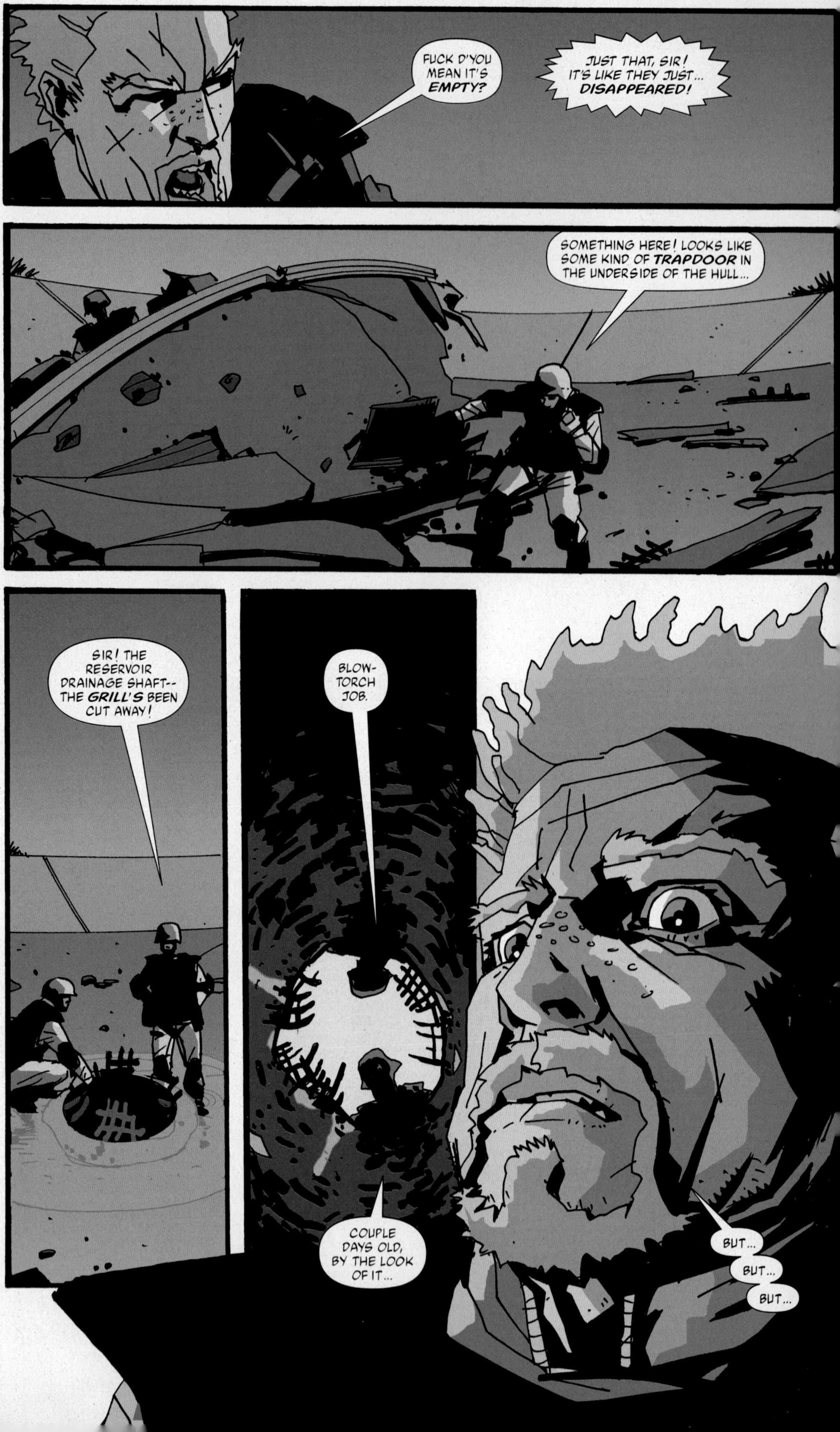
FUCK D'YOU MEAN IT'S EMPTY?
JUST THAT, SIR! IT'S LIKE THEY JUST... DISAPPEARED!
SOMETHING HERE! LOOKS LIKE SOME KIND OF TRAPDOOR IN THE UNDERSIDE OF THE HULL...
SIR! THE RESERVOIR DRAINAGE SHAFT-- THE GRILL'S BEEN CUT AWAY!
BLOW-TORCH JOB.
COUPLE DAYS OLD, BY THE LOOK OF IT...
BUT...
BUT...
BUT...

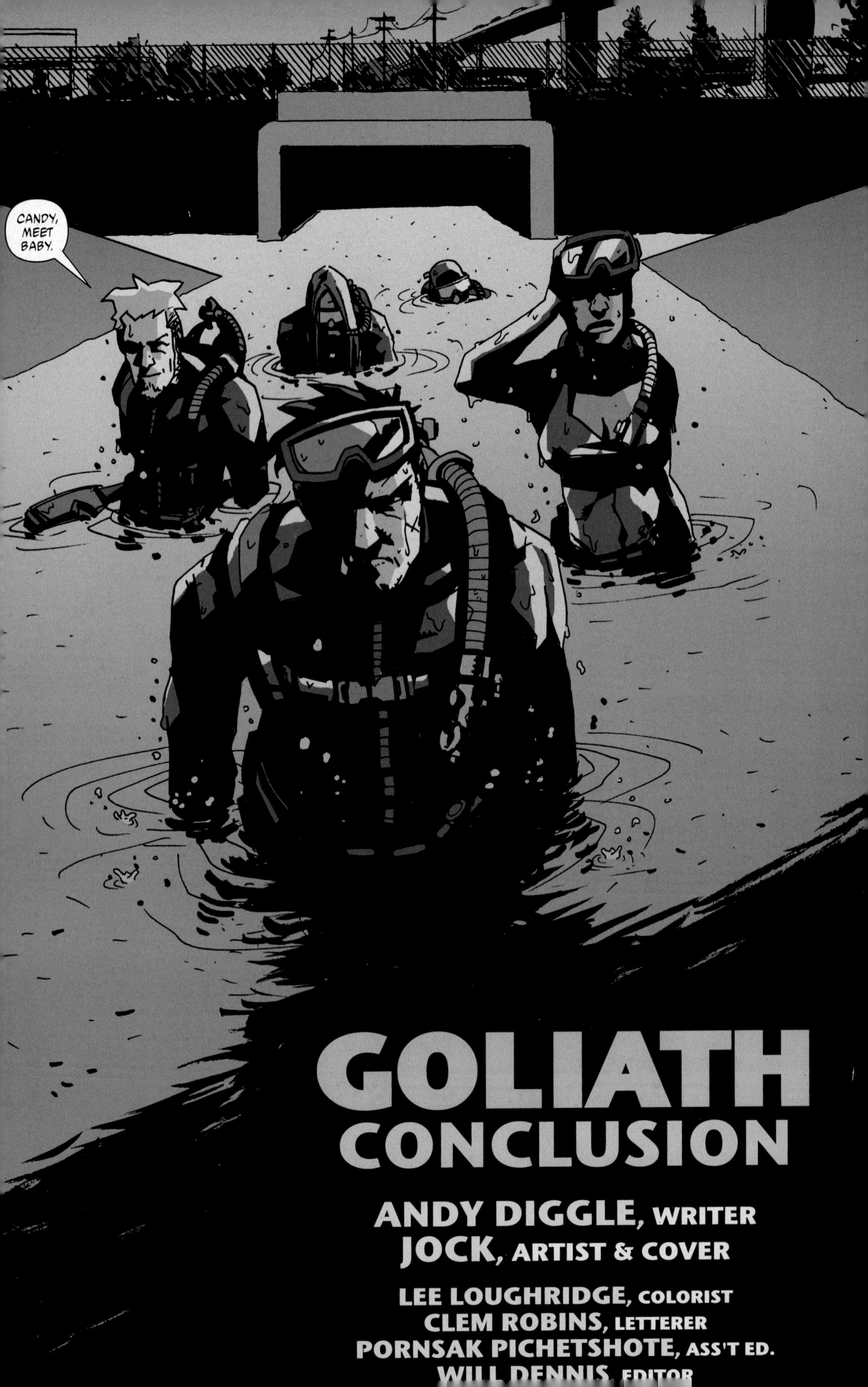
CANDY, MEET BABY.

GOLIATH
CONCLUSION

ANDY DIGGLE, WRITER
JOCK, ARTIST & COVER

LEE LOUGHRIDGE, COLORIST
CLEM ROBINS, LETTERER
PORNSAK PICHETSHOTE, ASS'T ED.
WILL DENNIS, EDITOR

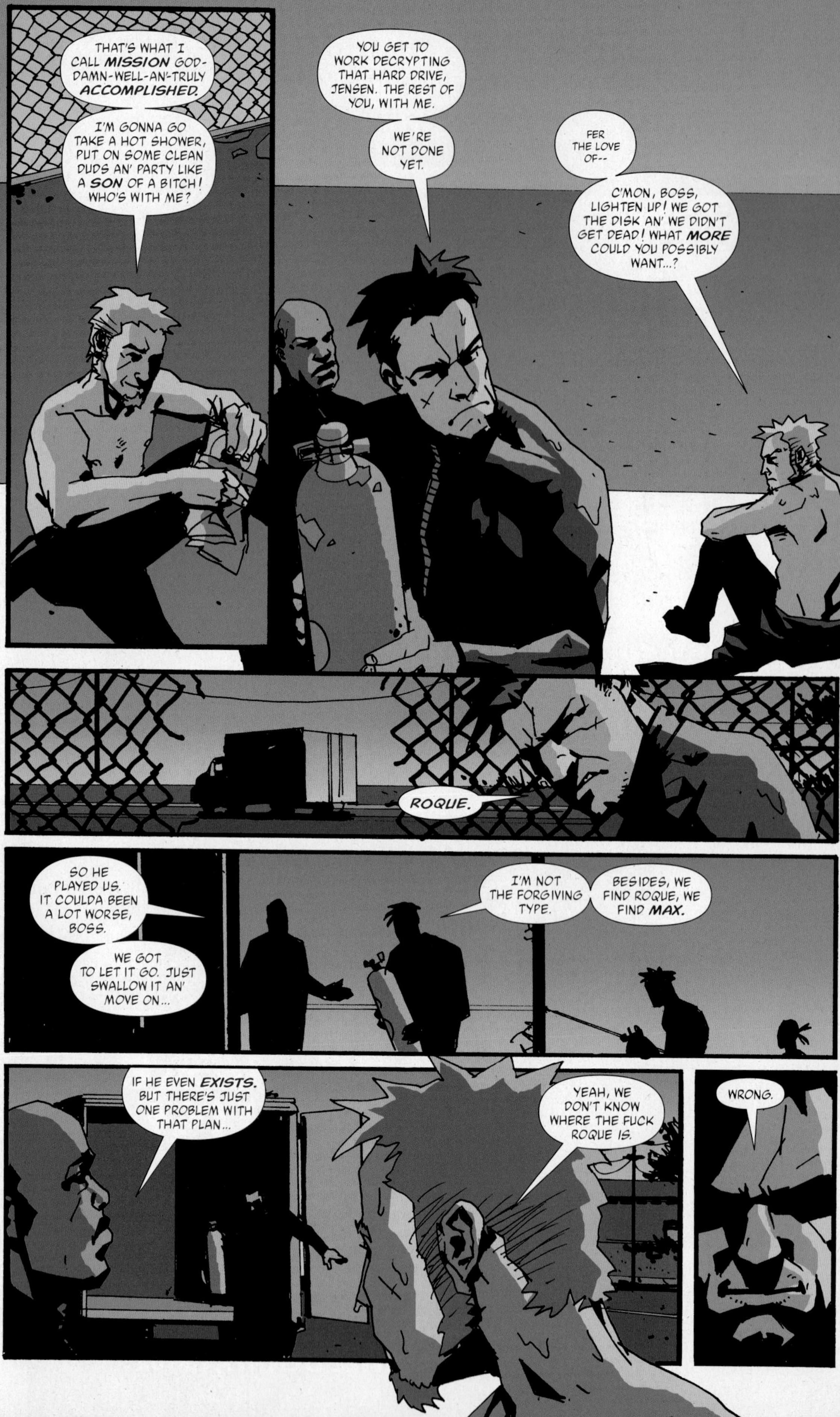

THAT'S WHAT I CALL **MISSION** GOD-DAMN-WELL-AN'-TRULY **ACCOMPLISHED.**
I'M GONNA GO TAKE A HOT SHOWER, PUT ON SOME CLEAN DUDS AN' PARTY LIKE A **SON** OF A BITCH! WHO'S WITH ME?
YOU GET TO WORK DECRYPTING THAT HARD DRIVE, JENSEN. THE REST OF YOU, WITH ME.
WE'RE NOT DONE YET.
FER THE LOVE OF--
C'MON, BOSS, LIGHTEN UP! WE GOT THE DISK AN' WE DIDN'T GET DEAD! WHAT **MORE** COULD YOU POSSIBLY WANT...?
ROQUE.
SO HE PLAYED US. IT COULDA BEEN A LOT WORSE, BOSS.
WE GOT TO LET IT GO. JUST SWALLOW IT AN' MOVE ON...
I'M NOT THE FORGIVING TYPE.
BESIDES, WE FIND ROQUE, WE FIND **MAX.**
IF HE EVEN **EXISTS.** BUT THERE'S JUST ONE PROBLEM WITH THAT PLAN...
YEAH, WE DON'T KNOW WHERE THE FUCK ROQUE IS.
WRONG.

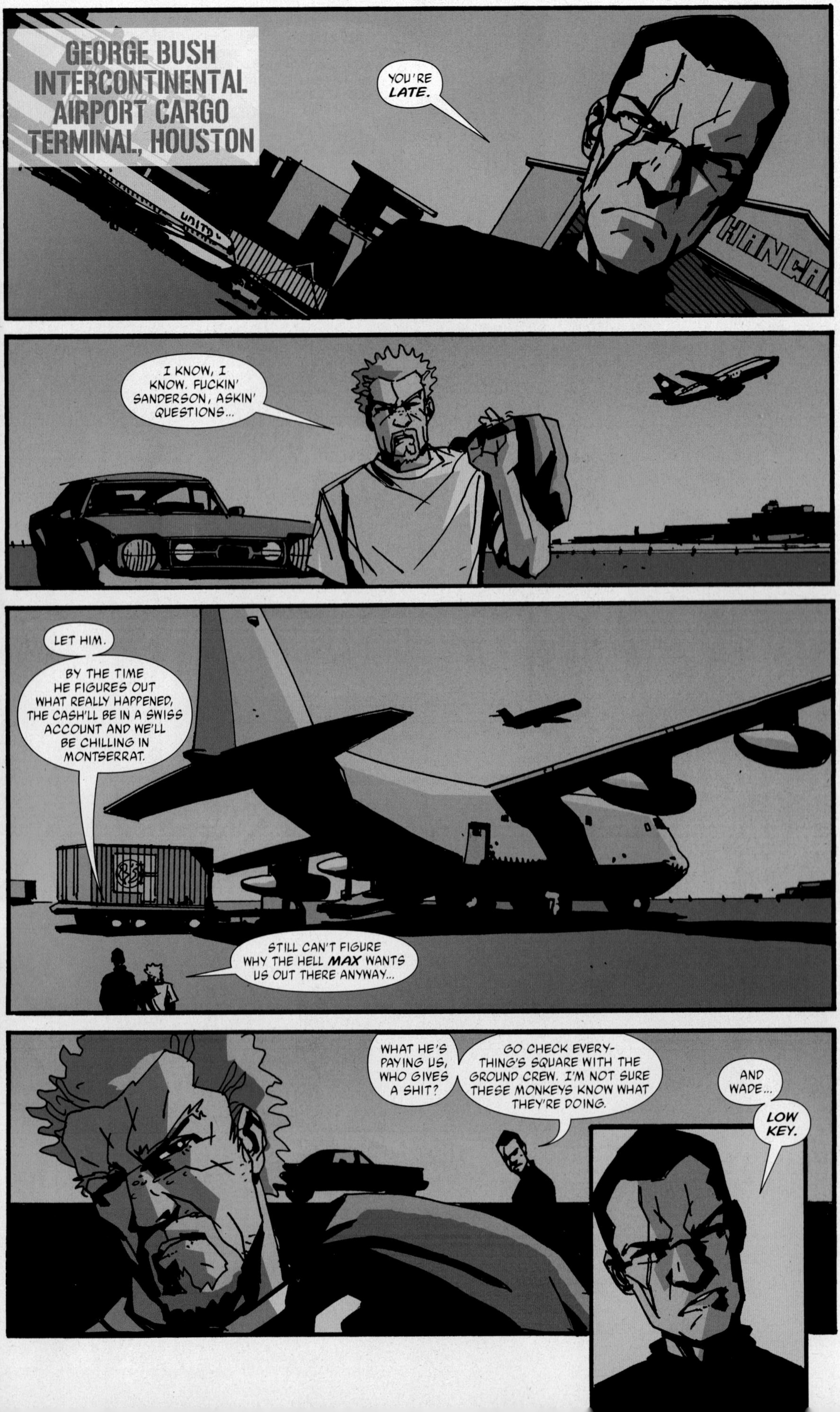
GEORGE BUSH INTERCONTINENTAL AIRPORT CARGO TERMINAL, HOUSTON
YOU'RE LATE.
I KNOW, I KNOW. FUCKIN' SANDERSON, ASKIN' QUESTIONS...
LET HIM.
BY THE TIME HE FIGURES OUT WHAT REALLY HAPPENED, THE CASH'LL BE IN A SWISS ACCOUNT AND WE'LL BE CHILLING IN MONTSERRAT.
STILL CAN'T FIGURE WHY THE HELL MAX WANTS US OUT THERE ANYWAY...
WHAT HE'S PAYING US, WHO GIVES A SHIT?
GO CHECK EVERY-THING'S SQUARE WITH THE GROUND CREW. I'M NOT SURE THESE MONKEYS KNOW WHAT THEY'RE DOING.
AND WADE...
LOW KEY.

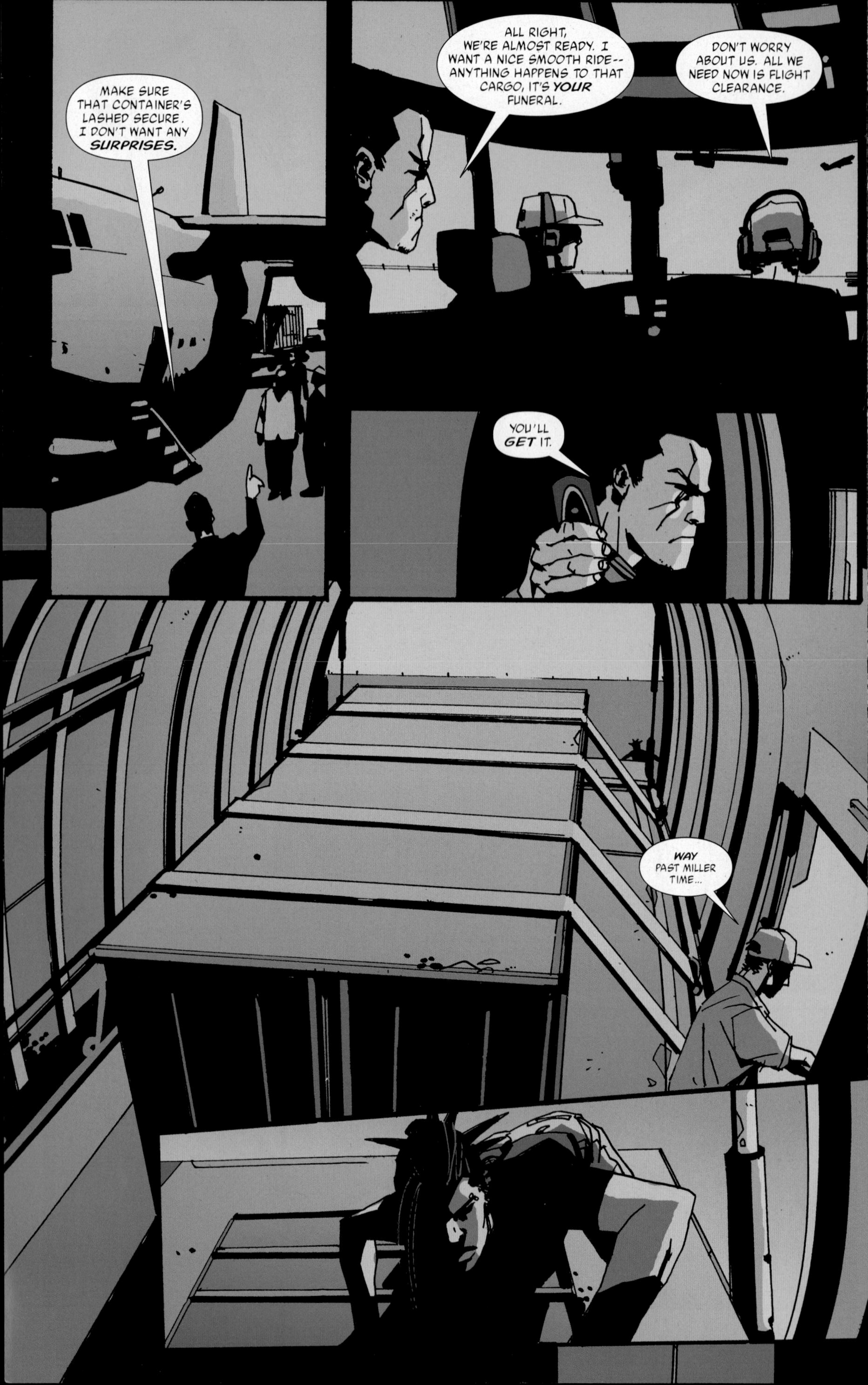
MAKE SURE THAT CONTAINER'S LASHED SECURE. I DON'T WANT ANY SURPRISES.
ALL RIGHT, WE'RE ALMOST READY. I WANT A NICE SMOOTH RIDE-- ANYTHING HAPPENS TO THAT CARGO, IT'S YOUR FUNERAL.
DON'T WORRY ABOUT US. ALL WE NEED NOW IS FLIGHT CLEARANCE.
YOU'LL GET IT.
WAY PAST MILLER TIME...

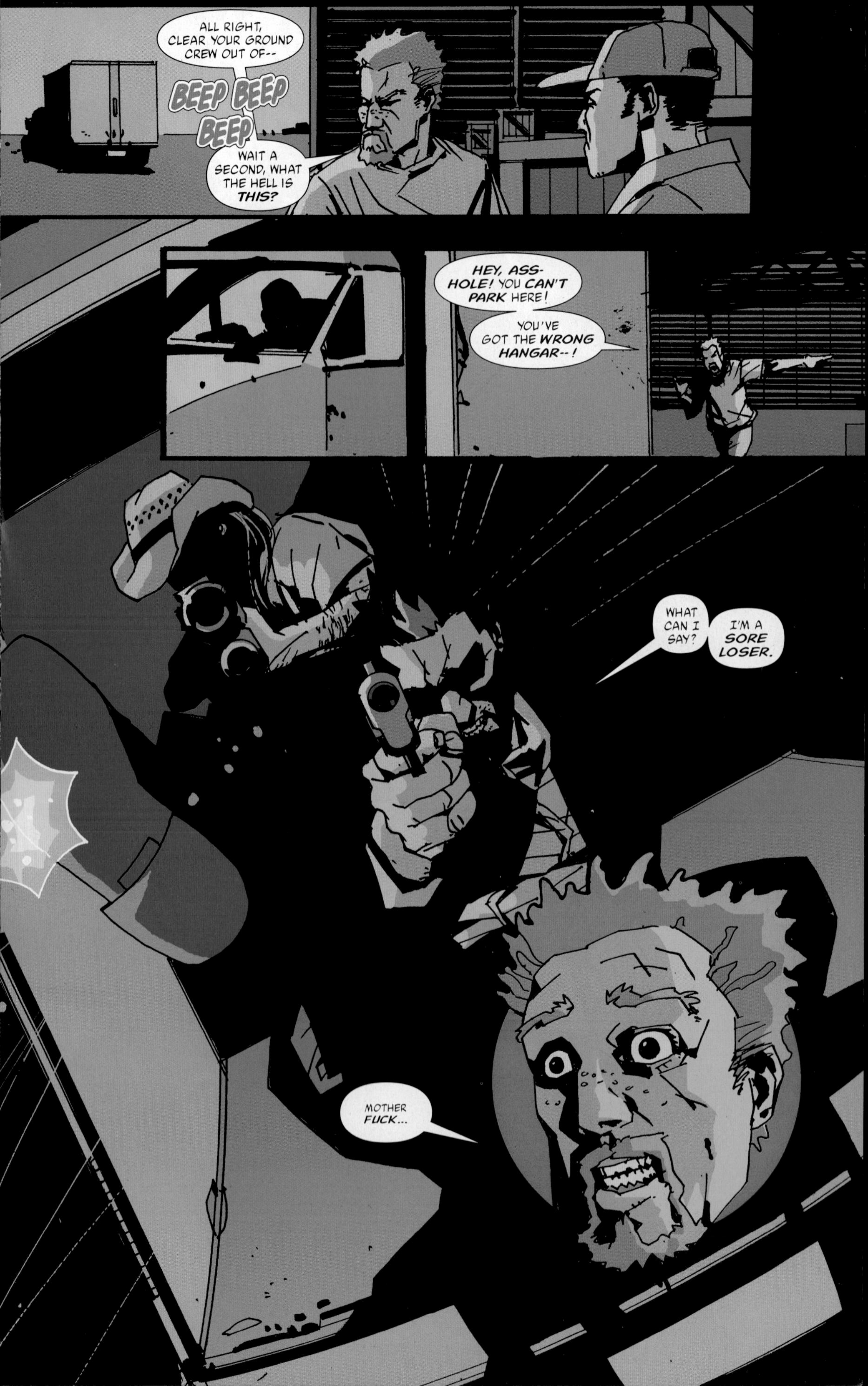
ALL RIGHT, CLEAR YOUR GROUND CREW OUT OF--
BEEP BEEP BEEP
WAIT A SECOND, WHAT THE HELL IS THIS?
HEY, ASS-HOLE! YOU CAN'T PARK HERE!
YOU'VE GOT THE WRONG HANGAR--!
WHAT CAN I SAY?
I'M A SORE LOSER.
MOTHER FUCK...

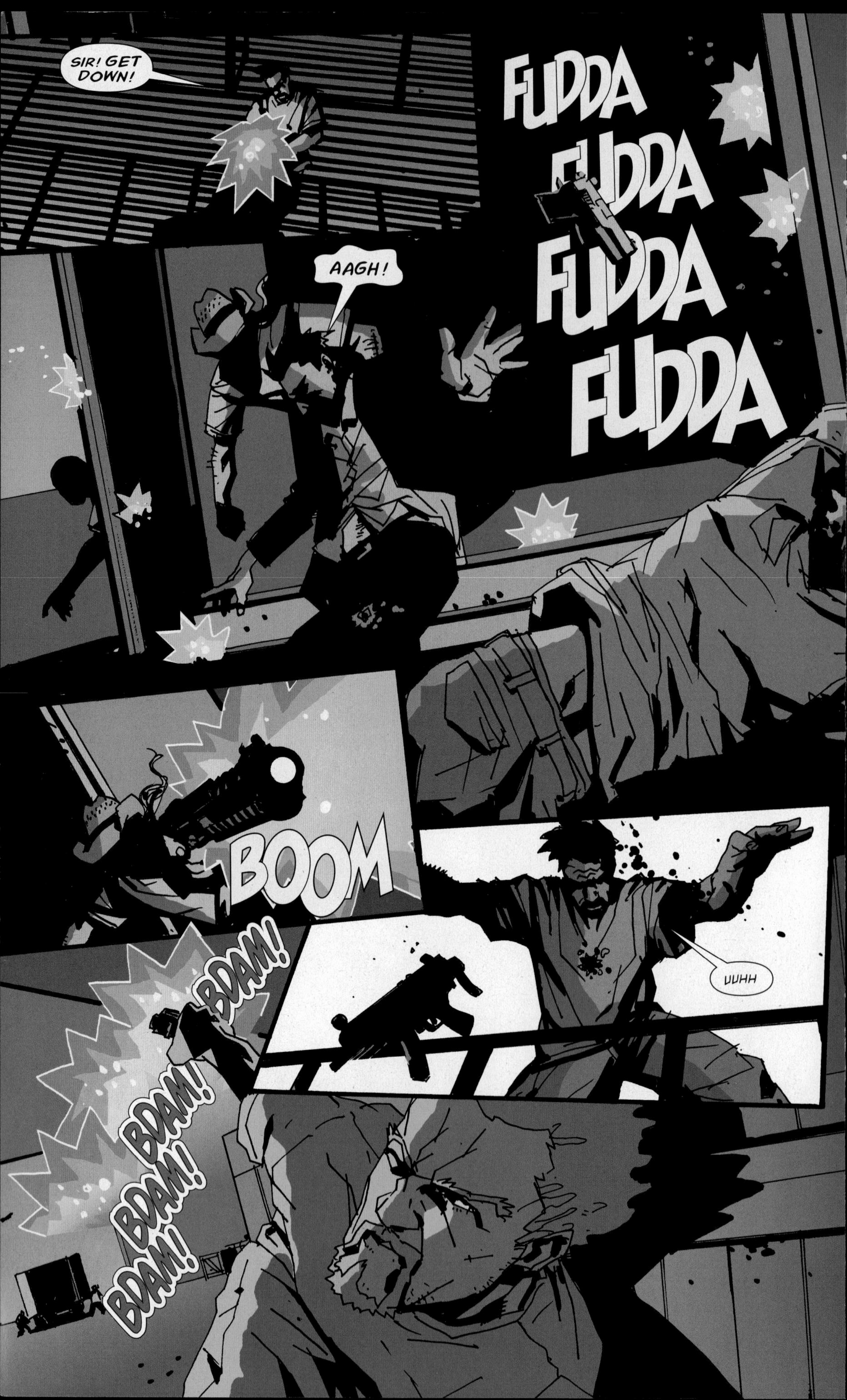
SIR! GET DOWN!
FUDDA FUDDA FUDDA FUDDA
AAGH!
BOOM
UUHH
BDAM! BDAM! BDAM! BDAM!

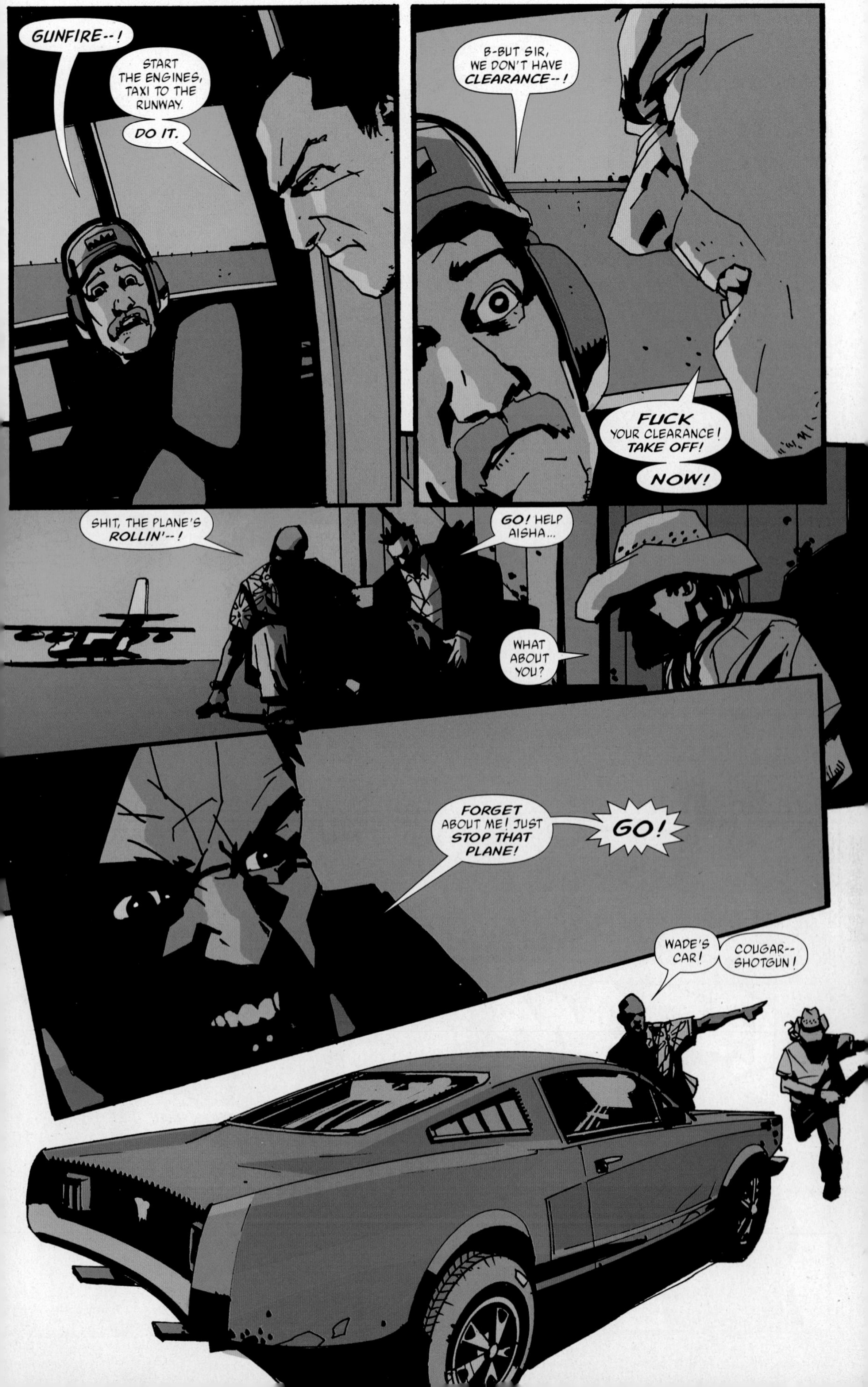
GUNFIRE--!
START THE ENGINES, TAXI TO THE RUNWAY.
DO IT.
B-BUT SIR, WE DON'T HAVE CLEARANCE--!
FUCK YOUR CLEARANCE! TAKE OFF!
NOW!
SHIT, THE PLANE'S ROLLIN'--!
GO! HELP AISHA...
WHAT ABOUT YOU?
FORGET ABOUT ME! JUST STOP THAT PLANE!
GO!
WADE'S CAR!
COUGAR-- SHOTGUN!

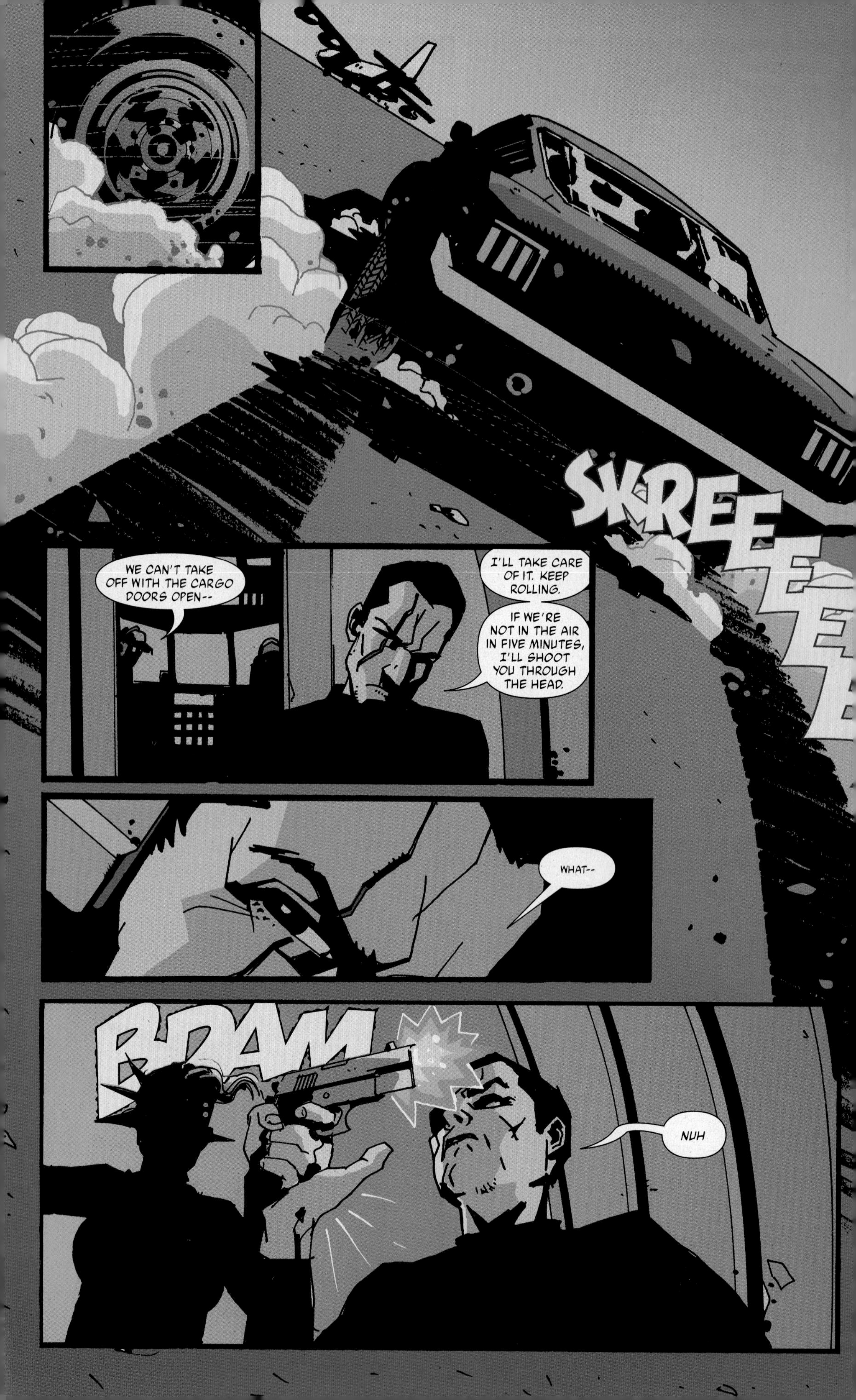
SKREEEEEE
WE CAN'T TAKE OFF WITH THE CARGO DOORS OPEN--
I'LL TAKE CARE OF IT. KEEP ROLLING.
IF WE'RE NOT IN THE AIR IN FIVE MINUTES, I'LL SHOOT YOU THROUGH THE HEAD.
WHAT--
BRAM
NUH

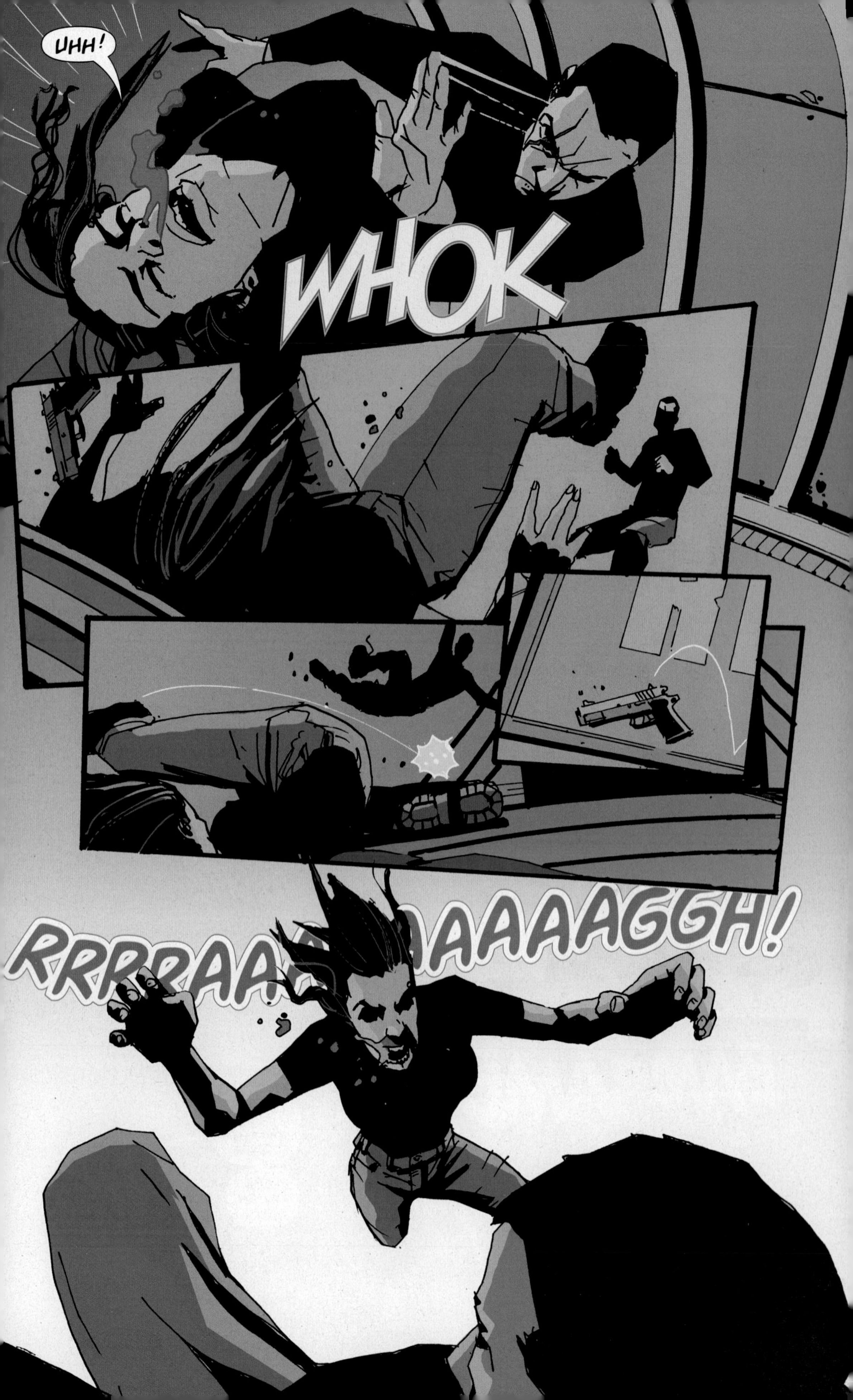
UHH!
WHOK
RRRRAAAAAAAAAAGGH!

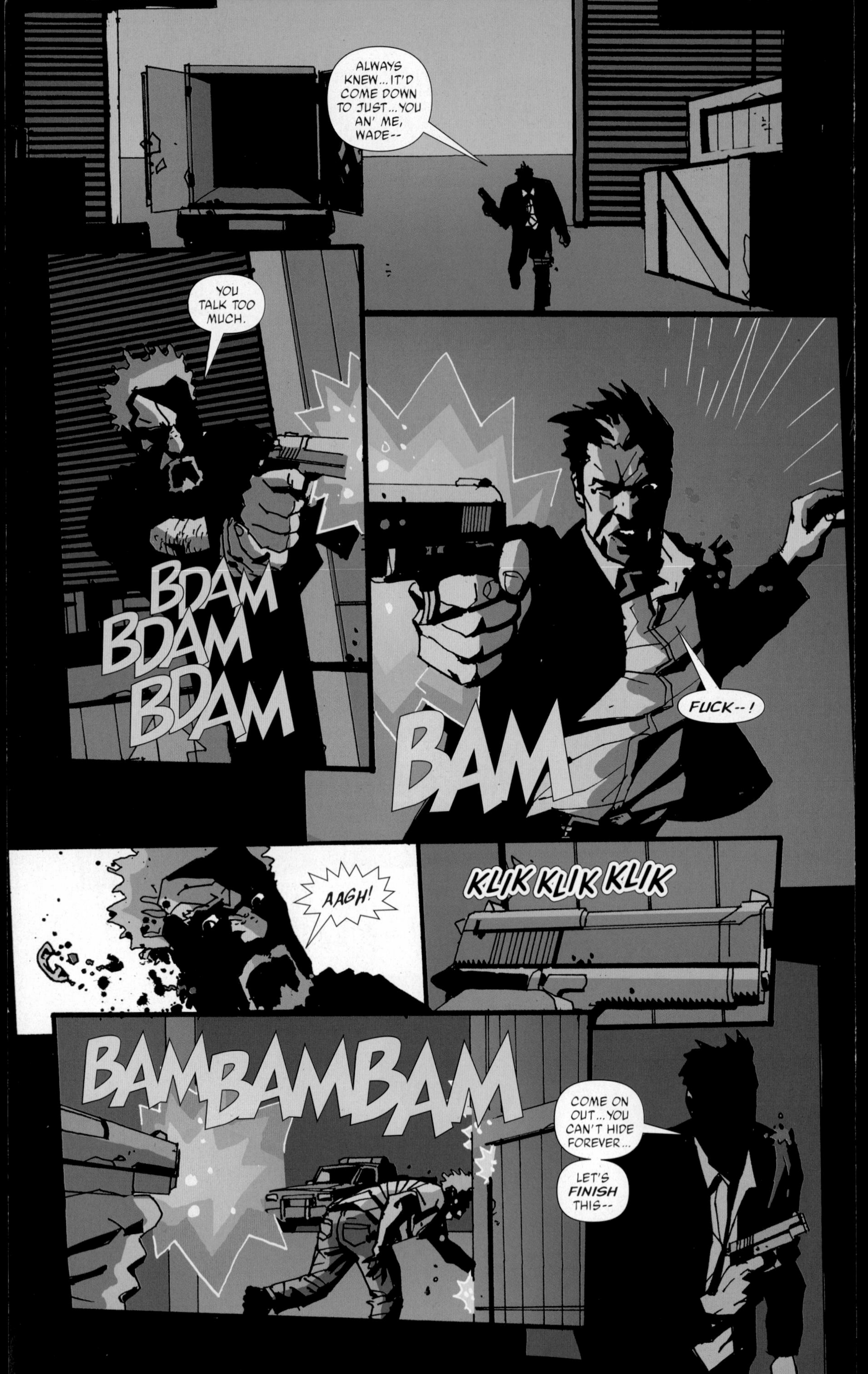
ALWAYS KNEW... IT'D COME DOWN TO JUST... YOU AN' ME, WADE--
YOU TALK TOO MUCH.
BDAM BDAM BDAM
BAM
FUCK--!
AAGH!
KLIK KLIK KLIK
BAMBAMBAM
COME ON OUT... YOU CAN'T HIDE FOREVER...
LET'S FINISH THIS--

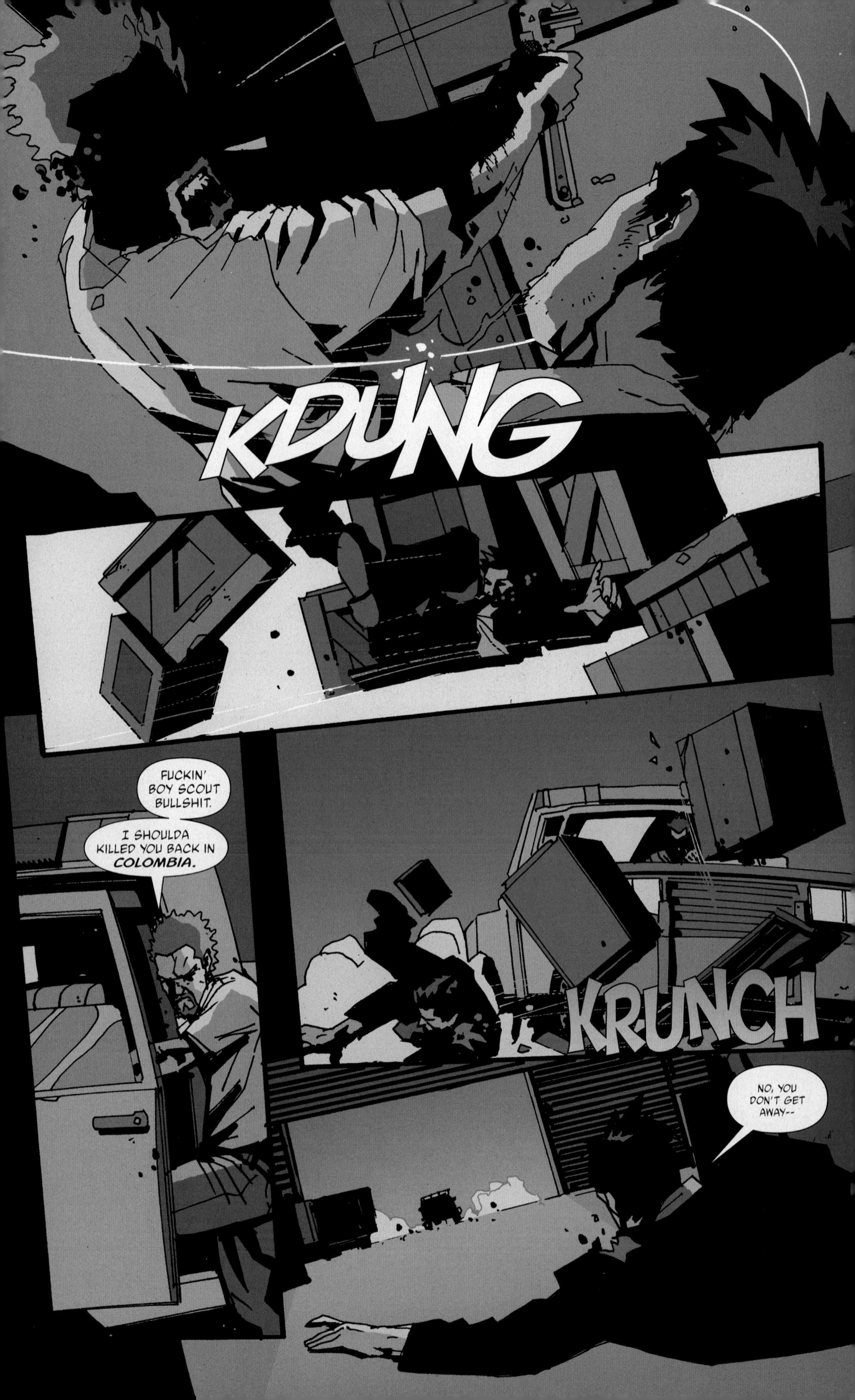
KDUNG
FUCKIN' BOY SCOUT BULLSHIT.
I SHOULDA KILLED YOU BACK IN COLOMBIA.
KRUNCH
NO, YOU DON'T GET AWAY--

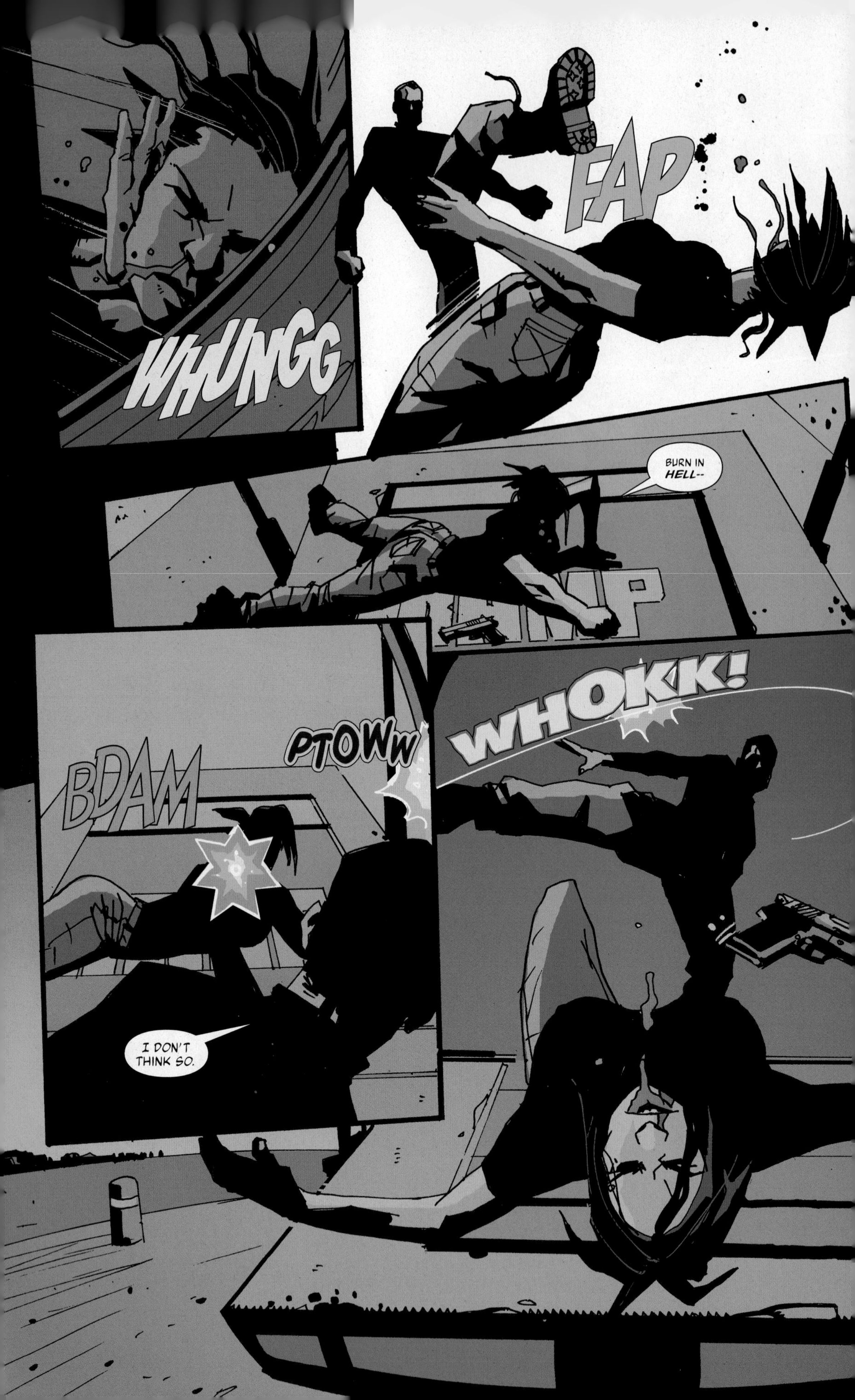
WHUNGG
FAP
BURN IN HELL--
BDAM
PTOWW
I DON'T THINK SO.
WHOKK!

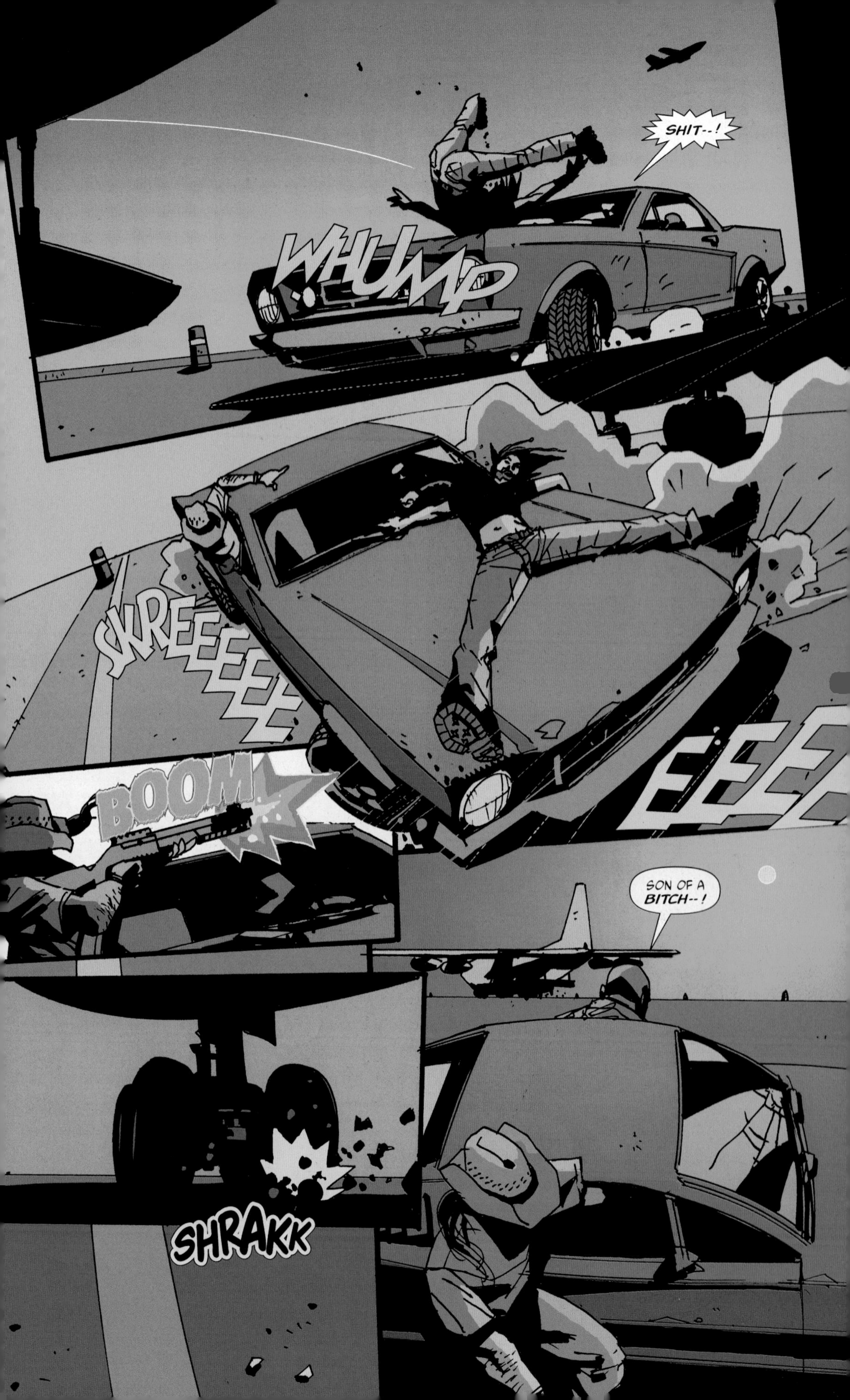
SHIT--!
WHUMP
SKREEEEEEEEEEEEE
BOOM
SON OF A BITCH--!
SHRAKK

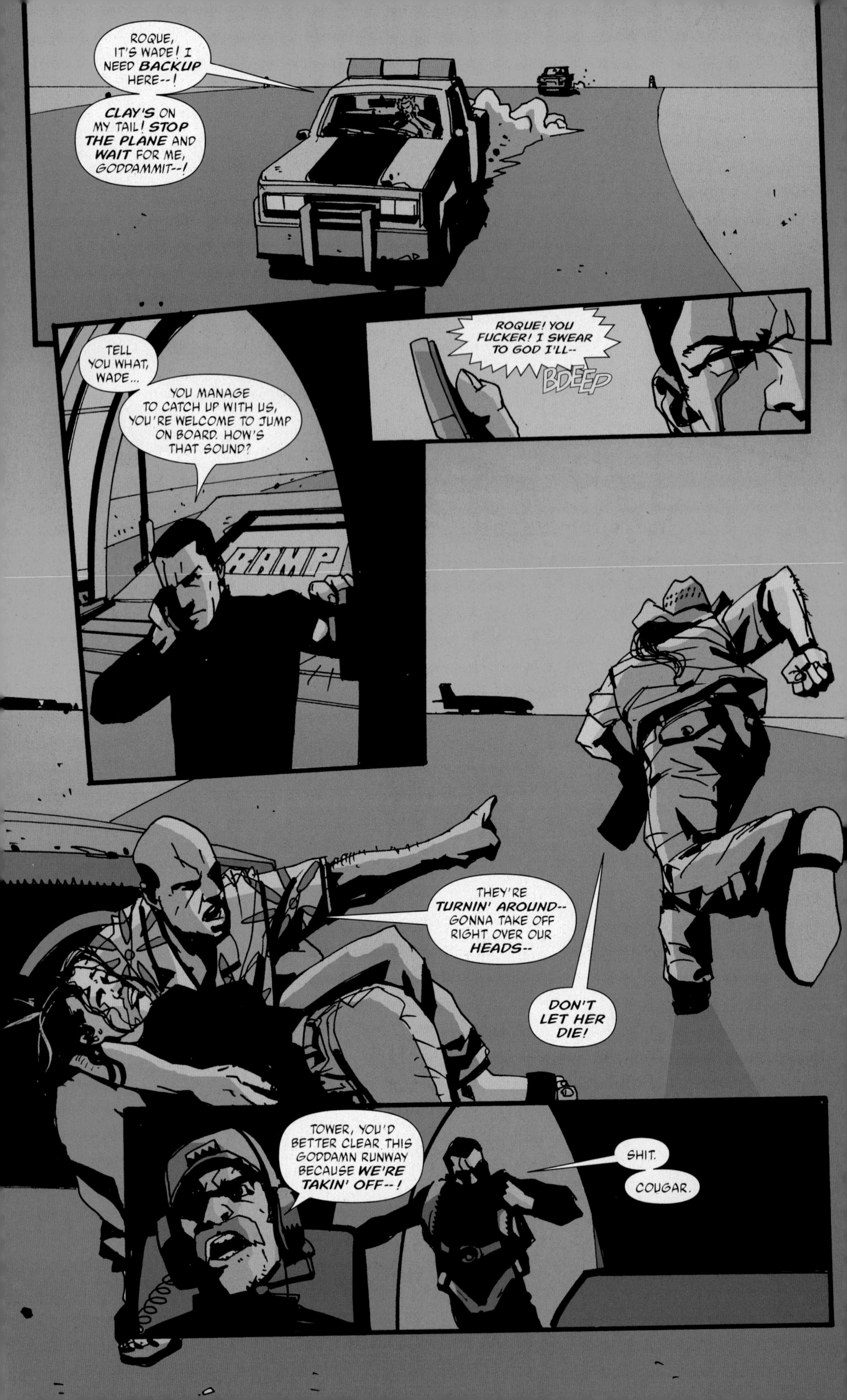
ROQUE, IT'S WADE! I NEED BACKUP HERE--!
CLAY'S ON MY TAIL! STOP THE PLANE AND WAIT FOR ME, GODDAMMIT--!
TELL YOU WHAT, WADE...
YOU MANAGE TO CATCH UP WITH US, YOU'RE WELCOME TO JUMP ON BOARD. HOW'S THAT SOUND?
RAMP
ROQUE! YOU FUCKER! I SWEAR TO GOD I'LL--
BDEEP
THEY'RE TURNIN' AROUND-- GONNA TAKE OFF RIGHT OVER OUR HEADS--
DON'T LET HER DIE!
TOWER, YOU'D BETTER CLEAR THIS GODDAMN RUNWAY BECAUSE WE'RE TAKIN' OFF--!
SHIT.
COUGAR.

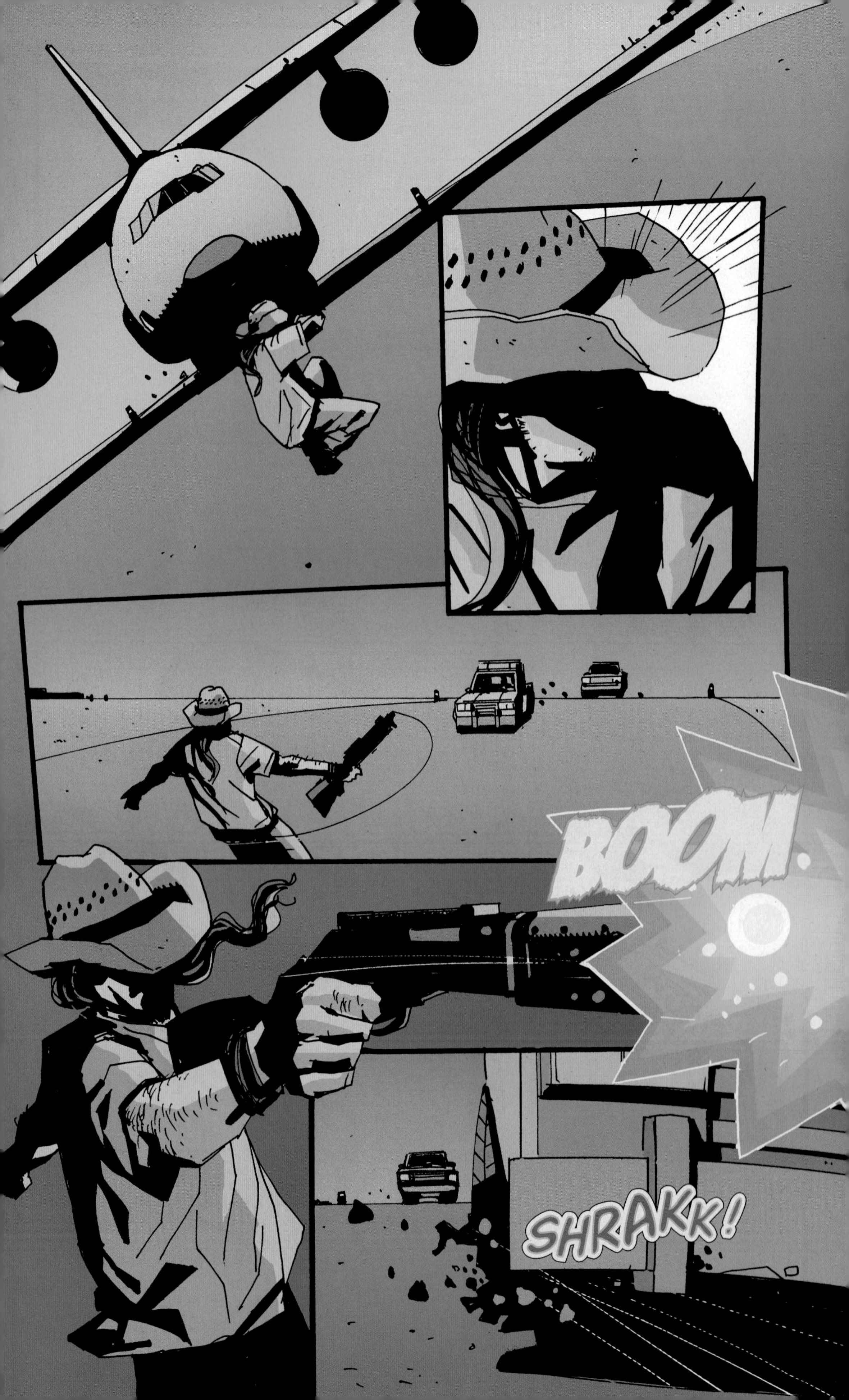
BOOM
SHRAKK!

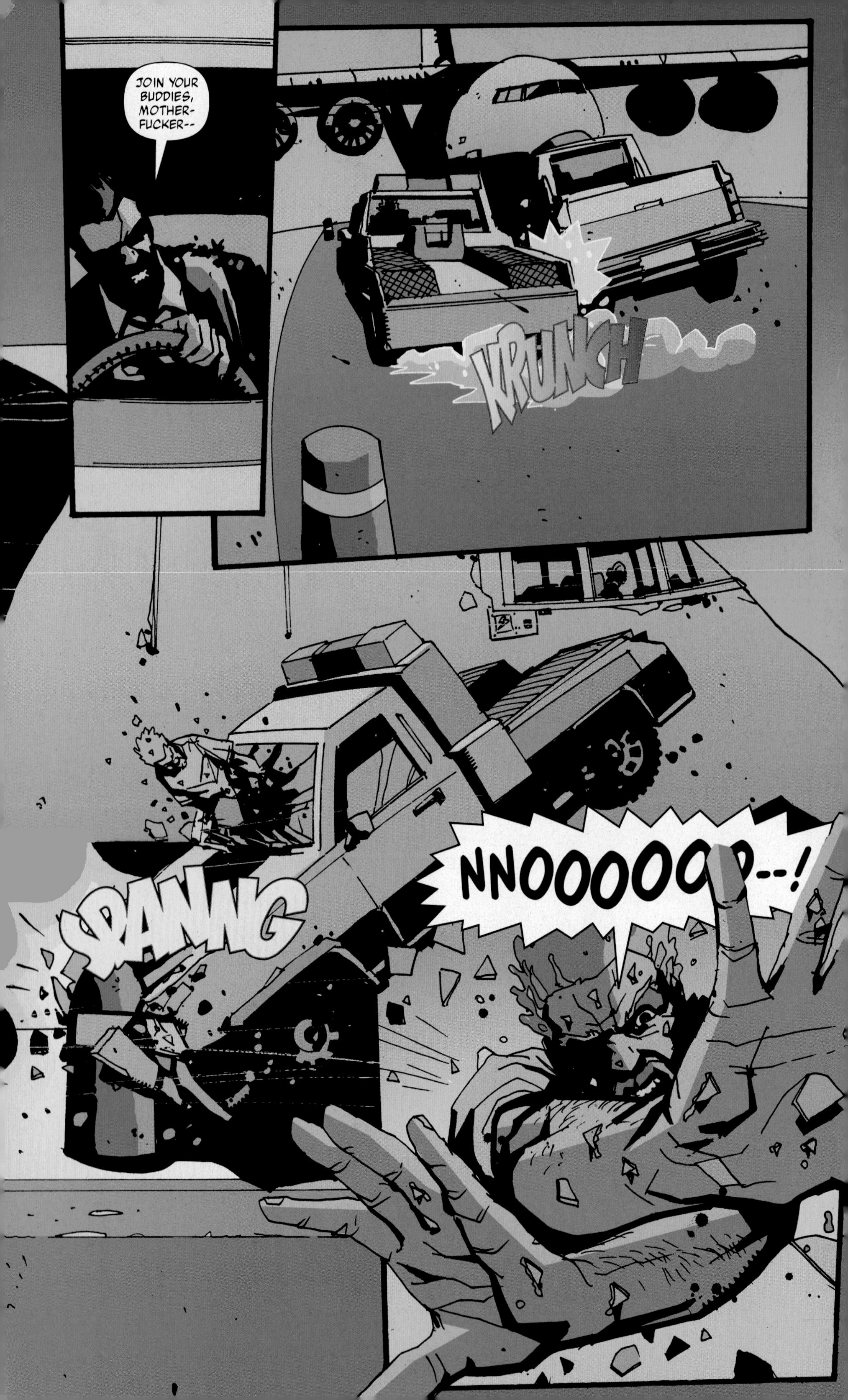
JOIN YOUR BUDDIES, MOTHER-FUCKER--
KRUNCH
SPANNG
NNOOOOOOO--!

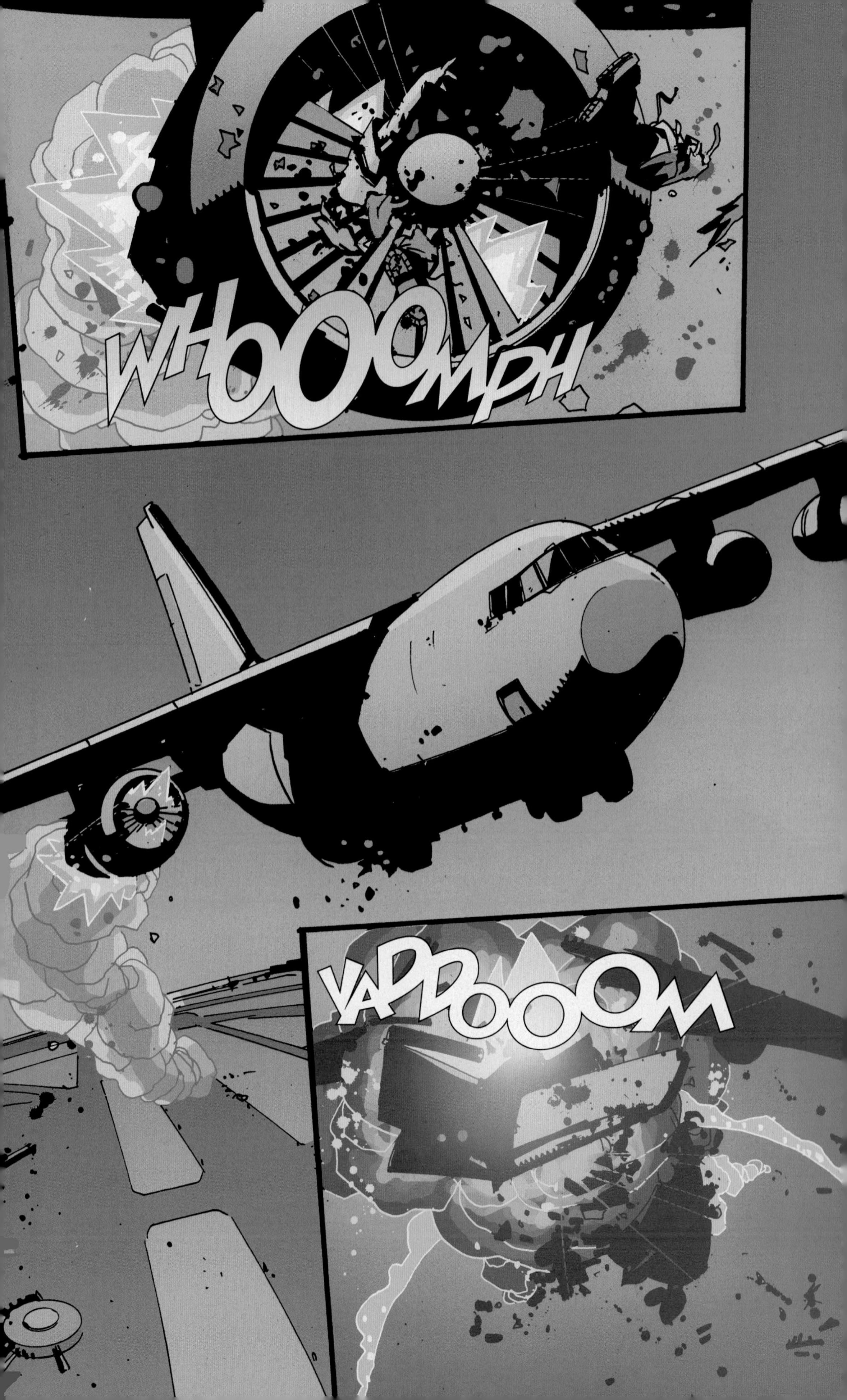
WHOOOMPH
VADDOOOM

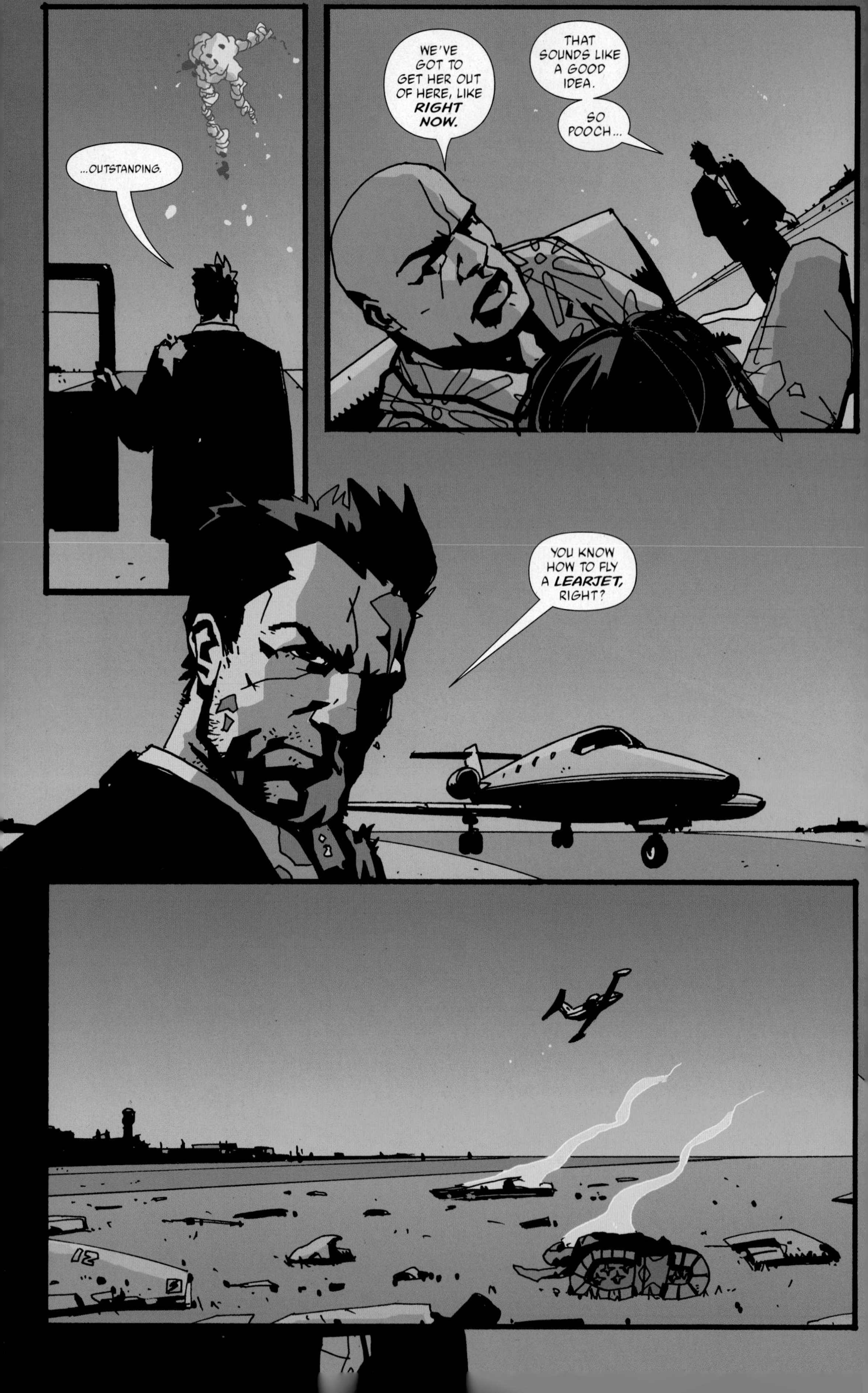
...OUTSTANDING.
WE'VE GOT TO GET HER OUT OF HERE, LIKE **RIGHT NOW.**
THAT SOUNDS LIKE A GOOD IDEA.
SO POOCH...
YOU KNOW HOW TO FLY A **LEARJET,** RIGHT?

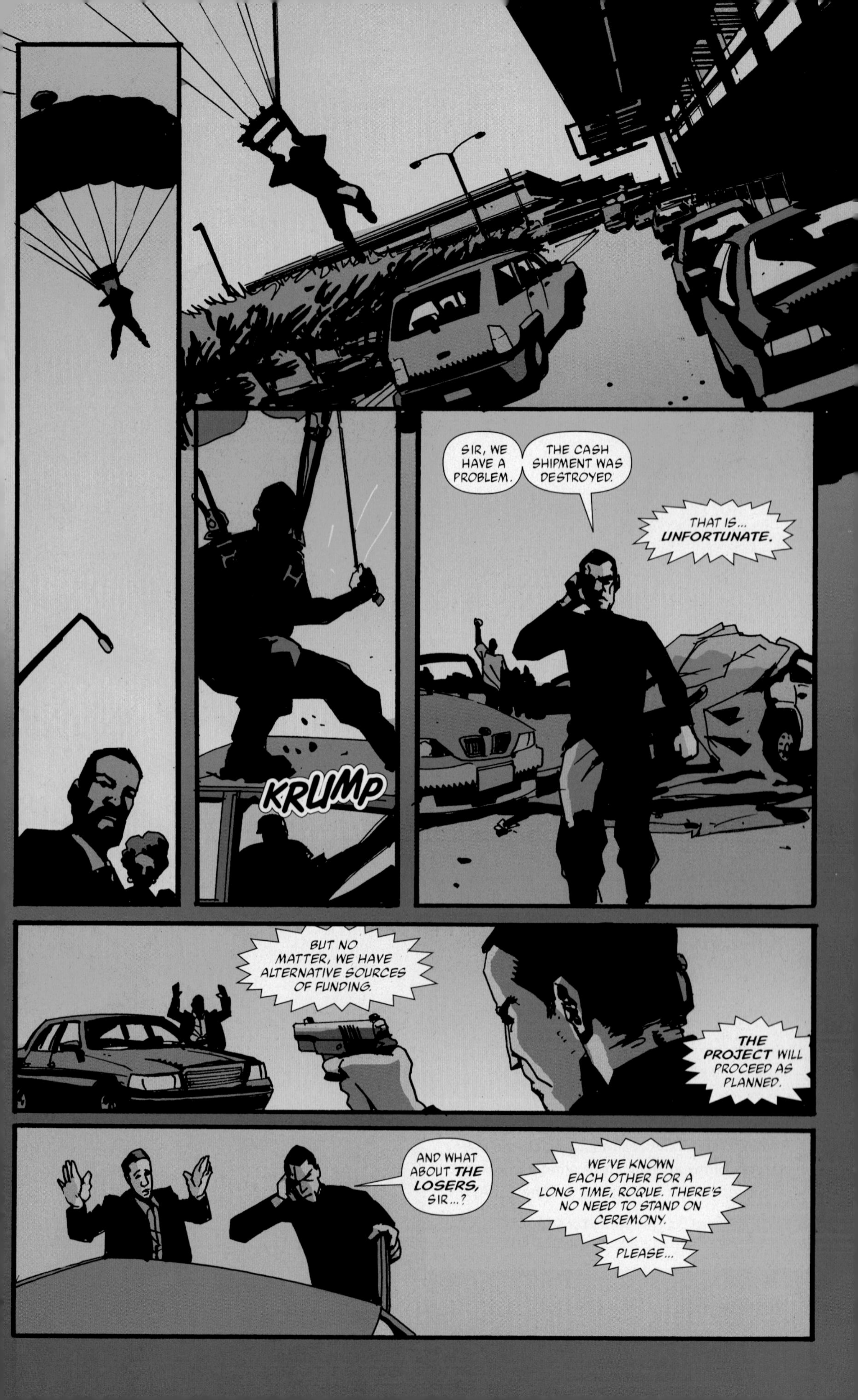
KRUMP
SIR, WE HAVE A PROBLEM.
THE CASH SHIPMENT WAS DESTROYED.
THAT IS... UNFORTUNATE.
BUT NO MATTER, WE HAVE ALTERNATIVE SOURCES OF FUNDING.
THE PROJECT WILL PROCEED AS PLANNED.
AND WHAT ABOUT THE LOSERS, SIR...?
WE'VE KNOWN EACH OTHER FOR A LONG TIME, ROQUE. THERE'S NO NEED TO STAND ON CEREMONY.
PLEASE...

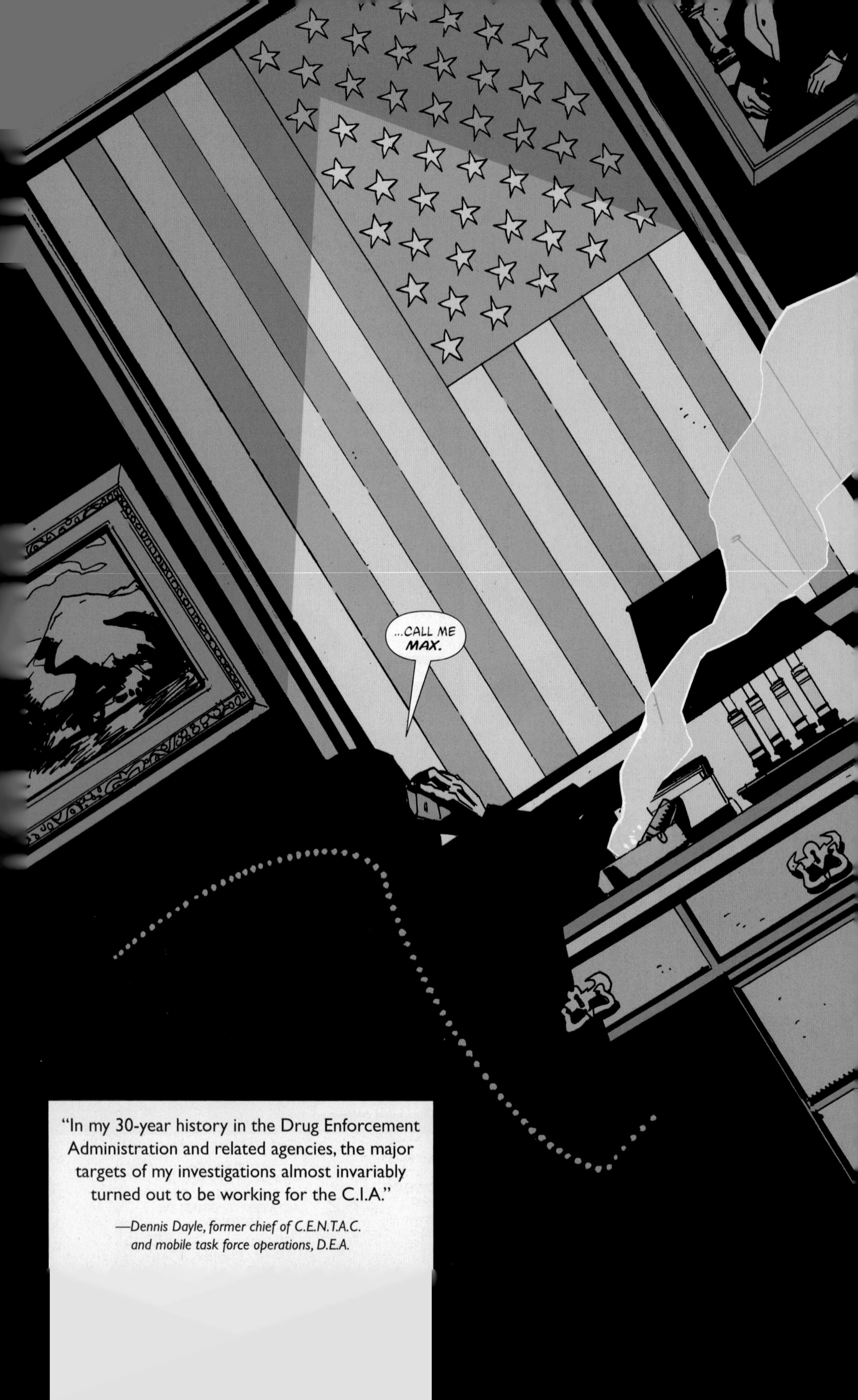
...CALL ME MAX.

"In my 30-year history in the Drug Enforcement Administration and related agencies, the major targets of my investigations almost invariably turned out to be working for the C.I.A."

—Dennis Dayle, former chief of C.E.N.T.A.C. and mobile task force operations, D.E.A.

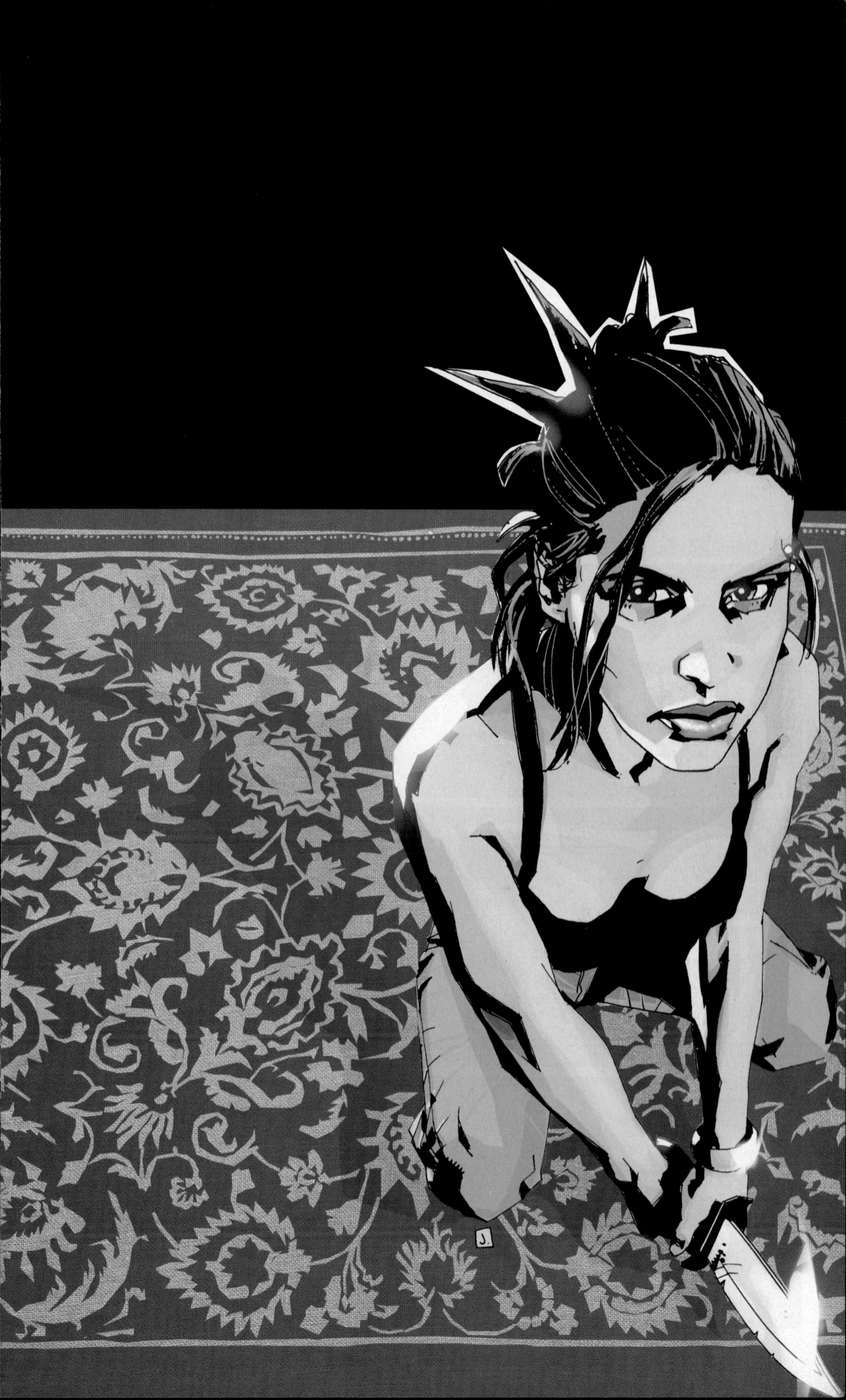

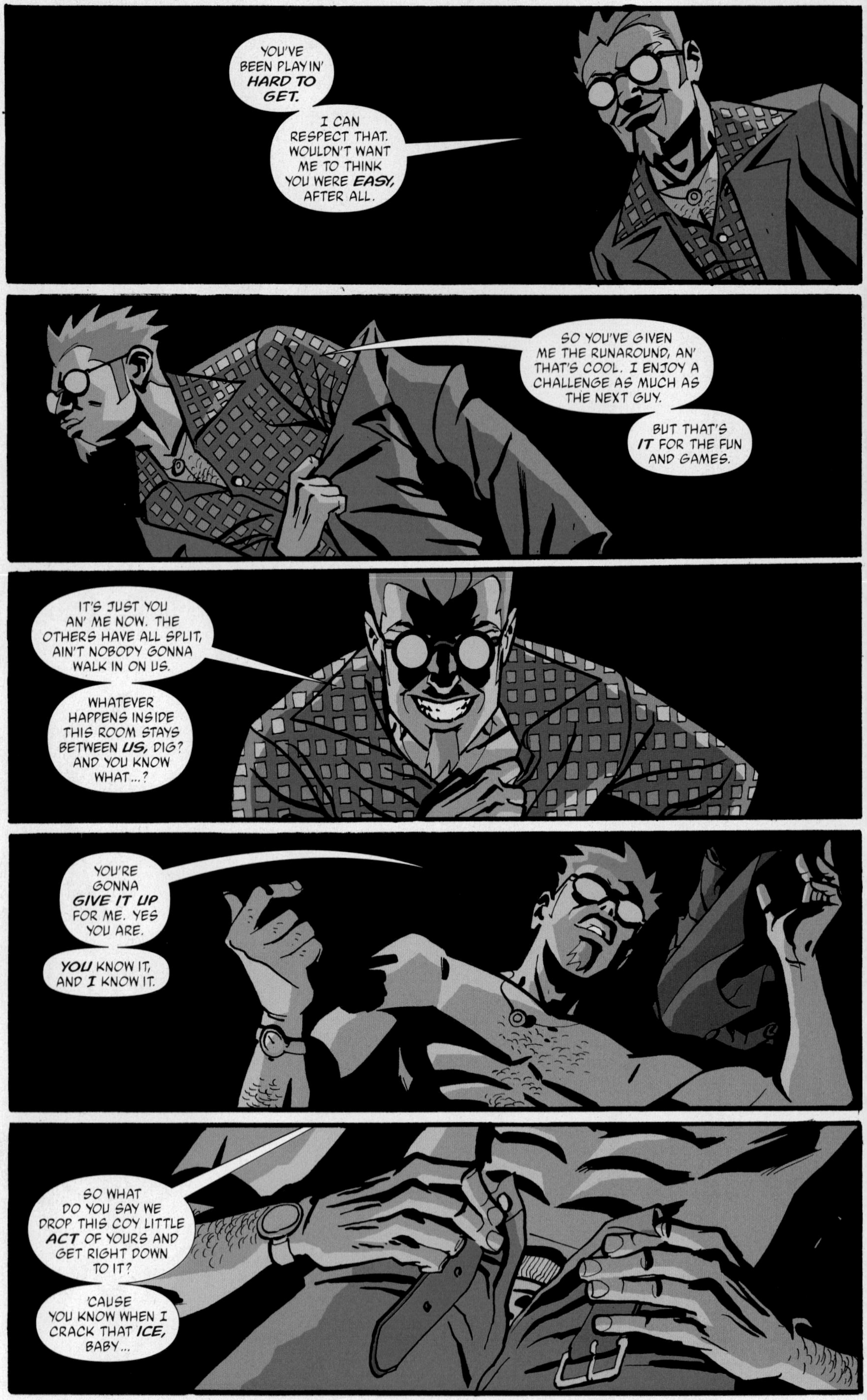

YOU'VE BEEN PLAYIN' HARD TO GET.
I CAN RESPECT THAT. WOULDN'T WANT ME TO THINK YOU WERE EASY, AFTER ALL.
SO YOU'VE GIVEN ME THE RUNAROUND, AN' THAT'S COOL. I ENJOY A CHALLENGE AS MUCH AS THE NEXT GUY.
BUT THAT'S IT FOR THE FUN AND GAMES.
IT'S JUST YOU AN' ME NOW. THE OTHERS HAVE ALL SPLIT, AIN'T NOBODY GONNA WALK IN ON US.
WHATEVER HAPPENS INSIDE THIS ROOM STAYS BETWEEN US, DIG? AND YOU KNOW WHAT...?
YOU'RE GONNA GIVE IT UP FOR ME. YES YOU ARE.
YOU KNOW IT, AND I KNOW IT.
SO WHAT DO YOU SAY WE DROP THIS COY LITTLE ACT OF YOURS AND GET RIGHT DOWN TO IT?
'CAUSE YOU KNOW WHEN I CRACK THAT ICE, BABY...

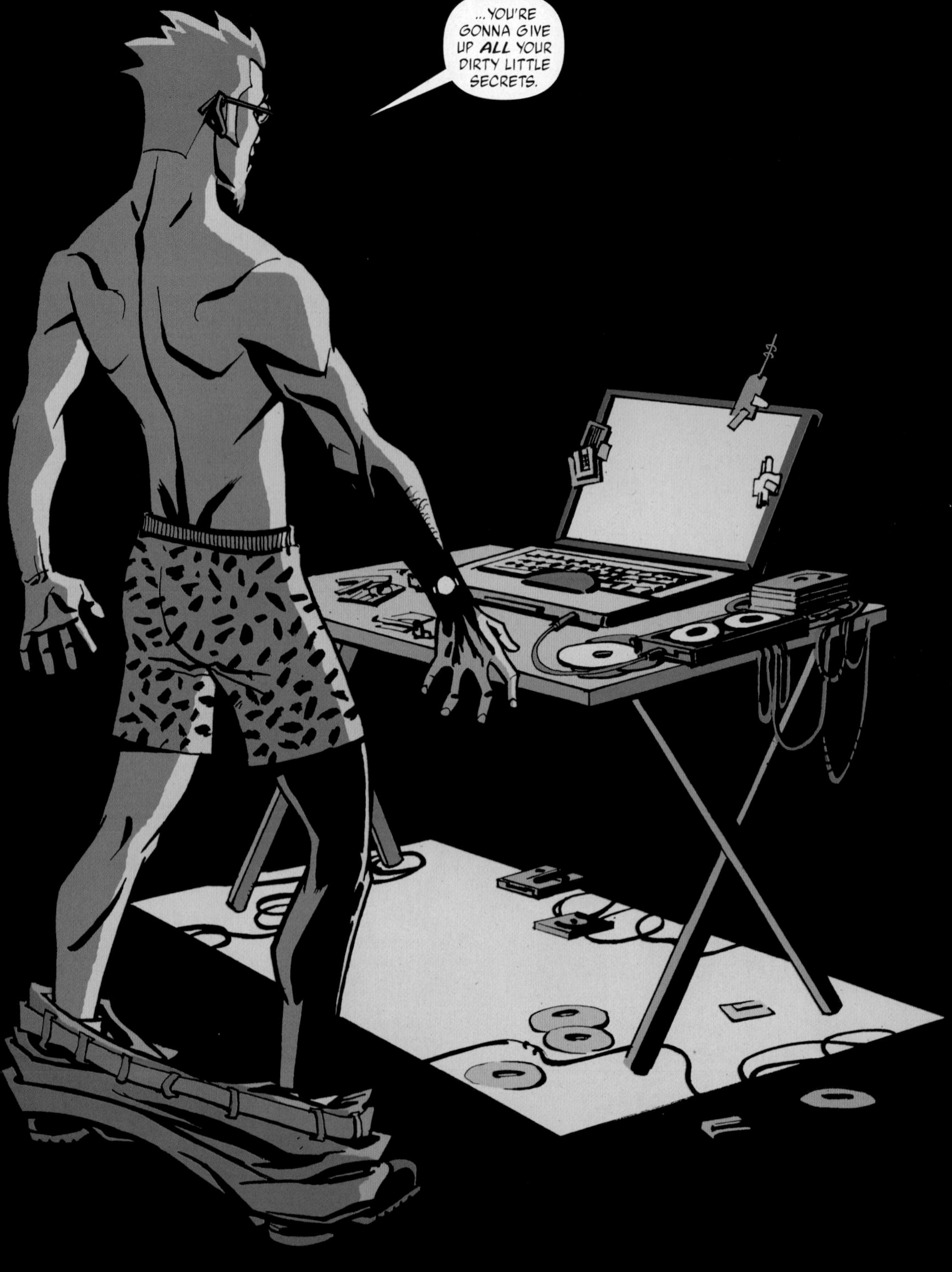
...YOU'RE GONNA GIVE UP ALL YOUR DIRTY LITTLE SECRETS.

DOWNTIME

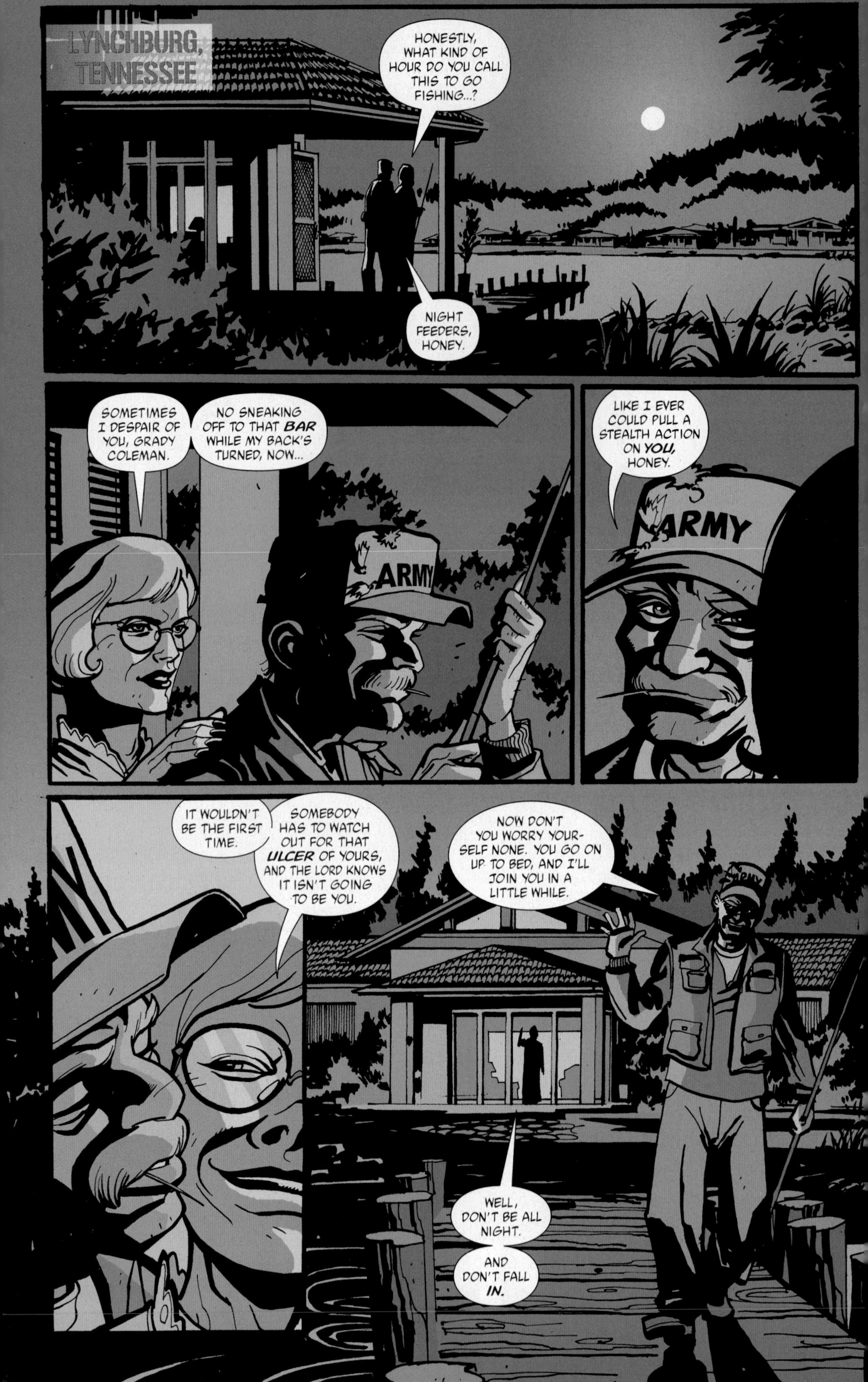
LYNCHBURG, TENNESSEE
HONESTLY, WHAT KIND OF HOUR DO YOU CALL THIS TO GO FISHING...?
NIGHT FEEDERS, HONEY.
SOMETIMES I DESPAIR OF YOU, GRADY COLEMAN.
NO SNEAKING OFF TO THAT BAR WHILE MY BACK'S TURNED, NOW...
ARMY
LIKE I EVER COULD PULL A STEALTH ACTION ON YOU, HONEY.
ARMY
IT WOULDN'T BE THE FIRST TIME.
SOMEBODY HAS TO WATCH OUT FOR THAT ULCER OF YOURS, AND THE LORD KNOWS IT ISN'T GOING TO BE YOU.
NOW DON'T YOU WORRY YOURSELF NONE. YOU GO ON UP TO BED, AND I'LL JOIN YOU IN A LITTLE WHILE.
WELL, DON'T BE ALL NIGHT.
AND DON'T FALL IN.

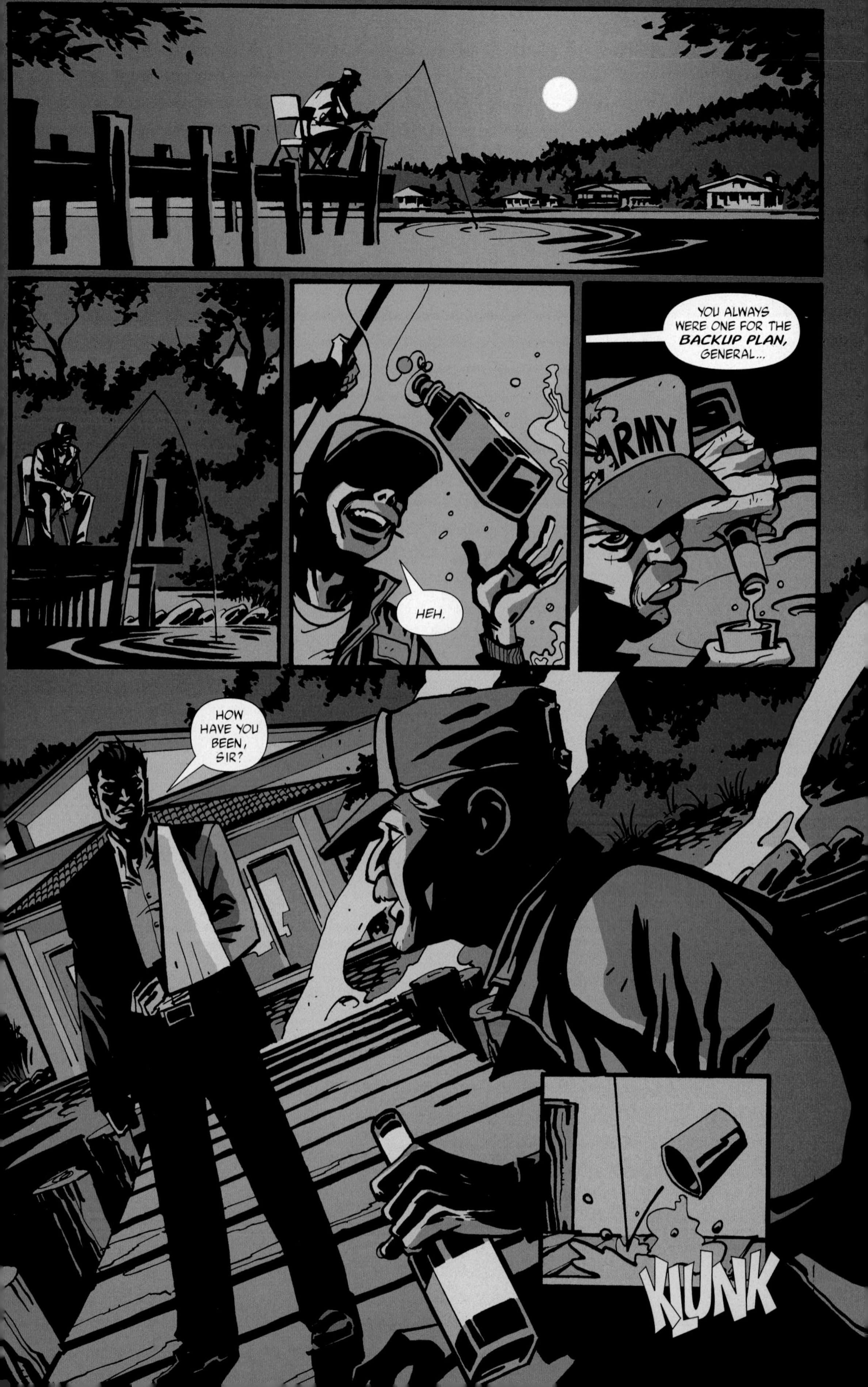
YOU ALWAYS WERE ONE FOR THE BACKUP PLAN, GENERAL...
HEH.
HOW HAVE YOU BEEN, SIR?
KLUNK

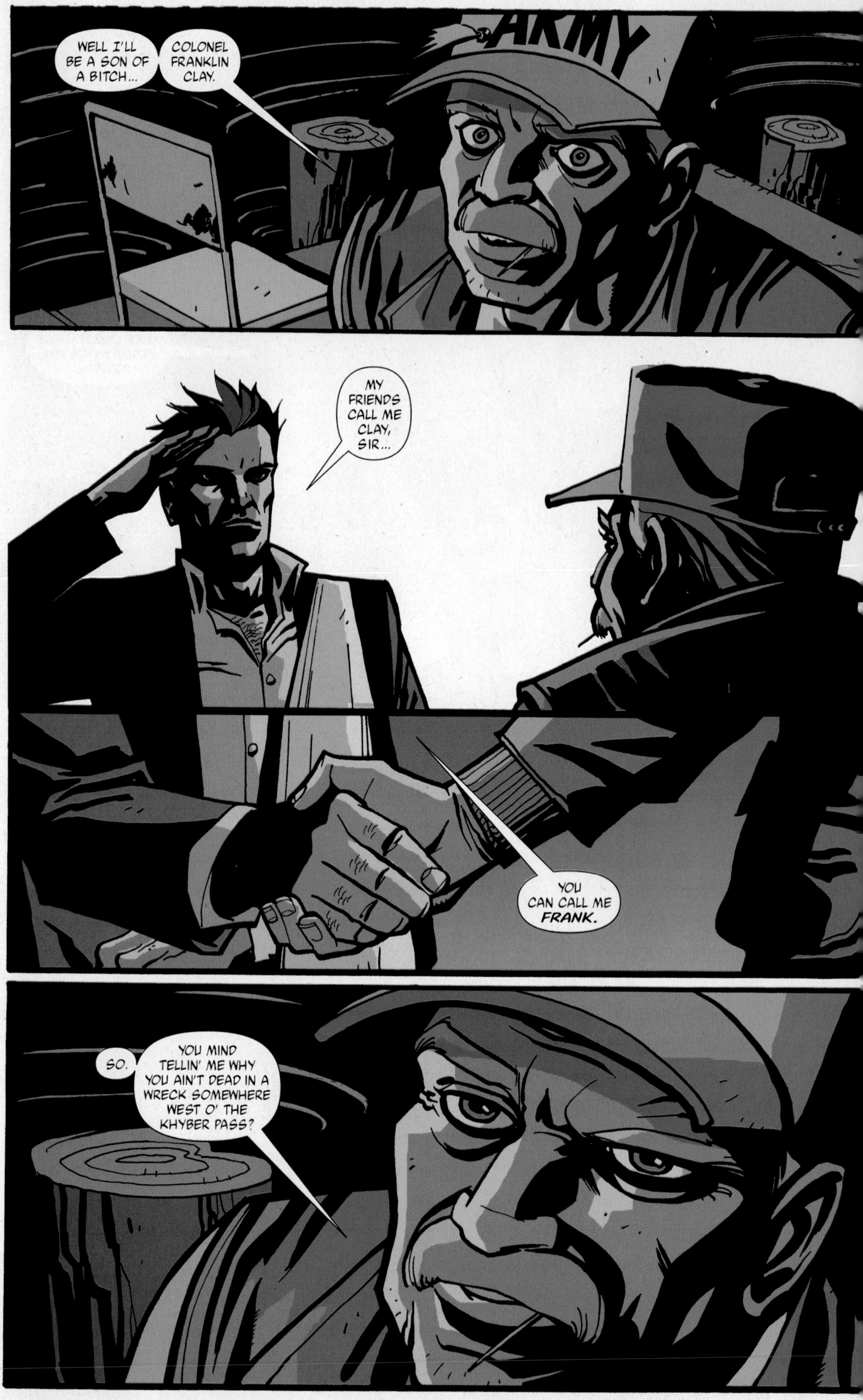
WELL I'LL BE A SON OF A BITCH...
COLONEL FRANKLIN CLAY.
MY FRIENDS CALL ME CLAY, SIR...
YOU CAN CALL ME FRANK.
SO.
YOU MIND TELLIN' ME WHY YOU AIN'T DEAD IN A WRECK SOMEWHERE WEST O' THE KHYBER PASS?
ARMY

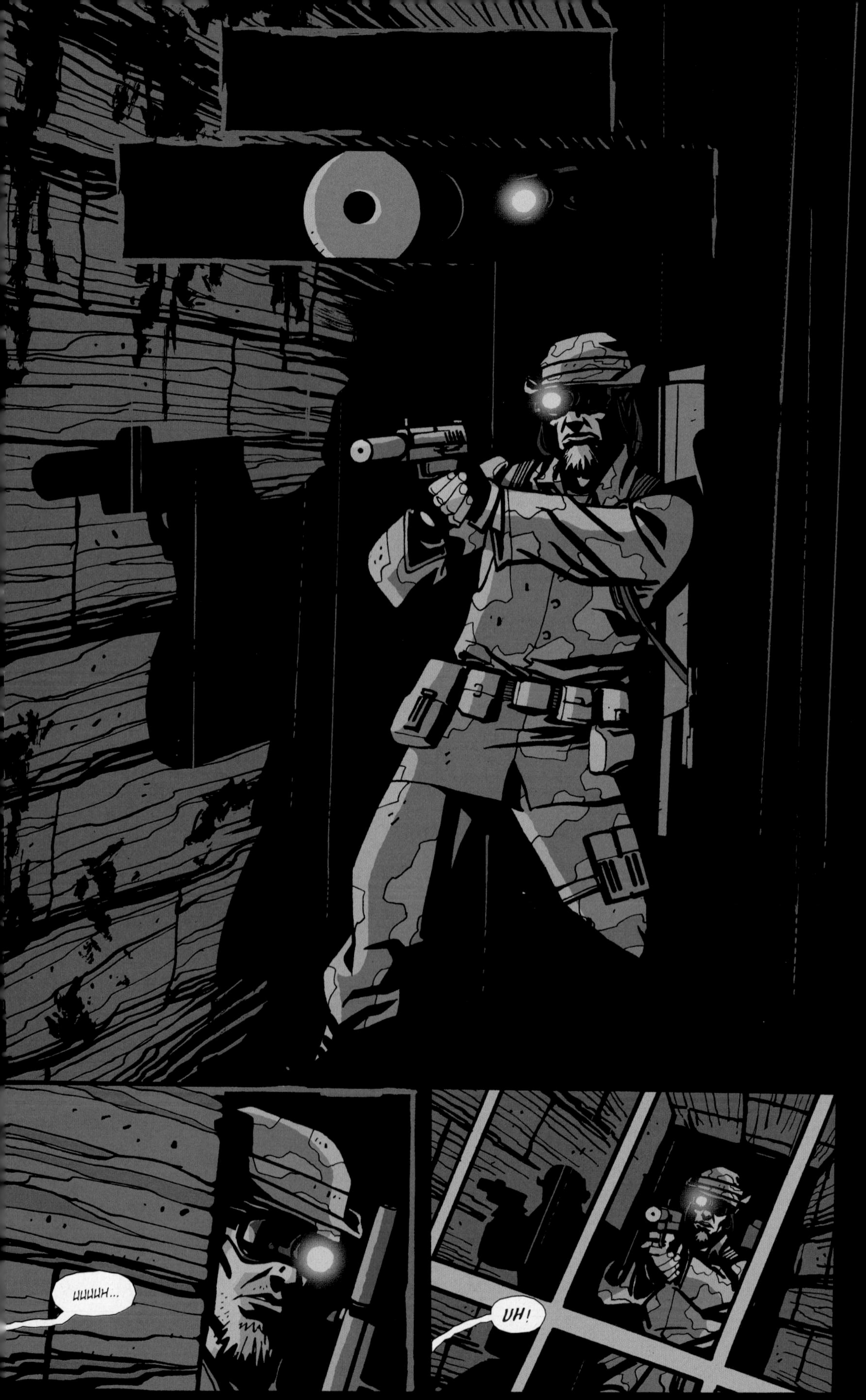
UUUUH...
UH!

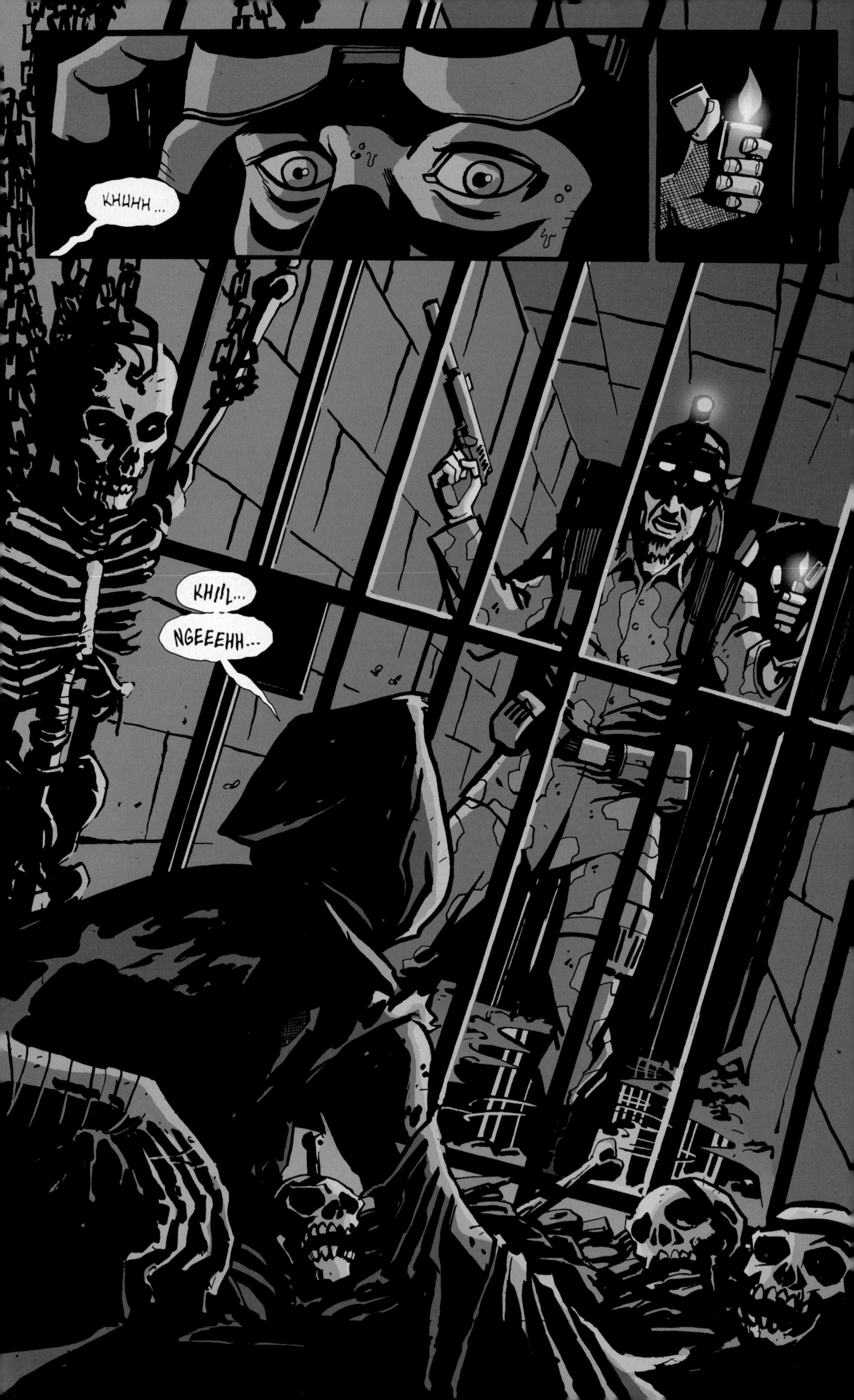
KHUHH...
KHI/L...
NGEEEHH...

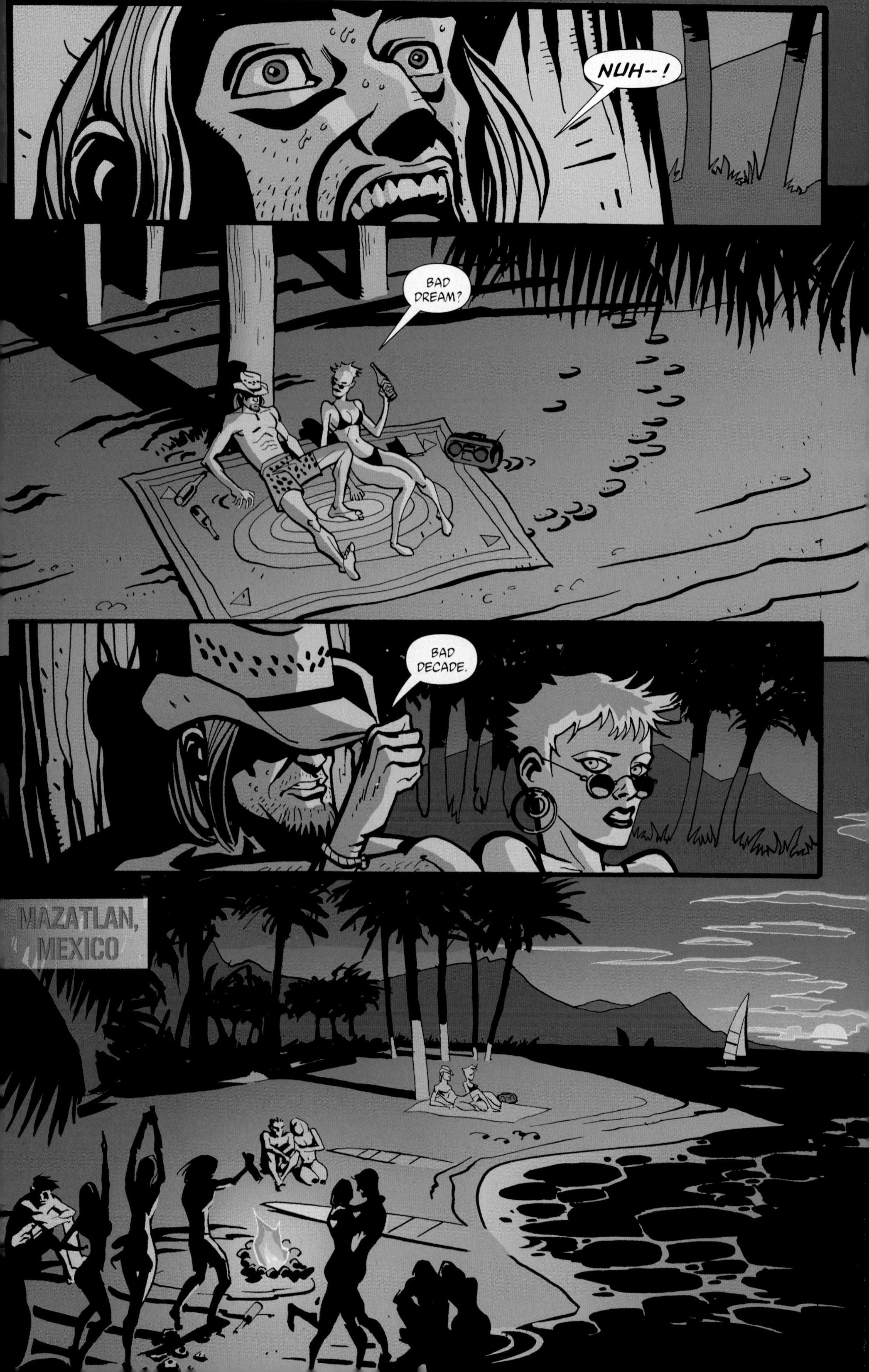
NUH--!
BAD DREAM?
BAD DECADE.
MAZATLAN, MEXICO

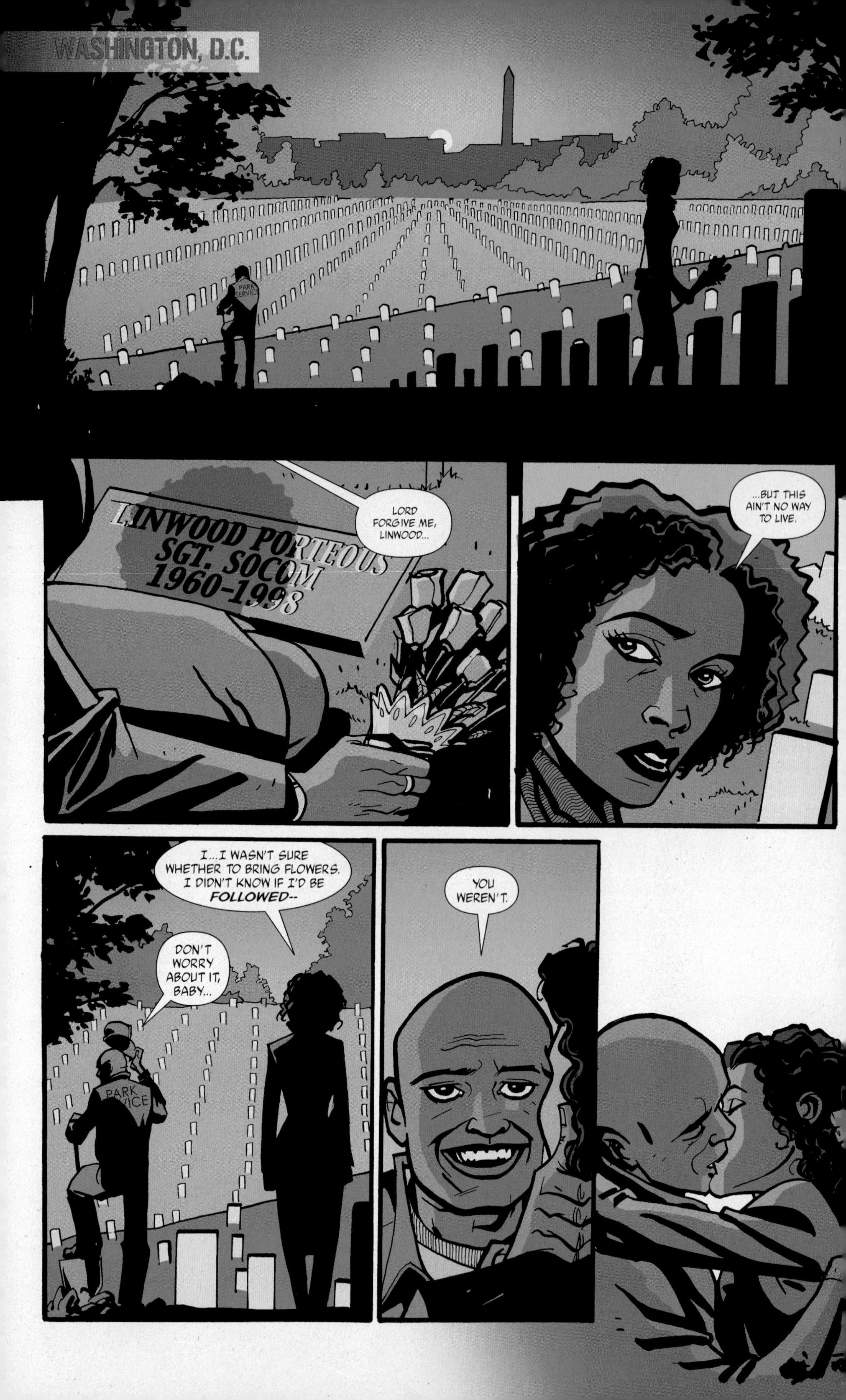
WASHINGTON, D.C.
PARK SERVICE
LINWOOD PORTEOUS SGT. SOCOM 1960-1998
LORD FORGIVE ME, LINWOOD...
...BUT THIS AIN'T NO WAY TO LIVE.
I...I WASN'T SURE WHETHER TO BRING FLOWERS. I DIDN'T KNOW IF I'D BE FOLLOWED--
DON'T WORRY ABOUT IT, BABY...
YOU WEREN'T.

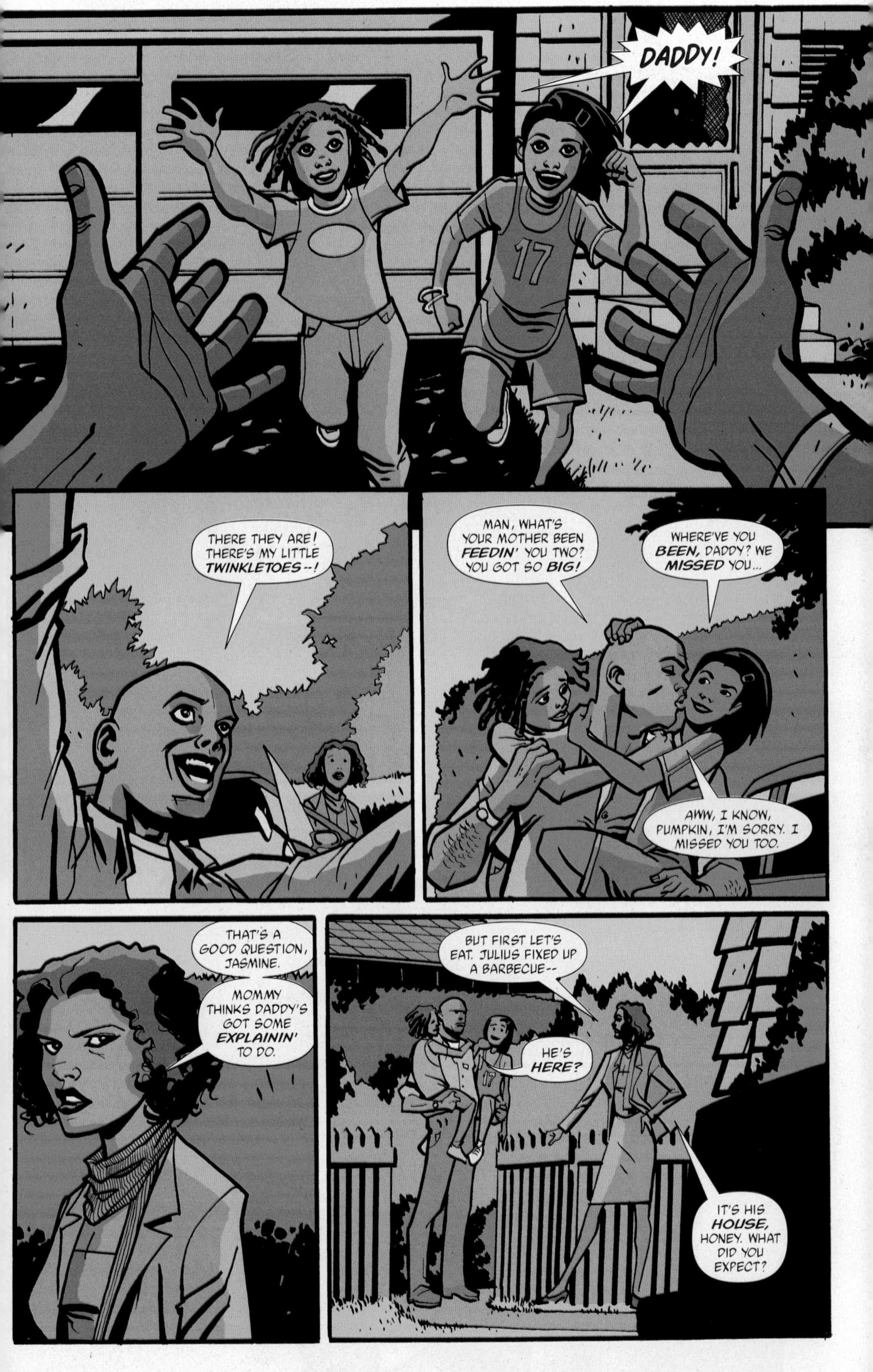
DADDY!
THERE THEY ARE! THERE'S MY LITTLE TWINKLETOES--!
MAN, WHAT'S YOUR MOTHER BEEN FEEDIN' YOU TWO? YOU GOT SO BIG!
WHERE'VE YOU BEEN, DADDY? WE MISSED YOU...
AWW, I KNOW, PUMPKIN, I'M SORRY. I MISSED YOU TOO.
THAT'S A GOOD QUESTION, JASMINE.
MOMMY THINKS DADDY'S GOT SOME EXPLAININ' TO DO.
BUT FIRST LET'S EAT. JULIUS FIXED UP A BARBECUE--
HE'S HERE?
IT'S HIS HOUSE, HONEY. WHAT DID YOU EXPECT?

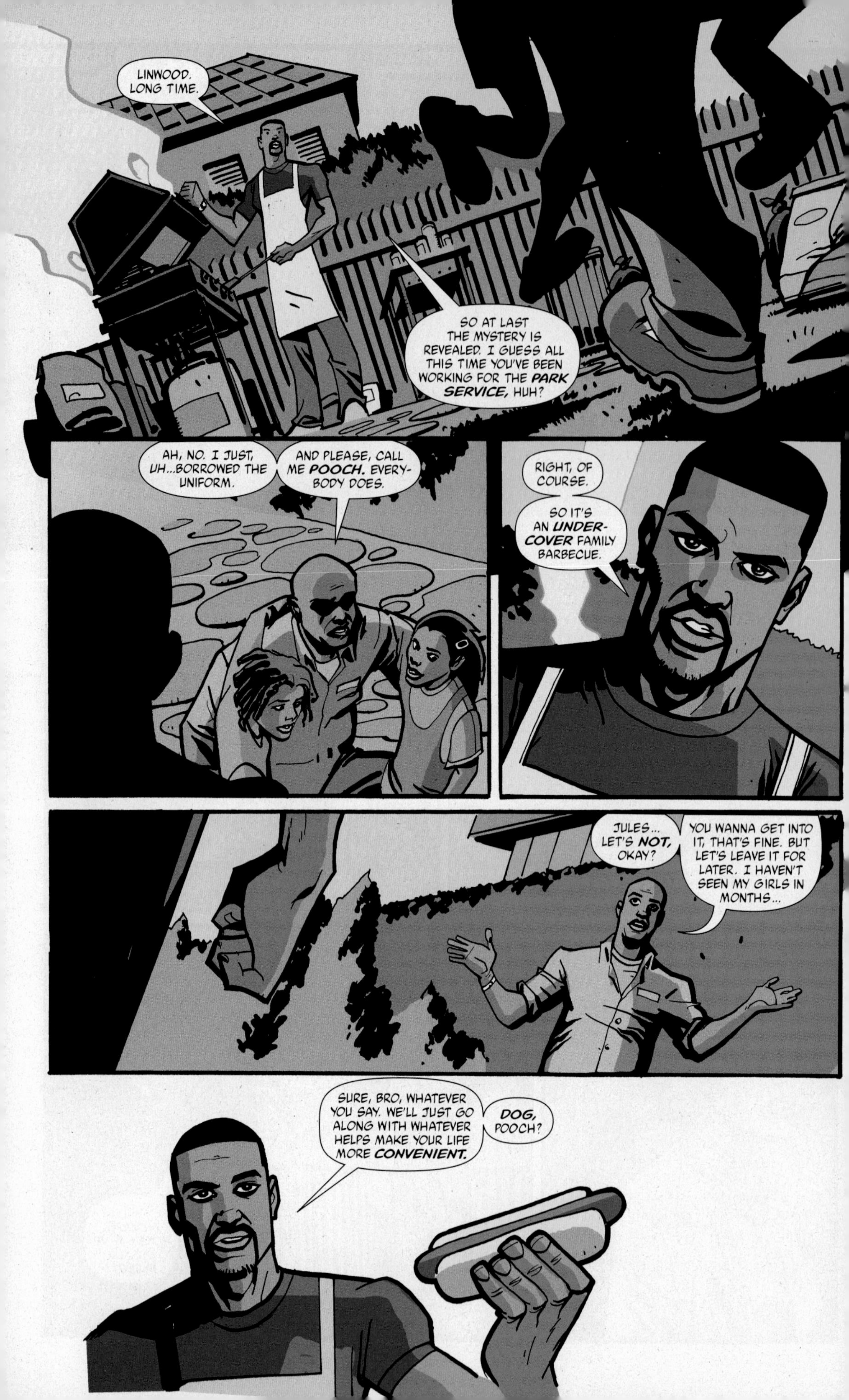

LINWOOD. LONG TIME.
SO AT LAST THE MYSTERY IS REVEALED. I GUESS ALL THIS TIME YOU'VE BEEN WORKING FOR THE **PARK SERVICE,** HUH?
AH, NO. I JUST, UH...BORROWED THE UNIFORM.
AND PLEASE, CALL ME **POOCH.** EVERY-BODY DOES.
RIGHT, OF COURSE.
SO IT'S AN **UNDER-COVER** FAMILY BARBECUE.
JULES... LET'S **NOT,** OKAY?
YOU WANNA GET INTO IT, THAT'S FINE. BUT LET'S LEAVE IT FOR LATER. I HAVEN'T SEEN MY GIRLS IN MONTHS...
SURE, BRO, WHATEVER YOU SAY. WE'LL JUST GO ALONG WITH WHATEVER HELPS MAKE YOUR LIFE MORE **CONVENIENT.**
DOG, POOCH?

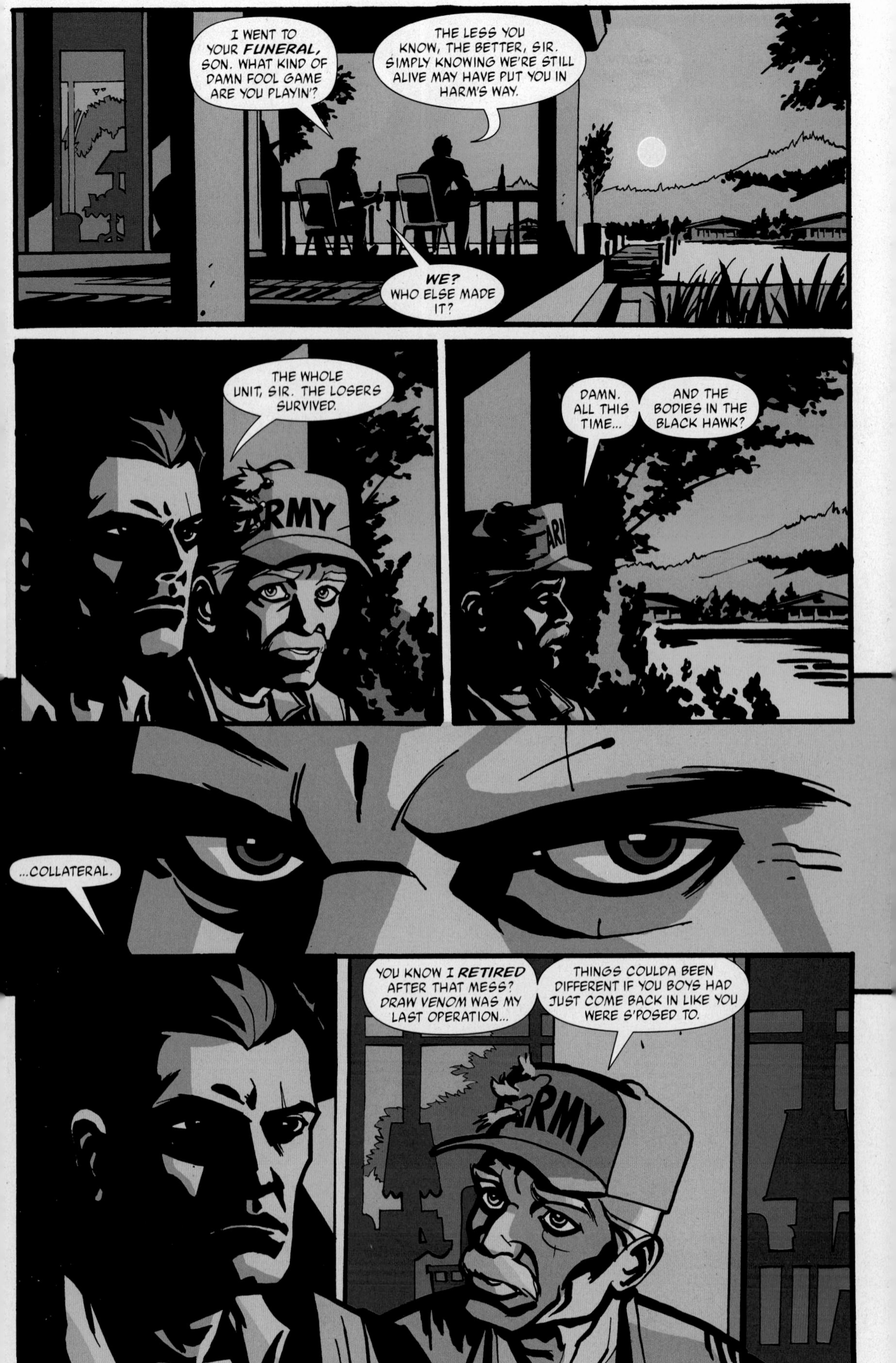
I WENT TO YOUR FUNERAL, SON. WHAT KIND OF DAMN FOOL GAME ARE YOU PLAYIN'?
THE LESS YOU KNOW, THE BETTER, SIR. SIMPLY KNOWING WE'RE STILL ALIVE MAY HAVE PUT YOU IN HARM'S WAY.
WE? WHO ELSE MADE IT?
THE WHOLE UNIT, SIR. THE LOSERS SURVIVED.
ARMY
DAMN. ALL THIS TIME...
AND THE BODIES IN THE BLACK HAWK?
...COLLATERAL.
YOU KNOW I RETIRED AFTER THAT MESS? DRAW VENOM WAS MY LAST OPERATION...
THINGS COULDA BEEN DIFFERENT IF YOU BOYS HAD JUST COME BACK IN LIKE YOU WERE S'POSED TO.
ARMY

WE *COULDN'T* COME BACK IN.

IT WASN'T SOME HAIRY-ASSED TRIBESMAN WITH AN *R.P.G.* BROUGHT DOWN OUR BLACK HAWK, SIR. IT WAS A PAKISTANI *MIRAGE* OUT OF PESHAWAR, ACTING UNDER AGENCY ORDERS.

THAT'S ONE HELL OF AN ALLEGATION, SON. CAN YOU BACK IT UP?

WE INTERCEPTED THE STRIKE CALL.

WE SAW SOMETHING WE SHOULDN'T HAVE. OUR HANDLER DIDN'T WANT IT GETTING OUT.

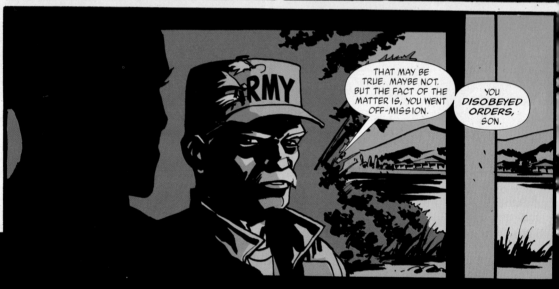

THAT MAY BE TRUE. MAYBE NOT. BUT THE FACT OF THE MATTER IS, YOU WENT OFF-MISSION.

YOU *DISOBEYED ORDERS*, SON.

WITH RESPECT, SIR, MY GRANDFATHER *DIED* FIGHTING AN AXIS THAT WAS "JUST FOLLOWING ORDERS."

EVERY SOLDIER MAKES A CHOICE.

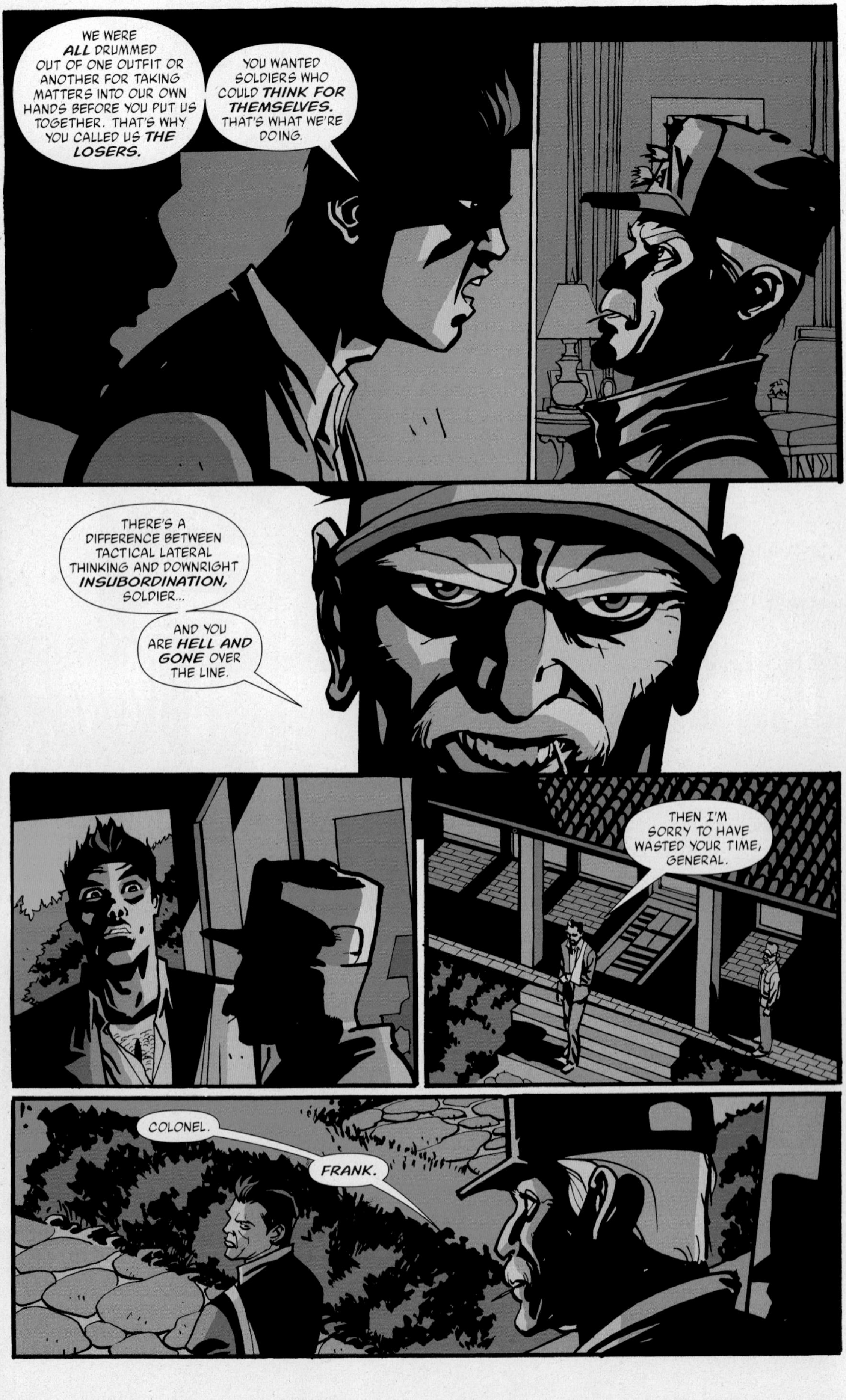
WE WERE ALL DRUMMED OUT OF ONE OUTFIT OR ANOTHER FOR TAKING MATTERS INTO OUR OWN HANDS BEFORE YOU PUT US TOGETHER. THAT'S WHY YOU CALLED US THE LOSERS.
YOU WANTED SOLDIERS WHO COULD THINK FOR THEMSELVES. THAT'S WHAT WE'RE DOING.
THERE'S A DIFFERENCE BETWEEN TACTICAL LATERAL THINKING AND DOWNRIGHT INSUBORDINATION, SOLDIER...
AND YOU ARE HELL AND GONE OVER THE LINE.
THEN I'M SORRY TO HAVE WASTED YOUR TIME, GENERAL.
COLONEL.
FRANK.

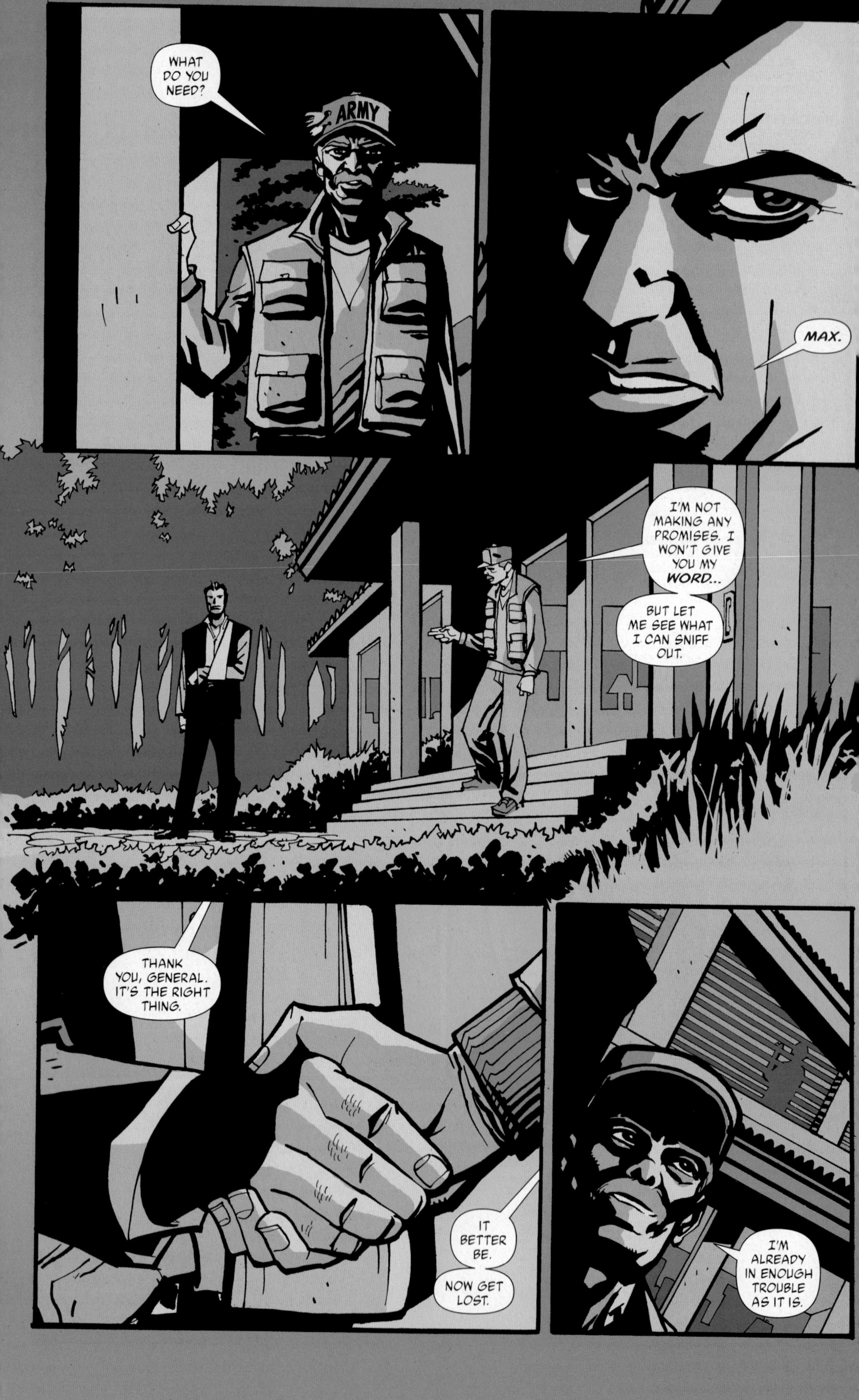
WHAT DO YOU NEED?
MAX.
I'M NOT MAKING ANY PROMISES. I WON'T GIVE YOU MY **WORD...**
BUT LET ME SEE WHAT I CAN SNIFF OUT.
THANK YOU, GENERAL. IT'S THE RIGHT THING.
IT BETTER BE.
NOW GET LOST.
I'M ALREADY IN ENOUGH TROUBLE AS IT IS.

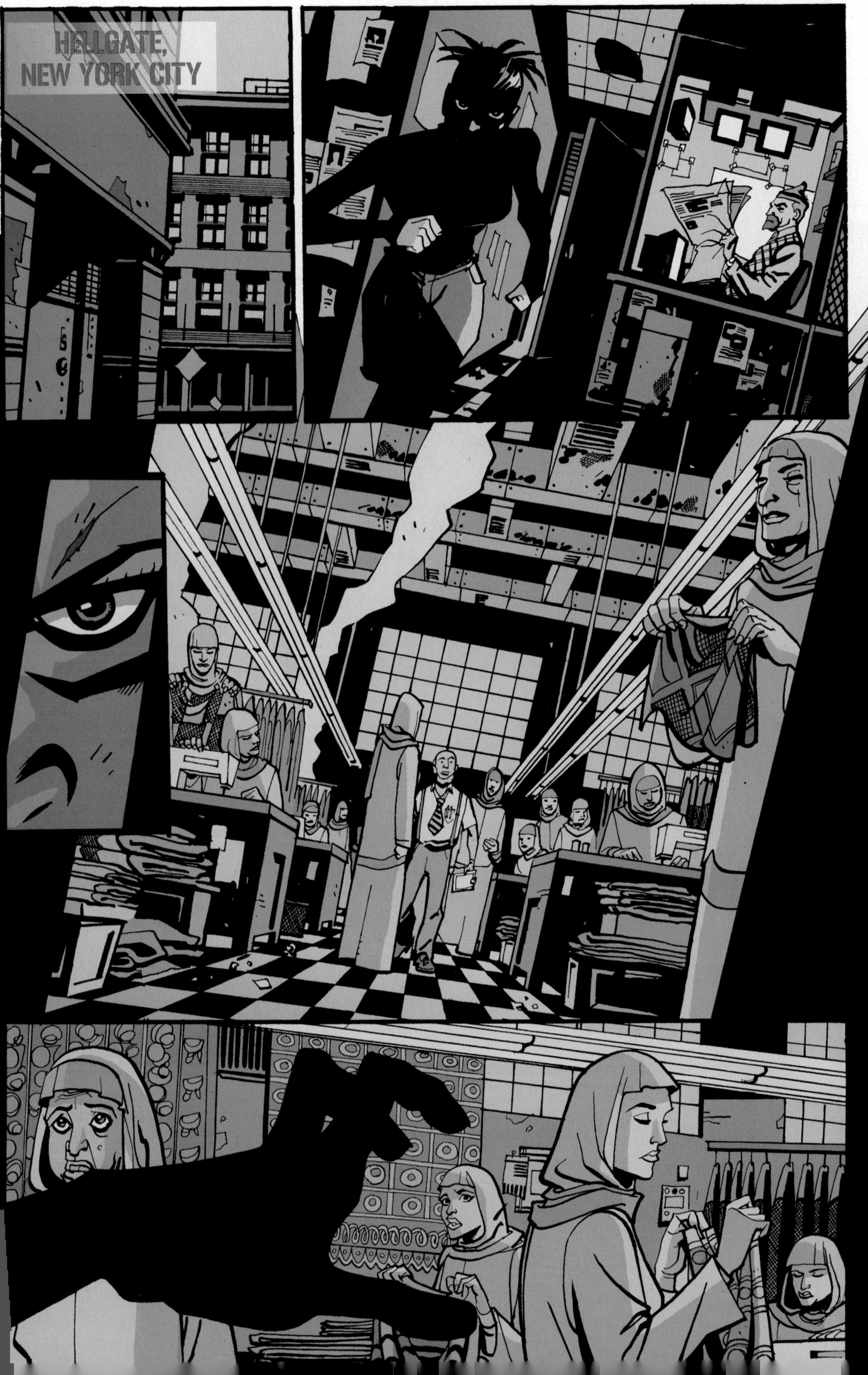
HELLGATE, NEW YORK CITY

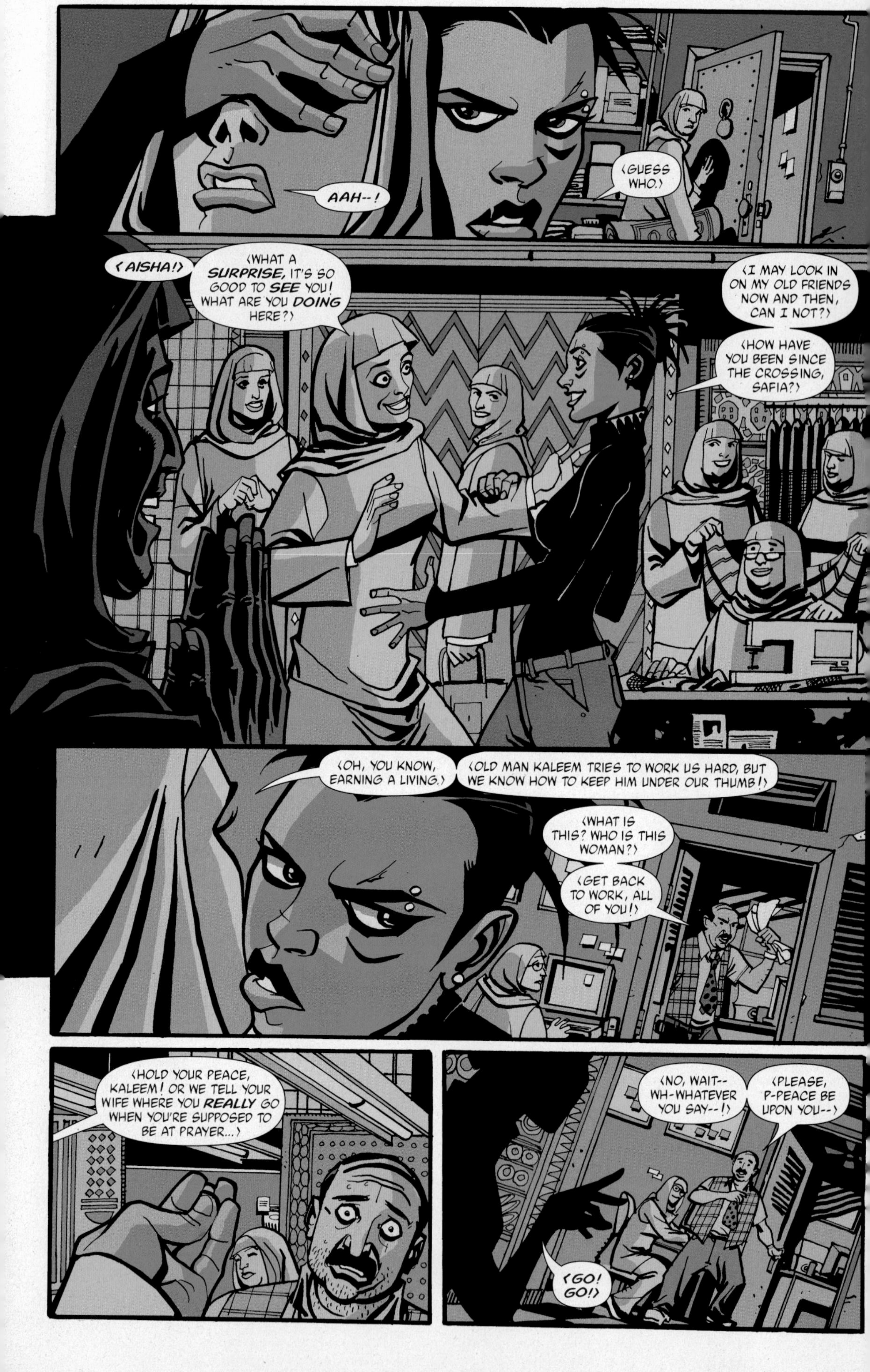

AAH--!
‹GUESS WHO.›
‹AISHA!›
‹WHAT A SURPRISE, IT'S SO GOOD TO SEE YOU! WHAT ARE YOU DOING HERE?›
‹I MAY LOOK IN ON MY OLD FRIENDS NOW AND THEN, CAN I NOT?›
‹HOW HAVE YOU BEEN SINCE THE CROSSING, SAFIA?›
‹OH, YOU KNOW, EARNING A LIVING.›
‹OLD MAN KALEEM TRIES TO WORK US HARD, BUT WE KNOW HOW TO KEEP HIM UNDER OUR THUMB!›
‹WHAT IS THIS? WHO IS THIS WOMAN?›
‹GET BACK TO WORK, ALL OF YOU!›
‹HOLD YOUR PEACE, KALEEM! OR WE TELL YOUR WIFE WHERE YOU REALLY GO WHEN YOU'RE SUPPOSED TO BE AT PRAYER...›
‹NO, WAIT-- WH-WHATEVER YOU SAY--!›
‹PLEASE, P-PEACE BE UPON YOU--›
‹GO! GO!›

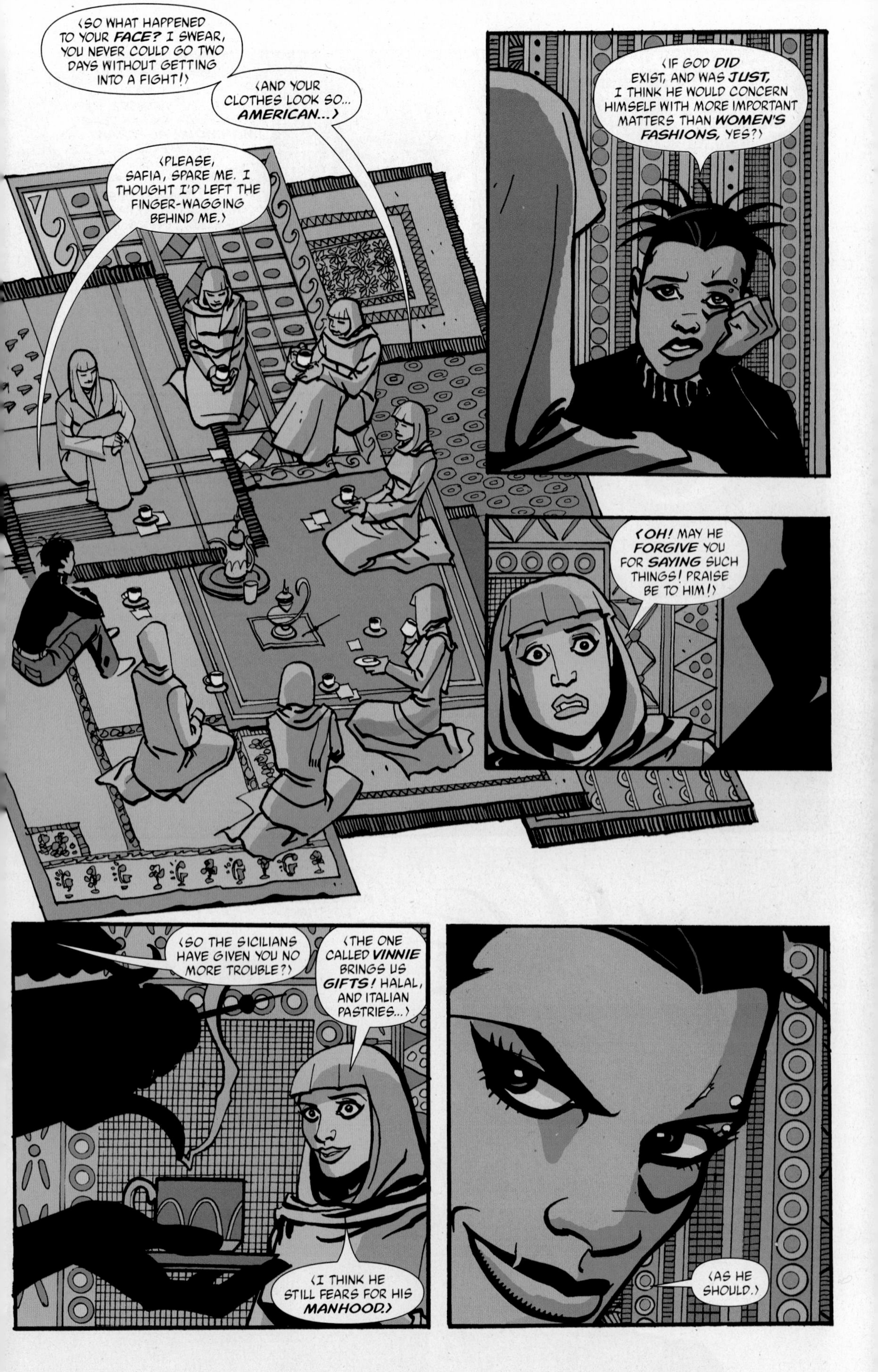
<SO WHAT HAPPENED TO YOUR FACE? I SWEAR, YOU NEVER COULD GO TWO DAYS WITHOUT GETTING INTO A FIGHT!>
<AND YOUR CLOTHES LOOK SO... AMERICAN...>
<PLEASE, SAFIA, SPARE ME. I THOUGHT I'D LEFT THE FINGER-WAGGING BEHIND ME.>
<IF GOD DID EXIST, AND WAS JUST, I THINK HE WOULD CONCERN HIMSELF WITH MORE IMPORTANT MATTERS THAN WOMEN'S FASHIONS, YES?>
<OH! MAY HE FORGIVE YOU FOR SAYING SUCH THINGS! PRAISE BE TO HIM!>
<SO THE SICILIANS HAVE GIVEN YOU NO MORE TROUBLE?>
<THE ONE CALLED VINNIE BRINGS US GIFTS! HALAL, AND ITALIAN PASTRIES...>
<I THINK HE STILL FEARS FOR HIS MANHOOD.>
<AS HE SHOULD.>

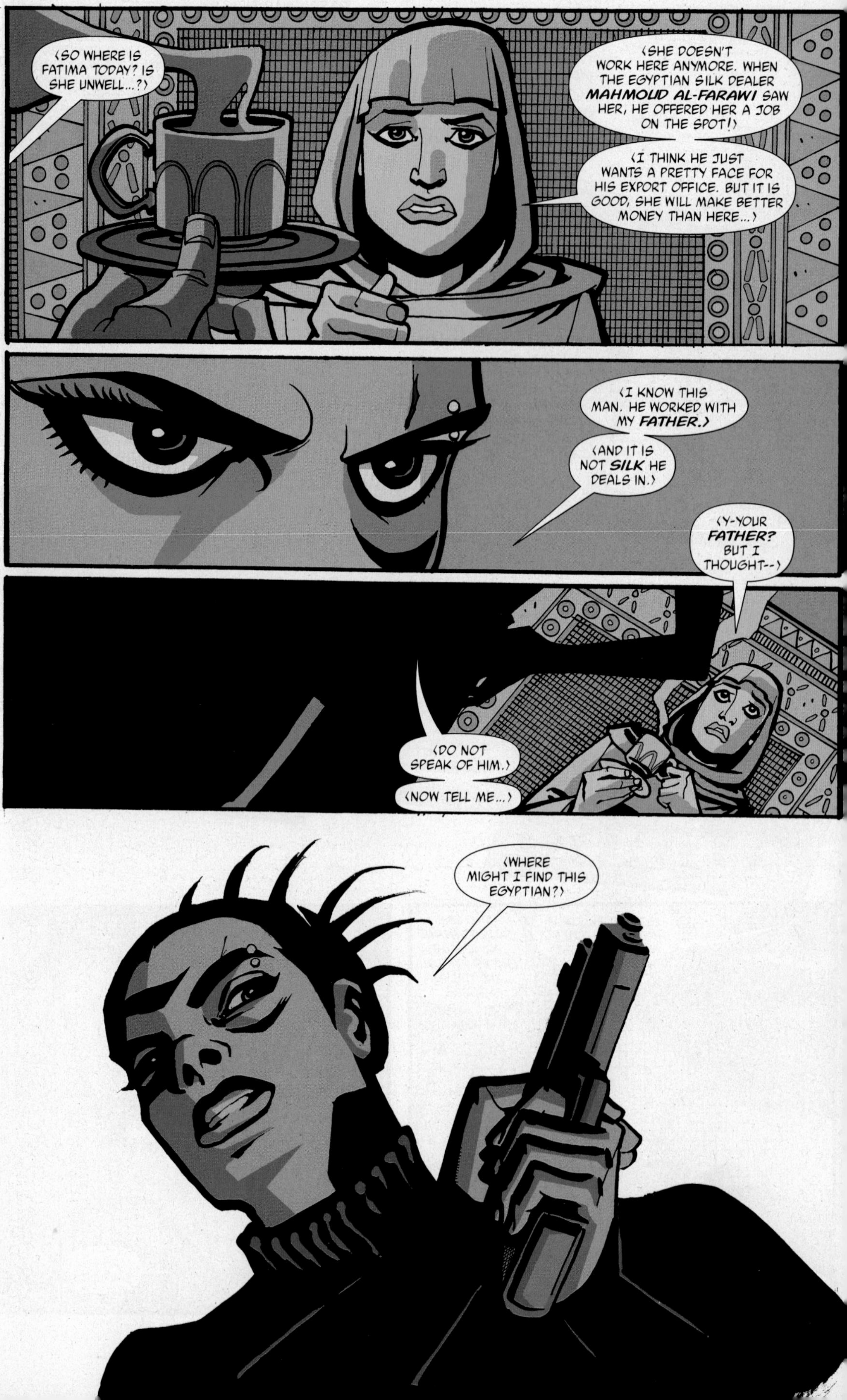
‹SO WHERE IS FATIMA TODAY? IS SHE UNWELL...?›
‹SHE DOESN'T WORK HERE ANYMORE. WHEN THE EGYPTIAN SILK DEALER MAHMOUD AL-FARAWI SAW HER, HE OFFERED HER A JOB ON THE SPOT!›
‹I THINK HE JUST WANTS A PRETTY FACE FOR HIS EXPORT OFFICE. BUT IT IS GOOD, SHE WILL MAKE BETTER MONEY THAN HERE...›
‹I KNOW THIS MAN. HE WORKED WITH MY FATHER.›
‹AND IT IS NOT SILK HE DEALS IN.›
‹Y-YOUR FATHER? BUT I THOUGHT--›
‹DO NOT SPEAK OF HIM.›
‹NOW TELL ME...›
‹WHERE MIGHT I FIND THIS EGYPTIAN?›

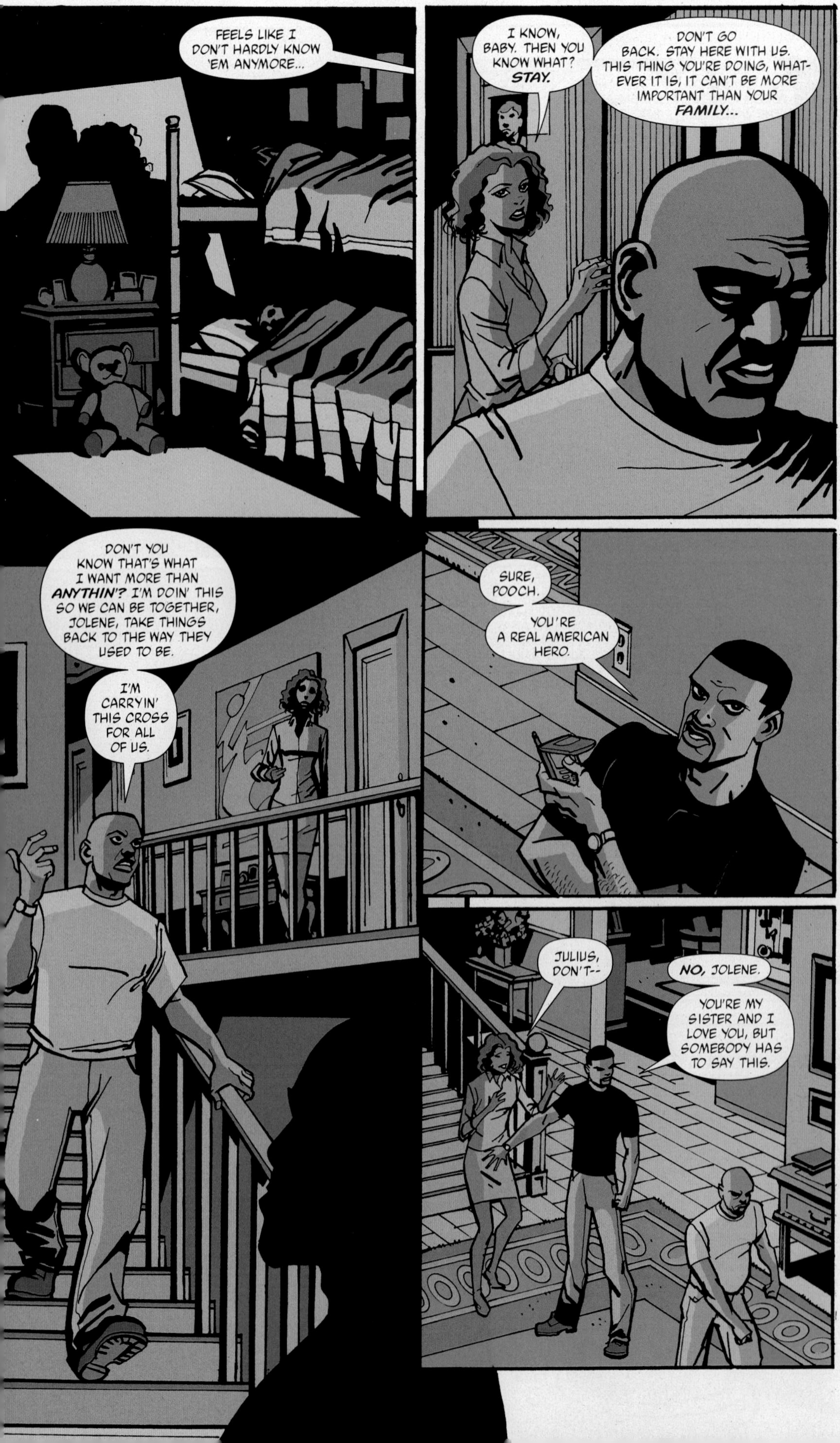
FEELS LIKE I DON'T HARDLY KNOW 'EM ANYMORE...
I KNOW, BABY. THEN YOU KNOW WHAT? STAY.
DON'T GO BACK. STAY HERE WITH US. THIS THING YOU'RE DOING, WHATEVER IT IS, IT CAN'T BE MORE IMPORTANT THAN YOUR FAMILY...
DON'T YOU KNOW THAT'S WHAT I WANT MORE THAN ANYTHIN'? I'M DOIN' THIS SO WE CAN BE TOGETHER, JOLENE, TAKE THINGS BACK TO THE WAY THEY USED TO BE.
I'M CARRYIN' THIS CROSS FOR ALL OF US.
SURE, POOCH.
YOU'RE A REAL AMERICAN HERO.
JULIUS, DON'T--
NO, JOLENE.
YOU'RE MY SISTER AND I LOVE YOU, BUT SOMEBODY HAS TO SAY THIS.

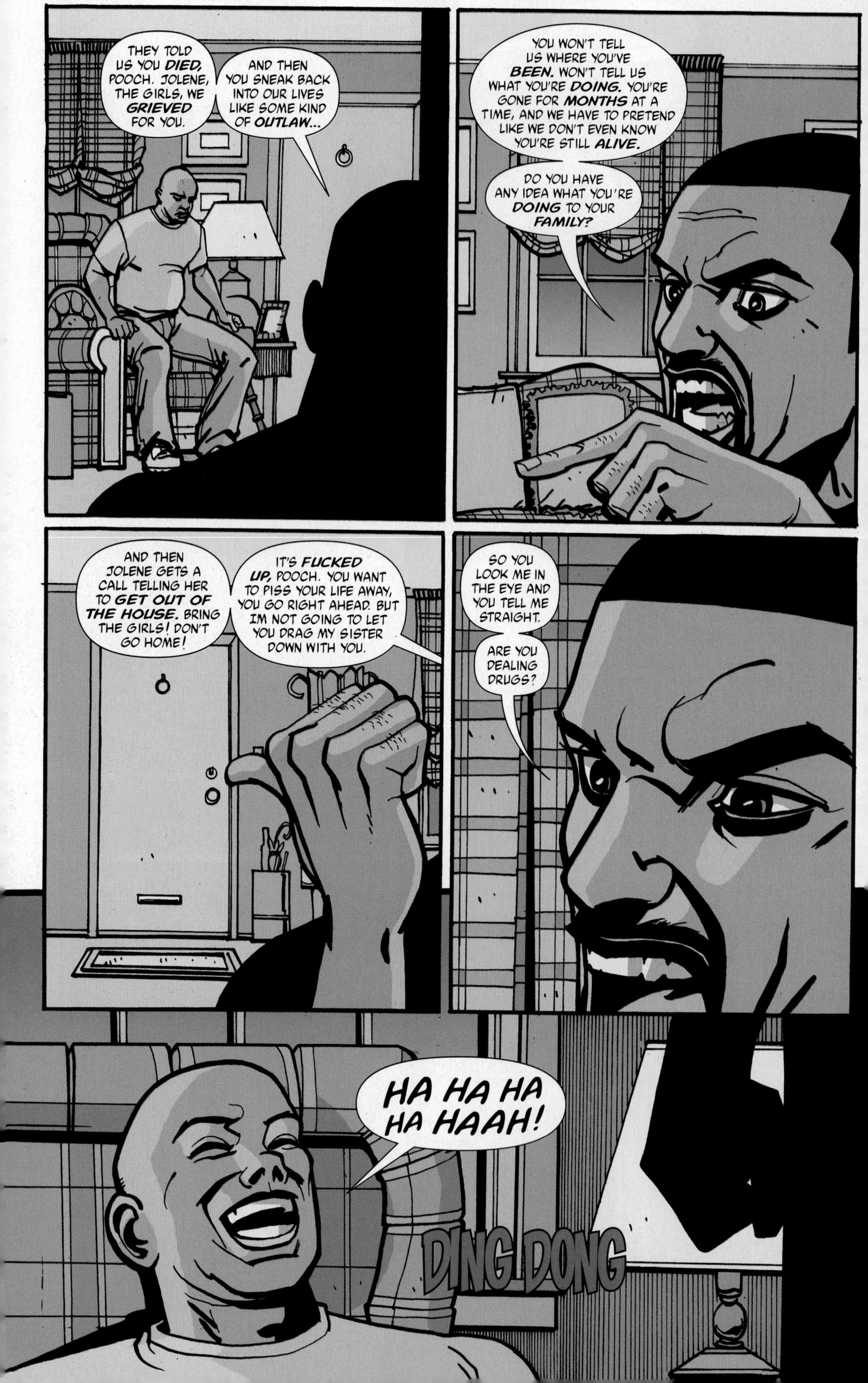
THEY TOLD US YOU DIED, POOCH. JOLENE, THE GIRLS, WE GRIEVED FOR YOU.
AND THEN YOU SNEAK BACK INTO OUR LIVES LIKE SOME KIND OF OUTLAW...
YOU WON'T TELL US WHERE YOU'VE BEEN. WON'T TELL US WHAT YOU'RE DOING. YOU'RE GONE FOR MONTHS AT A TIME, AND WE HAVE TO PRETEND LIKE WE DON'T EVEN KNOW YOU'RE STILL ALIVE.
DO YOU HAVE ANY IDEA WHAT YOU'RE DOING TO YOUR FAMILY?
AND THEN JOLENE GETS A CALL TELLING HER TO GET OUT OF THE HOUSE. BRING THE GIRLS! DON'T GO HOME!
IT'S FUCKED UP, POOCH. YOU WANT TO PISS YOUR LIFE AWAY, YOU GO RIGHT AHEAD. BUT I'M NOT GOING TO LET YOU DRAG MY SISTER DOWN WITH YOU.
SO YOU LOOK ME IN THE EYE AND YOU TELL ME STRAIGHT.
ARE YOU DEALING DRUGS?
HA HA HA HA HAAH!
DING DONG

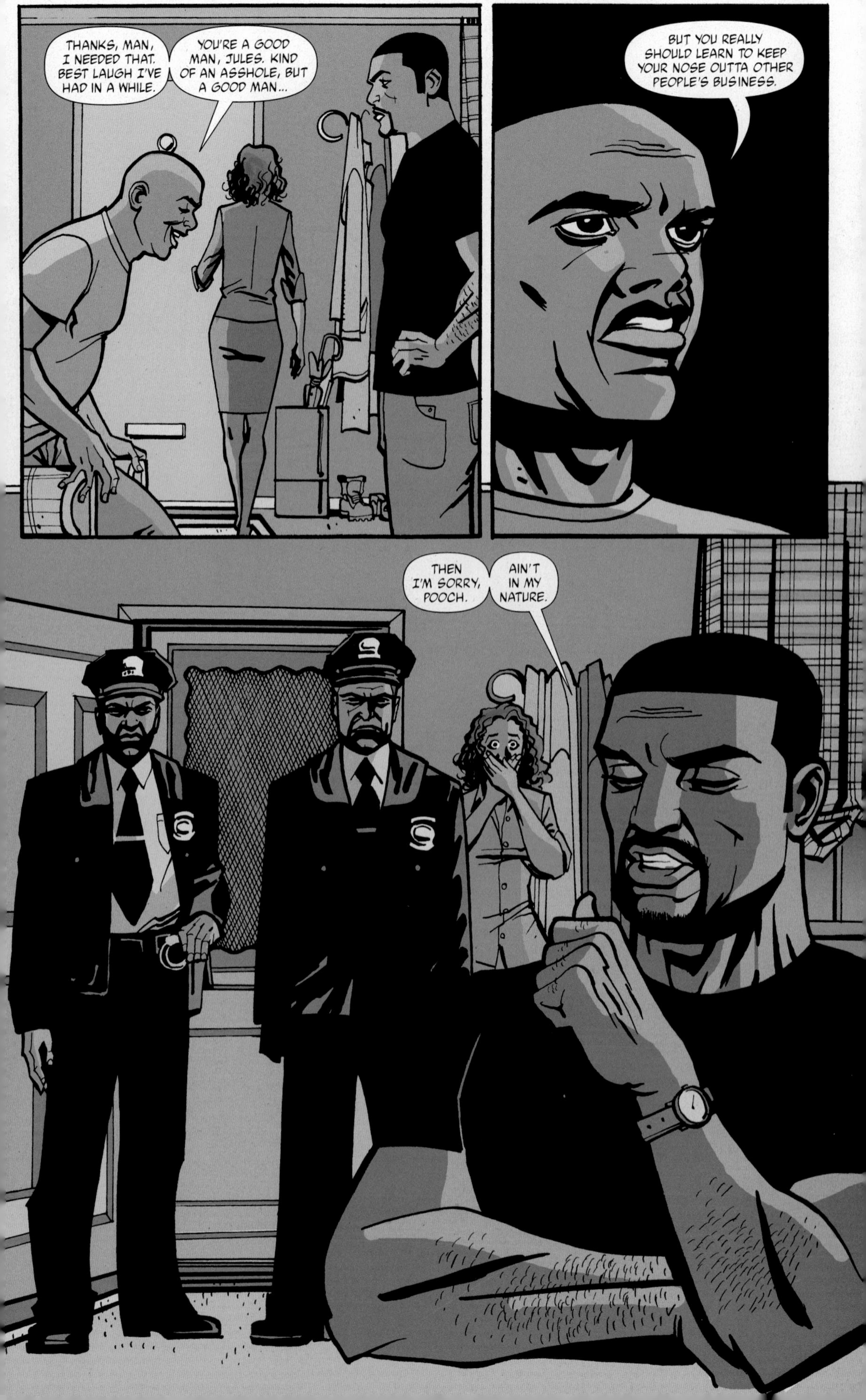
THANKS, MAN, I NEEDED THAT. BEST LAUGH I'VE HAD IN A WHILE.
YOU'RE A GOOD MAN, JULES. KIND OF AN ASSHOLE, BUT A GOOD MAN...
BUT YOU REALLY SHOULD LEARN TO KEEP YOUR NOSE OUTTA OTHER PEOPLE'S BUSINESS.
THEN I'M SORRY, POOCH.
AIN'T IN MY NATURE.

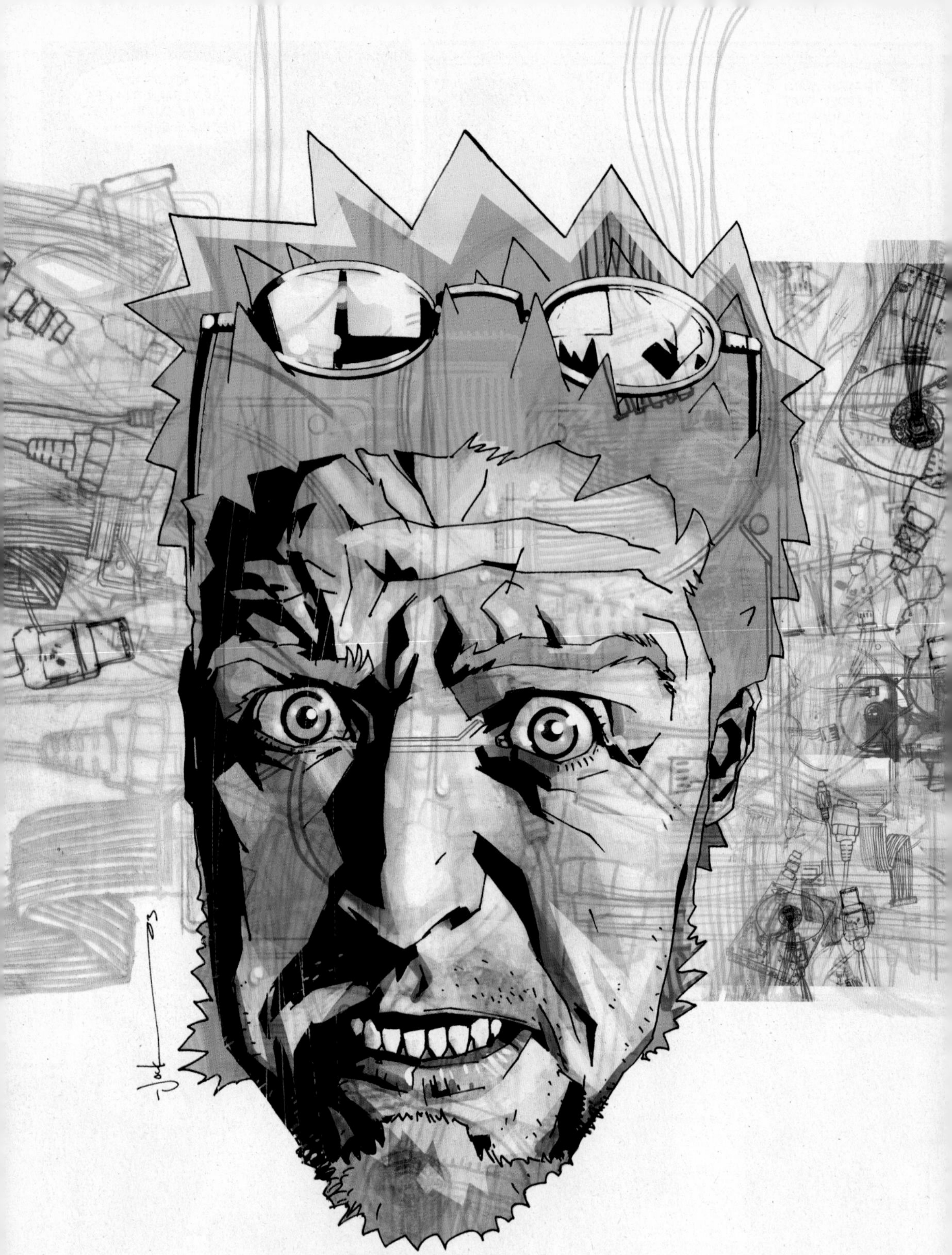

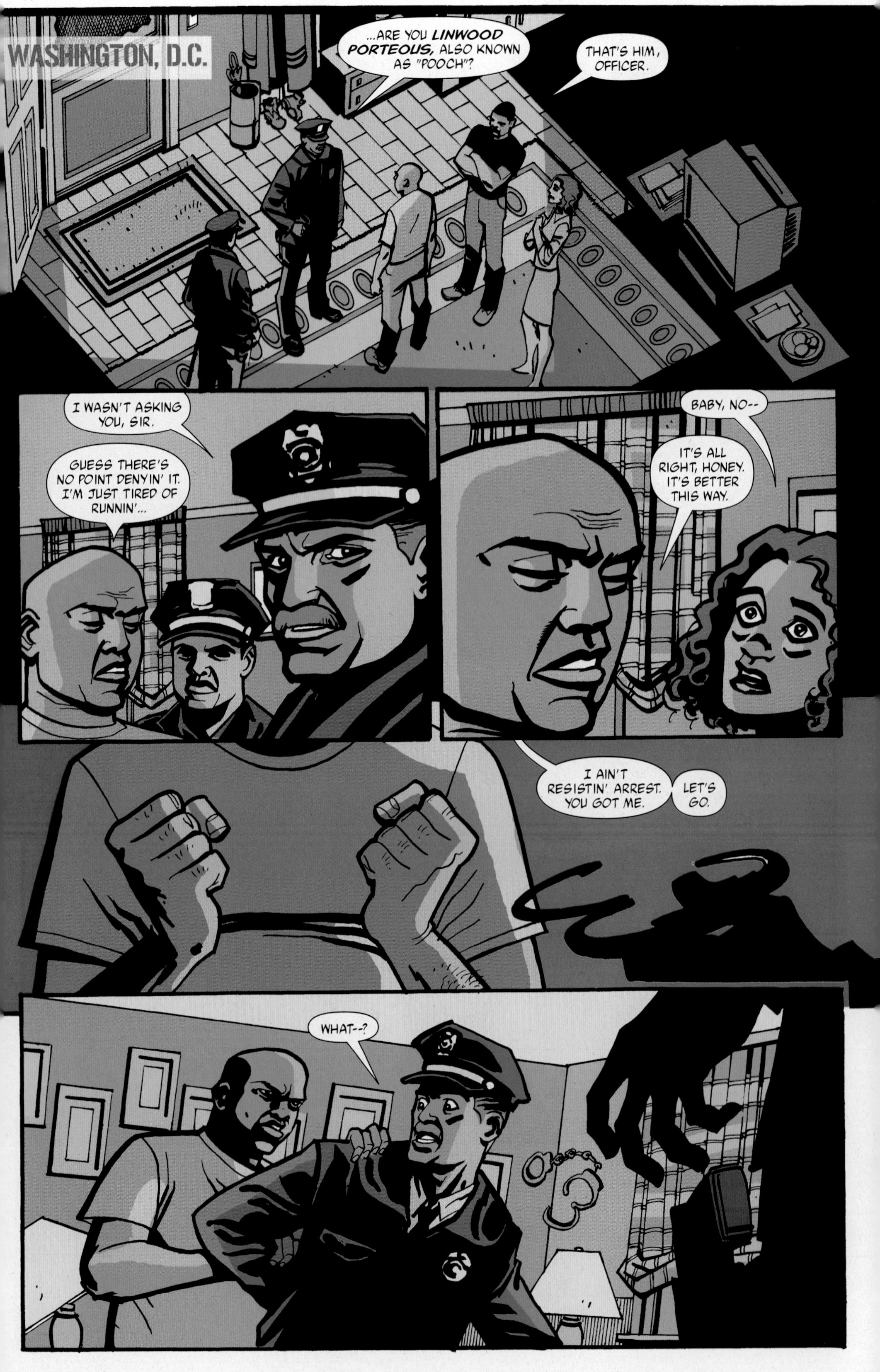
WASHINGTON, D.C.
...ARE YOU **LINWOOD PORTEOUS,** ALSO KNOWN AS "POOCH"?
THAT'S HIM, OFFICER.
I WASN'T ASKING YOU, SIR.
GUESS THERE'S NO POINT DENYIN' IT. I'M JUST TIRED OF RUNNIN'...
BABY, NO--
IT'S ALL RIGHT, HONEY. IT'S BETTER THIS WAY.
I AIN'T RESISTIN' ARREST. YOU GOT ME.
LET'S GO.
WHAT--?

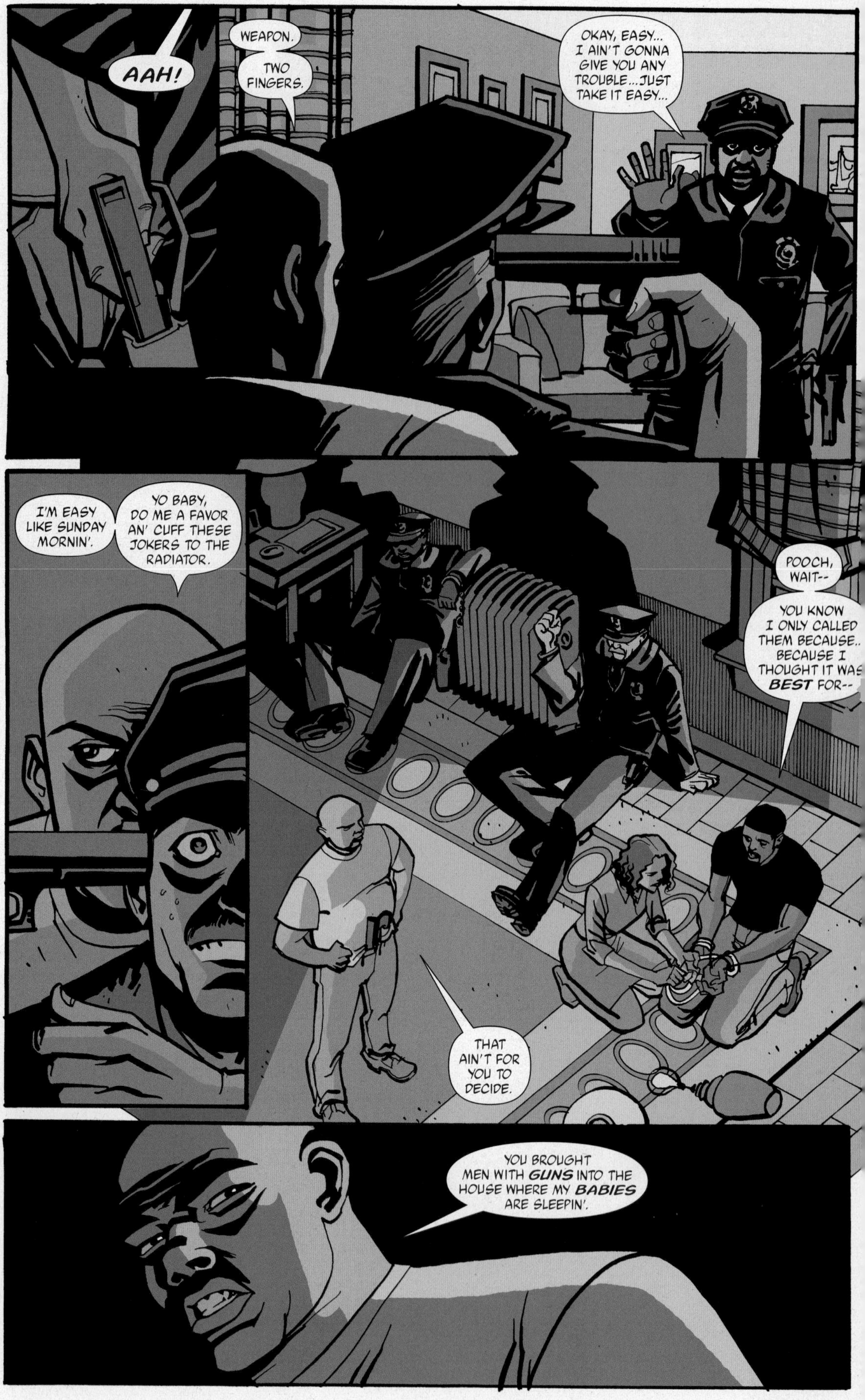
AAH!
WEAPON.
TWO FINGERS.
OKAY, EASY... I AIN'T GONNA GIVE YOU ANY TROUBLE...JUST TAKE IT EASY...
I'M EASY LIKE SUNDAY MORNIN'.
YO BABY, DO ME A FAVOR AN' CUFF THESE JOKERS TO THE RADIATOR.
POOCH, WAIT--
YOU KNOW I ONLY CALLED THEM BECAUSE.. BECAUSE I THOUGHT IT WAS BEST FOR--
THAT AIN'T FOR YOU TO DECIDE.
YOU BROUGHT MEN WITH GUNS INTO THE HOUSE WHERE MY BABIES ARE SLEEPIN'.

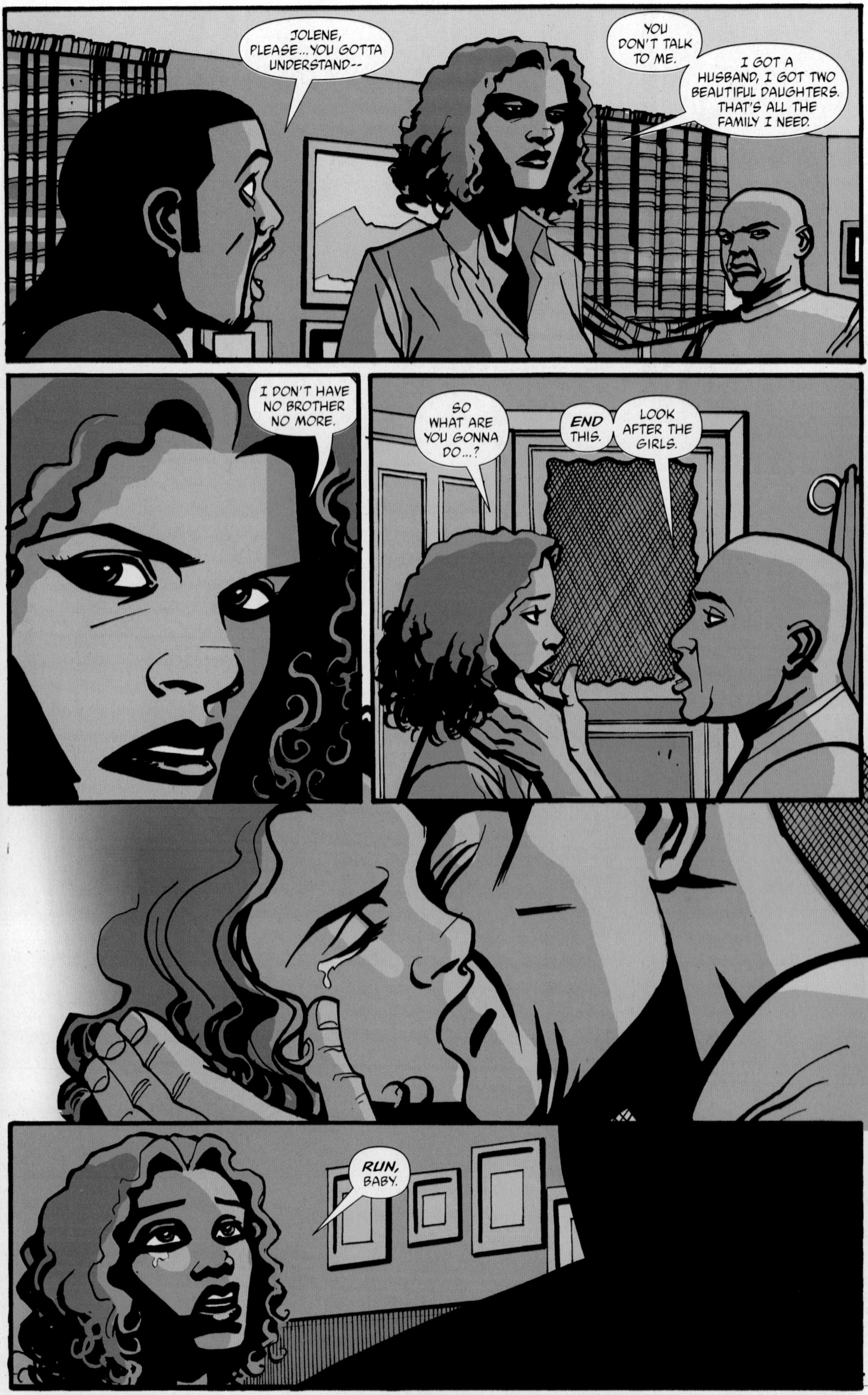
JOLENE, PLEASE... YOU GOTTA UNDERSTAND--
YOU DON'T TALK TO ME.
I GOT A HUSBAND, I GOT TWO BEAUTIFUL DAUGHTERS. THAT'S ALL THE FAMILY I NEED.
I DON'T HAVE NO BROTHER NO MORE.
SO WHAT ARE YOU GONNA DO...?
END THIS.
LOOK AFTER THE GIRLS.
RUN, BABY.

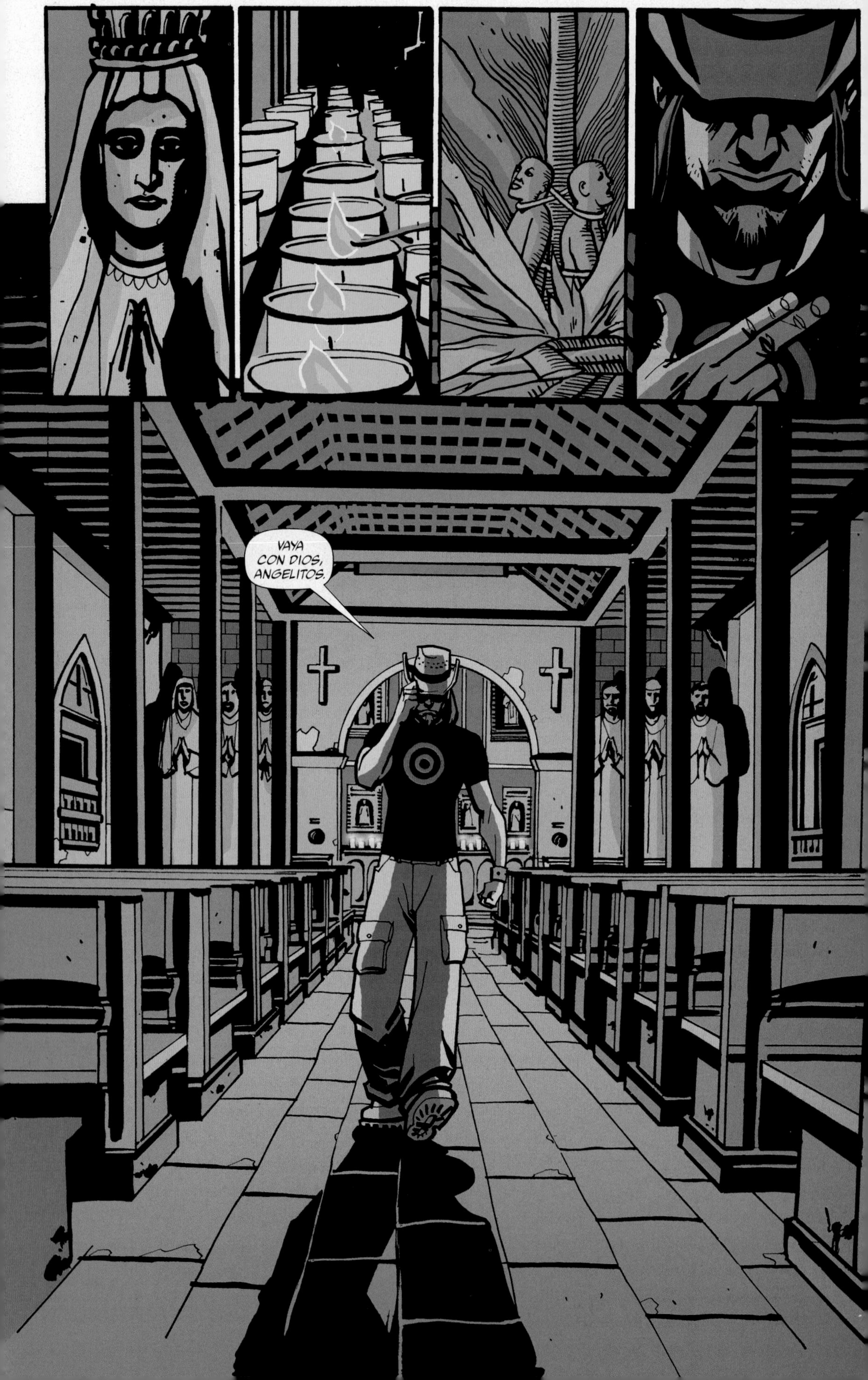
VAYA CON DIOS, ANGELITOS.

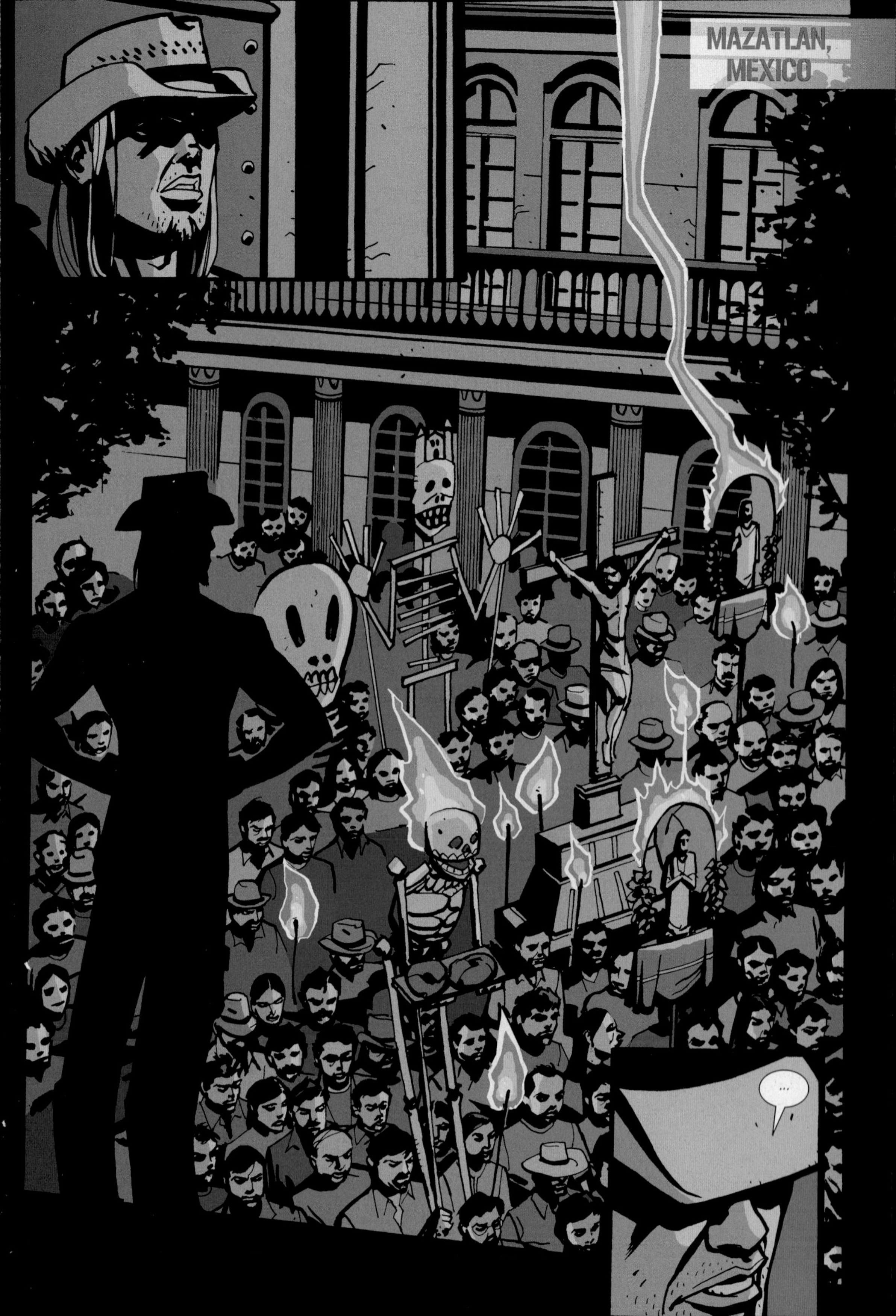
MAZATLAN, MEXICO
...

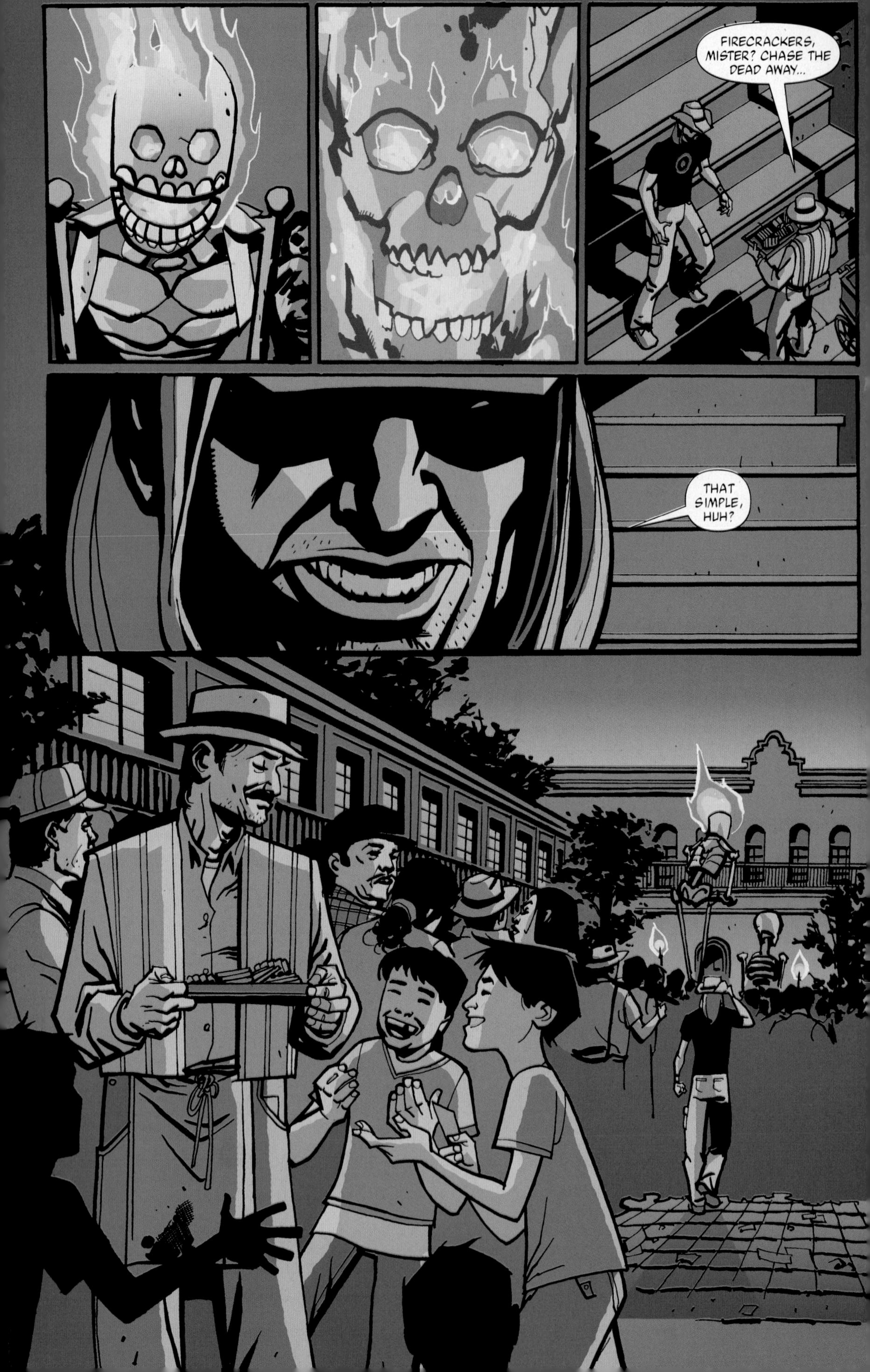
FIRECRACKERS, MISTER? CHASE THE DEAD AWAY...
THAT SIMPLE, HUH?

LYNCHBURG, TENNESSEE

PHILLIP

WHAT DO YOU SAY, SIR?

I'D SAY YOU **STEPPED** IN SOMETHIN', SOLDIER, AN' THE STINK CARRIES ALL THE WAY TO **WASHINGTON.**

CLAY, I'VE DONE SOME DIGGIN'. I MAY BE OUT OF THE GAME THESE DAYS, BUT THERE'S STILL A FEW OLD-TIMERS IN **STATE** OWE ME FAVORS.

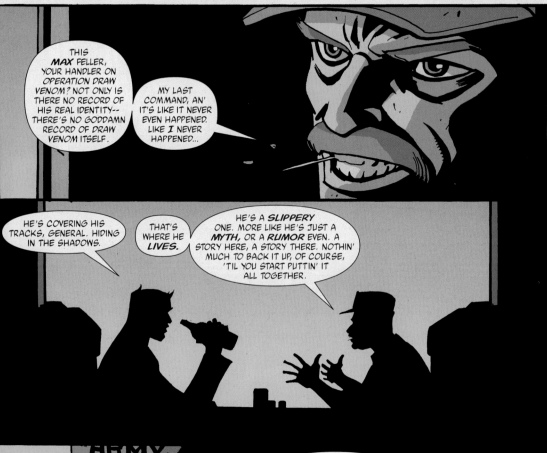

THIS **MAX** FELLER, YOUR HANDLER ON OPERATION DRAW VENOM? NOT ONLY IS THERE NO RECORD OF HIS REAL IDENTITY-- THERE'S NO GODDAMN RECORD OF DRAW VENOM ITSELF.

MY LAST COMMAND, AN' IT'S LIKE IT NEVER EVEN HAPPENED. LIKE **I** NEVER HAPPENED...

HE'S COVERING HIS TRACKS, GENERAL. HIDING IN THE SHADOWS.

THAT'S WHERE HE **LIVES.**

HE'S A **SLIPPERY** ONE. MORE LIKE HE'S JUST A **MYTH,** OR A **RUMOR** EVEN. A STORY HERE, A STORY THERE. NOTHIN' MUCH TO BACK IT UP, OF COURSE, 'TIL YOU START PUTTIN' IT ALL TOGETHER.

ARMY

NEAR AS I CAN TELL, THE MAX CODENAME GOES BACK AS FAR AS THE AGENCY ITSELF.

FURTHER, EVEN...

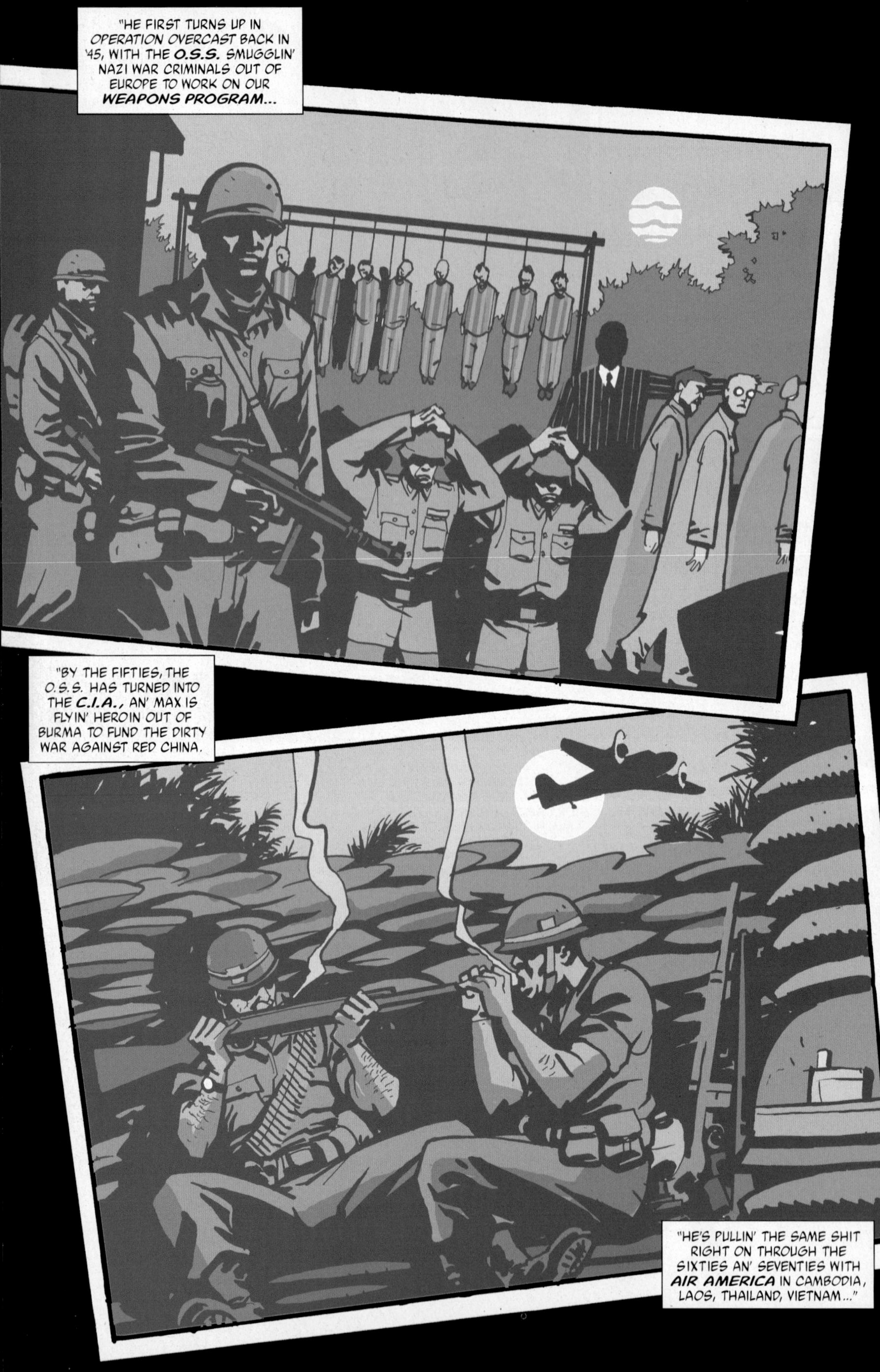
"HE FIRST TURNS UP IN OPERATION OVERCAST BACK IN '45, WITH THE O.S.S. SMUGGLIN' NAZI WAR CRIMINALS OUT OF EUROPE TO WORK ON OUR WEAPONS PROGRAM...
"BY THE FIFTIES, THE O.S.S. HAS TURNED INTO THE C.I.A., AN' MAX IS FLYIN' HEROIN OUT OF BURMA TO FUND THE DIRTY WAR AGAINST RED CHINA.
"HE'S PULLIN' THE SAME SHIT RIGHT ON THROUGH THE SIXTIES AN' SEVENTIES WITH AIR AMERICA IN CAMBODIA, LAOS, THAILAND, VIETNAM..."

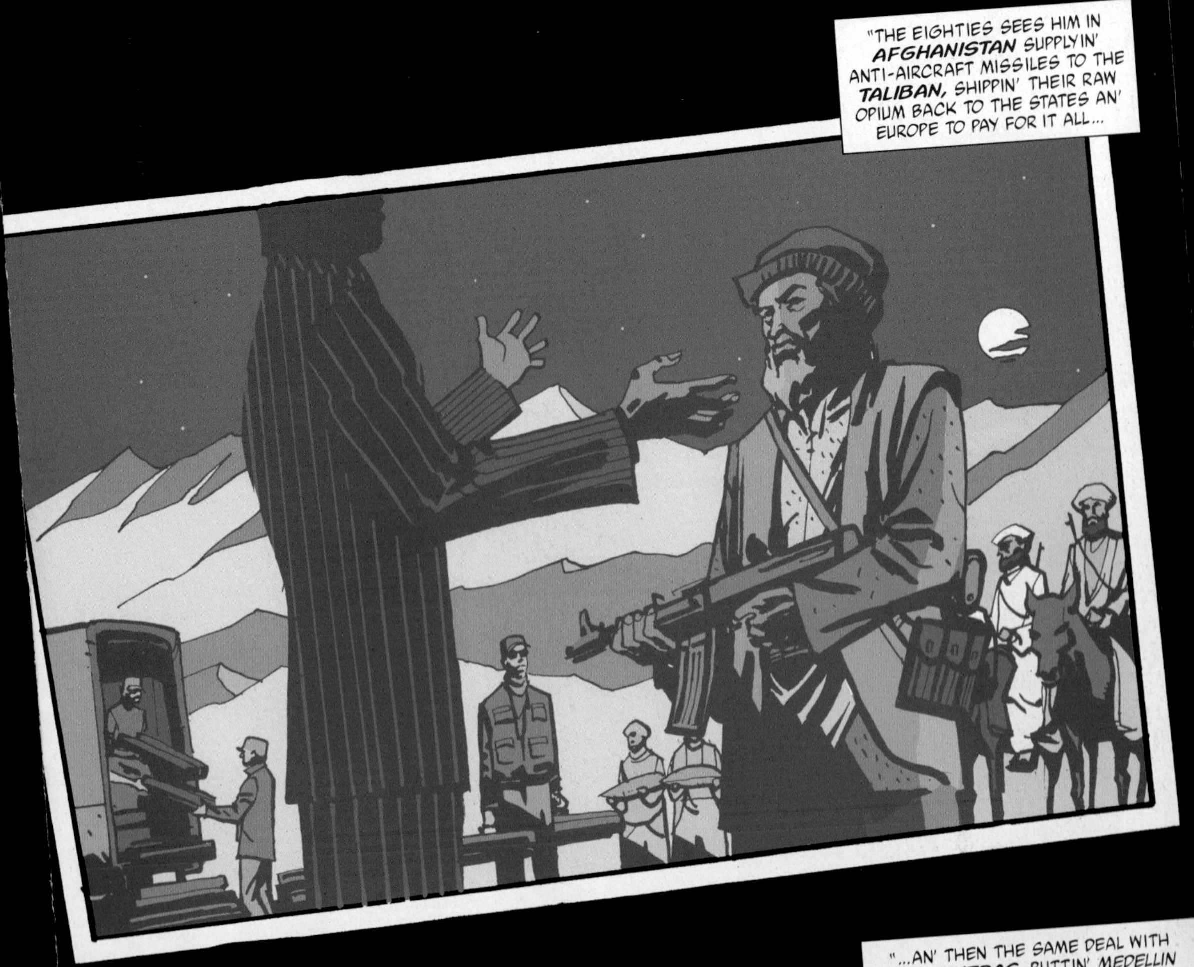
"THE EIGHTIES SEES HIM IN **AFGHANISTAN** SUPPLYIN' ANTI-AIRCRAFT MISSILES TO THE **TALIBAN,** SHIPPIN' THEIR RAW OPIUM BACK TO THE STATES AN' EUROPE TO PAY FOR IT ALL...

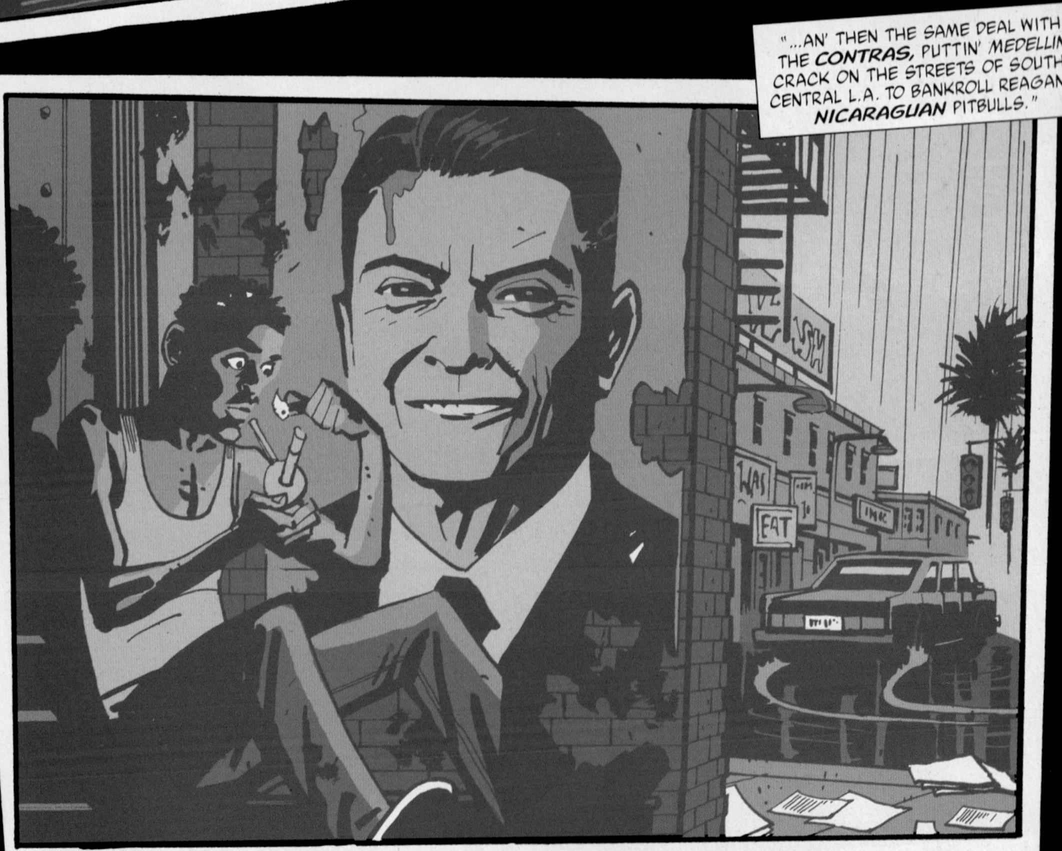
"...AN' THEN THE SAME DEAL WITH THE **CONTRAS,** PUTTIN' MEDELLIN CRACK ON THE STREETS OF SOUTH-CENTRAL L.A. TO BANKROLL REAGAN'S **NICARAGUAN** PITBULLS."
EAT

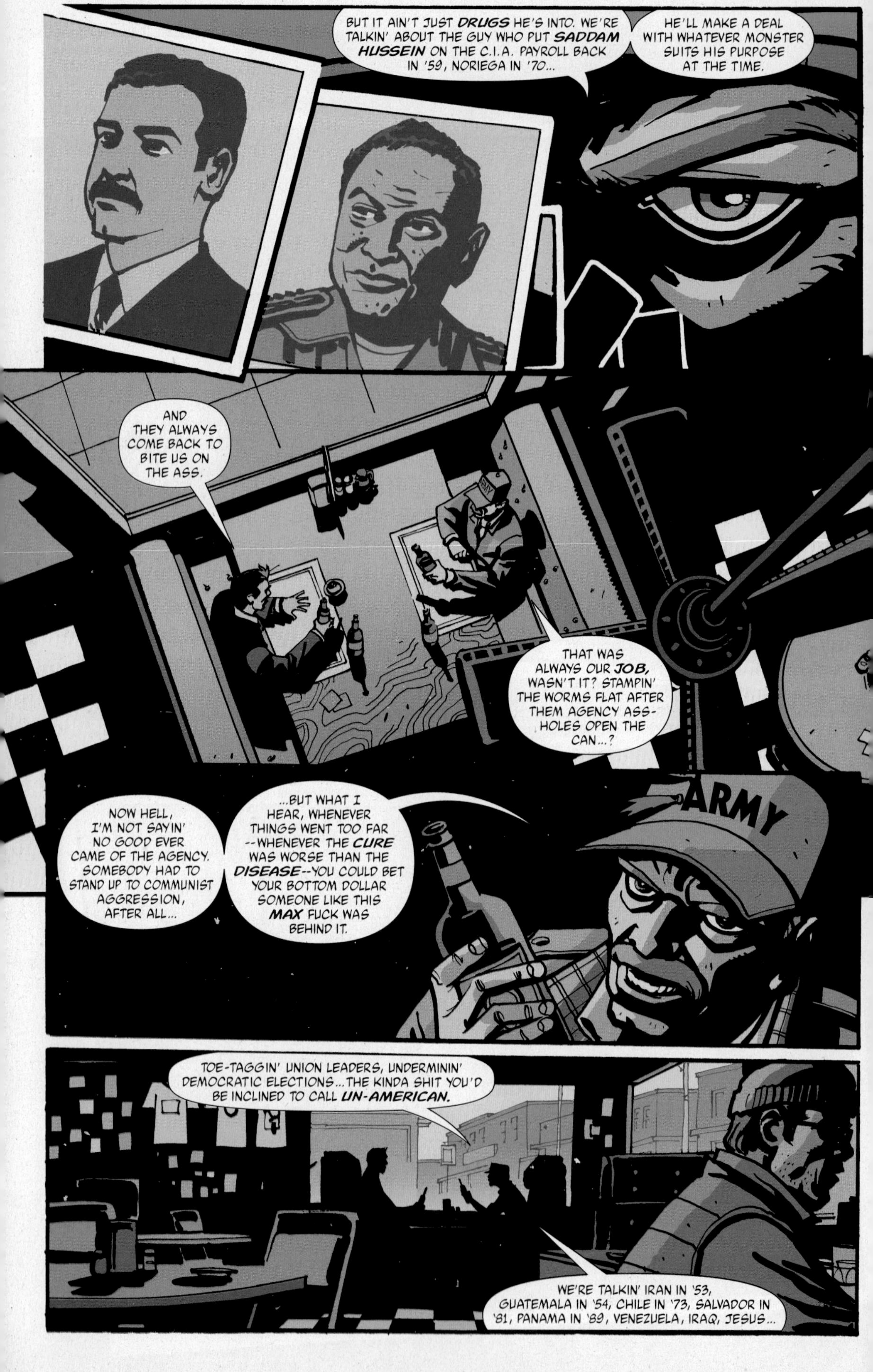
BUT IT AIN'T JUST DRUGS HE'S INTO. WE'RE TALKIN' ABOUT THE GUY WHO PUT SADDAM HUSSEIN ON THE C.I.A. PAYROLL BACK IN '59, NORIEGA IN '70...
HE'LL MAKE A DEAL WITH WHATEVER MONSTER SUITS HIS PURPOSE AT THE TIME.
AND THEY ALWAYS COME BACK TO BITE US ON THE ASS.
ARMY
THAT WAS ALWAYS OUR JOB, WASN'T IT? STAMPIN' THE WORMS FLAT AFTER THEM AGENCY ASS-HOLES OPEN THE CAN...?
NOW HELL, I'M NOT SAYIN' NO GOOD EVER CAME OF THE AGENCY. SOMEBODY HAD TO STAND UP TO COMMUNIST AGGRESSION, AFTER ALL...
...BUT WHAT I HEAR, WHENEVER THINGS WENT TOO FAR --WHENEVER THE CURE WAS WORSE THAN THE DISEASE--YOU COULD BET YOUR BOTTOM DOLLAR SOMEONE LIKE THIS MAX FUCK WAS BEHIND IT.
ARMY
TOE-TAGGIN' UNION LEADERS, UNDERMININ' DEMOCRATIC ELECTIONS... THE KINDA SHIT YOU'D BE INCLINED TO CALL UN-AMERICAN.
WE'RE TALKIN' IRAN IN '53, GUATEMALA IN '54, CHILE IN '73, SALVADOR IN '81, PANAMA IN '89, VENEZUELA, IRAQ, JESUS...

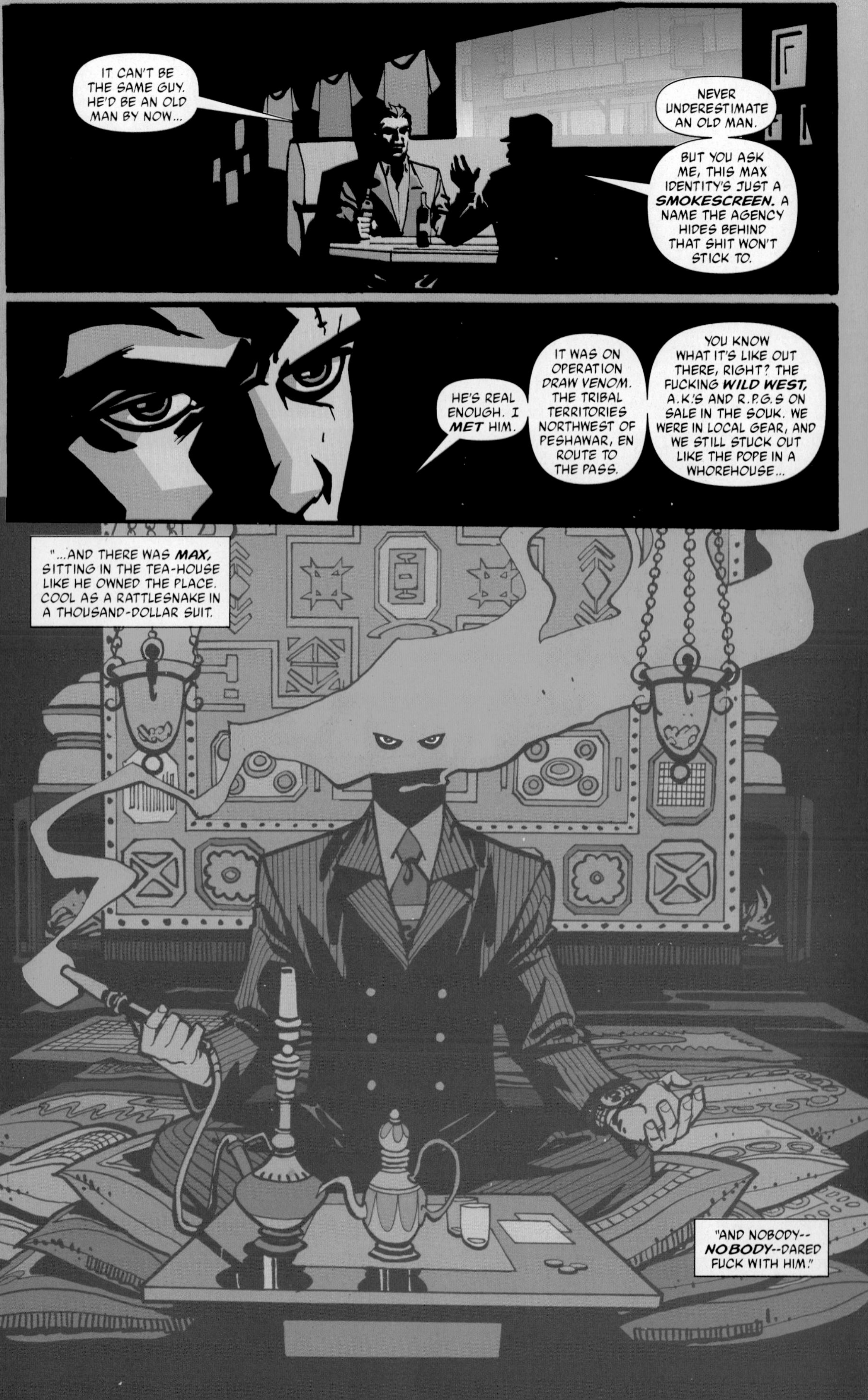

IT CAN'T BE THE SAME GUY. HE'D BE AN OLD MAN BY NOW...
NEVER UNDERESTIMATE AN OLD MAN.
BUT YOU ASK ME, THIS MAX IDENTITY'S JUST A **SMOKESCREEN.** A NAME THE AGENCY HIDES BEHIND THAT SHIT WON'T STICK TO.
HE'S REAL ENOUGH. I **MET** HIM.
IT WAS ON OPERATION DRAW VENOM. THE TRIBAL TERRITORIES NORTHWEST OF PESHAWAR, EN ROUTE TO THE PASS.
YOU KNOW WHAT IT'S LIKE OUT THERE, RIGHT? THE FUCKING **WILD WEST,** A.K.'S AND R.P.G.S ON SALE IN THE SOUK. WE WERE IN LOCAL GEAR, AND WE STILL STUCK OUT LIKE THE POPE IN A WHOREHOUSE...
"...AND THERE WAS **MAX,** SITTING IN THE TEA-HOUSE LIKE HE OWNED THE PLACE. COOL AS A RATTLESNAKE IN A THOUSAND-DOLLAR SUIT.
"AND NOBODY-- **NOBODY**--DARED FUCK WITH HIM."

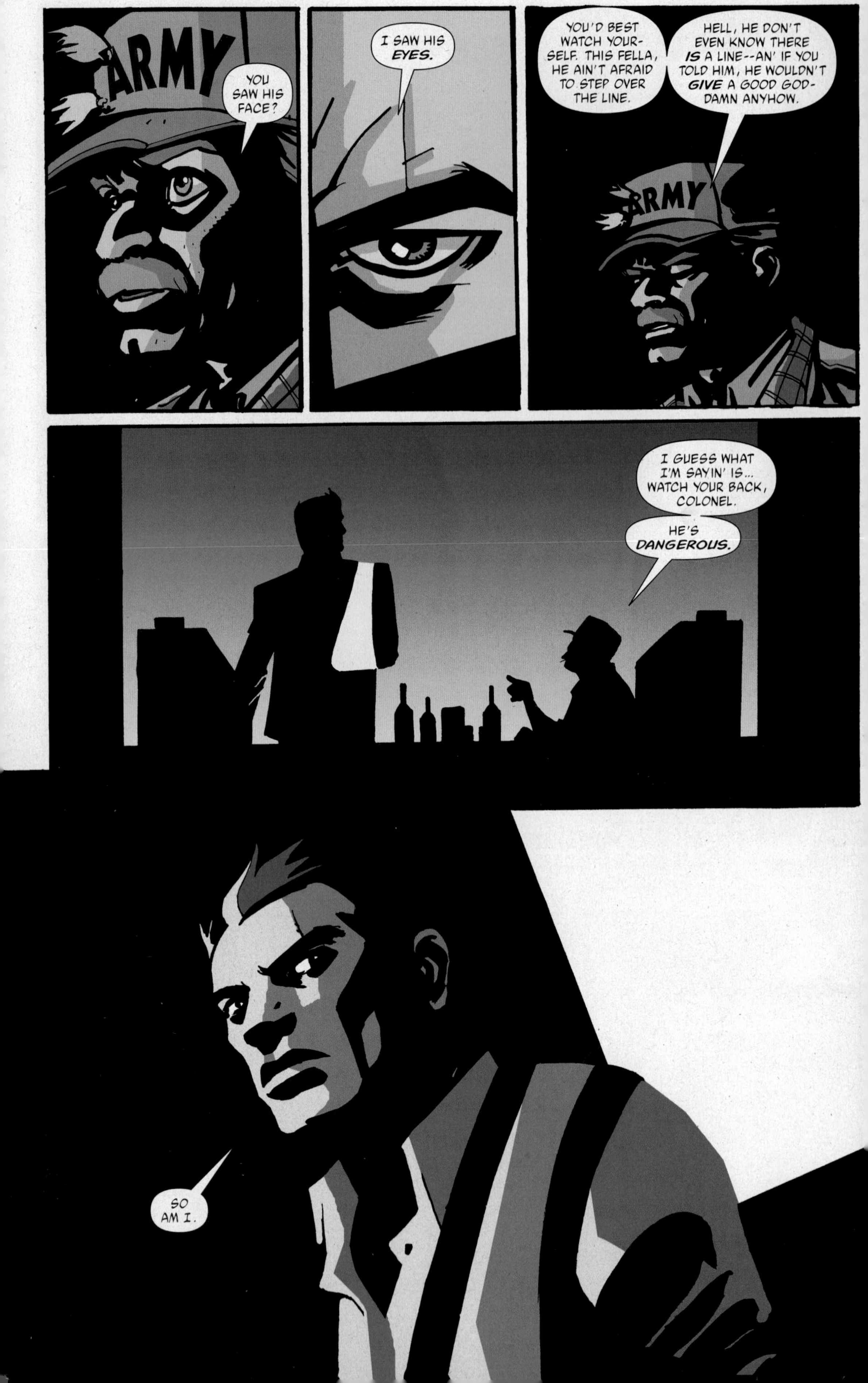
ARMY
YOU SAW HIS FACE?
I SAW HIS *EYES.*
YOU'D BEST WATCH YOUR-SELF. THIS FELLA, HE AIN'T AFRAID TO STEP OVER THE LINE.
HELL, HE DON'T EVEN KNOW THERE *IS* A LINE--AN' IF YOU TOLD HIM, HE WOULDN'T *GIVE* A GOOD GOD-DAMN ANYHOW.
ARMY
I GUESS WHAT I'M SAYIN' IS... WATCH YOUR BACK, COLONEL.
HE'S *DANGEROUS.*
SO AM I.

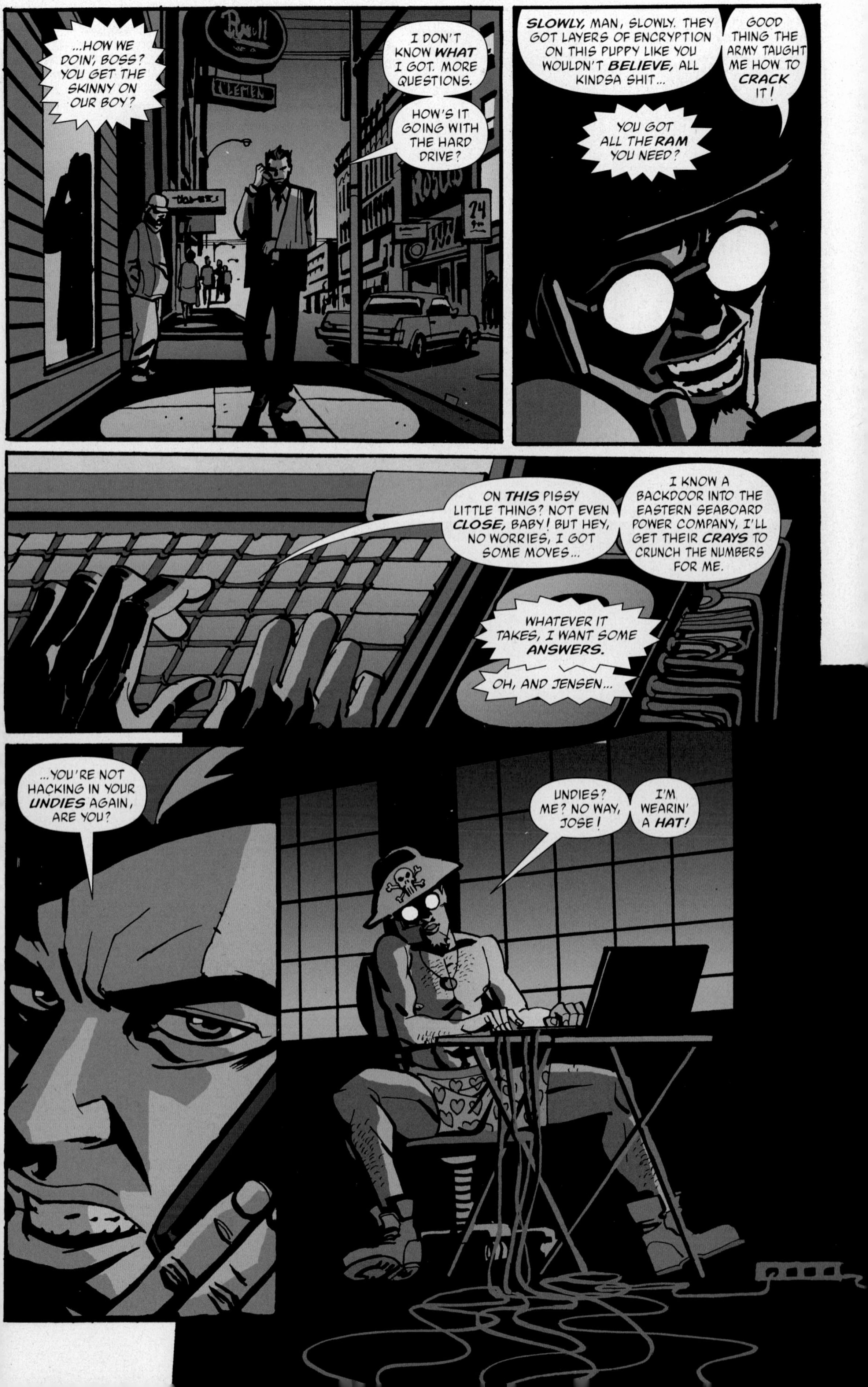
...HOW WE DOIN', BOSS? YOU GET THE SKINNY ON OUR BOY?
I DON'T KNOW WHAT I GOT. MORE QUESTIONS.
HOW'S IT GOING WITH THE HARD DRIVE?
SLOWLY, MAN, SLOWLY. THEY GOT LAYERS OF ENCRYPTION ON THIS PUPPY LIKE YOU WOULDN'T BELIEVE, ALL KINDSA SHIT...
GOOD THING THE ARMY TAUGHT ME HOW TO CRACK IT!
YOU GOT ALL THE RAM YOU NEED?
ON THIS PISSY LITTLE THING? NOT EVEN CLOSE, BABY! BUT HEY, NO WORRIES, I GOT SOME MOVES...
I KNOW A BACKDOOR INTO THE EASTERN SEABOARD POWER COMPANY, I'LL GET THEIR CRAYS TO CRUNCH THE NUMBERS FOR ME.
WHATEVER IT TAKES, I WANT SOME ANSWERS.
OH, AND JENSEN...
...YOU'RE NOT HACKING IN YOUR UNDIES AGAIN, ARE YOU?
UNDIES? ME? NO WAY, JOSE!
I'M WEARIN' A HAT!

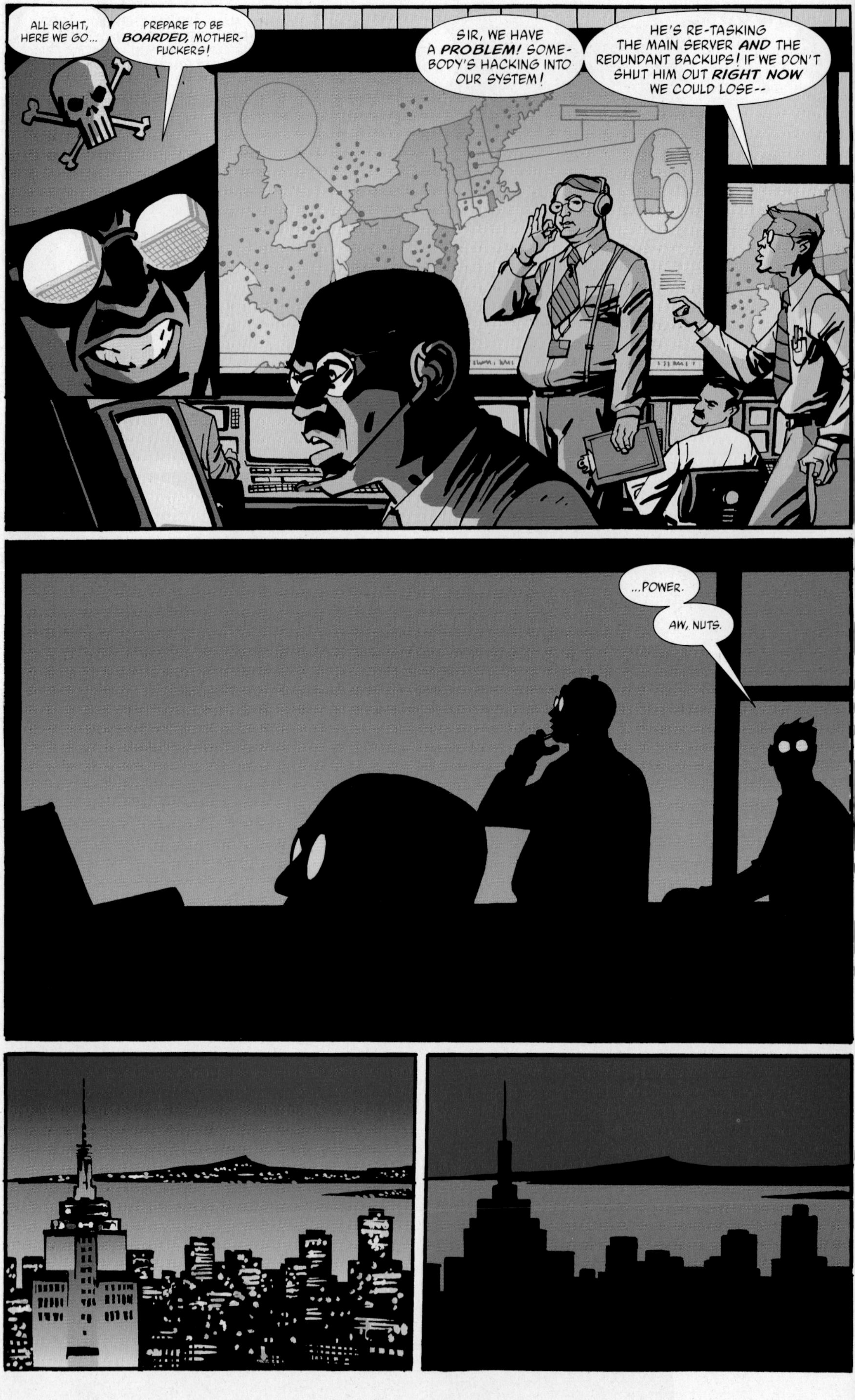
ALL RIGHT, HERE WE GO...
PREPARE TO BE **BOARDED,** MOTHER-FUCKERS!
SIR, WE HAVE A **PROBLEM!** SOMEBODY'S HACKING INTO OUR SYSTEM!
HE'S RE-TASKING THE MAIN SERVER **AND** THE REDUNDANT BACKUPS! IF WE DON'T SHUT HIM OUT **RIGHT NOW** WE COULD LOSE--
...POWER.
AW, NUTS.

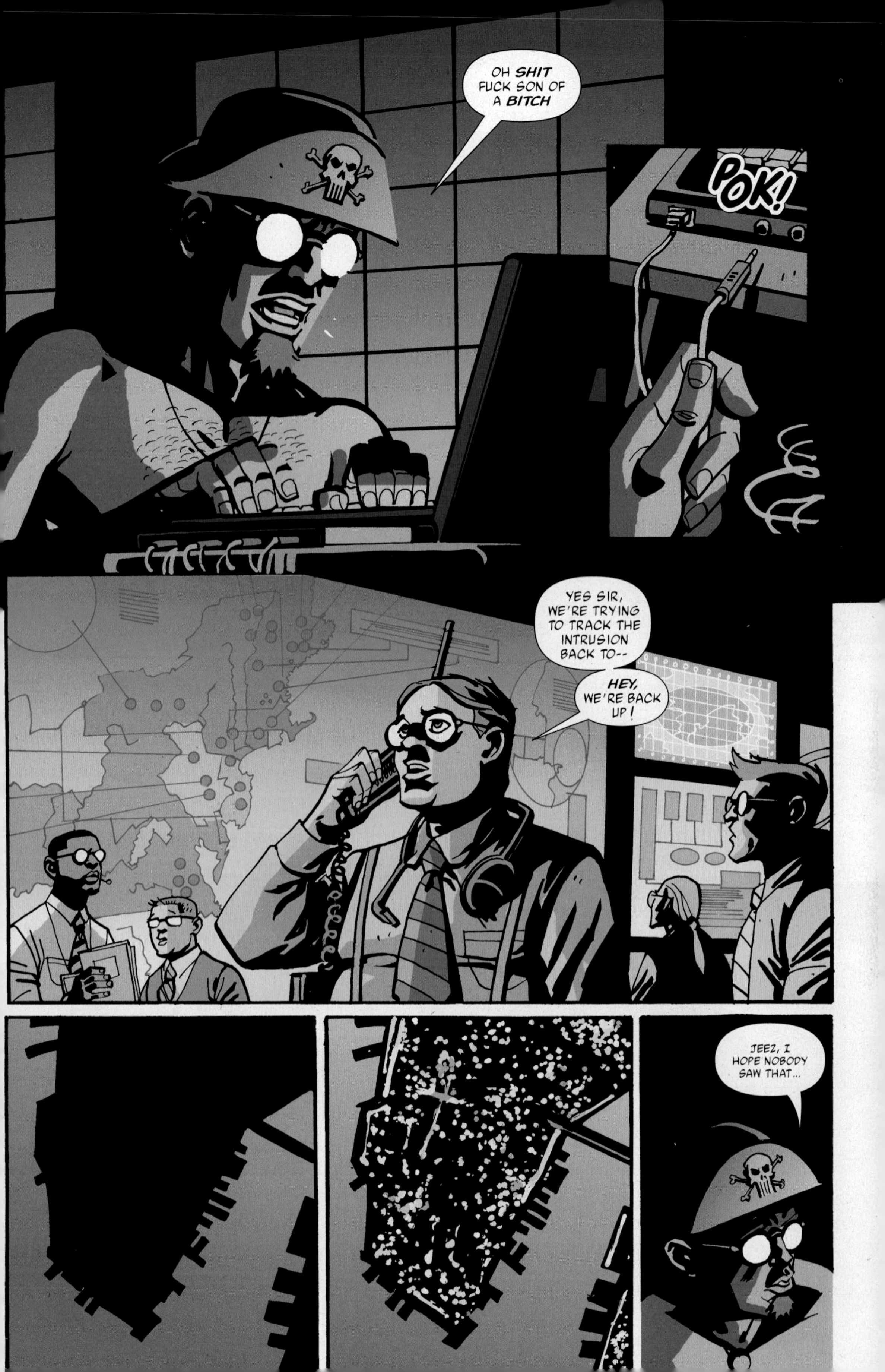
OH SHIT FUCK SON OF A BITCH
POK!
YES SIR, WE'RE TRYING TO TRACK THE INTRUSION BACK TO--
HEY, WE'RE BACK UP!
JEEZ, I HOPE NOBODY SAW THAT...

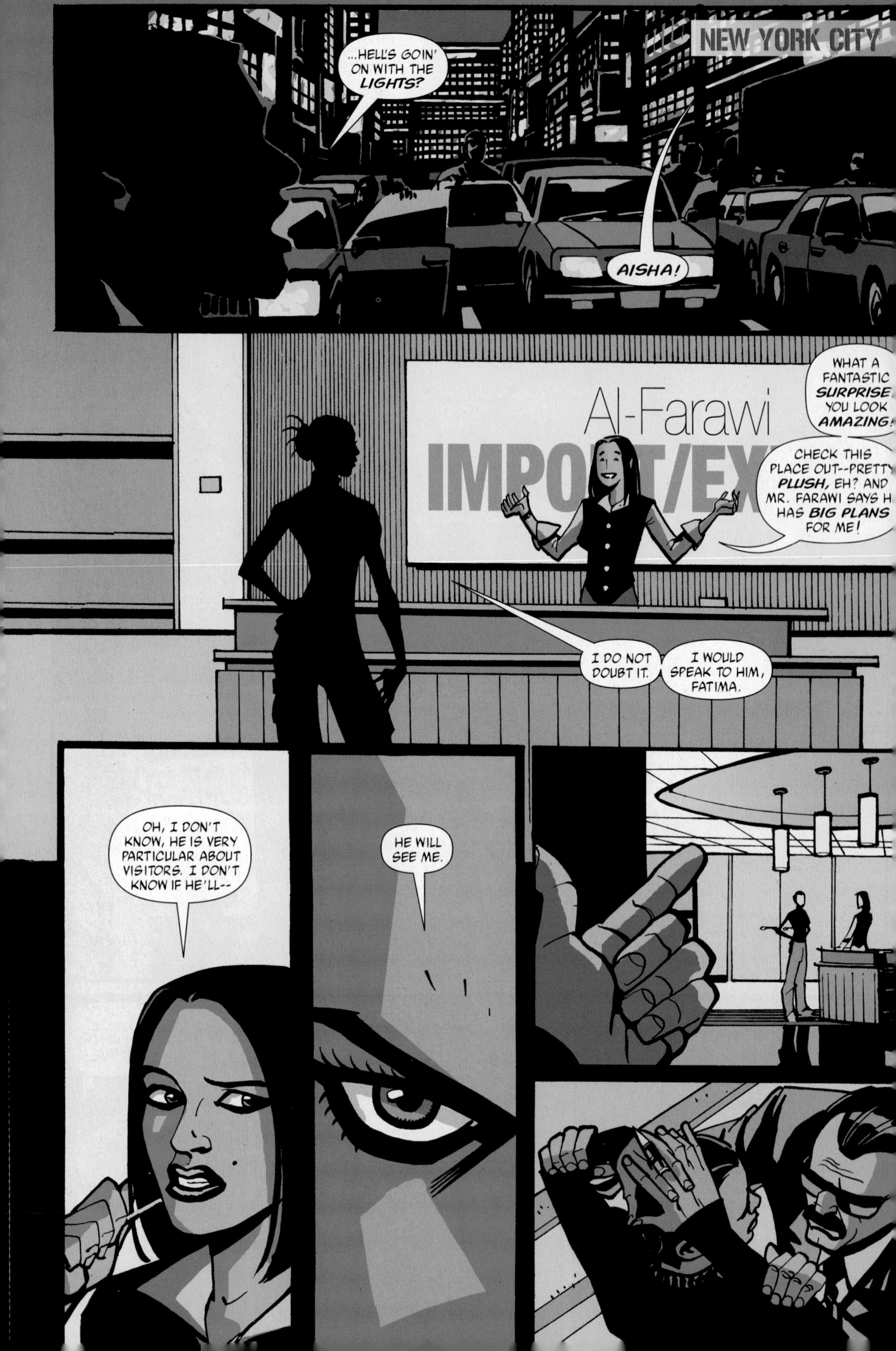
NEW YORK CITY
...HELL'S GOIN' ON WITH THE LIGHTS?
AISHA!
Al-Farawi
IMPORT/EX
WHAT A FANTASTIC SURPRISE! YOU LOOK AMAZING!
CHECK THIS PLACE OUT--PRETTY PLUSH, EH? AND MR. FARAWI SAYS HE HAS BIG PLANS FOR ME!
I DO NOT DOUBT IT.
I WOULD SPEAK TO HIM, FATIMA.
OH, I DON'T KNOW, HE IS VERY PARTICULAR ABOUT VISITORS. I DON'T KNOW IF HE'LL--
HE WILL SEE ME.

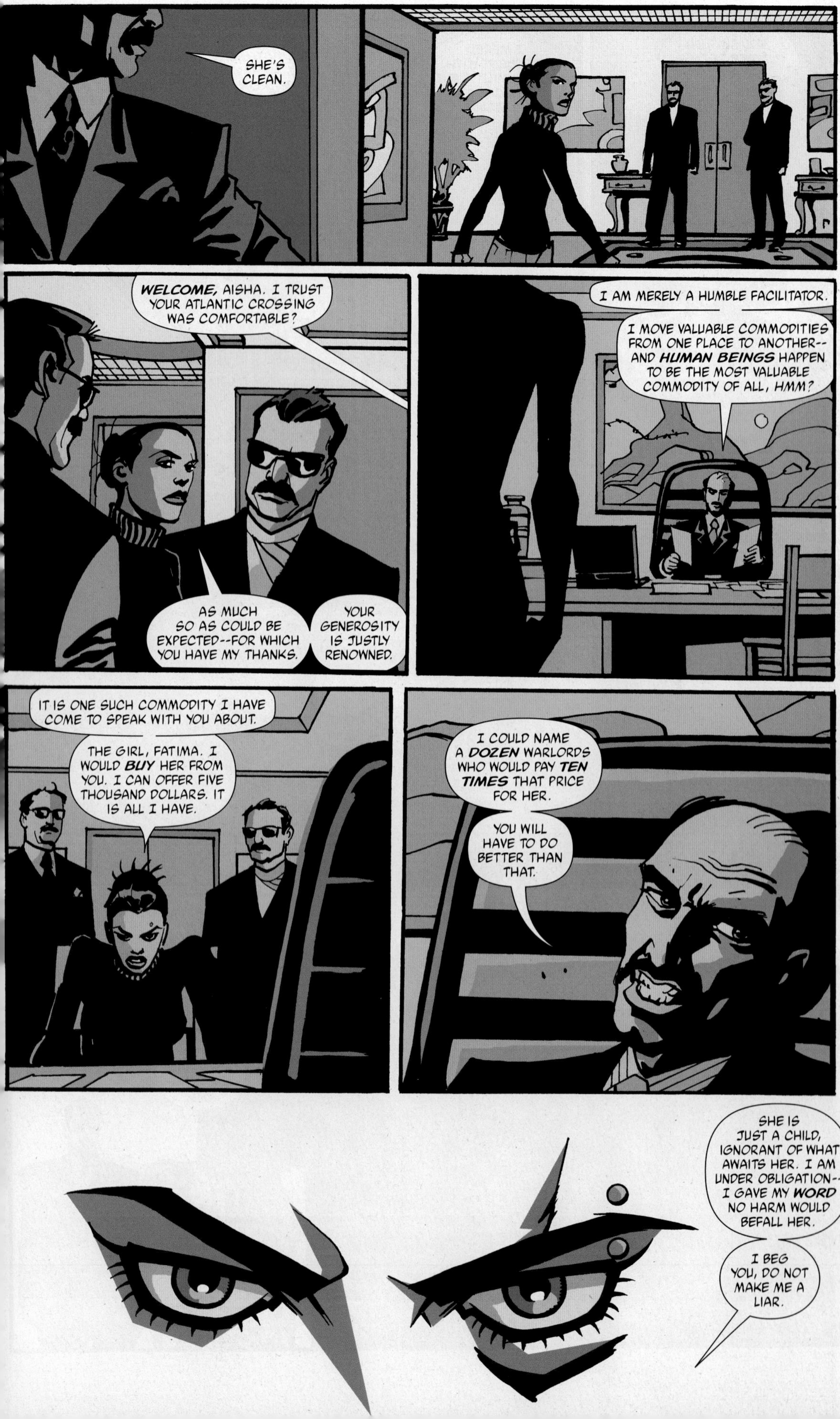
SHE'S CLEAN.
WELCOME, AISHA. I TRUST YOUR ATLANTIC CROSSING WAS COMFORTABLE?
AS MUCH SO AS COULD BE EXPECTED--FOR WHICH YOU HAVE MY THANKS.
YOUR GENEROSITY IS JUSTLY RENOWNED.
I AM MERELY A HUMBLE FACILITATOR.
I MOVE VALUABLE COMMODITIES FROM ONE PLACE TO ANOTHER--AND HUMAN BEINGS HAPPEN TO BE THE MOST VALUABLE COMMODITY OF ALL, HMM?
IT IS ONE SUCH COMMODITY I HAVE COME TO SPEAK WITH YOU ABOUT.
THE GIRL, FATIMA. I WOULD BUY HER FROM YOU. I CAN OFFER FIVE THOUSAND DOLLARS. IT IS ALL I HAVE.
I COULD NAME A DOZEN WARLORDS WHO WOULD PAY TEN TIMES THAT PRICE FOR HER.
YOU WILL HAVE TO DO BETTER THAN THAT.
SHE IS JUST A CHILD, IGNORANT OF WHAT AWAITS HER. I AM UNDER OBLIGATION--I GAVE MY WORD NO HARM WOULD BEFALL HER.
I BEG YOU, DO NOT MAKE ME A LIAR.

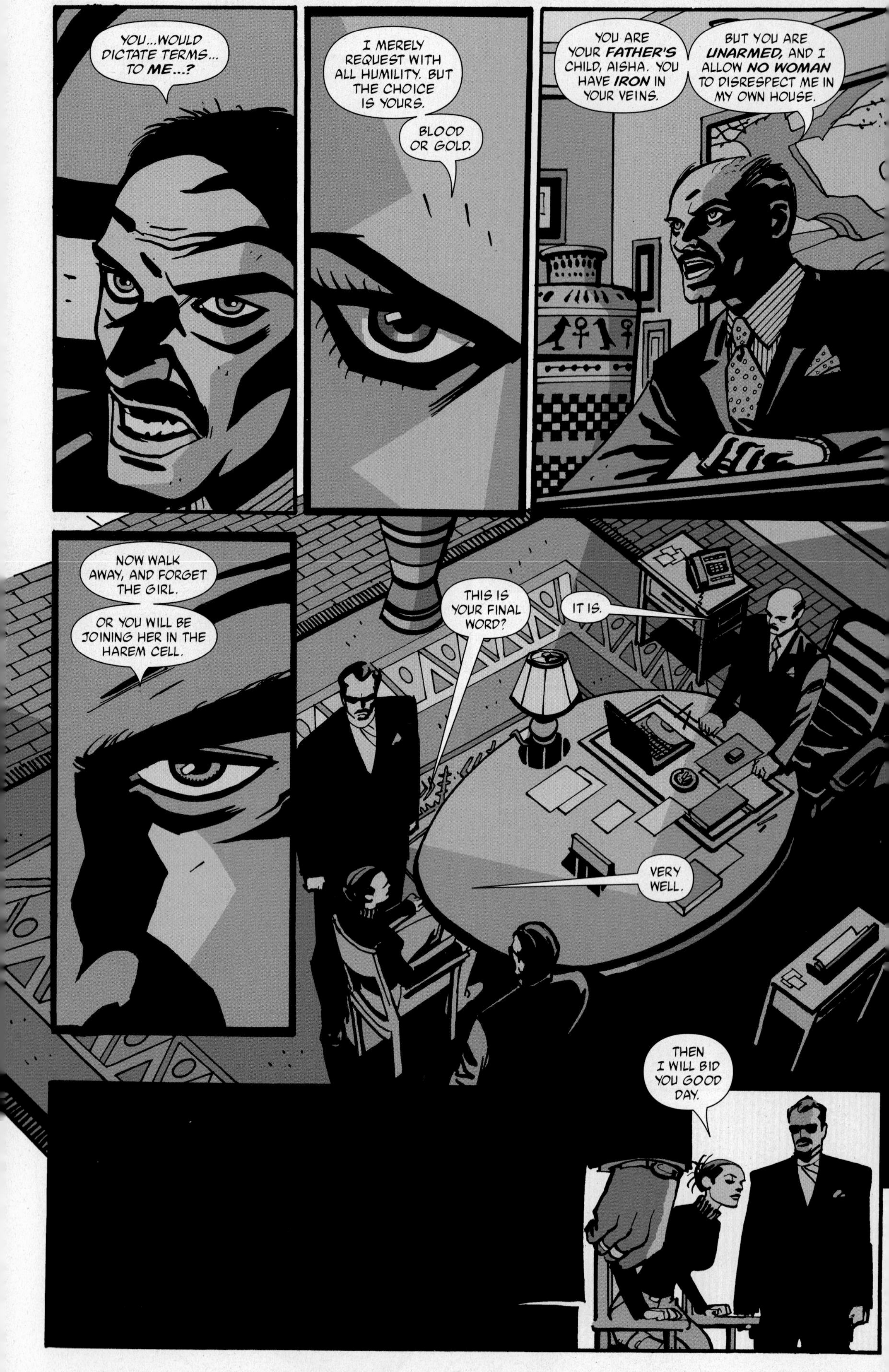
YOU...WOULD DICTATE TERMS... TO **ME...?**
I MERELY REQUEST WITH ALL HUMILITY. BUT THE CHOICE IS YOURS.
BLOOD OR GOLD.
YOU ARE YOUR **FATHER'S** CHILD, AISHA. YOU HAVE **IRON** IN YOUR VEINS.
BUT YOU ARE **UNARMED,** AND I ALLOW **NO WOMAN** TO DISRESPECT ME IN MY OWN HOUSE.
NOW WALK AWAY, AND FORGET THE GIRL.
OR YOU WILL BE JOINING HER IN THE HAREM CELL.
THIS IS YOUR FINAL WORD?
IT IS.
VERY WELL.
THEN I WILL BID YOU GOOD DAY.

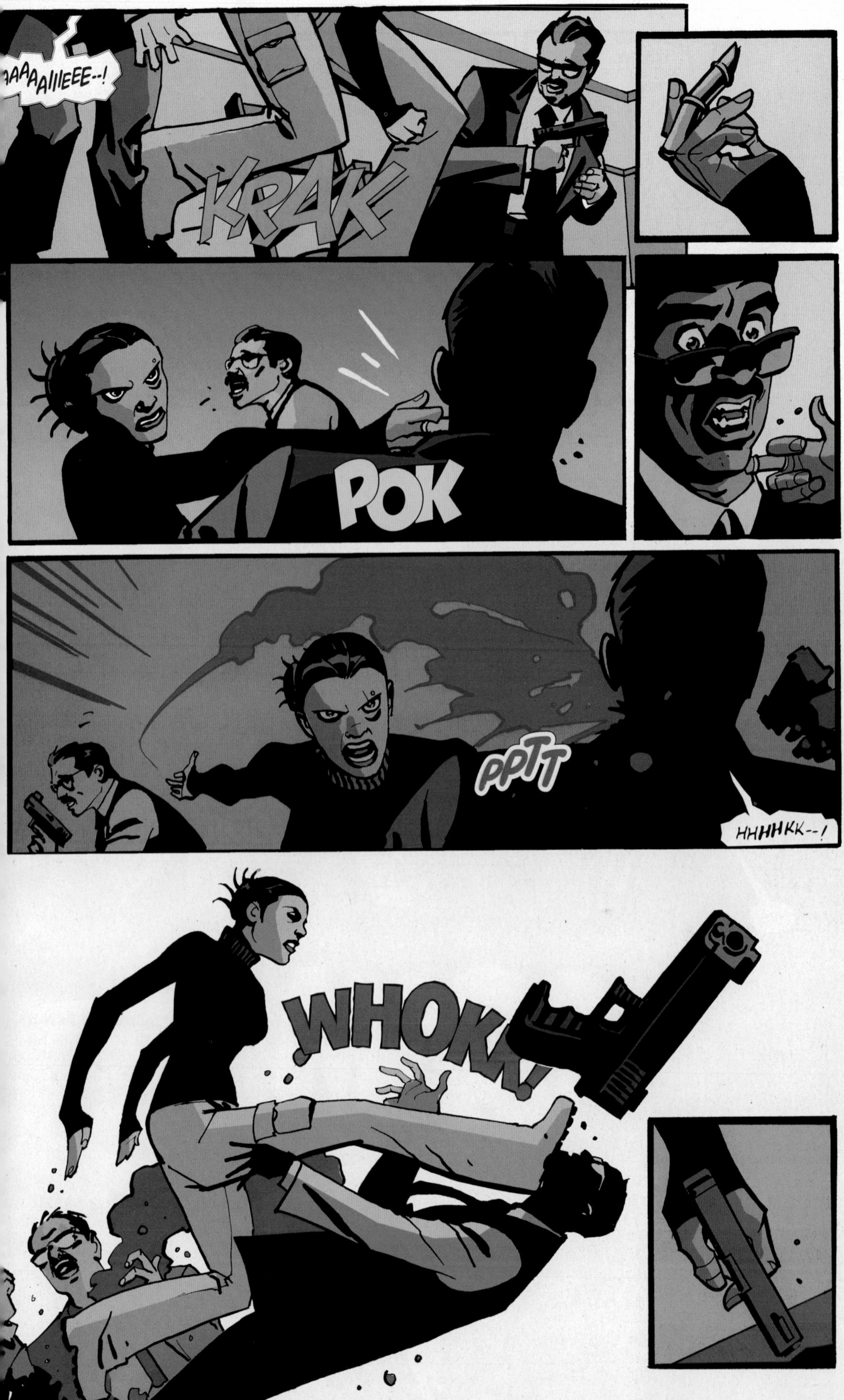
AAAAAIIIEEE--!
KRAK
POK
PPTT
HHHHKK--!
WHOKK!

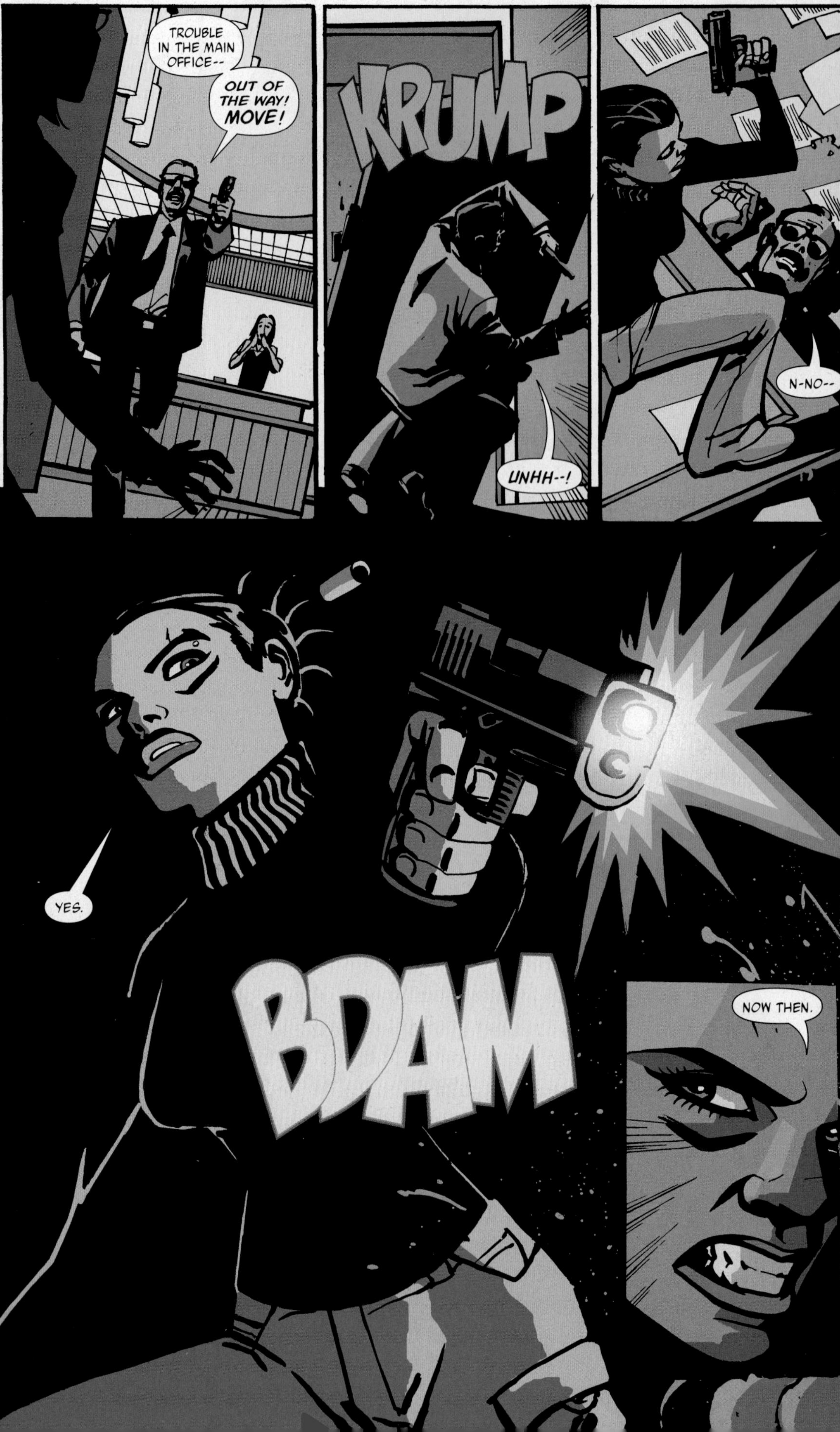
TROUBLE IN THE MAIN OFFICE--
OUT OF THE WAY! MOVE!
KRUMP
UNHH--!
N-NO--
YES.
BDAM
NOW THEN.

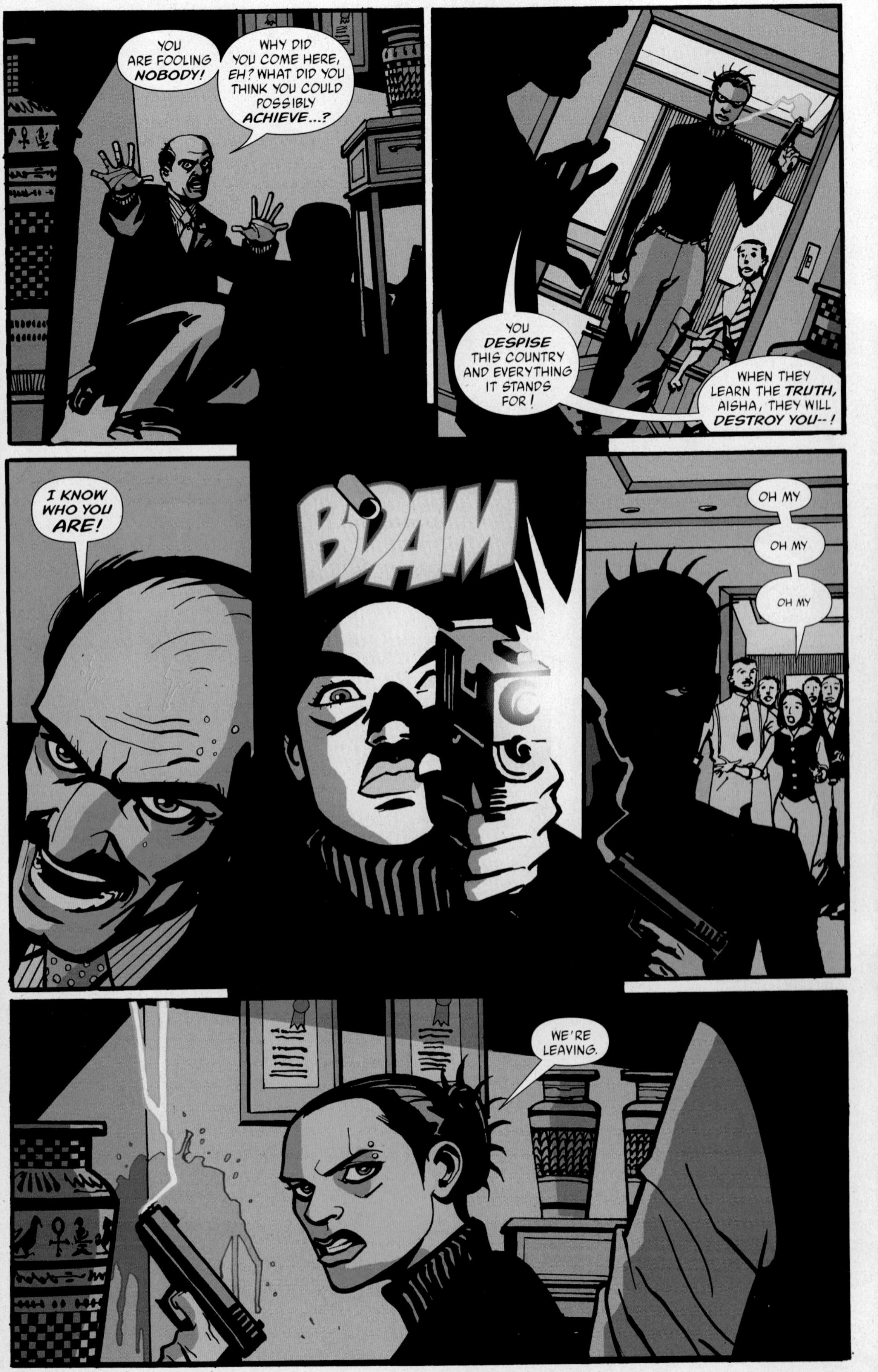
YOU ARE FOOLING NOBODY!
WHY DID YOU COME HERE, EH? WHAT DID YOU THINK YOU COULD POSSIBLY ACHIEVE...?
YOU DESPISE THIS COUNTRY AND EVERYTHING IT STANDS FOR!
WHEN THEY LEARN THE TRUTH, AISHA, THEY WILL DESTROY YOU--!
I KNOW WHO YOU ARE!
BLAM
OH MY
OH MY
OH MY
WE'RE LEAVING.

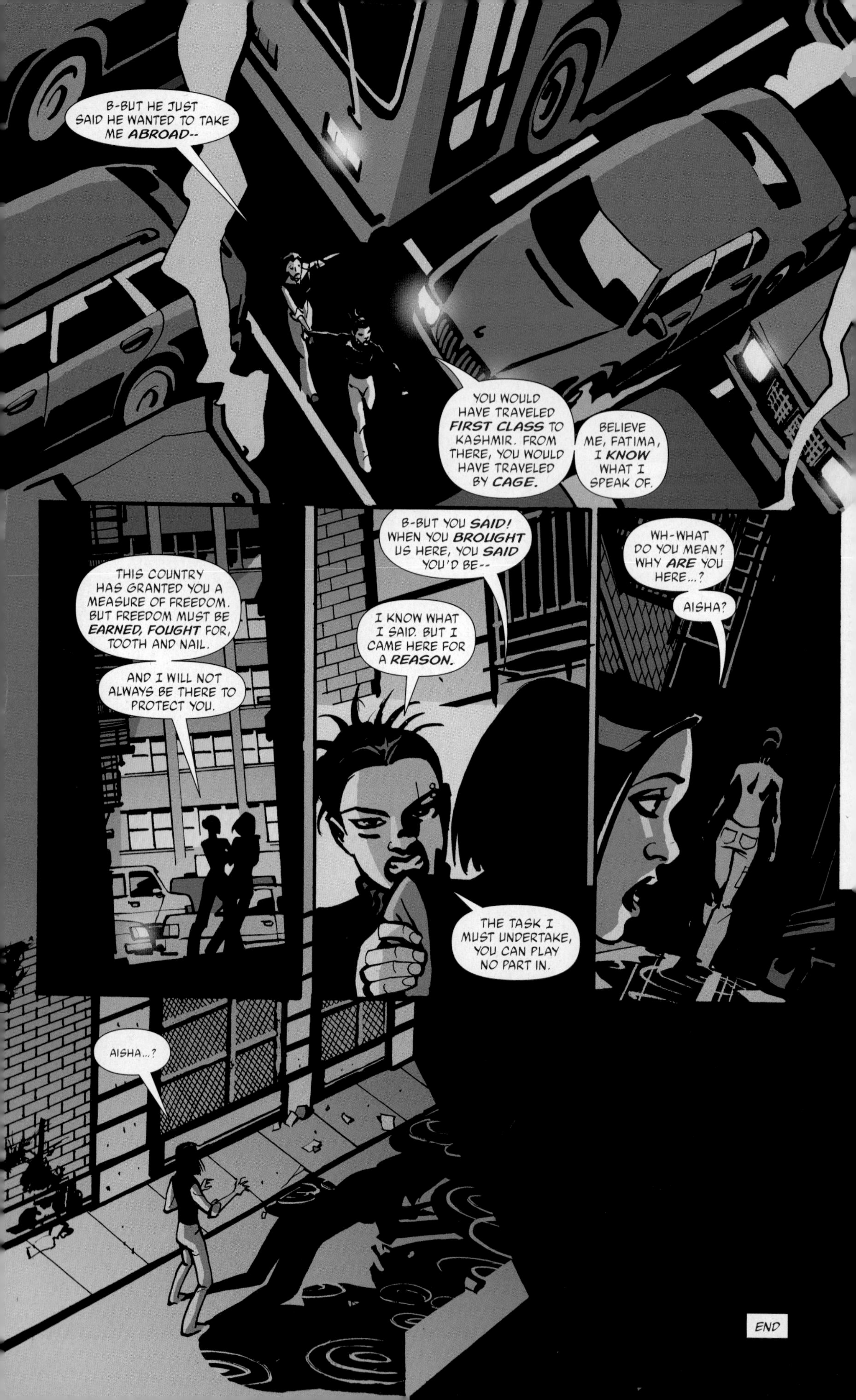
B-BUT HE JUST SAID HE WANTED TO TAKE ME ABROAD--
YOU WOULD HAVE TRAVELED FIRST CLASS TO KASHMIR. FROM THERE, YOU WOULD HAVE TRAVELED BY CAGE.
BELIEVE ME, FATIMA, I KNOW WHAT I SPEAK OF.
THIS COUNTRY HAS GRANTED YOU A MEASURE OF FREEDOM. BUT FREEDOM MUST BE EARNED, FOUGHT FOR, TOOTH AND NAIL.
AND I WILL NOT ALWAYS BE THERE TO PROTECT YOU.
B-BUT YOU SAID! WHEN YOU BROUGHT US HERE, YOU SAID YOU'D BE--
I KNOW WHAT I SAID. BUT I CAME HERE FOR A REASON.
THE TASK I MUST UNDERTAKE, YOU CAN PLAY NO PART IN.
WH-WHAT DO YOU MEAN? WHY ARE YOU HERE...?
AISHA?
AISHA...?
END

Jock

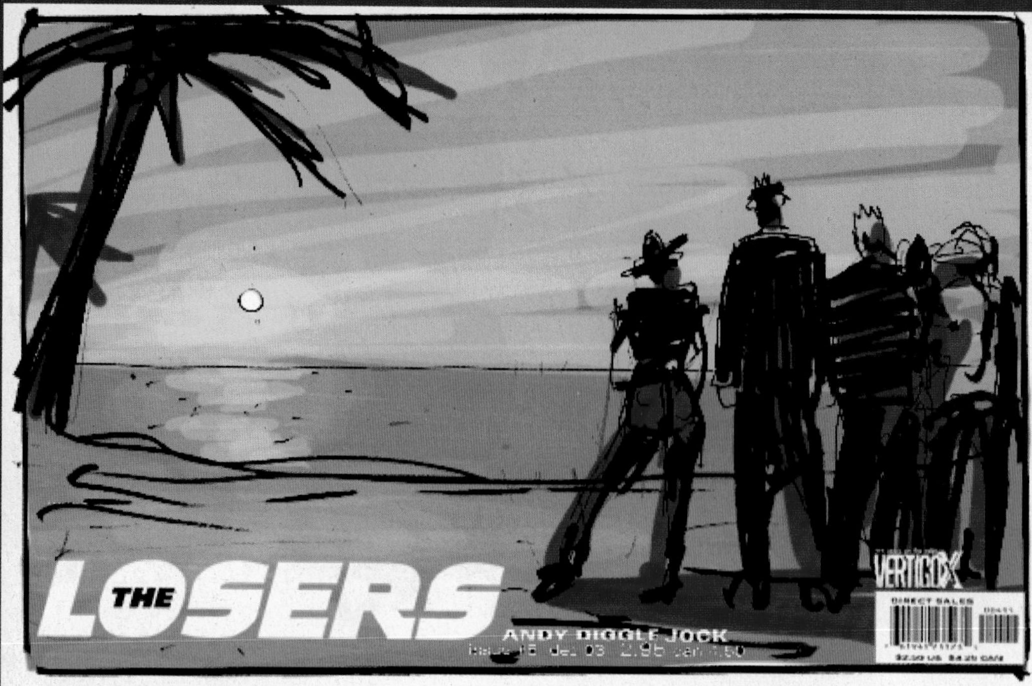
THE LOSERS
ANDY DIGGLE JOCK
VERTIGO
DIRECT SALES

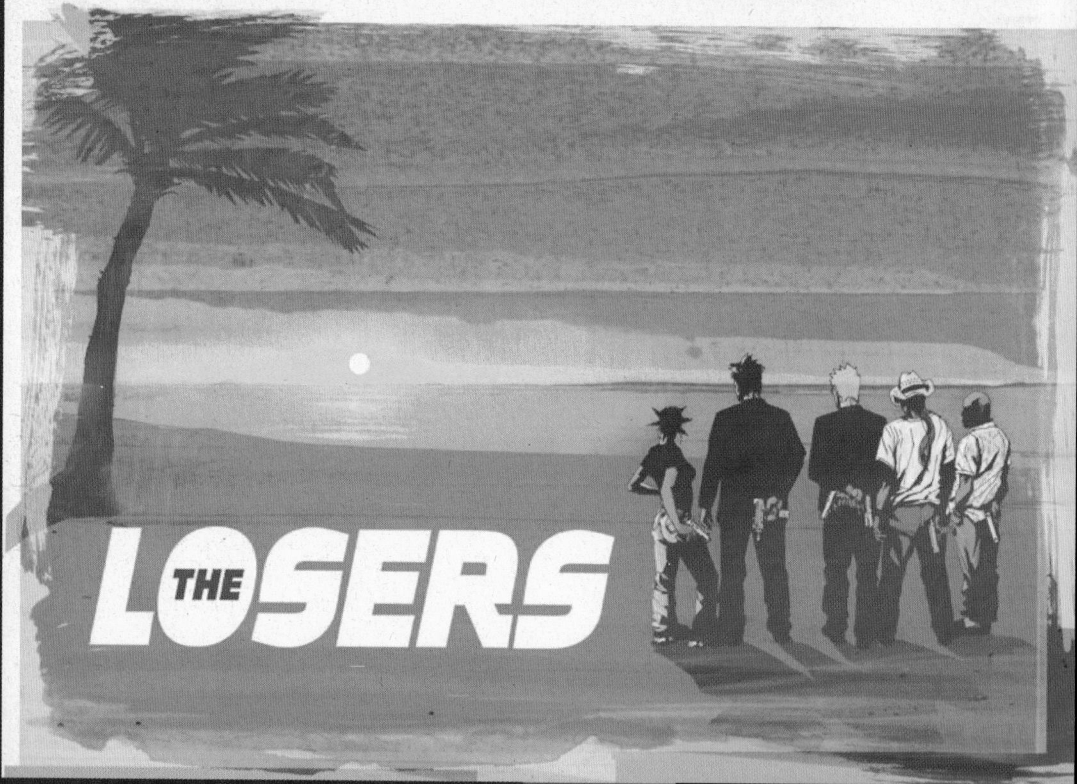
THE LOSERS

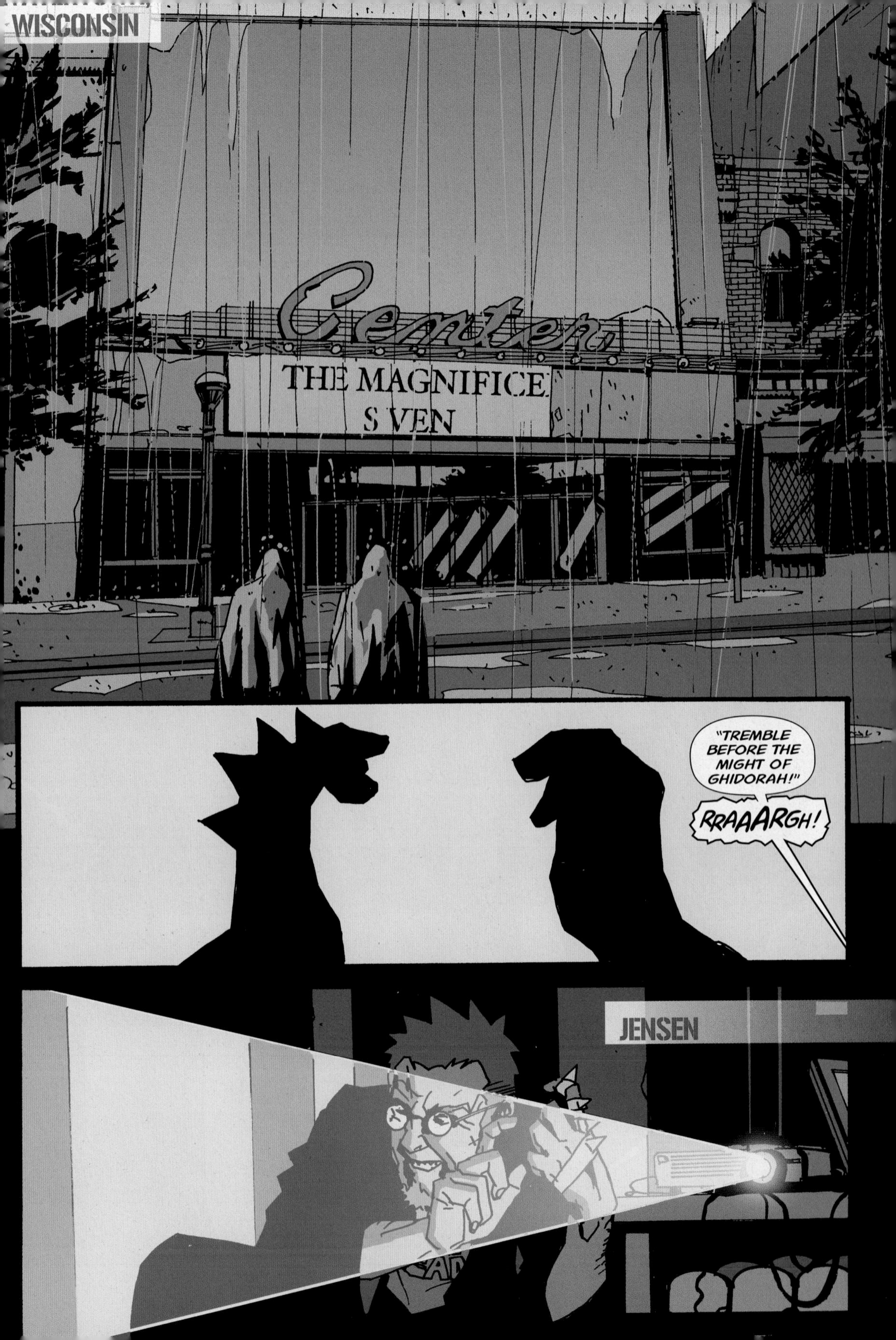
WISCONSIN
Center
THE MAGNIFICE
S VEN
"TREMBLE BEFORE THE MIGHT OF GHIDORAH!"
RRAAARGH!
JENSEN

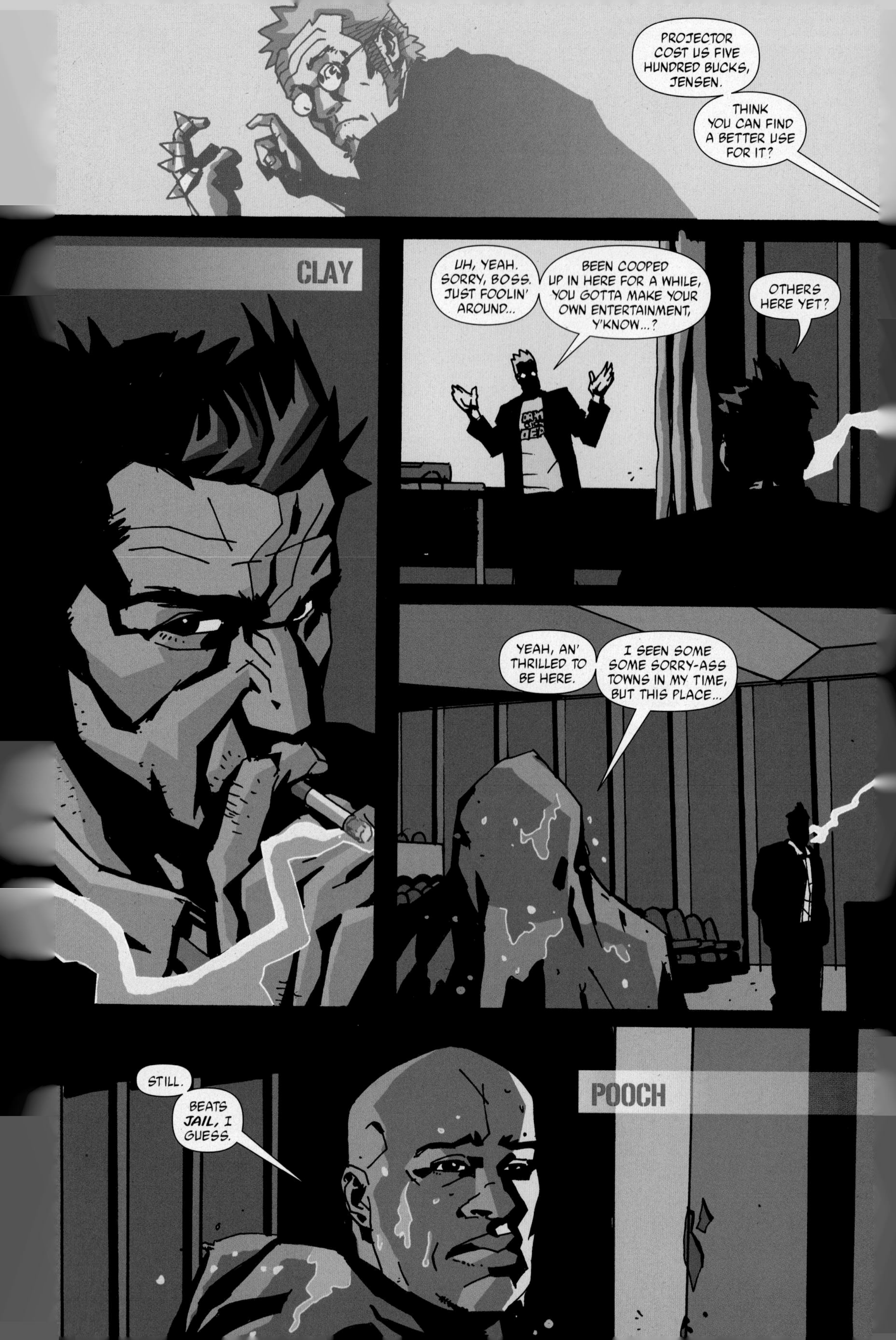
PROJECTOR COST US FIVE HUNDRED BUCKS, JENSEN.
THINK YOU CAN FIND A BETTER USE FOR IT?
CLAY
UH, YEAH. SORRY, BOSS. JUST FOOLIN' AROUND...
BEEN COOPED UP IN HERE FOR A WHILE, YOU GOTTA MAKE YOUR OWN ENTERTAINMENT, Y'KNOW...?
OTHERS HERE YET?
YEAH, AN' THRILLED TO BE HERE.
I SEEN SOME SOME SORRY-ASS TOWNS IN MY TIME, BUT THIS PLACE...
POOCH
STILL.
BEATS JAIL, I GUESS.

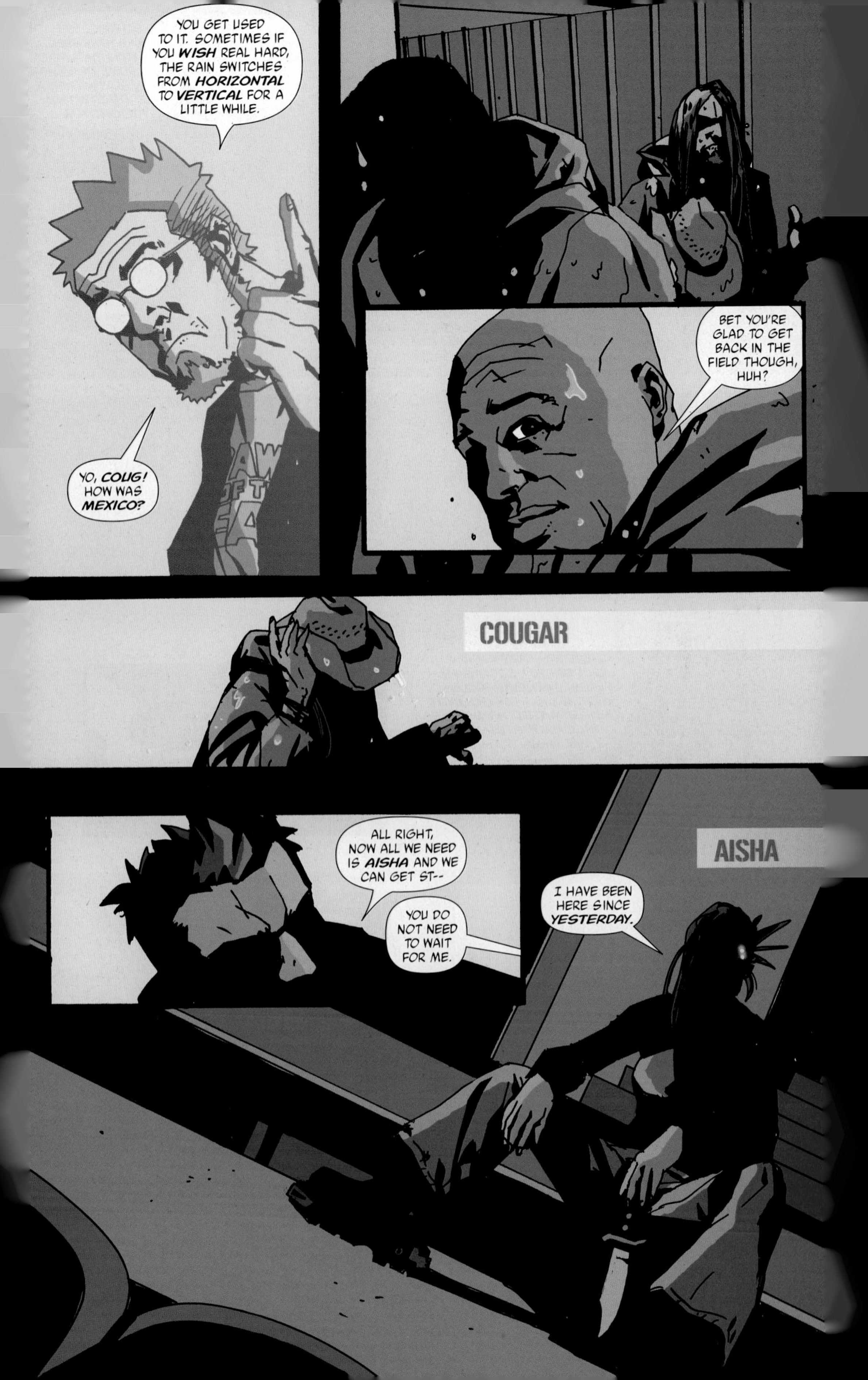
YOU GET USED TO IT. SOMETIMES IF YOU WISH REAL HARD, THE RAIN SWITCHES FROM HORIZONTAL TO VERTICAL FOR A LITTLE WHILE.
YO, COUG! HOW WAS MEXICO?
BET YOU'RE GLAD TO GET BACK IN THE FIELD THOUGH, HUH?
COUGAR
ALL RIGHT, NOW ALL WE NEED IS AISHA AND WE CAN GET ST--
YOU DO NOT NEED TO WAIT FOR ME.
AISHA
I HAVE BEEN HERE SINCE YESTERDAY.

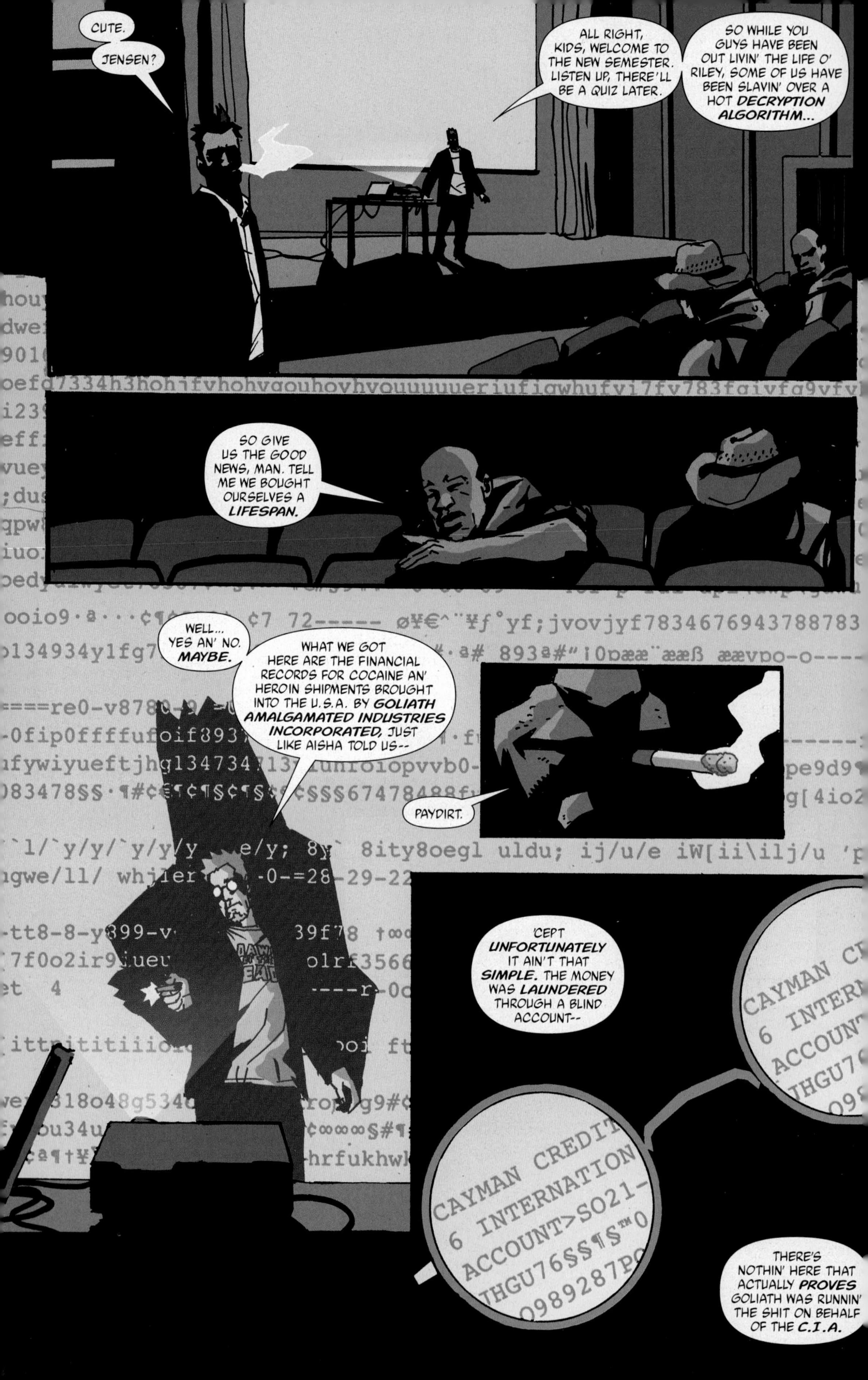
CUTE.
JENSEN?
ALL RIGHT, KIDS, WELCOME TO THE NEW SEMESTER. LISTEN UP, THERE'LL BE A QUIZ LATER.
SO WHILE YOU GUYS HAVE BEEN OUT LIVIN' THE LIFE O' RILEY, SOME OF US HAVE BEEN SLAVIN' OVER A HOT DECRYPTION ALGORITHM...
SO GIVE US THE GOOD NEWS, MAN. TELL ME WE BOUGHT OURSELVES A LIFESPAN.
WELL... YES AN' NO. MAYBE.
WHAT WE GOT HERE ARE THE FINANCIAL RECORDS FOR COCAINE AN' HEROIN SHIPMENTS BROUGHT INTO THE U.S.A. BY GOLIATH AMALGAMATED INDUSTRIES INCORPORATED, JUST LIKE AISHA TOLD US--
PAYDIRT.
'CEPT UNFORTUNATELY IT AIN'T THAT SIMPLE. THE MONEY WAS LAUNDERED THROUGH A BLIND ACCOUNT--
CAYMAN CREDIT
6 INTERNATION
ACCOUNT>SO21-
THGU76§§¶§™0
O989287PO
THERE'S NOTHIN' HERE THAT ACTUALLY PROVES GOLIATH WAS RUNNIN' THE SHIT ON BEHALF OF THE C.I.A.

OPERATION WAS A WASTED EFFORT.

LIVES, SUFFER BETRAYAL AT THE HANDS OF YOUR OWN COMRADE...ALL FOR **NOTHING?**

ALMOST NOTHIN', AISHA, BUT NOT QUITE.

GUESS WHOSE NAME WAS ON THE MONEY TRANSFER AUTHORIZATIONS--

======re0-
=--0fip0ff
soufywiyueftjhg13473471
43083478$$·¶#¢€¶¢¶$¢¶$¢$$
q
x:``l/`y/y/`y/y/y qoe/y; 8y` 8it
reugwe/ll/ whjler0930-0
2
2--tt8-8-y899-v--
ew[7f0o2ir9iueu
fiet 4   49
g
34[ittpit
piwero31
wgfyiou3
'¶$#¢$¶†

HS^MAX

NO WONDER HE WANTED US OUTTA THE WAY, HUH?

THIS DATA'S WORTHLESS UNLESS WE CAN TIE THESE SHIPMENTS TO THE AGENCY. AND **MAX** IS THE **KEY.**

BUT HOW WE SUPPOSED TO EVEN FIND HIM? ROQUE'S **DEAD,** AN' THAT AGENCY SUIT **SANDERSON** SAID MAX DOESN'T EVEN--

WE HUNT THAT LITTLE FUCKER DOWN, WE MAKE 'EM **DANCE.**

MONTSERRAT.

SAY WHAT?

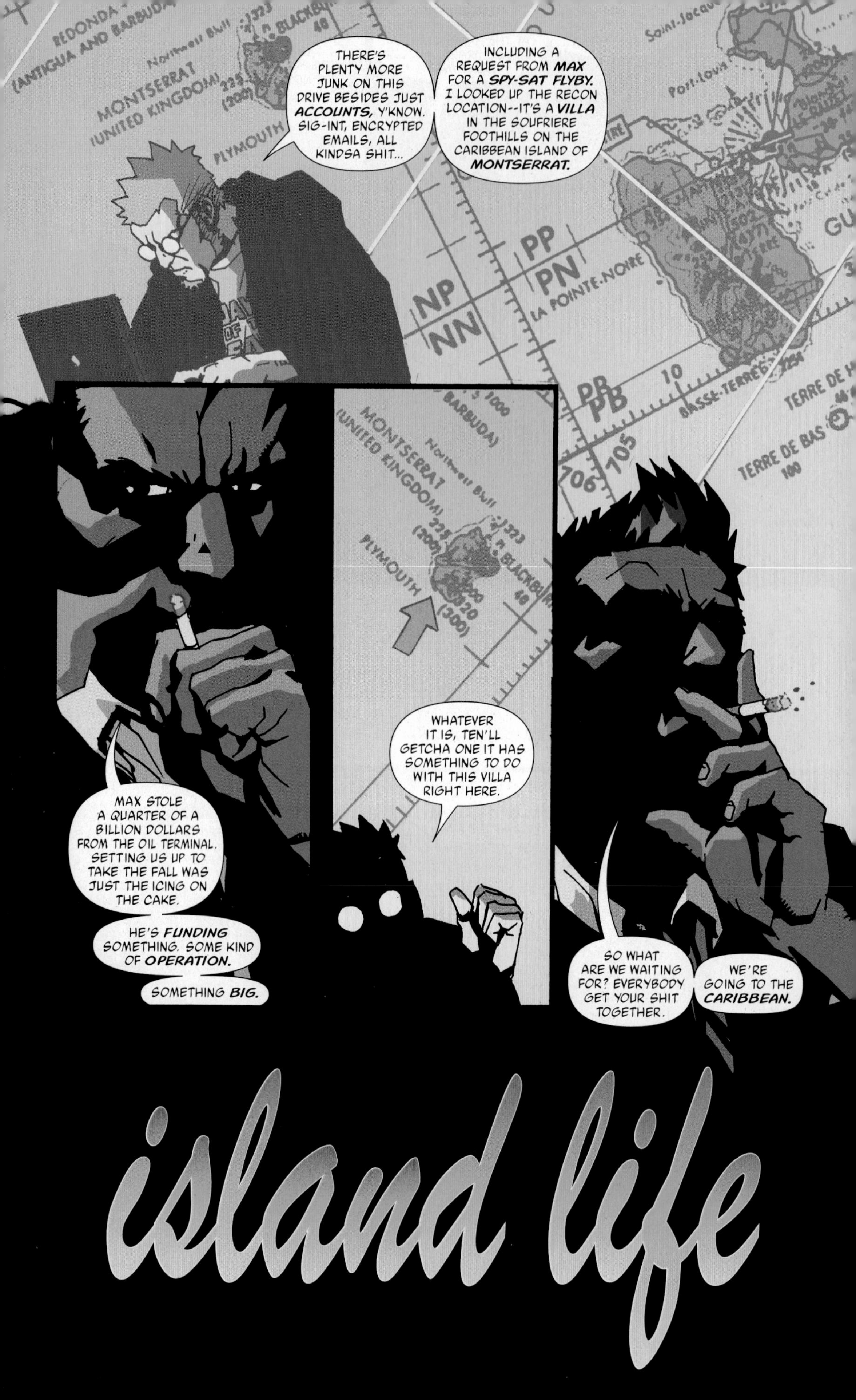
THERE'S PLENTY MORE JUNK ON THIS DRIVE BESIDES JUST **ACCOUNTS,** Y'KNOW. SIG-INT, ENCRYPTED EMAILS, ALL KINDSA SHIT...
INCLUDING A REQUEST FROM **MAX** FOR A **SPY-SAT FLYBY.** I LOOKED UP THE RECON LOCATION--IT'S A **VILLA** IN THE SOUFRIERE FOOTHILLS ON THE CARIBBEAN ISLAND OF **MONTSERRAT.**
MONTSERRAT (UNITED KINGDOM)
PLYMOUTH
REDONDA
(ANTIGUA AND BARBUDA)
LA POINTE-NOIRE
BASSE-TERRE
TERRE DE BAS
MAX STOLE A QUARTER OF A BILLION DOLLARS FROM THE OIL TERMINAL. SETTING US UP TO TAKE THE FALL WAS JUST THE ICING ON THE CAKE.
HE'S **FUNDING** SOMETHING. SOME KIND OF **OPERATION.**
SOMETHING **BIG.**
WHATEVER IT IS, TEN'LL GETCHA ONE IT HAS SOMETHING TO DO WITH THIS VILLA RIGHT HERE.
SO WHAT ARE WE WAITING FOR? EVERYBODY GET YOUR SHIT TOGETHER.
WE'RE GOING TO THE **CARIBBEAN.**
island life

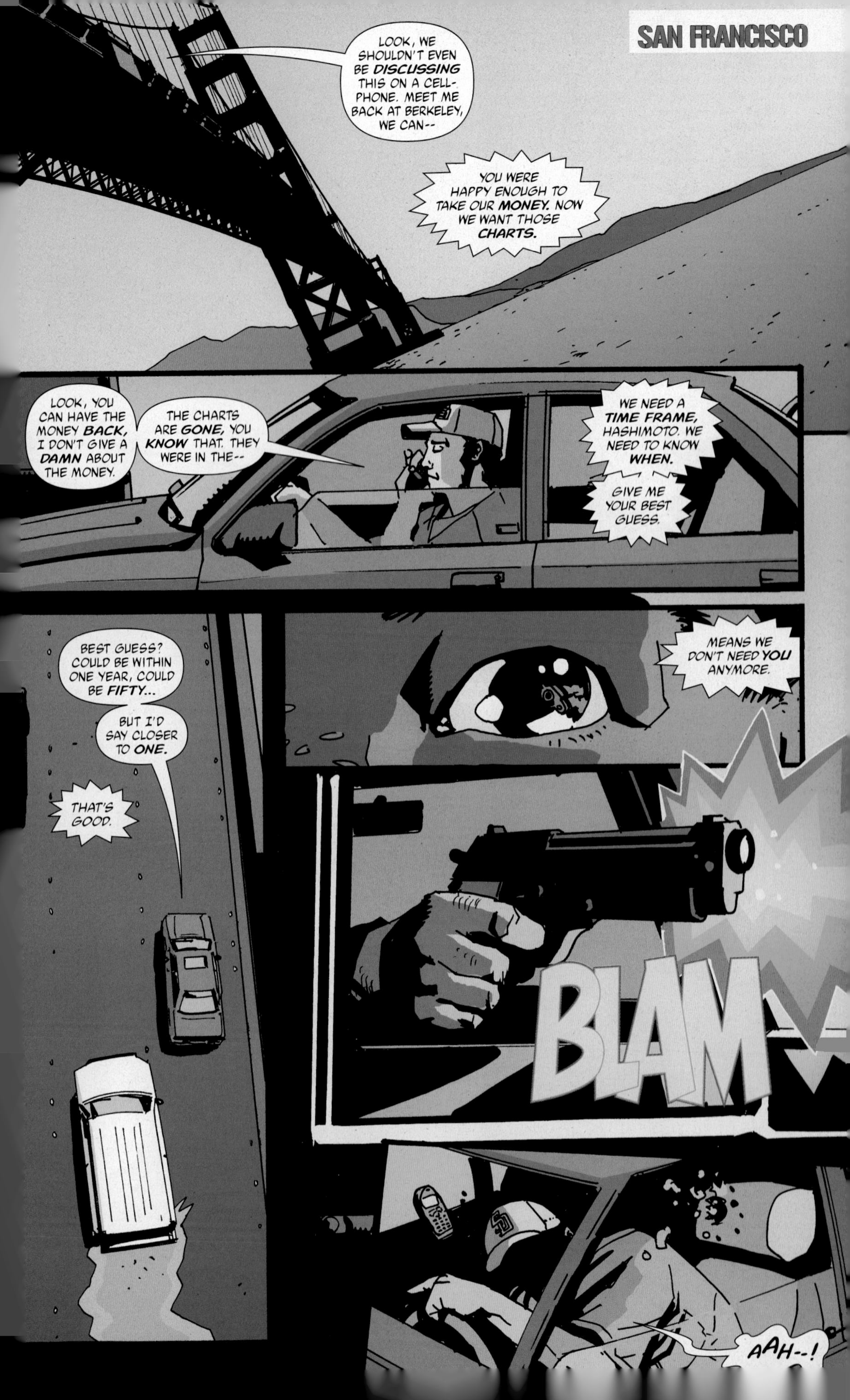

SAN FRANCISCO
LOOK, WE SHOULDN'T EVEN BE DISCUSSING THIS ON A CELL-PHONE. MEET ME BACK AT BERKELEY, WE CAN--
YOU WERE HAPPY ENOUGH TO TAKE OUR MONEY. NOW WE WANT THOSE CHARTS.
LOOK, YOU CAN HAVE THE MONEY BACK, I DON'T GIVE A DAMN ABOUT THE MONEY.
THE CHARTS ARE GONE, YOU KNOW THAT. THEY WERE IN THE--
WE NEED A TIME FRAME, HASHIMOTO. WE NEED TO KNOW WHEN.
GIVE ME YOUR BEST GUESS.
BEST GUESS? COULD BE WITHIN ONE YEAR, COULD BE FIFTY...
BUT I'D SAY CLOSER TO ONE.
THAT'S GOOD.
MEANS WE DON'T NEED YOU ANYMORE.
BLAM
AAH--!

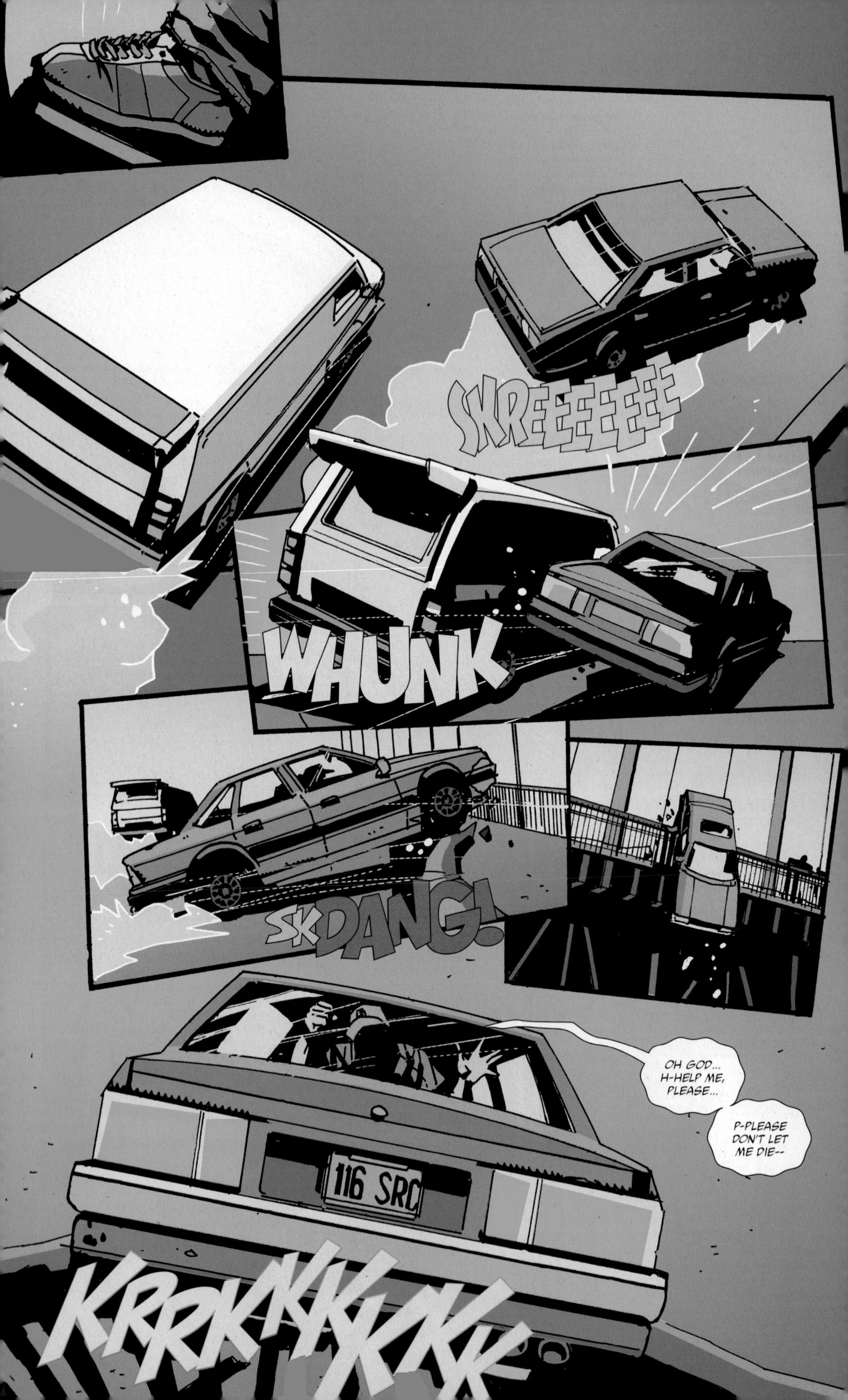
SKREEEEEEE
WHUNK
SKDANG!
OH GOD... H-HELP ME, PLEASE...
P-PLEASE DON'T LET ME DIE--
116 SRC
KRRKKKKKKK

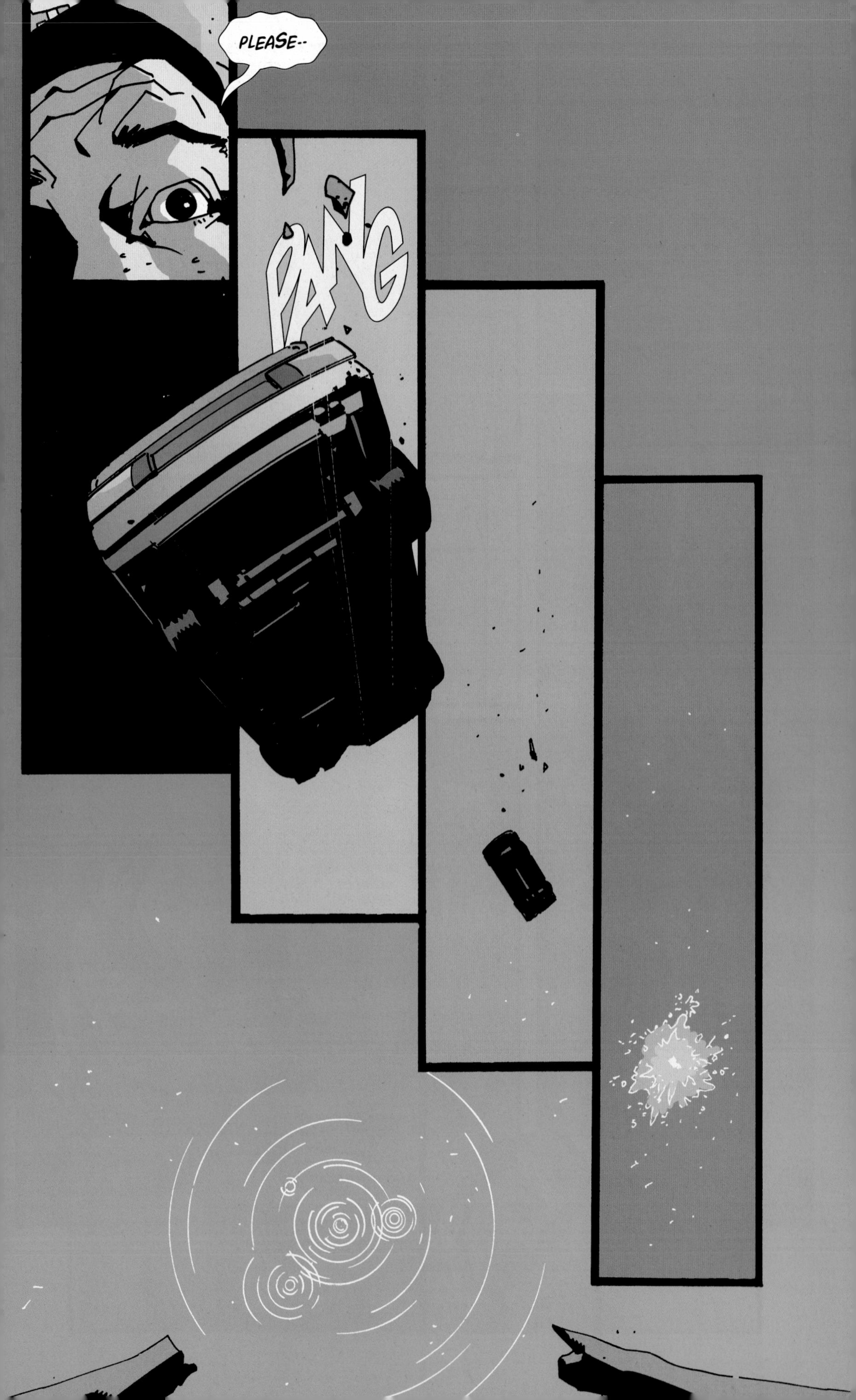
PLEASE--
PANG

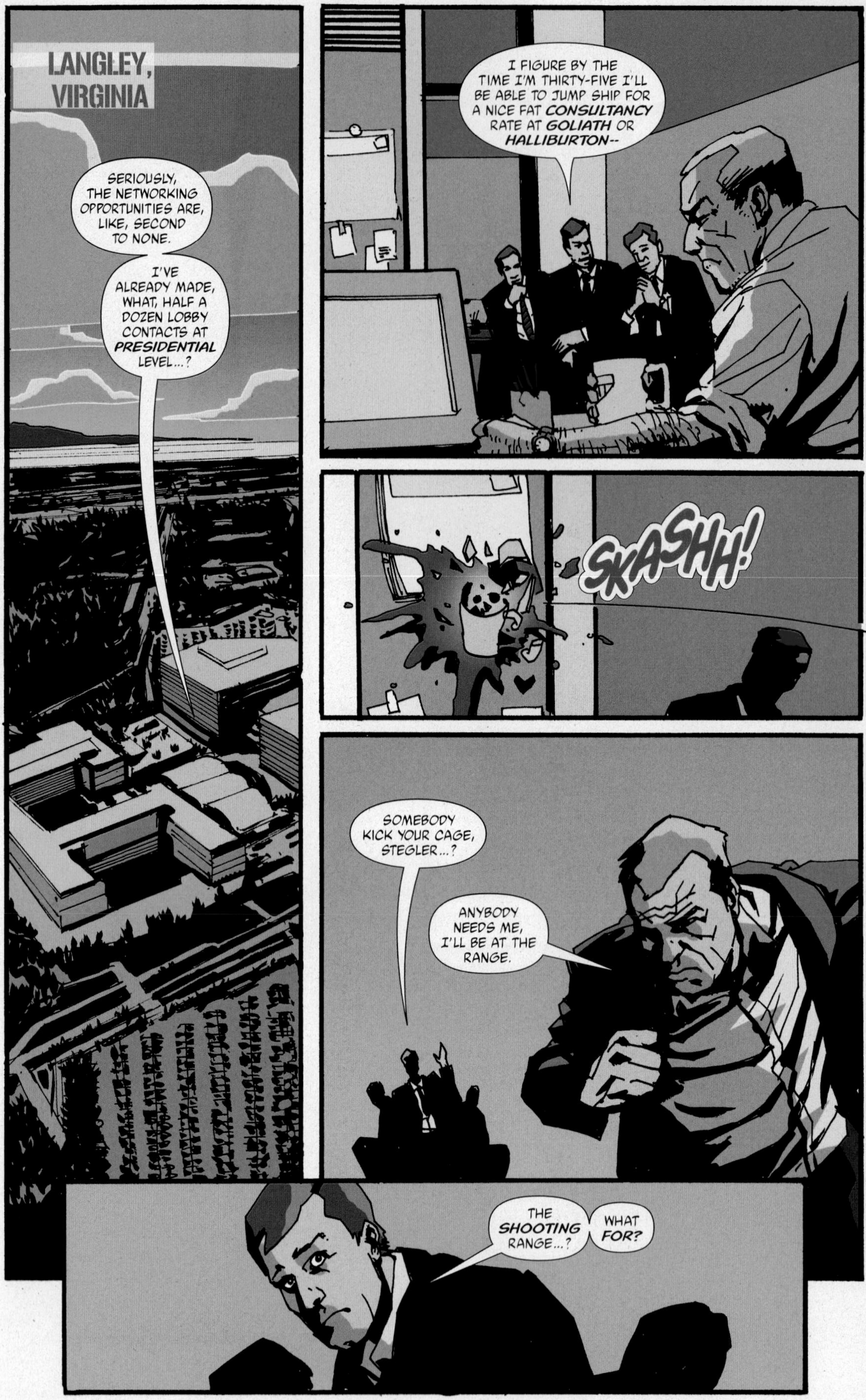
LANGLEY, VIRGINIA
SERIOUSLY, THE NETWORKING OPPORTUNITIES ARE, LIKE, SECOND TO NONE.
I'VE ALREADY MADE, WHAT, HALF A DOZEN LOBBY CONTACTS AT PRESIDENTIAL LEVEL...?
I FIGURE BY THE TIME I'M THIRTY-FIVE I'LL BE ABLE TO JUMP SHIP FOR A NICE FAT CONSULTANCY RATE AT GOLIATH OR HALLIBURTON--
SKASHH!
SOMEBODY KICK YOUR CAGE, STEGLER...?
ANYBODY NEEDS ME, I'LL BE AT THE RANGE.
THE SHOOTING RANGE...?
WHAT FOR?

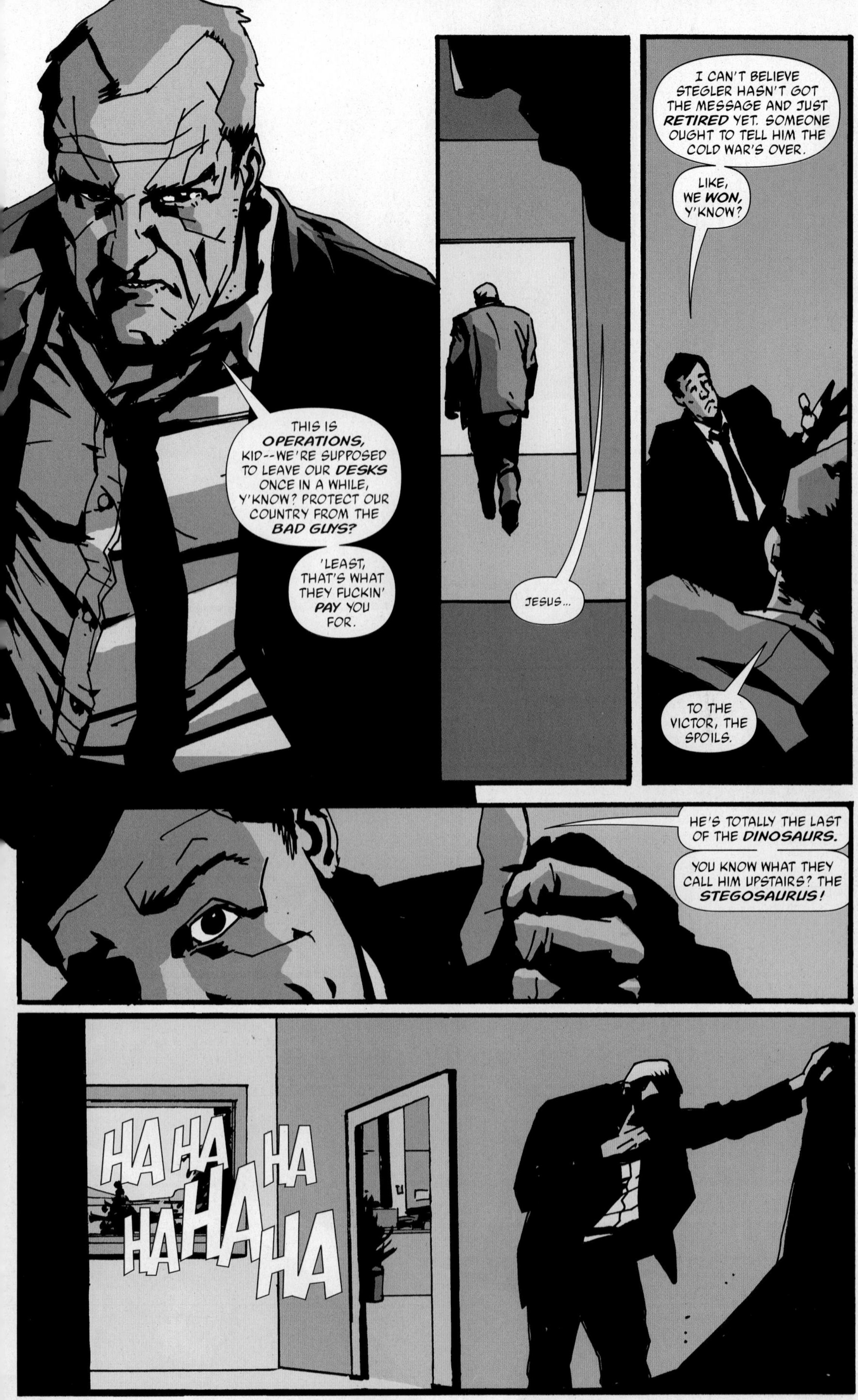
THIS IS OPERATIONS, KID--WE'RE SUPPOSED TO LEAVE OUR DESKS ONCE IN A WHILE, Y'KNOW? PROTECT OUR COUNTRY FROM THE BAD GUYS?
'LEAST, THAT'S WHAT THEY FUCKIN' PAY YOU FOR.
JESUS...
I CAN'T BELIEVE STEGLER HASN'T GOT THE MESSAGE AND JUST RETIRED YET. SOMEONE OUGHT TO TELL HIM THE COLD WAR'S OVER.
LIKE, WE WON, Y'KNOW?
TO THE VICTOR, THE SPOILS.
HE'S TOTALLY THE LAST OF THE DINOSAURS.
YOU KNOW WHAT THEY CALL HIM UPSTAIRS? THE STEGOSAURUS!
HA HA HA HA HA HA HA HA

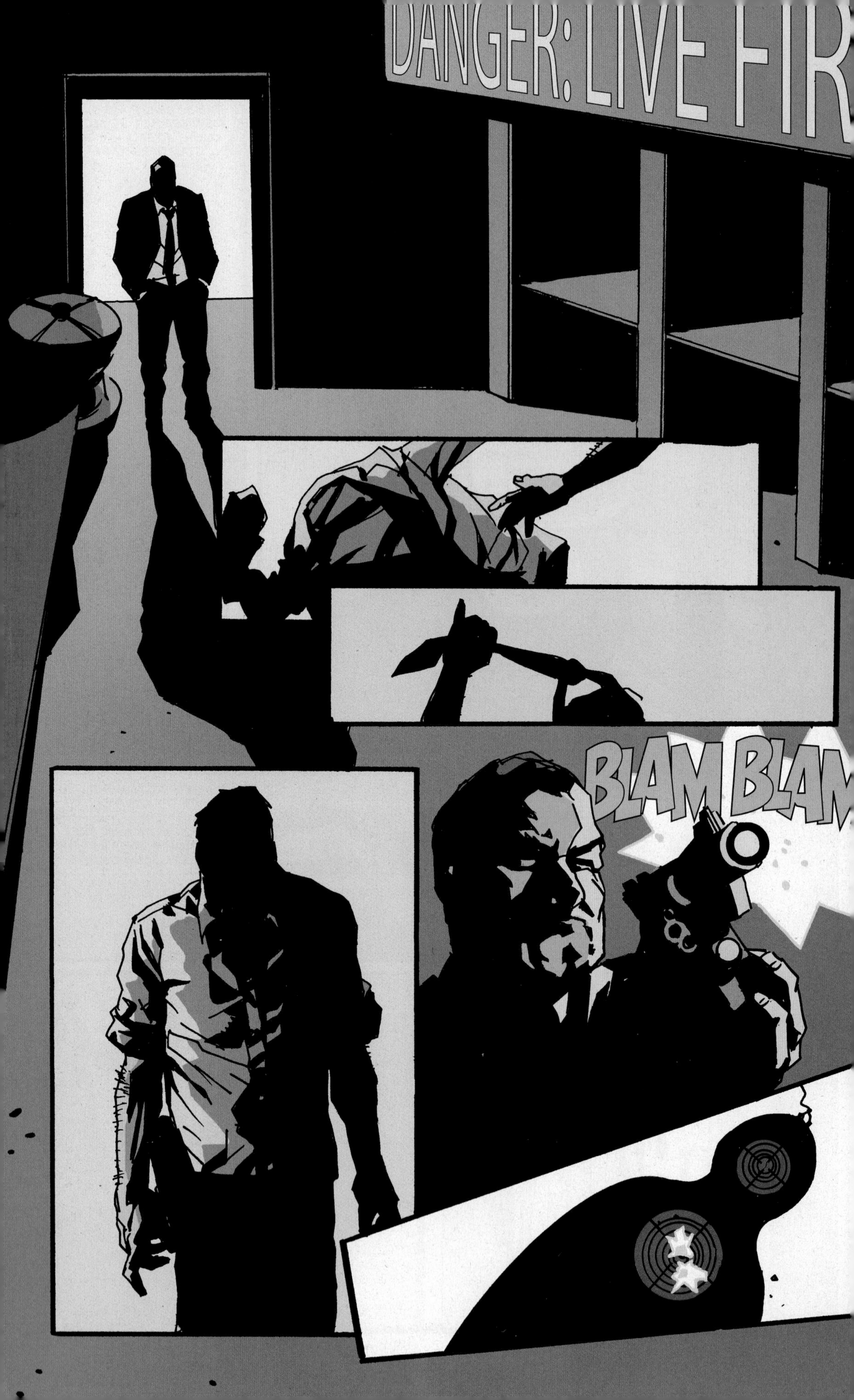

DANGER: LIVE FIR
BLAM BLAM

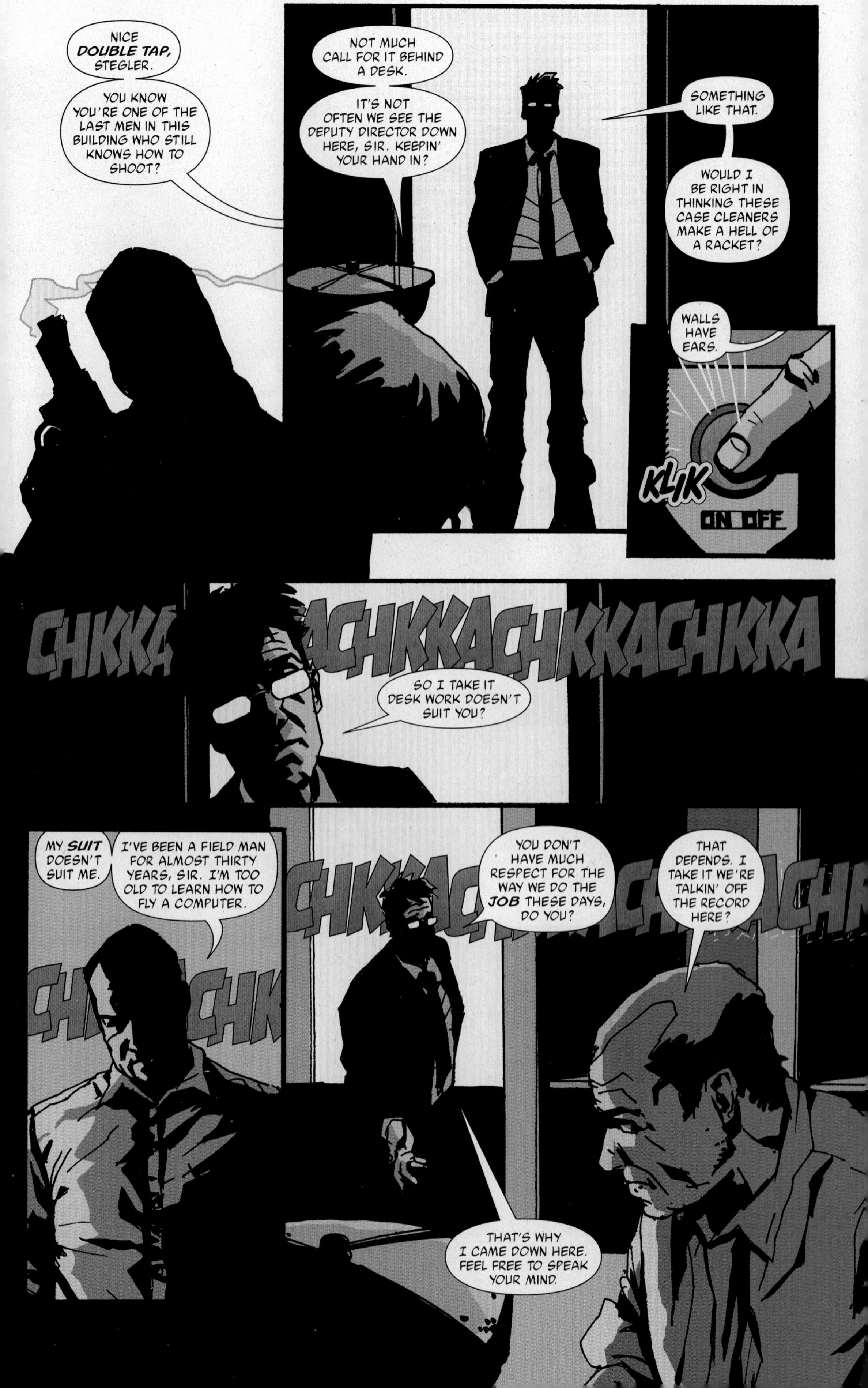
NICE DOUBLE TAP, STEGLER.
YOU KNOW YOU'RE ONE OF THE LAST MEN IN THIS BUILDING WHO STILL KNOWS HOW TO SHOOT?
NOT MUCH CALL FOR IT BEHIND A DESK.
IT'S NOT OFTEN WE SEE THE DEPUTY DIRECTOR DOWN HERE, SIR. KEEPIN' YOUR HAND IN?
SOMETHING LIKE THAT.
WOULD I BE RIGHT IN THINKING THESE CASE CLEANERS MAKE A HELL OF A RACKET?
WALLS HAVE EARS.
KLIK
ON OFF
CHKKACHKKACHKKACHKKA
SO I TAKE IT DESK WORK DOESN'T SUIT YOU?
MY SUIT DOESN'T SUIT ME.
I'VE BEEN A FIELD MAN FOR ALMOST THIRTY YEARS, SIR. I'M TOO OLD TO LEARN HOW TO FLY A COMPUTER.
YOU DON'T HAVE MUCH RESPECT FOR THE WAY WE DO THE JOB THESE DAYS, DO YOU?
THAT DEPENDS. I TAKE IT WE'RE TALKIN' OFF THE RECORD HERE?
THAT'S WHY I CAME DOWN HERE. FEEL FREE TO SPEAK YOUR MIND.

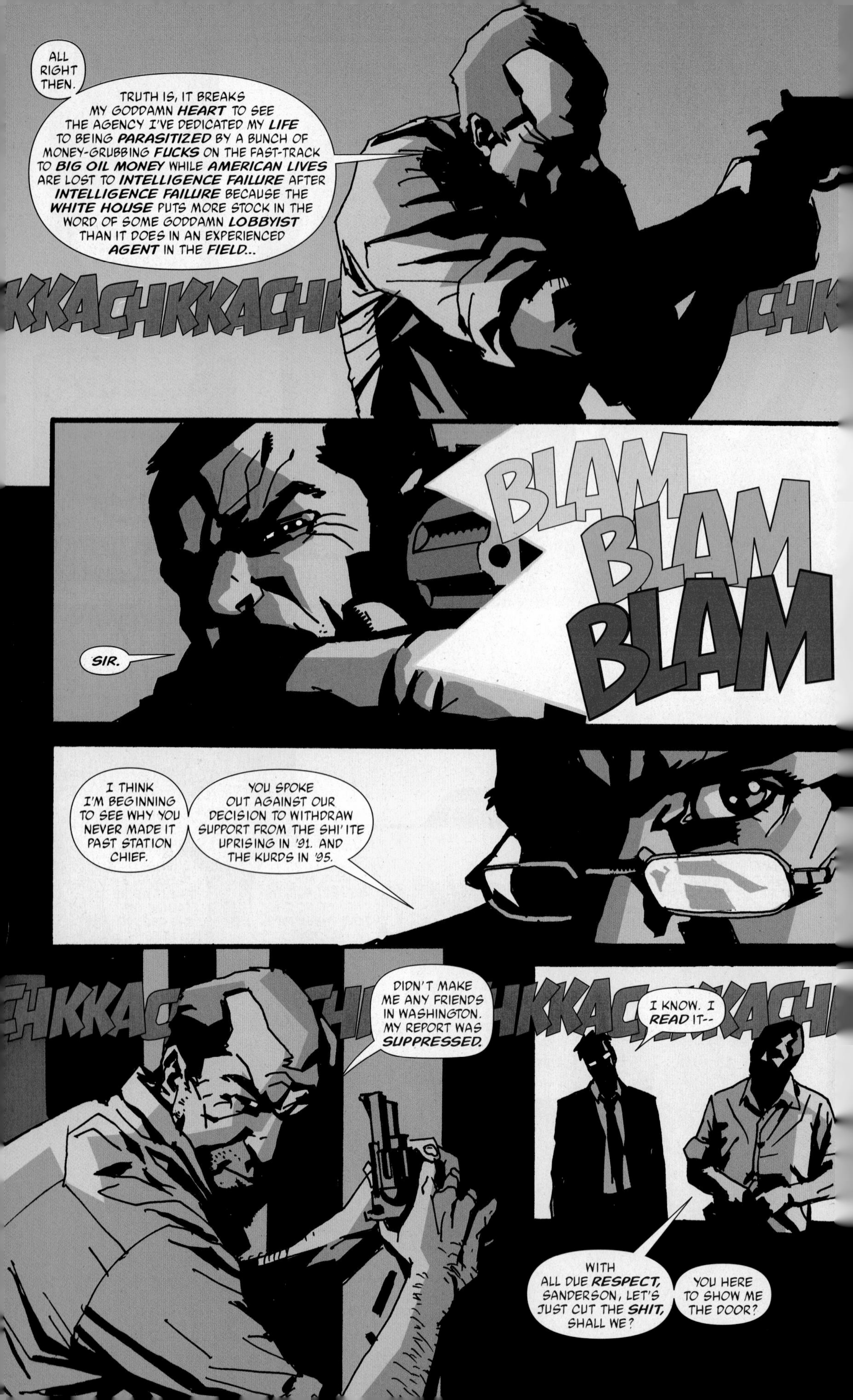
ALL RIGHT THEN.
TRUTH IS, IT BREAKS MY GODDAMN HEART TO SEE THE AGENCY I'VE DEDICATED MY LIFE TO BEING PARASITIZED BY A BUNCH OF MONEY-GRUBBING FUCKS ON THE FAST-TRACK TO BIG OIL MONEY WHILE AMERICAN LIVES ARE LOST TO INTELLIGENCE FAILURE AFTER INTELLIGENCE FAILURE BECAUSE THE WHITE HOUSE PUTS MORE STOCK IN THE WORD OF SOME GODDAMN LOBBYIST THAN IT DOES IN AN EXPERIENCED AGENT IN THE FIELD...
KKACHKKACH
BLAM
BLAM
BLAM
SIR.
I THINK I'M BEGINNING TO SEE WHY YOU NEVER MADE IT PAST STATION CHIEF.
YOU SPOKE OUT AGAINST OUR DECISION TO WITHDRAW SUPPORT FROM THE SHI'ITE UPRISING IN '91. AND THE KURDS IN '95.
DIDN'T MAKE ME ANY FRIENDS IN WASHINGTON. MY REPORT WAS SUPPRESSED.
I KNOW. I READ IT--
WITH ALL DUE RESPECT, SANDERSON, LET'S JUST CUT THE SHIT, SHALL WE?
YOU HERE TO SHOW ME THE DOOR?

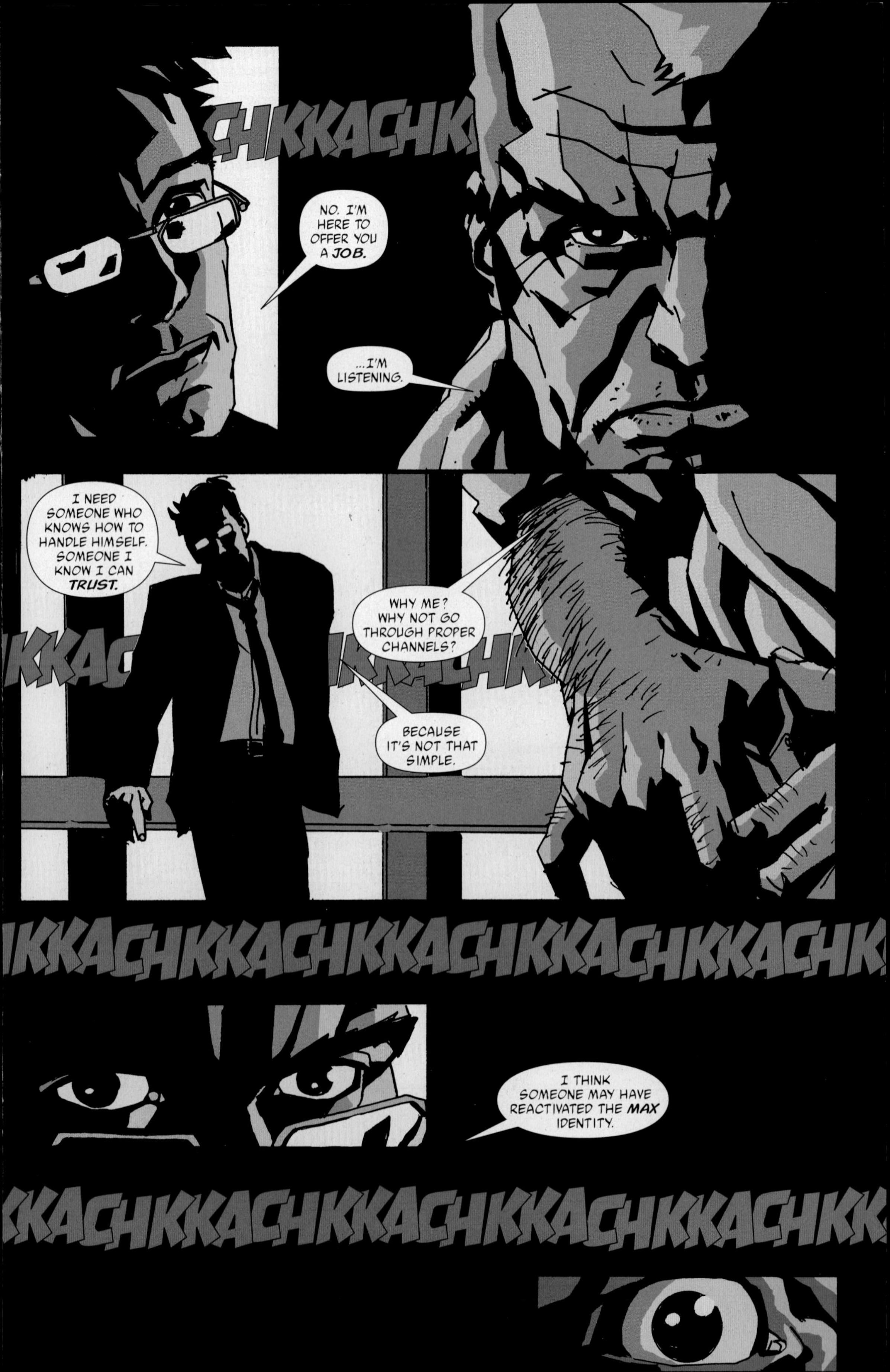
CHKKACHK
NO. I'M HERE TO OFFER YOU A JOB.
...I'M LISTENING.
I NEED SOMEONE WHO KNOWS HOW TO HANDLE HIMSELF. SOMEONE I KNOW I CAN TRUST.
WHY ME? WHY NOT GO THROUGH PROPER CHANNELS?
BECAUSE IT'S NOT THAT SIMPLE.
KKACHKKACHKKACHKKACHK
I THINK SOMEONE MAY HAVE REACTIVATED THE MAX IDENTITY.
KACHKKACHKKACHKKACHK

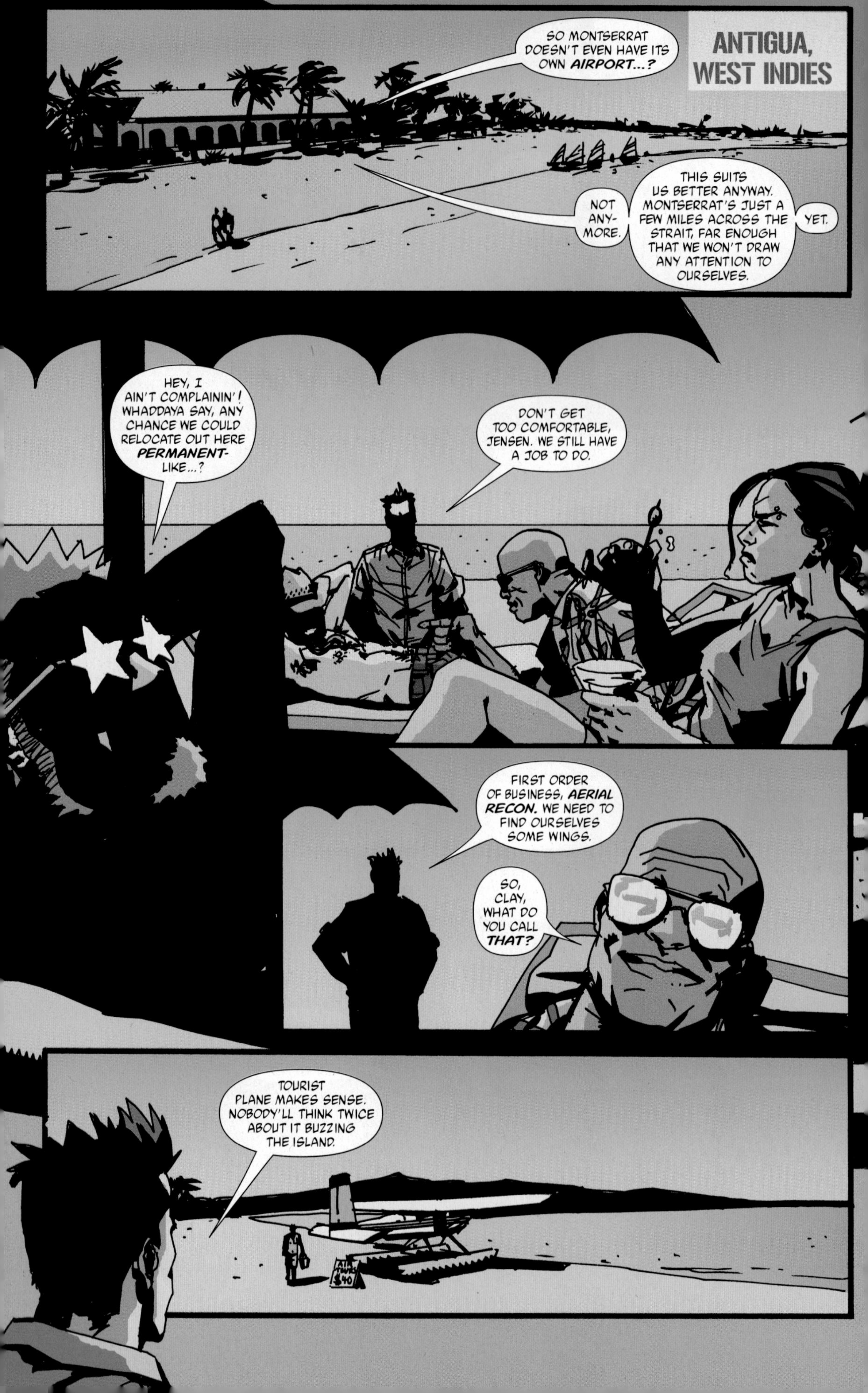
ANTIGUA, WEST INDIES
SO MONTSERRAT DOESN'T EVEN HAVE ITS OWN AIRPORT...?
NOT ANY-MORE.
THIS SUITS US BETTER ANYWAY. MONTSERRAT'S JUST A FEW MILES ACROSS THE STRAIT, FAR ENOUGH THAT WE WON'T DRAW ANY ATTENTION TO OURSELVES.
YET.
HEY, I AIN'T COMPLAININ'! WHADDAYA SAY, ANY CHANCE WE COULD RELOCATE OUT HERE PERMANENT-LIKE...?
DON'T GET TOO COMFORTABLE, JENSEN. WE STILL HAVE A JOB TO DO.
FIRST ORDER OF BUSINESS, AERIAL RECON. WE NEED TO FIND OURSELVES SOME WINGS.
SO, CLAY, WHAT DO YOU CALL THAT?
TOURIST PLANE MAKES SENSE. NOBODY'LL THINK TWICE ABOUT IT BUZZING THE ISLAND.

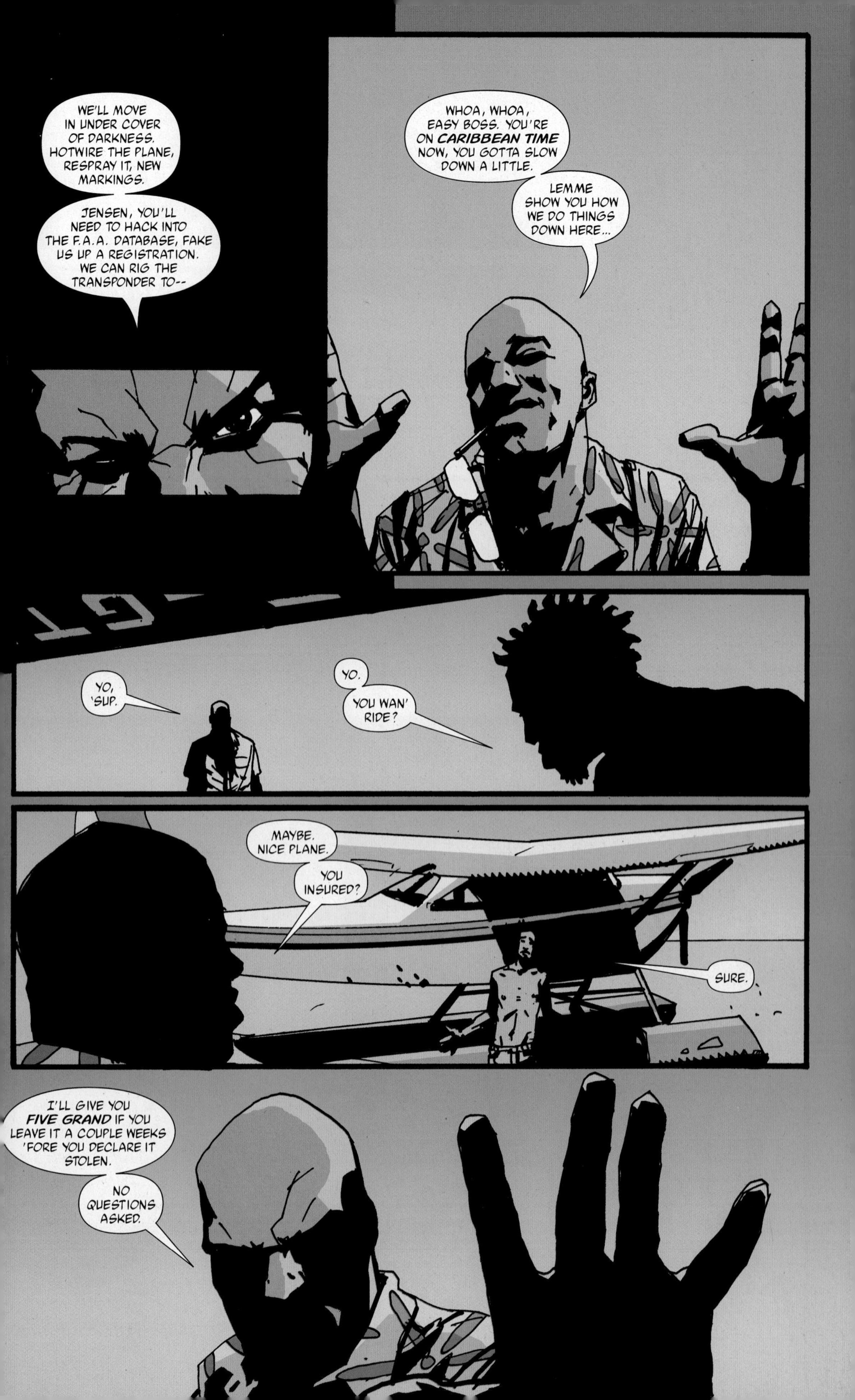
WE'LL MOVE IN UNDER COVER OF DARKNESS. HOTWIRE THE PLANE, RESPRAY IT, NEW MARKINGS.
JENSEN, YOU'LL NEED TO HACK INTO THE F.A.A. DATABASE, FAKE US UP A REGISTRATION. WE CAN RIG THE TRANSPONDER TO--
WHOA, WHOA, EASY BOSS. YOU'RE ON **CARIBBEAN TIME** NOW, YOU GOTTA SLOW DOWN A LITTLE.
LEMME SHOW YOU HOW WE DO THINGS DOWN HERE...
YO, 'SUP.
YO.
YOU WAN' RIDE?
MAYBE. NICE PLANE.
YOU INSURED?
SURE.
I'LL GIVE YOU **FIVE GRAND** IF YOU LEAVE IT A COUPLE WEEKS 'FORE YOU DECLARE IT STOLEN.
NO QUESTIONS ASKED.

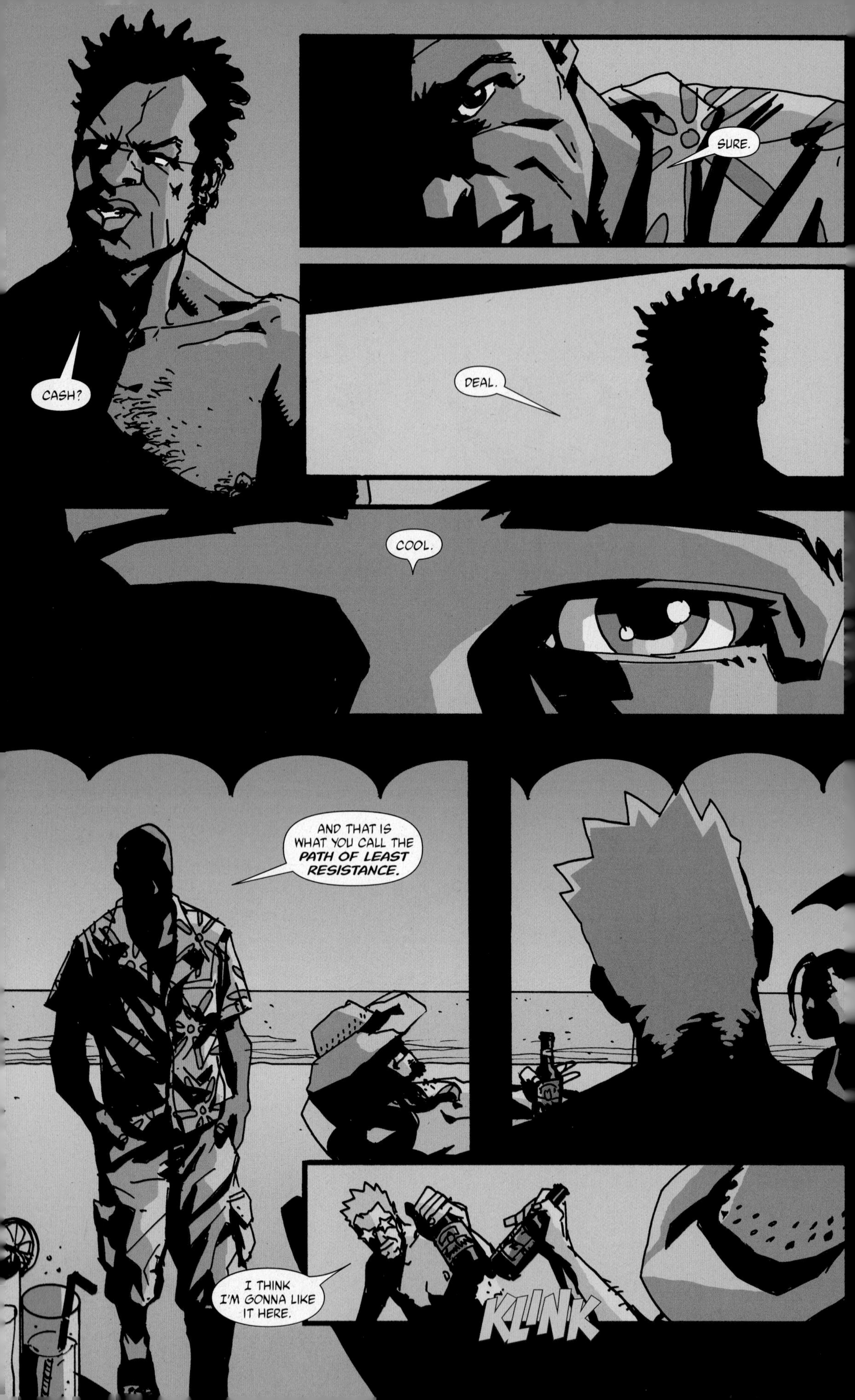
CASH?
SURE.
DEAL.
COOL.
AND THAT IS WHAT YOU CALL THE *PATH OF LEAST RESISTANCE.*
I THINK I'M GONNA LIKE IT HERE.
KLINK

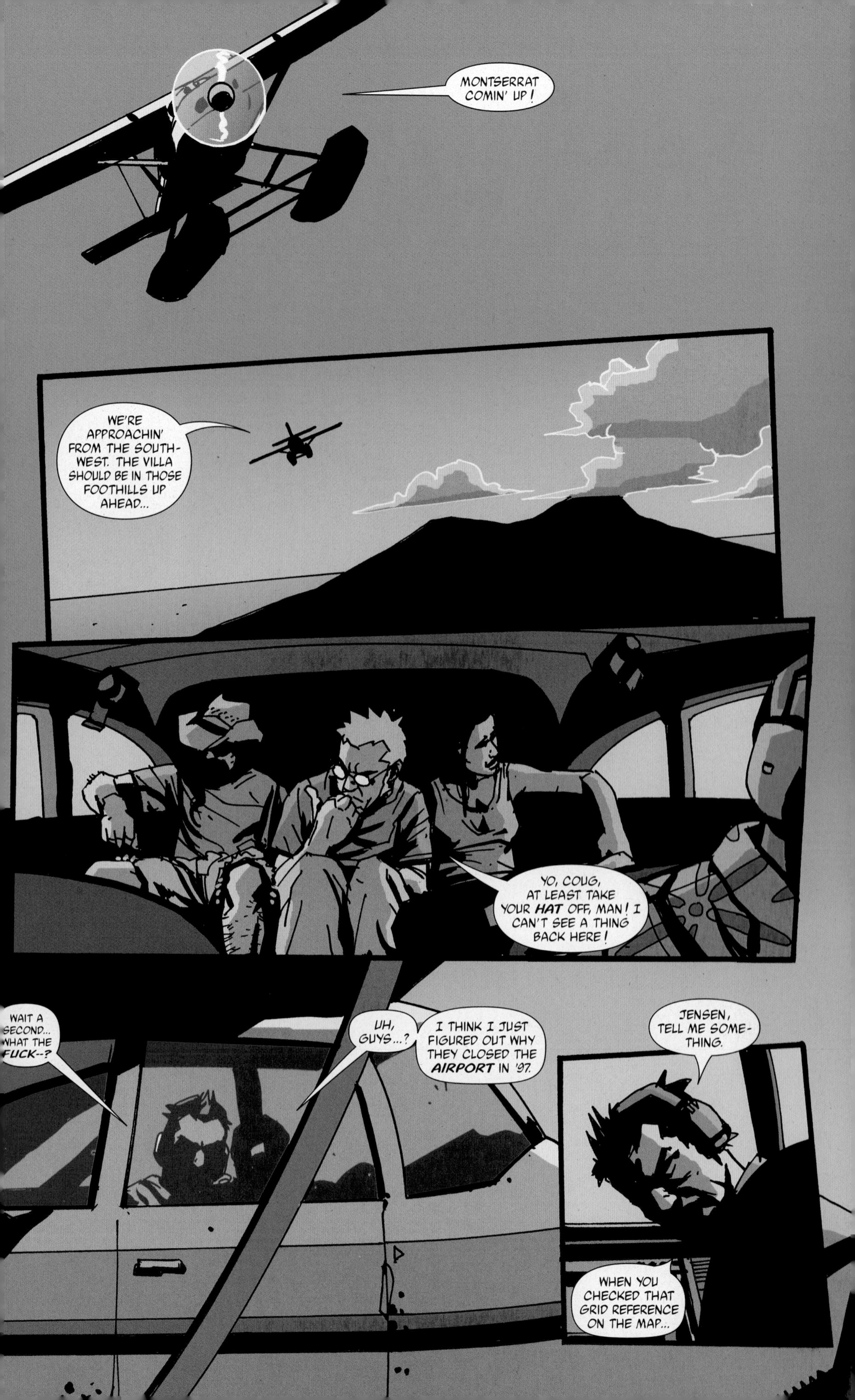
MONTSERRAT COMIN' UP!
WE'RE APPROACHIN' FROM THE SOUTH-WEST. THE VILLA SHOULD BE IN THOSE FOOTHILLS UP AHEAD...
YO, COUG, AT LEAST TAKE YOUR HAT OFF, MAN! I CAN'T SEE A THING BACK HERE!
WAIT A SECOND... WHAT THE FUCK--?
UH, GUYS...?
I THINK I JUST FIGURED OUT WHY THEY CLOSED THE AIRPORT IN '97.
JENSEN, TELL ME SOME-THING.
WHEN YOU CHECKED THAT GRID REFERENCE ON THE MAP...

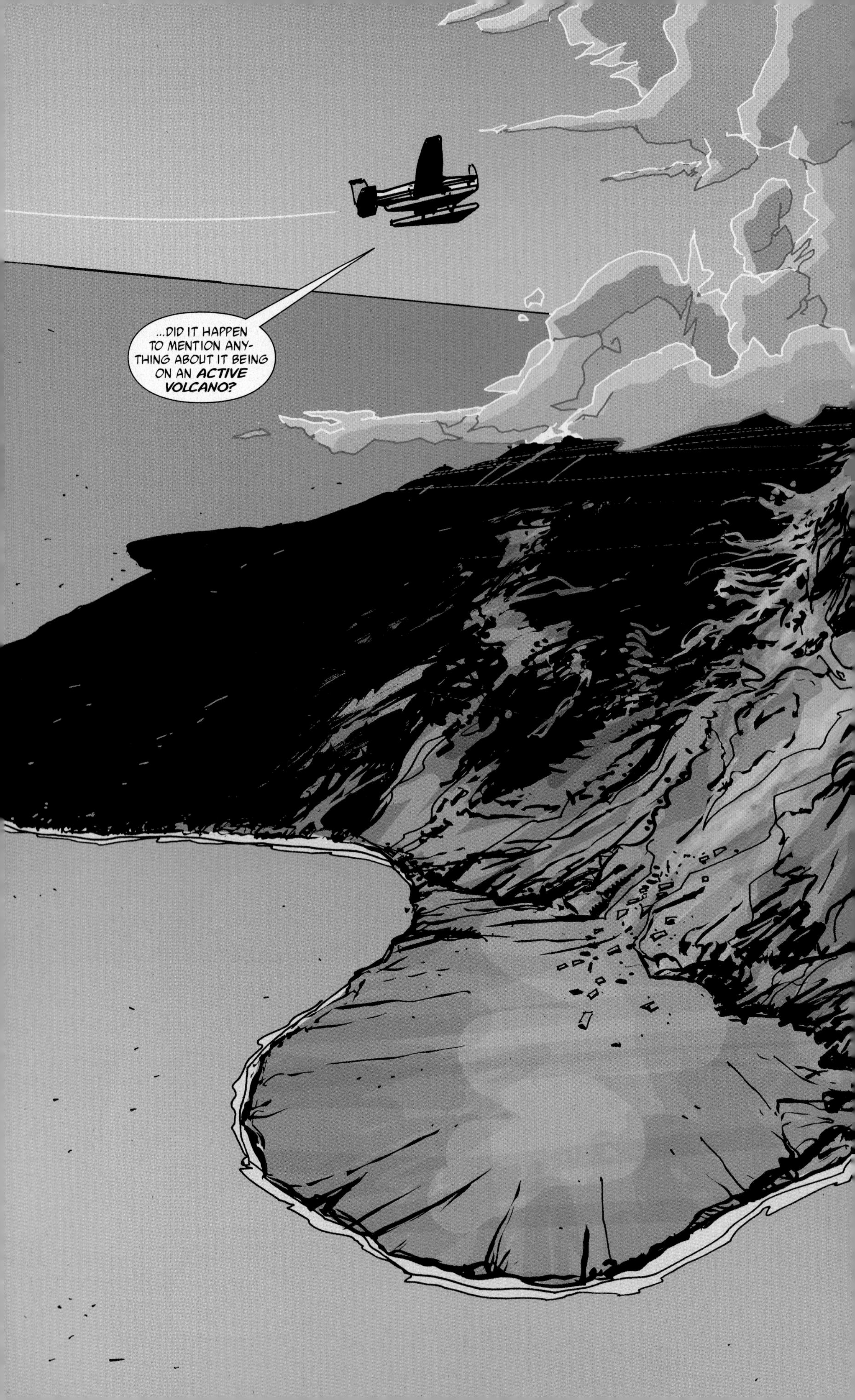
...DID IT HAPPEN TO MENTION ANY-THING ABOUT IT BEING ON AN *ACTIVE VOLCANO?*

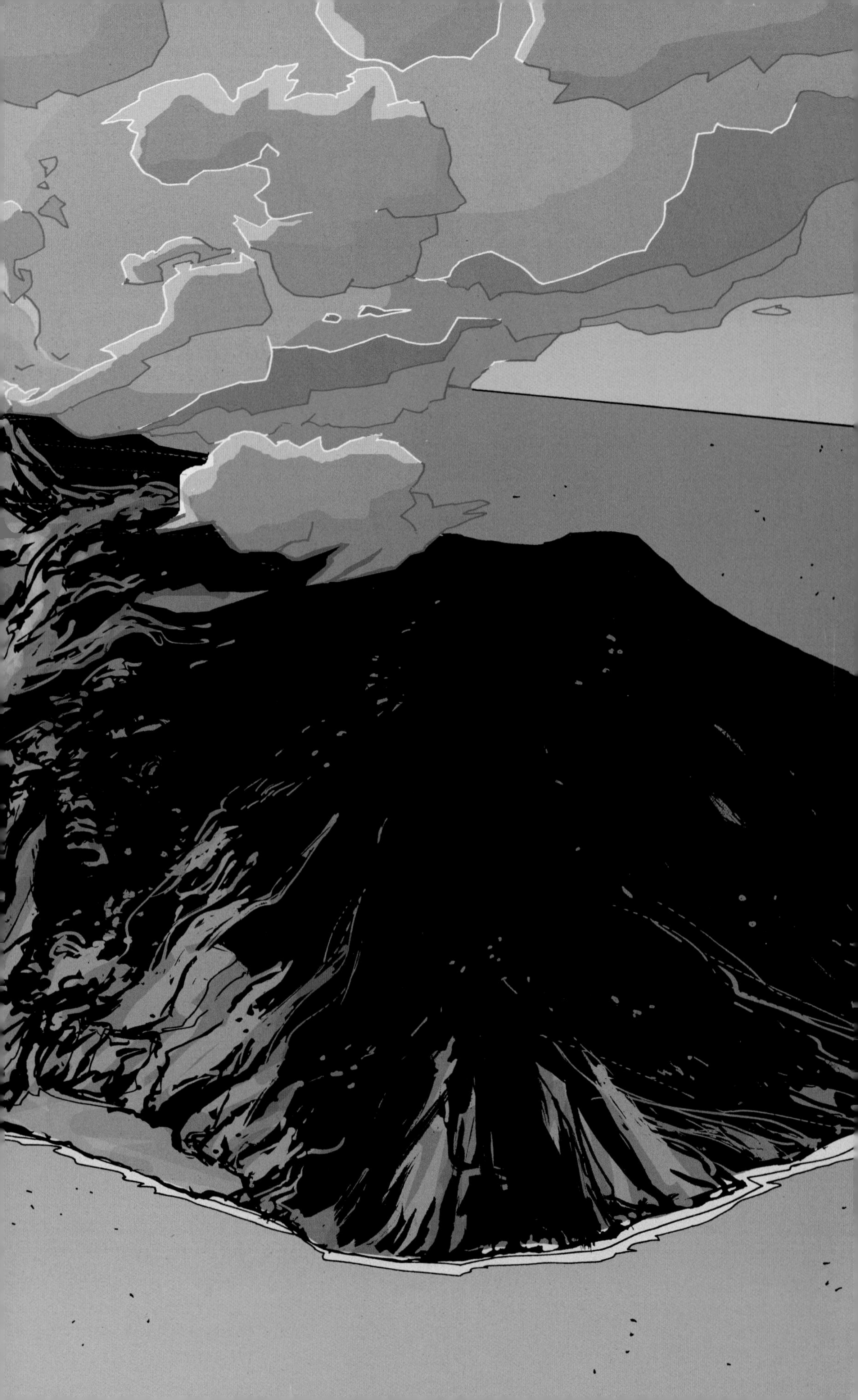

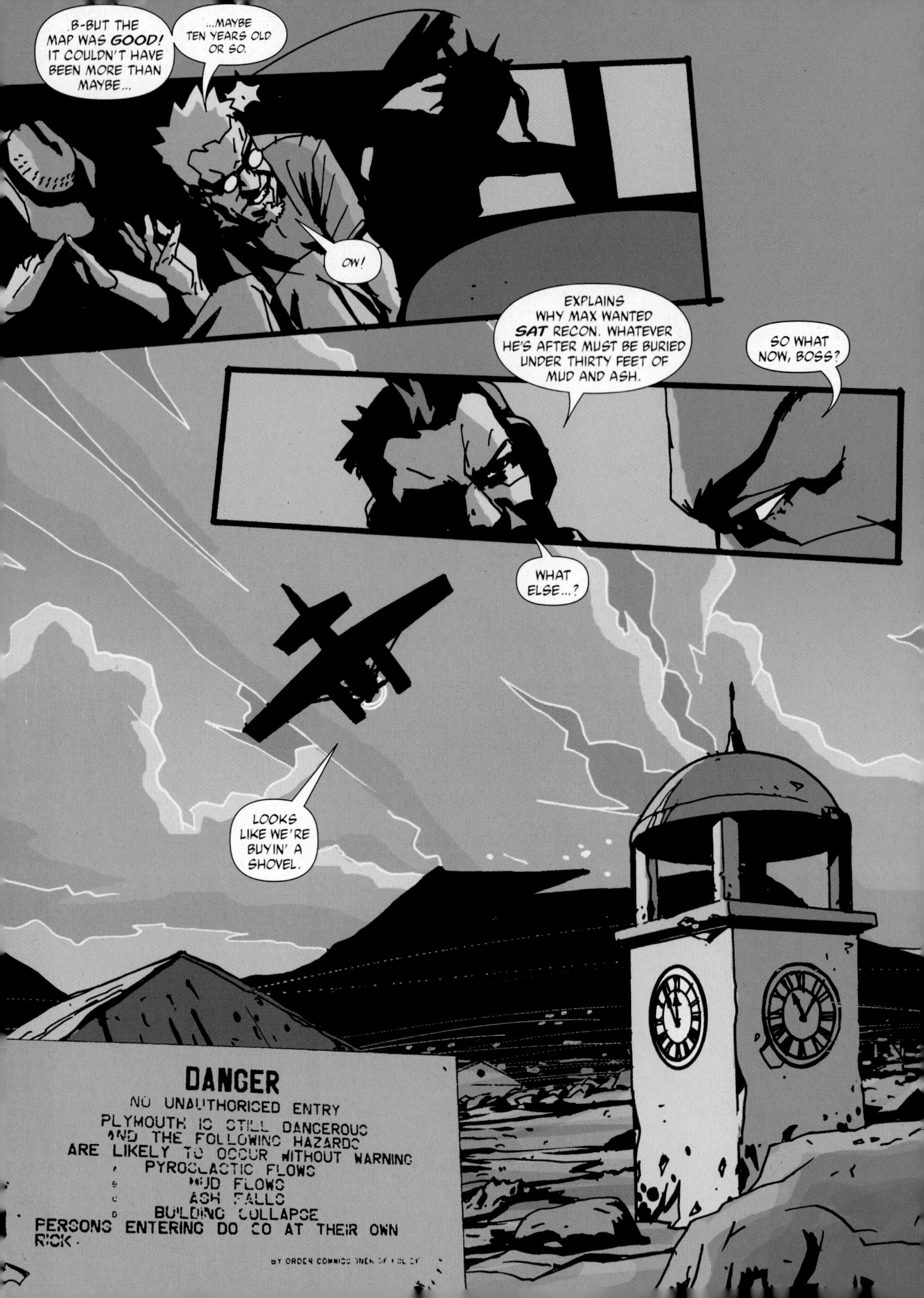
B-BUT THE MAP WAS GOOD! IT COULDN'T HAVE BEEN MORE THAN MAYBE...
...MAYBE TEN YEARS OLD OR SO.
OW!
EXPLAINS WHY MAX WANTED SAT RECON. WHATEVER HE'S AFTER MUST BE BURIED UNDER THIRTY FEET OF MUD AND ASH.
SO WHAT NOW, BOSS?
WHAT ELSE...?
LOOKS LIKE WE'RE BUYIN' A SHOVEL.
DANGER
NO UNAUTHORICED ENTRY
PLYMOUTH IS STILL DANGEROUS
AND THE FOLLOWING HAZARDS
ARE LIKELY TO OCCUR WITHOUT WARNING
PYROCLASTIC FLOWS
MUD FLOWS
ASH FALLS
BUILDING COLLAPSE
PERSONS ENTERING DO SO AT THEIR OWN RISK.

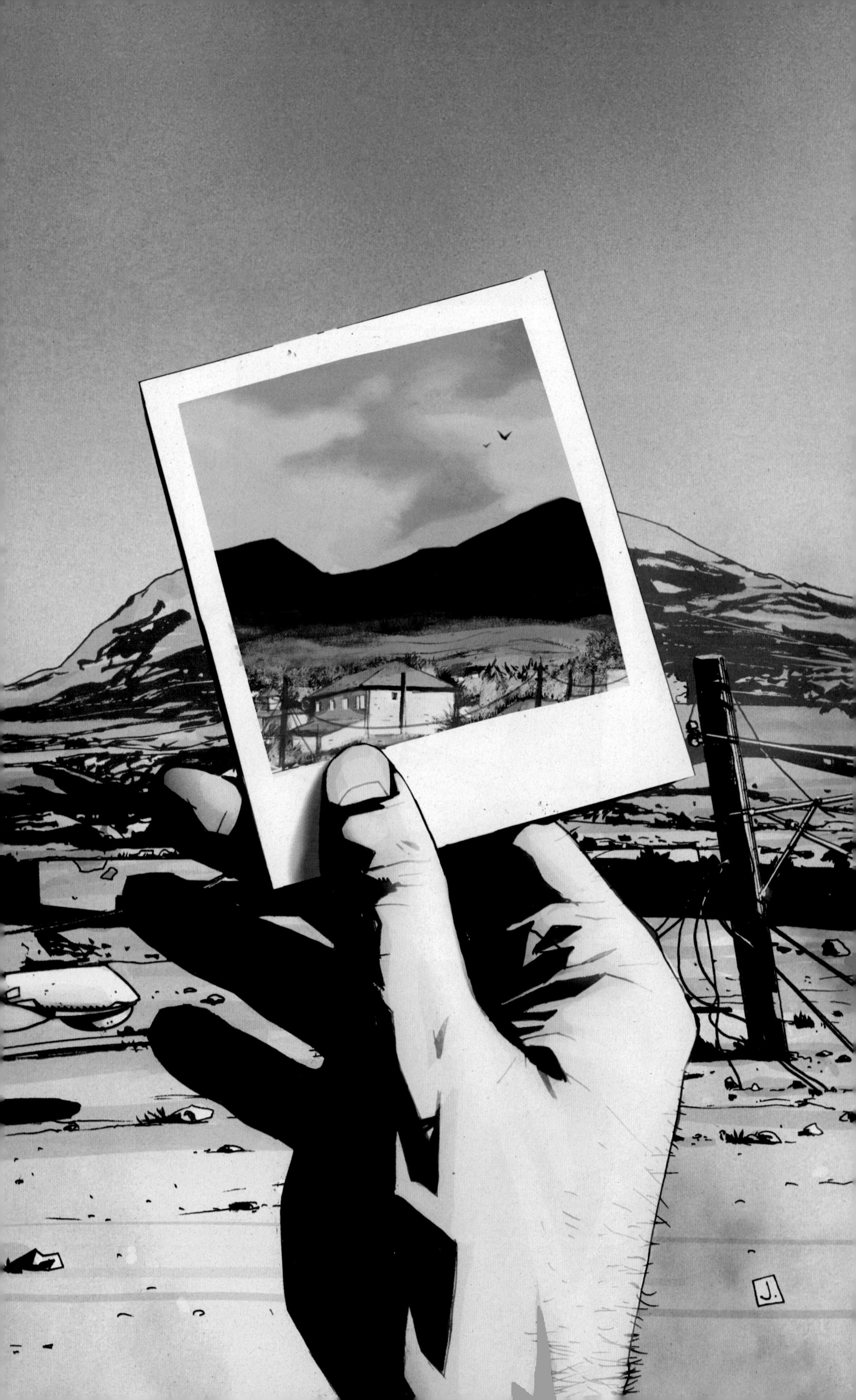
J.

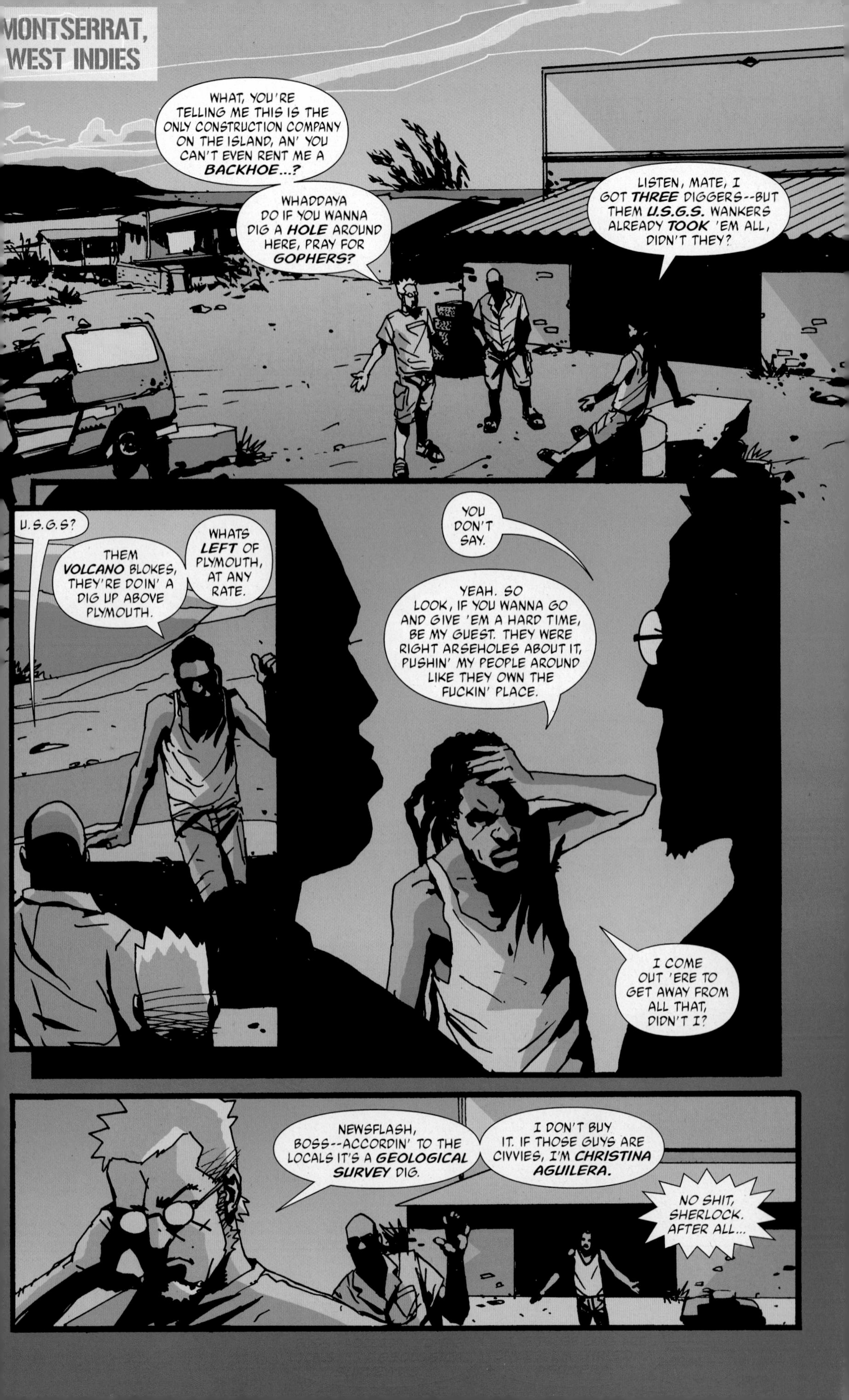
MONTSERRAT, WEST INDIES
WHAT, YOU'RE TELLING ME THIS IS THE ONLY CONSTRUCTION COMPANY ON THE ISLAND, AN' YOU CAN'T EVEN RENT ME A BACKHOE...?
WHADDAYA DO IF YOU WANNA DIG A HOLE AROUND HERE, PRAY FOR GOPHERS?
LISTEN, MATE, I GOT THREE DIGGERS--BUT THEM U.S.G.S. WANKERS ALREADY TOOK 'EM ALL, DIDN'T THEY?
U.S.G.S?
THEM VOLCANO BLOKES, THEY'RE DOIN' A DIG UP ABOVE PLYMOUTH.
WHATS LEFT OF PLYMOUTH, AT ANY RATE.
YOU DON'T SAY.
YEAH. SO LOOK, IF YOU WANNA GO AND GIVE 'EM A HARD TIME, BE MY GUEST. THEY WERE RIGHT ARSEHOLES ABOUT IT, PUSHIN' MY PEOPLE AROUND LIKE THEY OWN THE FUCKIN' PLACE.
I COME OUT 'ERE TO GET AWAY FROM ALL THAT, DIDN'T I?
NEWSFLASH, BOSS--ACCORDIN' TO THE LOCALS IT'S A GEOLOGICAL SURVEY DIG.
I DON'T BUY IT. IF THOSE GUYS ARE CIVVIES, I'M CHRISTINA AGUILERA.
NO SHIT, SHERLOCK. AFTER ALL...

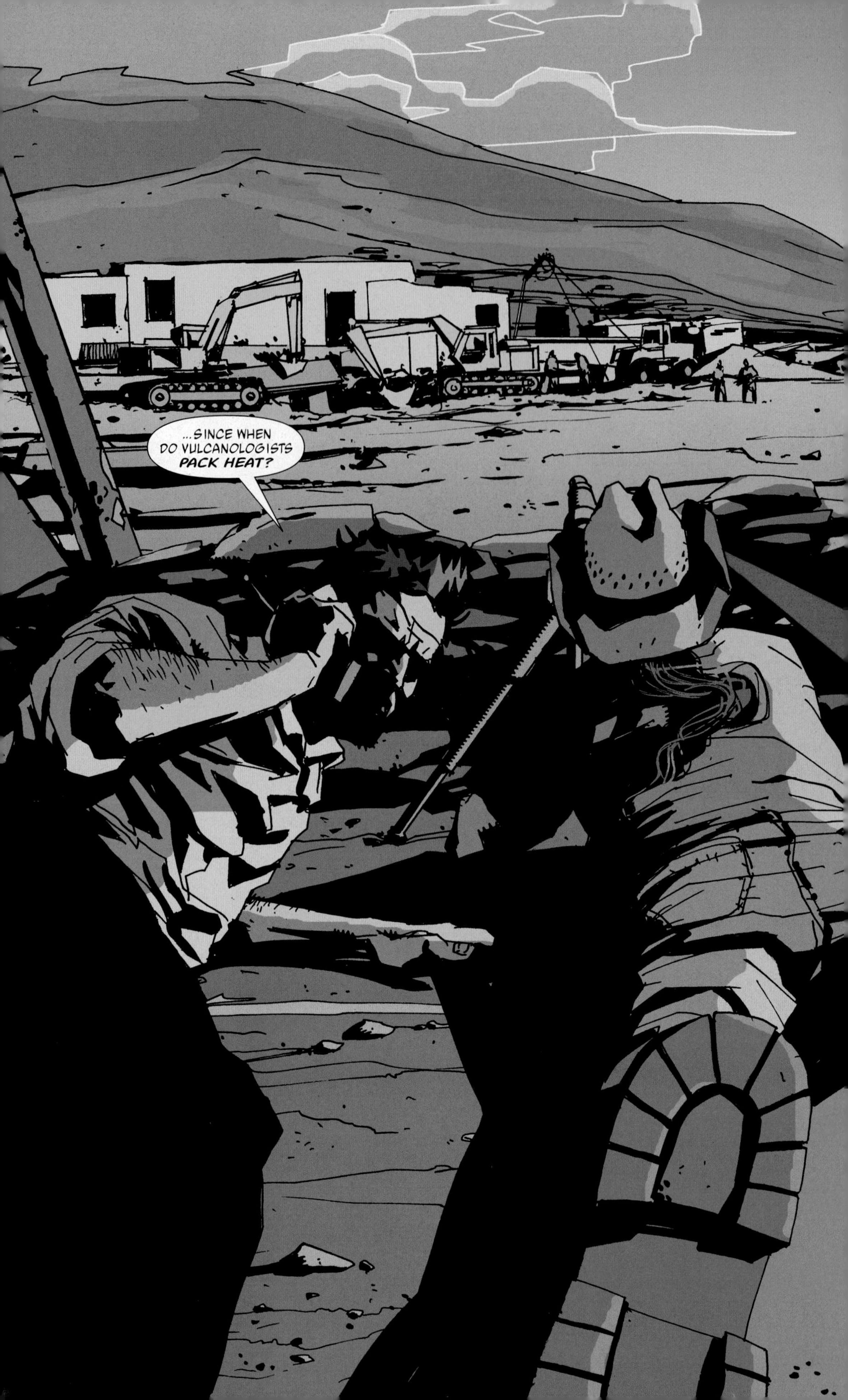
...SINCE WHEN DO VULCANOLOGISTS PACK HEAT?

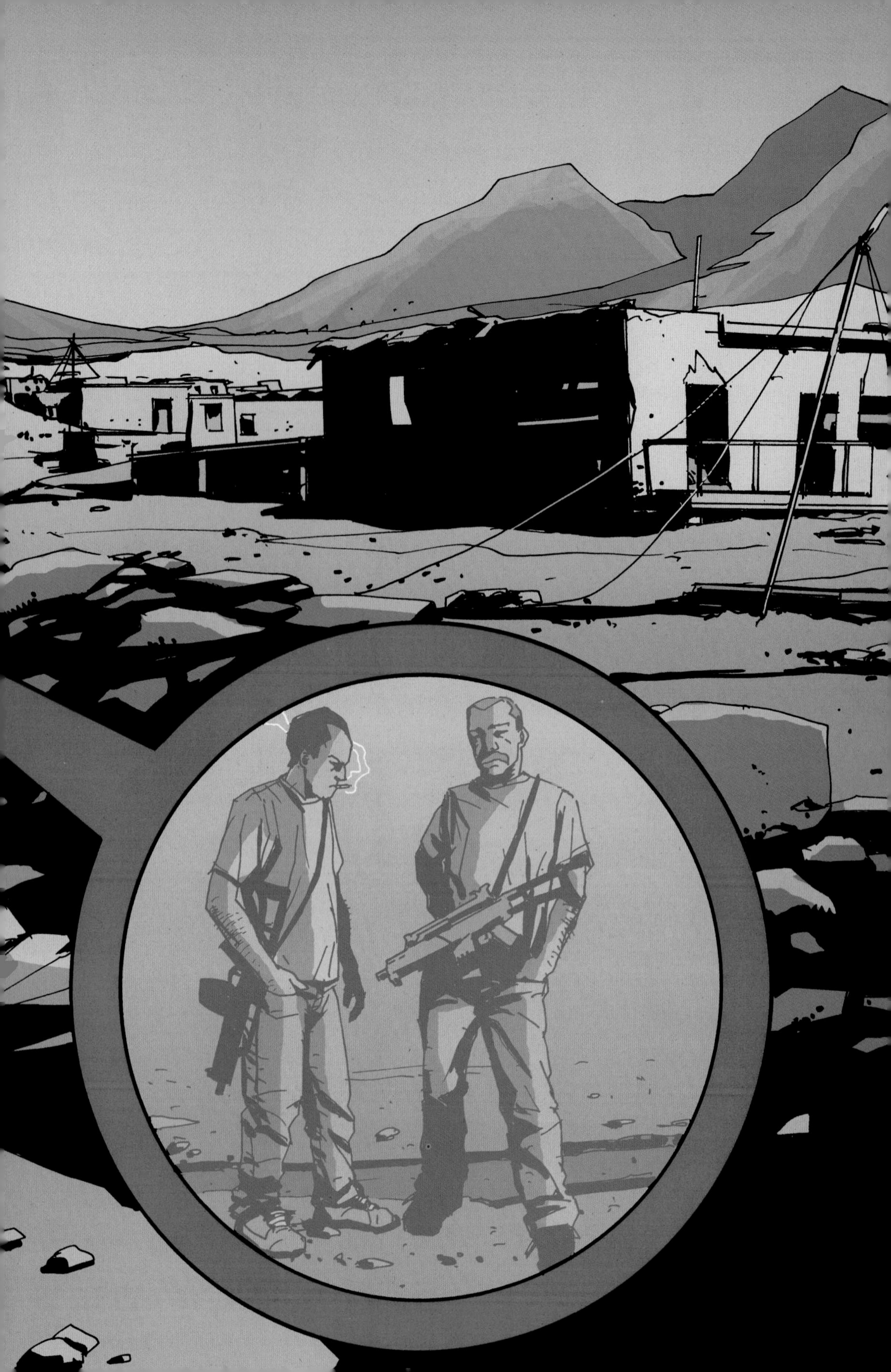

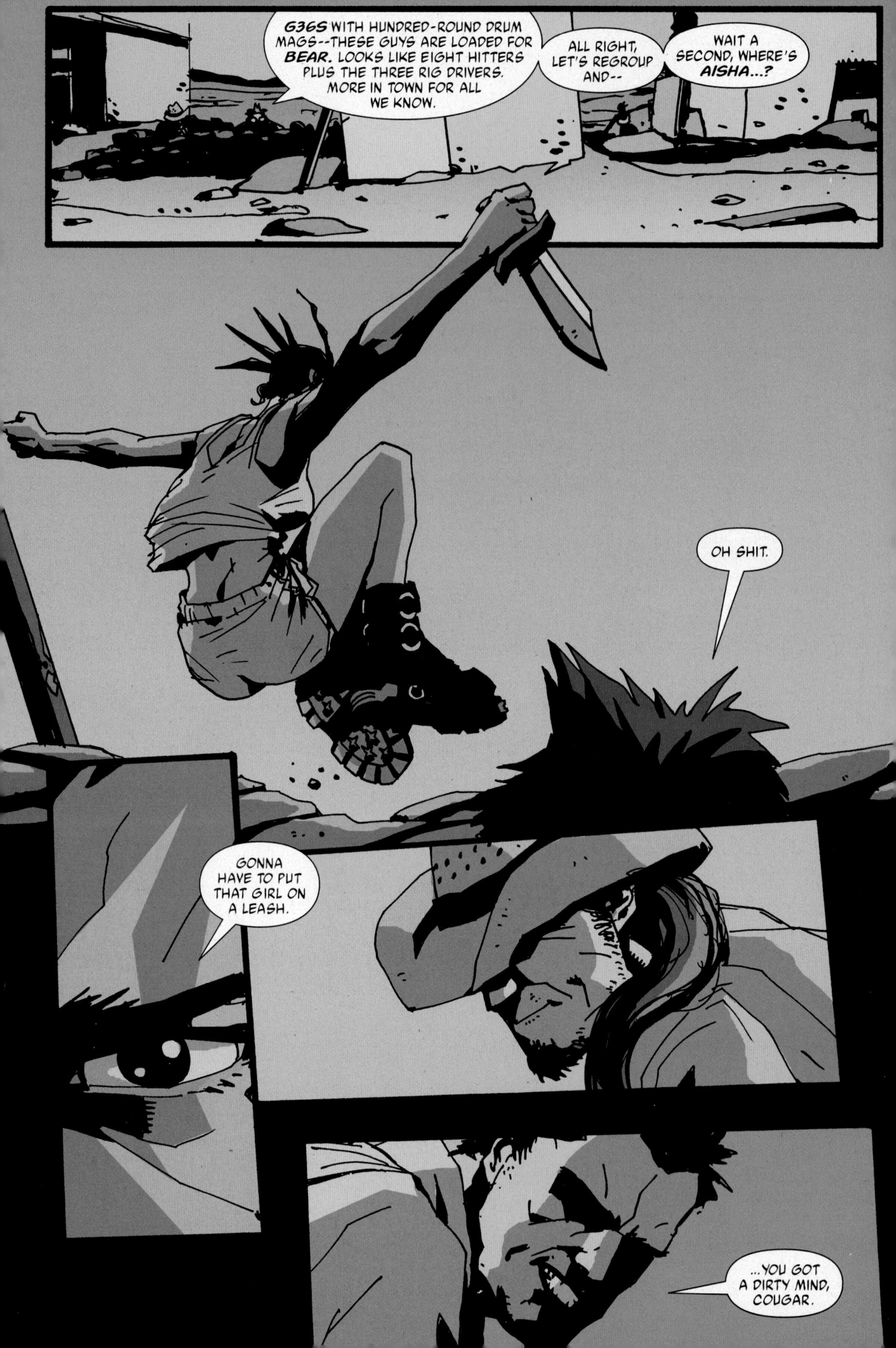
G36S WITH HUNDRED-ROUND DRUM MAGS--THESE GUYS ARE LOADED FOR BEAR. LOOKS LIKE EIGHT HITTERS PLUS THE THREE RIG DRIVERS. MORE IN TOWN FOR ALL WE KNOW.
ALL RIGHT, LET'S REGROUP AND--
WAIT A SECOND, WHERE'S AISHA...?
OH SHIT.
GONNA HAVE TO PUT THAT GIRL ON A LEASH.
...YOU GOT A DIRTY MIND, COUGAR.

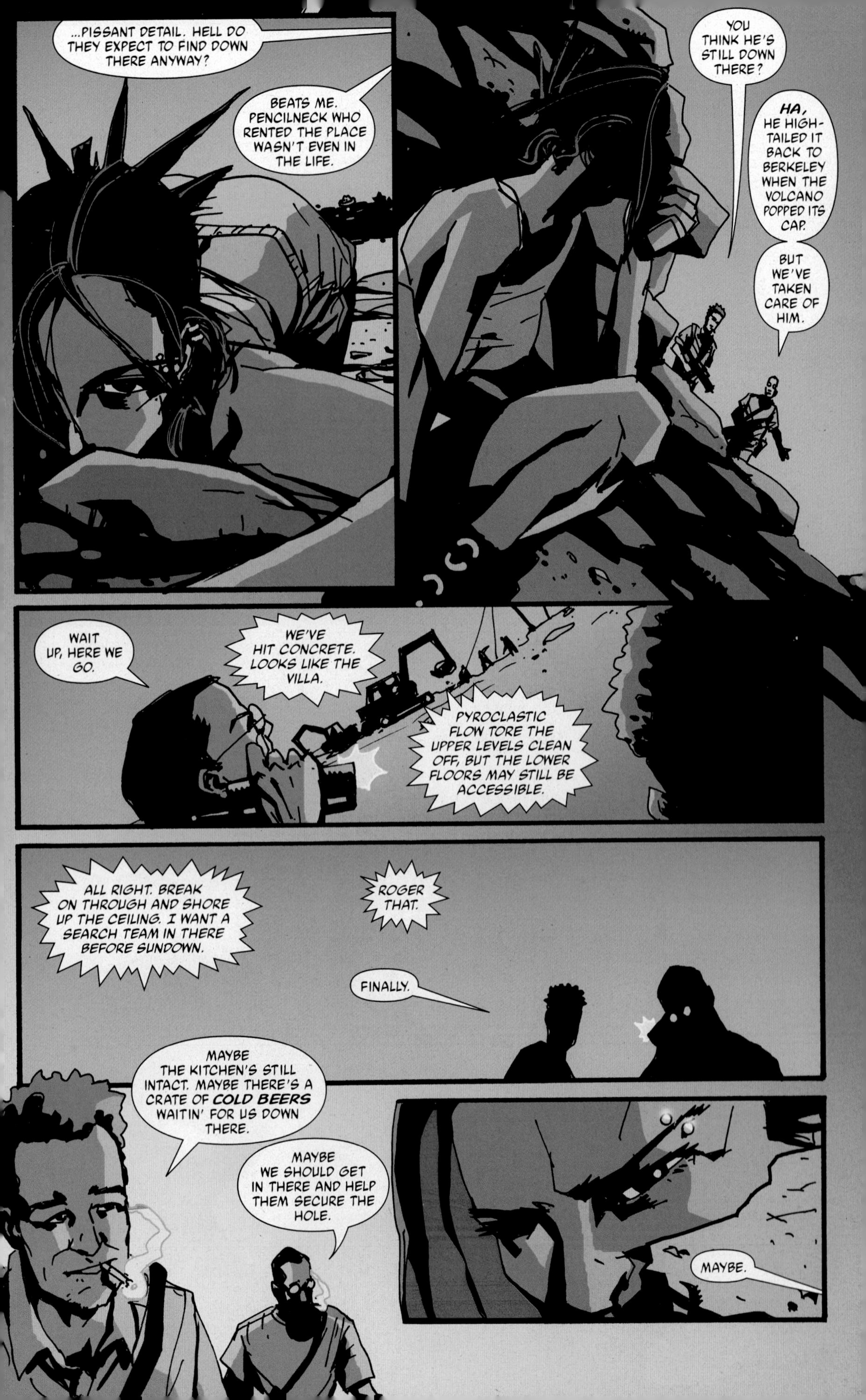
...PISSANT DETAIL. HELL DO THEY EXPECT TO FIND DOWN THERE ANYWAY?
BEATS ME. PENCILNECK WHO RENTED THE PLACE WASN'T EVEN IN THE LIFE.
YOU THINK HE'S STILL DOWN THERE?
HA, HE HIGH-TAILED IT BACK TO BERKELEY WHEN THE VOLCANO POPPED ITS CAP.
BUT WE'VE TAKEN CARE OF HIM.
WAIT UP, HERE WE GO.
WE'VE HIT CONCRETE. LOOKS LIKE THE VILLA.
PYROCLASTIC FLOW TORE THE UPPER LEVELS CLEAN OFF, BUT THE LOWER FLOORS MAY STILL BE ACCESSIBLE.
ALL RIGHT. BREAK ON THROUGH AND SHORE UP THE CEILING. I WANT A SEARCH TEAM IN THERE BEFORE SUNDOWN.
ROGER THAT.
FINALLY.
MAYBE THE KITCHEN'S STILL INTACT. MAYBE THERE'S A CRATE OF COLD BEERS WAITIN' FOR US DOWN THERE.
MAYBE WE SHOULD GET IN THERE AND HELP THEM SECURE THE HOLE.
MAYBE.

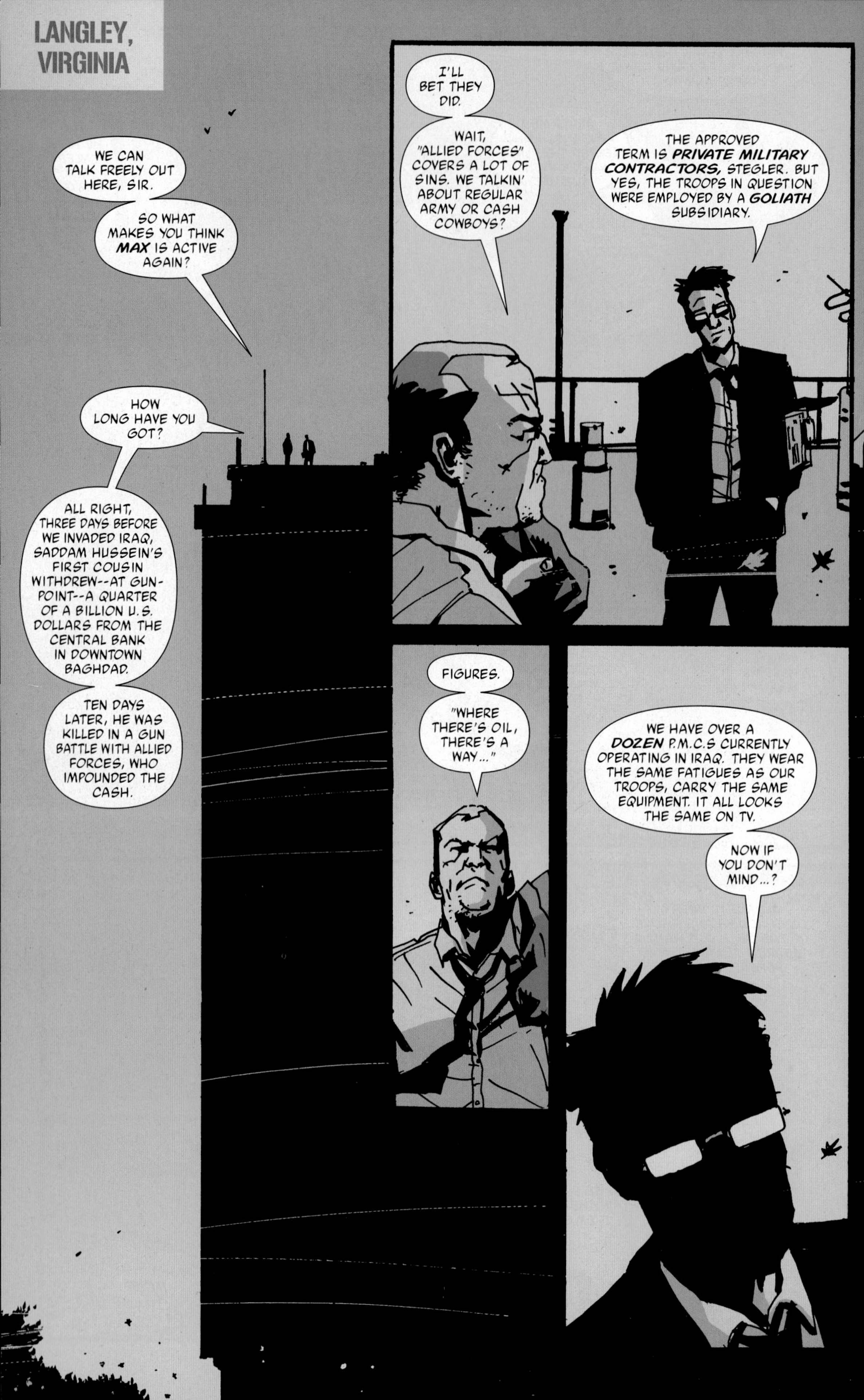
LANGLEY, VIRGINIA
WE CAN TALK FREELY OUT HERE, SIR.
SO WHAT MAKES YOU THINK MAX IS ACTIVE AGAIN?
HOW LONG HAVE YOU GOT?
ALL RIGHT, THREE DAYS BEFORE WE INVADED IRAQ, SADDAM HUSSEIN'S FIRST COUSIN WITHDREW--AT GUN-POINT--A QUARTER OF A BILLION U.S. DOLLARS FROM THE CENTRAL BANK IN DOWNTOWN BAGHDAD.
TEN DAYS LATER, HE WAS KILLED IN A GUN BATTLE WITH ALLIED FORCES, WHO IMPOUNDED THE CASH.
I'LL BET THEY DID.
WAIT, "ALLIED FORCES" COVERS A LOT OF SINS. WE TALKIN' ABOUT REGULAR ARMY OR CASH COWBOYS?
THE APPROVED TERM IS PRIVATE MILITARY CONTRACTORS, STEGLER. BUT YES, THE TROOPS IN QUESTION WERE EMPLOYED BY A GOLIATH SUBSIDIARY.
FIGURES.
"WHERE THERE'S OIL, THERE'S A WAY..."
WE HAVE OVER A DOZEN P.M.C.S CURRENTLY OPERATING IN IRAQ. THEY WEAR THE SAME FATIGUES AS OUR TROOPS, CARRY THE SAME EQUIPMENT. IT ALL LOOKS THE SAME ON TV.
NOW IF YOU DON'T MIND...?

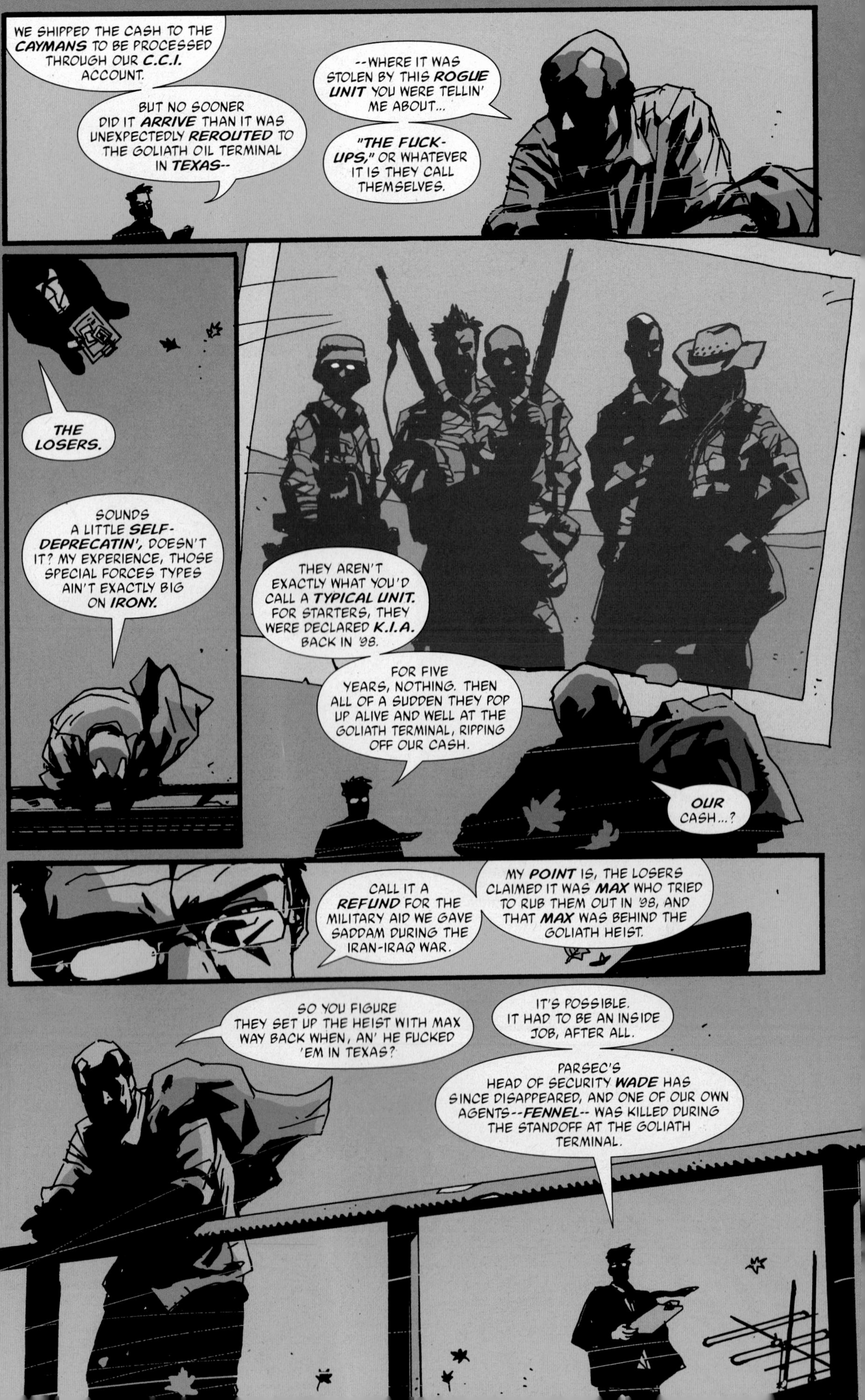
WE SHIPPED THE CASH TO THE CAYMANS TO BE PROCESSED THROUGH OUR C.C.I. ACCOUNT.
BUT NO SOONER DID IT ARRIVE THAN IT WAS UNEXPECTEDLY REROUTED TO THE GOLIATH OIL TERMINAL IN TEXAS--
--WHERE IT WAS STOLEN BY THIS ROGUE UNIT YOU WERE TELLIN' ME ABOUT...
"THE FUCK-UPS," OR WHATEVER IT IS THEY CALL THEMSELVES.
THE LOSERS.
SOUNDS A LITTLE SELF-DEPRECATIN', DOESN'T IT? MY EXPERIENCE, THOSE SPECIAL FORCES TYPES AIN'T EXACTLY BIG ON IRONY.
THEY AREN'T EXACTLY WHAT YOU'D CALL A TYPICAL UNIT. FOR STARTERS, THEY WERE DECLARED K.I.A. BACK IN '98.
FOR FIVE YEARS, NOTHING. THEN ALL OF A SUDDEN THEY POP UP ALIVE AND WELL AT THE GOLIATH TERMINAL, RIPPING OFF OUR CASH.
OUR CASH...?
CALL IT A REFUND FOR THE MILITARY AID WE GAVE SADDAM DURING THE IRAN-IRAQ WAR.
MY POINT IS, THE LOSERS CLAIMED IT WAS MAX WHO TRIED TO RUB THEM OUT IN '98, AND THAT MAX WAS BEHIND THE GOLIATH HEIST.
SO YOU FIGURE THEY SET UP THE HEIST WITH MAX WAY BACK WHEN, AN' HE FUCKED 'EM IN TEXAS?
IT'S POSSIBLE. IT HAD TO BE AN INSIDE JOB, AFTER ALL.
PARSEC'S HEAD OF SECURITY WADE HAS SINCE DISAPPEARED, AND ONE OF OUR OWN AGENTS--FENNEL-- WAS KILLED DURING THE STANDOFF AT THE GOLIATH TERMINAL.

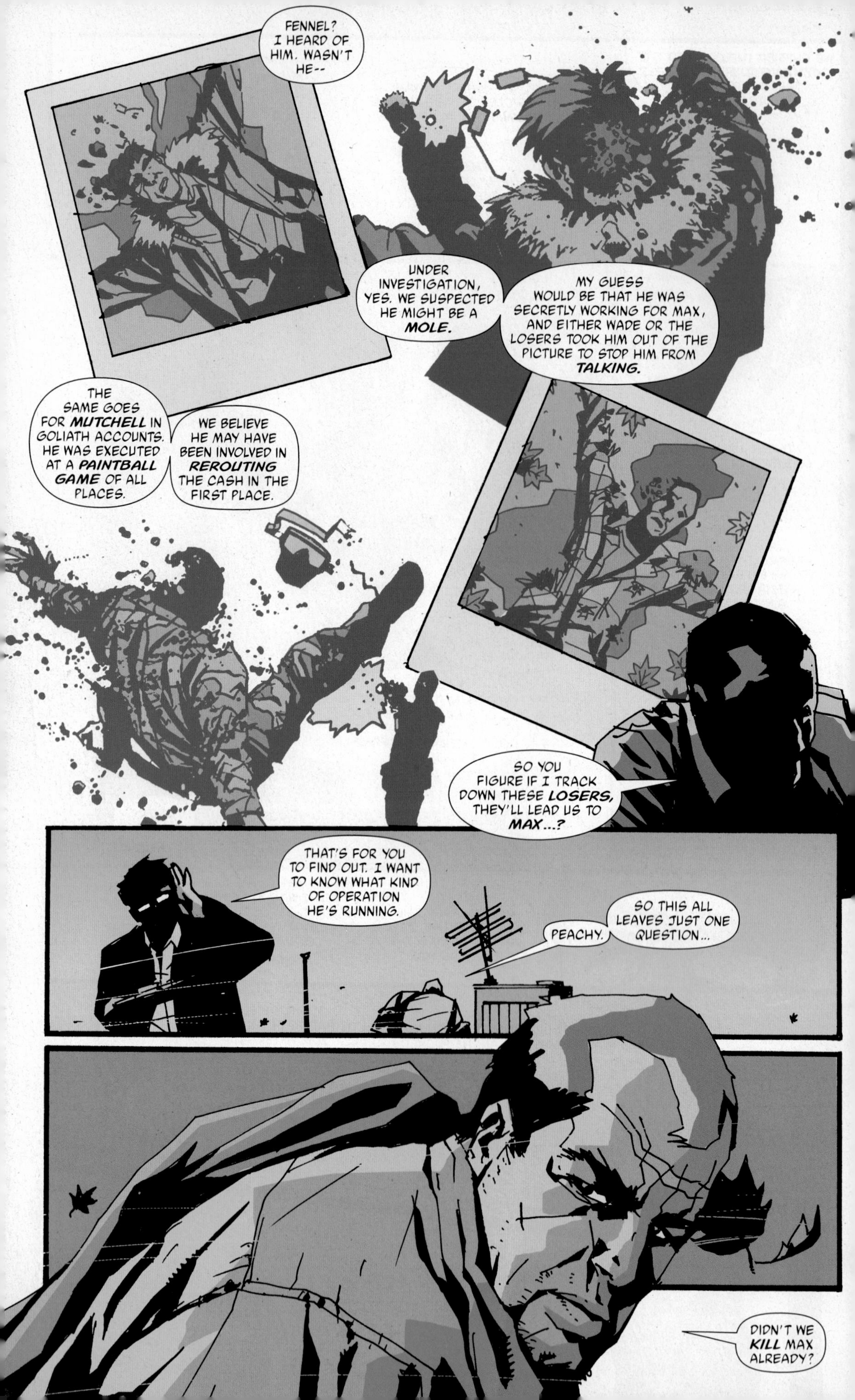
FENNEL? I HEARD OF HIM. WASN'T HE--
UNDER INVESTIGATION, YES. WE SUSPECTED HE MIGHT BE A MOLE.
MY GUESS WOULD BE THAT HE WAS SECRETLY WORKING FOR MAX, AND EITHER WADE OR THE LOSERS TOOK HIM OUT OF THE PICTURE TO STOP HIM FROM TALKING.
THE SAME GOES FOR MUTCHELL IN GOLIATH ACCOUNTS. HE WAS EXECUTED AT A PAINTBALL GAME OF ALL PLACES.
WE BELIEVE HE MAY HAVE BEEN INVOLVED IN REROUTING THE CASH IN THE FIRST PLACE.
SO YOU FIGURE IF I TRACK DOWN THESE LOSERS, THEY'LL LEAD US TO MAX...?
THAT'S FOR YOU TO FIND OUT. I WANT TO KNOW WHAT KIND OF OPERATION HE'S RUNNING.
PEACHY.
SO THIS ALL LEAVES JUST ONE QUESTION...
DIDN'T WE KILL MAX ALREADY?

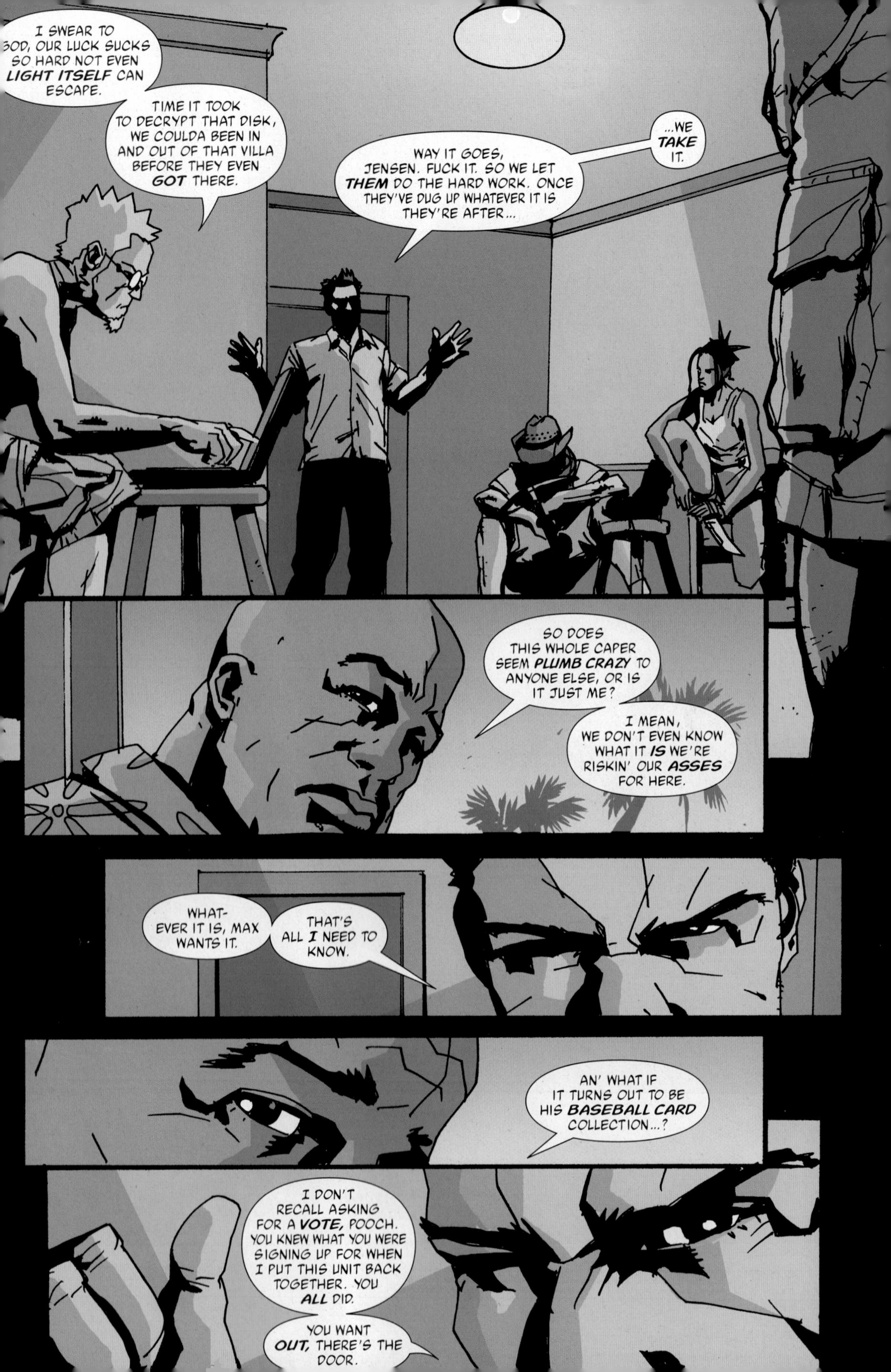
I SWEAR TO GOD, OUR LUCK SUCKS SO HARD NOT EVEN LIGHT ITSELF CAN ESCAPE.
TIME IT TOOK TO DECRYPT THAT DISK, WE COULDA BEEN IN AND OUT OF THAT VILLA BEFORE THEY EVEN GOT THERE.
WAY IT GOES, JENSEN. FUCK IT. SO WE LET THEM DO THE HARD WORK. ONCE THEY'VE DUG UP WHATEVER IT IS THEY'RE AFTER...
...WE TAKE IT.
SO DOES THIS WHOLE CAPER SEEM PLUMB CRAZY TO ANYONE ELSE, OR IS IT JUST ME?
I MEAN, WE DON'T EVEN KNOW WHAT IT IS WE'RE RISKIN' OUR ASSES FOR HERE.
WHAT-EVER IT IS, MAX WANTS IT.
THAT'S ALL I NEED TO KNOW.
AN' WHAT IF IT TURNS OUT TO BE HIS BASEBALL CARD COLLECTION...?
I DON'T RECALL ASKING FOR A VOTE, POOCH. YOU KNEW WHAT YOU WERE SIGNING UP FOR WHEN I PUT THIS UNIT BACK TOGETHER. YOU ALL DID.
YOU WANT OUT, THERE'S THE DOOR.

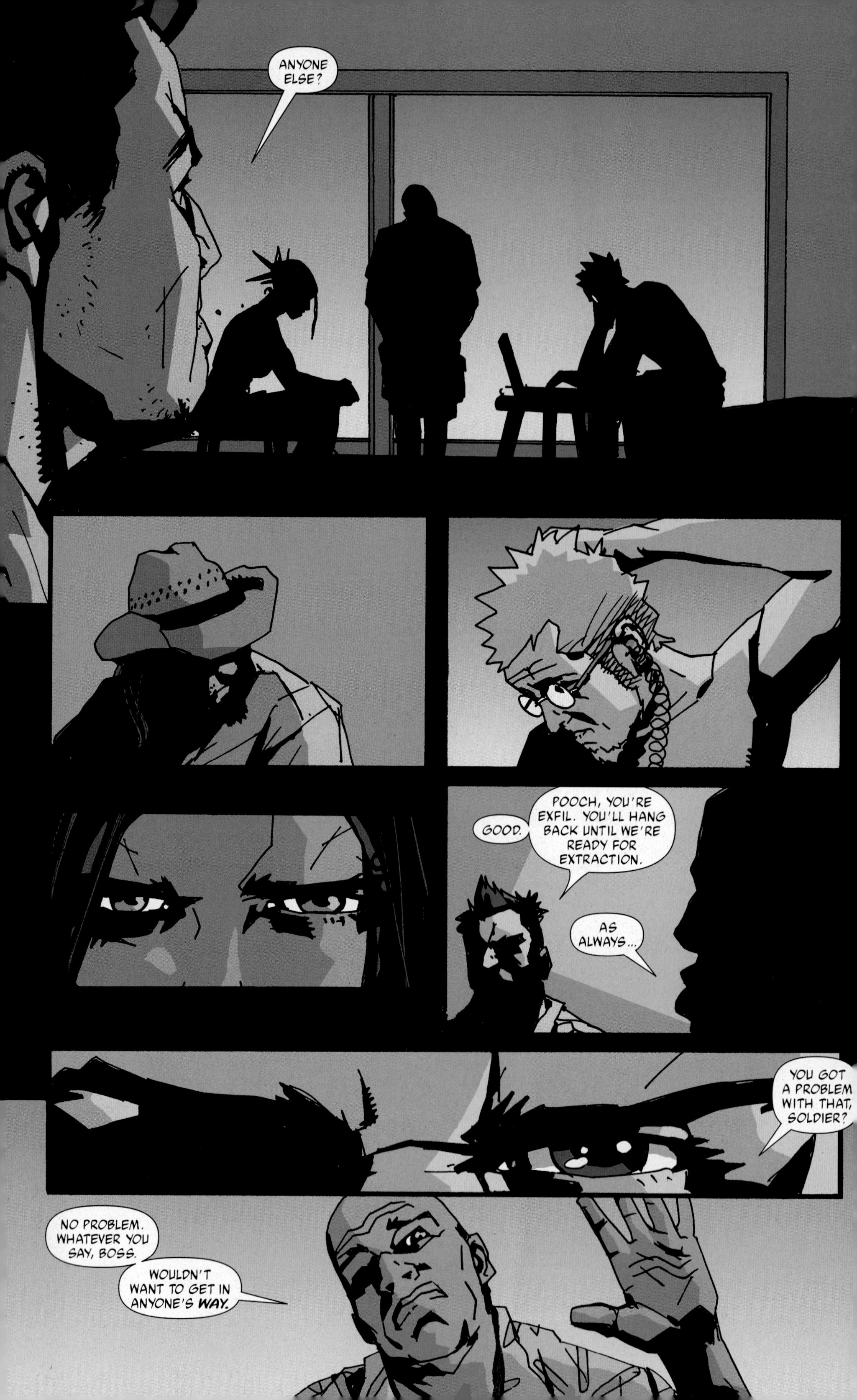
ANYONE ELSE?
GOOD.
POOCH, YOU'RE EXFIL. YOU'LL HANG BACK UNTIL WE'RE READY FOR EXTRACTION.
AS ALWAYS...
YOU GOT A PROBLEM WITH THAT, SOLDIER?
NO PROBLEM. WHATEVER YOU SAY, BOSS.
WOULDN'T WANT TO GET IN ANYONE'S **WAY.**

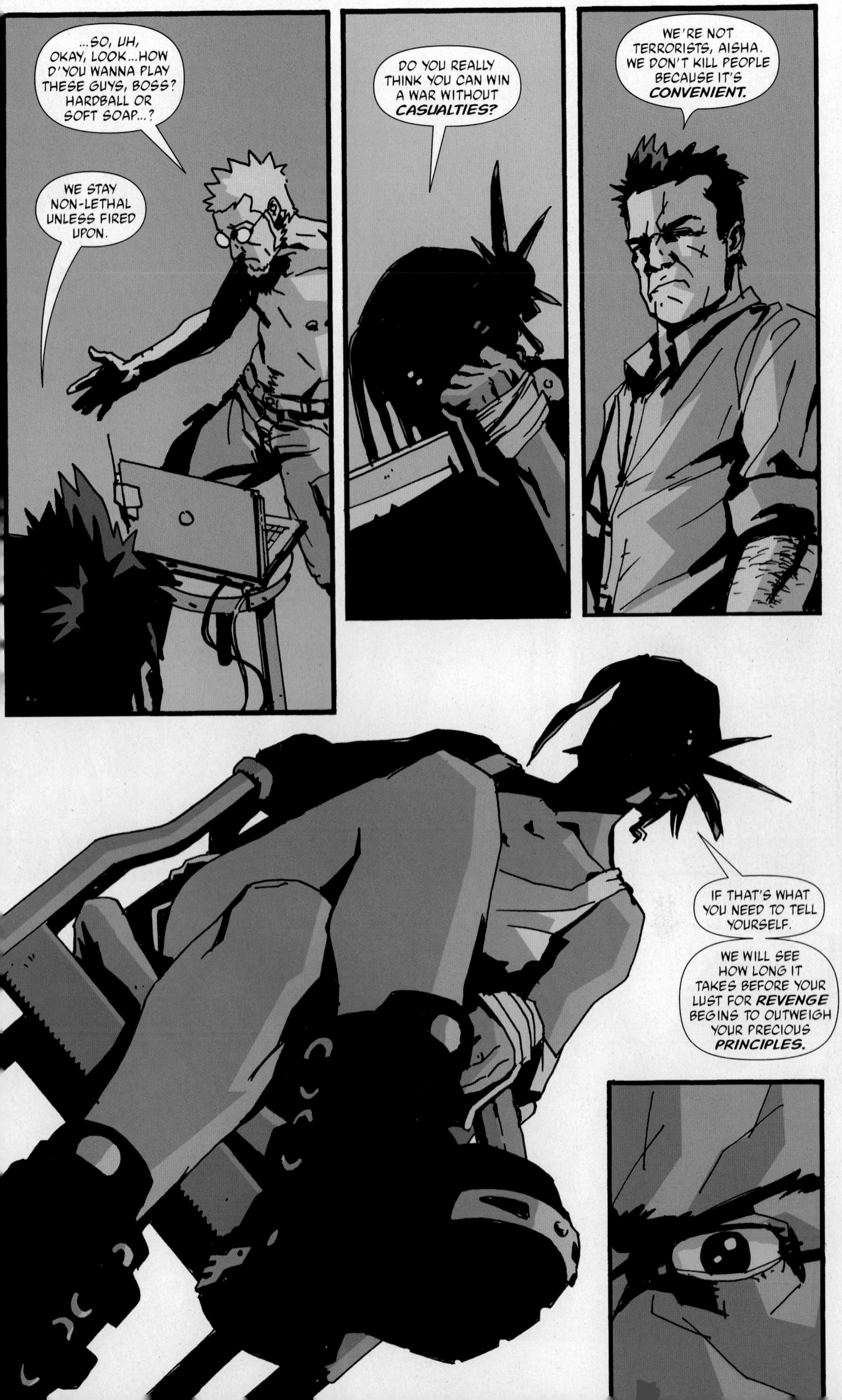
...SO, UH, OKAY, LOOK...HOW D'YOU WANNA PLAY THESE GUYS, BOSS? HARDBALL OR SOFT SOAP...?
WE STAY NON-LETHAL UNLESS FIRED UPON.
DO YOU REALLY THINK YOU CAN WIN A WAR WITHOUT CASUALTIES?
WE'RE NOT TERRORISTS, AISHA. WE DON'T KILL PEOPLE BECAUSE IT'S CONVENIENT.
IF THAT'S WHAT YOU NEED TO TELL YOURSELF.
WE WILL SEE HOW LONG IT TAKES BEFORE YOUR LUST FOR REVENGE BEGINS TO OUTWEIGH YOUR PRECIOUS PRINCIPLES.

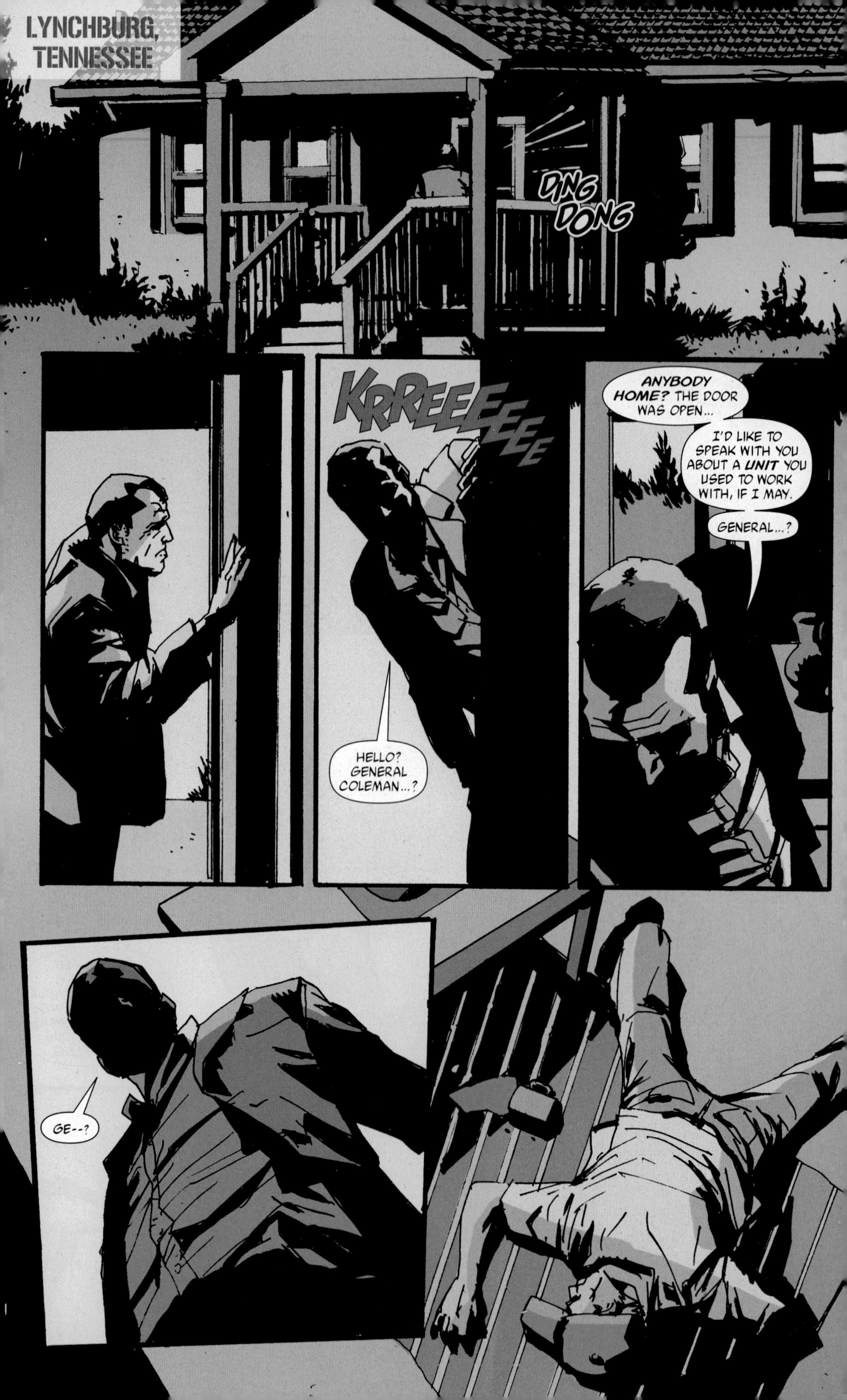
LYNCHBURG, TENNESSEE
DING DONG
KRREEEEEEE
HELLO? GENERAL COLEMAN...?
ANYBODY HOME? THE DOOR WAS OPEN...
I'D LIKE TO SPEAK WITH YOU ABOUT A UNIT YOU USED TO WORK WITH, IF I MAY.
GENERAL...?
GE--?

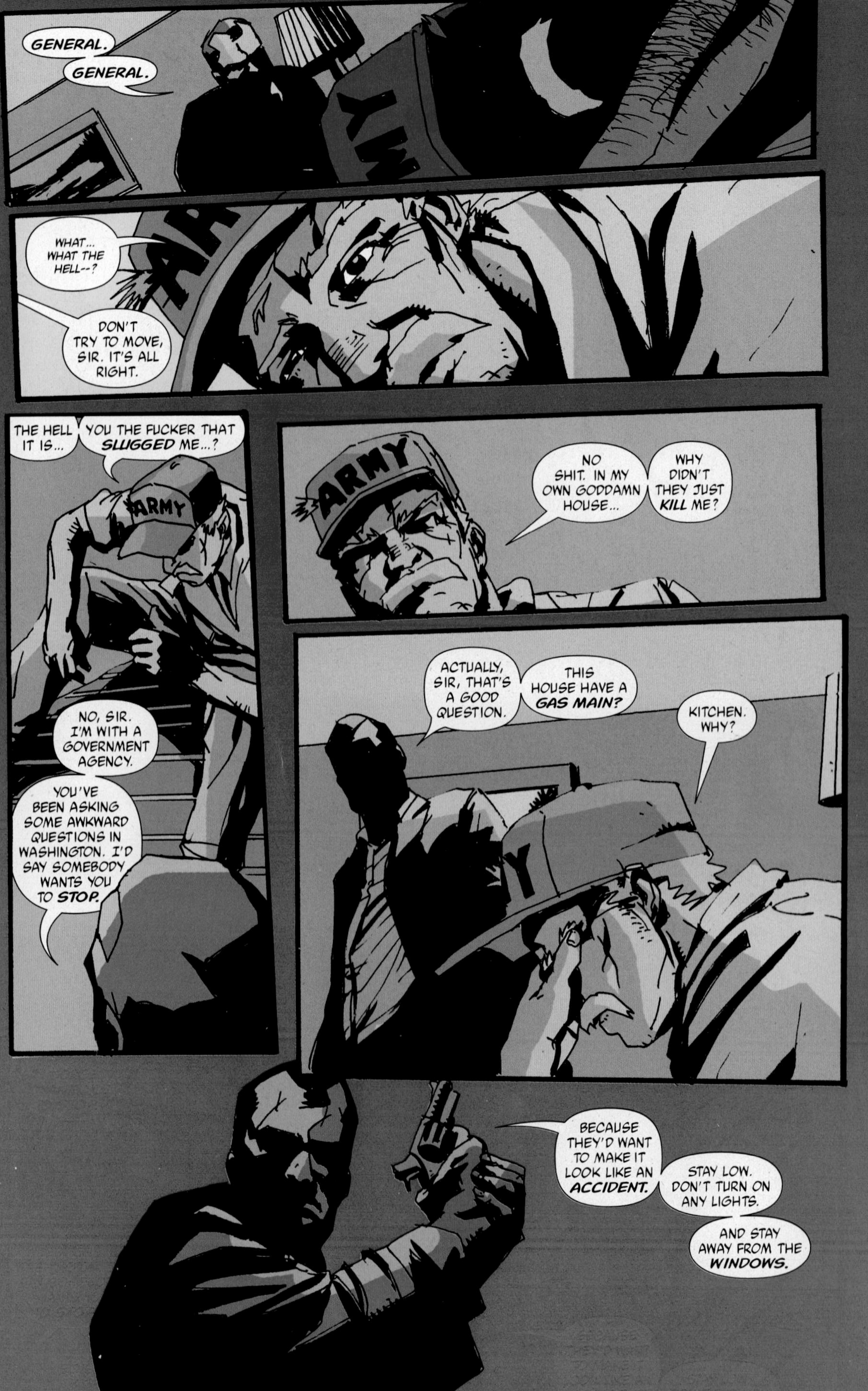
GENERAL.
GENERAL.
WHAT... WHAT THE HELL--?
DON'T TRY TO MOVE, SIR. IT'S ALL RIGHT.
THE HELL IT IS...
YOU THE FUCKER THAT SLUGGED ME...?
NO, SIR. I'M WITH A GOVERNMENT AGENCY.
YOU'VE BEEN ASKING SOME AWKWARD QUESTIONS IN WASHINGTON. I'D SAY SOMEBODY WANTS YOU TO STOP.
NO SHIT. IN MY OWN GODDAMN HOUSE...
WHY DIDN'T THEY JUST KILL ME?
ACTUALLY, SIR, THAT'S A GOOD QUESTION.
THIS HOUSE HAVE A GAS MAIN?
KITCHEN. WHY?
BECAUSE THEY'D WANT TO MAKE IT LOOK LIKE AN ACCIDENT.
STAY LOW. DON'T TURN ON ANY LIGHTS.
AND STAY AWAY FROM THE WINDOWS.

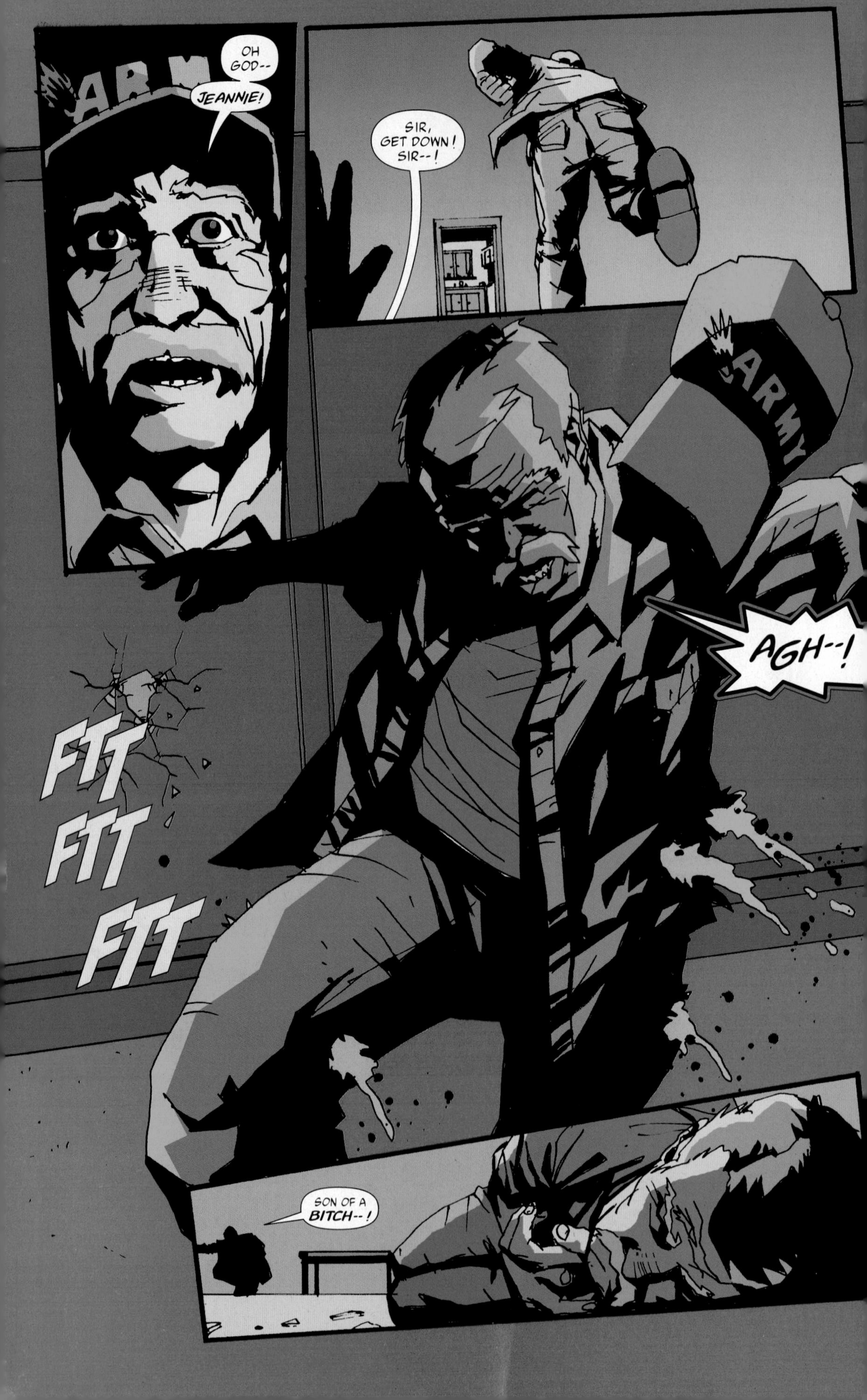
OH GOD--
JEANNIE!
SIR, GET DOWN! SIR--!
FTT
FTT
FTT
AGH--!
SON OF A BITCH--!

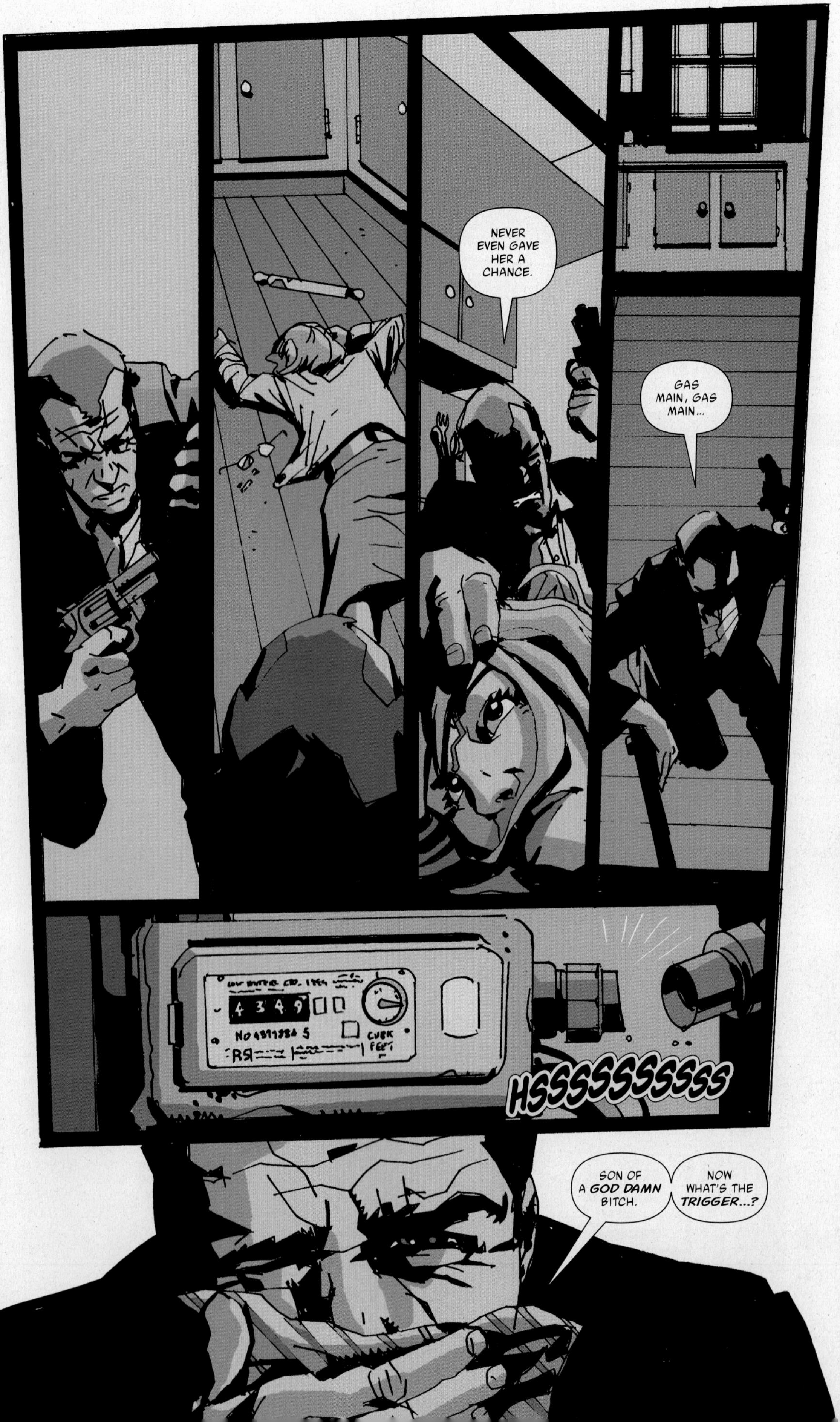
NEVER EVEN GAVE HER A CHANCE.
GAS MAIN, GAS MAIN...
HSSSSSSSSSS
SON OF A GOD DAMN BITCH.
NOW WHAT'S THE TRIGGER...?

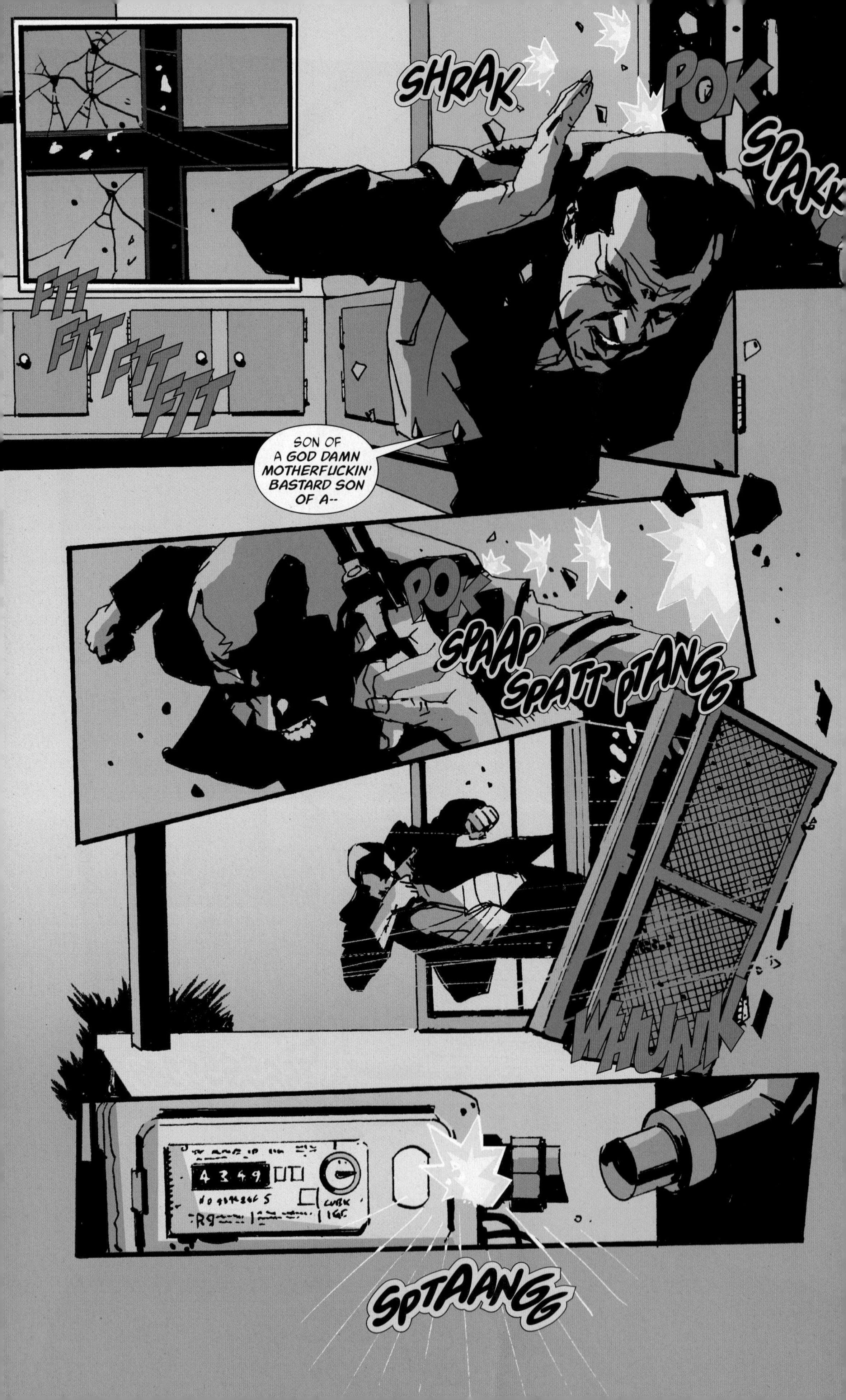
SHRAK
POK
SPAKK
FTT FTT FTT FTT
SON OF A GOD DAMN MOTHERFUCKIN' BASTARD SON OF A--
POK
SPAAP
SPATT PTANGG
WHUNK
SPTAANGG

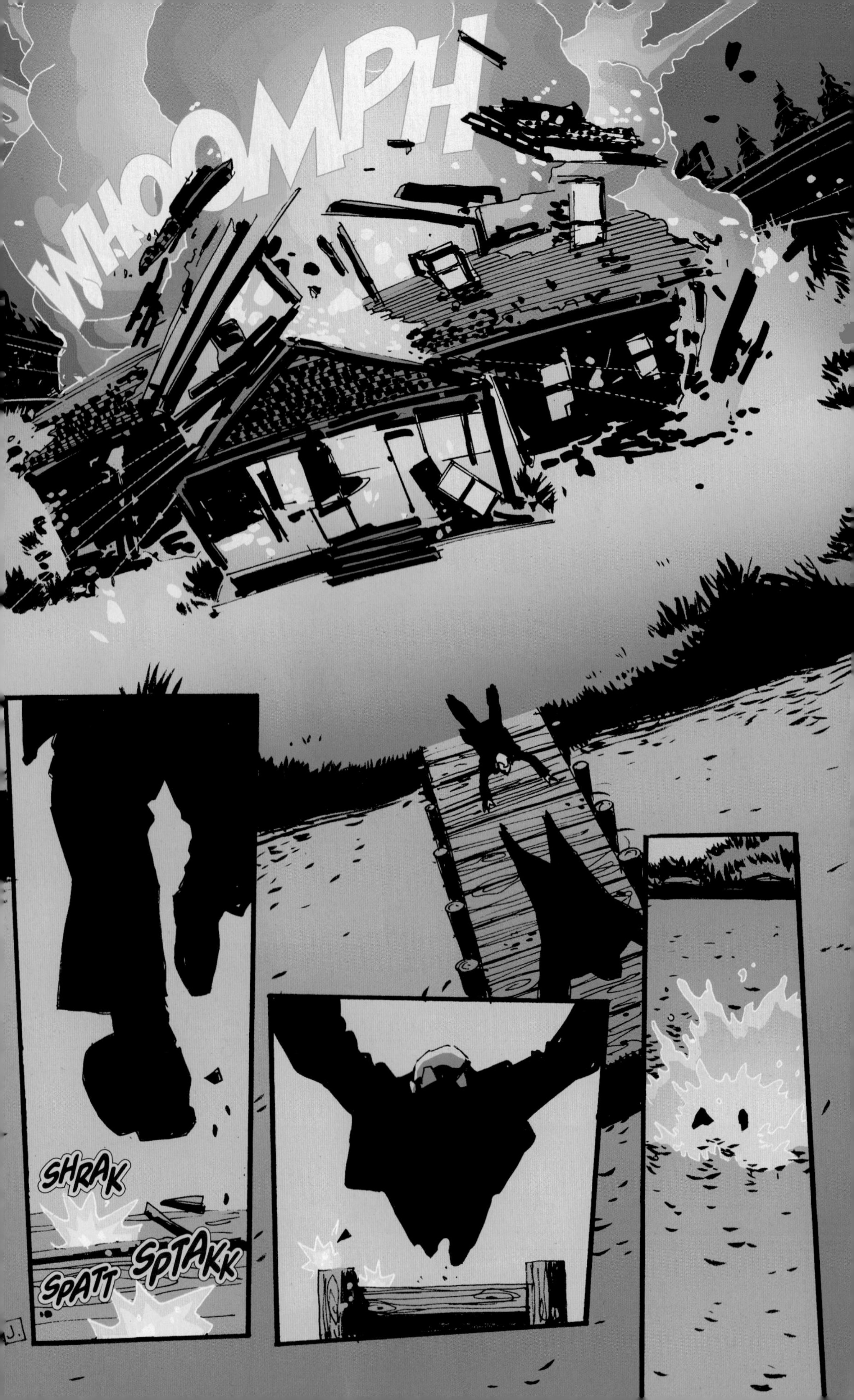
WHOOOMPH
SHRAK
SPTAKK
SPATT
J.

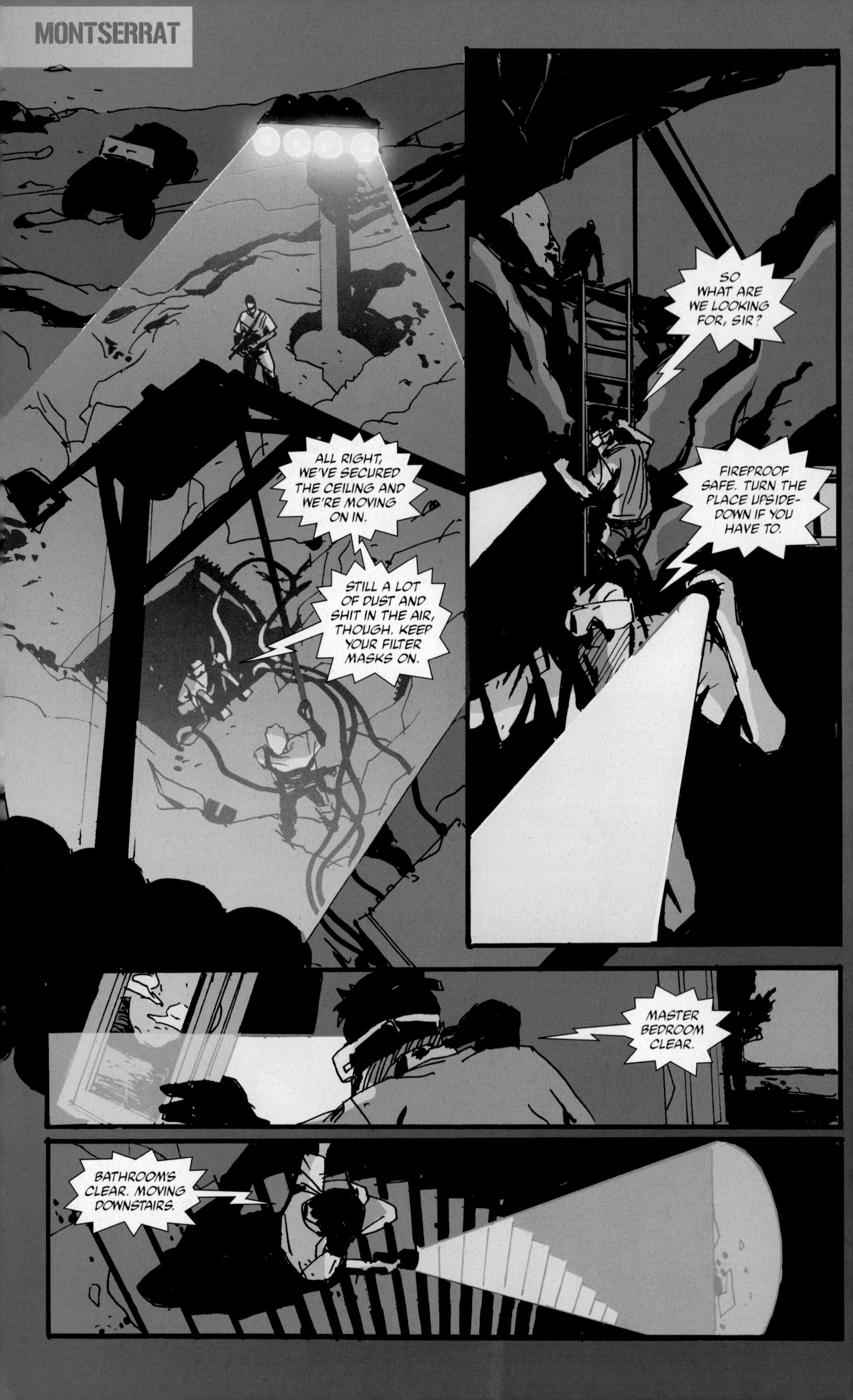
MONTSERRAT
ALL RIGHT, WE'VE SECURED THE CEILING AND WE'RE MOVING ON IN.
STILL A LOT OF DUST AND SHIT IN THE AIR, THOUGH. KEEP YOUR FILTER MASKS ON.
SO WHAT ARE WE LOOKING FOR, SIR?
FIREPROOF SAFE. TURN THE PLACE UPSIDE-DOWN IF YOU HAVE TO.
MASTER BEDROOM CLEAR.
BATHROOM'S CLEAR. MOVING DOWNSTAIRS.

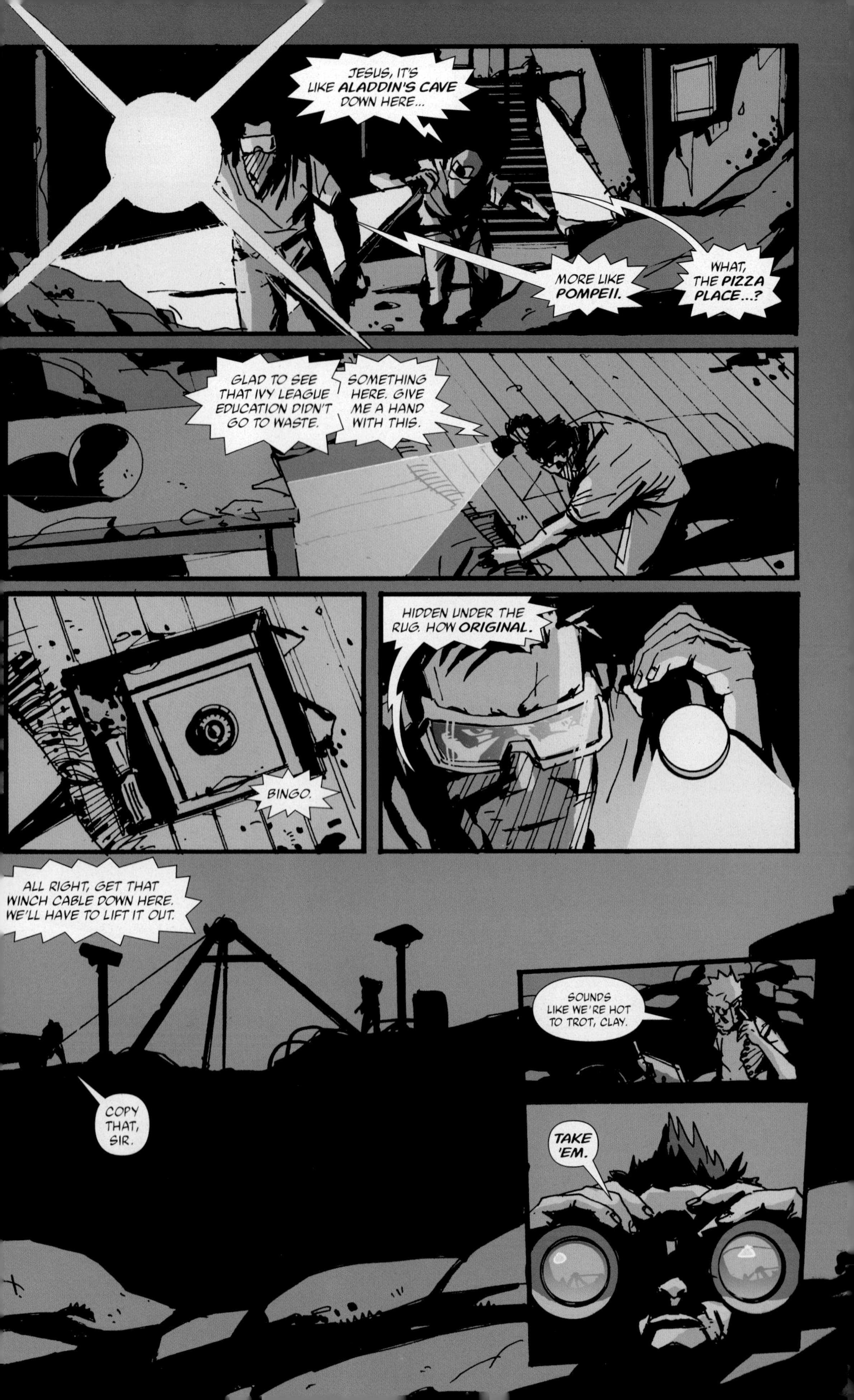
JESUS, IT'S LIKE ALADDIN'S CAVE DOWN HERE...
MORE LIKE POMPEII.
WHAT, THE PIZZA PLACE...?
GLAD TO SEE THAT IVY LEAGUE EDUCATION DIDN'T GO TO WASTE.
SOMETHING HERE. GIVE ME A HAND WITH THIS.
BINGO.
HIDDEN UNDER THE RUG. HOW ORIGINAL.
ALL RIGHT, GET THAT WINCH CABLE DOWN HERE. WE'LL HAVE TO LIFT IT OUT.
SOUNDS LIKE WE'RE HOT TO TROT, CLAY.
COPY THAT, SIR.
TAKE 'EM.

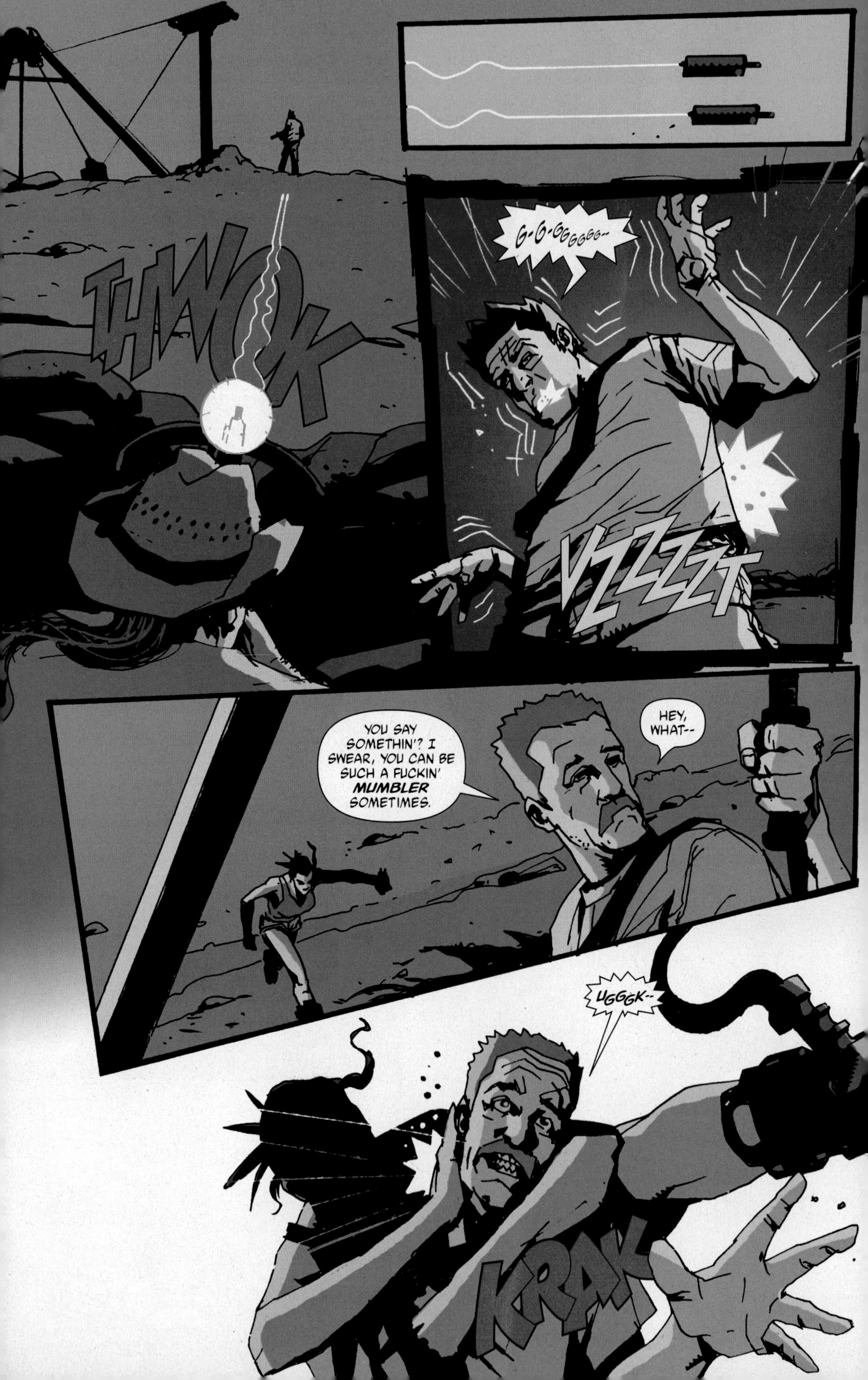

THWOK
G-G-GGGGGG--
VZZZZT
YOU SAY SOMETHIN'? I SWEAR, YOU CAN BE SUCH A FUCKIN' **MUMBLER** SOMETIMES.
HEY, WHAT--
UGGGK--
KRAK

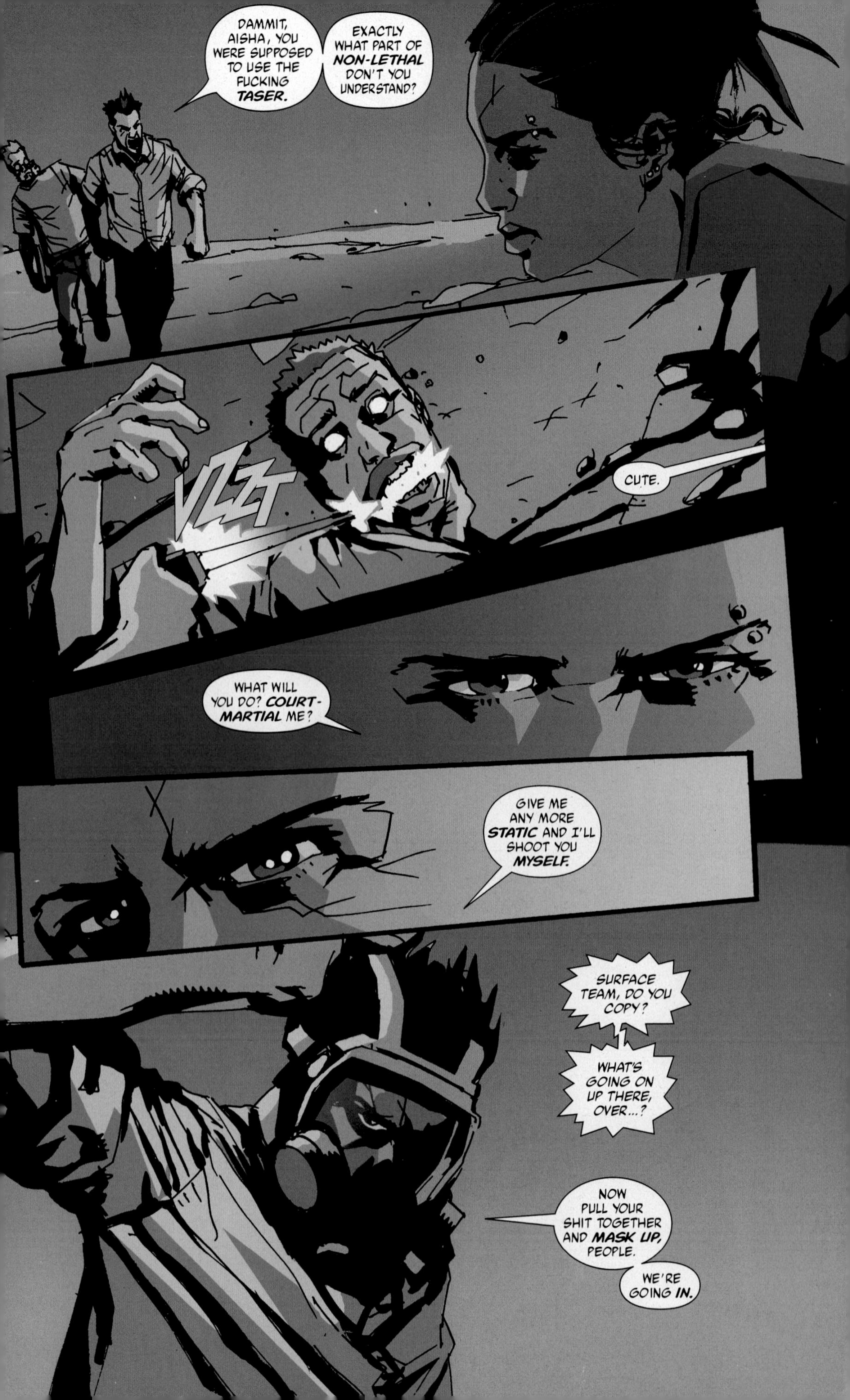
DAMMIT, AISHA, YOU WERE SUPPOSED TO USE THE FUCKING TASER.
EXACTLY WHAT PART OF NON-LETHAL DON'T YOU UNDERSTAND?
VZZT
CUTE.
WHAT WILL YOU DO? COURT-MARTIAL ME?
GIVE ME ANY MORE STATIC AND I'LL SHOOT YOU MYSELF.
SURFACE TEAM, DO YOU COPY?
WHAT'S GOING ON UP THERE, OVER...?
NOW PULL YOUR SHIT TOGETHER AND MASK UP, PEOPLE.
WE'RE GOING IN.

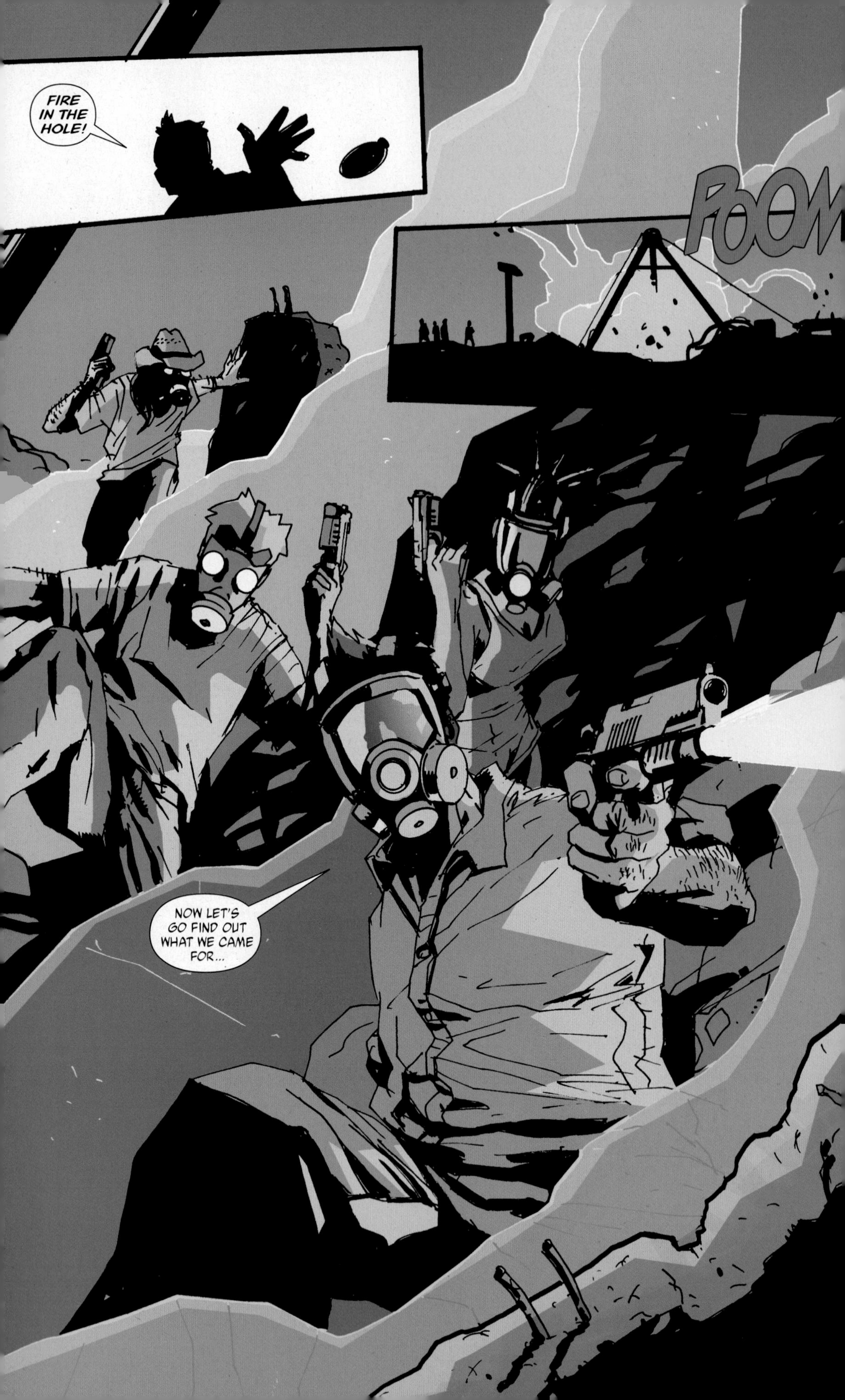
FIRE IN THE HOLE!
POOM
NOW LET'S GO FIND OUT WHAT WE CAME FOR...

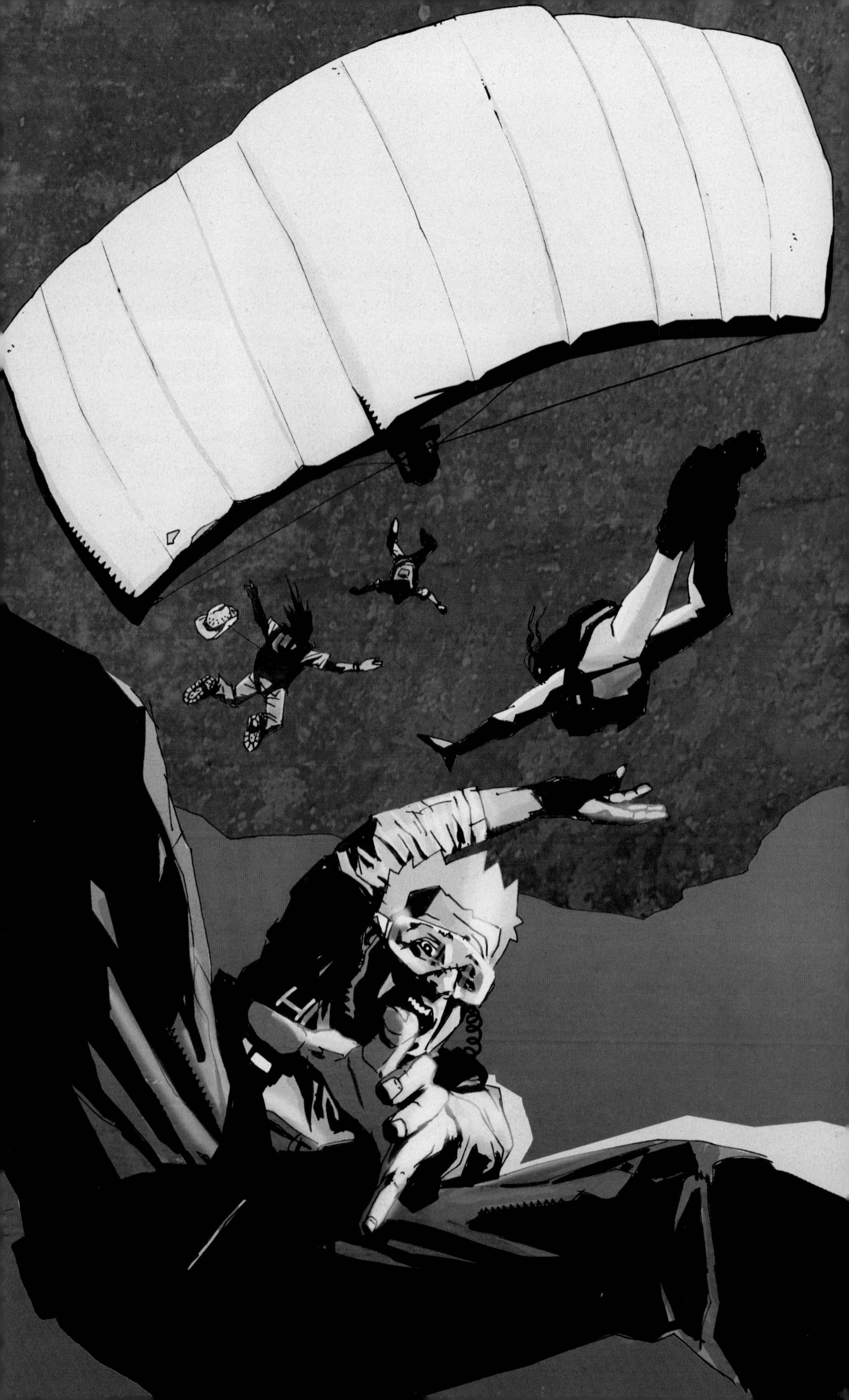

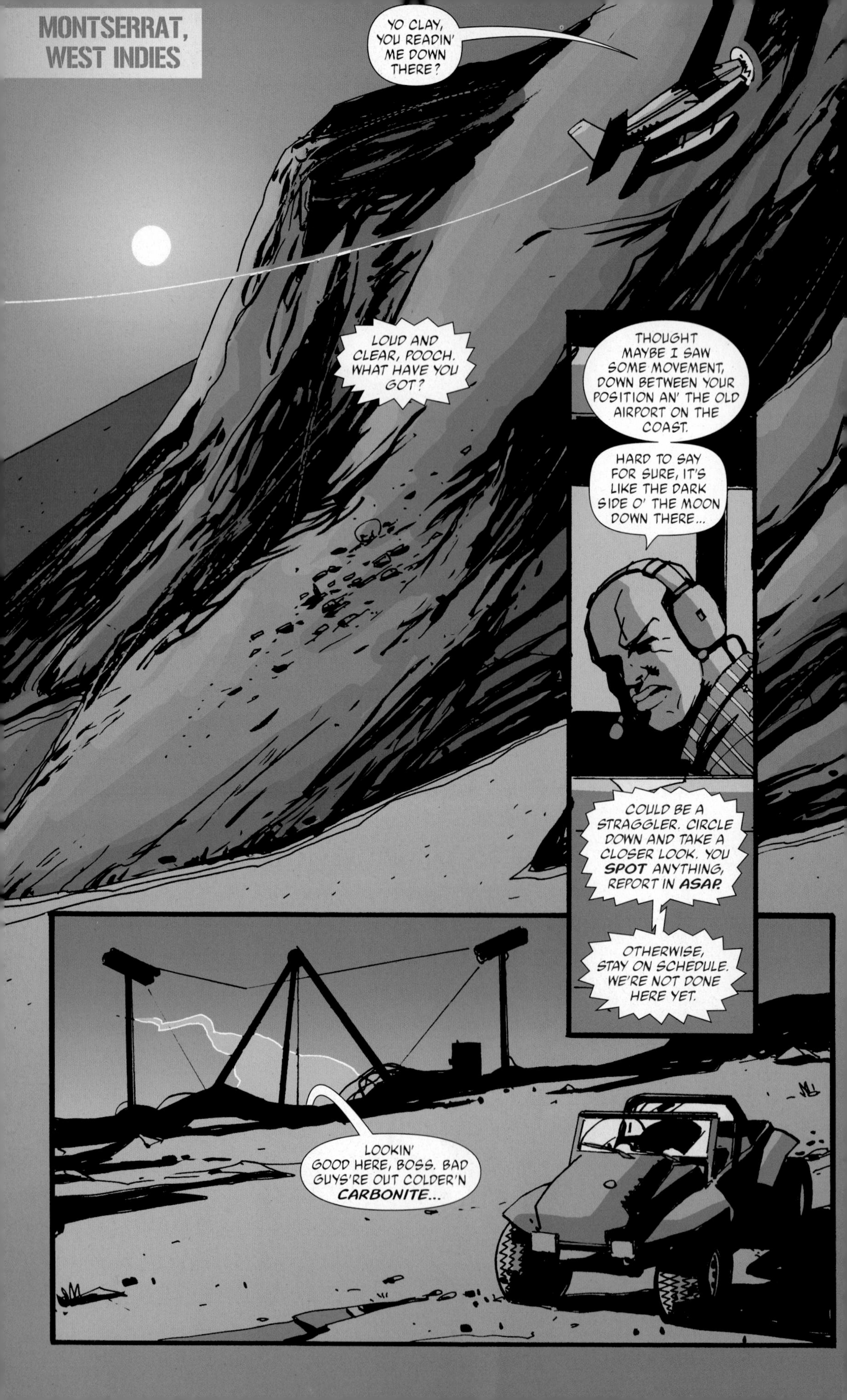
MONTSERRAT, WEST INDIES
YO CLAY, YOU READIN' ME DOWN THERE?
LOUD AND CLEAR, POOCH. WHAT HAVE YOU GOT?
THOUGHT MAYBE I SAW SOME MOVEMENT, DOWN BETWEEN YOUR POSITION AN' THE OLD AIRPORT ON THE COAST.
HARD TO SAY FOR SURE, IT'S LIKE THE DARK SIDE O' THE MOON DOWN THERE...
COULD BE A STRAGGLER. CIRCLE DOWN AND TAKE A CLOSER LOOK. YOU SPOT ANYTHING, REPORT IN ASAP.
OTHERWISE, STAY ON SCHEDULE. WE'RE NOT DONE HERE YET.
LOOKIN' GOOD HERE, BOSS. BAD GUYS'RE OUT COLDER'N CARBONITE...

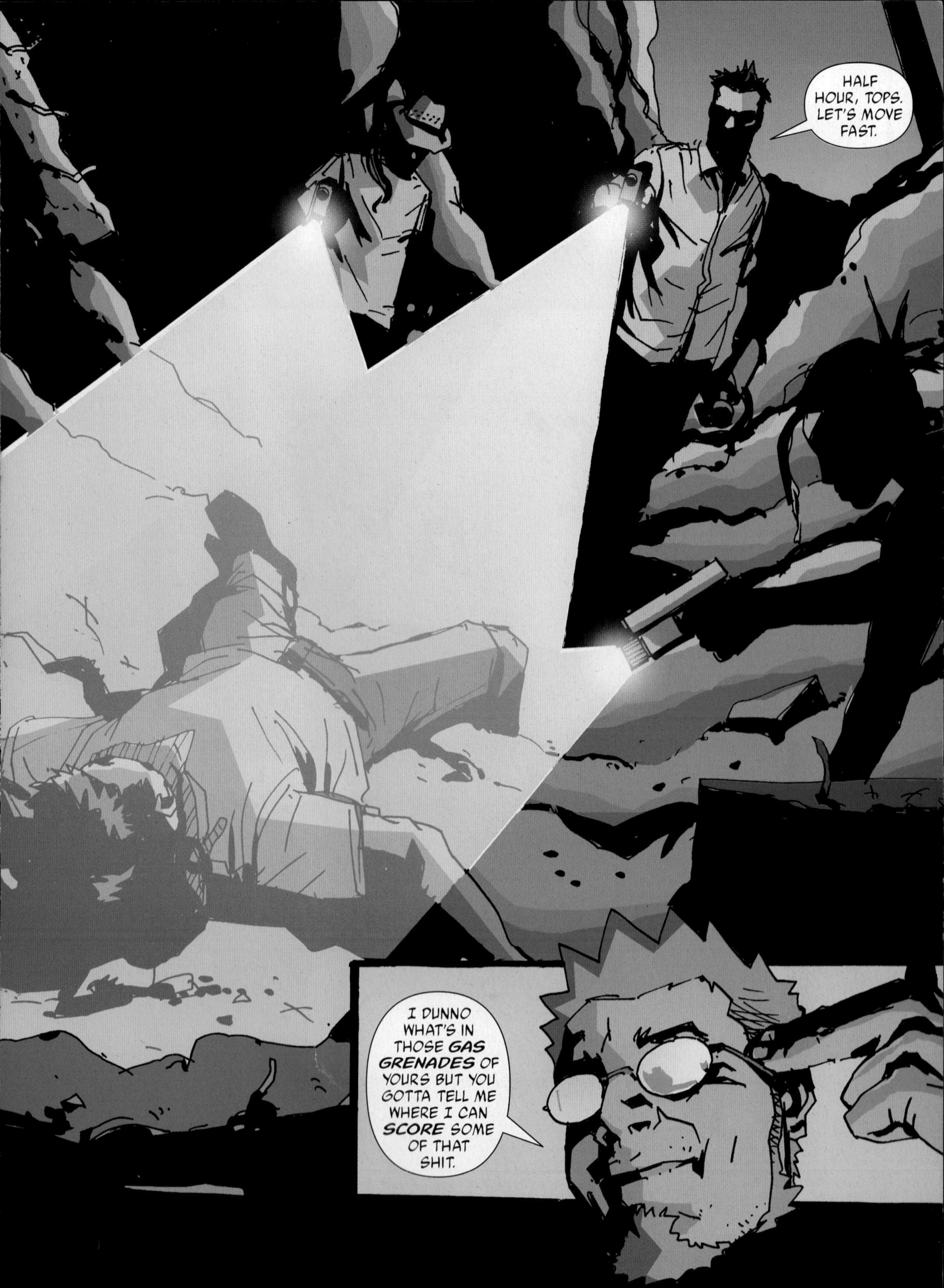
HALF HOUR, TOPS. LET'S MOVE FAST.
I DUNNO WHAT'S IN THOSE **GAS GRENADES** OF YOURS BUT YOU GOTTA TELL ME WHERE I CAN **SCORE** SOME OF THAT SHIT.

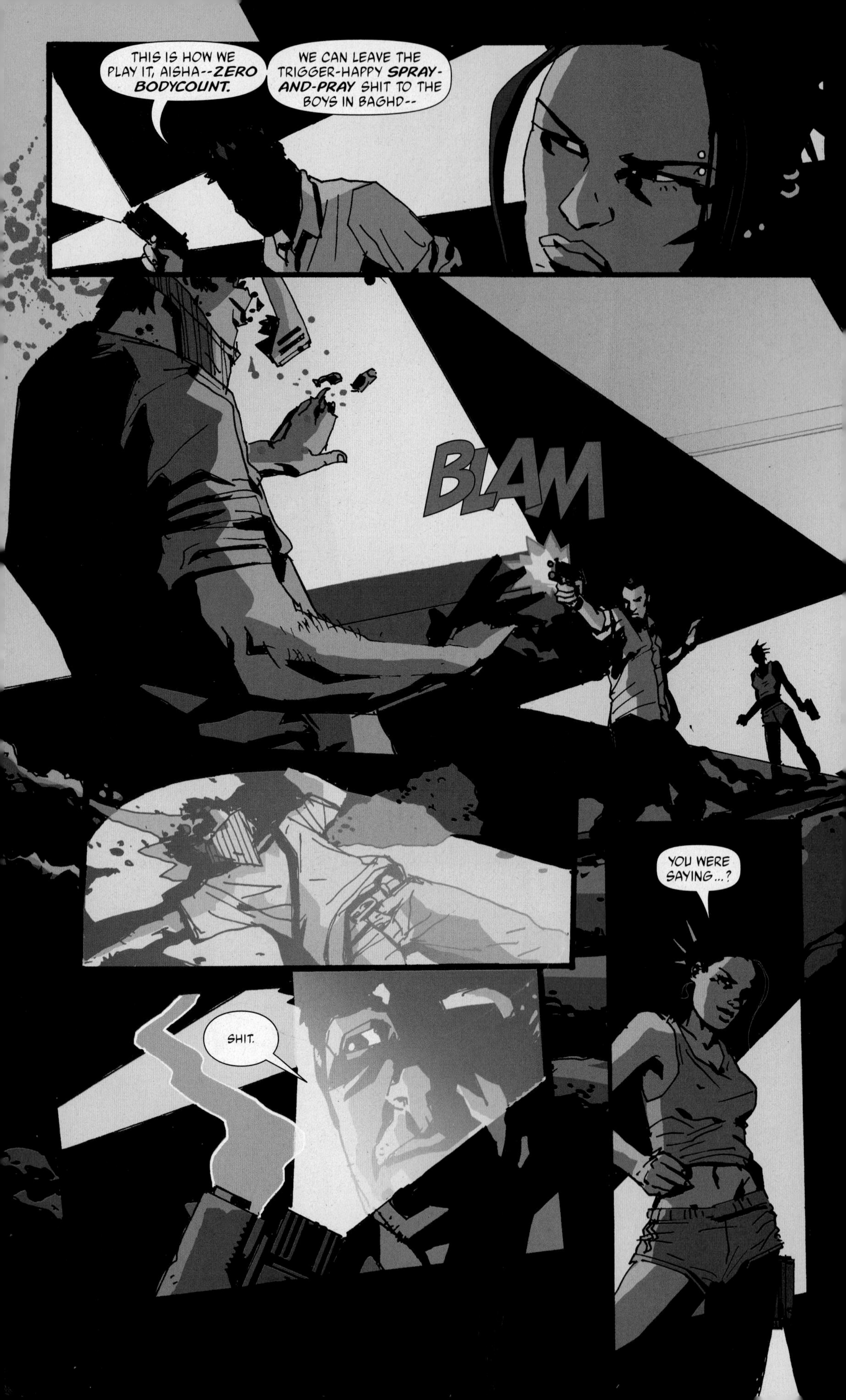
THIS IS HOW WE PLAY IT, AISHA--ZERO BODYCOUNT.
WE CAN LEAVE THE TRIGGER-HAPPY SPRAY-AND-PRAY SHIT TO THE BOYS IN BAGHD--
BLAM
YOU WERE SAYING...?
SHIT.

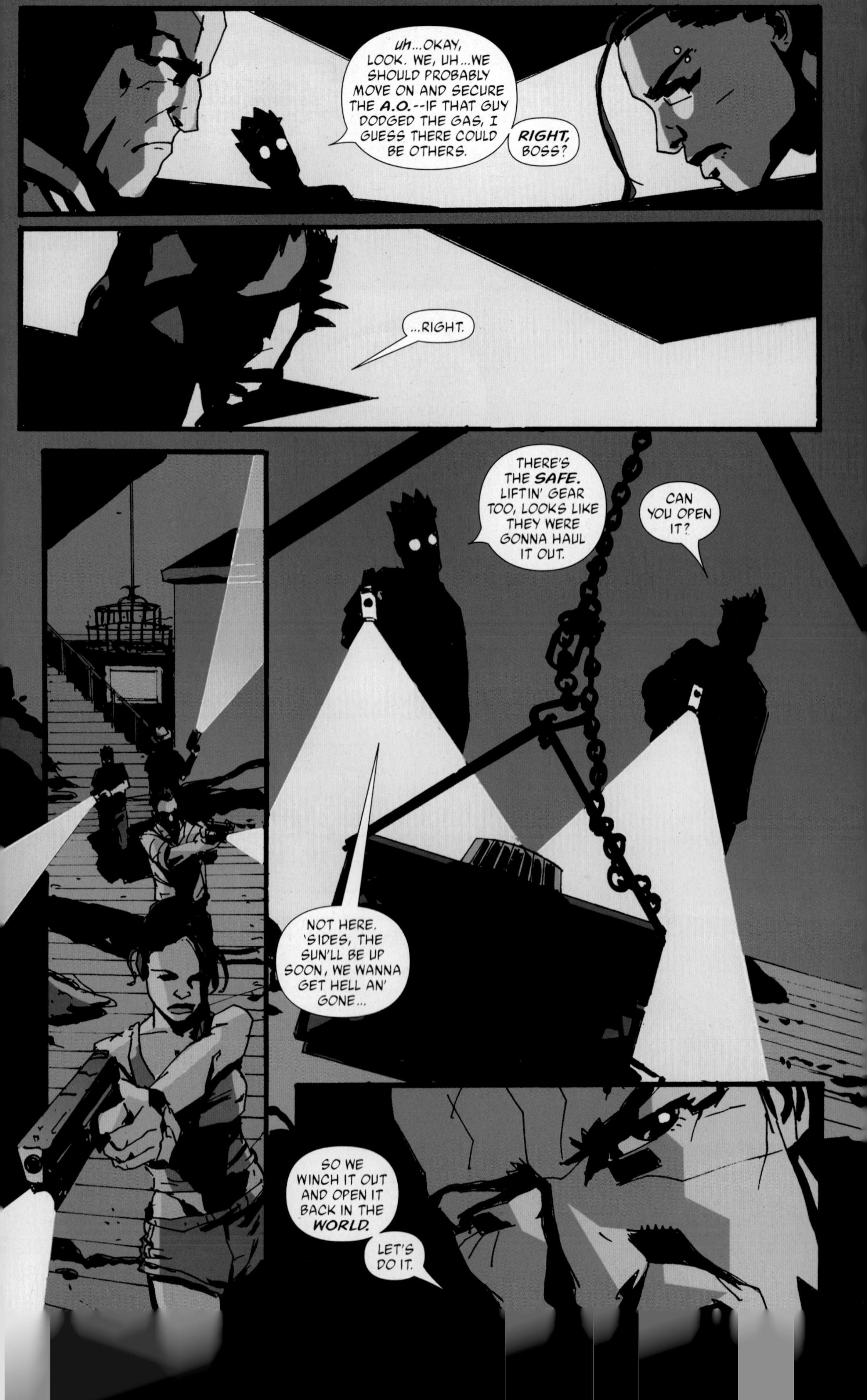
uh...OKAY, LOOK. WE, UH...WE SHOULD PROBABLY MOVE ON AND SECURE THE A.O.--IF THAT GUY DODGED THE GAS, I GUESS THERE COULD BE OTHERS.
RIGHT, BOSS?
...RIGHT.
THERE'S THE SAFE. LIFTIN' GEAR TOO, LOOKS LIKE THEY WERE GONNA HAUL IT OUT.
CAN YOU OPEN IT?
NOT HERE. 'SIDES, THE SUN'LL BE UP SOON, WE WANNA GET HELL AN' GONE...
SO WE WINCH IT OUT AND OPEN IT BACK IN THE WORLD.
LET'S DO IT.

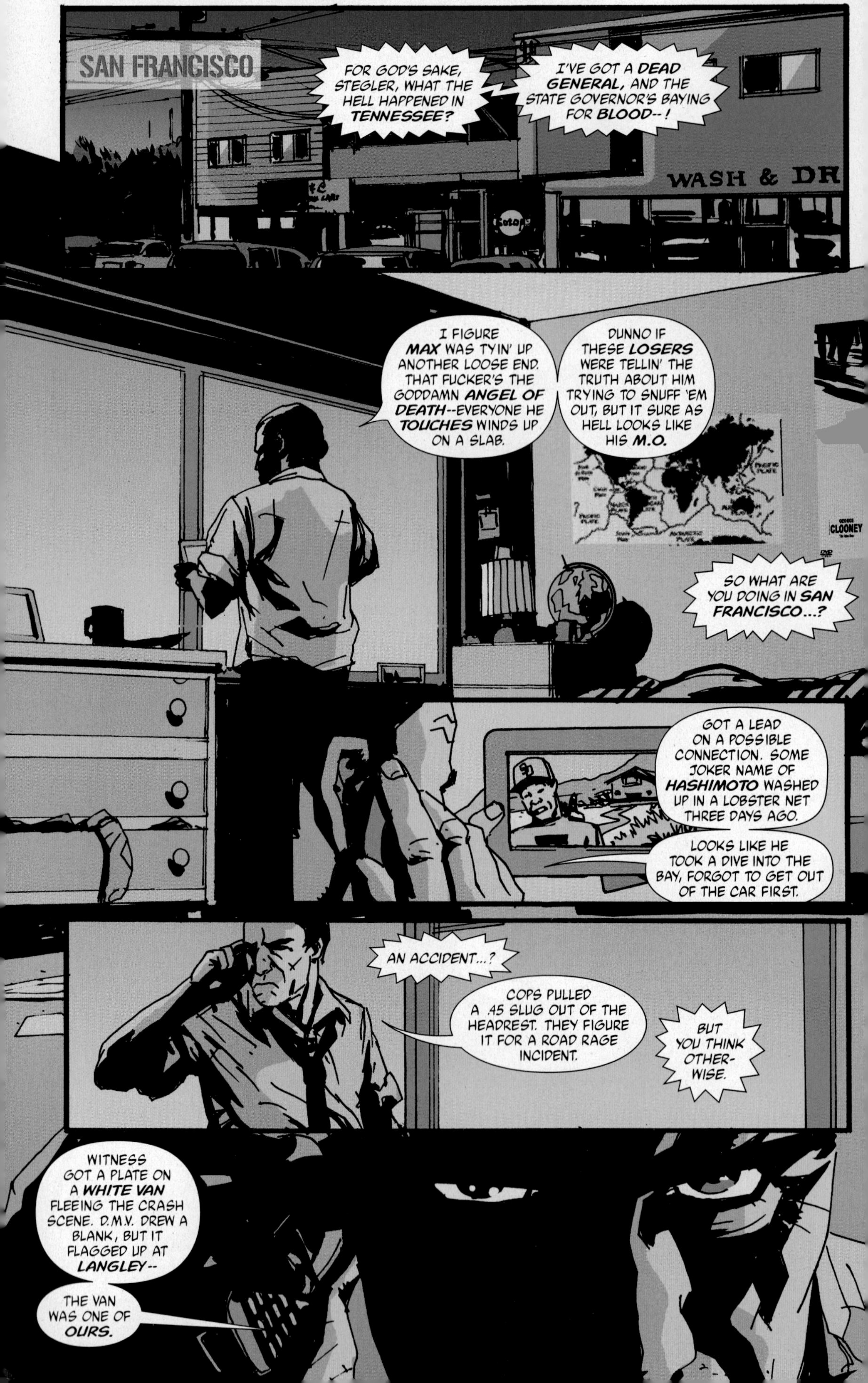
SAN FRANCISCO
FOR GOD'S SAKE, STEGLER, WHAT THE HELL HAPPENED IN TENNESSEE?
I'VE GOT A DEAD GENERAL, AND THE STATE GOVERNOR'S BAYING FOR BLOOD--!
WASH & DR
I FIGURE MAX WAS TYIN' UP ANOTHER LOOSE END. THAT FUCKER'S THE GODDAMN ANGEL OF DEATH--EVERYONE HE TOUCHES WINDS UP ON A SLAB.
DUNNO IF THESE LOSERS WERE TELLIN' THE TRUTH ABOUT HIM TRYING TO SNUFF 'EM OUT, BUT IT SURE AS HELL LOOKS LIKE HIS M.O.
CLOONEY
SO WHAT ARE YOU DOING IN SAN FRANCISCO...?
GOT A LEAD ON A POSSIBLE CONNECTION. SOME JOKER NAME OF HASHIMOTO WASHED UP IN A LOBSTER NET THREE DAYS AGO.
LOOKS LIKE HE TOOK A DIVE INTO THE BAY, FORGOT TO GET OUT OF THE CAR FIRST.
AN ACCIDENT...?
COPS PULLED A .45 SLUG OUT OF THE HEADREST. THEY FIGURE IT FOR A ROAD RAGE INCIDENT.
BUT YOU THINK OTHER-WISE.
WITNESS GOT A PLATE ON A WHITE VAN FLEEING THE CRASH SCENE. D.M.V. DREW A BLANK, BUT IT FLAGGED UP AT LANGLEY--
THE VAN WAS ONE OF OURS.

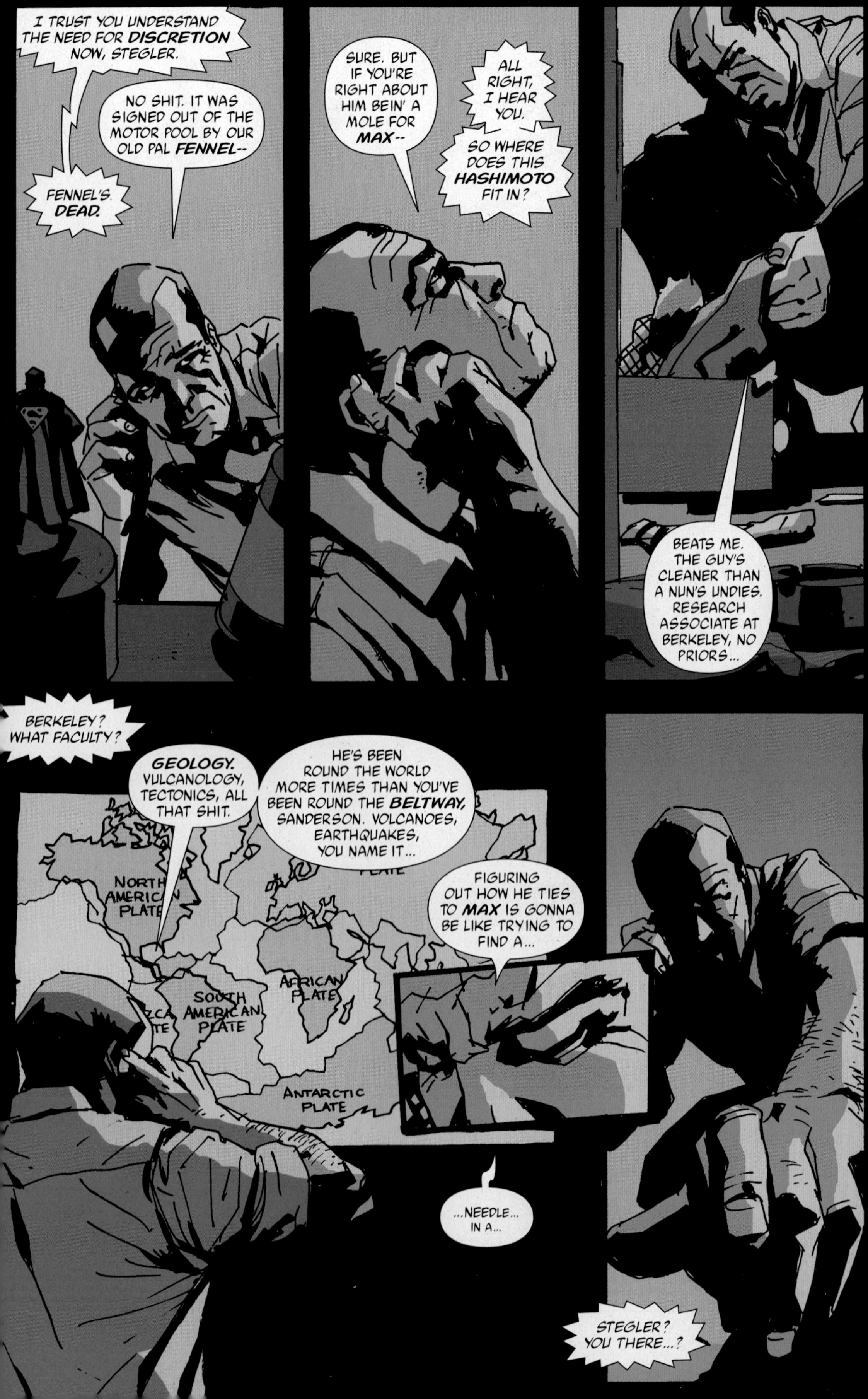
I TRUST YOU UNDERSTAND THE NEED FOR DISCRETION NOW, STEGLER.
NO SHIT. IT WAS SIGNED OUT OF THE MOTOR POOL BY OUR OLD PAL FENNEL--
FENNEL'S DEAD.
SURE. BUT IF YOU'RE RIGHT ABOUT HIM BEIN' A MOLE FOR MAX--
ALL RIGHT, I HEAR YOU.
SO WHERE DOES THIS HASHIMOTO FIT IN?
BEATS ME. THE GUY'S CLEANER THAN A NUN'S UNDIES. RESEARCH ASSOCIATE AT BERKELEY, NO PRIORS...
BERKELEY? WHAT FACULTY?
GEOLOGY. VULCANOLOGY, TECTONICS, ALL THAT SHIT.
HE'S BEEN ROUND THE WORLD MORE TIMES THAN YOU'VE BEEN ROUND THE BELTWAY, SANDERSON. VOLCANOES, EARTHQUAKES, YOU NAME IT...
NORTH AMERICAN PLATE
SOUTH AMERICAN PLATE
AFRICAN PLATE
ANTARCTIC PLATE
FIGURING OUT HOW HE TIES TO MAX IS GONNA BE LIKE TRYING TO FIND A...
...NEEDLE... IN A...
STEGLER? YOU THERE...?

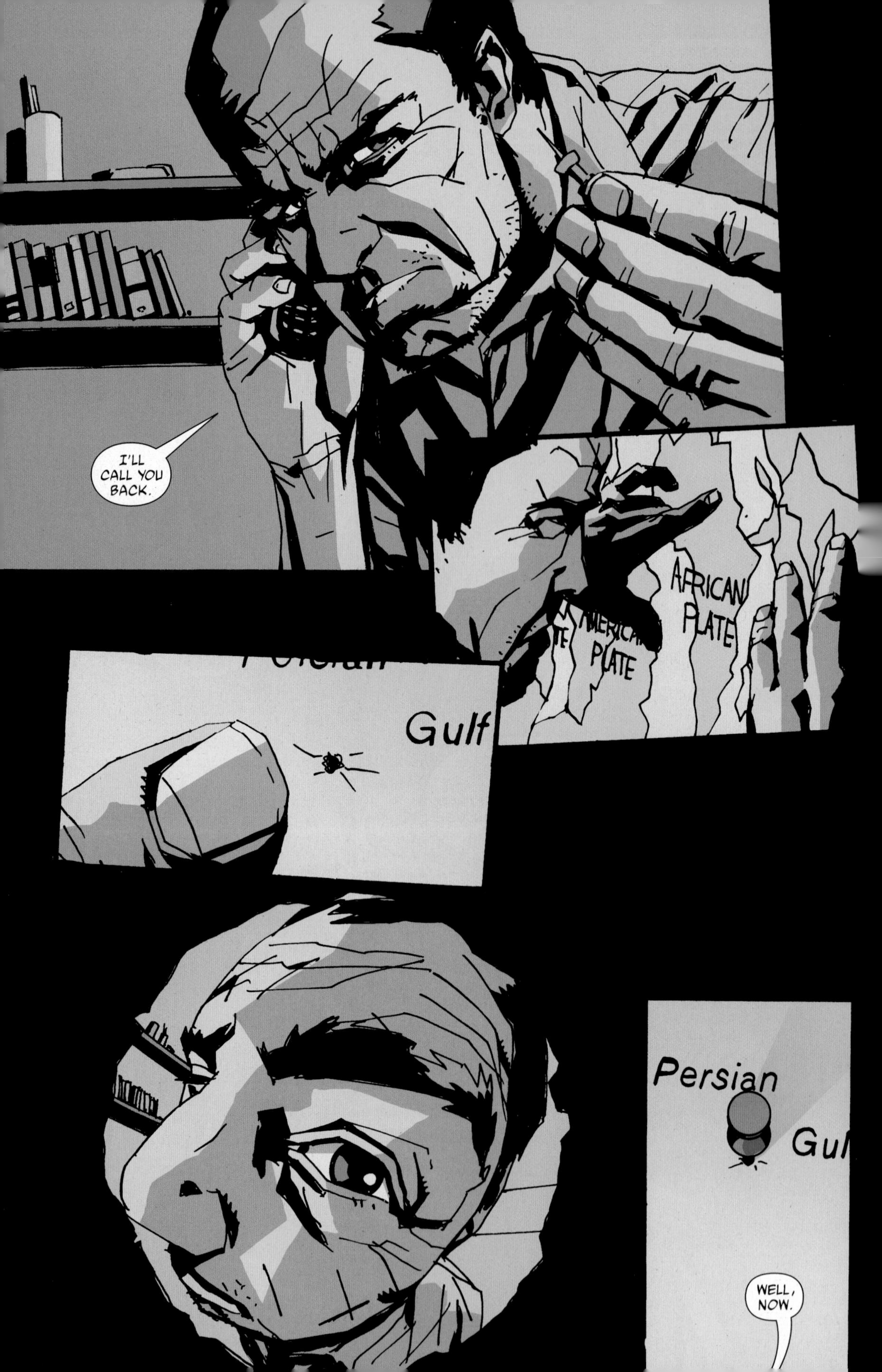
I'LL CALL YOU BACK.
AFRICAN PLATE
AMERICAN PLATE
Gulf
Persian
Gul
WELL, NOW.

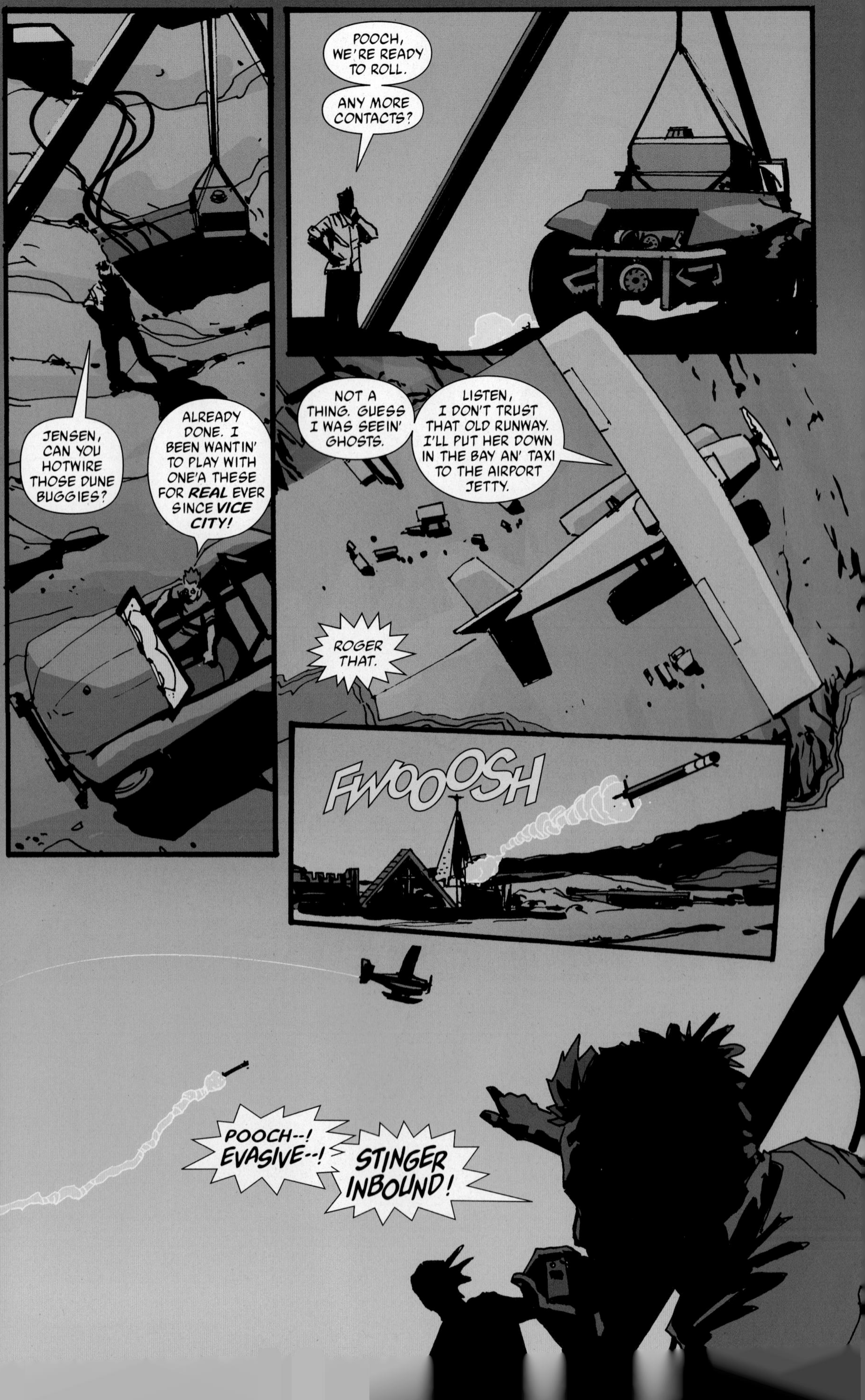

POOCH, WE'RE READY TO ROLL.
ANY MORE CONTACTS?
JENSEN, CAN YOU HOTWIRE THOSE DUNE BUGGIES?
ALREADY DONE. I BEEN WANTIN' TO PLAY WITH ONE'A THESE FOR REAL EVER SINCE VICE CITY!
NOT A THING. GUESS I WAS SEEIN' GHOSTS.
LISTEN, I DON'T TRUST THAT OLD RUNWAY. I'LL PUT HER DOWN IN THE BAY AN' TAXI TO THE AIRPORT JETTY.
ROGER THAT.
FWOOOSH
POOCH--! EVASIVE--!
STINGER INBOUND!

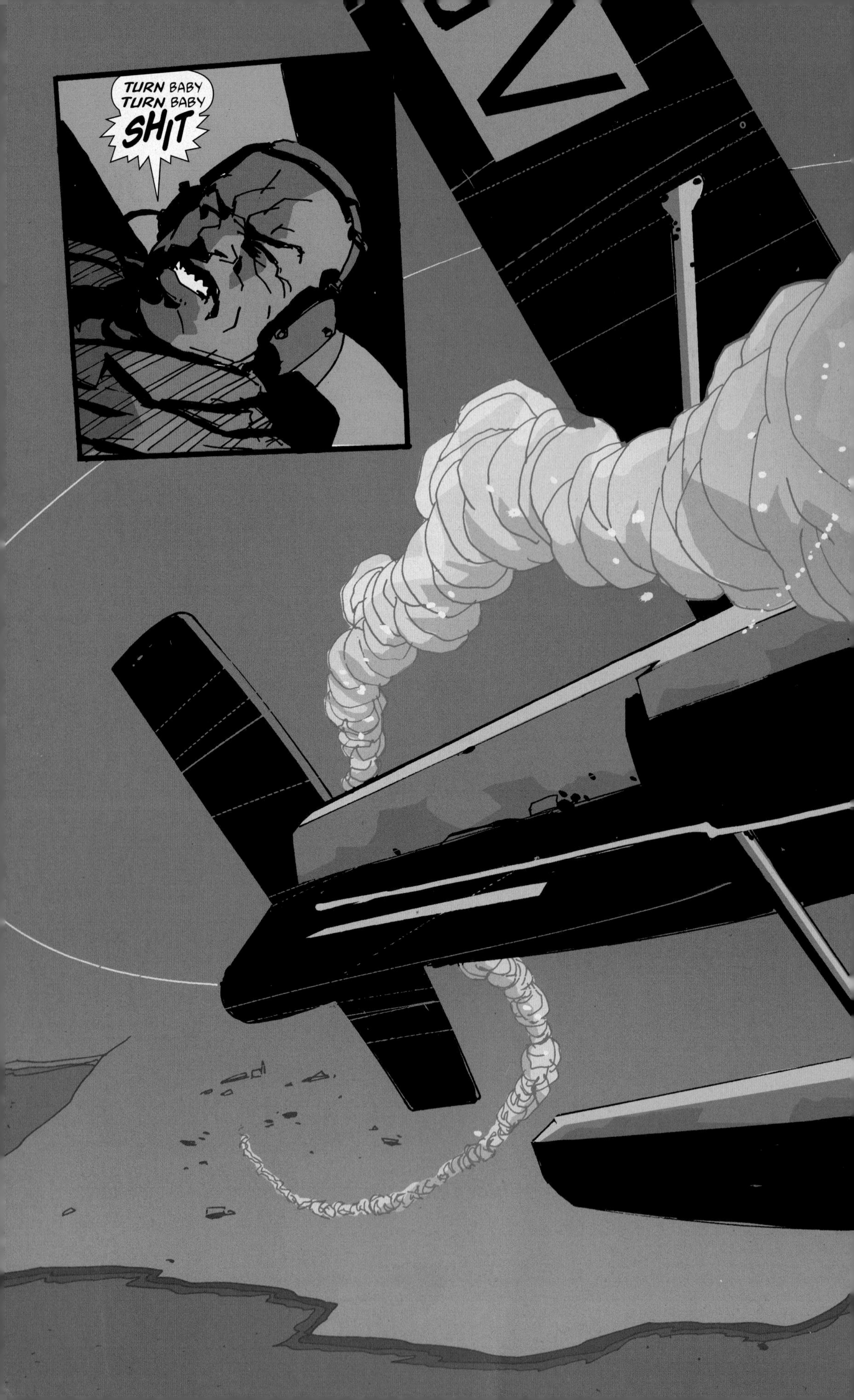
TURN BABY
TURN BABY
SHIT

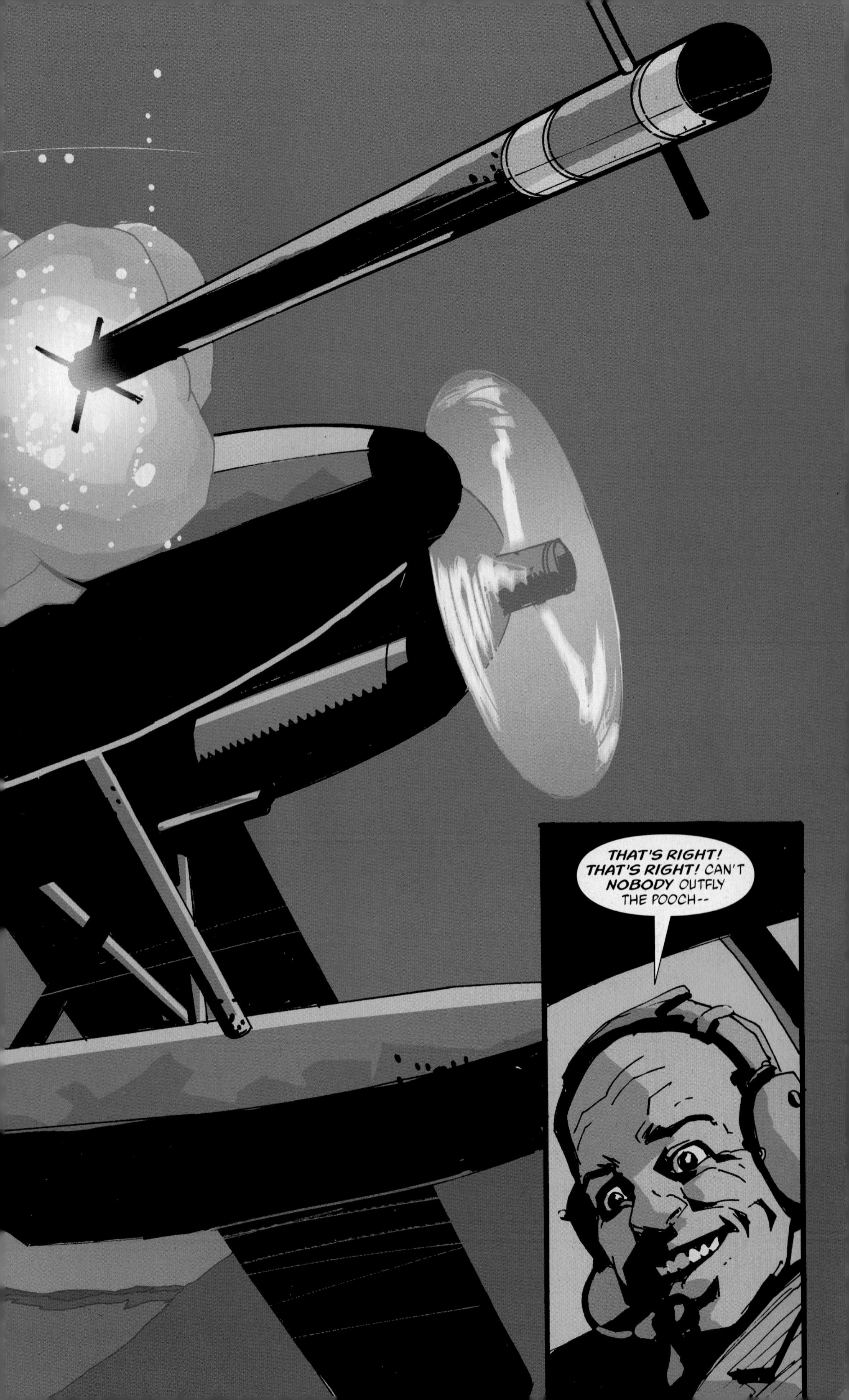
THAT'S RIGHT! THAT'S RIGHT! CAN'T NOBODY OUTFLY THE POOCH--

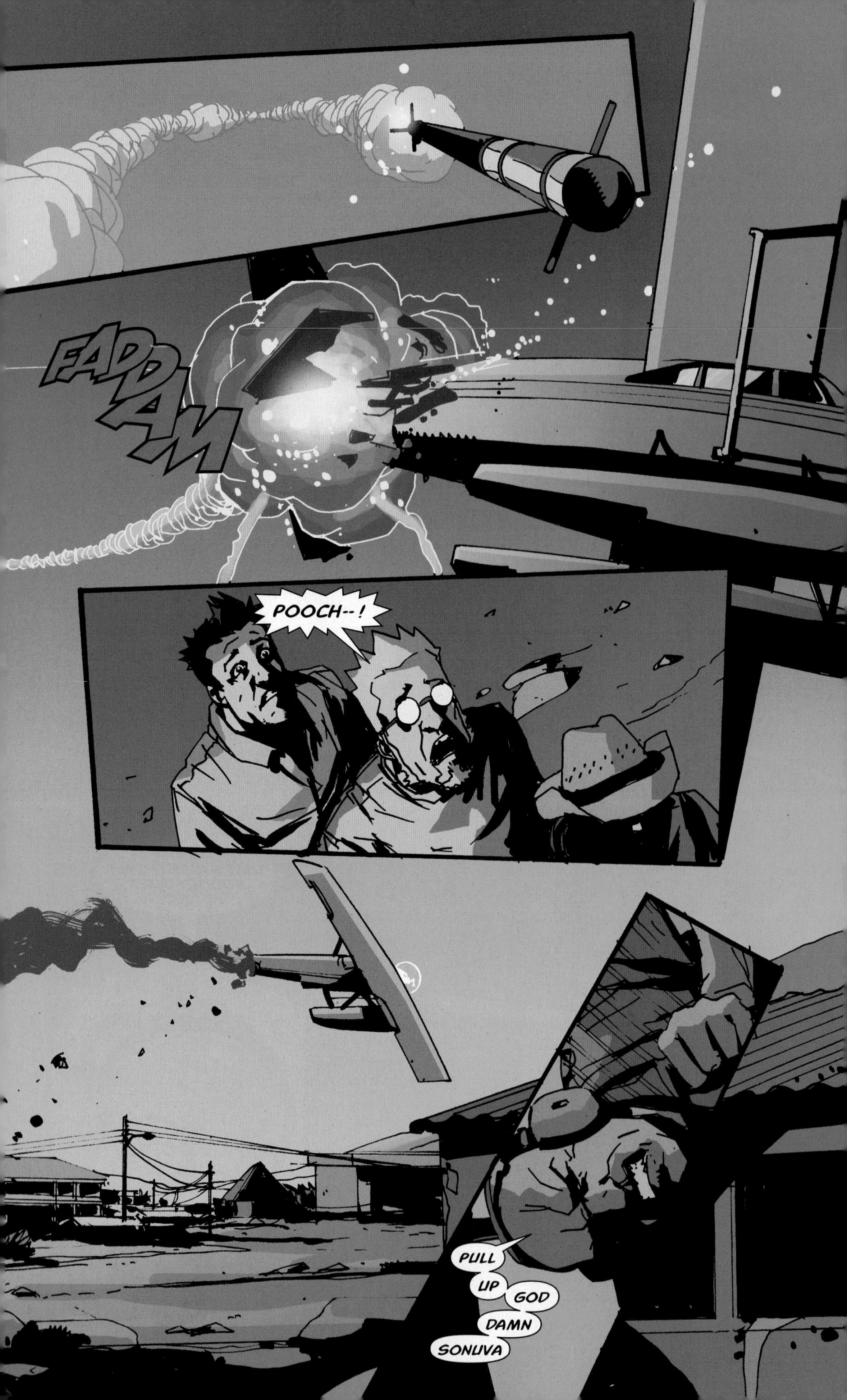
FADDAM
POOCH--!
PULL
UP
GOD
DAMN
SONUVA

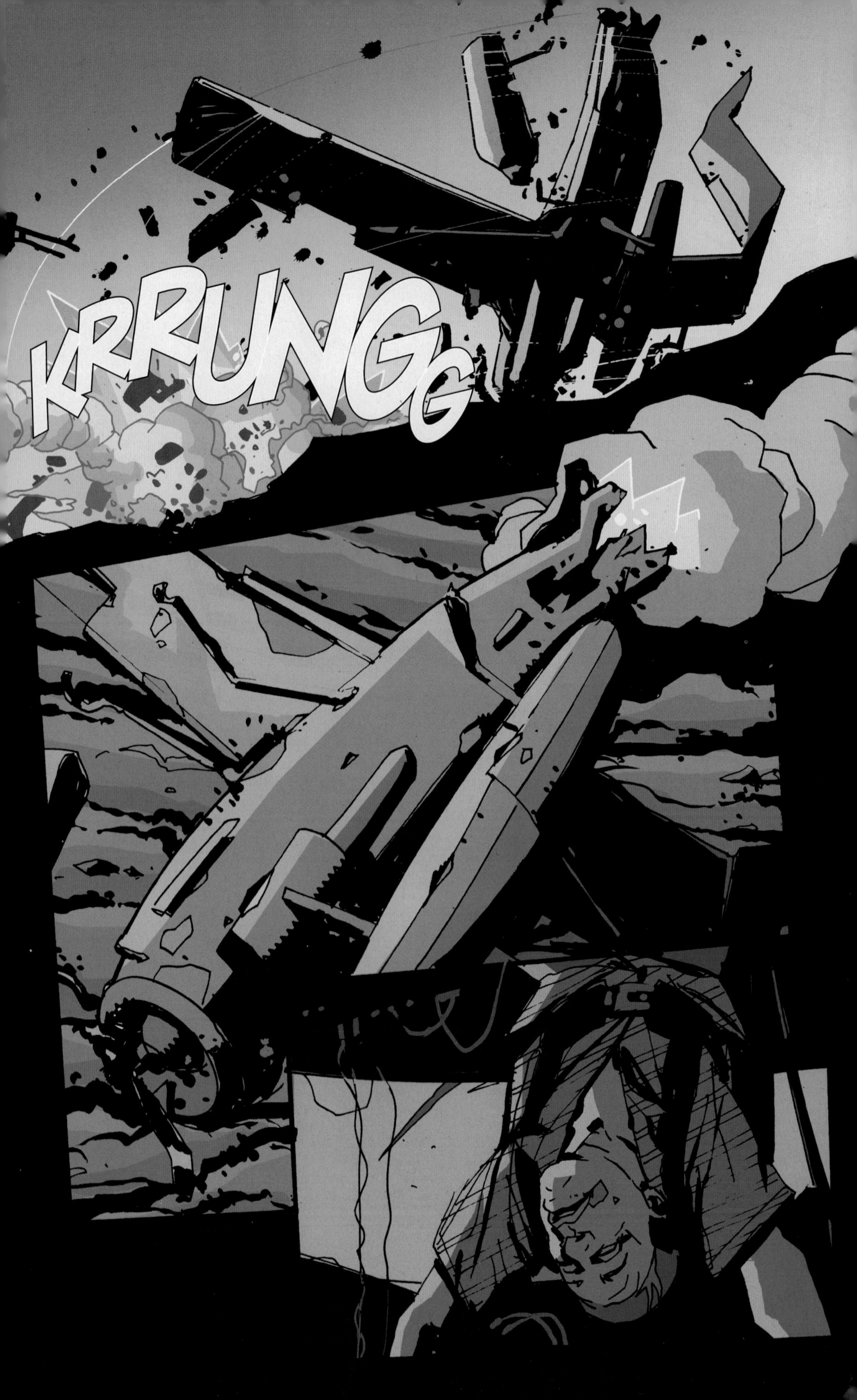
KRRUNGG

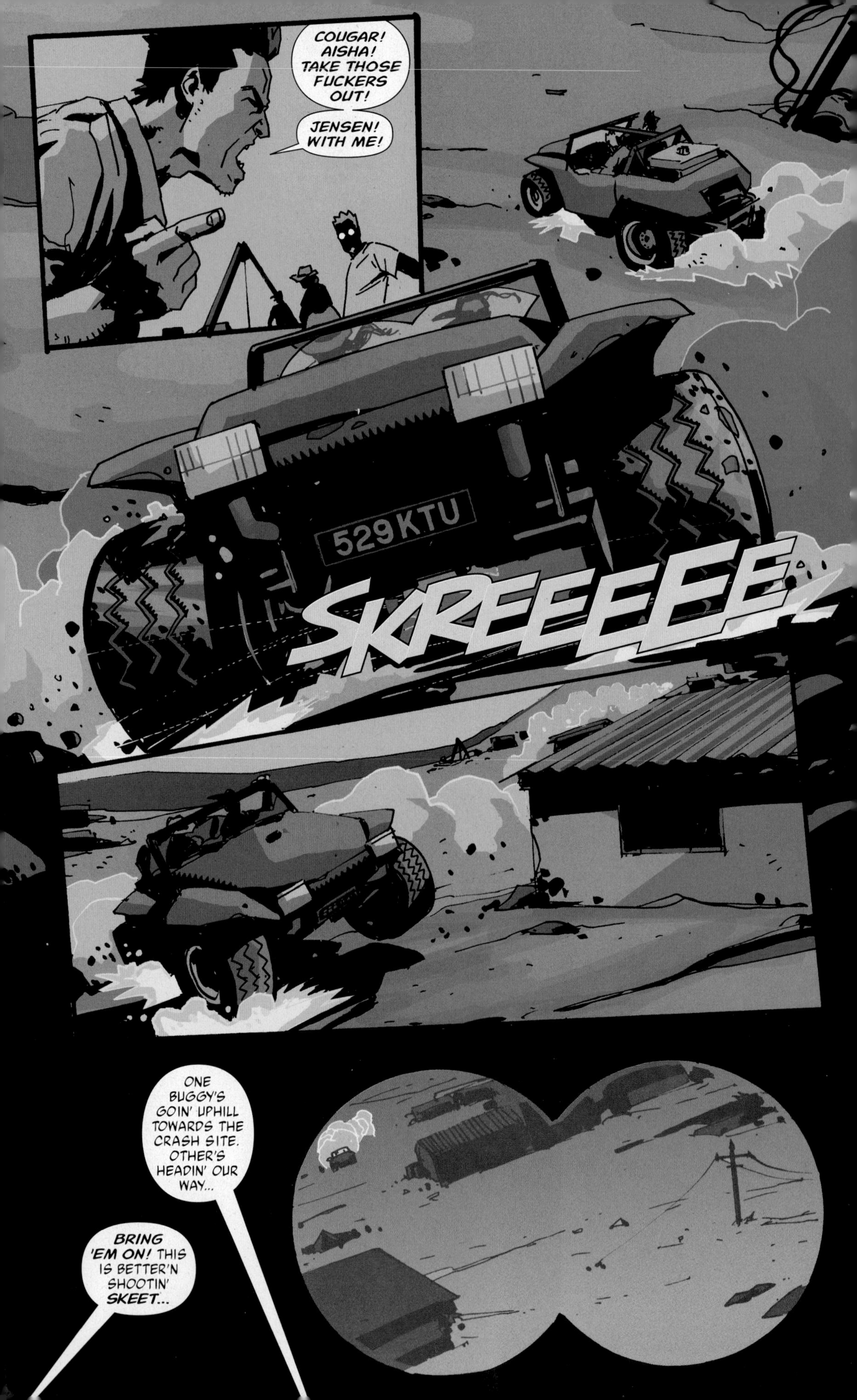
COUGAR! AISHA! TAKE THOSE FUCKERS OUT!
JENSEN! WITH ME!
529 KTU
SKREEEEEE
ONE BUGGY'S GOIN' UPHILL TOWARDS THE CRASH SITE. OTHER'S HEADIN' OUR WAY...
BRING 'EM ON! THIS IS BETTER'N SHOOTIN' SKEET...

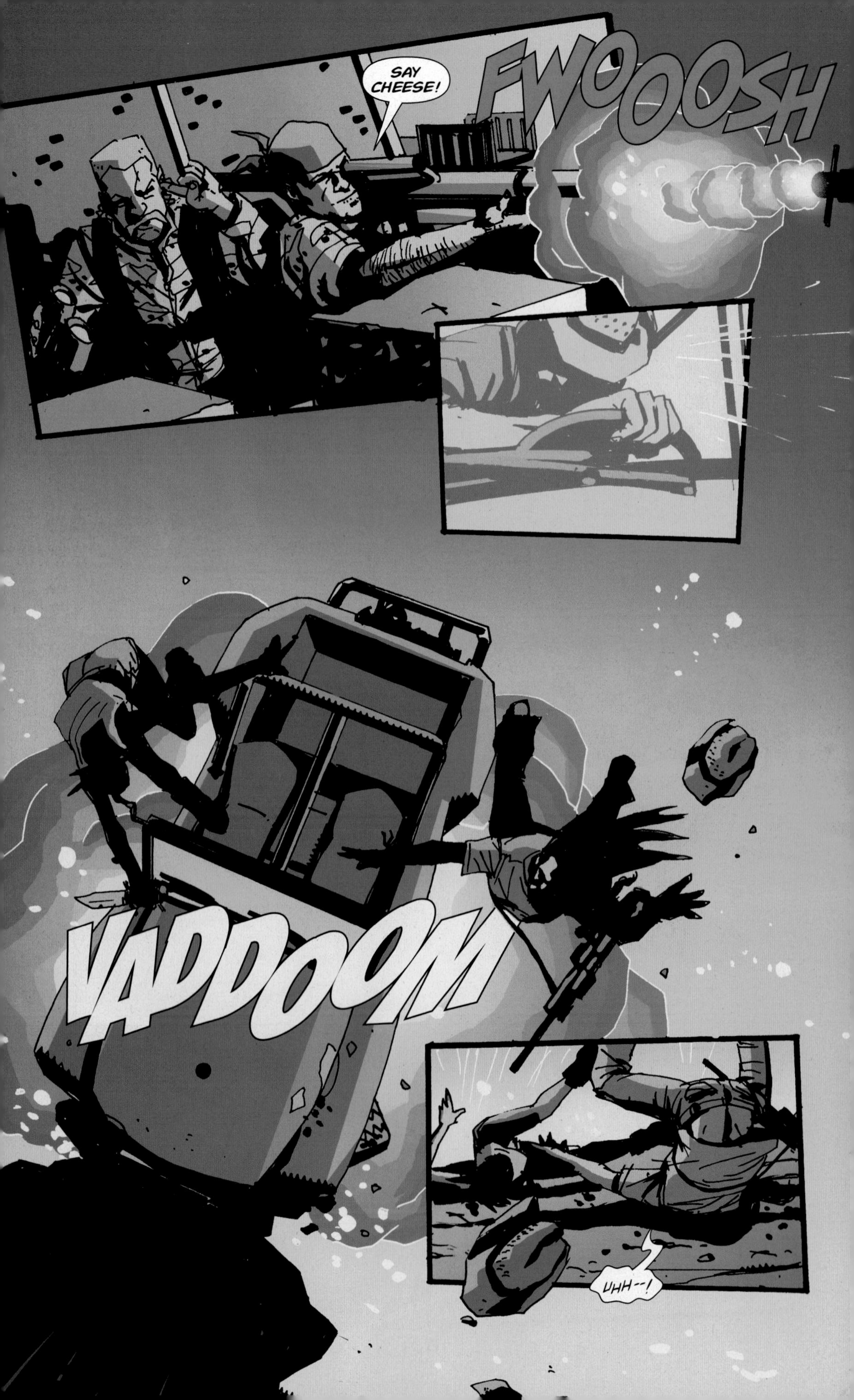
SAY CHEESE!
FWOOOSH
VADDOOM
UHH--!

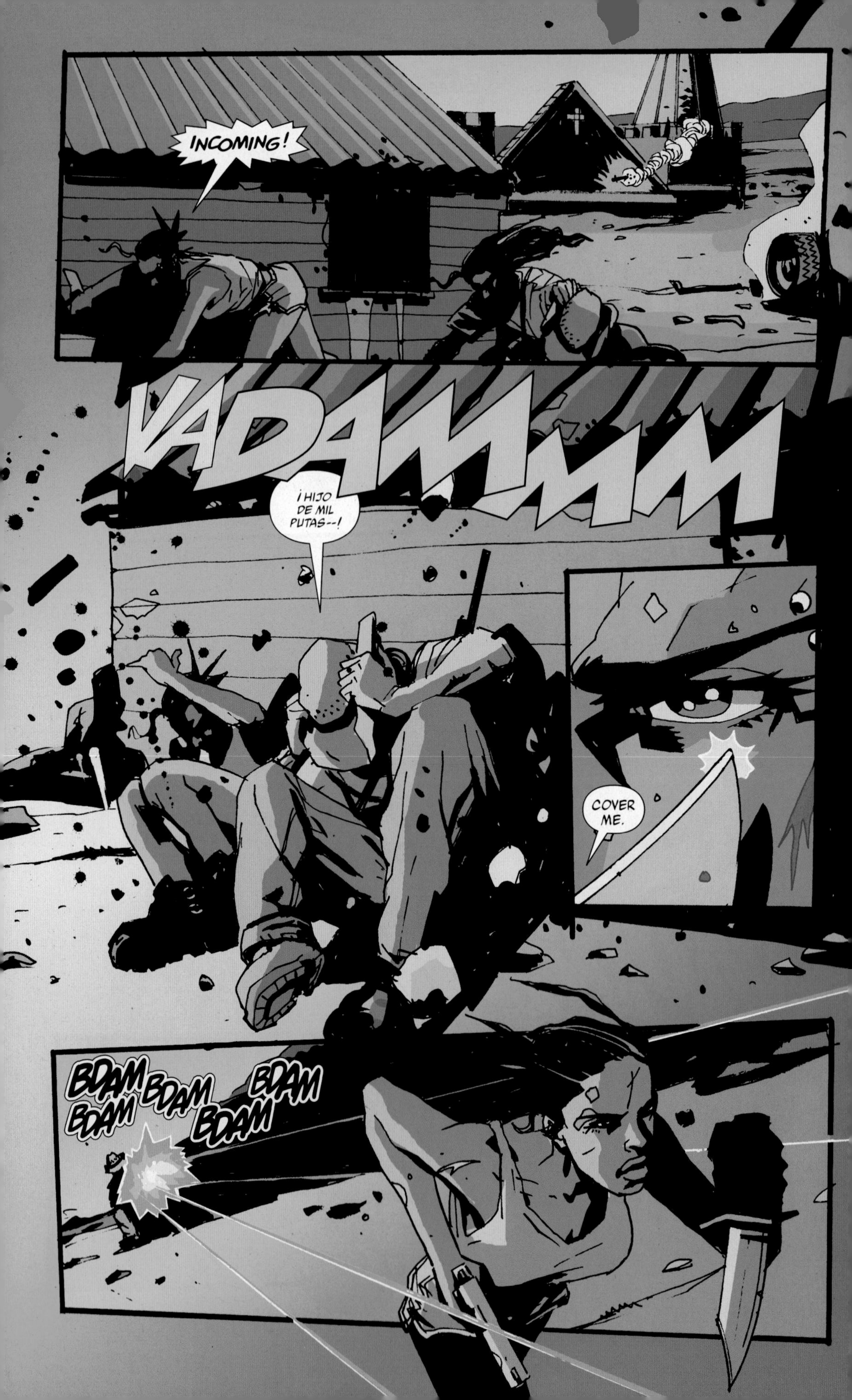
INCOMING!
VADAMMM
¡HIJO DE MIL PUTAS--!
COVER ME.
BDAM BDAM BDAM BDAM BDAM

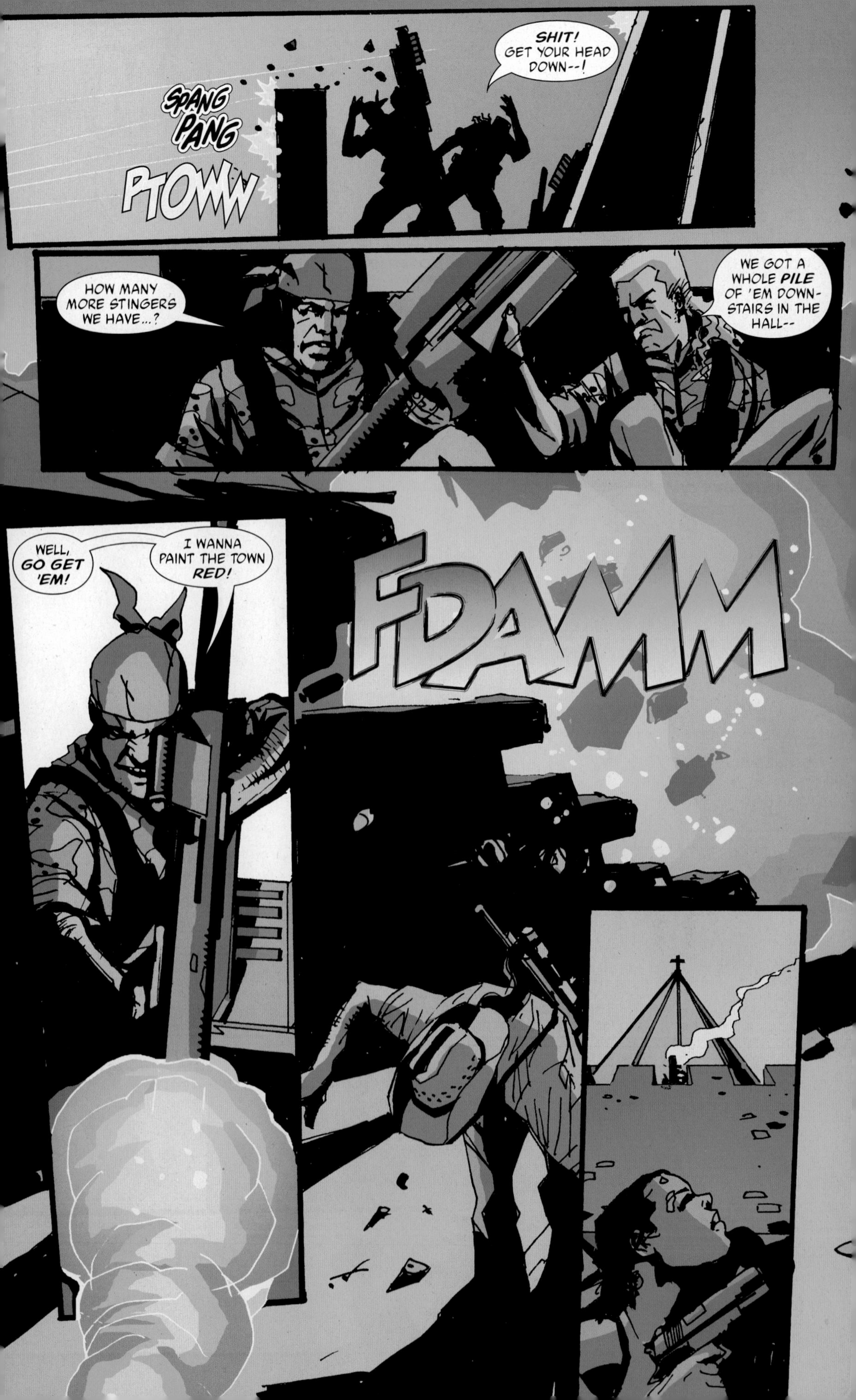
SHIT! GET YOUR HEAD DOWN--!
SPANG PANG
PTOWW
HOW MANY MORE STINGERS WE HAVE...?
WE GOT A WHOLE PILE OF 'EM DOWN-STAIRS IN THE HALL--
WELL, GO GET 'EM!
I WANNA PAINT THE TOWN RED!
FDAMM

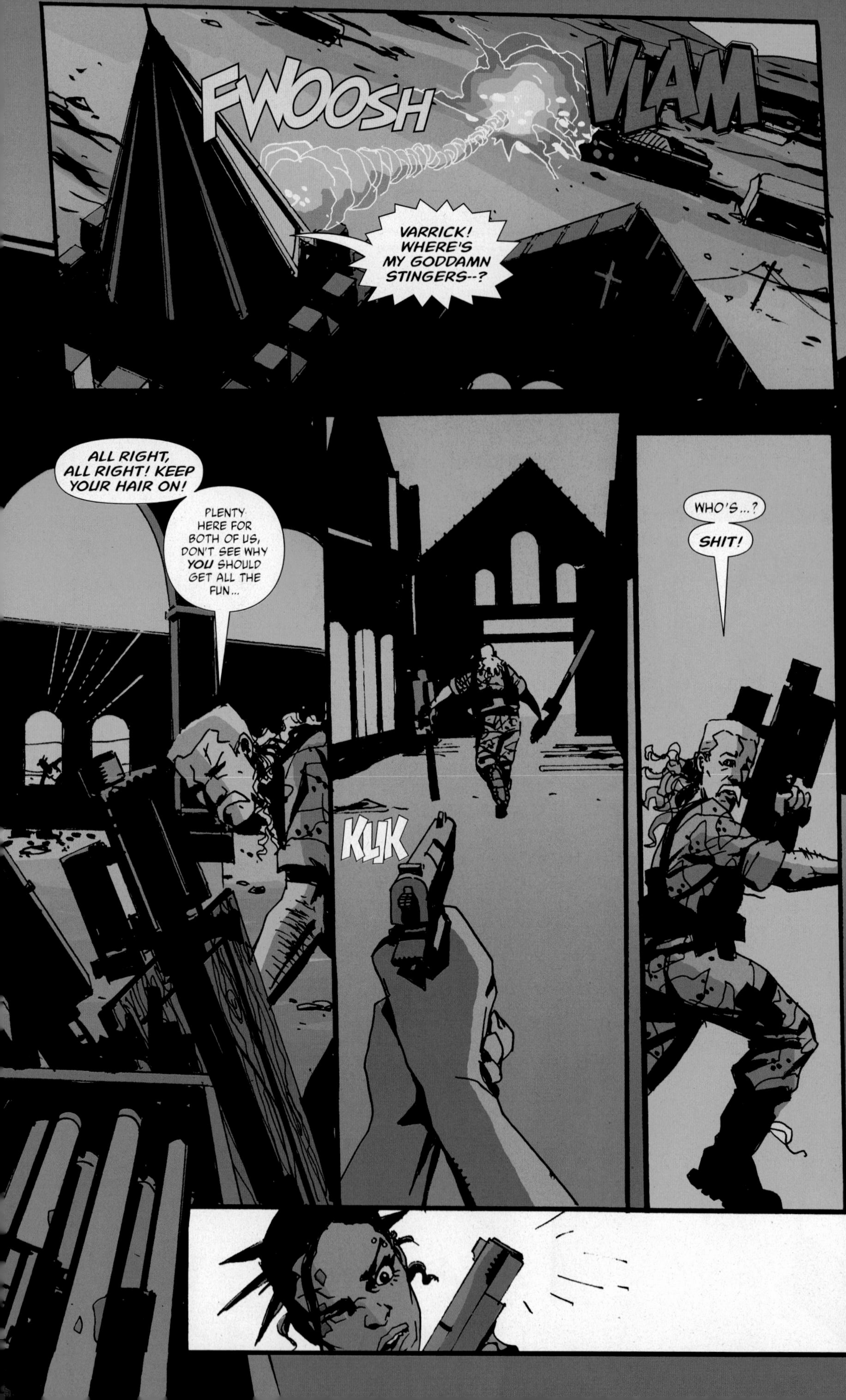
FWOOSH
VLAM
VARRICK! WHERE'S MY GODDAMN STINGERS--?
ALL RIGHT, ALL RIGHT! KEEP YOUR HAIR ON!
PLENTY HERE FOR BOTH OF US, DON'T SEE WHY YOU SHOULD GET ALL THE FUN...
KLIK
WHO'S...?
SHIT!

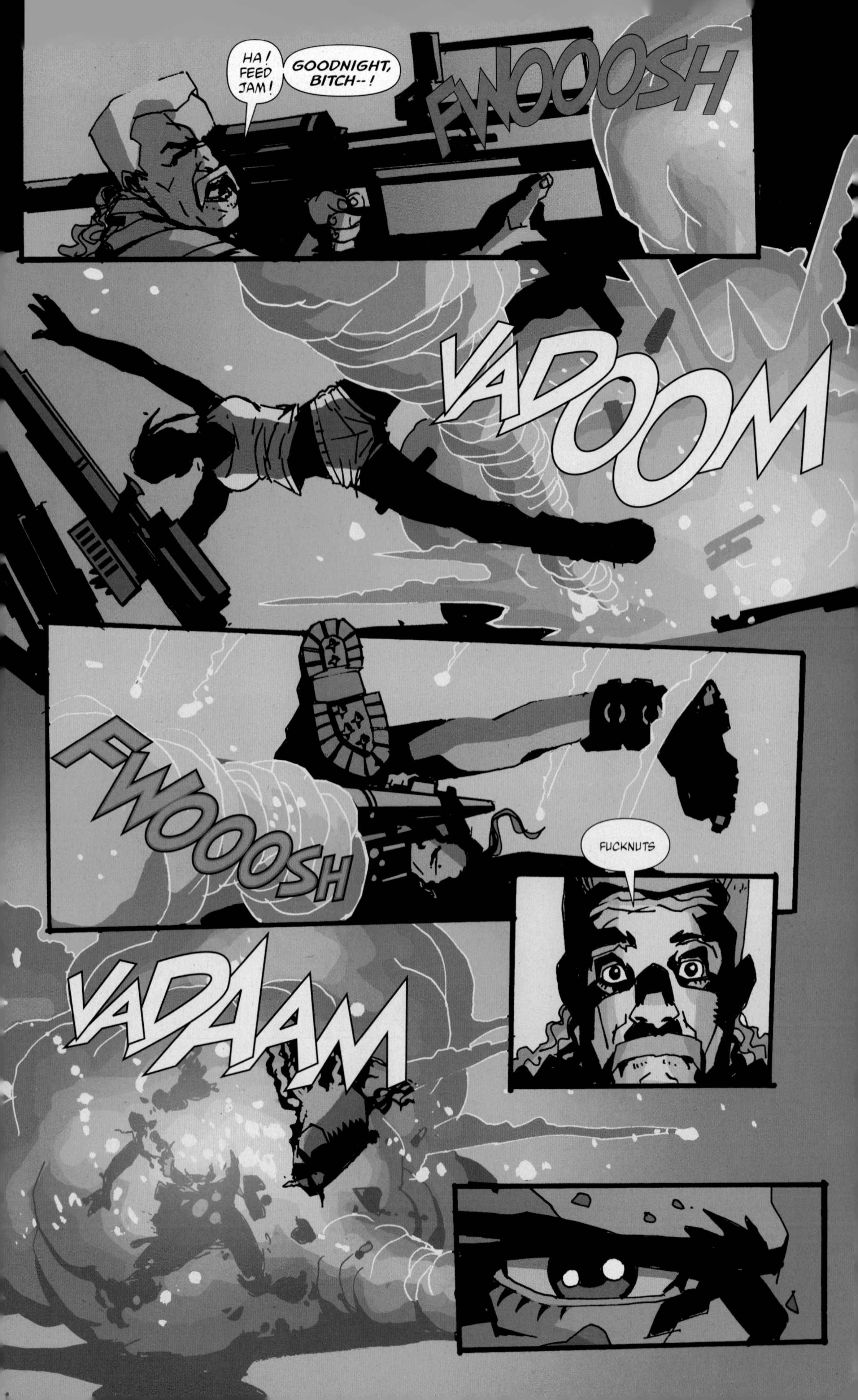

HA! FEED JAM!
GOODNIGHT, BITCH--!
FWOOOSH
VADOOOM
FWOOOSH
FUCKNUTS
VADAAM

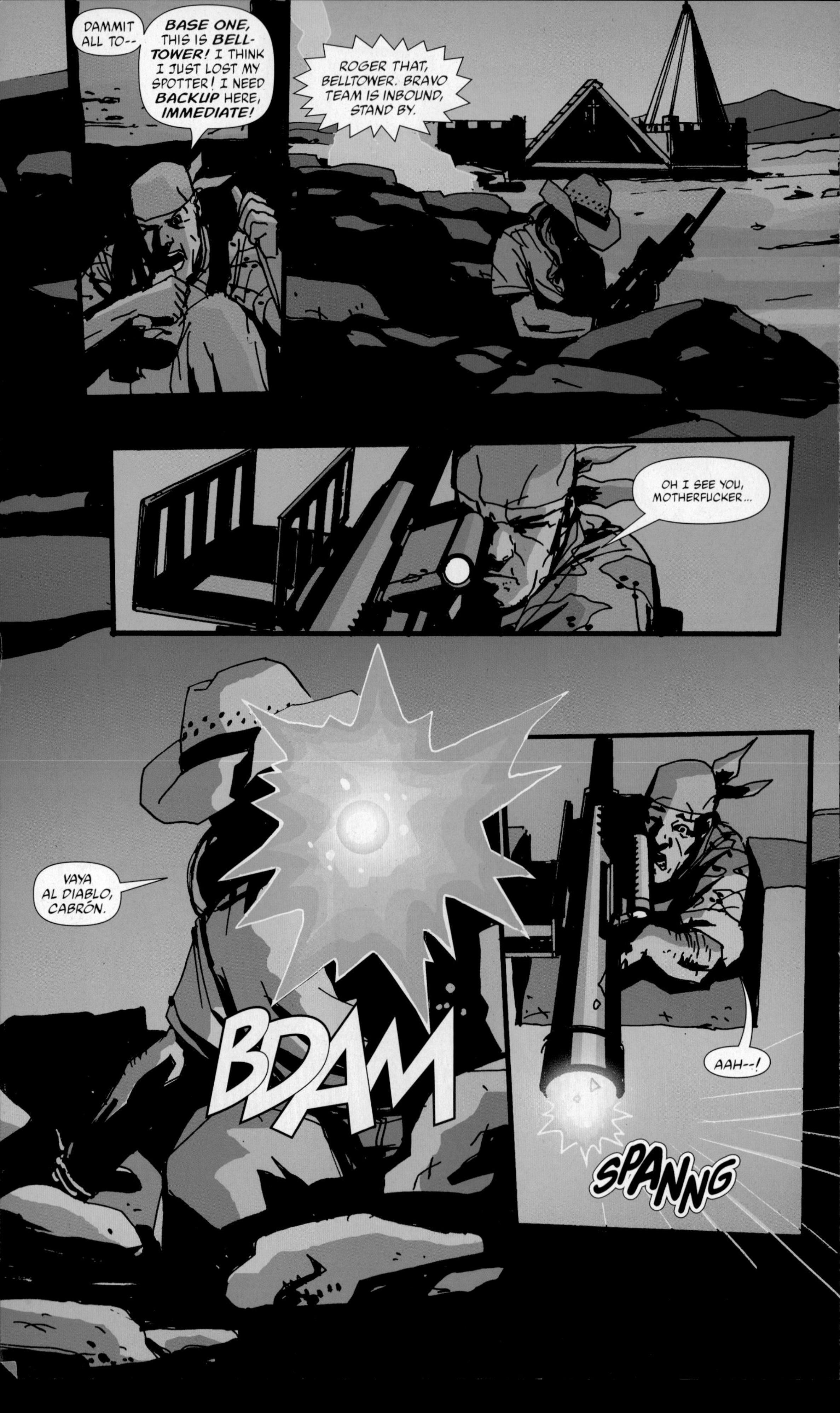
DAMMIT ALL TO--
BASE ONE, THIS IS BELL-TOWER! I THINK I JUST LOST MY SPOTTER! I NEED BACKUP HERE, IMMEDIATE!
ROGER THAT, BELLTOWER. BRAVO TEAM IS INBOUND, STAND BY.
OH I SEE YOU, MOTHERFUCKER...
VAYA AL DIABLO, CABRÓN.
BDAM
AAH--!
SPANNG

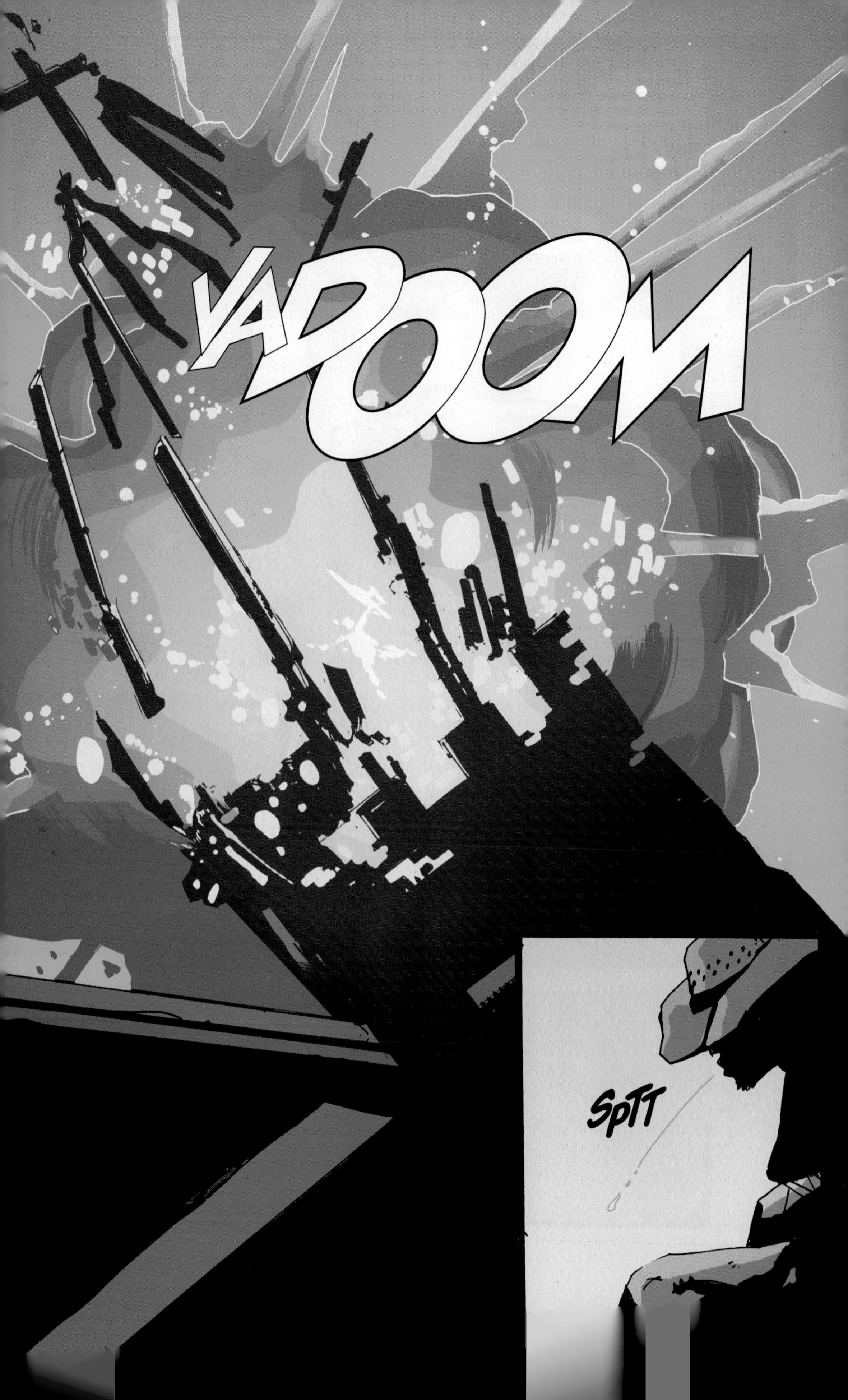
VADOOM
SPTT

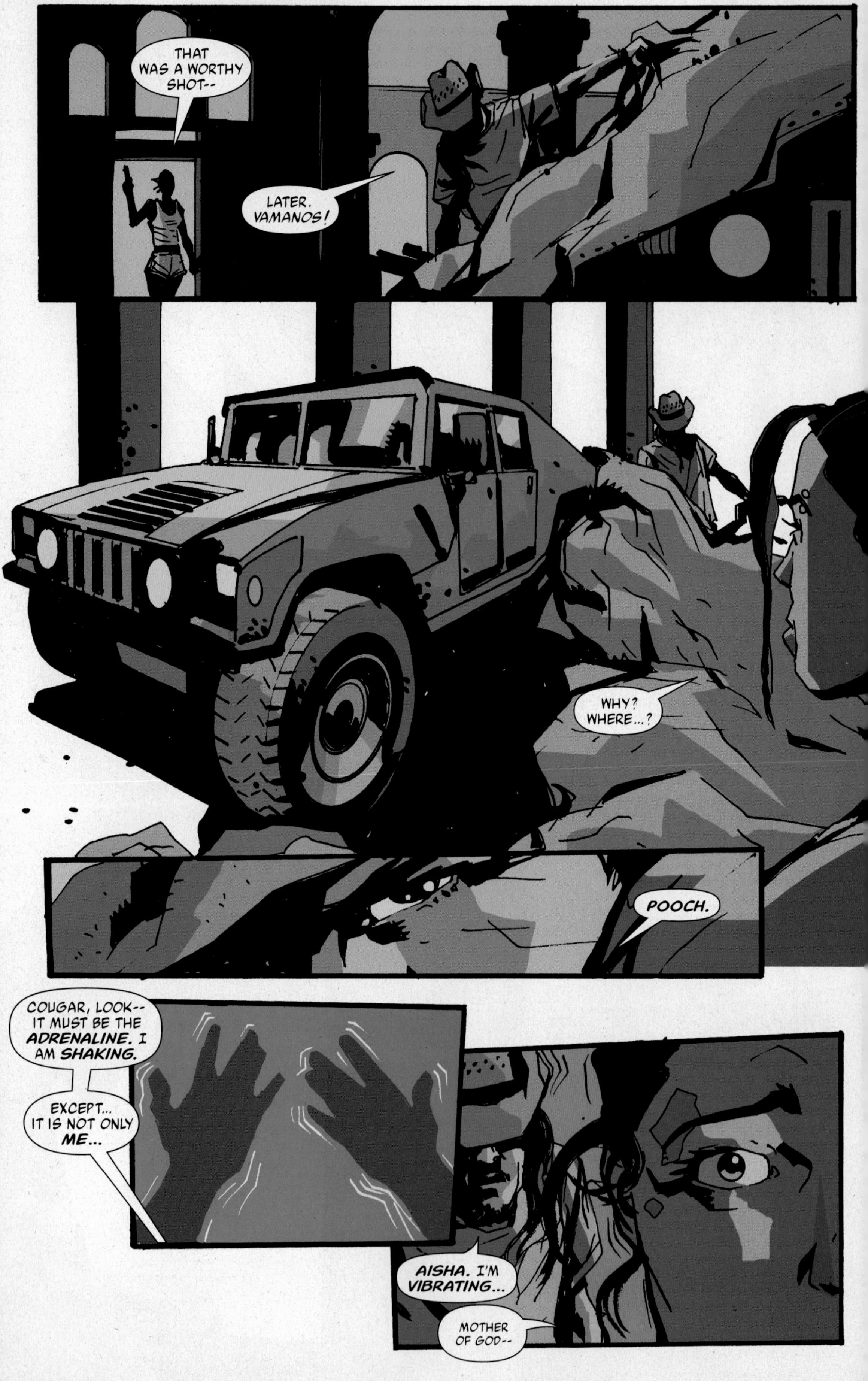
THAT WAS A WORTHY SHOT--
LATER. VAMANOS!
WHY? WHERE...?
POOCH.
COUGAR, LOOK-- IT MUST BE THE ADRENALINE. I AM SHAKING.
EXCEPT... IT IS NOT ONLY ME...
AISHA. I'M VIBRATING...
MOTHER OF GOD--

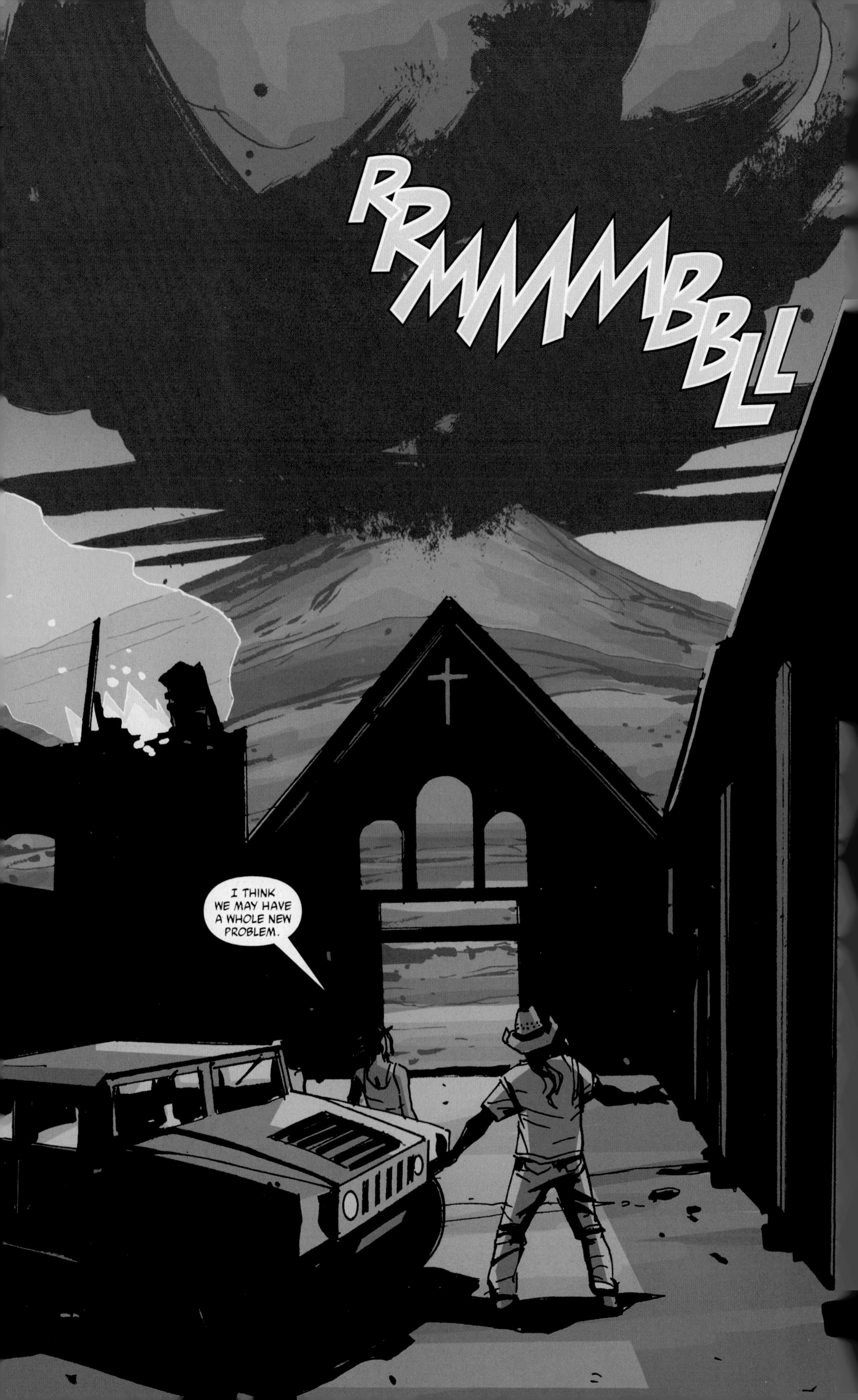
RRMMMMBBLL
I THINK WE MAY HAVE A WHOLE NEW PROBLEM.

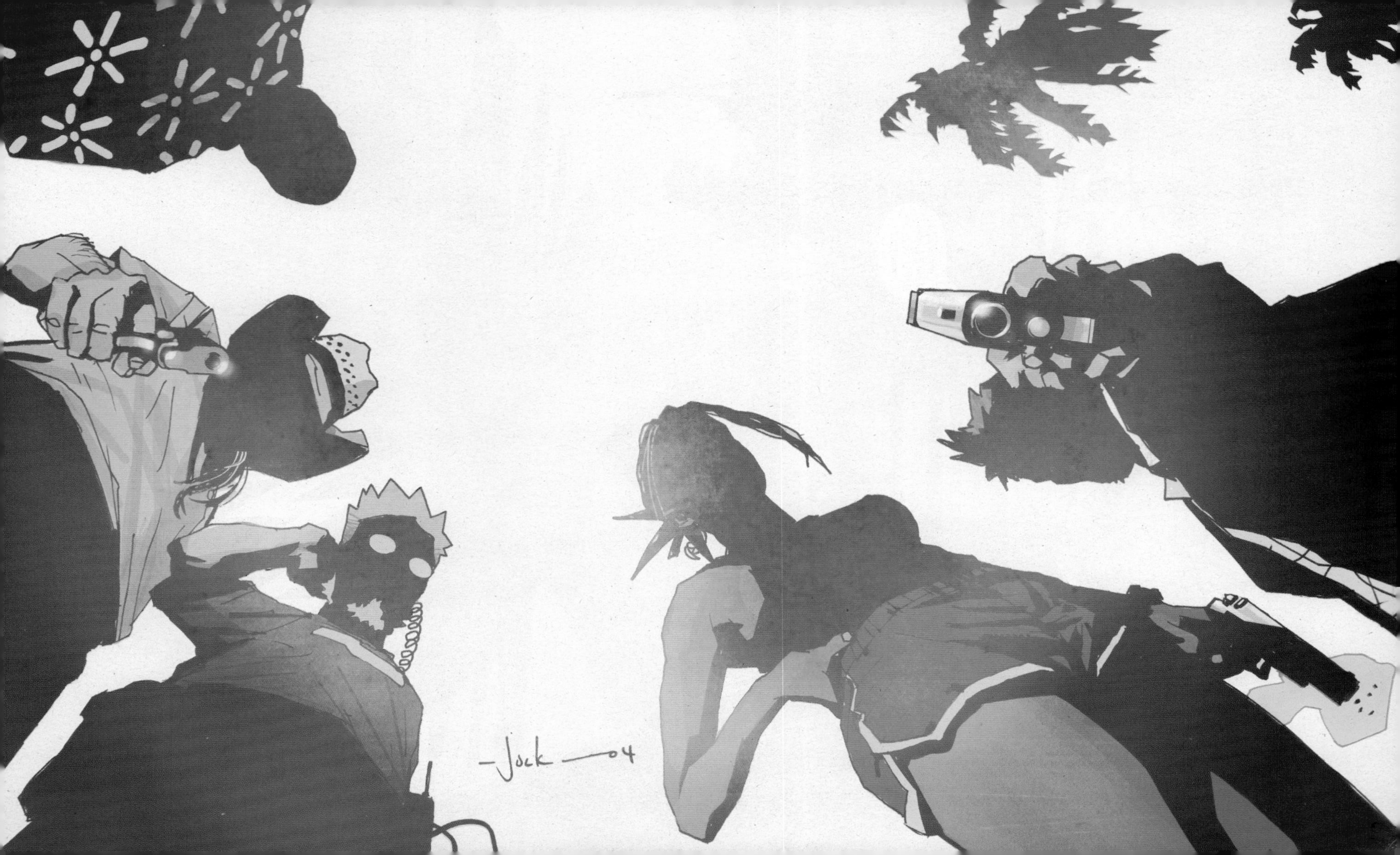
-Jock —04

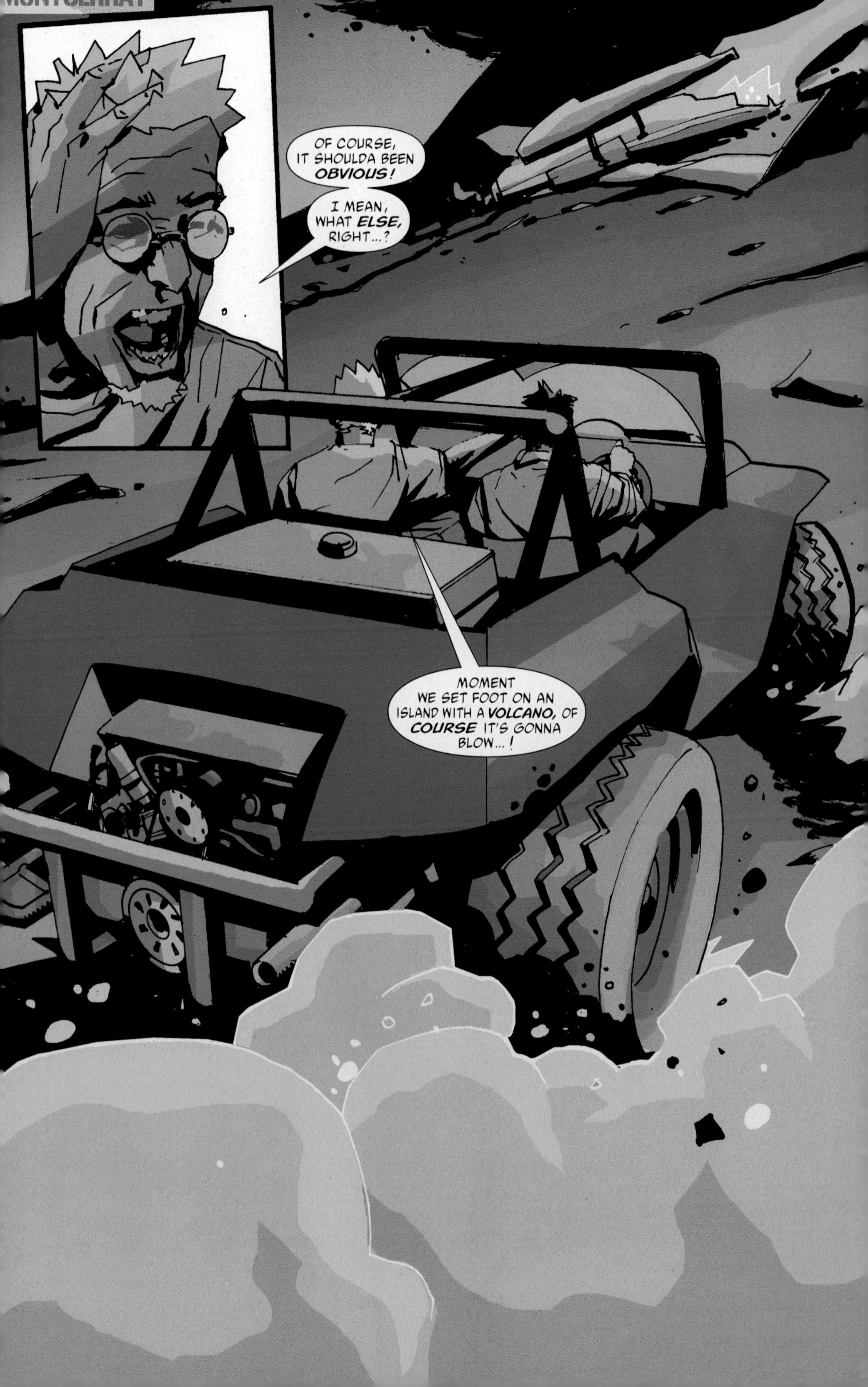

OF COURSE, IT SHOULDA BEEN **OBVIOUS!**
I MEAN, WHAT **ELSE,** RIGHT...?
MOMENT WE SET FOOT ON AN ISLAND WITH A **VOLCANO,** OF **COURSE** IT'S GONNA BLOW...!

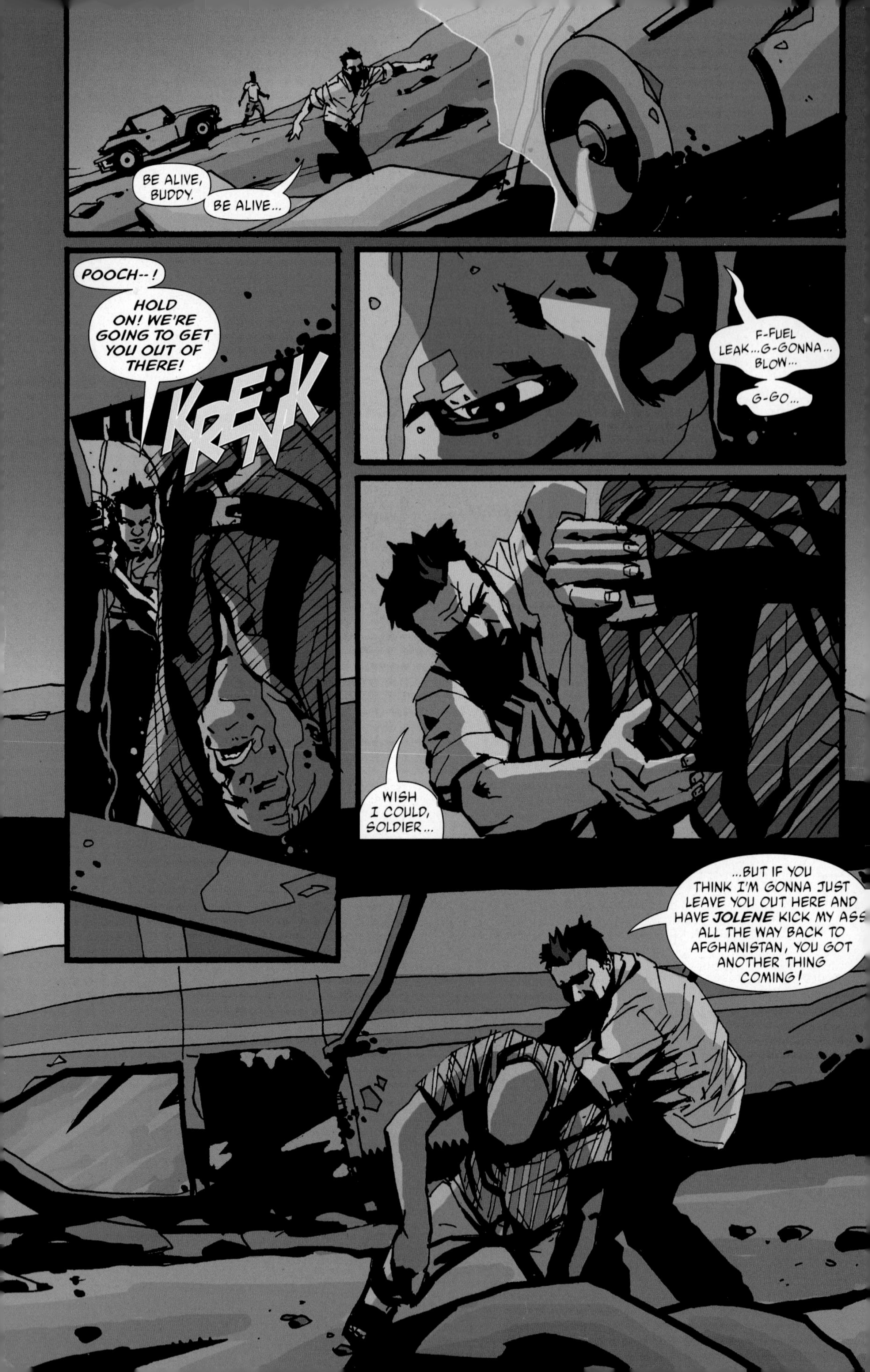
BE ALIVE, BUDDY.
BE ALIVE...
POOCH--!
HOLD ON! WE'RE GOING TO GET YOU OUT OF THERE!
KRENK
F-FUEL LEAK...G-GONNA... BLOW...
G-GO...
WISH I COULD, SOLDIER...
...BUT IF YOU THINK I'M GONNA JUST LEAVE YOU OUT HERE AND HAVE JOLENE KICK MY ASS ALL THE WAY BACK TO AFGHANISTAN, YOU GOT ANOTHER THING COMING!

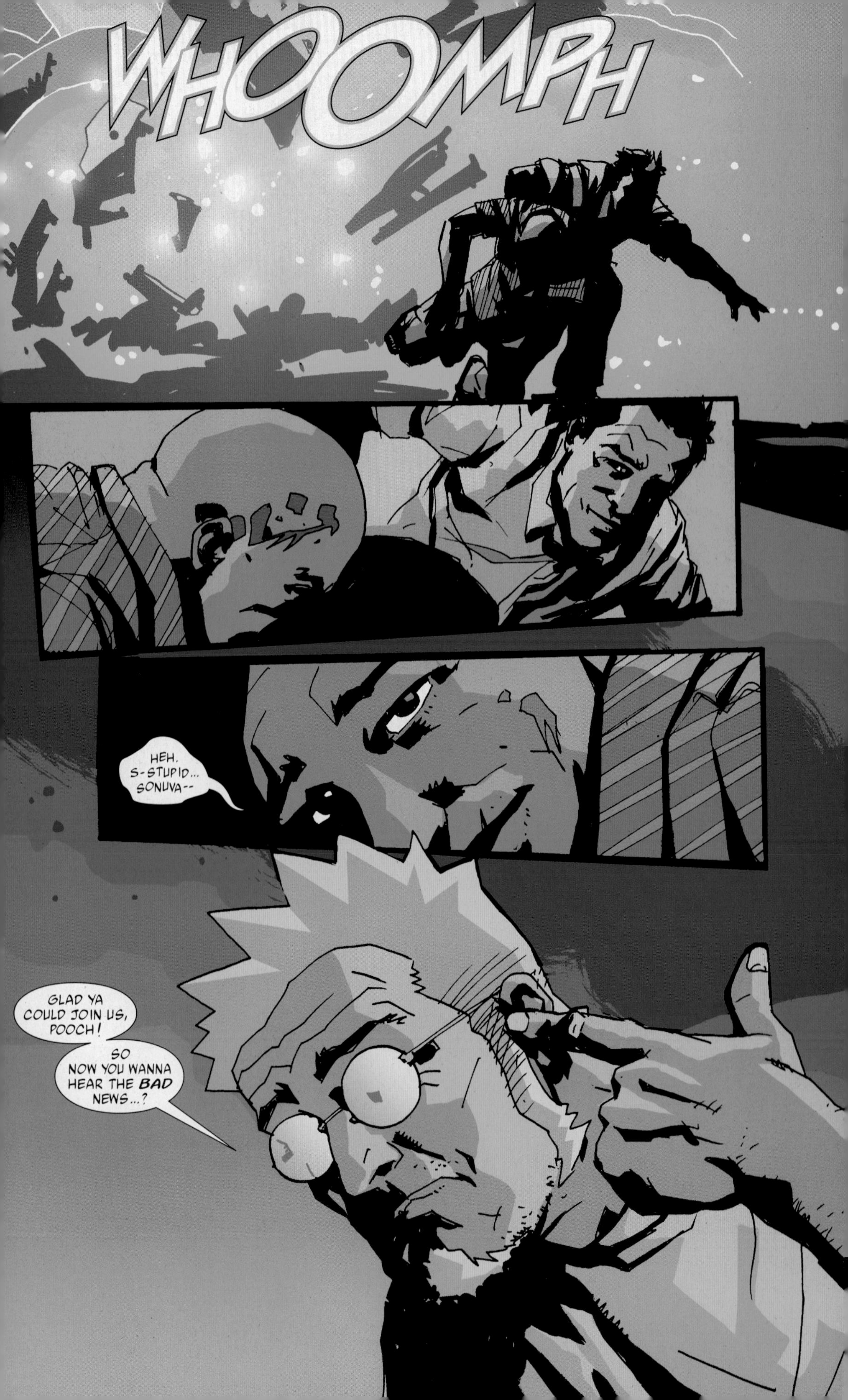
WHOOMPH
HEH. S-STUPID... SONUVA--
GLAD YA COULD JOIN US, POOCH!
SO NOW YOU WANNA HEAR THE BAD NEWS...?

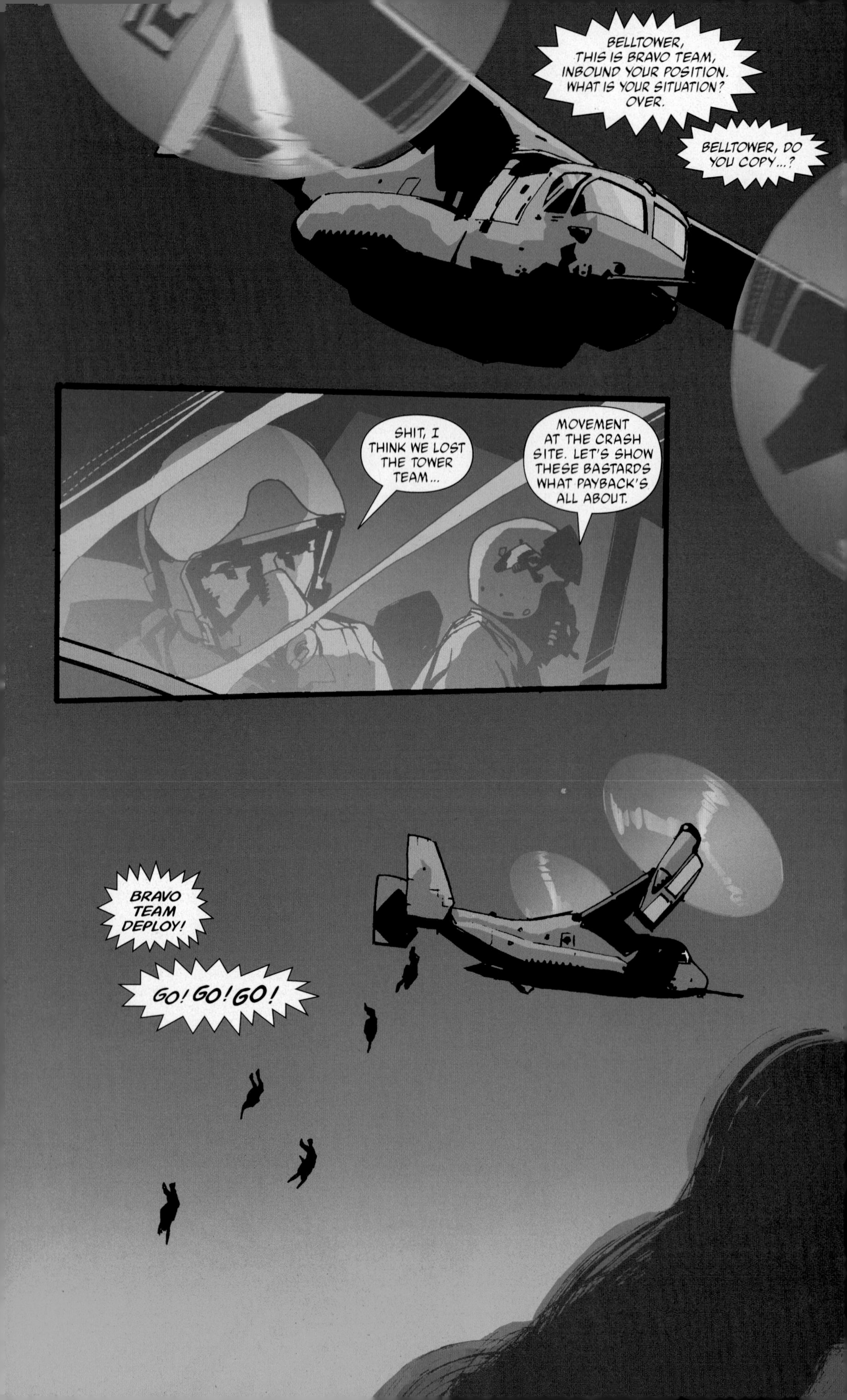
BELLTOWER, THIS IS BRAVO TEAM, INBOUND YOUR POSITION. WHAT IS YOUR SITUATION? OVER.
BELLTOWER, DO YOU COPY...?
SHIT, I THINK WE LOST THE TOWER TEAM...
MOVEMENT AT THE CRASH SITE. LET'S SHOW THESE BASTARDS WHAT PAYBACK'S ALL ABOUT.
BRAVO TEAM DEPLOY!
GO! GO! GO!

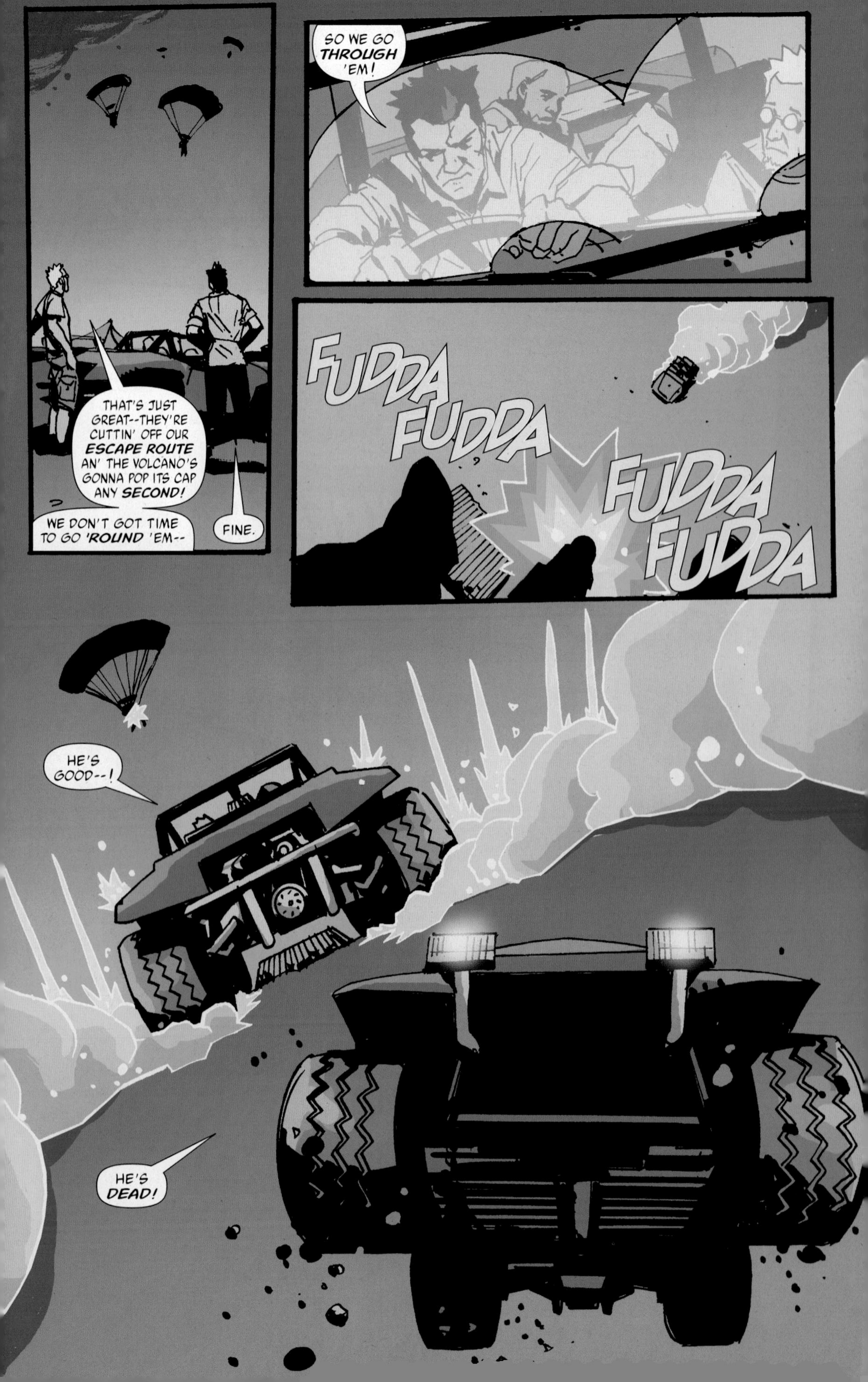
THAT'S JUST GREAT--THEY'RE CUTTIN' OFF OUR ESCAPE ROUTE AN' THE VOLCANO'S GONNA POP ITS CAP ANY SECOND!
WE DON'T GOT TIME TO GO 'ROUND 'EM--
FINE.
SO WE GO THROUGH 'EM!
FUDDA FUDDA
FUDDA FUDDA
HE'S GOOD--!
HE'S DEAD!

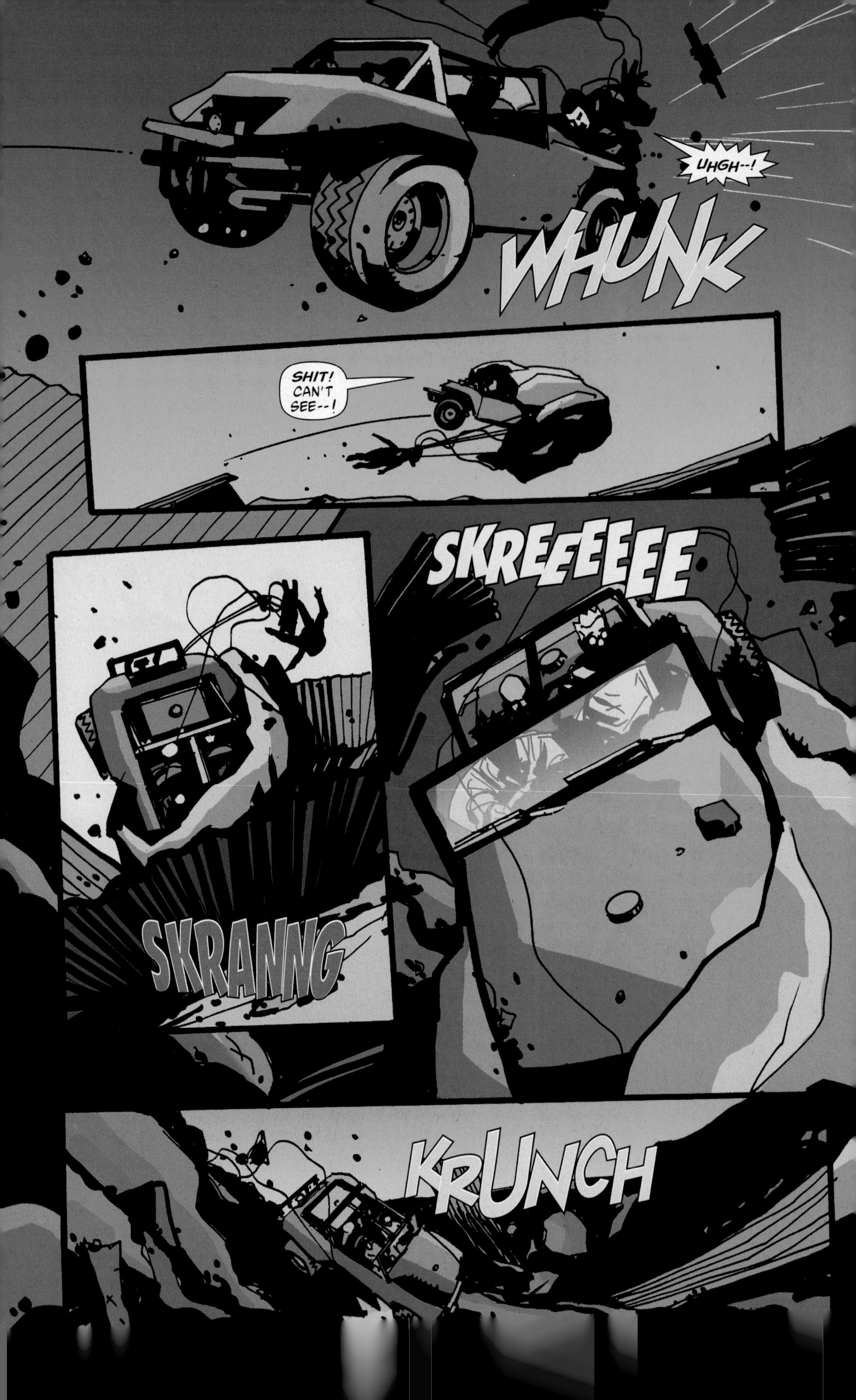
UHGH--!
WHUNK
SHIT! CAN'T SEE--!
SKREEEEEE
SKRANNG
KRUNCH

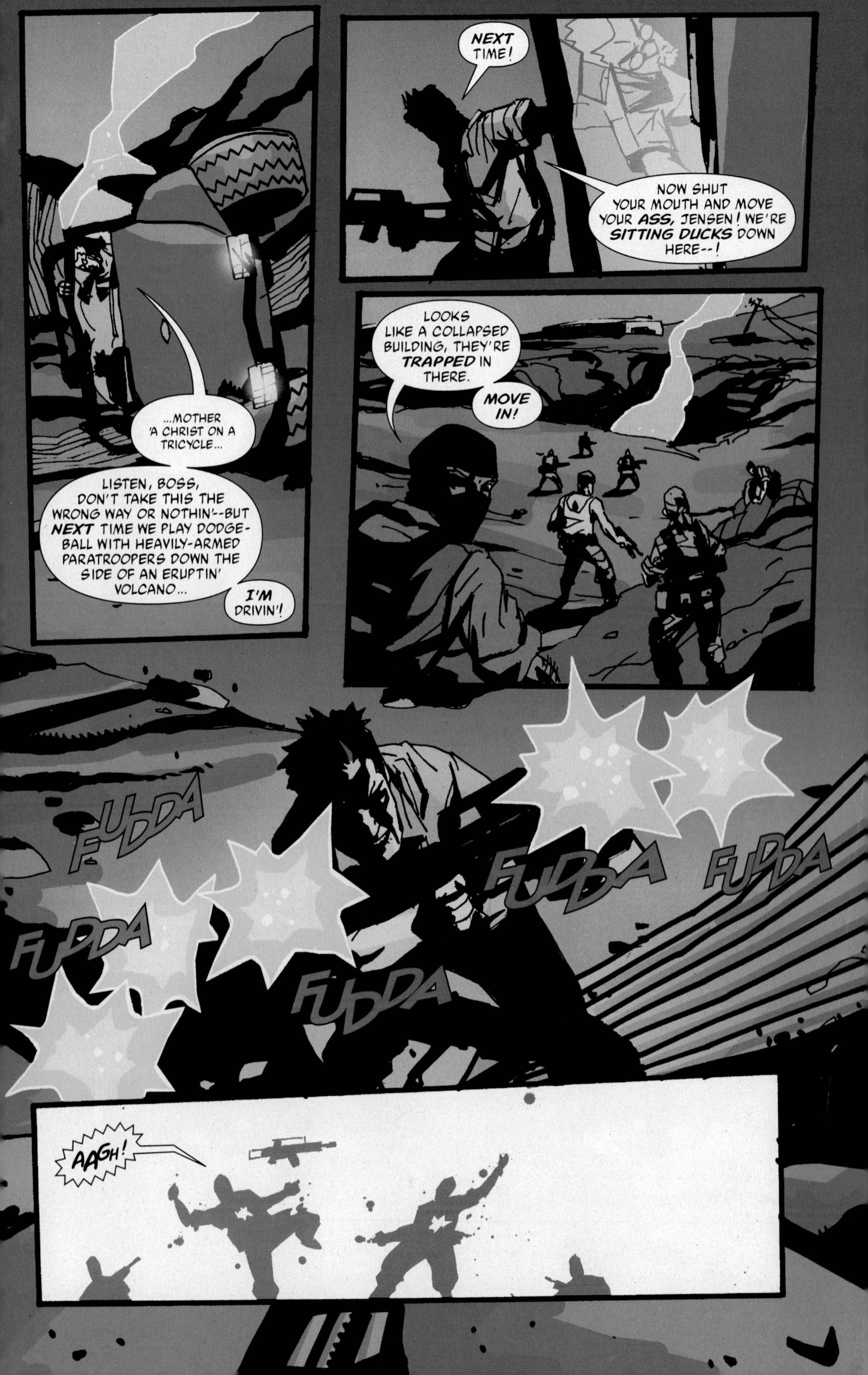

...MOTHER 'A CHRIST ON A TRICYCLE...
LISTEN, BOSS, DON'T TAKE THIS THE WRONG WAY OR NOTHIN'--BUT NEXT TIME WE PLAY DODGE-BALL WITH HEAVILY-ARMED PARATROOPERS DOWN THE SIDE OF AN ERUPTIN' VOLCANO...
I'M DRIVIN'!
NEXT TIME!
NOW SHUT YOUR MOUTH AND MOVE YOUR ASS, JENSEN! WE'RE SITTING DUCKS DOWN HERE--!
LOOKS LIKE A COLLAPSED BUILDING, THEY'RE TRAPPED IN THERE.
MOVE IN!
FUDDA
FUDDA
FUDDA
FUDDA
FUDDA
AAGH!

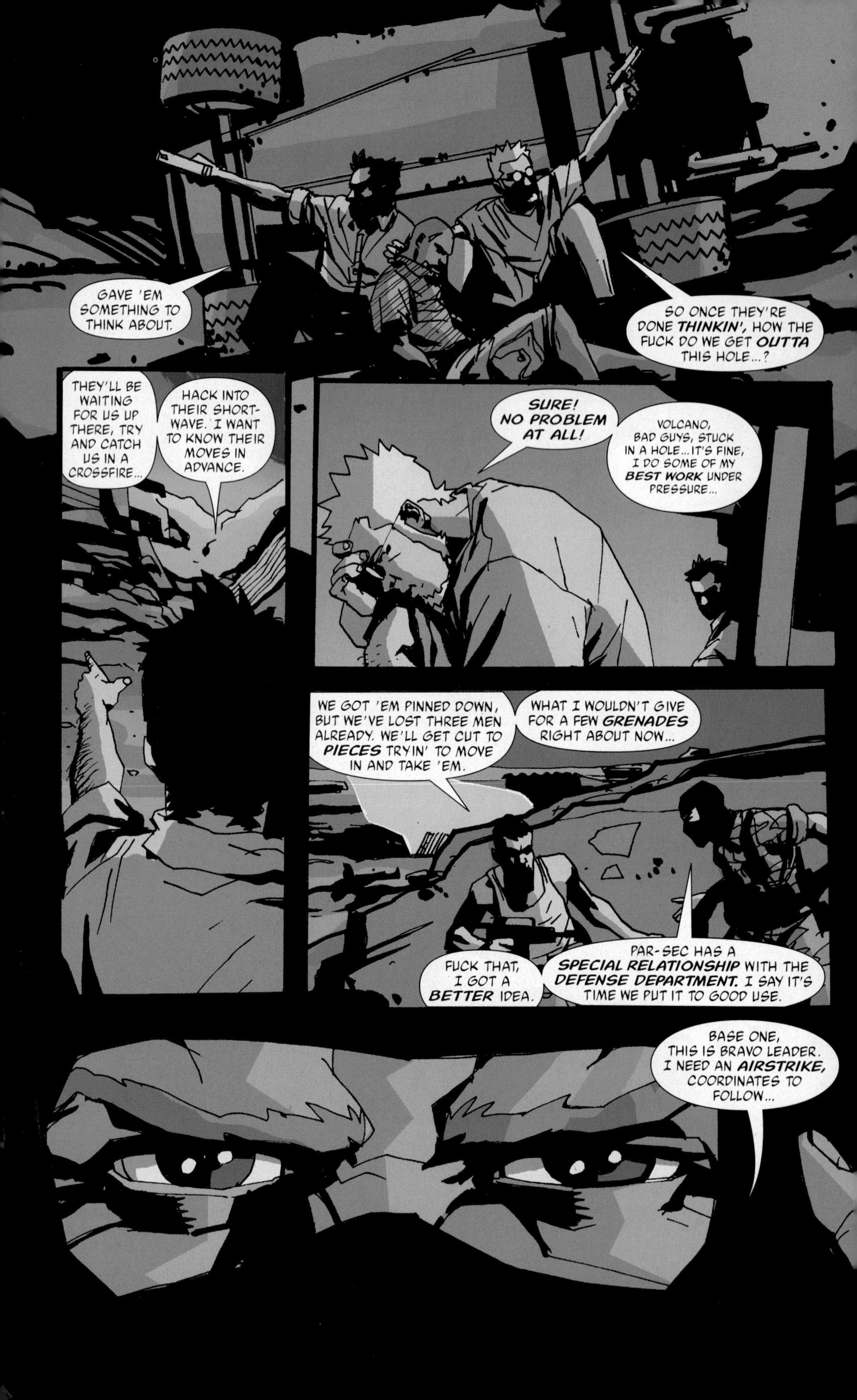
GAVE 'EM SOMETHING TO THINK ABOUT.
SO ONCE THEY'RE DONE **THINKIN'**, HOW THE FUCK DO WE GET **OUTTA** THIS HOLE...?
THEY'LL BE WAITING FOR US UP THERE, TRY AND CATCH US IN A CROSSFIRE...
HACK INTO THEIR SHORT-WAVE. I WANT TO KNOW THEIR MOVES IN ADVANCE.
SURE! NO PROBLEM AT ALL!
VOLCANO, BAD GUYS, STUCK IN A HOLE... IT'S FINE, I DO SOME OF MY **BEST WORK** UNDER PRESSURE...
WE GOT 'EM PINNED DOWN, BUT WE'VE LOST THREE MEN ALREADY. WE'LL GET CUT TO **PIECES** TRYIN' TO MOVE IN AND TAKE 'EM.
WHAT I WOULDN'T GIVE FOR A FEW **GRENADES** RIGHT ABOUT NOW...
FUCK THAT, I GOT A **BETTER** IDEA.
PAR-SEC HAS A **SPECIAL RELATIONSHIP** WITH THE **DEFENSE DEPARTMENT.** I SAY IT'S TIME WE PUT IT TO GOOD USE.
BASE ONE, THIS IS BRAVO LEADER. I NEED AN **AIRSTRIKE,** COORDINATES TO FOLLOW...

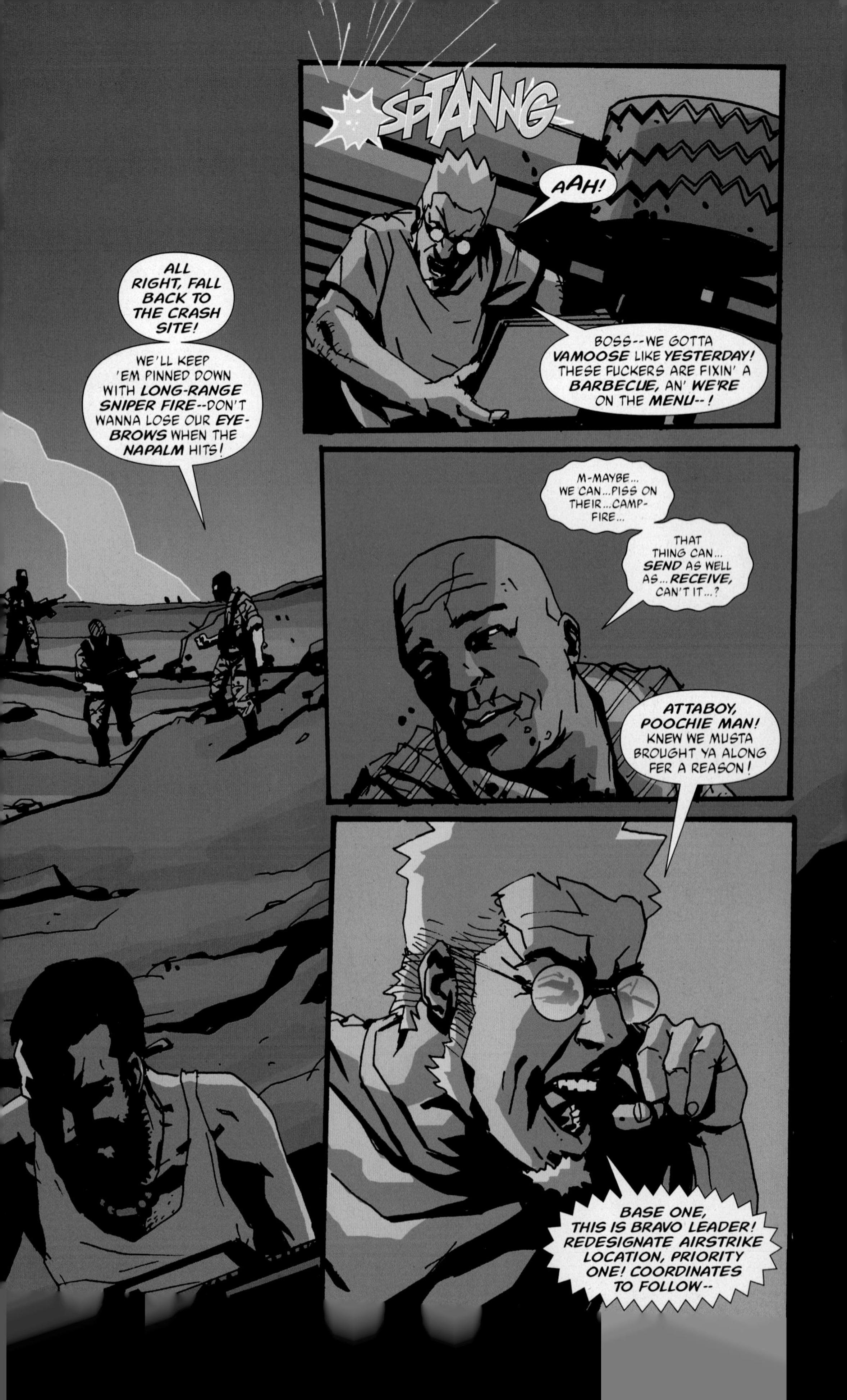
SPTANNG
AAH!
BOSS--WE GOTTA VAMOOSE LIKE YESTERDAY! THESE FUCKERS ARE FIXIN' A BARBECUE, AN' WE'RE ON THE MENU--!
ALL RIGHT, FALL BACK TO THE CRASH SITE!
WE'LL KEEP 'EM PINNED DOWN WITH LONG-RANGE SNIPER FIRE--DON'T WANNA LOSE OUR EYE-BROWS WHEN THE NAPALM HITS!
M-MAYBE... WE CAN...PISS ON THEIR...CAMP-FIRE...
THAT THING CAN... SEND AS WELL AS...RECEIVE, CAN'T IT...?
ATTABOY, POOCHIE MAN! KNEW WE MUSTA BROUGHT YA ALONG FER A REASON!
BASE ONE, THIS IS BRAVO LEADER! REDESIGNATE AIRSTRIKE LOCATION, PRIORITY ONE! COORDINATES TO FOLLOW--

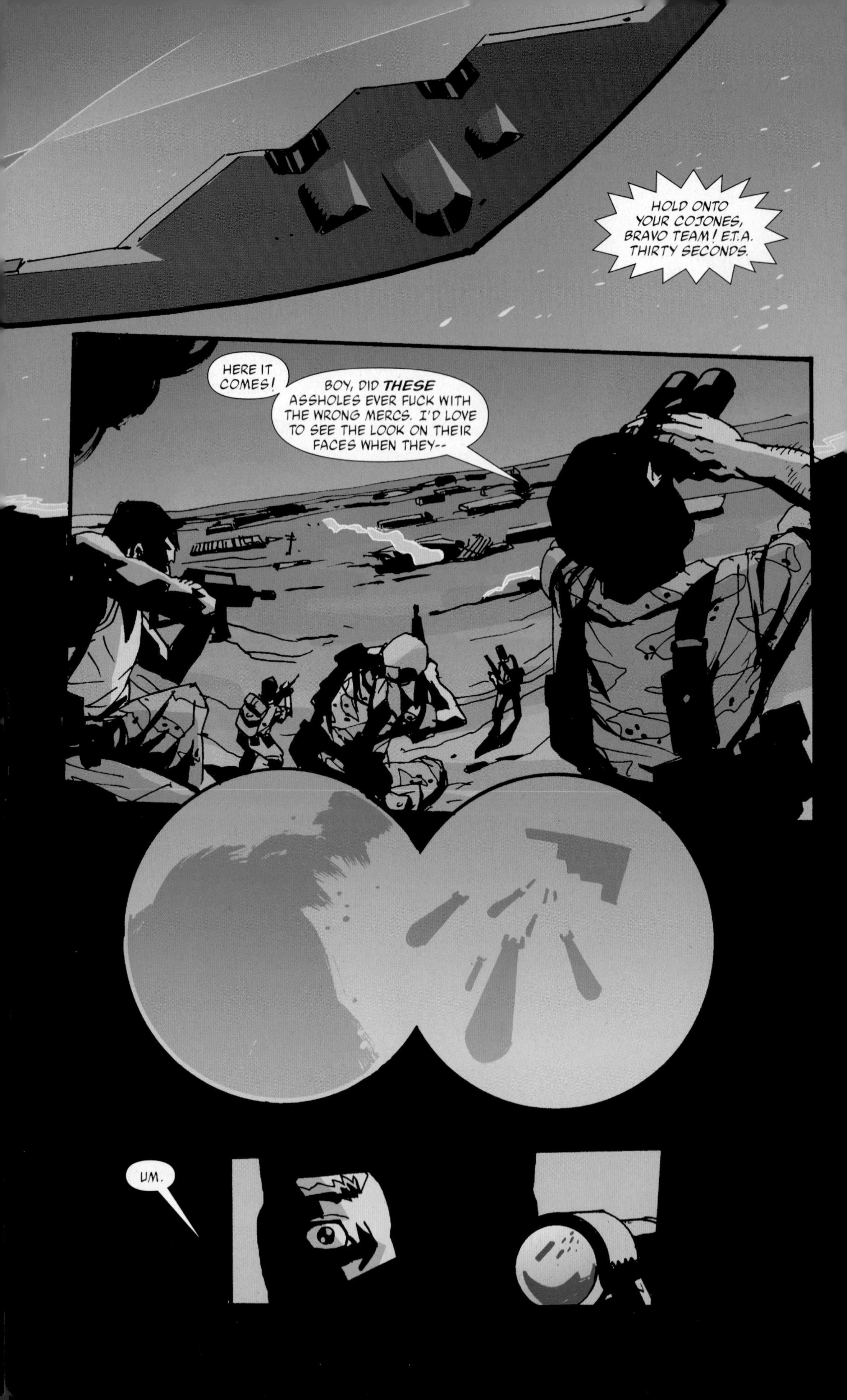
HOLD ONTO YOUR COJONES, BRAVO TEAM! E.T.A. THIRTY SECONDS.
HERE IT COMES!
BOY, DID THESE ASSHOLES EVER FUCK WITH THE WRONG MERCS. I'D LOVE TO SEE THE LOOK ON THEIR FACES WHEN THEY--
UM.

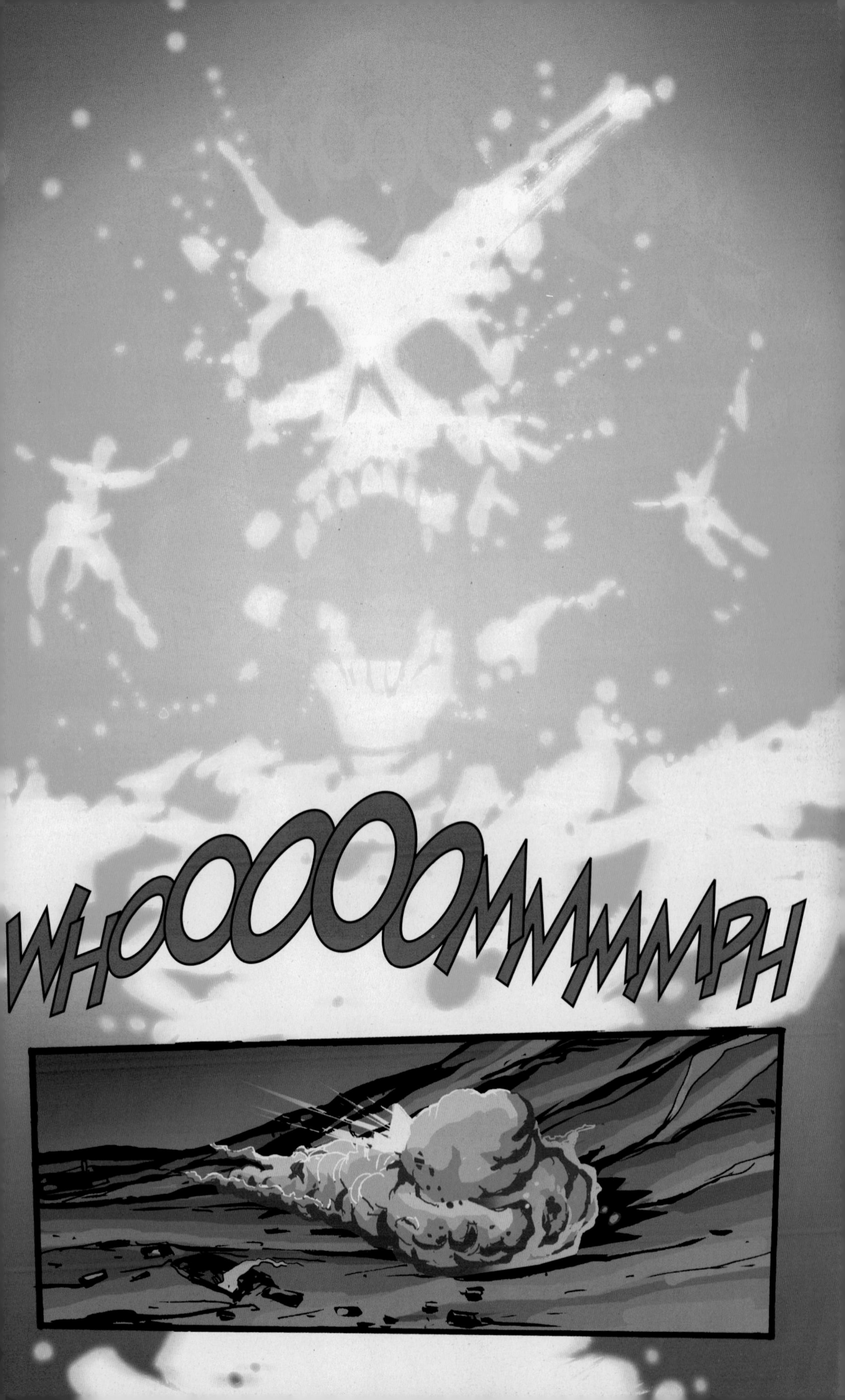
WHOOOOOMMMMPH

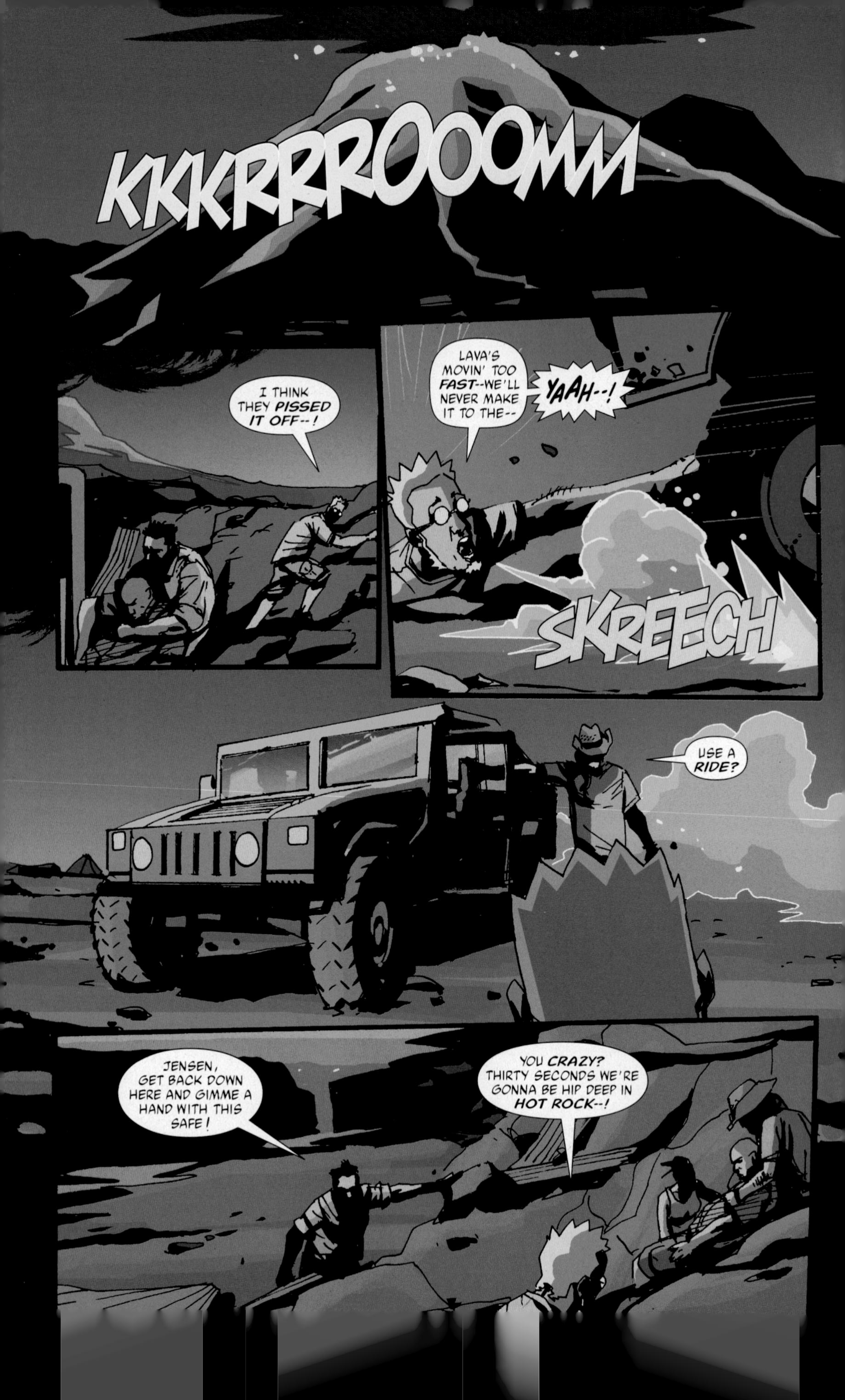
KKKRRROOOMM
I THINK THEY PISSED IT OFF--!
LAVA'S MOVIN' TOO FAST--WE'LL NEVER MAKE IT TO THE--
YAAH--!
SKREECH
USE A RIDE?
JENSEN, GET BACK DOWN HERE AND GIMME A HAND WITH THIS SAFE!
YOU CRAZY? THIRTY SECONDS WE'RE GONNA BE HIP DEEP IN HOT ROCK--!

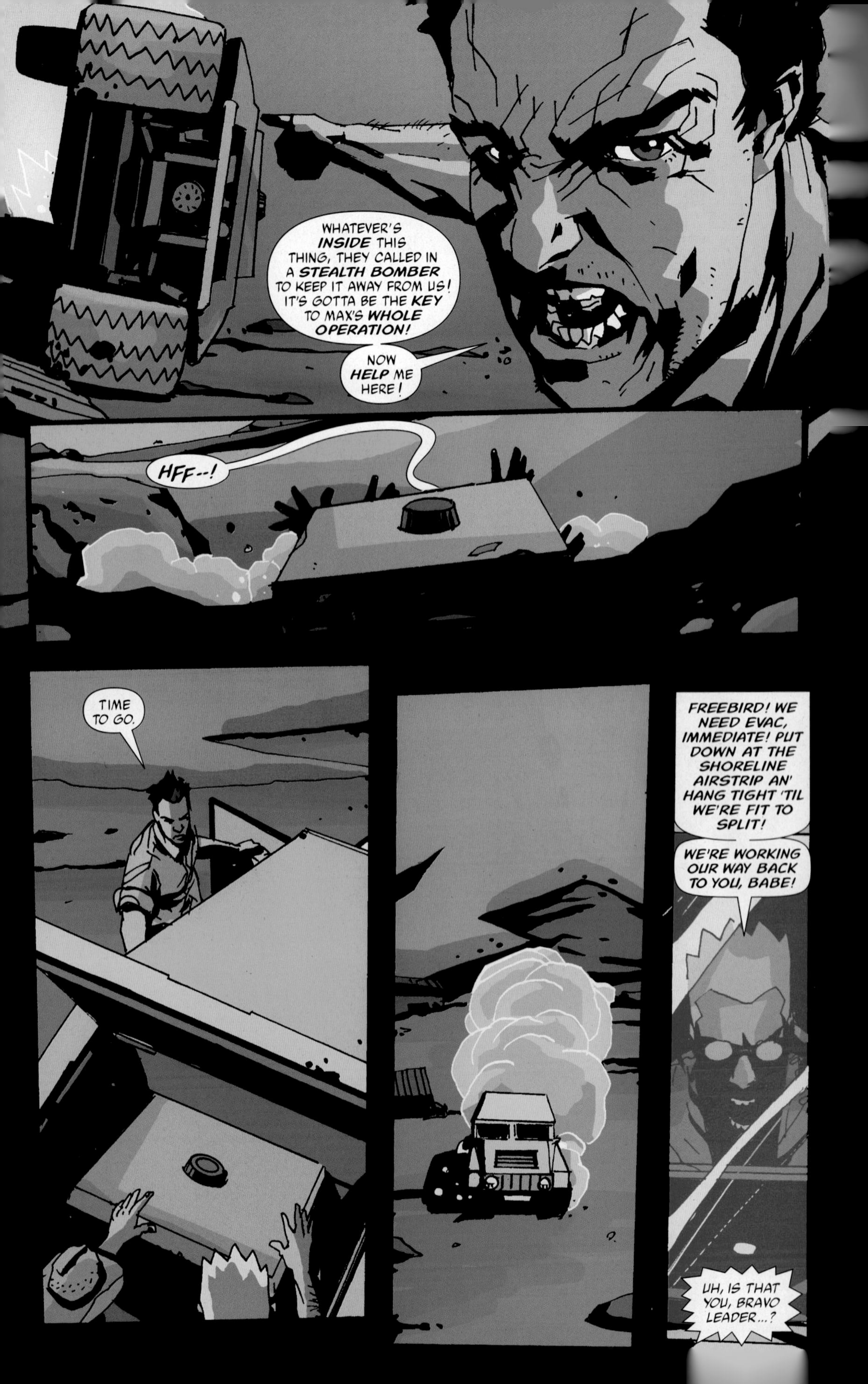
WHATEVER'S INSIDE THIS THING, THEY CALLED IN A STEALTH BOMBER TO KEEP IT AWAY FROM US! IT'S GOTTA BE THE KEY TO MAX'S WHOLE OPERATION!
NOW HELP ME HERE!
HFF--!
TIME TO GO.
FREEBIRD! WE NEED EVAC, IMMEDIATE! PUT DOWN AT THE SHORELINE AIRSTRIP AN' HANG TIGHT 'TIL WE'RE FIT TO SPLIT!
WE'RE WORKING OUR WAY BACK TO YOU, BABE!
UH, IS THAT YOU, BRAVO LEADER...?

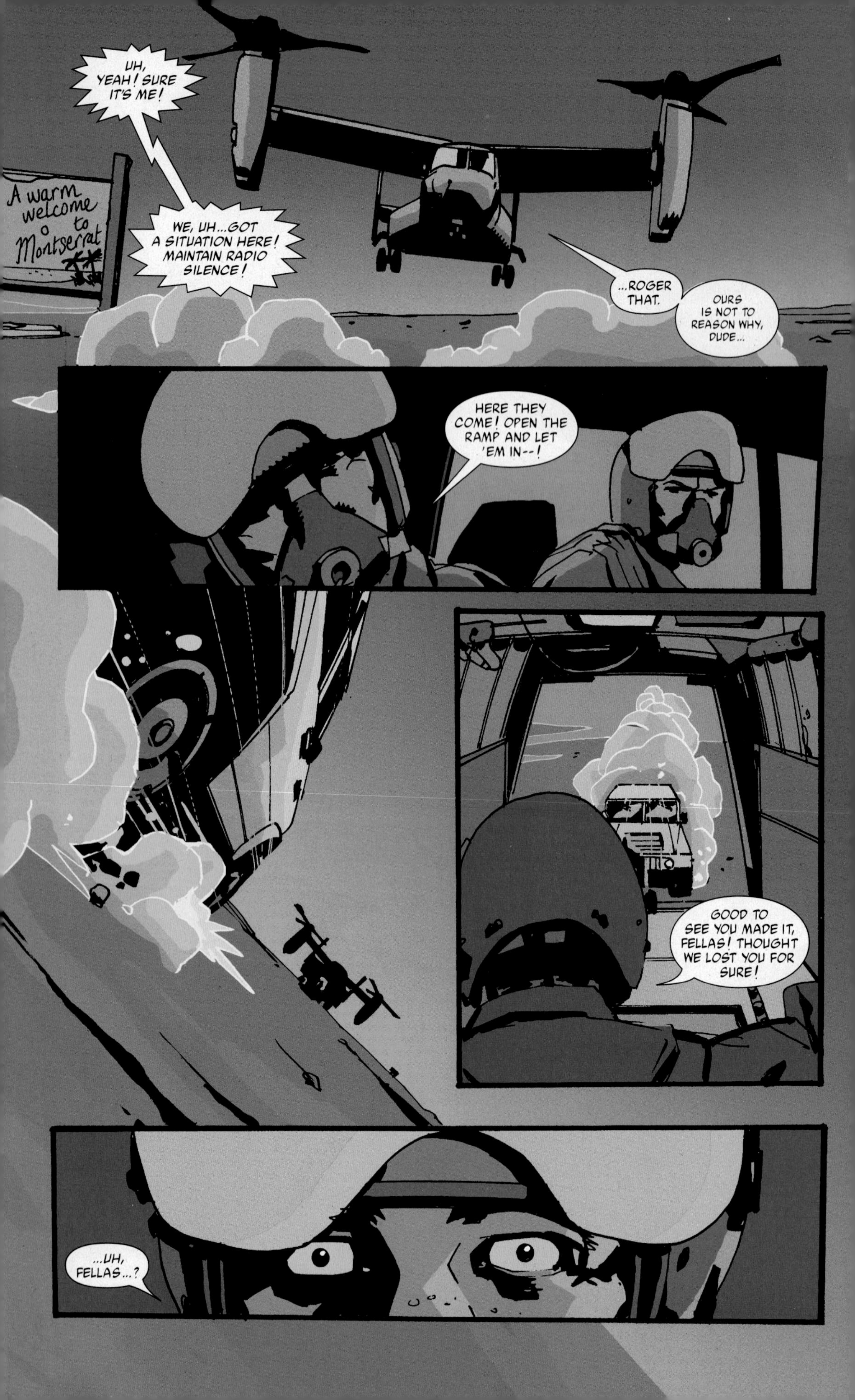
UH, YEAH! SURE IT'S ME!
A warm welcome to Montserrat
WE, UH...GOT A SITUATION HERE! MAINTAIN RADIO SILENCE!
...ROGER THAT.
OURS IS NOT TO REASON WHY, DUDE...
HERE THEY COME! OPEN THE RAMP AND LET 'EM IN--!
GOOD TO SEE YOU MADE IT, FELLAS! THOUGHT WE LOST YOU FOR SURE!
...UH, FELLAS...?

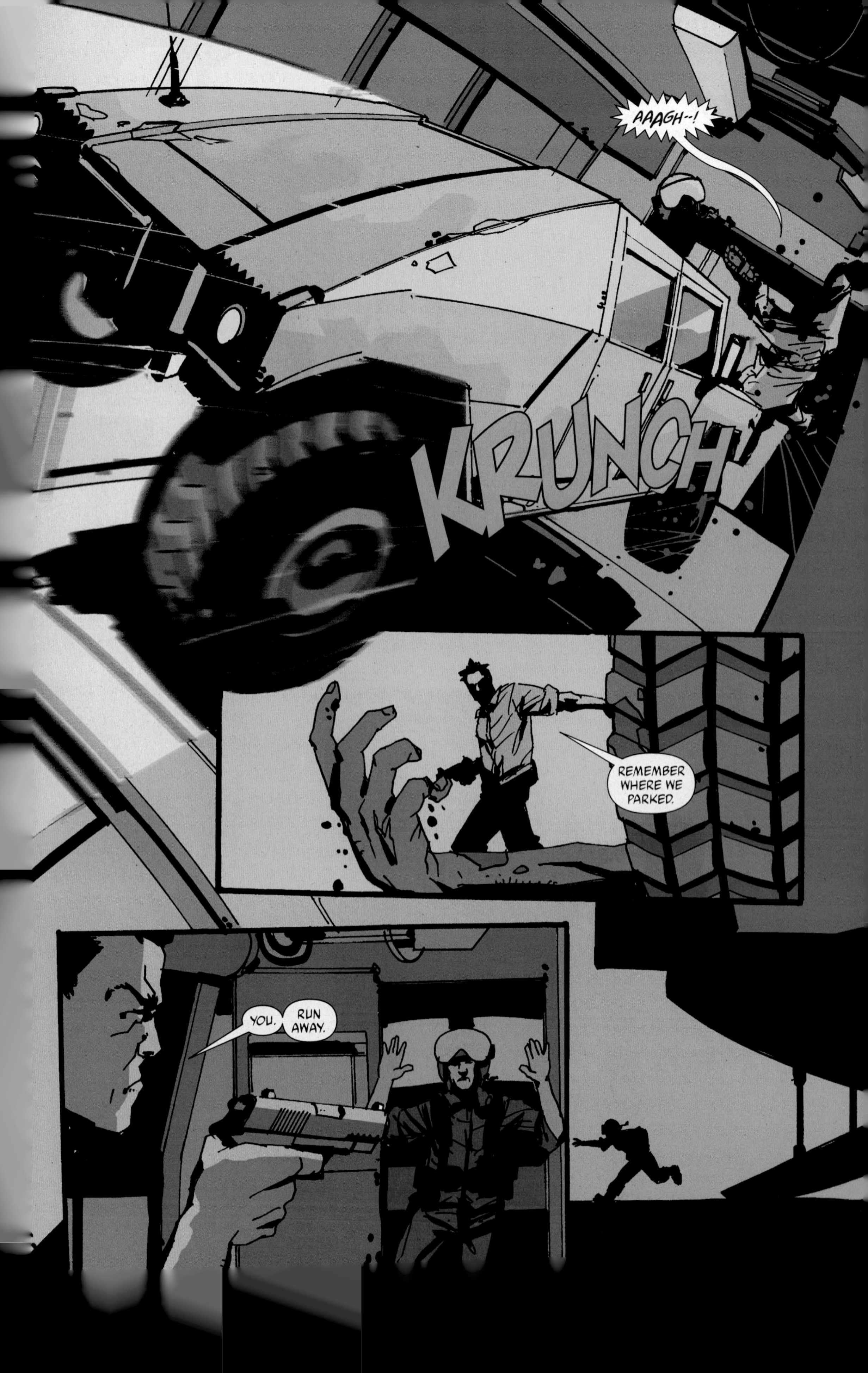
AAAGH--!
KRUNCH
REMEMBER WHERE WE PARKED.
YOU.
RUN AWAY.

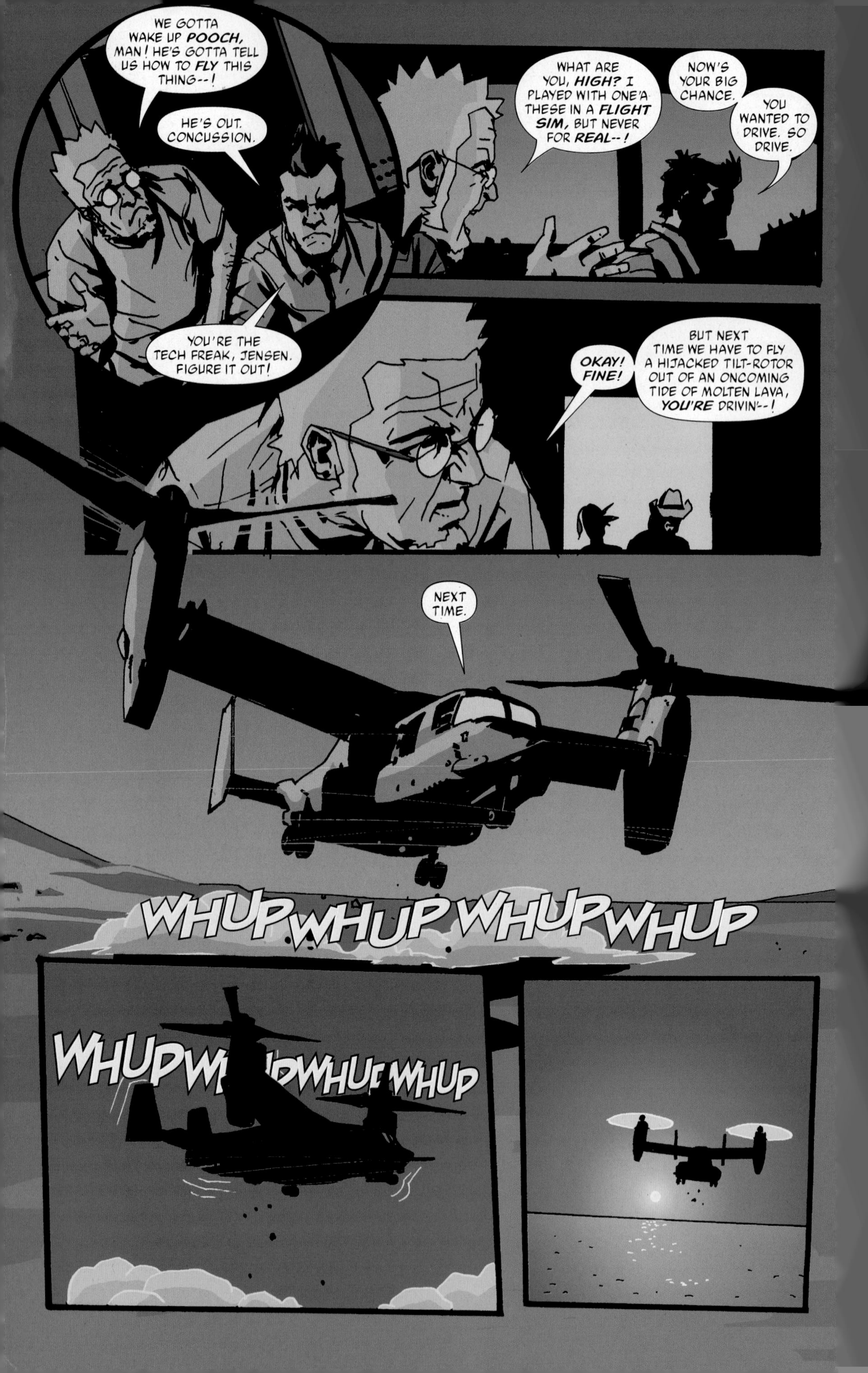
WE GOTTA WAKE UP **POOCH**, MAN! HE'S GOTTA TELL US HOW TO **FLY** THIS THING--!
HE'S OUT. CONCUSSION.
YOU'RE THE TECH FREAK, JENSEN. FIGURE IT OUT!
WHAT ARE YOU, **HIGH?** I PLAYED WITH ONE'A THESE IN A **FLIGHT SIM,** BUT NEVER FOR **REAL**--!
NOW'S YOUR BIG CHANCE.
YOU WANTED TO DRIVE. SO DRIVE.
OKAY! FINE!
BUT NEXT TIME WE HAVE TO FLY A HIJACKED TILT-ROTOR OUT OF AN ONCOMING TIDE OF MOLTEN LAVA, **YOU'RE** DRIVIN'--!
NEXT TIME.
WHUP WHUP WHUP WHUP
WHUP

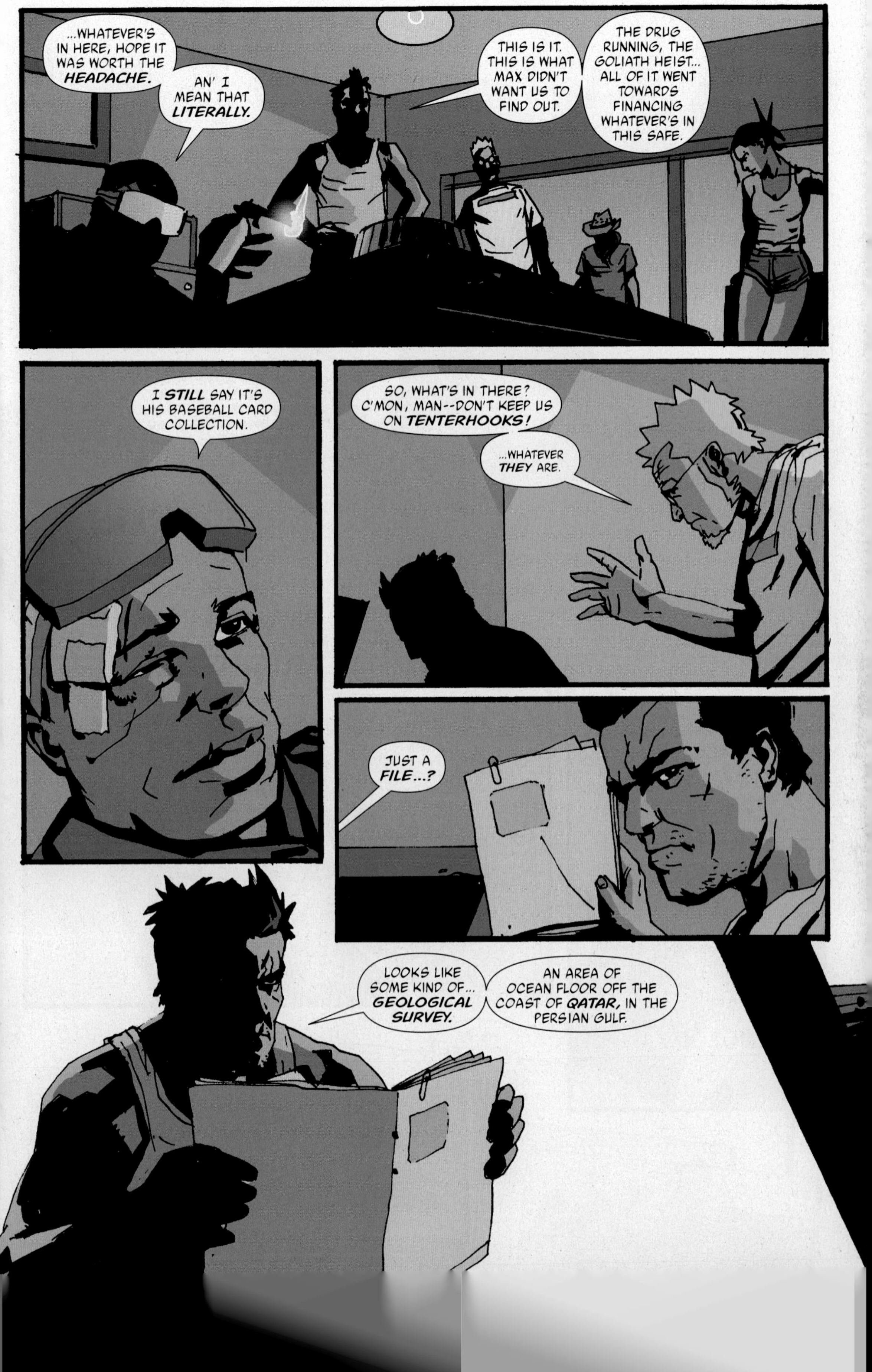
...WHATEVER'S IN HERE, HOPE IT WAS WORTH THE **HEADACHE**.
AN' I MEAN THAT **LITERALLY.**
THIS IS IT. THIS IS WHAT MAX DIDN'T WANT US TO FIND OUT.
THE DRUG RUNNING, THE GOLIATH HEIST... ALL OF IT WENT TOWARDS FINANCING WHATEVER'S IN THIS SAFE.
I **STILL** SAY IT'S HIS BASEBALL CARD COLLECTION.
SO, WHAT'S IN THERE? C'MON, MAN--DON'T KEEP US ON **TENTERHOOKS!**
...WHATEVER **THEY** ARE.
JUST A **FILE...?**
LOOKS LIKE SOME KIND OF... **GEOLOGICAL SURVEY.**
AN AREA OF OCEAN FLOOR OFF THE COAST OF **QATAR,** IN THE PERSIAN GULF.

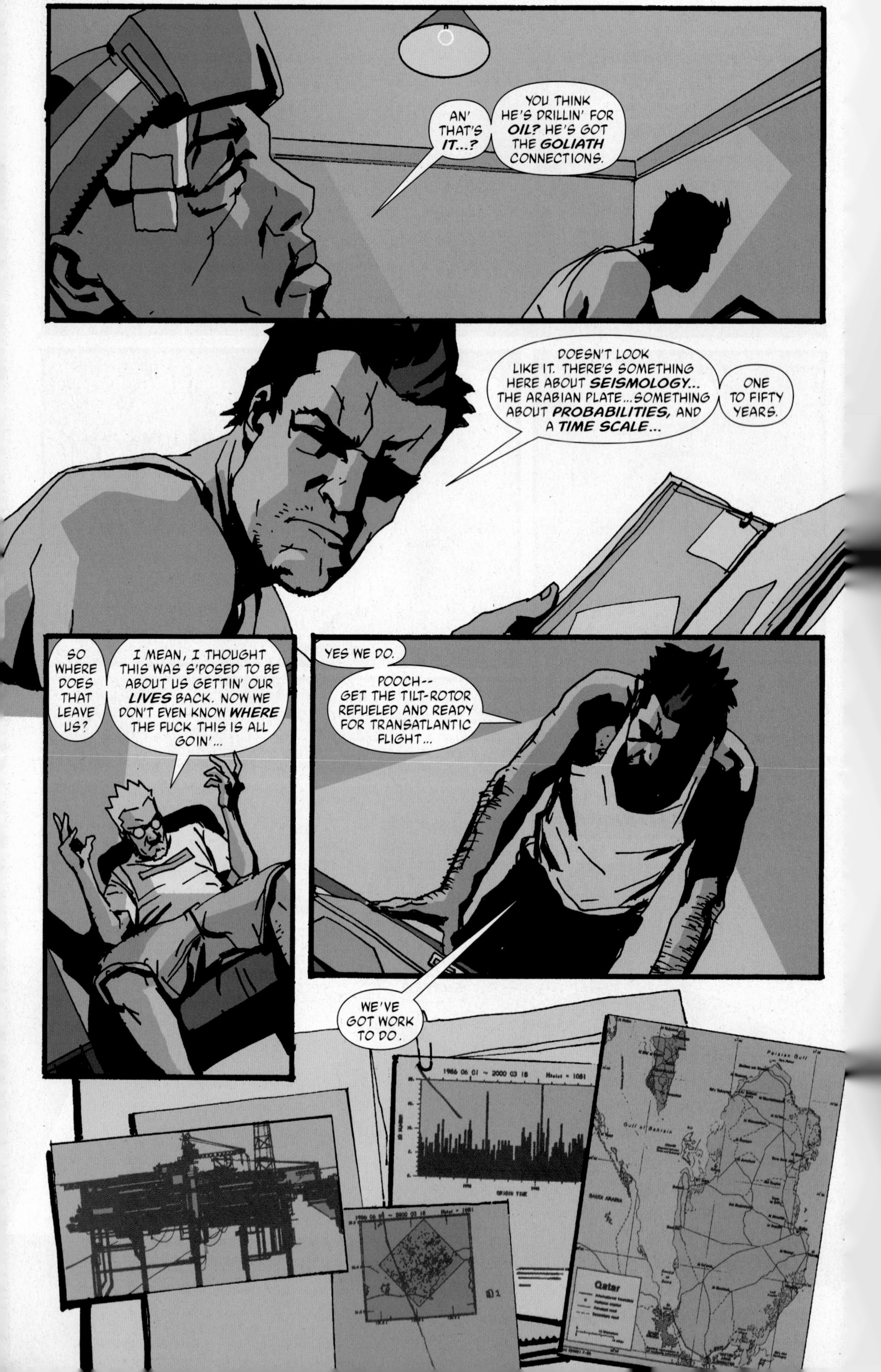
YOU THINK HE'S DRILLIN' FOR OIL? HE'S GOT THE GOLIATH CONNECTIONS.
AN' THAT'S IT...?
DOESN'T LOOK LIKE IT. THERE'S SOMETHING HERE ABOUT SEISMOLOGY... THE ARABIAN PLATE...SOMETHING ABOUT PROBABILITIES, AND A TIME SCALE...
ONE TO FIFTY YEARS.
SO WHERE DOES THAT LEAVE US?
I MEAN, I THOUGHT THIS WAS S'POSED TO BE ABOUT US GETTIN' OUR LIVES BACK. NOW WE DON'T EVEN KNOW WHERE THE FUCK THIS IS ALL GOIN'...
YES WE DO.
POOCH-- GET THE TILT-ROTOR REFUELED AND READY FOR TRANSATLANTIC FLIGHT...
WE'VE GOT WORK TO DO.
Qatar
Persian Gulf
Gulf of Bahrain
SAUDI ARABIA
ORIGIN TIME

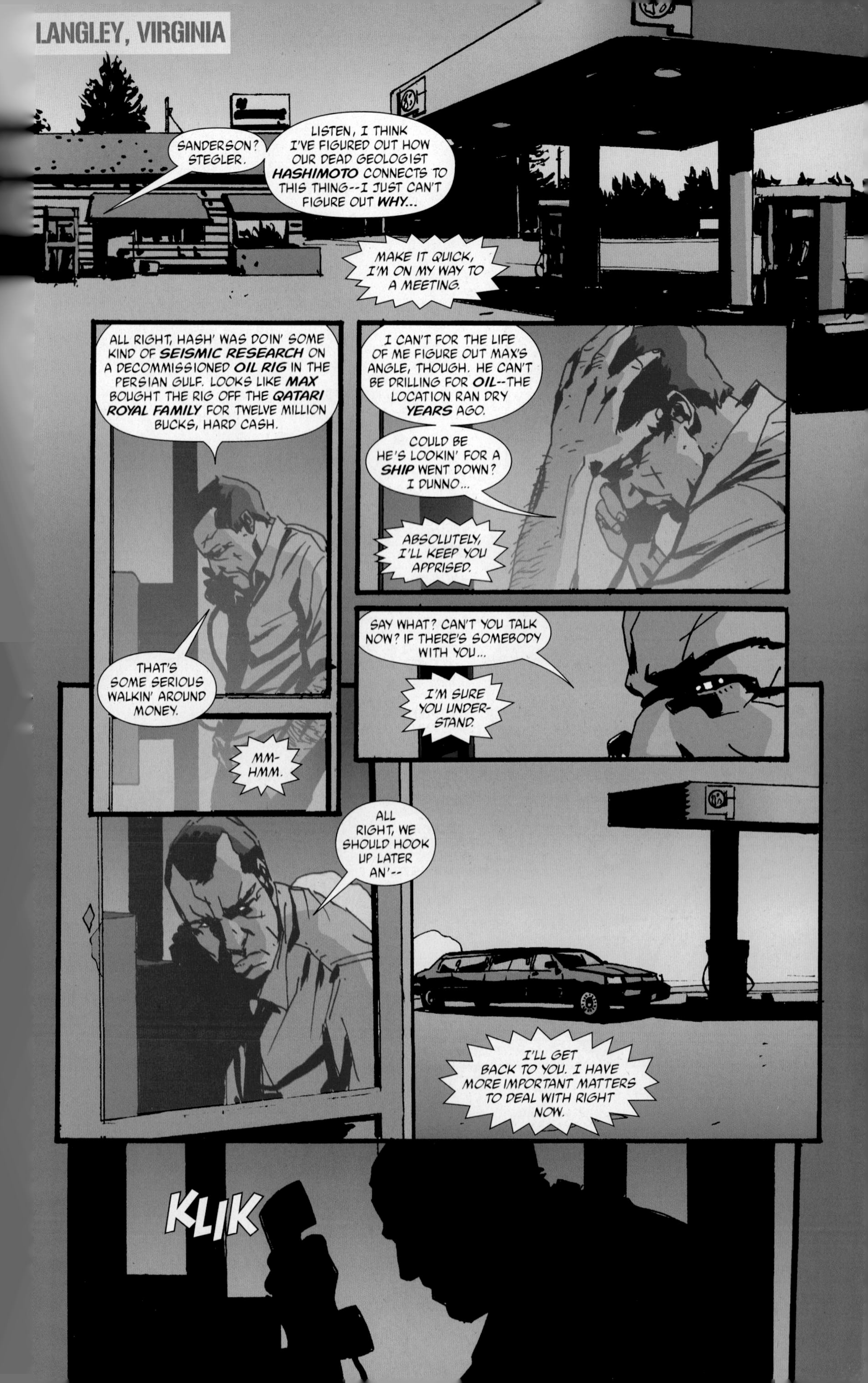
LANGLEY, VIRGINIA
SANDERSON? STEGLER.
LISTEN, I THINK I'VE FIGURED OUT HOW OUR DEAD GEOLOGIST HASHIMOTO CONNECTS TO THIS THING--I JUST CAN'T FIGURE OUT WHY...
MAKE IT QUICK, I'M ON MY WAY TO A MEETING.
ALL RIGHT, HASH' WAS DOIN' SOME KIND OF SEISMIC RESEARCH ON A DECOMMISSIONED OIL RIG IN THE PERSIAN GULF. LOOKS LIKE MAX BOUGHT THE RIG OFF THE QATARI ROYAL FAMILY FOR TWELVE MILLION BUCKS, HARD CASH.
THAT'S SOME SERIOUS WALKIN' AROUND MONEY.
MM-HMM.
I CAN'T FOR THE LIFE OF ME FIGURE OUT MAX'S ANGLE, THOUGH. HE CAN'T BE DRILLING FOR OIL--THE LOCATION RAN DRY YEARS AGO.
COULD BE HE'S LOOKIN' FOR A SHIP WENT DOWN? I DUNNO...
ABSOLUTELY, I'LL KEEP YOU APPRISED.
SAY WHAT? CAN'T YOU TALK NOW? IF THERE'S SOMEBODY WITH YOU...
I'M SURE YOU UNDERSTAND.
ALL RIGHT, WE SHOULD HOOK UP LATER AN'--
I'LL GET BACK TO YOU. I HAVE MORE IMPORTANT MATTERS TO DEAL WITH RIGHT NOW.
KLIK

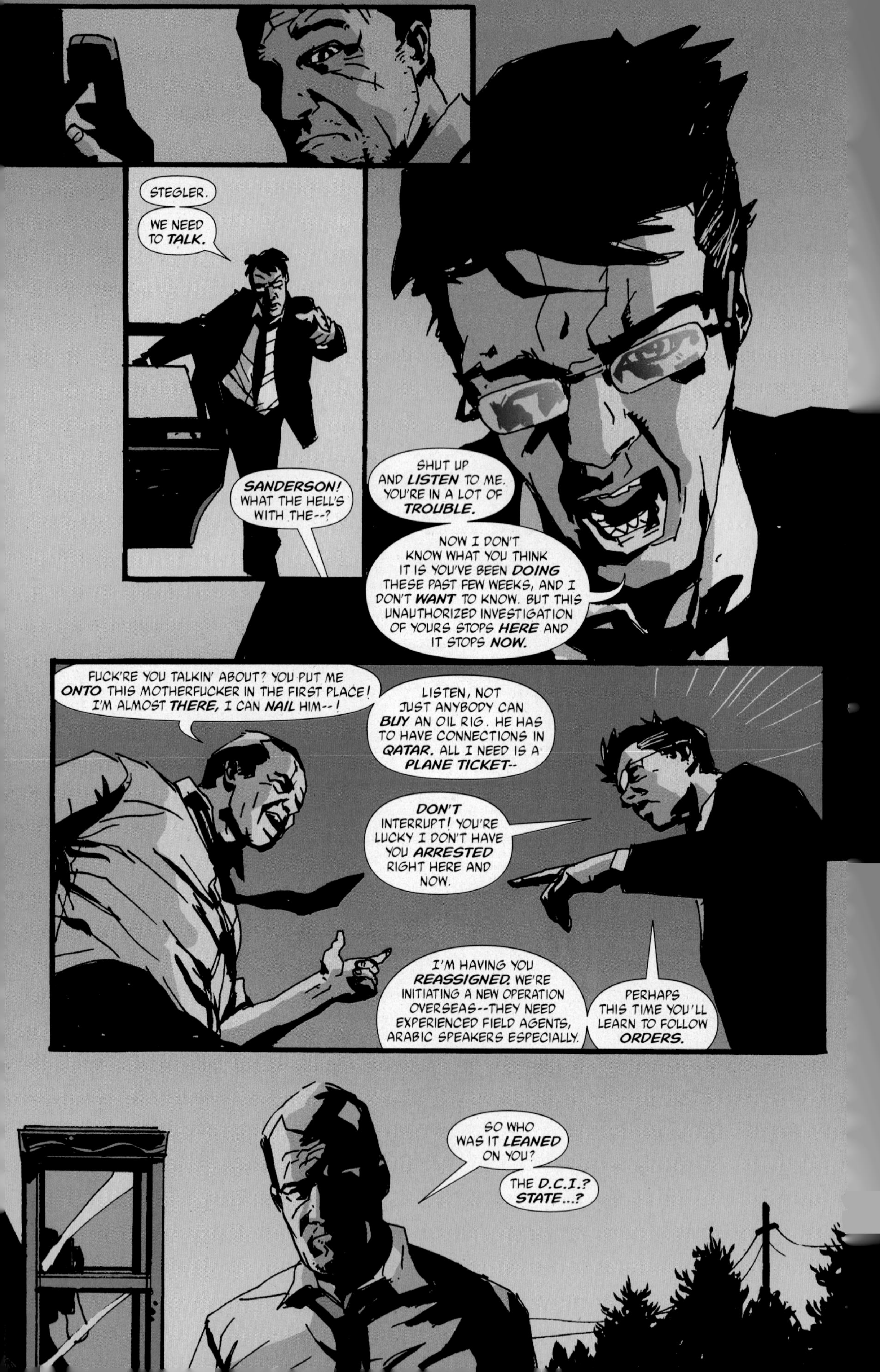
STEGLER.
WE NEED TO TALK.
SANDERSON! WHAT THE HELL'S WITH THE--?
SHUT UP AND LISTEN TO ME. YOU'RE IN A LOT OF TROUBLE.
NOW I DON'T KNOW WHAT YOU THINK IT IS YOU'VE BEEN DOING THESE PAST FEW WEEKS, AND I DON'T WANT TO KNOW. BUT THIS UNAUTHORIZED INVESTIGATION OF YOURS STOPS HERE AND IT STOPS NOW.
FUCK'RE YOU TALKIN' ABOUT? YOU PUT ME ONTO THIS MOTHERFUCKER IN THE FIRST PLACE! I'M ALMOST THERE, I CAN NAIL HIM--!
LISTEN, NOT JUST ANYBODY CAN BUY AN OIL RIG. HE HAS TO HAVE CONNECTIONS IN QATAR. ALL I NEED IS A PLANE TICKET--
DON'T INTERRUPT! YOU'RE LUCKY I DON'T HAVE YOU ARRESTED RIGHT HERE AND NOW.
I'M HAVING YOU REASSIGNED. WE'RE INITIATING A NEW OPERATION OVERSEAS--THEY NEED EXPERIENCED FIELD AGENTS, ARABIC SPEAKERS ESPECIALLY.
PERHAPS THIS TIME YOU'LL LEARN TO FOLLOW ORDERS.
SO WHO WAS IT LEANED ON YOU?
THE D.C.I.? STATE...?

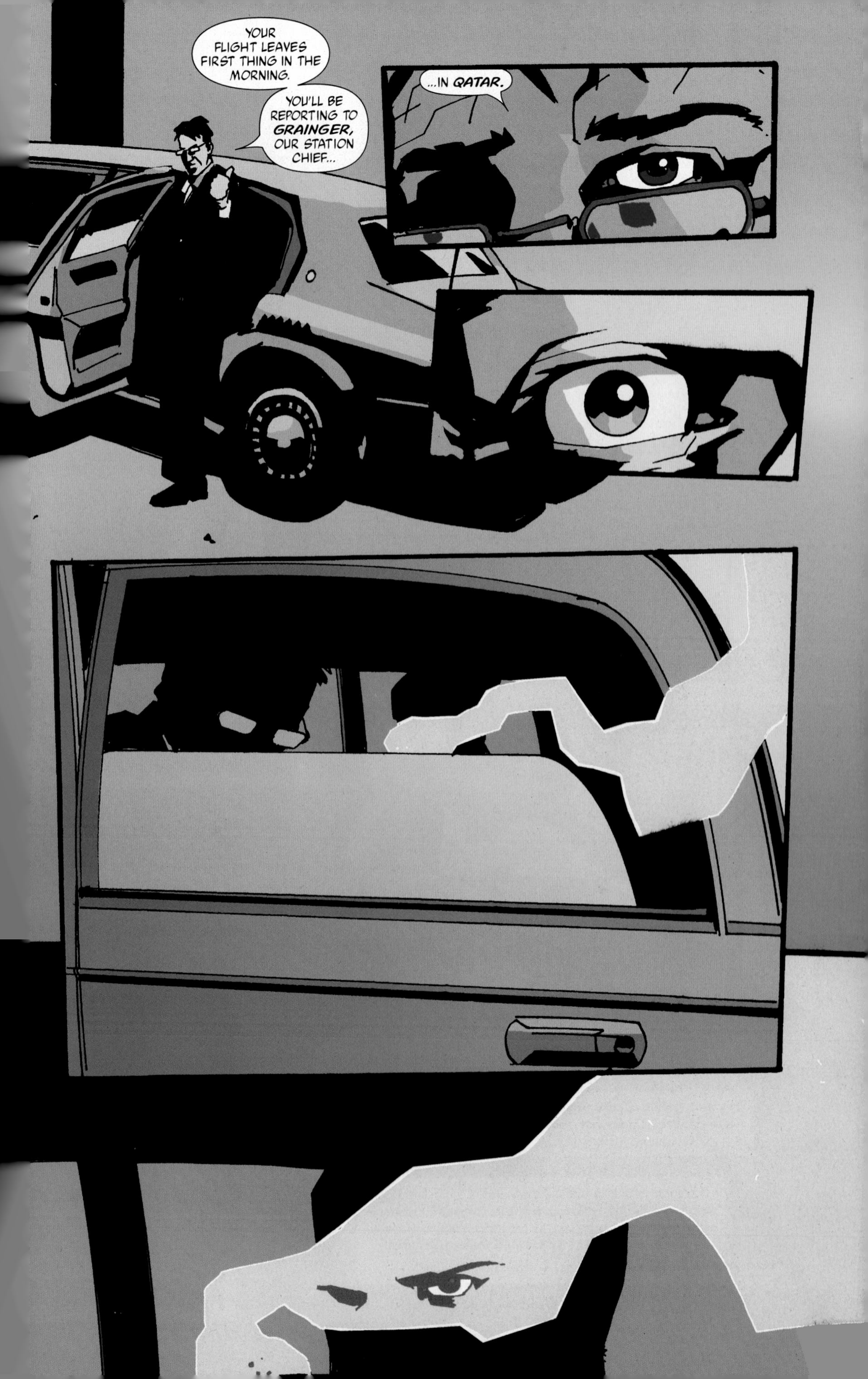
YOUR FLIGHT LEAVES FIRST THING IN THE MORNING.
YOU'LL BE REPORTING TO GRAINGER, OUR STATION CHIEF...
...IN QATAR.

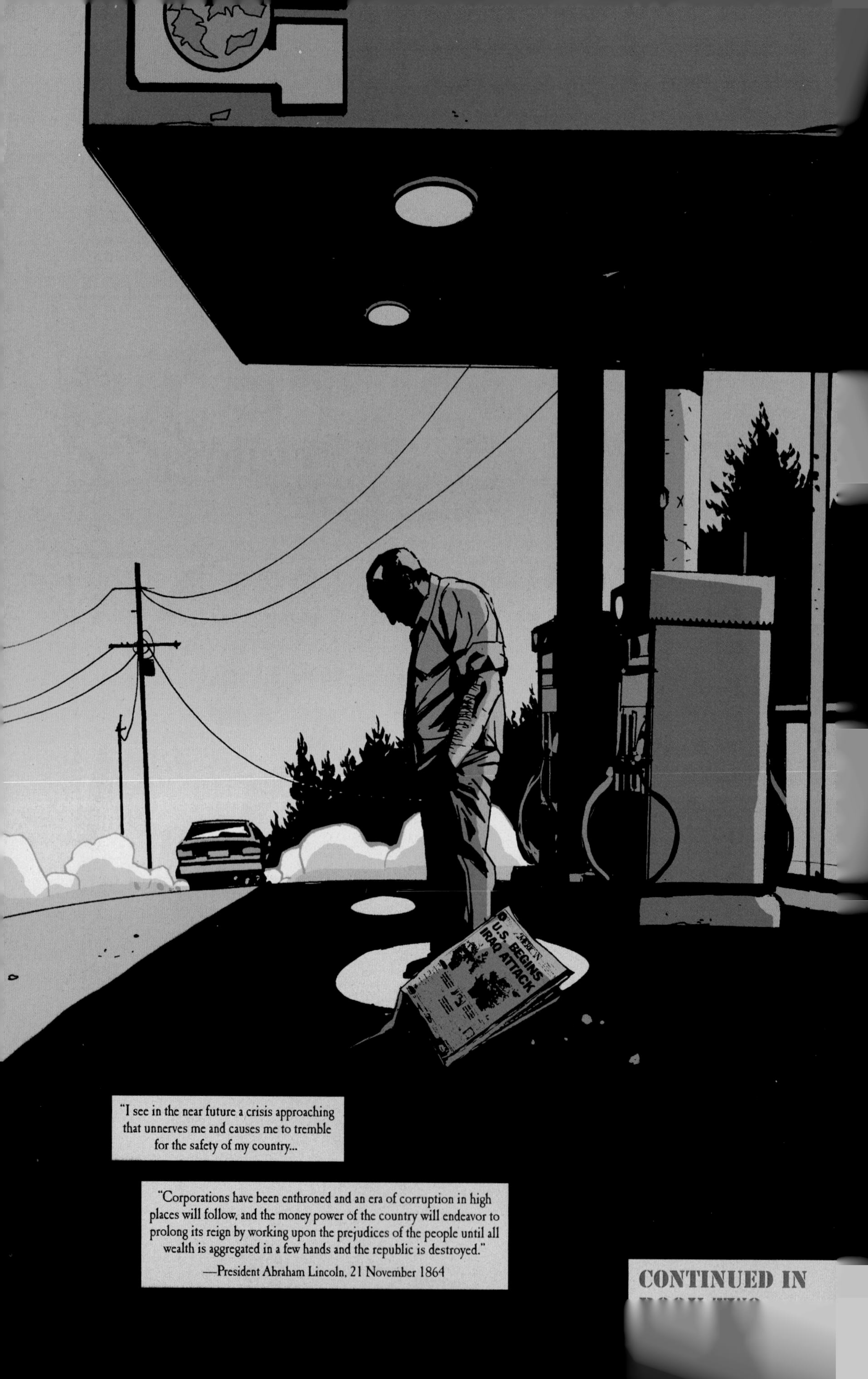
U.S. BEGINS IRAQ ATTACK
"I see in the near future a crisis approaching that unnerves me and causes me to tremble for the safety of my country...
"Corporations have been enthroned and an era of corruption in high places will follow, and the money power of the country will endeavor to prolong its reign by working upon the prejudices of the people until all wealth is aggregated in a few hands and the republic is destroyed."
—President Abraham Lincoln, 21 November 1864
CONTINUED IN

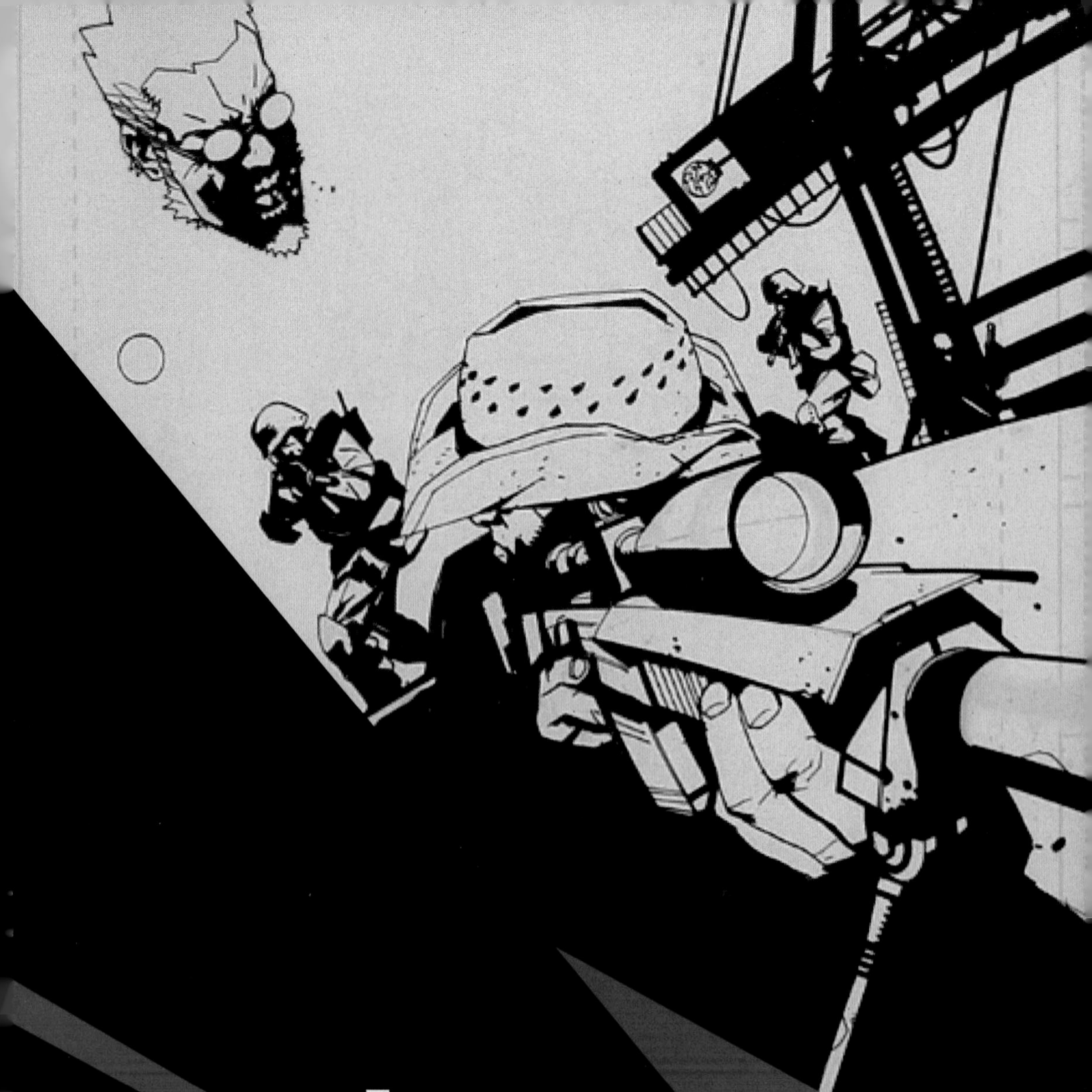

losers, guns and money

Preliminary designs and sketches by **jock**

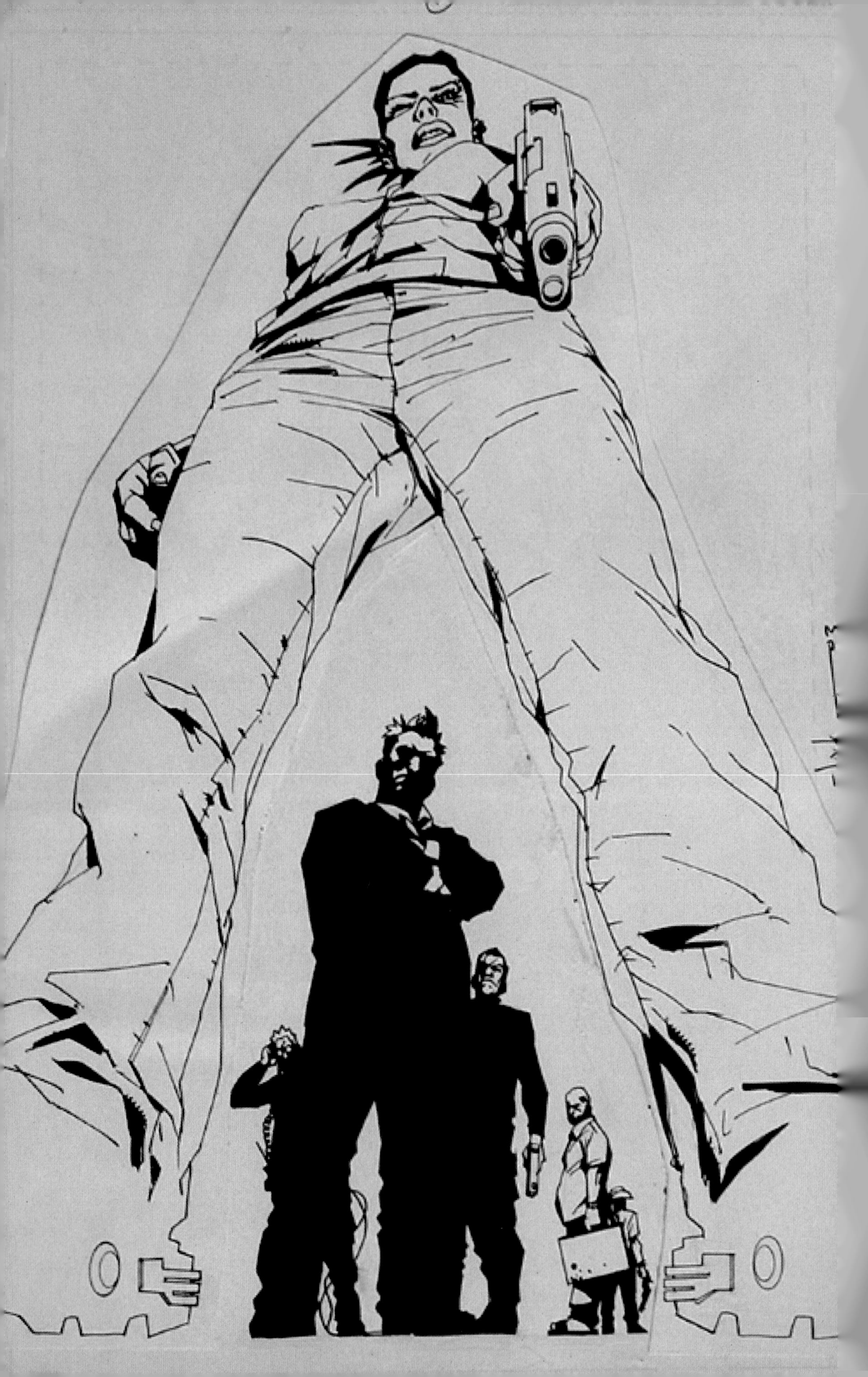

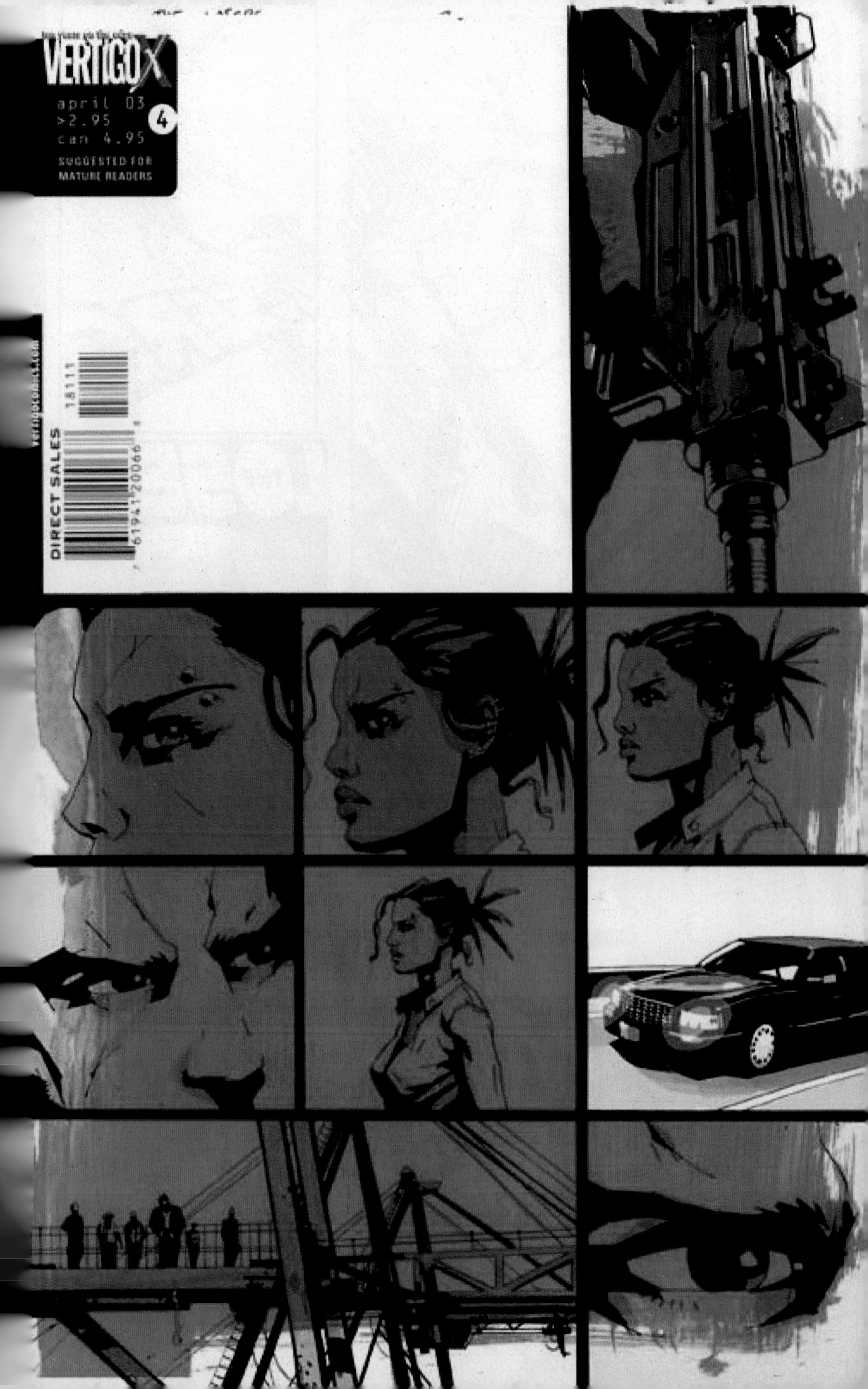
VERTIGO X
april 03
>2.95
can 4.95
4
SUGGESTED FOR MATURE READERS
vertigocomics.com
DIRECT SALES

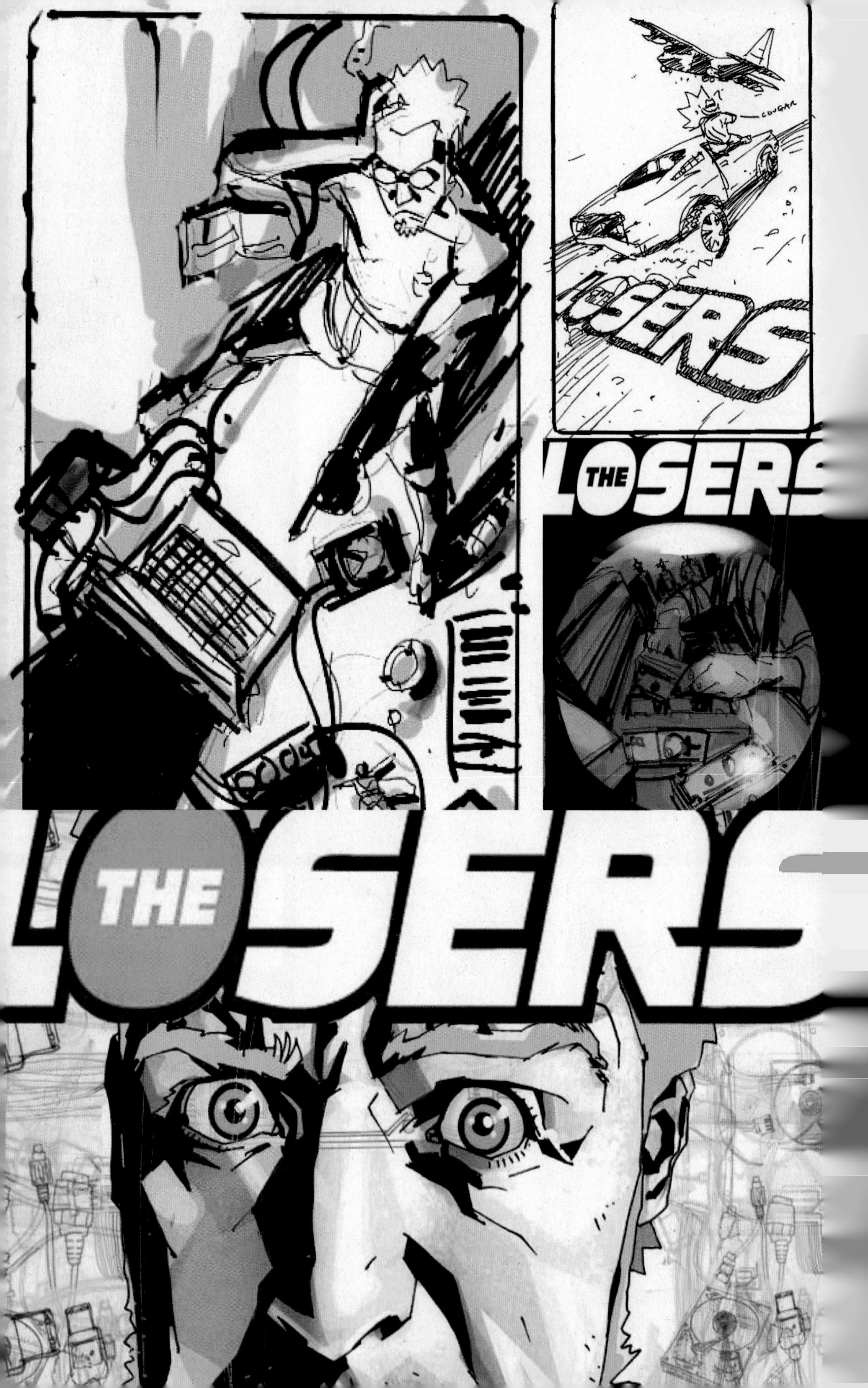
COUGAR
THE LOSERS

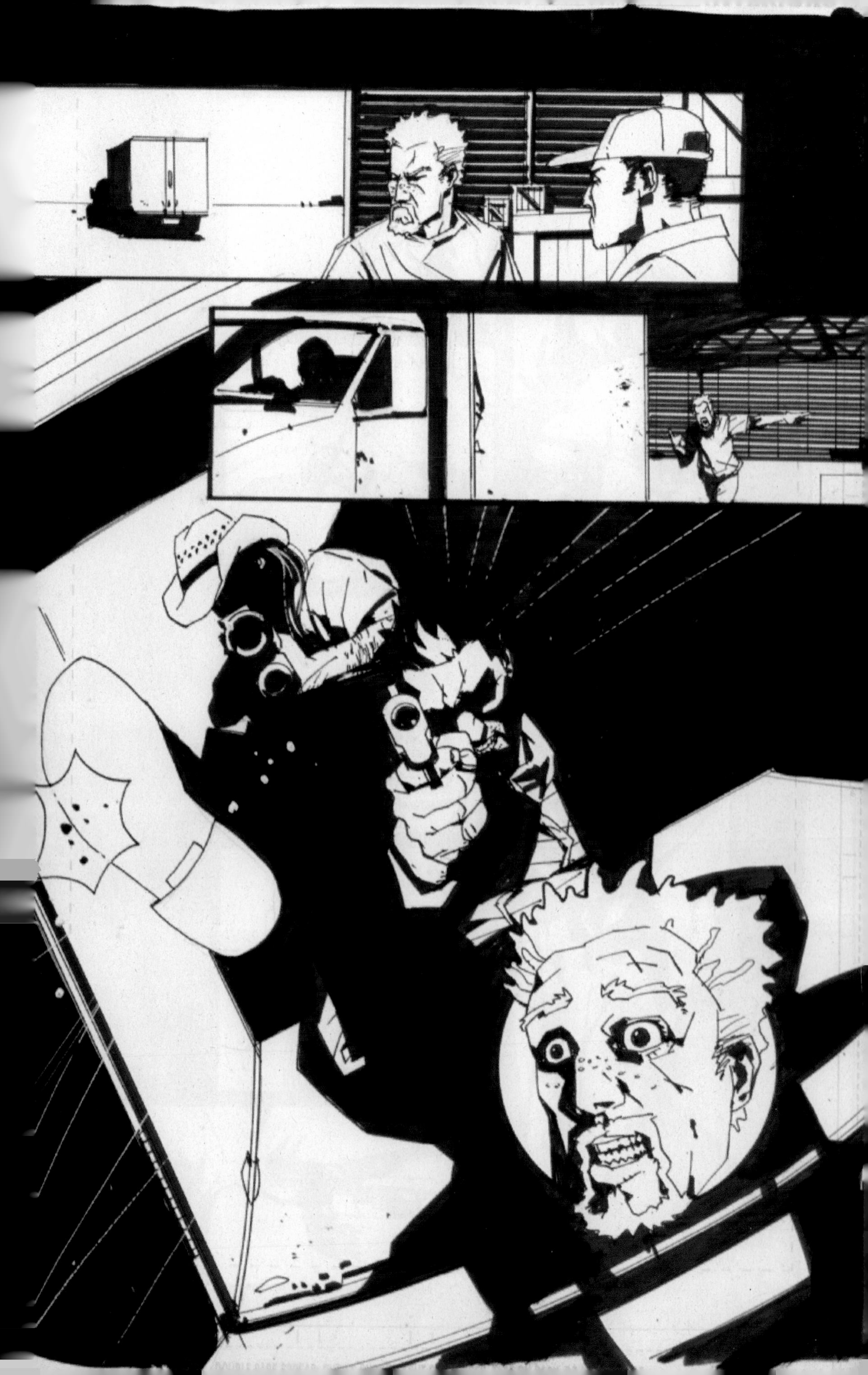

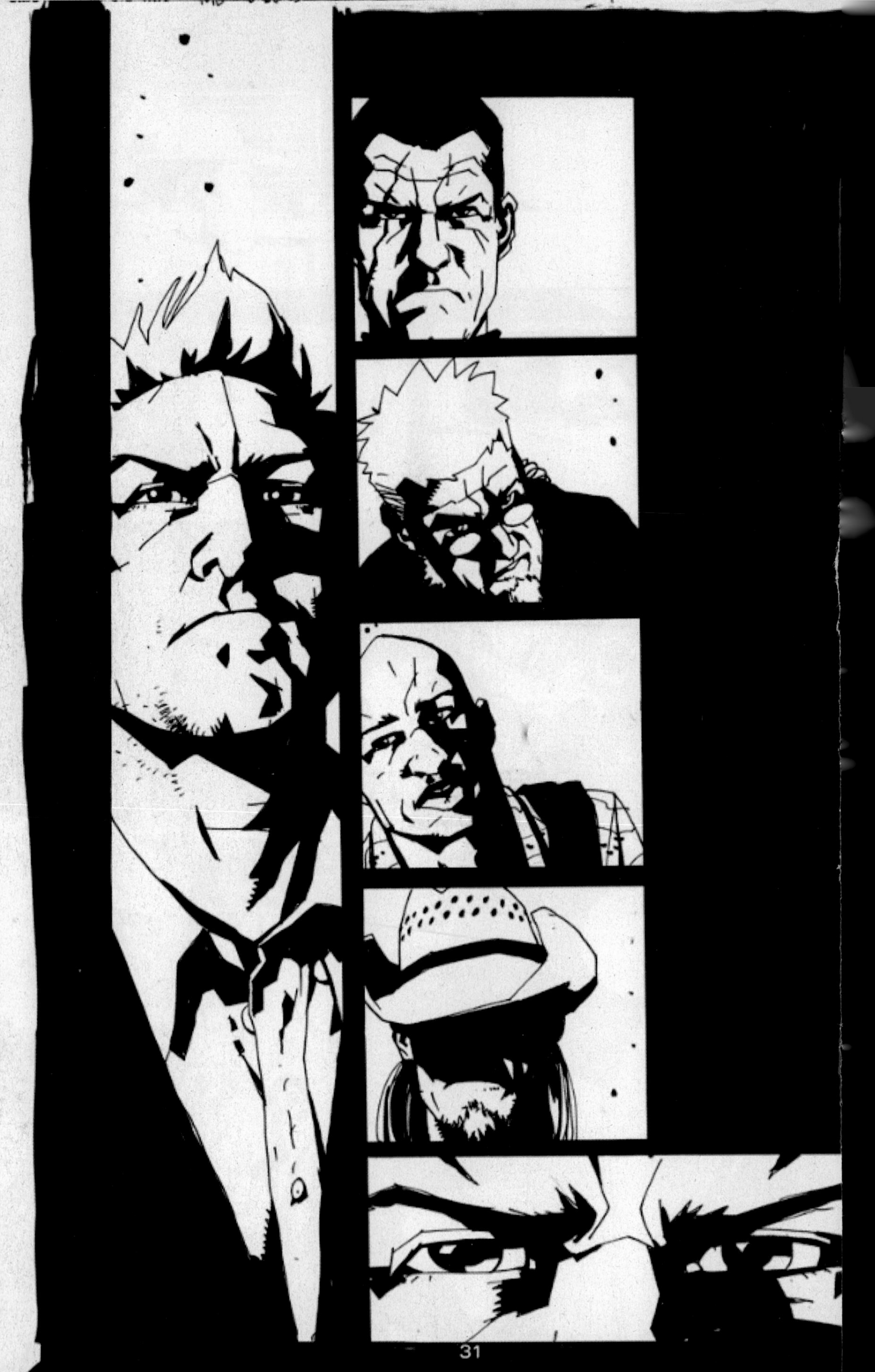

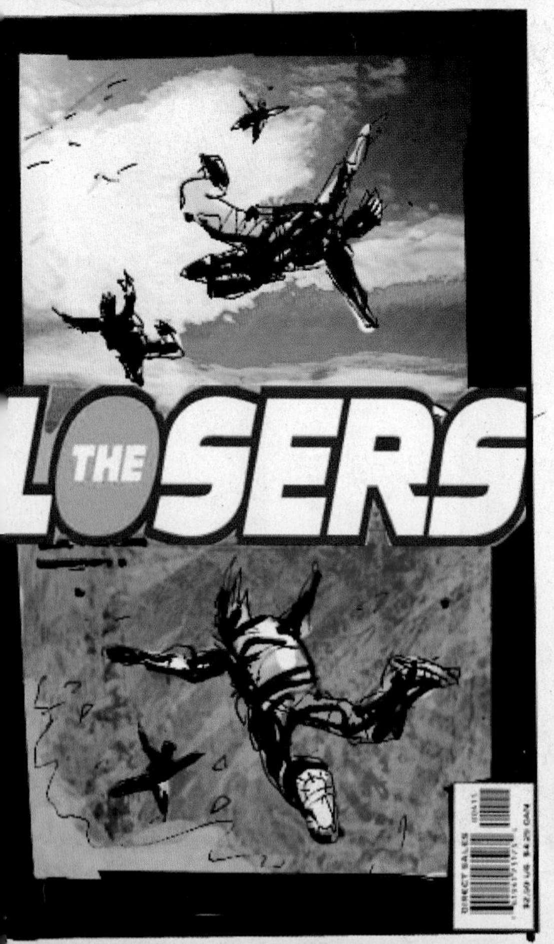
THE LOSERS
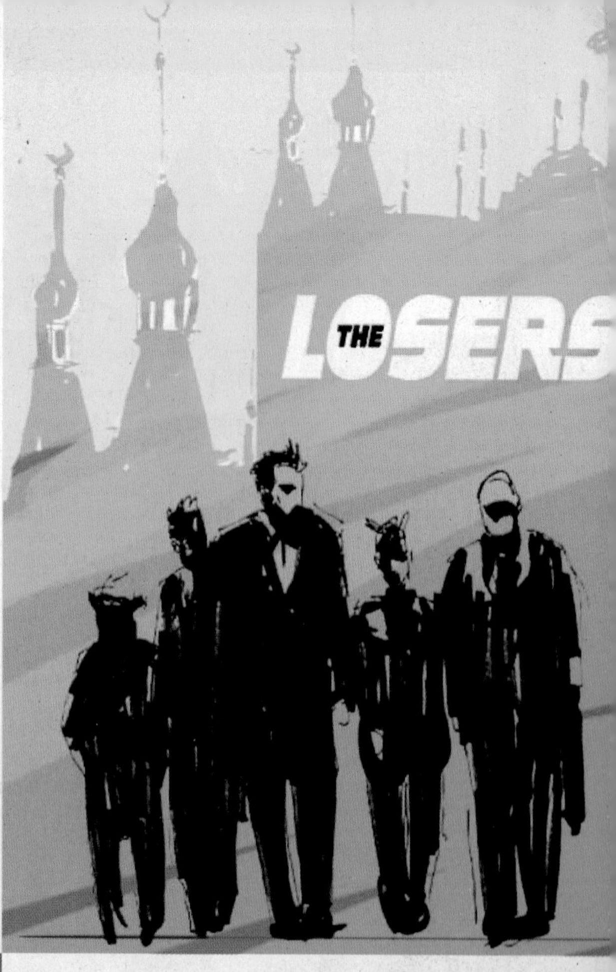
THE LOSERS
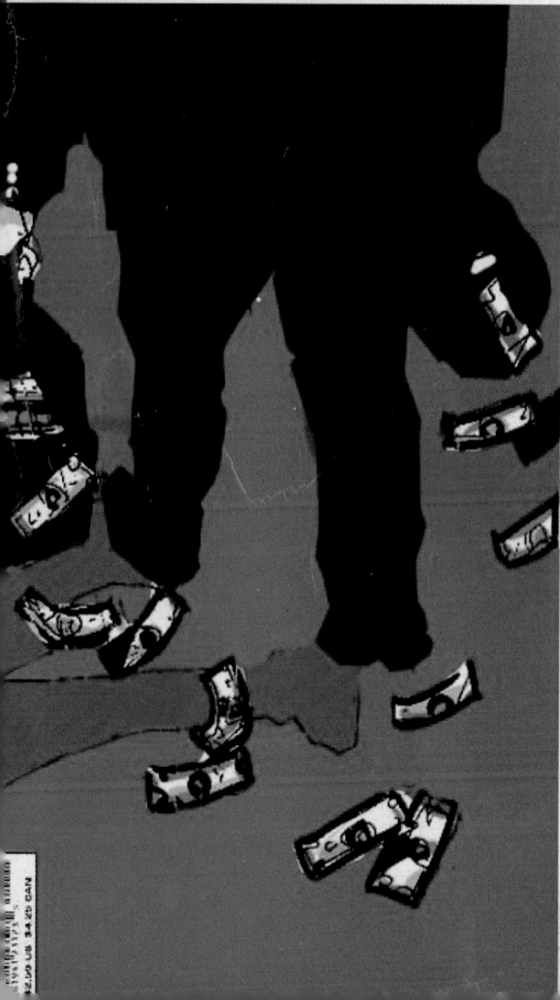
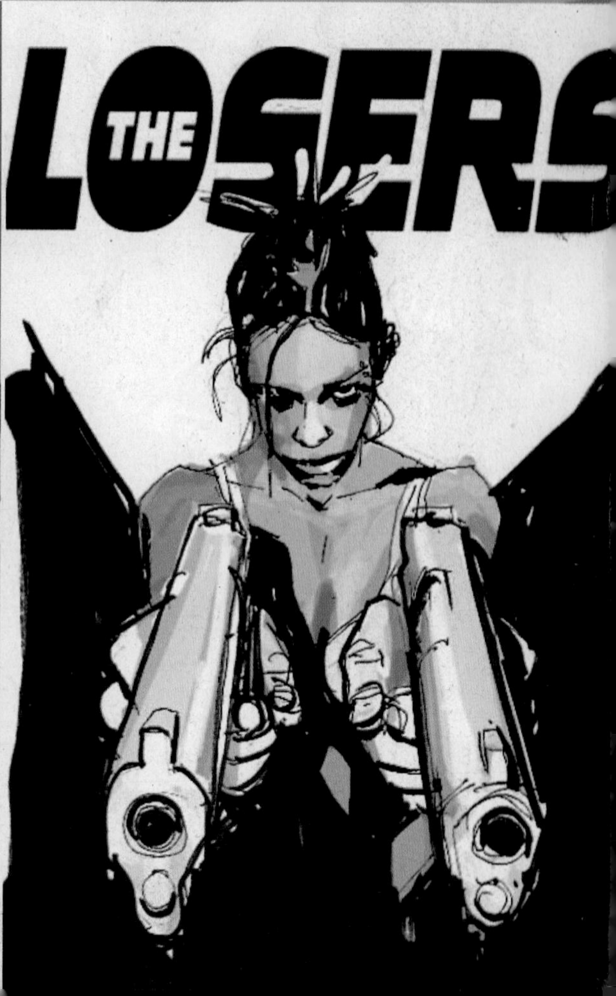
THE LOSERS

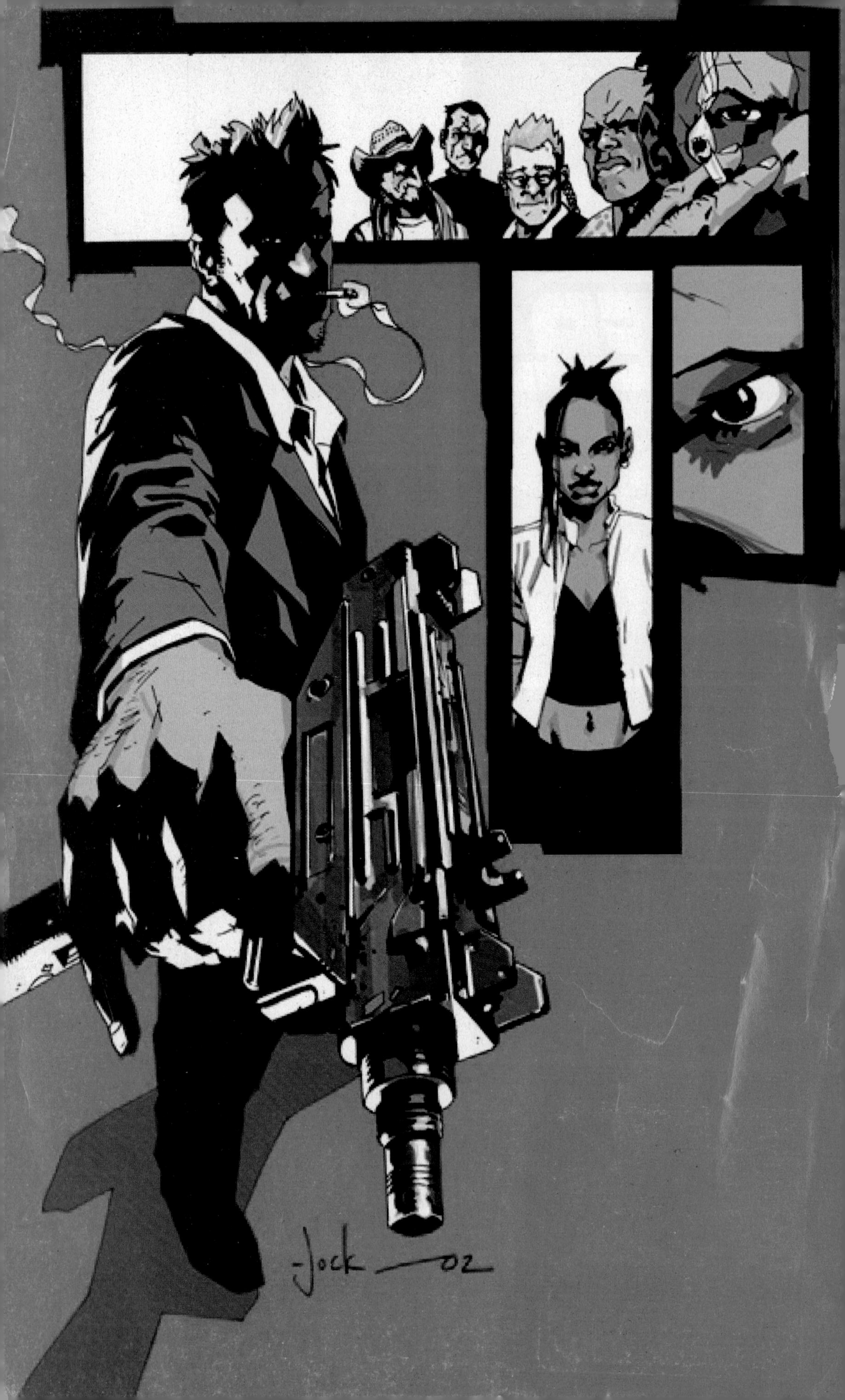
Jock — 02